Human
Resource
Management

PRENTICE HALL BUSINESS PUBLISHING
MANAGEMENT TITLES FOR 2001

Bowin/Harvey: Human Resource Management: An Experiential Approach 2/e
Caproni: The Practical Coach: Management Skills for Everyday Life 1/e
Carrell/Heavrin: Labor Relations and Collective Bargaining 6/e
Coulter: Strategic Management in Action 2/e
Coutler: Entrepreneurship in Action 1/e
Daniels/Radebaugh: International Business 9/e
David: Strategic Management: Concepts and Cases 8/e
David: Cases in Strategic Management 8/e
David: Concepts in Strategic Management 8/e
Dessler: Management: Leading People and Organizations in the 21st Century 2/e
DiBella: Learning Practices: Assessment and Action for Organizational Improvement (OD Series)
Ghemawat: Strategy and the Business Landscape: Core Concepts 1/e
Gomez-Mejia/Balkin/Cardy: Managing Human Resources 3/e
Greer: Strategic Human Resource Management 2/e
Harvey/Brown: Experiential Approach to Organization Development 6/e
Hersey/Blanchard/Johnson: Management of Organizational Behavior: Leading Human Resources 8/e
Howell/Costley: Understanding Behaviors for Effective Leadership 1/e
Hunger/Wheelen: Essentials of Strategic Management 2/e
Hunsaker: Training in Managerial Skills 1/e
Jones: Organizational Theory 3/e
Mische: Strategic Renewal: Becoming and High-Performance Organization 1/e
Martocchio: Strategic Compensation 2/e
Narayanan: Managing Technology and Innovation for Competitive Advantage 1/e
Osland/Kolb/Rubin: The Organizational Behavior Reader 7/e
Osland/Kolb/Rubin: Organizational Behavior: An Experiential Approach 7/e
Robbins: Organizational Behavior 9/e
Robbins/DeCenzo: Fundamentals of Management 3/e
Sanyal: International Management 1/e
Sloane/Whitney: Labor Relations 10/e
Thompson: The Mind and Heart of the Negotiator 2/e
Tompkins: Cases in Management and Organizational Behavior Vol. I 1/e
Wexley/Latham: Developing and Training Human Resources in Organizations 3/e

Other Books of Interest

Dessler: Human Resources Management 8/e
Dessler: Essentials of Human Resource Management 1/e
Mondy/Noe/Premeux: Human Resource Management 7/e
Henderson: Compensation Management 8/e
Blanchard/Thacker: Effective Training Systems: Strategies and Practices 1/e
Feldacker: Labor Guide to Labor Law 4/e
Sovereign: Personnel Law 4/e

Human Resource Management

An Experiential Approach
Second Edition

Robert Bruce Bowin, Emeritus Professor of Management
Don Harvey, Professor of Management

School of Business and Public Administration
California State University, Bakersfield

Prentice Hall

Upper Saddle River, NJ 07458

Bowin, Robert Bruce, 1931–
    Human resource management : an experiential approach/
    Robert Bruce Bowin, Don Harvey.—2nd ed.
      p. cm.
    Harvey's name appears first on the earlier edition.
    Includes bibliographical references and index.
    ISBN 0–13–017788–1
    1. Personnel management.   I. Harvey, Donald F., 1931–   II. Title.
HF5549 .H3443 2000
658.3—dc21   00-035950

VP/Editorial Director: James C. Boyd
Acquisitions Editor: Melissa Steffens
Editorial Assistant: Samantha Steel
Assistant Editor: Jessica Sabloff
Executive Marketing Manager: Michael Campbell
Permissions Coordinator: Suzanne Grappi
Media Project Manager: Michele Faranda
Director of Production: Michael Weinstein
Manager, Production: Gail Steier de Acevedo
Production Coordinator: Kelly Warsak
Manufacturing Buyer: Natacha St. Hill Moore
Associate Director, Manufacturing: Vincent Scelta
Cover Design: Bruce Kenselaar
Full Service Composition: BookMasters, Inc.

10 9 8 7 6 5 4 3 2 1
ISBN 0-13-017788-1

Dedication

To my parents—Mildred W. and Robert Bowin, Sr.

To Viola Higgins for her patience and support.

To my mentors—John B. Miner
        Emeritus Professor
        State University of New York–Buffalo

        Robert Dubin
        Emeritus Professor
        University of California–Irvine

        James Reinmuth
        Emeritus Dean
        University of Oregon

        Donald Parker
        Emeritus Dean
        Portland State University

—R. B.

To my sons—Scott and Dave Harvey.

To the memory of Dawn Zimmer.

—D. H.

BRIEF CONTENTS

CONTENTS

Contents

PART V   THE SUCCESS SYSTEM: MAINTAINING A HIGH-PERFORMING WORKFORCE   323

Preface

In the past, managers aimed for success in a relatively stable and predictable world. Today, however, in the hyperturbulent environment of the twenty-first century, managers confront accelerating change. They are facing constant innovation in computer and information technology and a chaotic world of changing markets and consumer lifestyles. Today's organization must be able to transform and renew to meet these changing forces.

This is a book about human resource management (also known as HRM). HRM is a management discipline aimed at improving organizational effectiveness by utilizing a firm's human resources. It is also about managing in a changing world. We have tried to make this the most "user-friendly" text available. *Human Resource Management: An Experiential Approach* offers a practical and realistic approach to the study of human resource management. Through the applications of a new procedure—the Success System Model—each of the functions is described from the standpoint of its relationship to the overall program of human resource management. This book is written primarily for students who are learning about human resource management for the first time. The text relates the student to the real world through the use of numerous illustrations and company examples, showing how human resource management is being applied in today's organizations.

HRM is an emerging behavioral science discipline that provides a set of methodologies for systematically bringing about high-performing organizations. The goals of HRM are to make an organization more effective and to enhance the opportunity for the individual to develop their potential. It is our view that these HRM goals can be accomplished best by using the experiential approach to learning.

This text differs from most HRM texts by providing both conceptual and experiential approaches to the study of HRM. A revolution is underway in how individuals use education to improve their performance. Our approach is to focus on the development of interpersonal skills. Students are provided with a conceptual framework necessary to understand the relevant issues in HRM. In addition, individuals will be actively participating in individual and team exercises that require the application of chapter content to specific organizational situations. This approach is aimed at developing those critical interpersonal skills needed to manage in a changing world.

This text is the first to directly relate student learning experiences in HRM with those skills judged by experts to be essential for potential HR managers. As noted in chapter 1, recent studies have been critical of recent business graduates for deficiencies in a number of areas, including communication skills, problem solving, decision-making ability, and leadership potential. This is the first approach to provide coverage of HRM topics while also developing student skills in a "learn-by-doing" context.

OBJECTIVES

The basic objective is to provide the student and practicing manager with an integrated and comprehensive view of the field of HRM. We hope to present, in a clear and organized manner, the newest approaches, concepts, and techniques of this discipline. We have attempted to include most of the current state-of-the-art HRM techniques of this discipline. The stages of the Success System Model are presented so as to provide a step-by-step description of the various techniques and problems involved in organization HRM efforts.

Our second objective is to present HRM from an experiential learning approach; that is, the student not only reads the concepts but also practices and experiments by doing and using these techniques in a simulated organizational situation.

There is much evidence to support the success of this approach. Our own experience and student evaluations support this. Students report an enhanced level of learning, greater course satisfaction, and rate the overall course learning higher than in more traditional courses.

The HRM concepts, techniques, and skills that make up this book were selected because of their usefulness to practitioners. To achieve this goal, we have integrated materials from a diverse set of approaches. Our strategy has been to try and integrate these various approaches to provide a comprehensive view of HRM.

Every successful HRM program is the result of a concerted group effort, and each failure is a failure for all organization members. Therefore, people—as agents of change, not forces or structures—determine whether the HR manager will manage change effectively. Because the HR practitioners' effectiveness results not only from the concepts learned but also from their managerial style and the way they influence others, our emphasis in this book is on the experiential approach to learning.

As students progress in the book, the simulations will allow them to continually utilize growing knowledge and experience, thereby building a foundation of management skills to carry forward into their managerial career. By analyzing successes and failures, students begin to develop the ability to learn from experience and to develop insights into organizational functioning that would normally take years to acquire.

METHODOLOGIES

This HRM text is designed to present the complex and fascinating world of managing people in a easy-to-grasp, user-friendly way. In addition to its comprehensive, innovative coverage, the text provides an HR practitioner a managerial approach to the field. It provides a rich depth of practical examples and applications, showing the major problems that managers face in their efforts to change organizations to meet a changing environment.

Each chapter presents an HRM skill application, a major example describing actual company situations, practical examples, a case, and a behavioral problem-solving simulation. Finally, this HRM text makes learning this discipline easy and enjoyable. Its writing style and level are well suited to the beginning HRM student.

The text sets forth incidents that reveal the drama of today's HR manager, such as how Apple Computer's culture focuses not just on products, but also on the hopes and dreams of its members; Walt Disney's legendary emphasis on making the customer happy; and Johnson & Johnson's attempt to change to an entrepreneurial culture.

The manager of the future will probably be acting as a people manager and will be involved in initiating, designing, or implementing organization-change programs. The material in the text will provide the manager with new methodologies and techniques for implementing HRM programs, as well as an opportunity for personal growth and development. The book is designed so that each one may assess their own behavior and begin setting some personal development goals. Also, opportunities are created for feedback on the effectiveness of one's behavioral style, which encourages greater effectiveness.

The text is designed so that the instructor may incorporate new methodologies into the learning situation, including simulations and cases. All of the experiential skill exercises in this text were designed to focus on critical personal skills in the HRM field.

The text is organized to present an overview of HRM concepts and theories and provides behavioral skill simulations for each major stage of an HRM program. This book may be used as an independent study guide for those wanting to learn more about organization change or as a comprehensive set of materials on how to initiate HR programs for the practicing HRM or operating manager.

FEATURES

This HRM text gives the student a comprehensive, innovative, and practical introduction to the field. Its style and extensive use of applications and exercises make the book straightforward, easy to read, and enjoyable.

The text contains 19 chapters to fit a one semester course and has been thoroughly edited to improve readability. Illustrations and figures add to the book's visual appeal. All tables, facts, figures, references, and dozens of current examples are provided within the text materials. Chapter objectives and a list of key terms are supplied for each chapter to enhance learning.

Human Resource Management: An Experiential Approach, Second Edition offers coverage on several important topics: organization renewal, changing the corporate culture, self-managed work teams, organization compensation, managing diversity, total quality management, and empowerment.

The text has many significant features that we have included to promote the readability and understanding of important human resource management concepts.

1. The Success System Model presents a visual, graphic display of the major stages relating all human resource management topics. We believe that the model (in each section) will serve as an excellent teaching device.
2. The approach is dynamic rather than static. Time is considered as a significant variable in changing organizations.
3. Case studies involving human resource management are provided at the end of each chapter to provide for discussion of the major topics.

4. HRM in Action examples are included in many chapters. These examples allow the student to become involved in situations that are occurring in the business world.

5. A comprehensive exercise called HRM Skills Simulation is provided for each chapter. These exercises provide for extensive class participation.

This book was designed to provide a variety of learning methods. The skill exercises are fun and involving, cases often make the concepts more understandable, and text readings provide a set of concepts to be applied and challenged. The book can be used as the primary text or as a supplemental text for college courses at the junior or senior level. We have successfully used the material with undergraduate students, as well as with students from many fields, including communications, public administration, engineering, administration, and health care. The material has also been used for management training and executive development programs in a variety of fields with bankers, engineers, nurses, teachers, public administrators, military officers, production managers, and marketing managers, and at a variety of levels from first-line supervision to top management teams.

TOPICS

Corporate culture, goal setting, organizational compensation, empowerment, and self-managed work teams are the subject of chapters. These chapters represent recent theory, research, and applications in literature.

Each case emphasizes a particular HRM issue or managerial technique. They cover a variety of different types and sizes of organizations and include problems at all levels of management.

The HRM in Action segments have been enthusiastically received by students and instructors. They report actual applications of concepts and theories presented in the chapter and appear at the exact point in the text where the concept or theory is being discussed. Many chapters in this second edition contain an HRM in Action application. Through the identification of actual organizational applications of text materials, the gap between the classroom and the real world can hopefully be narrowed.

We have also added an international emphasis by including Our Changing World of HRM sections to present the application HRM concepts in a global context.

In addition, we have included a number of self-report questionnaires for the reader to complete. These questionnaires allow students a close look at personal style, attitudes, and behavior patterns.

LEARNING AIDS

Many learning aids are provided within this book to help students learn about HRM. The main ones are:

• Chapter objectives. Each chapter presents objectives that prepare the student for the chapter material and point out learning goals.

• Figures and illustrations. Throughout each chapter, key concepts and applications are illustrated with strong, visual materials.

• HRM applications/highlights. Current examples of HRM practices and important information are highlighted in boxed exhibits throughout the text.

• HRM international applications/highlights. Current examples of HRM topics focusing upon global changes.

- Summaries. Each chapter ends with a summary that wraps up the main points and concepts.
- Review questions. Each chapter has a set of review questions covering the main chapter points.
- Key terms. Key terms are highlighted within each chapter, and a list of key terms is provided at the end of each chapter.
- HRM skills (exercises). These self-learning experiential exercises include both individual and team learning. The exercises take theories and principles covered in the text and bring them to life in team activities. This hands-on team interaction serves to generate feedback, lively discussion, the testing of personal ideas, and sharing of information.
- Case studies. Cases for class discussion, written assignment, or self study are provided throughout the text. The cases challenge students to apply HRM principles to real companies in real situations.
- Index. A subject index helps students quickly find information and examples in the book.

We are grateful to the many people who contributed to this edition. Special thanks go to Professor John Hulpke, University of Technology, Hong Kong, for Our Changing World sections, and to Dean Ron Eaves, California State University–Bakersfield, School of Business and Public Administration, for their support. Many students and managers have been involved in the development of the simulations and cases.

Special thanks go to Johanna Alexander of the California State University–Bakersfield, Walter E. Stiern Library for her splendid research efforts. It was a delight to work with one so knowledgeable and enthusiastic to help.

We would like to thank our typist, Carolyn Gomez, for her skill and dedication in meeting publication deadlines. Her accuracy and attention to detail is appreciated.

Our sincere appreciation is also extended to Natalie Anderson, Melissa Steffens, and Samantha Steel of Prentice Hall for their support and assistance.

The authors would like to thank the following reviewers

Carol Carnevale, Ithaca College

Wallace Duvall, Wayland Baptist University

Mark Wesolowski, Miami University

Roger Weikle, Winthrop University

Robert Figler, University of Akron

Vishwanath Baba, Concordia University

Philip Quaglieri, University of Massachusetts

Dennis Dosset, University of Missouri–St. Louis

Craig Tunwall, Ithaca College

Ann Cowden, California State University–Sacramento

David A. Gray, The University of Texas–Arlington

Tom Anastasi, Boston University

James C. Wimbush, Indiana University

Satish P. Deshpande, Western Michigan University

Don Harvey would like to thank his sons Scott and Dave who have contributed in more ways than he can enumerate—not just in allowing the time for writing but in a form of involvement that can never be fully appreciated or repaid.

Both authors have jointly contributed and reviewed the 19 chapters of this second edition. As a result of our special interests we have concentrated on certain chapters. R. B. chose chapters 2, 4, 5, 6, 7, 10, 11, 12, 13, and 14; D. H. chose Chapters 1, 3, 8, 9, 15, 16, 17, 18, and 19.

We would appreciate hearing your suggestions and comments for improving any future editions. Please contact R. B. at P.O. Box 235, Glenedon Beach, OR 97388 (April–October) or 78121 Labrook Drive, Palm Desert, CA 92211 (November–March). Please contact D. H. at California State University–Bakersfield, School of Business and Public Administration, Department of Management and Marketing, 9001 Stockdale Highway, Bakersfield, CA 93311-1099.

MEMO

To: *Our Readers*

From: *The Authors*

Subject: *Use of This "User-Friendly" Text*

Perhaps we can reflect on some of the things we tried to develop in this book to make your task easier. Because our major goal is to present knowledge (and yours, we hope, to acquire it), we thought it would be helpful to preview some of the learning tools so that you can use them as you progress. First, there is a set of behavioral objectives at the beginning of each chapter. These are general guides to the major points in each chapter and relate to the review questions provided at the end of each chapter.

In addition, throughout the text we have identified key terms and concepts for you to remember. There are HRM terms and concepts that you should be able to use as you complete each chapter. For motivation: Exams are often designed around these key concepts, so when a concept is introduced and defined, it will appear in boldface in the text. Also, at the end of each chapter, many key concepts will be listed with space for you to note the pages on which they are defined. In review, you can scan the text, define each concept for yourself, and—if you are unsure—move back into the text to clarify the meaning. Also, you can review the questions at the end of each chapter and then go back into the text for those you may have missed.

We hope these aids will be helpful to you.

R. B.
D. H.

Part I

The Success System: Anticipating Success

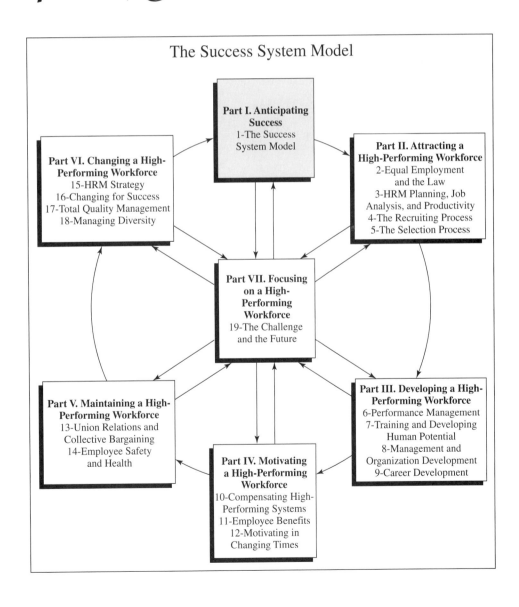

The Success System Model

Part I. Anticipating Success
1-The Success System Model

Part II. Attracting a High-Performing Workforce
2-Equal Employment and the Law
3-HRM Planning, Job Analysis, and Productivity
4-The Recruiting Process
5-The Selection Process

Part III. Developing a High-Performing Workforce
6-Performance Management
7-Training and Developing Human Potential
8-Management and Organization Development
9-Career Development

Part IV. Motivating a High-Performing Workforce
10-Compensating High-Performing Systems
11-Employee Benefits
12-Motivating in Changing Times

Part V. Maintaining a High-Performing Workforce
13-Union Relations and Collective Bargaining
14-Employee Safety and Health

Part VI. Changing a High-Performing Workforce
15-HRM Strategy
16-Changing for Success
17-Total Quality Management
18-Managing Diversity

Part VII. Focusing on a High-Performing Workforce
19-The Challenge and the Future

Chapter 1

Human Resource Management: The Success System Model

Objectives

Upon completing this chapter, you will be able to:

1. Define the concept of human resource management, identify the underlying approaches, and recognize the need for this emerging field.
2. Describe organization culture and understand its impact on the behavior of individuals in an organization.
3. Understand the expectations of the psychological contract formed on joining an organization.
4. Identify and describe the major HRM functions in the Success System Model.

Premeeting preparation

1. Read chapter 1.
2. Prepare for HRM Skills Simulation 1.1. Review steps.
3. Prepare for HRM Skills Simulation 1.2. Review steps.
4. Read Case 1.1: Precision Products, Inc. Answer questions.

THE WORKOUT: KEY TO ORGANIZATION AND HUMAN RESOURCE CHANGES AT GE?[1]

Croton-on-Hudson, New York

Just inside the entrance to the main building at General Electric Company's sprawling management development center is an amphitheater-like classroom known affectionately—and officially—as The Pit. Several times a month, GE Chairman John F. Welch Jr. comes to stand at the foot of The Pit and fields tough questions from GE managers taking courses at the center. Protected by the anonymity of numbers, the several dozen participants at the session pitch gripes and opinions at the chairman.

Welch, who gives as good as he gets, has long relished these sessions as a way to take the pulse of his huge company. Two years ago, he hit upon a way to put the format to a constructive use in rethinking GE.

Employee Input

Traveling back to GE's headquarters in Fairfield, Connecticut, aboard a company helicopter, Welch and James Baughman, GE's manager of corporate management development, were marvelling over the particularly pitched nature of that day's session with 150 GE managers in The Pit. "These people were pretty outspoken about 'Why can't we get the money to fix this?'" Welch recalled. "They were quite specific about their business—'Why aren't we doing this in our business?'"

Baughman said, "We seemed to have found a way to open them up and get them talking about the things that had been bugging them over the years, particularly about the slowness of the pace of our ability to make changes and move into new market areas."

Over the swirl of the helicopter rotors on the short trip, Welch and Baughman wondered "if we could only find a mechanism where [employees] could get in front of their leadership and not have retribution," Welch recalled. By the time the helicopter had touched down, the two men had dreamed up a unique program called "Workout."

Challenge to Employees

Welch is challenging GE's 300,000 employees to use Workout to fundamentally question the way the company conducts its business and implements change programs. GE employees are examining all sorts of company practices and programs with promises of no retribution and immediate feedback—and action—by management. GE is continually reinventing the organization.

People: Leading to Success

People: They are the lifeblood of every organization. Every day, managers like those at GE are confronting massive accelerating change. They must deal with a chaotic world of new competitors and constant innovation. Tom Peters, in *Thriving on Chaos*, suggests that "the time for 10 percent staff cuts and 20 percent quality improvement is past . . . the rate of change demanded . . . and the boldness of goals suggested will be unfailingly new—and frightening.[2]

Human resource decisions are critical to the economic success as well as the financial and psychological well-being of individual employees and organizations like GE. Recruiting, training, **compensation** (monetary reward), and employee relations are all major areas of human resource management (HRM). Although many human resource (HR) decisions are being made by HR managers, most are being made by operating-level managers. HR decisions are among the most difficult but important decisions that organizations make because they affect the organization's future and people's lives.

Because people are becoming such a critical factor, in the future the only winning organizations will be those that respond quickly to change and are able to manage their human resources effectively.[3] Preparing managers to cope with today's accelerating rate of change in the management of people is the central concern of this book. The modern manager must not only be flexible and adaptive in a changing environment, but must also be proactive in diagnosing human resource problems and implementing new programs.[4] The management of human resource activities will play a crucial role in the performance of organizations into the twenty-first century.

Using the Success System Model

The Success System Model presented in this book is aimed at accomplishing these goals in several ways. First, all managers must be human resource managers. For example, at organizations such as Hewlett-Packard, every manager is expected to set goals for the development and satisfaction of subordinates. Second, employees are viewed as resources, just like the plant and machinery. A high-performing workforce is what gives a company its competitive advantage. Third, HRM is a process of integrating the corporate goals with individual needs.

Organizations are never completely static. They are in continuous interaction with external forces (see Figure 1.1). Changing consumer lifestyles, emerging employee needs, and technological breakthroughs all act on the organization to cause it to change. The degree of change may vary from one organization to another, but all face the need for adaptation to external forces. Many of these changes are forced upon the organization by forces outside the organizations, such as fuel shortages and labor problems; others are generated internally. Because change is occurring so rapidly, there is a need for new ways to manage.

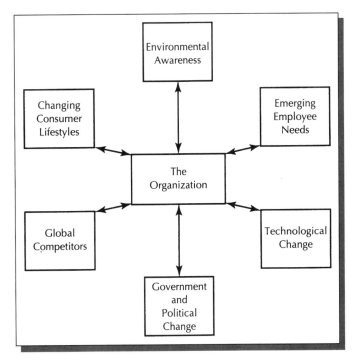

Figure 1.1
Forces of change upon the corporation

Human resource management (HRM) is the field involving the effective management of human resources as a key factor in helping organizations adapt to environmental changes. HRM is aimed not only at improving the organization's effectiveness, but also at enhancing the development of the organization's employees: its human resources.

This book introduces the practicing manager and the student to the concepts of human resource management and the Success System Model. The purpose is twofold: (1) to create an awareness of the changing environmental forces confronting the modern manager and (2) to provide a systematic approach for developing the knowledge and skills necessary for those with the goal of becoming a human resource management professional. Does this mean that this book is only for those planning to specialize in the HRM field? Not at all. Every manager at every level will be involved in the issues to be discussed.

Organizations are using HRM techniques to increase their effectiveness and adaptiveness to changing conditions. In this chapter, you will learn:

- The definition of HRM;

- Why HRM has emerged; and

- Some basic concepts about using the Success System Model in organizations.

You will be introduced to the experiential approach to learning and will be given an overview of the field of study.

WHAT IS HUMAN RESOURCE MANAGEMENT?

What makes one organization a winner whereas another fails to make use of the same opportunities? Management gurus Thomas J. Peters, in *Thriving on Chaos*, and Robert H. Waterman, in *The Renewal Factor*, confirm what has long been suspected: The key to survival and success lies not in the rational, quantitative approaches, but rather in a commitment to irrational, difficult-to-measure things like people, quality, customer service, and most importantly, developing the flexibility to meet changing conditions.[5] Richard E. Dutton, for example, examined the "high-tech—high touch" phenomenon at Citicorp and found that the crucial component in adapting to technological change was the human factor.[6] The true key to successful change is employee involvement and commitment.

In the process of human resource management, there is an increasing emphasis on the personal needs of the organization and its members. How effectively employees contribute to organization goals depends in a major sense upon the ability of its HR managers. The challenge is to develop an organization in which the individual can grow and develop. Such an environment may be termed a "healthy" organization, and this is what human resource management is all about: making organizations healthier and more effective. These HRM concepts apply to all types of organizations, including schools, churches, military, government, hospitals, and industrial concerns.

A DEFINITION OF HUMAN RESOURCE MANAGEMENT (HRM)

Human Resource Management (HRM) can be defined as the management of activities undertaken to attract, develop, motivate, and maintain a high-performing workforce within the organization.[7] HRM involves moving towards corporate excellence by integrating the desires of individuals for growth and development with organizational goals.

People design and produce the goods and services, maintain quality, market the goods or services, use financial resources, and develop strategies and objectives for the organization. Without an effective workforce, it would be impossible for an organization to achieve its objectives. The HR manager's role is to develop an effective relationship between the organization and its employees.

Human resource management efforts, then, are planned, systematic approaches to improving organizational performance. They involve HRM programs aimed at the total organization or to relatively large segments of it. The purpose of HRM programs is to increase the effectiveness of the system and also to develop the potential of all individual members. HRM also emphasizes that HR planning needs to be closely related to the organization's strategic goals and plans. Finally, there are a series of planned HRM activities which will ultimately influence the productivity of the organization. These human resource activities are described in succeeding chapters of this text.

THE SUCCESS SYSTEM MODEL (SSM)

Human resource management is an increasingly important element in organizations. Robert Reich suggests that in the future, the organization's ability to attract, develop, and retain a talented workforce will be a critical factor in developing a high-performance organization.[8]

An HRM program is a continuing process of long-term organizational improvement involving a series of functions or activities as shown in Figure 1.2. The Success System Model involves the application of the systems approach to the basic technical and human relationships in an organization. This model, based upon a series of interviews with key HRM professionals, emphasizes a systematic analysis of HRM activities and a top management which is committed to a high-performing organization.[9]

We present the Success System Model to show the process of developing an effective, high-performing workforce in an organization. Only by anticipating the future need for employees and developing specific human resource plans to obtain the appropriate number and type of employees can organizations meet the future with a reasonable expectation of success. This evolving Success System Model is based upon the current, state-of-the-art practices of HRM professionals.

An essential element of this model is developing a master **HRM strategy** and shared vision in order to provide a positive, future-oriented direction to all HRM activities. As noted in Figure 1.2, each of the HRM functions has an influence on the others. The success of the recruiting and selection process, for example, will determine the type and level of people that the organization will hire, which will in turn impact the type and amount of training and development activities required, the kinds of incentive systems needed, and so forth.

Part One: The Success System: Anticipating Success

The first stage in developing an effective HRM system involves anticipating future changes, identifying new trends, and developing new programs to meet changing conditions. The failure of current management to anticipate and cope with change is one of the major causes of low productivity in American industry.

Part Two: Attracting a High-Performing Workforce

The second stage focuses on the HRM activities of ensuring that the organization is able to staff its workforce with the necessary quality and quantity of skilled personnel.[10] People are the engine that drive the organization. In this section, we

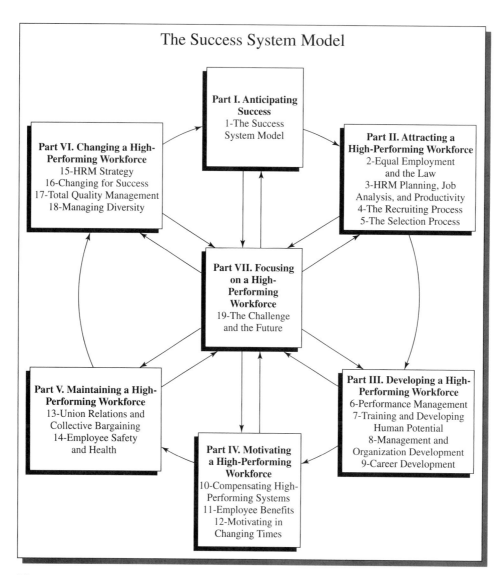

The Success System Model

Part I. Anticipating Success
1-The Success System Model

Part II. Attracting a High-Performing Workforce
2-Equal Employment and the Law
3-HRM Planning, Job Analysis, and Productivity
4-The Recruiting Process
5-The Selection Process

Part VI. Changing a High-Performing Workforce
15-HRM Strategy
16-Changing for Success
17-Total Quality Management
18-Managing Diversity

Part VII. Focusing on a High-Performing Workforce
19-The Challenge and the Future

Part III. Developing a High-Performing Workforce
6-Performance Management
7-Training and Developing Human Potential
8-Management and Organization Development
9-Career Development

Part V. Maintaining a High-Performing Workforce
13-Union Relations and Collective Bargaining
14-Employee Safety and Health

Part IV. Motivating a High-Performing Workforce
10-Compensating High-Performing Systems
11-Employee Benefits
12-Motivating in Changing Times

Figure 1.2
The success system model

present the staffing, recruiting and selection functions, beginning with the legal issues of hiring: Equal Employment Opportunity (EEO). At Walt Disney World, instilling the Disney vision and philosophy into new recruits is an important and continuous process.

Part Three: Developing a High-Performing Workforce

Once an organization has recruited a quality workforce, it must then continue to develop this resource to achieve a high level of performance. This includes performance management, or the training and development of its employees and managers. Many large companies budget thousands of dollars annually for training and development. Motorola and IBM, for example, spend some $2 billion annually on training and development.[11] **Training** includes the orientation of new employees, training of employees in job performance, and retraining as job needs change.

Part Four: Motivating a High-Performing Workforce

One key element in developing a high-performing system is an understanding of the motivational forces leading to productivity. HRM develops the organization's pay system relative to its competition, determines proper pay differences among employees, and determines whether raises should be based on individual, team, or organization performance measures.

Labor costs are a substantial part of the operating costs of an organization. These costs are a function of the number of employees, their wages and benefits, plus the costs of training, recruiting, and providing services. In the past, managers focused on pay scales and the number of employees as crucial cost control factors. Increasingly, HRM is moving to focus on total labor costs and the relationship between pay and productivity. Effective managers realize that the Success System Model approach to HRM yields Total Quality Management results.

Here we examine approaches to motivation that can lead to increased productivity including rewards, compensation, incentives, benefits, and various employee involvement programs. At Levi Strauss and Company, for example, all 37,000 employees are involved in a profit-sharing plan.

Part Five: Maintaining a High-Performing Workforce

The HR manager must maintain effective employee management relations with open communications. **Labor relations** activities are important because they affect employees, managers, and the performance of many HRM activities. Labor relations take on added complexity when workers are represented by unions. Contact between a union and an employer occurs at several levels. At the formal organizational level, the union is the agent representing a group of employees in an organization. A labor contract must be negotiated through union-organization discussion and collective bargaining—a negotiating process in which behavioral considerations play a vital role. General Motors must deal with the United Auto Workers' union in trying to increase their productivity per each autoworker.

Part Six: Changing a High-Performing Workforce

In a changing environment, HRM provides an approach to developing new strategies, changing the organization culture, and managing an increasingly diverse workforce.

The global marketplace often requires shifts in organizational strategy, which necessitates changes to structure, culture, and managerial processes.[12] Every organization must continuously update its workforce skills, costs, and productivity on a global basis. HRM plays an important role in managing these changes. Changing the corporate culture starts with developing a shared vision, the empowerment of employees, and the development of a trust relationship within the workforce. Microsoft, for example, is constantly developing innovative ways of managing teams of talented people.

In the future, HRM will be involved in managing a more diverse workforce, which will require changing attitudes, values, and procedures. During the next decade, significant numbers of women and minorities will be moving into previously white, male-dominated jobs. Developing a high-performing workforce from this diversity will be an emerging challenge for HRM. Strategic change has become increasingly important and often influences the survival of the organization in a volatile environment.

Information, communications, and research systems are also vital to the coordination of HRM activities. The development and use of computerized human resource information systems are necessary for HRM departments to do better recordkeeping and HRM research. Creating and maintaining HRM databases and systems are critical aspects of the new strategic role of HR management.[13] This may seem obvious, especially if you are thinking about large organizations. However, computers may be just as essential to manage human resources in the small business also. When one manager wears many hats, the computer can be the manager's best friend.

Part Seven: Focusing on a High-Performing Workforce

Measuring HR effectiveness is done by evaluating how well HR activities are being performed in an organization. Various means can be used, ranging from attitude surveys to formal HR audits. HR managers must be able to work directly with line managers in creating a competitive advantage through people.

The HR manager must be able to take a proactive role in changing the organization to meet a new set of conditions. Increasingly, HR managers need to be involved in strategic planning and in anticipating trends that may require changes in HRM programs or policies.[14]

Human Resource Management as a Career Field

Effective management of human resource activities requires a professional approach. As these activities become more involved, the level of education and expertise required of individuals who enter the HRM field will also increase. In the 1990s, there were over 450,000 people in the HRM field in the United States, a number that is growing by about 5 percent per year.[15] This number, however, does not completely represent the changing forces in this field. As we said before and will say again, it is not just the **HR specialists** who manage human resources. Every manager who supervises at least one person should know the human resources Success System Model. Most businesses are small businesses without the luxury of HR specialists. But even in the smallest organization, HRM is a critical skill.

In larger businesses, agencies, and organizations (even though every manager has HR responsibilities), an HRM specialist facilitates this effort. This person providing HR expertise is usually given the position of Vice President of human resources, or some similar position. A survey of corporate executives found that most HR managers report directly to the CEO, and almost half (43 percent) were given the title of vice president.[16]

As previously noted, these HR managers in the twenty-first century should be professionals in terms of skills and performance. Today a number of organizations represent HRM; the largest (over 50,000 members) is the Society for Human Resource Management (SHRM). SHRM also offers professional certification for meeting the following:

1. *Professional in Human Resources (PHR)*—Four years professional HR experience or 2 years and a related bachelors degree, or 1 year of experience and a related graduate degree.
2. *Senior Professional in Human Resources (SPHR)*—Eight years professional HR experience or 6 years and a related bachelors degree, or 5 years experience and a related graduate degree.

To meet these requirements, an applicant must provide verification of work experience in the HR field and pass an intensive 4-hour written examination to demonstrate a mastery of basic HR knowledge.

WHY HUMAN RESOURCE MANAGEMENT?

Why is HRM so important? Organizations are designed to accomplish some purpose or function and to continue doing so for as long as possible. Because of this, organizations are not necessarily intended to change. Only recently have companies begun looking to the HRM function as a means to attaining their bottom line goals.

Competitive changes are affecting all types of organizations, from giants like IBM to the smallest business. No one can escape change, which is why managers must be skilled in human resource management techniques. As M.I.T. professor Richard Beckhard notes, "Corporations are so hard up for answers these days that I'd say there's a $3 billion or $4 billion market for transformational (HRM) consulting out there." There are a number of reasons why HRM is becoming more important:

- *Changing Employee Needs.* Employees are demanding that organizations become more responsive to their personal needs by developing such programs as flextime work schedules, parental leave, child care, sabbaticals, elderly-care assistance, and job sharing. The human resource manager is responsible for developing and implementing policies designed to reduce possible conflicts between organizational demands and family responsibilities. They must also be aware of the effect that "downsizing" and "restructuring" have on the loyalty of employees.

- *Increased Complexity.* Management in the twenty-first century is becoming increasingly complex for many reasons. These include emerging foreign competition, changing technology, expanding scientific innovation, and an accelerating rate of change. As a result, organizations need human resource managers to be involved in making strategic decisions and in developing the distinctive competencies of the organization's human resources. Top executives depend upon the expertise of human resource management in recruitment, productivity, performance evaluation, quality, compensation, and other human resource activities.

- *Increasing Legal Complexity.* The enactment of new state and federal laws is contributing to the importance of human resource managers. The added reporting requirements of these new laws are so extensive that compliance requires increasing human resource expertise. The activities most influenced by governmental legislation include equal employment, compensation, safety, and labor relations. If an organization fails to comply with these laws, it runs the risk of costly legal actions and possibly severe financial penalties.

- *Developing Human Resource Policies.* Human resource policies are designed to create consistency and equity within an organization. These policies are particularly important in hiring, compensation, promotion, and termination decisions. At Walt Disney, for example, all employees go through an initial orientation program, "Traditions I." Given that everyone starts with a common base, it should not be surprising that a majority of promotions come from within. [17] Compensation guidelines need to be made within the human resources framework, so that the salary structure is completely fair and equitable. Promotion procedures also need to be developed and coordinated by human resource managers to ensure equity throughout the organization. In the twenty-first century, with organizations increasing in size and complexity and with new laws prescribing even greater equality in the rights of employees, the human resource manager's role in developing and implementing changing policies will become increasingly important.

- *Human Resource Information Systems.* In the high-tech world of the future, more human resource activities will be requiring specialized expertise. As an example, many organizations are developing computerized expert systems for making employee-selection decisions. These systems integrate interview data, test scores, and application-blank information. Similarly, many organizations are developing compensation systems with elaborate cafeteria-style benefit packages (explained in detail later, see chapter 11) to replace simple hourly pay or piece-rate incentive systems. Many organizations are also developing sophisticated databases to centralize all human resource information to provide real time information for strategic manpower planning and other reporting activities.

- *Human Resource Cost-Effectiveness.* Human resource activities have become increasingly important because of the high investment in human resources and the costs associated with employee problems. The largest single cost in most organizations is labor. Labor costs are often too high as a result of problems involving absenteeism, tardiness, turnover, slowdowns, sabotage, or drug dependencies. Having the right person in the wrong job also means unnecessary costs. Good HRM is good management.

- *Other HRM Trends.* Other HRM trends include changing the corporate culture, helping employees become more adaptive to change, increasing organizational competitiveness and productivity, achieving Total Quality Management, and employee involvement. At IBM, for example, changing conditions are forcing

---

HRM IN ACTION
BIG CHANGES AT BIG BLUE[18]

IBM, once America's premier growth company, is now talking mostly about downsizing and layoffs. To come to grips with a changing marketplace and years of lackluster performance, by the 1990s it became common for IBM to announce staff cuts of 10,000, 20,000, and even 25,000 employees.

Many industry analysts feel that IBM has been slow to react to changes in the computer industry. IBM was dogged by a series of manufacturing problems and product delays, and its results were devastated by a huge charge resulting from the company's decision to consolidate operations and pare its workforce.

New CEO Lou Gerstner said that the new measures should lead IBM to substantial improvement, but that if costs had to be cut further, he would cut them. He also emphasized the prospects for growth, mainly overseas, but also in the United States where IBM's business has been in the doldrums for years.

INDUSTRY CHANGES

The moves by CEO Lou Gerstner to cut costs and consolidate operations illustrate how quickly the industry that IBM once owned is changing. Mainframes used to be a simple business; IBM had 80 to 90 percent of the business locked up. But technology began changing so fast that IBM decided it had to start selling hardware lest its rental equipment become obsolete overnight. Now IBM must grind out $60 billion in sales every year just to maintain its current size. Consequently, changes will need to be made in both HRM policies and programs.

TOUGHER COMPETITION—WAVING A SAMURAI SWORD

Over the past few years, as other makers of IBM-compatible mainframes have gained credibility and cut prices, IBM's response has been to get tough. When that didn't work, they got even tougher.

One survey found that nearly a third of IBM customers are getting discounts on their mainframes. One large customer says he found he could get a better price just by taking a large Japanese Samurai sword off the wall, waving it over his head, and yelling the name of a Japanese computer company.

Amdahl, one of IBM's biggest competitors, uses what it terms the "million dollar coffee mug;" they tell customers to just leave an Amdahl coffee mug on their desk when an IBM salesman comes calling and they will get $1 million knocked off the IBM price.

However, for all the changes CEO Lou Gerstner is trying to initiate and despite price discounts, IBM is losing market share.

THE BIG BLUE CORPORATE CULTURE

Top management's central challenge may be to transform and renew one of America's most deliberate, slow-moving management structures into a lean, aggressive, market-driven team. Among the challenges are the following.

Increasing the Rate of Technological Innovation

In a high-tech market, IBM is almost absent from two of the industry's hottest segments. IBM was late entering the laptop and notebook computer market, even though that $2 billion segment is growing at 40 percent per year. Similarly, in engineering workstations, a $4.3 billion market that is growing at 30 percent a year, IBM has only a 2 percent market share. Even with its new workstations, it may take years for IBM to catch up with market leaders such as Sun Microsystems, Hewlett-Packard, and Digital Equipment. This means HRM needs to recruit and develop the technical expertise IBM needs to regain its leadership role.

Faster Decisions

IBM is still missing out on some product development opportunities, and needs to cut the time required to get a product to the personal computer and workstation markets, where it has had some well-publicized problems. In fact, in the two fastest growing desktop markets—laptops and workstations—IBM has almost no presence. IBM researchers spend months analyzing and defining the market; product plans must fit with other operations, and that often slows product development projects. One manager notes, "it takes you ten months to figure out what you want to do, and if you go through six changes of direction, you can expect a 34-month development process." IBM has improved this decision process with a new internal slogan of "just say yes," so that IBM can offer price quotes in hours instead of days or weeks. HRM can provide training in leadership, communication, and problem-solving skills to develop faster decision making.

SUMMARY

In summary, top management is faced with changing IBM's human resources to meet new competitive forces. Many analysts feel that current changes have not increased IBM's competitiveness in the marketplace: That they should also be talking new products, not only accounting changes. So far, IBM has not demonstrated the ability to manage **organization renewal** and streamline its business fast enough to keep up with tougher competition.

QUESTIONS

1. Do you agree that IBM needs to make changes? What kind?

2. Can human resource management programs be appropriate here?

3. What human resource changes would you recommend?

the firm to become more effective in order to remain competitive. (See HRM in Action.) In the coming decades, changes in the external environment will be occurring so rapidly that organizations will need HRM techniques just to keep pace with the accelerated rate of innovation.

While many organizations have been able to keep pace with changes in information technology, few firms have been able to adapt to changing social and cultural conditions. In a dynamic environment, change is unavoidable. The pace of change has become so rapid today that it is difficult to adjust or compensate for one change before another is necessary. The technological, social, and economic environment is rapidly changing, and an organization will be able to survive only if its employees can effectively respond to these changing demands. As we move into the twenty-first century, increases in productivity of 500 percent, not 10 percent, will be required for corporations to compete effectively.[19]

Robin Burns, for example, abandoned Calvin Klein Cosmetics—where she helped develop the fragrance "Obsession,"—to become president and CEO of Estee Lauder, USA, a top competitor.[20] Ms. Burns' new job is to plan strategy for her new company's growth into the twenty-first century. She left Calvin Klein for a new, more challenging position. In this case, Calvin Klein lost a valuable manager because top management failed to perceive the need to allow individuals to fulfill personal objectives as well as attaining company goals. The loss of key managers is one HRM issue that can greatly affect the performance of an organization and alter its ability to attract and develop new effective human resources leadership.

Many management theorists suggest that for a firm to be successful in the twenty-first century, changes will be required, as shown in Figure 1.3. They suggest that predictability is a thing of the past and that the shape of tomorrow's winning organization is becoming increasingly clear, based upon quality, innovation, and flexibility.[21] Former baseball great Yogi Berra, echoing this sentiment, reportedly once said, "The future ain't what it used to be."

These successful firms will share common traits, including:

- *Action-Oriented:* Faster—more responsive to innovation and change. Today's HRM emphasizes solving organizational problems to facilitate employee satisfaction and high-performance.

- *Individual-Oriented:* A total commitment to treat each employee as an individual and offer services and programs to improve each individual's job satisfaction and morale.

- *Employee Involvement-Oriented:* Adding value through human resources. The most important task of HRM is to elicit peak performance from the organization's employees. People need to have a stake in their work.

- *Globally Oriented:* Creating professionally managed organizations around the world that treat people equitably and fairly, with respect and sensitivity to cultural differences. (See Our Changing World of HRM.)

- *Quality-Oriented:* Consistently geared towards complete customer satisfaction through a comprehensive program, ensuring that every job is done right the first time. Total Quality Management, or TQM, is discussed later in this text.

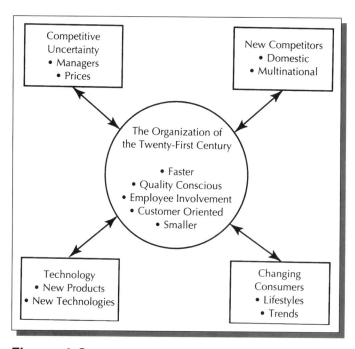

Figure 1.3
The changing organization of the twenty-first century

In the 1940s, it was Lionel or American Flyer model trains under the American Christmas tree, or maybe a Schwinn bicycle. By the 1960s, Barbie dolls and Playskool toys found their way under the tree on Christmas Eve. Luke Skywalker action figures, Holly Hobby dolls, and a host of other goodies helped make toys an important American industry. But in the twenty-first century, will any Americans at all work in this $14 billion industry? The answers have something to do with public policy, but they also depend on how well human resource managers, here and in the rest of the world, do their jobs.

Fisher Price moved much of its toy making to Tijuana, Mexico, in 1973. Now Barbie dolls, Swamp Things, Disney stuffed toys, and even miniature John Deere tractors come off the Tijuana assembly lines for companies such as Mattel, Hasbro, Kenner, and Erdl.

Mexico, however big it may seem compared to the toy-making business in the United States, is still puny by global standards.

Mexico "produces only about 15 percent of the toys," said Jody Levine, a spokeswoman for the Toy Manufacturers of America. "About a third are manufactured in China, and a third in other Asian countries."

Toys are, of course, just one industry. Fourteen billion dollars may seem like quite a bit, but compared to a national gross domestic product of somewhere around 5 or 6 trillion dollars, it doesn't amount to much. But are toys the only industry affected by growing globalization? It is the contention of this book that *every* industry is impacted by gut-wrenching, massive change. This change almost always is related to changing world economic patterns. Will the pattern of change lessen? Will a period of stability return, so managers can plan on tomorrow being more or less like today? It just won't happen. The pace of change will pick up, and HR managers had better be ready for a tomorrow radically different from today. The one constant will be change. That is why the Success System Model is essential. No one part of the program is enough. Learn it all, or be cut out of the action in a dynamic future. It's a changing world.

QUESTIONS

1. How are industries other than toys affected by globalization? Name some specific industries and indicate their problems.

2. What will be the impact upon human resource management departments as globalization continues to grow? Will HRM be the "hot seat"?

HRM AND TOTAL QUALITY MANAGEMENT

Total Quality Management (TQM) is a top management philosophy that emphasizes the continuous improvement of the processes which result in goods or services. Its ultimate goal is customer satisfaction. Instead of being content with the status quo, employees at all levels continually seek alternative methods or technologies that will improve existing processes. TQM provides a strategy for reducing the causes of poor quality and thereby increasing productivity.

TQM originated with the pioneering work of Walter A. Shewart, who acted as a mentor to W. Edwards Deming. Deming applied Shewart's principles of statistical process control in Japan following World War II. As a result, the Japanese were able to improve quality and productivity, capture world market share, add jobs, and improve the standard of living in their country.

Because TQM is related to organizational and individual change, HRM is increasingly becoming involved in this area. The TQM approach focuses on continuously improving process quality over the long run. In the short run, once each of the linked processes within a firm is operating at or above a desired level of quality, reliance on costly inspection practices can be reduced or eliminated altogether. Attention can then be turned to monitoring the overall process to determine the sources of variation still present. If these sources are also eliminated, then the process can be more precise and fewer defects or errors will be produced. In the view of the ultimate customer, quality will have exceeded the expected level. The customer will be more satisfied and will probably continue to buy the firm's products.

Today's HR managers exist in shifting organizational structures and can be the central force in initiating change and establishing the means for adaptation. Most organizations strive to be creative, efficient, and highly competitive, maintaining a leading edge in their respective fields rather than following trends set by others. Effective managers are vital to the continuing self-renewal and ultimate survival of the organization.

The HR manager must recognize when changes are occurring in the external environment and possess the necessary competence to bring about a more responsive workforce when it is needed. The manager must also be aware of the internal system and recognize that the major element in a flexible workforce is the **organization culture:** the feelings, norms, and behavior of its members.

The human resource manager knows that an effective culture will have bottom-line impact. A recent study by Charles O'Reilly, Jennifer Chatman, and David Caldwell reported that job commitment, job satisfaction, and employee turnover are greatly affected by the fit between the individual's values and the organizational culture.[23]

STAGE ONE: ANTICIPATING CHANGE: THE ORGANIZATION CULTURE

One important element of an organization's human resource system in adapting to change is the organization culture. The term **culture** refers to a specific civilization, society, or group that shares distinguishing characteristics. As B. F. Skinner has commented: "A culture is not the behavior of the people 'living in it'; it is the 'it' in which they live—contingencies of social reinforcement which generate and sustain their behavior."[24]

The organization culture may be defined as a system of shared meaning, including the language, dress, patterns of behavior, value system, feelings, attitudes, interactions, and group norms of the members. Examine the patterns of behavior on your campus or in your company. How do people dress or wear their hair? What jargon or unique terms are used? (See B.C. cartoon.) These are the elements that make up a culture: the accepted patterns of behavior.[25]

One example is the culture at Federal Express, carefully crafted by Fred Smith, the chairman, to reflect a combat situation. Flights are called "missions" and competitors are "enemies." Fred Smith, a Vietnam veteran, gives a Bravo Zulu award (Navy jargon meaning "job well done"), and his managers are sometimes called "Ho Chi Minh's Guerrillas."[26] This provides a set of values and behavioral norms for the organization.

Norms are the organized and shared ideas regarding what members should do and feel, how this behavior should be regulated, and what sanctions should be applied when behavior does not coincide with social expectations. The values and behaviors of each organization are also unique, as shown by Oliver Stone's movie *Wall Street*, which examines the cultural norms of investment banking firms, or John Sculley's book *Odyssey*, a description of the high-tech computer industry culture. Some patterns of behavior may be functional and may facilitate the accomplishment of organization goals. Other patterns of behavior or cultural norms may actually inhibit or restrict the accomplishment of organization goals. Several studies have found that the fit between individual preferences and the organization culture affected commitment, job satisfaction, and turnover.[27]

Source: B.C. by permission of Johnny Hart and Creators Syndicate, Inc.

It is helpful to look at the types of norms that exist in an organization to gain a better understanding of the culture of that organization. Norms generally are enforced only for behaviors that are viewed as most important by most group members.[28] Norms essential to accomplishing the organization's objectives are called **pivotal norms.** Norms that support and contribute to the pivotal norms but are not essential to the organization's objects are called **peripheral norms;** for example, norms requiring a student to conform to a certain dress code are peripheral. Pivotal and peripheral norms constantly confront an individual in an organization, and he or she must decide whether or not to conform. The pressure to conform to these norms varies, allowing individuals some degree of freedom in responding to these organizational pressures depending on how they perceive the rewards or punishments. The organization also has latitude in the degree of conformity it requires of its members. One method to ensure organizational commitment is through training programs that fulfill trainee's expectations and desires.

THE SOCIALIZATION PROCESS

Even though an organization does an effective job of recruiting, new employees must still adjust to the organizational culture. Because they are not aware of the culture, new employees are likely to disagree with or question the customs and values that exist. **Socialization** may be defined as the process that adapts employees to the organization's culture.[29] (See Figure 1.4.)

To function effectively, a manager or a member must be aware of the norms within the organization. He or she must recognize how sharply norms are defined and how strongly they are enforced. The individual's initial entry into any new situation often results in some degree of anxiety or stress. The more closely an individual can relate the new situation to previous situations, the less anxiety will be felt. The less the individual can relate a situation to other situations, the greater the feelings are of anxiety and discomfort.

One example of organizational norms can be seen at Bain and Company. Like many other companies, the cultural atmosphere at Bain & Co. (a Boston consulting firm) reflects many of the values of its founder, Bill Bain. For example, desks are kept clear. Any paper left on desks overnight is shredded. Partners have offices, but other employees work in open areas designed to increase team morale. The company tries to hire only the "best and brightest" young MBAs and expects them to dress in the company uniform, the so-called "power suit"—dark suit, handmade shirt, and bright but conservative tie—or its female equivalent.[30]

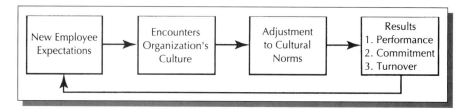

Figure 1.4
The socialization process

While the individual is experiencing a new situation, the organization may be attempting to influence the person. If a new member comes to an organization expecting to find a certain set of norms, he or she is looking for those expectations to be affirmed. If these expectations reflect the actual norms of that organization, then the transition is relatively painless. Although overall work satisfaction and organizational commitment are related, it appears overall work satisfaction has a stronger effect upon organizational commitment than organizational commitment has upon overall work satisfaction.

The new member often finds that the norms are unclear, confusing, and restrictive. As a result, he or she may react in several different ways when entering an organization. (See Figure 1.5.) At one extreme, the new member may choose to conform to all the norms of the organization, resulting in uniformity of behavior and complete acceptance of organization values. In an organization, this conformity may result in stagnation, nonresponsiveness, and a loss of creativeness. At the other extreme, the new member may choose to rebel, to reject all values, or to leave the organization altogether.

Another less obvious alternative is for the new members to accept the pivotal norms and seriously question the peripheral norms, which Schein has termed **creative individualism.** This would be the ideal behavior for a healthy and effective organization, but it is often difficult for a newcomer to correctly determine which norms are peripheral and which are pivotal. What may be a pivotal norm in one department may be peripheral or not a norm at all in another department of the same organization. Since norms are changing and dynamic, it requires an awareness on the part of the organization member to discern the differences between pivotal and peripheral norms.

Only the more healthy organizations allow their members to challenge the norms. The aim of HRM is to develop an organization climate that is appropriate to its mission and its members. In a sense, HRM involves changing the culture of organizations and work groups so that a more effective means of interacting, relating, and problem solving will result. HRM is involved in developing an organization to the point that it feels comfortable in allowing its members to openly examine the norms, both pivotal and peripheral, with the ultimate goal of building a more effective organization. The reaction of the individual to these norms results in the formation of an unwritten agreement with the organization.

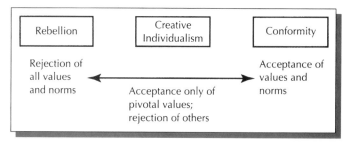

Figure 1.5
Basic responses to socialization

Part I   The Success System: Anticipating Success

THE PSYCHOLOGICAL CONTRACT

Psychological contract may be defined as an unwritten agreement between individuals and the organization of which they are members.[31] It describes certain expectations that the organization has of the individual and the individual's expectations of the organization. Because the two parties are growing and changing, the contract must be open-ended, so that old issues and new issues may be renegotiated.

An organization has certain expectations of its members. If it is a business organization, certain expectations of member behavior will probably be spelled out very clearly. It undoubtedly expects its members to be on the job during certain hours of the day. It is probably concerned with quality and quantity of work, loyalty, appearance, and various other things unique to the organization. For the organization to be satisfied, the individual will need to comply to some degree with the expectations. In other words, the organization has certain requirements, and the individual must do certain things to meet those requirements if there is to be a lasting and healthy relationship. In many instances, these unfulfilled expectations result in high turnover, absenteeism, sabotage, and worker alienation.[32]

Similarly, the individual has certain expectations of the organization. An individual may expect to gain work experience, security, and advancement. The individual probably expects to have an opportunity to meet people, make friends, and form social relationships and undoubtedly expects remuneration from the organization. For the individual to be satisfied and stay, the organization will have to meet the individual's expectations. It has been found that employee familiarity with their jobs, coworkers, and work environment has a positive effect, with lower familiarity resulting in lower productivity.

When either the organization's or individual's expectations are not being satisfied adequately by the other party, friction and difficulties may develop. If these problems cannot be solved, they may culminate in the individual leaving the organization by either his or her or the organization's choice. All too often, the problem is solved by not solving it; it takes too much effort to reach a real solution, so both parties just continue with a tenuous and unharmonious relationship. Employees in autonomous work groups have more favorable work attitudes than nonautonomous groups plus less absenteeism and turnover.

In some psychological contracts between the organization and the individual, key expectations may not even be addressed. One or both of these parties may assume that the other party agrees to some unstated expectations. The phrase "it is intuitively obvious to the most casual observer" may be the underlying assumption of one or both parties. Such unstated or assumed expectations can lead to an organization staffed by individuals who feel cheated or managers who feel disappointed in their subordinates. To avoid such misunderstandings, it is suggested that both parties—the employees and the managers—form a psychological contract that is continually being renegotiated.

AN OVERVIEW OF THE FIELD OF STUDY

In this book, we present the field of human resource management—both theory and practice. The material has been selected to provide you with most of what is known at this time about the HRM field: the current state of the art. This includes issues, critiques, and controversies as well, for the knowledge of HRM is itself evolving and being questioned.

The book is intended to assist the participant, the manager, and the practitioner in understanding the strategies and techniques of HRM, and moves from the more basic elements to the more complex. The topic contents coverage is shown in Figure 1.3 (shown earlier in this chapter), which also identifies the chapters within which each topic area is discussed. The arrows and feedback loops show the notion of interrelationship among the various sections.

Part I: The Success System: Anticipating Success presents an overview of the field of HRM, the definition of HRM, why it is important, and the Success System Model as framework for learning HRM.

Part II: The Success System: Attracting a High-Performing Workforce introduces the concepts of recruitment, selection, and staffing the organization. This includes the basic techniques of recruiting and selection, the importance of good recruiting, and an overview of the basic recruiting process as a framework for building an effective workforce.

Part III: The Success System: Developing a High-Performing Workforce presents the training and development of human resources including management, career and organization development, and performance management.

Part IV: The Success System: Motivating a High-Performing Workforce examines the motivational systems and processes of the HRM practitioner. This includes the nature and role of the compensation and benefit systems.

Part V: The Success System: Maintaining a High-Performing Workforce covers in considerable detail the HRM employee management relations techniques and their application in HRM programs, including the Success System Model, areas concerning unions, labor relations, collective bargaining, and employee safety and health.

Part VI: The Success System: Changing a High-Performing Workforce presents several newer HRM approaches including changing corporate culture, strategic HRM planning, Total Quality Management, and managing diversity.

Part VII: The Success System: Focusing on a High-Performing Workforce examines future challenges and trends in the HRM process.

We hope you find this approach interesting, and that it answers some significant questions about HRM and raises additional questions regarding this dynamic field. Basically, this is an opportunity for you to improve your human resource management skills, gain an overall grasp of HRM, and learn to make better predictions about the implications and consequences of any future HRM activities that you may undertake or be involved in.

SUMMARY

Human resource management is an important subject. It is important because human resources are the critical element to the organization. People make decisions, determine objectives, and produce and sell the products, goods, or services.

The Success System Model provides a framework for combining theoretical and practical knowledge with the experiential approach. In this model, the key elements in human resource decisions influence the organization's ability to achieve its objectives. These objectives include organizational efficiency and productivity.

Today, organizations operate in a dynamic and changing environment and consequently must be adaptive. You have been introduced to the emerging field of human resource management and the ways it is used to improve organizational effectiveness.

HRM refers to the management of activities involving the human resources of an organization. HRM represents new techniques and approaches to performing the old personnel functions. In the future, a proactive role for HR managers will become increasingly important as they will be more involved in strategic planning and changing the corporate culture. The major HRM functions have been described in the Success System Model including recruiting, developing, rewarding and maintaining an effective workforce.

You, as a **human resource manager,** must be sensitive to changes in markets, people, and competition and be aware of the need for an adaptive and flexible organization. You have had an opportunity to experience the need for human resource skills in this class meeting. Students frequently complain about the lack of effectiveness and learning in the classroom. In HRM, we call this the awareness of a human resource problem. The university environment is changing, and today's student is not the same as the student who attended a university 10 or 20 years ago. Today's students' backgrounds, their motivation, and their expectations are different, but they face basically the same learning environment that students experienced 20 years ago.

Entering a class for the first time is very similar to the first day on the job. You may decide to rebel and reject the classroom norms, you may conform by accepting classroom norms, or you may respond with creative individualism.

In this class, your role will be active. You will be an active participant, and your degree of learning and that of your fellow class members depends to a large degree upon your involvement and contributions. In this session, you have become aware of the potential within other individuals and within yourself, and of the factors of organization culture and norms. We create and maintain the culture and norms, and we can change them. Frequently, organizations must change these attitudes, values, beliefs, and behaviors if they are to become more effective.

In the classroom, students often feel that a course is boring, dull, and unsatisfying. Instructors often feel similarly—that students are lazy, apathetic, and immature. It is often easier to sit back passively and complain rather than attempt to change the situation. Students become accustomed to placing full responsibility for learning upon the instructor. When they are confronted with an opportunity to express expectations and to participate in setting learning goals, students may become confused, suspicious, or frustrated. Yet both students and instructor share objectives and responsibility for the learning environment.

By using the Success System Model, you will examine the organization culture and the norms. In the HRM Skills, you will experience the formation of a psychological contract. As a result of the contract formation process, many underlying expectations will be brought out into the open and explained, and the interdependence and shared responsibility of student and instructor will be demonstrated.

Human resource management is the discipline that applies a behavioral approach to management problems. Since the essential task of management is to deal with change, it is the purpose of this book to better prepare students and future human resource managers for this task. We have found that this can best be accomplished by using the **experiential approach**—an approach that differs significantly from the traditional lecture-exam approach. We think you will enjoy it.

REVIEW QUESTIONS

1. How would you define "human resource management"?
2. Present examples of how HRM activities are used in organizations you have worked for.
3. Identify and demonstrate the uses of the psychological contract.
4. Contrast the difference between pivotal and peripheral norms.
5. Discuss and explain the basic HRM functions and the Success System Model.
6. Explain three basic responses an individual has to socialization.
7. Read a book or view a video movie and identify organization culture and norms.

KEY WORDS AND CONCEPTS

Define and be able to use the following:

- Compensation
- Culture
- Creative Individualism
- Experiential Approach
- Human Resources Management (HRM)
- Human Resource Manager

- HRM Specialists
- HRM Strategy
- Labor Relations
- Norms
- Organization Renewal
- Organization Culture
- Peripheral Norms

- Pivotal Norms
- Psychological Contract
- Socialization
- Success System Model
- Total Quality Management (TQM)
- Training

**HRM SKILLS SIMULATION 1.1:
AUDITIONING FOR "THE TONIGHT SHOW WITH JAY
LENO" GUEST HOST SPOT**

Total time suggested: 1 hour.

A. PURPOSE

The goal of this exercise is to begin building trust within the group by sharing information about yourself with others and exploring group member's values and norms. You will gain experience interviewing another person, which is a key skill for a potential HRM.

B. PROCEDURES

Step 1. Members form into dyads (pairs).

Step 2. Each dyad member (A) interviews their partner (B) to find out who he or she is. The purpose is for you to gain enough information to introduce the other person to the group with an emphasis on behavior. The partners then reverse roles, with (B) interviewing (A). A set of questions are provided as a departure point for your discussion on the interview format.

Time suggested for Steps 1 and 2: 20 minutes.

INTERVIEW FORMAT

Name of Person
Interviewed _____

1. Tell me a little bit about yourself.
   a.
   b.
   c.

2. How would you describe the strengths you bring to the group?
   a.
   b.
   c.

3. What do you consider your past accomplishments or highlights?
   a.
   b.
   c.

4. What are your hobbies, interests, and astrological sign?

5. What is your favorite:
   Color _____
   Music _____
   Car _____
   Food _____
   TV Star _____
   Other _____

6. What are your goals for this class?
   a.
   b.
   c.

7. What resources can you contribute?

8. Is there anything else we've not covered?

Step 3. The total group is reformed. Each person (A) then introduces her or his partner. Introduce your partner to the class with a focus on positive accomplishments, yet add some humor and demonstrate your own "guest host" style. The class may ask questions to find more relevant information about (B). This proceeds around the class until each partner has been introduced.

At the end of the introductions, how many potential guest hosts did you discover?

Step 4. Meeting with the entire class, discuss the following questions:

1. Based on the introductions, can you foresee the formation of any norms?
2. In the introduction process, did you learn more about the person being introduced or the person doing the introduction?
3. What seems to be the type and level of participation of the members?

Time suggested for Steps 3 and 4: 40 minutes.

HRM SKILLS SIMULATION 1.2:
THE PSYCHOLOGICAL CONTRACT

Total time suggested: 1 hour, 25 minutes.

A. PURPOSE

The goal of this exercise is to make explicit and share some of the major expectations and obligations between students and instructor.[33] It provides an opportunity for the instructor to find out what the class expects and for the students to learn what the instructor expects.

B. PROCEDURES

Part A. Instructor's Interview of Students

Step 1. The class forms into groups of four or five persons.

Step 2. Each group elects one person as representative.

Step 3. Each group prepares its representative for the interview, and should be sure that they understand the group's position. (See the Suggested Question Guide for Instructor's Interview of Students.)

Time suggested for Steps 1 to 3: 15 minutes.

Step 4. The representatives, one from each group, meet with the instructor. The instructor interviews them about their expectations while the rest of the class observes.

Time suggested for Step 4: 20 minutes.

Part B. Students' Interview of Instructor

Step 1. The class forms into the same groups.

Step 2. Each group elects a different representative.

Step 3. Each group discusses any questions it would like its representative to ask the instructor. He or she makes sure they understand the group's questions and concerns. (See the Suggested Question Guide for Students' Interview of Instructor.)

Time suggested for Steps 1 to 3: 15 minutes.

Step 4. The representatives, one from each group, interview the instructor to clarify the instructor's expectations of the class.

Time suggested for Step 4: 20 minutes.

It might be helpful to incorporate into Step 4 the following: The representatives and the instructor should write the consensus of course objectives for a visual review. This will not only reaffirm and support objectives listed in the syllabus (by allowing the class to come up with the objectives), but will let the students and instructor delete or add other objectives which they feel may be important to the HRM learning process.

SUGGESTED QUESTION GUIDE FOR INSTRUCTOR'S INTERVIEW OF STUDENTS

1. What are your objectives for this course?
   a. To learn theories.
   b. To reach some desired level of knowledge.
   c. To learn new skills.
   d. To gain new behaviors.
   e. To get a good grade.
   f. To get required credit hours.
2. How can the instructor best help you to achieve your goals?
   a. By giving lectures.
   b. By assigning and discussing readings.
   c. By giving exams.
   d. By leading seminar discussions.
   e. By relating personal experiences.
   f. By letting you work on your own.
   g. By being a stern taskmaster.
   h. By being warm and supportive.
3. How can other class members help you achieve your goals?
   a. By sharing prior experiences.
   b. By participating in group discussions.
   c. By coming to class prepared.
   d. By sharing educational background.
   e. By doing nothing.
   f. By being enthusiastic and supportive.
   g. By being critical.
   h. By being flattering.
   i. By giving honest appraisals.
4. How should class members be evaluated?
   a. By quizzes, exams, and tests.
   b. By instructor.
   c. By peers.
   d. By quantity or quality of work.
5. How should the class be motivated and how would you in reality act toward this motivation?
   a. By self-motivation.
   b. By peer pressure.
   c. By instructor pressure.
   d. By class interest.
   e. By grade pressure.
6. What is the best thing that could happen in this class?

SUGGESTED QUESTION GUIDE FOR STUDENTS' INTERVIEW OF INSTRUCTOR

You may ask the instructor any questions you feel are relevant to effective learning. Some areas you may want to discuss are:

1. How do people learn?
2. What are expectations about attendance?
3. What is the philosophy of evaluation? How are students evaluated?
4. What is the instructor's role in the class?
5. What stereotypes about students are held?
6. Is there anything else that you feel is important?

Part C. Identifying and Establishing Norms

Step 1. Meeting in plenary session, do or discuss the following:

1. Identify the pivotal and peripheral norms that are being established.
2. Which of these norms are functional or dysfunctional to the class?

3. Which of these norms would you like to change?
4. Do you have any additional behaviors you would like to see become norms?
5. How much trust is being developed among students and between students and instructors?

Step 2. For the norms you would like to change, make some specific plans for the changes.

Time suggested for Steps 1 and 2: 15 minutes.

CASE ANALYSIS GUIDELINES

Why Use Cases?

Case studies allow a learning-by-doing approach. The material in the case provides the data for analysis and decision making. Cases require you to diagnose and make decisions about the situation and to defend those decisions to your peers. There are cases in the text which will provide you with opportunities to use this learning technique.

Objectives of the Case Method:

1. Help you acquire the skills of putting textbook knowledge about management into practice.
2. Get you out of the habit of being a receiver of facts, concepts, and techniques and into the habit of diagnosing problems, analyzing and evaluating alternatives, and formulating workable plans of action.
3. Train you to work out answers and solutions for yourself, as opposed to relying upon the authoritative crutch of the professor or a textbook.
4. Provide you with exposure to a range of firms and managerial situations (which might take a lifetime to experience personally), thus offering you a basis for comparison when you begin your own management career.

How to Prepare a Case

1. Begin your analysis by reading the case once for familiarity.
2. On the second reading, attempt to gain full command of the facts, organizational goals, objectives, strategies, policies, symptoms of problems, problems, basic causes of problems, unresolved issues, and roles of key individuals.
3. Who are the key players in this situation? What are their roles? Their styles?
4. Arrive at a solid evaluation of the organization based on the information in the case. Developing an ability to evaluate organizations and size up their situations is the key to case analysis.
5. Decide what you think the organization needs to do to improve its performance and to set forth a workable plan of action.

Case 1.1   Precision Products, Inc.

You are about to meet Personnel Manager Helen Brown and learn about this company. At the end of each chapter, you will be asked to help Helen respond to problems from her organization involving HRM issues. So enjoy yourselves and learn about the exciting, and challenging, field of human resource management. You may find that you want to go into a rewarding career in HRM.

Helen Brown is the personnel manager of Precision Products Company, although the more contemporary title

is human resource manager. Personnel is on the secondary level of the company, and does not report directly to the president (as do administration, engineering, manufacturing, and marketing). To gain the attention of their immediate boss, the vice president of administrative services, personnel must compete with the demands of finance, purchasing, credit, and printing. Perhaps indicative of the status of the personnel function at Precision Products is that George Hoffman, the previous retired personnel manager, had been with the company 25 years in manufacturing before being laterally "promoted" to personnel manager. His college degree was a Bachelor of Science in mechanical engineering.

The organization employs a total of 1,753 employees who produce a variety of parts for the automotive and truck industry. The main plant is located on a 40-acre site outside a city of 350,000 people. The one branch is located in a rural area 50 miles away with 511 employees. The company was founded in 1912, but it wasn't until the arrival of the present ambitious chairman of the board that Precision Products experienced a period of rapid growth. The company is publicly owned, with the stock trading on the American Stock Exchange at a moderate 12 times earnings. The production workers are represented by a national union of skilled craftsmen, and the office workers are represented by a clerical union. Both the company and the union have the reputation of being tough negotiators, with several unpleasant strikes occurring during the past decade.

Helen Brown has been in her present job slightly less than a year. The previous manager opted for early retirement and Helen was the compromise replacement. The final decision was determined by Howard J. Peterson, Jr., the recently hired dynamic CEO and president of Precision Products. The transition has been smooth, and Helen appears to be doing everything right. She joined the company 15 months ago upon graduation from State University with a Bachelor of Arts degree in business administration, majoring in human resource management. Her accumulative grade point average of 3.64 attracted several interesting employment offers. Helen finally accepted a position with Precision Products because of the possibility of rapid promotion. Now at age 27, with a yearly salary close to $27,000, Helen looks forward to further mobility within Precision Products or with a larger company. Her unique application of "hands-on" and participative management appears to be working.

Helen has thought about organizing the personnel functions as she sees it for the future. This will result in an upgrading of the personnel department both in status and number of employees. At present, too few people are wearing too many hats, with the result that many functions are not being done as thoroughly as they should be. This is not the fault of the personnel staff (all of whom are dedicated and effective), but rather results from the current system. The present way of operating is probably costing Precision Products some rather sizable hidden costs, and Helen has been quietly collecting data to support this contention with numbers.

On the home front, Helen is divorced with one daughter, Kim, in the second grade, who announced at the breakfast table this morning that she now wants to be an Internet entrepreneur. ■

QUESTIONS

1. Would you join Precision Products Company in an entry-level HRM position? In your answer, include the company culture and any appropriate historical data.

2. What reasons do you believe led to Helen's promotion to personnel manager after having joined the company only 15 months ago?

3. Do you think George Hoffman, the retired personnel manager who Helen replaced, had the necessary qualifications (25 years in manufacturing) to head the personnel department? In your presentation, include both pros and cons.

ENDNOTES

1. John Byrne, "How Jack Welch Runs GE," *Business Week* (June 8, 1998): 76.
2. Thomas J. Peters, *Thriving on Chaos* (New York: Alfred A. Knopf, 1987), xi. Also see Rosabeth Moss Kanter, "Championing Change," *Harvard Business Review* (January-February 1991): 119–30.
3. D. Ulrich, "A New Mandate for Human Resources," *Harvard Business Review* (January-February, 1998): 124.
4. M. A. Hitt, B. W. Keats, and S. M. Demarley, "Navigating in the New Competitive Landscape," *Academy of Management Executive* 12, no. 4 (1998): 4.
5. Thomas J. Peters, *Thriving on Chaos* (New York: Alfred A. Knopf, 1987); Robert H. Waterman, Jr., *The Renewal Factor* (New York: Bantam Books, 1987).
6. Richard E. Dutton, "High Technology with the Human Touch," paper presented at Academy of Management, Washington, DC, 1989. Also see Brian Dumaine, "Creating a New Company Culture," *Fortune;* (January 15, 1990): 127–31.
7. J. T. Hoeg, "Human Resources versus Personnel," *Personnel* 64, no. 5 (May 1987): 72–73.
8. Robert B. Reich, "The Company of the Future," *Fast Company* (November 1998): 124.
9. J. A. Neal and C. L. Thrombley, "From Incremental Change to Retrofit, Creating High-Performance Systems," *Academy of Management Executive* (1995): 42–54.
10. P. B. Doesinger, *Turbulence in the Workplace* (New York: Oxford Press, 1991).
11. K. Kelley, "Motorola: Training for the Millennium," *Business Week* (March 1993): 158.
12. S. Greenbard, "When HRMs Goes Global," *Personnel Journal* (June 1995): 91.

13. S. A. Snell and J. W. Dean, "Integrated Manufacturing and HRM," *Academy of Management Journal* 35 (1992): 467–504.

14. D. McCann and C. Mangerism, "Managing High Performance Teams," *Training and Development Journal* (November 1989): 52–60.

15. D. Ulrich, "Managing Human Resources: Anonymously," *Human Resource Management* 36 (1997): 303–20.

16. Ibid., p. 311.

17. Michelle N. Martinez, "Disney Training Works Magic," *HRM Magazine* 37, no. 5 (May 1992): 53.

18. "Big Blue Will Make Deep Cuts—But Precisely Where?" *New York Times,* 1 August 1993, sec. 3, p. 2. Also Mark Stahlman, "Creative Destruction at IBM," *Wall Street Journal,* 6 January 1993, p. A12; "IBM Chief Akers Announces Revamp," *San Diego Union,* 5 December 1991, E2; John W. Verity, "What's Ailing IBM?" *Business Week* (October 16, 1989): 75; Michael Schrage, "Innovation . . .", *Los Angeles Times,* 16 November 1989, p. B1; Geoff Lewis, "Big Changes at Big Blue," *Business Week* (February 15, 1988): 91–98; Joel Drefus, "The New IBM," *Fortune* (August 14, 1988): 31.

19. Russell Mitchell, "Masters of Innovation," *Business Week* (April 10, 1989): 58–63.

20. Kathleen Deveny, "Cosmetic Move: R. Burns Walks," *Wall Street Journal,* 12 January 1990, p. B1.

21. Robert S. Reich, "The Company of the Future," *Fast Company* (November 1998): 126.

22. Diane Lindquist, "Hecho En Mexico," *San Diego Union,* 3 December 1991, p. D1.

23. Charles A. O'Reilly, Jennifer Chatman, and David F. Caldwell, "People and organizational culture: A profile comparison approach to assessing person-organization fit," *Academy of Management Journal* 34 (September 1991): 487–516.

24. See Don Harvey, R. Bowin, and J. Hulpke, "The Success System Approach in HRM," Working Paper, 1994.

25. Edgar H. Schein, "Coming to a New Awareness of Organizational Culture," *Sloan Management Review* (Winter 1984): 3–16; Daniel C. Feldman, "The Development of Group Norms," *Academy of Management Review* 9, no. 1 (1984): 47–53.

26. Peter Waldman, "Federal Express Faces Test of Pilot's Loyalty Since Purchasing Tiger," *Wall Street Journal,* 23 October 1989, p. A1.

27. Edward E. Lawler, "HRM: Meeting the New Challenges," *Personnel* (January 1988): 24.

28. Edgar H. Schein, "Coming to a New Awareness of Organizational Culture," *Sloan Management Review* 25, no. 2 (Winter 1984): 3–16; Daniel C. Feldman, "The Development of Group Norms," *Academy of Management Journal* 9, no. 1 (June 1986): 262–79.

29. See, for example, J. E. Hebden, "Adopting an Organization's Culture," *Organizational Dynamics* (Summer 1986): 54–72; and G. R. Jones, "Socialization Tactics," *Academy of Management Journal* (June 1986): 262–79.

30. Nancy J. Perry, "A Consulting Firm Too Hot To Handle," *Fortune* (April 27, 1987): 91.

31. H. G. Baker, "The Unwritten Contract," *Personnel Journal* 64, no. 7 (July 1985): 37–41. See also Edgar H. Schein, *Organizational Psychology* (Upper Saddle River, NJ: Prentice-Hall, Inc., 1970), 76–79.

32. Robert W. Goddard, "The Psychological Contract," *Management World* 13, no. 7 (August 1984): 12.

33. D. A. Kolb observes: "Managerial education will not be improved by eliminating theoretical analysis or relevant case problems. Improvement will come through integration of the scholarly and practical learning styles." See "Management and the Learning Process," *California Management Review* 18, no. 3 (Spring 1976): 21–31. Several management schools experimenting with ways of encouraging intuitive and creative approaches to management because of feelings that systematic and logical thinking can lead only so far. See "B-School Buzzword: Creativity," *Business Week* (August 8, 1977): 66.

Part II

The Success System: Attracting a High-Performing Workforce

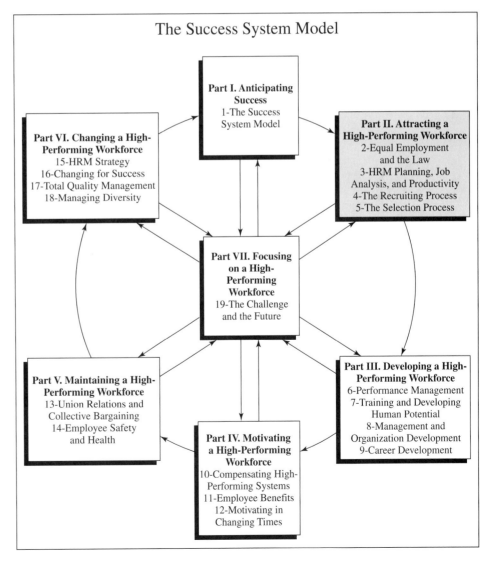

The Success System Model

Part I. Anticipating Success
1-The Success System Model

Part II. Attracting a High-Performing Workforce
2-Equal Employment and the Law
3-HRM Planning, Job Analysis, and Productivity
4-The Recruiting Process
5-The Selection Process

Part III. Developing a High-Performing Workforce
6-Performance Management
7-Training and Developing Human Potential
8-Management and Organization Development
9-Career Development

Part IV. Motivating a High-Performing Workforce
10-Compensating High-Performing Systems
11-Employee Benefits
12-Motivating in Changing Times

Part V. Maintaining a High-Performing Workforce
13-Union Relations and Collective Bargaining
14-Employee Safety and Health

Part VI. Changing a High-Performing Workforce
15-HRM Strategy
16-Changing for Success
17-Total Quality Management
18-Managing Diversity

Part VII. Focusing on a High-Performing Workforce
19-The Challenge and the Future

Chapter 2

The Success System: Equal Employment and the Law

Objectives

Upon completing this chapter, you will be able to:

1. Understand and explain the influence of equal employment practices in an organization.
2. Identify and describe the major equal employment opportunity legislation and understand its importance.
3. Describe the steps in developing and implementing an affirmative action program and understand its impact on the behavior of individuals in an organization.
4. Define the concept of disparate impact and recognize how this can be applied in an organization.

Premeeting preparation

1. Read chapter 2.
2. Prepare for HRM Skills Simulation 2.1. Read and complete Steps 1 and 2.
3. Prepare for HRM Skills Simulation 2.2. Read and complete Part B, Step 1.
4. Prepare for HRM Skills Simulation 2.3. Read and complete Part B, Step 1.
5. Read Case 2.1: Precision Products, Inc. Answer questions.

In the twenty-first century, one of the most important HRM issues will be the area of equal employment. Every day, managers are confronting complex legal problems, from top executives to the first line supervisor, from the biggest firms to the smallest. They must deal with a chaotic world of new legislation and constant innovation. There are a myriad of legal requirements which necessitate that managers must comply with new laws and guidelines.[1] Put it another way: There are many ways a manager can get into trouble, but violating Equal Employment Opportunity (EEO) laws is probably the quickest and easiest way.

An example is the situation Hyundai Semiconductor America found itself in on the west coast. The company apparently ordered an employment recruiter to stop referring women for work at one of their plants. A California jury found Hyundai violated the state's anti-discrimination law by telling the recruiter not to send women candidates. He continued to do so and was fired. The jury's judgment against Hyundai was $14.2 million. The company has filed motions for a new trial, asking for a reduction in the jury's award.[2]

In the future, successful companies will be those that respond quickly to changing conditions and increasing workforce diversity (see chapter 18) and are able to face the critical issue of discrimination-related problems.[3] Understanding the complex legal issues in the management of people is the central concern of this chapter. In an unprecedented decision affecting the operation of human resource management functions, BP Amoco has turned its human resources operations over to an outside consulting firm. Although other companies have turned parts of its HRM functions over to outside consulting firms, the BP Amoco decision sets an unique precedent.[4] Although the reason given was cost cutting, there is always the possibility of the complex legal issues. Regardless of BP Amoco, most HR managers must also be able to recognize and comply with all legal requirements in developing new HRM programs. However, it is not just the HR manager who must keep the organization in line.

Every manager or supervisor with power to hire, fire, promote, discipline, or transfer an employee can get the business in hot water. An employee with no supervisory responsibility at all may cause the organization to face—and lose— a **sexual harassment** lawsuit. The entire area is of massive importance. It may seem complex and difficult to learn, but it is important. The organization's records must be accurate and complete on everything from pay to discipline. Thus, all administrative personnel and whoever handles the books share joint responsibility. Equal Employment Opportunity is the law—and, it applies to everyone in the organization.

A survey in 1999 by the polling firm Zogby International asked adults aged 18 to 29 years old whether it was acceptable if races are "basically separate." Approximately one-half of these young white adults believed separation of the races is acceptable providing there are equal opportunities for everyone. Although this is only one survey, if it does represent a general consensus, this complicates the work for HRM.[5]

The management of Equal Employment Opportunity practices will play a key role in the performance of organizations in the twenty-first century. The purpose of this chapter is to provide an understanding of this part of the Success System Model. In this chapter, we present an overview of major Equal Employment Opportunity legislation, discuss human resource activities of implementing an **affirmative action** program, and discuss basic EEO complaints and defenses and the implications for HRM.

The employment practices of American businesses have been based on the freedom of individual choice. In earlier times, the government did little to infringe upon the actions of business. One result was the growth of a world power with the highest standard of living for its citizens. However, as in all societies, inequities developed, with some people not receiving their fair share of the pie. The inequities seem to run deep, and cause disparities in areas you might not expect. For example, some women's issues advocates have advised women to avoid discrimination in the workplace by starting their own firms. But even this may not work: academic researchers looking into this issue report that small businesses headed by women are more likely to be unsuccessful or go out of business than those headed by men. So even when a way to sidestep the inequity is found, it seems new inequities are discovered.[6] Perhaps one explanation for the failure of small businesses headed by women is their difficulty in obtaining venture capital financing. Women entrepreneurs are starting almost twice as many new businesses as men; however, the money is mostly going to companies started by men. Because women are not yet connected to the old boy's network, they suffer from the old stereotype they are not as technically qualified as men.[7] In addition, evidence suggests that inequities based on culture and tradition are hard to overcome. Even as women move into traditionally male jobs, their roles at home often remain unchanged.[8]

Employment discrimination may be present in numerous ways, and there are varying methods for employees to seek equity through the courts. The laws to be discussed are designed to protect employees from discrimination based on race, gender, disability, or age. The focus is on developing a fair and equitable system and preventing potential legal liability.

LEGISLATION: AN OVERVIEW

Today, federal and state legislation prohibits any business policies or practices that adversely affect designated protected minority groups. Any business violating this legislation can be brought before the legal system by these protected groups to obtain remedy and compensation. Three major forces seem to have influenced this situation:

1. An emerging awareness of discriminatory practices;
2. Changing attitudes among voting groups toward employment discrimination;
3. Investigative reports emphasizing the economic disparities among minorities, women, the disabled, and older employees.

Top management needs to be aware of how costly EEO violations can be. In many cases, millions of dollars may be lost due to inefficient personnel practices. Table 2.1 provides a summary of major legislation which will be discussed in the next section.

U.S. Constitution

The laws against discrimination in this country have a long history. They begin with the Thirteenth Amendment to the United States Constitution that freed the slaves. The **Civil Rights Act** of 1866 followed this amendment and allowed all persons, regardless of race, the rights to sue and to engage in contracts.

Table 2.1
Summary of major EEO legislation

LEGISLATION	INTENT
Fifth Amendment, U.S. Constitution	Protects against federal violation of "due process"
Thirteenth Amendment, U.S. Constitution	Abolishes slavery
Fourteenth Amendment, U.S. Constitution	Protects against state violations of "due process"
Civil Rights Act, 1866	Establishes the right of all citizens to make and enforce contracts
Civil Rights Act, 1871	Makes citizens liable for suits
Equal Pay Act, 1963	Prohibits sex discrimination in wages and salary: equal pay for equal work
Civil Rights Act, 1964 (Title VII), as amended in 1991	Declares all discriminatory employment practices unlawful
Age Discrimination in Employment Act (ADEA), 1967, as amended in 1978 and 1986	Prohibits discrimination against persons age 40 and older
Equal Employment Opportunity Act, 1972	Extends coverage of the 1964 Civil Rights Act to include both public and private sectors, educational institutions, labor organizations, and employment agencies
Rehabilitation Act, 1973	Protects persons with disabilities against discrimination (public sector)
Americans with Disabilities Act (ADA), 1990	Prohibits discrimination against persons with disabilities
Executive Orders 11246 and 11375	Prohibits discrimination by contractors and subcontractors of federal agencies
Family and Medical Leave Act, 1993	Protects and mandates equal opportunity programs

The Fourteenth Amendment to the Constitution prohibited the states from denying persons life, liberty, or property without due process of law and the equal protection of laws. This amendment was followed by the Civil Rights Act of 1871 that protects individuals from employment discrimination resulting from state law, custom, or use that dilutes the rights granted by federal laws.

Executive Orders

Although there were few important federal employment laws for almost three-quarters of a century after 1871, there finally were a number of presidential executive orders to promote affirmative action and equal opportunity. Executive Order 8802, issued in 1941, required fair employment in U.S. defense industries. A similar order, Executive Order 9345, extended fair employment provisions to all government contractors. However, both of these orders expired at the end of Word War II.

Executive Order 11246, issued in 1965, states that in organizations with federal contracts, persons have a right to employment regardless of color, creed, national origin, or race. This executive order still applies today, although it was strengthened by another presidential executive order a few years later. Executive Order 11375, issued in 1968, covers procedures for practicing equal employment opportunities, requiring the implementation of affirmative action programs and prohibiting discrimination based on race, color, national origin, religion, sex, age, or handicap. This executive order basically applies to "government contractors" having 50 or more employees, but since this means contractors and those who sell to the government and to their subcontractors, millions of businesses, both large and small, are affected. According to the Labor Department, over 95,000 companies with 27 million employees are covered by this order.

Fair Labor Standards Act of 1938

Although the Fair Labor Standards Act is not strictly speaking an "equal opportunity" law, any discussion of employment legislation must begin with this foundation law. From the beginning of the United States of America until the twentieth century, employment issues were typically considered private matters between the employer and the employee, or perhaps an issue for individual states to address. In 1938, however, an important precedent was set: The federal government enacted legislation covering virtually all employment in America.

This law has been amended many times, but, is still on the books, and to a certain extent it is familiar to every American. You probably know it as the Minimum Wage Law, the law that is described on the minimum wage poster on the wall where you work. The minimum wage today is a far cry from the 25 cents per hour set in 1938, but other provisions of the law still have important implications for employers today. Employees working more than 40 hours a week must be paid time-and-a-half for each hour after the first 40 (with a few exceptions such as managers with exempt status). This provision, written into law during the Great Depression of the 1930s, still has impact today: ask managers from Nordstrom's, the up-scale retail chain. This firm got into hot water because its sales staff were working long hours, and even though they seemed to be doing so voluntarily, the law applied. After a back pay settlement amounting to more than $20 million, you can be sure the firm is being a bit more careful about recording those hours worked.[9]

Although the Fair Labor Standards Act (FLSA) was not an equal opportunity law, it did set the stage: Employment conditions, even in private sector jobs, were within the purview of the Federal Government. Disadvantaged groups must also be protected: That is one reason the FLSA also severely restricted child labor in America.

In an interesting exception to the Fair Labor Standards Act, last year the Supreme Court in three separate rulings decreed states did not have to pay their employees overtime pay under the federal law. This decision was based on states' rights. However, while federal laws may not apply, state laws regarding pay issues will apply to overtime pay.[10]

Equal Pay Act of 1963

The Equal Pay Act prohibits discrimination in pay based upon a worker's gender. (See cartoon.) The final result of this act was to require equal pay for males and females in jobs requiring equal skill, effort, and responsibility under similar working conditions. For example, female and male flight attendants at American Airlines may not be paid differently because of gender. Other airlines may have differing pay rates but must still maintain equity among genders. Employers are not violating this law, however, when salary differences between male and female are based upon seniority, merit, incentive pay systems, or any factor other than sex.

Kidder Peabody, for example, has become the target of several sex, age, and racial discrimination lawsuits that could be very costly. According to reports, 15 former women employees, ranging from entry level to a managing director, claimed

Source: The Wizard of ID by Brant Parker and Johnny Hart, by permission of Creators Syndicate, Inc.

the company paid them less than their male counterparts.[11] Even if an organization such as Kidder Peabody is ultimately found innocent of charges it violated the Equal Pay Act, substantial sums of money are involved in legal fees. Organizations large and small should take notice. If it appears that men and women are paid differently for essentially the same jobs, somebody could end up in trouble.

The Civil Rights Act of 1964 and Title VII

One of the most important legislative acts relating to equal opportunity is the Civil Rights Act of 1964.

The 1964 Civil Rights Act has the distinction of being the broadest of anti-discrimination legislation. The act states that an employer cannot discriminate on the basis of race, color, religion, national origin, or sex.

The employment part of this act, commonly called Title VII, applies to employers, labor unions, apprenticeship committees, employment agencies, and both state and local governments. The act covers all firms that employ a minimum of 15 people for a period of at least 20 weeks and affect interstate commerce. The **Equal Employment Opportunity Commission (EEOC)** is the enforcement arm of the act, and all discrimination charges must begin with the EEOC or a state referral agency. Title VII also protects majority groups, as in religious freedom, because the constitutional provision did not apply to employment practices. The law requires that job applications, payroll records, and personnel files be kept a minimum of 6 months or until any personnel action is resolved. Realistically, most employers keep records much longer. Those employers with 100 or more employees must file annually the EEO-1 report inventorying employees' race, ethnic group, sex, job category, and pay. Unions must file a similar report, entitled EEO-3, with records kept 1 year after the report has been filed.

Charges of discrimination may be filed with the EEOC or a state agency working cooperatively with the EEOC by an individual, and the EEOC may file its own charges that may involve more than one person. The party charging discrimination (the plaintiff) must present reasonable evidence of the event, usually offering some form of statistical data. Once reasonable cause is shown, the burden of proof is transferred to the one being charged with discrimination (the defendant). Now the organization accused of discrimination begins the process of proving that no discrimination occurred. Often the firm presents data to try to show that the employment practice being questioned is a business necessity or is job-related. (See HRM in Action.)

One important point to note here is that this settlement cost Chevron $1.5 million, not including legal fees, and the case never even made it to trial. But without hard data to prove no discrimination had taken place, Chevron decided to settle. And, if you watch your local papers, you will no doubt see similar cases, involving employers large and small. Each case underscores the need for both fair employment and for good recordkeeping.

A federal judge has approved settlement of a discrimination suit by Chevron oil-field workers in the San Joaquin Valley despite objections by a majority of the workers in the suit. The settlement provides $1.5 million in compensation for lost promotions and emotional distress, to be divided among 179 workers, and requires Chevron U.S.A. to set numerical goals for promoting blacks and Hispanics. Most of the workers are in Kern County. In his ruling, Chief U.S. District Judge Thelton Henderson said he was approving the settlement despite opposition from 102 workers, or 57 percent of those affected. The objections quoted by Henderson included the absence of a finding that Chevron had discriminated, the leeway the company was given to fall short of its promotional goals and to set job criteria, the determination of individual damages by a court-appointed officer rather than a judge, and a complaint that workers had not been informed or allowed to provide input into decisions affecting their future. Henderson said a trial might yield more damages, but he was satisfied the terms of the settlement were "fair, reasonable, and adequate." The judge said the trial would have been long and complex, and the outcome uncertain. U.S. Supreme Court rulings have made it harder for workers to prove discrimination by statistics showing workforce disparities.

The suit was based on statistics showing virtually no minorities in management jobs, such as foreman, between 1980 and 1986; minorities made up 15 to nearly 30 percent of the pool from which those jobs were filled, said Henry Hewitt, a lawyer who negotiated the settlement on behalf of the entire group of workers. The settlement contains $800,000 for lost wages by blacks and Hispanics who were denied promotions between 1980 and 1986, and between $710,000 and $750,000 for blacks and Hispanics who can show they suffered emotional distress from the denial of a promotion. The company also is required to make good-faith efforts to promote minorities to management jobs at a rate that reflects the availability of qualified minority candidates.

QUESTIONS

1. Why did the federal judge approve a discrimination suit against Chevron despite the objections of the workers? Do you agree or disagree with the judge's ruling? Why?

2. How should the human resource management department respond to the emotional stress issue? Be specific.

Equal Employment Opportunity Act of 1972

In 1972, the Equal Employment Opportunity Act was passed, amending Title VII of the Civil Rights Act of 1964. Title VII was amended to cover all private employers with 15 or more employees, public and private schools, state and local governments, labor unions, and labor-management apprenticeship committees. The 1972 act also added to the EEOC's powers by permitting it to go directly to the courts for enforcement. Further, regional centers were established, complete with legal staffs, to implement the law and enforce court decisions.

Although the emphasis of Title VII is on unlawful discrimination, it does recognize three discriminatory practices that are legal. First, a **Bona Fide Occupational Qualification (BFOQ)** can be used to discriminate on the basis of national origin, religion, and sex, but not race or color. So a women's fashion designer could legally discriminate against men and hire only female models. Second, employers may use tests for hiring and promotion purposes if those tests have been validated on job-related performance criteria. Third, employers may also use seniority and performance appraisal systems to discriminate among employees, provided that these systems have not been designed to inhibit the intent of Title VII and that they are based on job-related criteria.

Civil Rights Act of 1991

In the years between 1972 and 1990, the U.S. Supreme Court had narrowed the interpretation of the Civil Rights Acts of 1964 and 1972 somewhat. Employers were finding the laws on equal opportunity were getting a bit easier to handle. On the other hand, individuals suffering from discrimination were finding it tougher to use the laws to fight back. All this changed with the passage of the Civil Rights Act of 1991.[13] This law amended the Civil Rights Act of 1964, and made changes to other laws as well. The key focus, however, was on those Supreme Court decisions.

The law addressed some of the issues which previous laws had left debatable, and in so doing, effectively overturned some half-dozen critical Supreme Court cases. The Wards Cove decision mentioned later in this chapter was one of these which fell by the wayside.

Bottom line? It is again tougher on businesses, large and small. Also, employees or job applicants suffering from discrimination can in many cases seek jury trials and ask for big damage awards. The key here is not just to play it safe—it is to follow the laws of the land. Discrimination? Not advised!

Age Discrimination in Employment Act of 1967 (Amended, 1986)

The Age Discrimination in Employment Act (ADEA) protects persons 40 years of age or older from **age discrimination** in selection, discharge, and job assignments. In one Department of Labor study, it was stated that by the year 2000, more than half of the workforce would be over 39 years of age.[14] The temptation for employers sometimes is to try to revitalize an organization by bringing in "new ideas" or "new blood." If the "new blood" brought in happens to be young, and someone over 40 is let go, watch out! If the phrase "younger blood" happens to get used, don't bother to try to defend yourself in court. Just settle.

Older employees may believe there is widespread age discrimination; however, experience indicates it is very difficult to prove. A study by the Equal Employment Opportunity Commission ruled 61 percent of 18,279 complaints filed in 1997 had "no reasonable cause." One study revealed that out of 325 cases filed in federal court, only 19 went before a jury. While the chances of getting an age discrimination case to court is slim, once there, damages can be very large.[15]

The media continues to report many unfilled jobs in information technology (IT). However, a large number of senior IT professionals claim they cannot find a job. The unemployment rate among IT workers over age 50 is 17 percent versus 2 percent within other U.S. industries. Some suggest this means the IT industry is among the most age discriminatory in the United States.[16]

The same problem is present in the computer industry where engineers over the age of 40 are having a difficult time finding jobs. Companies can protect themselves against charges of age discrimination by establishing their own training programs or by participating in funding a major industry-run retraining center.[17]

HRM IN ACTION
AGE DISCRIMINATION? THE $4 MILLION QUESTION[18]

Richard S. Gibson, Western regional sales manager for an Ohio manufacturing company, was suddenly given a choice: he could either take early retirement, or accept demotion to a job "one step behind where I had started." Gibson was told that he could no longer handle his duties as regional sales manager, yet his performance reviews were always very good to excellent and he got regular salary increases and bonuses. After declining the retirement offer, Gibson was demoted to an assistant district manager. His customers were shocked by his loss of status. "It was very degrading and humiliating," Gibson said. He sued his former employer and was awarded a $4 million settlement, one of the largest ever in an age discrimination case.

QUESTIONS

1. What does this situation suggest to the human resource management department regarding the company's performance appraisal program?

2. Why would a company act in a way that would promote an age discrimination suit? How could such a suit be avoided?

The Age Discrimination in Employment Act of 1967 protects persons over 40 from discrimination in selection, discharge, and job assignments. The law prohibits employers from replacing employees with younger workers, regardless of whether the purpose is to save money in wages, or to give the company a more youthful image. Some would argue the ADEA permits discrimination against those under age 40. Their position is that under 40 age discrimination is just as serious as the discrimination against other protected groups. If Congress does amend the ADEA to protect the under 40 age group, businesses would be faced with very high costs.[19]

A sharp increase in employee complaints and litigation involving the issue of age discrimination is forcing human resource managers, and those making employment decisions in smaller firms, to become more aware of this relatively new problem area. We know that there will be a significant increase in the number of persons in the protected age groups (40 and older) during the next decade.

Phillip Houghton, for example, was fired by the McDonnell Douglas Corporation. The stated reason: unsatisfactory performance in a new assignment. Houghton was certain the real reason was his age—52. He hired a lawyer and sued McDonnell Douglas under the Age Discrimination in Employment Act. An appeals court ruled that McDonnell Douglas had violated the federal law. The 1986 amendments to the Age Discrimination in Employment Act eliminate, with certain exceptions, the mandatory retirement age for all workers.

Similarly, Pan American World Airways in 1988 agreed to pay $17 million to 100 former pilots who charged that the firm's policy of barring them from serving as flight engineers after age 60 had no scientific basis.[20] However, a recent 5–4 decision by the Supreme Court removed federal protection against age discrimination for the nation's state employees including teachers and state employees. This decision limits the power of the federal government and supports the states as being independent sovereigns. While private sector employees can sue their employers for damages caused by age discrimination, state workers can no longer do so. Yet, some states do have strong state laws against age discrimination, and the Supreme Court decision will have little or no effect upon those states.[21]

A new area of concern to the EEOC regarding age occurs when a company decides to convert a traditional pension plan to a cash benefit plan. Their interest is that such a conversion reduces the benefits of the older employee. If the conversion reduces the benefit available in the short run when the older person is more apt to retire, the older person may lose part of their pension under the conversion. If this is the case, it is age discrimination. During the period of conversion, legislation is being proposed to advise employees that they may lose benefits.[22]

Vocational Rehabilitation Act of 1973

The **Rehabilitation Act** of 1973 requires federal agencies, federal contractors, federal grant recipients, and employers of federally assisted programs to demonstrate affirmative action in hiring the handicapped "who have a physical or mental impairment which substantially limits one or more of such person's life activities." All federal agencies are required to take affirmative action to hire qualified persons with disabilities. Under this act, a person with a disability is considered qualified for a job if it is determined that the person can "with reasonable accommodation" perform the job. This law had some impact in the working world, but many observers felt not enough was being done to provide opportunity for the disabled among us. Congress agreed and addressed the area with the following new law.

Americans with Disabilities Act of 1990

The American with Disabilities Act prohibits employers from discriminating against individuals with physical or mental handicaps or the chronically ill. An important but unclear issue with the **Americans with Disabilities Act (ADA)** is how it will interact with workers compensation. Richard Pimentel (1992) indicates the majority of ADA complaints will come from existing employees, and many of the complaints will be related to an industrial accident. This implies the clear potential for a disabilities discrimination claim in a workers compensation case.

In such a situation, if the individual worker satisfies the ADA's definitional tests of being disabled, the person will have the same rights under the act as other qualified individuals. An example of discrimination would be the failure to reassign a qualified worker to a vacant position with or without a reasonable accommodation.[23] The U.S. Census Bureau recently found that 21 percent of the population is considered disabled. The criteria for being disabled is needing a wheelchair or having difficulty with the functional activities of daily life.[24]

In a recent class-action suit charging a hospital with violating the ADA, it was claimed the hospital discriminated against 28 job applicants because they were all overweight. The federal district court ruled against the plaintiffs. The reasoning: When a person's weight hampers their ability to do a job, they are not discriminated against when they are not hired.[25]

The Americans with Disabilities Act imposes only one recordkeeping requirement on employers. A record must be kept of all requests for reasonable accommodations for a disability. The record will be maintained for both applicants and employees showing the process for considering the request, the action taken, and the rationale for the action. Further, in gathering information from the disabled person, many advisors suggest that the employer should not ask questions or keep notes on observations about disabilities, nor ask if the person will need an accommodation.

Employment decisions should be made fairly and in such a way to take full advantage of all our country's human resources, including those who are in one way or another "less abled." The key is, can the individual perform the essential functions of the job? If not, why? A safe and reasonable step is to not make inquiries regarding an applicant's disability status before making an offer of employment. Then, any request for a medical exam must be a post job offer and be a requirement for all entering employees for that position.[26]

There is still confusion regarding interpretation of the ADA. Nine years after the law was enacted, there remains many troubling aspects of the act, particularly how to make accommodations for someone with a disability.[27]

Legal Aspects of AIDS at Work

Another important issue facing every employer is the issue of AIDS. It is estimated that over 365,000 employees have been infected with the AIDS virus. Attorneys agree that under the ADA, it is illegal for most companies to fire or even reassign an employee solely because the person is HIV positive.[28] Although the ADA clearly has some impact on the AIDS issue, it will be up to the courts to define the nature of that impact.

The Vocational Rehabilitation Act and American with Disabilities Act have recently taken on added prominence because of the likelihood they can be used to prohibit discrimination against people with AIDS. In *School Board of Nassau County* v. *Arline*, the Supreme Court ruled in 1987 that persons with contagious diseases are covered by the act.[29] In this particular case, a school teacher (Arline) was dismissed because she had tuberculosis, an infectious respiratory disease. To that point in time, it was often assumed that merely having a contagious disease meant the person was left unprotected under the Rehabilitation Act.

In *Arline*, however, the Supreme Court held that the opposite was true: The fact that a disease is contagious can, by itself, place an employee under the protection of the act, since the mere fear of the disease (rather than its actual likelihood of being transmitted) might cause employers to discriminate against the ailing persons. In *Chalk* v. *U.S. District Court*, it was ruled that individuals with AIDS are also handicapped within the coverage of the Rehabilitation Act.[30] It therefore seems likely that a person with AIDS would be protected by the Rehabilitation Act, at least as long as the person is otherwise qualified to continue working and can be reasonably accommodated by the employer. (See HRM in Action.)

HRM IN ACTION
AIDS POLICIES[31]

According to a recent survey, few companies have policies that explicitly address the issue of AIDS. "Of *Fortune* 500 companies, about 20 percent have a formal policy and/or practice" for dealing with AIDS in the workplace, according to B. J. Stiles, president of the National Leadership Coalition on AIDS. The percentage is probably half of that if smaller firms are included. Companies with progressive policies include Levi Strauss, Kaiser Permanente, Wells Fargo, Bank of America, Digital Equipment Corporation, and General Motors.

In any case, numerous state laws now protect people with AIDS from discrimination. Furthermore, the guidelines issued by the Labor Department's Office of Federal Contract Compliance Programs also require that AIDS-type diseases be treated as covered by the Rehabilitation Act. The bottom line seems to be that, for many or most employers, discriminating against people with AIDS would be viewed by the courts and enforcement agencies as unlawful.[32]

Vietnam Era Veterans Readjustment Assistance Act of 1974

The Vietnam Era Veterans Readjustment Assistance Act of 1974 requires agencies and federal contractors with minimum contracts of $10,000 to demonstrate affirmative action in hiring Vietnam era veterans and also disabled veterans from all wars. As of March 1988, federal contractors who have contracts worth $10,000 or more must file a special form with the Department of Labor. The form lists the number of "special disabled" veterans and Vietnam era veterans they employ and related information.

Pregnancy Discrimination Act of 1978

Title VII of the Civil Rights Act of 1964 was also amended by the **Pregnancy Discrimination** Act of 1978. This amendment makes it illegal not to hire or to discharge women because they are pregnant. Under this act, it becomes illegal for employers to deny sick leave for morning sickness or related pregnancy illnesses, and pregnancy must receive the same benefits accorded other illnesses or disabilities. Basically, what the act says is that if an employer offers its employees disability coverage, pregnancy and childbirth must be treated like any other disability and must be included in the plan as a covered condition. This means that a woman is protected from being fired or refused a job or promotion because she is pregnant.

Further, the law prohibits discrimination in hiring, promotion, or termination because of pregnancy. In January 1987, the U.S. Supreme Court ruled in *California Federal Savings and Loan Association* v. *Guerra* that if an employer offers no disability leave to any of its employees it can (but need not necessarily) grant pregnancy leave to a woman who requests it when disabled for pregnancy, childbirth, or a related medical condition, although men get no comparable benefits.[33] Although later court decisions might well have changed this ruling, another law passed by Congress brought changes anyway. After 1993, either the wife or the husband might qualify for time off under the Family and Medical Leave Act of 1993.

Although the Pregnancy Discrimination Act of 1978 was designed to resolve pregnancy-related legal issues, it has failed to do so; plaintiffs are still looking for clarification as to what it means not to be discriminated against because of pregnancy and/or pregnancy-related conditions.[34]

Family and Medical Leave Act of 1993

Almost all employers with 50 or more workers are now subject to the Family and Medical Leave Act (FMLA). In these organizations, most full-time employees can request up to 12 weeks of leave for a large number of reasons: The individual worker may face a serious health problem; a parent, child, or spouse may need care; the family may be having a child, either through childbirth or adoption. In these and similar cases, the covered employee may request leave and the employer must grant it.[35]

Although implications of this law will be defined over time in the courts, it is clear that employers will have to adjust. According to most observers, organizations are finding that proportionally more women than men utilize the provisions of this law. In this sense, the FMLA may be seen as a law to help provide enhanced employment opportunities for women. However, that is not how the law reads: FMLA is truly an equal opportunity law, applying to men and women equally.

UNIFORM GUIDELINES ON EMPLOYEE SELECTION

One can well imagine the confusion resulting from the tangle of laws and executive orders. This problem was addressed in 1978 when the Equal Employment Opportunity Commission released the Uniform Guidelines on Employee Selection Procedures to assist affected parties in complying with federal laws prohibiting employment discrimination. Approximately 6 months later, in an attempt to clarify these guidelines, the Equal Employment Opportunity Commission issued 90 questions and answers to help clarify the guidelines. Then, after a 1 year interval, four more questions and answers were released.

The result of all this activity at clarifying the guidelines was generally met with employer dissatisfaction and confusion. Finally, in 1984, the chairman of the EEOC responded to employer complaints by stating it would be unwise to change them now since the courts had generally accepted the guidelines. Although subject to change from many angles, through legislation, executive action, or court decisions, it is still worth becoming familiar with the Uniform Guidelines.

Perhaps it would be valuable both from the viewpoint of a manager as well as a human resource management career choice to briefly review the guidelines on selection procedures. Our intent is not to memorize, but to be aware of the comprehensiveness and detail that will govern your conduct during your career in the world of business. An inexperienced HR manager can cause a firm to be fined, to be sued by employees, and to suffer serious internal problems of employee discontent resulting in further costs. Of course, for those who enter areas of management other than human resource management, a knowledge of EEO will also be necessary in order to avoid EEO problems.

Validity

One of the issues addressed in the Uniform Guidelines is validity of selection procedures. If an employer uses a test or other selection instrument to select individuals for employment, the employer must be able to prove that the selection instrument has a direct relation to job success. Many employers have stopped using written selection tests, because such tests are often tough to prove for validity that they actually test the trait needed for job success. However, just abandoning written tests is no solution: The new substituted procedure, such as interviews, should also be verifiably valid. Employers have now resumed using written tests, but following the test provider's instructions to help ensure validity.

DISPARATE IMPACT

What Is Disparate Impact?

In order for individuals to claim discrimination, they must establish that selection procedures resulted in a disparate or adverse impact on a protected class. **Disparate impact** may be defined as the rejection of a higher percentage of a protected class for employment, placement, or promotion. Up until the *Wards Cove Packing* v. *Antonio* decision in 1989, a person who felt unintentionally discriminated against needed only establish a prima facie case of discrimination: This meant showing that the employer's selection procedures had an **adverse impact** on a protected minority group. "Adverse impact" refers to the total employment process that results in a significantly higher percentage of a protected group in the candidate population being rejected for employment, placement, or promotion.[36] (For example, if 80 percent of the male applicants passed the test, but only 20 percent of the female applicants passed, a female applicant had a prima facie case showing adverse impact.)

Then, once the employee had established a case (such as in *Wards Cove Packing* case), the burden of proof shifted to the *employer*. It became the employer's task to prove that any test, application blank, interview, or other hiring procedure was a valid predictor of performance on the job (and that it was applied fairly and equitably to both minorities and nonminorities).

Wards Cove changed this situation. Before *Wards*, a plaintiff might just show statistically that all clerical jobs were filled by women and all higher level jobs by men. Then the employer had to prove its hiring practice (such as a test) was nondiscriminatory. After the *Wards Cove* decision, the burden of proof switched to the plaintiff. So much heat was generated by this decision that some claim *Wards Cove* was a major factor in adding to the passage of the Civil Rights Act of 1991, which moved things back to a tougher standard. As this illustrates, the job of keeping up never ends.

How Can Disparate Impact Be Proven?

Because the burden of proof is shifted to the plaintiff or employee, it means the plaintiff must prove his or her case. There are four basic approaches that can be used.

1. *Disparate Rejection Rates* (or **Four-Fifths Rule**). This involves comparing the rejection rates between a minority group and another group. The EEOC has adopted the four-fifths rule to determine: "Is there a disparity between the percentage of a protected group among those applying for a particular position and the percentage of the protected group among those hired for the position?" If the answer to either question is yes, the firm could be facing legal action.

   Federal agencies use a formula to determine when disparate rejection rates actually exist. Their guidelines state that "a selection rate for any racial, ethnic or gender group which is less than 4/5 or 80 percent of the rate for the group with the highest selection rate will generally be regarded as evidence of disparate impact, while a greater than 4/5 rate will generally not be regarded as evidence of disparate impact." For example, suppose 55 percent of male applicants are hired, but only 28 percent of female applicants are hired. Then, since the percentage of females hired to males (51 percent) is less than four-fifths), disparate impact exists.

2. *Restricted Policy.* This approach means demonstrating that the employer has (intentionally or unintentionally) been using a selection policy that excludes members of a protected group. Evidence of restricted policies (for example, against hiring women) is evidence of adverse impact.

3. *Population Comparisons.* This approach involves comparing the percentage of a protected class in a firm with the percentage of that protected class in the population in the surrounding community.

4. *Statistical Evidence.* This approach involves using statistical analysis to show underrepresentation of protected groups. It is used in situations of (intentional) disparate treatment rather than (unintentional) disparate impact (for which approaches 1 to 3 above are used). The following guidelines are set forth by the U.S. Supreme Court: **(a)** that he or she belongs to a protected class; **(b)** that he or she applied and was qualified for a job in which the employer was seeking applicants; **(c)** that, despite this qualification, he or she was rejected; and **(d)** that, after his or her rejection, the position remained open and the employer continued to seek applications from persons of complainant's qualifications. For example, in *Watson* v. *Fort Worth Bank*, the court ruled as proof of discrimination statistical evidence showing that white supervisors hired only 3.5 percent of blacks, while hiring 14.8 percent of white applicants. If all these conditions are met, then a prima facie case of disparate treatment is established.

OTHER ISSUES

Within this broad legal framework, there are several other issues which are of interest to HR managers, such as the possible employer liability in failing to screen applicants in the selection process. Many managers are unaware of their accountability for the actions of employees. Negligent hiring can result in being liable for employees' unlawful acts if the employer does not reasonably investigate their backgrounds. If, as the result of an inadequate investigation, the employee is put in a position to commit crimes harming others, the employer may be liable. Of prime importance to the question of employer liability is the nature of the job itself and its exposure to others. Many experts believe that an organization should obtain the applicant's written permission to conduct a thorough background investigation including references and, if appropriate, consumer credit reports.[37]

Of course, even a thorough background check may not provide much information, even with the applicant's written permission. Previous employers are often reluctant to say anything. Many employers are aware of decisions caused by "Words That May Later Haunt You." In one case, the court ordered Procter & Gamble to pay $15.5 million to Dan Hagerty after Procter & Gamble announced Dan had been fired for theft. Because Dan hadn't been tried and convicted, this was defamation of character, worth $15.5 million to Dan. No wonder former employers are often tight-lipped.[38]

Child Labor and Overtime

As competitive pressures increase, companies continue to find themselves in trouble with the Labor Department over claims of child labor and adult overtime violations.

Nordstrom's agreed to pay more than $20 million in back wages and legal fees to employees to settle a suit filed by the United Food and Commercial Workers that claimed employees were forced to work overtime without pay.[39] Watch your local newspapers or the *Wall Street Journal*. Without a doubt, there will be continuing reports of new violations. These laws continue to get employers in legal difficulties.

In the case of Nike, they voluntarily contacted the International Labor Organization about counterfeit Nike soccer balls believed to have been manufactured by an unauthorized factory in Pakistan. They suspected child labor was involved. The Nike spokesperson pointed out the use of child labor was a violation of their corporate practices and standards.[40]

Sexual Harassment

One area which has been of increasing interest since the 1980s is the issue of sexual situations in the work environment. There are a number of studies demonstrating the increase in sexual harassment legal actions, and in one study, some 42 percent of women and 14 percent of men said that they had experienced some form of sexual harassment on the job. According to one survey, sexual harassment costs the typical *Fortune* 500 company $6.7 million per year in employee turnover, absenteeism, and reduced productivity.[41]

Reporting of sexual harassment on the job is on the rise. In 1998 there were 9,908 such claims filed with the Equal Employment Opportunity Commission and state agencies. By comparison, in 1991 the number was 4,910. For the 7-year period, the number of cases doubled.

The number of sexual harassment cases can be expected to further increase as the Supreme Court has expanded employer liability. The result is employers are now facing a greater difficulty in persuading judges to dismiss race-harassment claims.

The Supreme Court will now hold an employer liable when a supervisor creates a hostile work environment. If in this hostile environment the employee is fired or demoted, or loses a significant job benefit, the employer is liable. Also, the EEOC has revised its guidelines to say the Supreme Court's sexual harassment standard applies to all types of harassment.[42]

One approach to limiting the legal problems associated with sexual harassment is to control incidents of sexual harassment by increasing employees' awareness of the problem. Such programs do result in more internal complaints, but also result in fewer formal charges. This is a positive development as court costs continue to escalate. Most companies welcome solving such problems internally rather than in the courts, even if the end result is dismissing a problem employee. Digital Equipment Corporation has a specific training program on sexual harassment open to all employees. Although the program has not eliminated the problem, there were only three formal complaints against Digital out of 116,000 employees worldwide.[43]

The EEOC has also issued interpretive guidelines on sexual harassment. However, one should always keep in mind that these EEOC guidelines have great influence, but they are not laws and do not have the power of laws. Although they are accepted in many courts, "federal courts have not always followed them."[44] These guidelines state that employers have an affirmative duty to maintain a workplace free of sexual harassment and intimidation. These and related guidelines state that harassment on the basis of sex is a violation of Title VII when such conduct has the purpose or effect of substantially interfering with a person's work performance or creating an intimidating, hostile, or offensive work environment.

The guidelines define sexual harassment as:

unwelcome sexual advances, requests for sexual favors, and other verbal or physical conduct of a sexual nature that takes place under any of the following conditions:

1. Submission to such conduct is made either explicitly or implicitly a term or condition of an individual's employment.
2. Submission or rejection of such conduct by an individual is used as the basis for employment decisions.
3. Such conduct has the effect of unreasonably interfering with the individual's performance or creating an intimidating or hostile work environment.

Concerted efforts by employers to abate sexual harassment have apparently not been totally unsuccessful. *Working Woman Magazine* surveyed large *Fortune* 500 companies in manufacturing and services. Detailed responses from 160 of them revealed that 76 percent had written policies banning sexual harassment, while an additional 16 percent had a general policy against discrimination, including sexual harassment.[45]

Nevertheless, the same survey disclosed that 90 percent of large companies have received complaints of sexual harassment, and one-third of them have been sued. Indeed, 15 percent of all female employees are sexually harassed in any one year, according to one source.[46]

The influential EEOC guidelines covering various aspects of sexual harassment were issued back in 1980. But it was not until 1986, in the Supreme Court's *Meritor Savings Bank* v. *Vinson* decision, that federal law explicitly outlined an employee's right to a work environment free from abusive, sexual harassment. Further court decisions have basically affirmed these ideas. *Harris* v. *Forklift Systems* (1993) broadens the victim's right to compensation to include cases where no actual emotional damage can be shown.[47] These cases indicate the general approach of the courts in sexual harassment cases so employers should know what they must do to be in compliance.

Despite the legislation against it, and all the court decisions, sexual harassment remains a problem in the workplace, and HR managers and all others responsible for employment policy must develop policies to prevent its occurrence. (See HRM in Action.)

The EEOC has recently issued guidelines for employers concerned about unlawful harassment by their supervisors. They are contained in a 29-page booklet called "Enforcement Guidance: Vicarious Employer Liability for Unlawful Harassment by Supervisors." The guide clarifies who qualifies as a supervisor and defines a tangible employment action. It also includes an explanation of the employer's responsibility to exercise reasonable care.[48]

While sometimes the emphasis seems to focus on laws and defensive measures, the effective human resource manager knows that a proactive approach is the way to go. For example, consider the following: One company that has been successful in promoting workforce diversity is U.S. West. For example, U.S. West now selects women for management jobs 52 percent of the time and minorities total

---

HRM IN ACTION
THE SWEDISH BIKINI TEAM LAWSUIT[49]

The "Swedish Bikini Team" advertisements for Stroh's Old Milwaukee beer contributed to sexual harassment at a company brewery, according to one lawsuit. The commercials show a team of blonde-wigged, bikini-clad women parachuting into a campsite with cases of beer for a group of men. Five female employees filed sexual harassment suits against Stroh Brewery Company. The five workers allege they were subjected to physical and verbal abuse at work—including an allegedly obscene poster listing reasons "why beer is better than women"—and that the ads created a climate of tolerance of such abuse. Stroh was telling its employees through its ads that "women are stupid, panting playthings," said Lori Peterson, the plaintiffs' attorney.

13 percent of management jobs. The top 125 corporate officers are evaluated on pluralism-related criteria based on their organizational profile and the overall pluralism profile of their geographical area. An example would be New Mexico, where 50 percent of U.S. West employees are Hispanic. If managers fail to hire or promote employees representative of their geographical diverse population base, their salaries may be reduced or they may lose their annual bonuses.[50]

In a same-sex harassment case filed by the EEOC, a Minnesota packing firm agreed to a $1.4 million settlement without admitting wrongdoing. The charges filed were disability-based harassment and men-on-men sexual harassment. The EEOC points out this resolves their first same-sex harassment class-action suit since the Supreme Court ruling in 1998. That ruling stated same-sex sexual harassment may violate the Civil Rights Act of 1964.[51]

BUSINESS NECESSITY

Another term sometimes comes up in discussions of employment discrimination. That term, **business necessity,** basically involves showing that there is an overriding business purpose for the discriminatory practice and that the practice is therefore acceptable.

It's not easy proving that a practice is required for "business necessity." The Supreme Court has made it clear that business necessity does not encompass such matters as inconvenience, annoyance, or expense to the employer.

The Civil Rights Act of 1991 requires employers to be more alert in avoiding discrimination in their employment practices. The new act reverses seven U.S. Supreme Court decisions and creates compensation and punitive damage rights plus the right for a jury trial. Most experts believe the act has increased litigation since charges are easier to prove and also, more lucrative damage awards are possible. The act requires the burden of proof to now be on the employer and not the employee. For example, the employer must prove that the ability to lift a certain amount of weight is not just business convenience, but is a business necessity.[52]

ENFORCING THE LAW: THE EEOC

Charges of discrimination may be filed with the EEOC by an individual, and the EEOC may file its own charges that may involve more than one person. The party charging discrimination (the plaintiff) must present reasonable evidence of the event, usually offering some form of statistical data. Once reasonable cause is shown, the burden of proof is transferred to the one being charged with discrimination (the defendant). Now the defendant presents data to try to show that the employment practice being questioned is a business necessity or is job-related.

First, the EEOC must attempt to bring the parties together to obtain a voluntary, out-of-court compliance with Title VII. If this fails, the EEOC may bring charges in the federal courts. If the employer is found guilty, the EEOC may require reinstatement of employees, back pay of up to 2 years prior to filing, attorneys' fees, and an affirmative action plan (AAP). The AAP shows the remedies offered and corrective measures to ensure that the discriminatory practices do not occur again.

RELIGION

In regard to religious practices of employees and prospective employees, employers must make reasonable efforts to accommodate them. Reasonableness is defined by cost. If the cost to the employer is minimal, then the employer will be expected to bear them. Areas of minimal cost might include recordkeeping costs incurred in new job assignments or shift assignments. Other minimal costs might result from flextime, staggered hours, flexible time off without pay, and substituting holidays.

The employer's defense is to show that any of the religious accommodations places an undue hardship upon the operation of the business. Such hardships that would justify denying the employee's religious request would include interfering with the rights of other employees under a seniority system or requiring the employer to pay excessive costs such as overtime, shift differentials, or days off with pay. A request for religious accommodation may also be denied where such accommodation would pose safety problems. For example, even if an employee would prefer to wear a turban rather than a safety hard hat in a construction zone, the employer can and should require wearing of necessary safety equipment.

PHYSICAL AND LANGUAGE DISCRIMINATION

The guidelines deny employers the right to discriminate against employees due to physical characteristics or language due to a particular national origin. Again, a bona fide occupational qualification would permit the employer to discriminate as would a job validation study or a business necessity. However, these last two exemptions become more difficult to validate. Some problem areas for the employer would be requiring fluency in English where it is not job-related, or unnecessary height and weight requirements. Employers are also responsible for the discriminatory actions of their employees and other persons who may frequent the place of employment.

RECRUITING

In recruiting, all advertisements must comply with fair employment laws. Once again, there can be no references in the ads for race, color, religion, sex, national origin, or age other than bona fide occupational qualification. That is, even the merest indication cannot be tolerated. For instance, an ad containing "newly graduated" would cause problems.

When the advertisement contains job qualifications, they must be job-related. Even when a job is usually associated with one sex, the ad must indicate either male or female is acceptable. Although only federal contractors are required to do so, a short statement that you are an equal employment opportunity company further adds to your case.

During recruitment, the company can expect a certain number of unsolicited applications. From an EEO standpoint, either acceptance or rejection of such applications requires careful attention. All unsolicited applicants must be treated courteously and, above all, fairly. However, fairness alone will not satisfy the EEO, if the mix of unsolicited applicants does not supply proportionate numbers of female and minority job candidates.

In all probability, the human resource department, or whoever makes employment decisions in the smaller organization, will have to review present recruitment techniques and expand them into new areas. This may require going out into the community and attempting nontraditional recruiting methods. The company may hold an open house and a job fair, specifically inviting underrepresented groups. Other organizations that could be contacted would be the local YMCA, YWCA, community centers, and the "Forty-Plus" Club.

Some businesses may attempt to circumvent Title VII through the practice of leasing employees from temporary employment agencies to assist with peak work periods or as substitutes for regular employees on vacations. However, while the leased employee is considered to be employed by the temporary employment agency, the business client is still subject to Title VII and the Age Discrimination in Employment Act. The business client may come under fire if it violates these laws in the firing or disciplining of leased employees.

The advent of the equal employment laws, both federal and state, have increased businesses' awareness of the problem resulting in concrete action. This is demonstrated by comparing data collected in 1975 with that of 1985:

- Black employment rose from 10.5% to 11.8%.
- Hispanic employment rose from 4.3% to 5.6%.
- Asian American employment rose from 0.9% to 2.7%.
- Female employment rose from 37.3% to 44.4%.

These figures are the result of personnel policies that mandate special efforts in the recruitment and hiring of females and minorities by businesses.[53]

Application Blank

Information gathered from the application blank frequently becomes the basis for questions during the interview. So, there may be some redundancy between this section and the interviewing section that follows.

Questions asked on the application blank can lead to EEO legal settlements. Companies are well aware of the EEO consequences regarding questions concerning race, color, national origin, sex, age, religion, and handicaps, and so have eliminated them from the application blank. However, there are countless seemingly appropriate questions still appearing on many application blanks that are equally as dangerous and costly. Some applications, for example, ask for date of high school graduation and location of high school. While firms using these forms may honestly support EEO principles, their application forms are indirectly collecting data on age and national origin. It will pay employers to inspect all forms used in the employee selection process to ensure no violations are occurring.

INTERVIEWING

Depending upon where the employment interview takes place, the interviewer (and possibly the personnel receptionist) will be the recruit's first official contact with the company. It is essential that these initial contacts are aware of the need to treat *all* applicants with equal courtesy and friendliness. Personnel who are uncomfortable with females and/or minority members, and who are unable to place them at ease and be fair, must not be allowed to participate in this sensitive first step.

Hiring standards need to be reviewed prior to the interview process to eliminate requirements that are not job-related. For instance, the requirement of a high school diploma might not be appropriate for the job opening. Cut-off test scores may need to be reevaluated. A high degree of English speaking ability may not be required for all jobs. It is only when the job has been carefully reviewed for unnecessary qualifications that a truly equal employment interview can begin.

The importance of the preceding statements cannot be overemphasized, since approximately 70 percent of the discrimination complaints based on EEO laws originate from interviews.

EEO and Discipline

The involvement of the human resource department with Equal Employment Opportunity will not end with the successful hiring of representative groups of women and minorities. There will be continuing problems with seniority issues, attendance, promotions, training, and discipline. While these problems will occur on the shop floor or within administrative offices, because of their EEO implications, the human resource department will become involved.

One of the unique responsibilities of the HR manager is the concern for fairness. While other managers also need to be concerned about fairness, this issue sometimes is pushed aside to meet the more pressing concern of productivity and schedules.

For instance, a worker may be disciplined either through time off without pay, demotion, or in rare circumstances, termination.[54] It is the responsibility of the HR manager to examine the issue of fairness. Picture a worker being disciplined for smoking in a nonsmoking area. Is this an open and shut case of violating a long-standing company rule, with the only decision being the length and severity of the discipline? Perhaps yes, but then again, perhaps no. The issue may be that the worker was not told about the no smoking rule. No smoking signs may not be clearly posted. Or, if they are posted, perhaps the area is littered with cigarette butts, indicating the no smoking rule was not being enforced.

The discipline issue will become more frequent and involved with the successful implementation of EEO selection programs. The purpose of EEO is to bring into the company people who either because of past discrimination or lack of training and education have been excluded from responsible jobs. While the company's discipline policies must be practiced fairly, consistently, and equitably to avoid discrimination charges, the company must be aware of the special problems of particular groups. (See Our Changing World.)

OUR CHANGING WORLD OF HRM
MEXICO'S SLEEPY BORDER TOWNS?[55]

Remember the sleepy little border towns of Tijuana, Ciudad Juarez, Nogalez, and Mexicali? Well, they're gone. Not the towns, but the "sleepy" aspect. The transformation along the U.S.-Mexico border points out once again that change is everywhere. Nearly 2,000 U.S. firms have set up assembly operations near Mexico's northern border, employing over 400,000 people. Maquiladoras, as the plants are called, provide Mexico with its second largest source of foreign exchange, just behind oil. Those benefiting the most are the workers and residents of what *Business Week* called "Mexico's Booming Northland." "There's no question that border towns are bustling today," agrees Don Nibbe, publisher of the El Paso, Texas, monthly publication *Twin Plant*. Not only U.S. firms are involved. Nissan, Hitachi, Sony, Philips, and Siemens are also taking advantage of the special duty forgiveness provisions of the U.S.-Mexico agreement that set up the program in the first place. Everybody wins, right?

Maybe. It depends on who you talk to. Once again, we see that organizational health is a day-to-day thing. What looked good yesterday may not fit at all today. What seems like an all-win situation in the maquiladoras may turn into massive headaches in years to come unless organizational climate is monitored with care and concern. Human resource management issues are causing severe headaches, at least partly because some maquiladoras are following personnel practices in Mexico that equal opportunity legislation and public opinion would make totally unthinkable elsewhere. In fact, one of the arguments in favor of NAFTA—the North American Free Trade Agreement—was that NAFTA would help limit the abuses of maquiladoras.

These human resource practices are not only targets of deserved criticism, but they may make maquiladoras ineffective as well. Workers are often not paid well, even by Mexican standards. Then there is the occasional ob-

---

vious mistake, like the firm Acapulco Fashions. Workers were so fed up with pay and conditions that they went out on strike. Acapulco Fashions simply pulled out, not even paying already-earned back pay. Too many maquiladoras seem to favor young unmarried female workers who are willing to accept low wages. When these same women get older, or marry, they tend to lose their jobs. Turnover stays high, approaching levels that Scandinavia worried about in the 1970s. But too few employers seem to care. It is as if the human resources management policy is to exploit people until burned out and then discard, according to some critics.

Most observers feel that the maquiladora program has the potential to help everyone concerned, if run right. Once again, we see why human resource management must be an ongoing process. No organization can remain static and stay effective. Maquiladoras, take note.

QUESTIONS

1. What are the causes of the problems, and what would you suggest to correct these problems?

2. How would you prevent such occurrences as the Acapulco Fashions problem?

3. Discuss the legal structure of a country that may allow this type of business behavior.

AFFIRMATIVE ACTION

Equal employment opportunity legislation requires organizations to provide the same opportunity to all job applicants regardless of race, color, religion, sex, national origin, or age. Affirmative action goes beyond equal employment opportunity. It requires the employer to put forth an extra effort to hire and promote those in any protected group. Affirmative action programs include those specific actions (in recruitment, hiring, promotions, and compensation) that are designed to eliminate the present effects of past discrimination.

According to the EEOC, the most important measure of an affirmative action program is whether it gets results. The program should result in "measurable, yearly improvements in hiring, training, and promotion of minorities and females" in all parts of the organization. The EEOC also notes that all company officials, managers, and supervisors should clearly understand their own responsibilities for carrying out equal employment opportunity and affirmative action as a basic part of their jobs.

The Basic Steps in an Affirmative Action Program

According to the EEOC, in an affirmative action program, the employer ideally takes eight steps, as follows:

1. Issues a written equal employment policy and affirmative action commitment.
2. Appoints a top official with responsibility and authority to direct and implement the program.
3. Publicizes the equal employment policy and affirmative action commitment.
4. Surveys present minority and female employment by department and job classification to determine where affirmative action programs are needed.
5. Develops goals and timetables to improve utilization of minorities and females in each area where problems have been identified.
6. Develops and implements specific programs to achieve these goals.
7. Establishes an internal audit and reporting system to monitor and evaluate progress in the program.
8. Develops support for the affirmative action program, both inside the company (among supervisors, for instance) and outside the company (in the community).

Affirmative Action: Current Issues

While many affirmative action programs have been successful, there are still important issues to be addressed: First, the realization that some employers only provide enough emphasis to avoid legal action; and second, a prevailing attitude that an affirmative action program may reduce productivity.

As organizations face the challenges of the twenty-first century, we will find women, minority, handicapped, and older employees in increasing numbers and diversity, and there will be increasing equal employment pressures in the future.

SUMMARY

EEO, stated in simple terms, means that everyone should receive an equal opportunity, or a level playing field, in employment decisions. Civil rights legislation has become one of the most critical and difficult functions in the HRM process. Developing an affirmative action program is a complex activity because of multiple factors which influence hiring decisions. Civil rights laws issued by state and federal agencies prohibit discrimination based on race, religion, national origin, age, sex, and physical disability. The skills of HR managers in this area are often critical to organizational success.

In this chapter, the major civil rights legislation and approaches have been described. In the HRM Skills, you will now have a chance to experience using information in an employment interview and making an equal employment decision. You may find that equal opportunity interviews are not a simple process because they involve the employee's needs, a set of values, and existing legal constraints.

The chapter has also described the important elements of an affirmative action program, and you will now have an opportunity to practice and apply these concepts and skills. Change is the name of the game in HRM today, requiring rapid solutions to complex issues. In the HRM Skills, you will have an opportunity to experience some of these complex issues.

REVIEW QUESTIONS

1. How would you define "affirmative action"?
2. Present examples of what employers can do to reduce chances of litigation in organizations you have worked for.
3. Identify and demonstrate the uses of adverse impact in an organization.
4. Contrast the difference between handling of discrimination and sexual harassment cases.
5. Discuss and explain the basic uses of BFOQ.
6. Explain three basic responses an organization might use to minimize the chances of sexual harassment charges.
7. Read a book or view a video movie, and identify an act that might fall under EEOC guidelines. (For example, *Mr. Mom, The Secret of My Success, Working Girl,* or *Nine-to-Five.*)

KEY WORDS AND CONCEPTS

Define and be able to use the following:

- Adverse Impact
- Affirmative Action
- Age Discrimination
- Americans with Disabilities Act (ADA)
- Bona Fide Occupational Qualification (BFOQ)

- Business Necessity
- Civil Rights Act
- Disparate Impact
- Equal Employment Opportunity Commission (EEOC)
- Four-Fifths Rule
- Pregnancy Discrimination
- Rehabilitation Act
- Sexual Harassment

**HRM SKILLS SIMULATION 2.1:
HR MANAGER BEHAVIOR PROFILE I—
THE EMPLOYMENT INTERVIEW**

Total time suggested: 65–75 minutes.

A. PURPOSE

In most organizations, there is a lot of untapped human potential. In an excellent, renewing organization, this potential can be released, resulting in personal growth for the individual. Personal development and organization renewal involve changes in attitudes and behavior which are related to your self-concept, role, goals, and values. In interviewing, the HR manager learns to use good interviewing skills.

The behavior profile which you will generate in this simulation is intended to illustrate some growth dimensions for interpersonal competence and career planning. By recognizing your strengths and accomplishments, you may be encouraged to improve your self-image and interpersonal skills. Hopefully, an honest self-appraisal may aid you in becoming a more effective individual and team member. During this course, you will be afforded additional opportunities to obtain information about yourself on how you behave in organizational situations. This feedback may provide the impetus for you to change, but the ultimate responsibility for that change is with you. Retain this completed survey as it will be used again in chapter 19.

B. PROCEDURES

Part A. The HRM Profile Survey

Step 1. Before class, complete your HRM Profile on the following survey. How you respond reflects how you view yourself, which in turn reveals something about your behavioral style. Based on the following scale, select the number to indicate the degree to which you feel each description is characteristic of you. Record your choice in the blank to the right. Retain this completed survey as it will be used again in Simulation 19.1.

Step 2. Complete Table 2.3, HRM Profile Form, by making a horizontal bar graph in the line marked "Chapter 2" for your behavior profile you have just completed. Note that the 30 descriptions have been reordered to fit into five categories. The profile provides information about your behavioral style and allows you to see where you stand in each category. It also lets you directly compare your score on different scales by looking at the difference in the bar graph. The profile may indicate items on which your score is less desirable than you would like. You may also find categories in which you have generally low ratings. These may suggest areas for improvement during this course and for assessing the kinds of changes you may wish to make in order to become a more effective HR manager.

Part B. Goal Setting—Personal Objectives for Course

Step 1. After completing Table 2.3, HRM Profile Form, outside of class list some of the *specific* objectives and expectations you have for this class on the Performance Objectives Form. These objectives should describe what you will be able to do and the time required. Refer to the HRM Profile Form you have just completed, and select some behaviors you would like to emphasize for change.

Sample: To develop more self-confidence in performing class presentations by doing three short presentations in class.

Try referring to the preceding objectives often and at least before coming to class for the remainder of the course. Do not hesitate to experiment with the new behaviors you would like to cultivate. You will be referring to these objectives again later in the book.

Step 2. The HRM Profile can be used as a feedback tool. You will be able to learn more about yourself by assessing the kinds of changes you may need to make in order to become more effective. Form into trios, with one person acting as the interviewer, a second as the interviewee, and the third as observer (see the HRM Profile Form and Observer Recording Form).

The interviewer will help you to develop a fuller understanding of how your styles play a part in your overall effectiveness, and how you may build on your strengths during this course. The interviewer will review the interviewee's HRM Profile Form and Performance Objectives Form for the following:

1. How accurate are the profile assessments relative to observations in class?
2. Are they a complete and challenging set of goals?
3. Are they realistic and feasible?
4. Are they specific and measurable?
5. Are they things the employee (student) can do and demonstrate by the end of the course?

The observer will study the interview style using the Observer Recording Form, and try to provide feedback on the interviewing style. At the end of each interview, the observer gives observations providing feedback to the interviewer using the Observer Recording Form. Then rotate roles, so that each person is in each of the three roles. Continue the simulation by switching roles until everyone has played each of the roles.

Time suggested for Step 2: 15–20 minutes per person (in each of the rotating roles)

Step 3. Meeting with the entire class, discuss:

1. How can we improve performance?
2. What interview skills seemed to work best?
3. Do we view change as positive or negative?
4. The role of the interviewer—Was it helpful? How?
5. How effective was our team?

Time suggested for Step 3: 15 minutes.

HRM PROFILE SURVEY

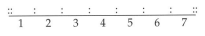

```
::   :   :   :   :   :   :  ::
 1   2   3   4   5   6   7
```

Not at All   Somewhat   Very
Characteristic   Characteristic Characteristic

1. Having the ability to communicate in a clear, concise, and persuasive manner   _____

2. Being spontaneous—saying and doing things that seem natural on the spur of the moment   _____

3. Doing things "by the book"—noticing appropriate rules and procedures and following them   _____

4. Being creative—having a lot of unusual, original ideas; thinking of new approaches to problems others do not often come up with   _____

5. Being competitive—wanting to win and be the best   _____

6. Being able to listen to and understand others   _____

7. Being aware of other people's moods and feelings   _____

8. Being careful in your work—taking pains to make sure everything is "just right"   _____

9. Being resourceful in coming up with possible ways of dealing with problems   _____

10. Being a leader—having other people look to you for direction; taking over when things are confused   _____

11. Having the ability to accept feedback without reacting defensively, becoming hostile, or withdrawing   _____

12. Having the ability to deal with conflict and anger   _____

13. Having written work neat and organized; making plans before starting on a difficult task; organizing details of work   _____

14. Thinking clearly and logically; attempting to deal with ambiguity, complexity, and confusion in a situation with thoughtful, logical analysis   _____

15. Having self-confidence when faced with a challenging situation   _____

16. Having the ability to level with others, to give feedback to others   _____

17. Doing new and different things; meeting new people; experimenting and trying out new ideas or activities   _____

18. Having a high level of aspiration; setting difficult goals   _____

19. Analyzing a situation carefully before acting; working out a course of action in detail before embarking on it   _____

20. Being effective at initiating projects and innovative ideas   _____

21. Seeking ideas from others; drawing others into discussion   _____

22. Having a tendency to seek close personal relationships while participating in social activities with friends; giving affection and receiving it from others   _____

23. Being dependable—staying on the job; doing what is expected   _____

24. Having the ability to work as a catalyst to stimulate and encourage others to develop their own resources for solving their own problems   _____

25. Taking responsibility; relying on your own abilities and judgment rather than those of others   _____

26. Selling your own ideas effectively   _____

27. Being the dominant person; having a strong need for control or recognition   _____

28. Getting deeply involved in your work; being extremely committed to ideas or work you are doing   _____

29. Having the ability to evaluate possible solutions critically   _____

30. Having the ability to work in unstructured situations, with little or no support and to continue to work effectively even if faced with lack of cooperation, resistance, or hostility   _____

Table 2.3
HRM profile form

		Score	NOT AT ALL CHARACTERISTIC			SOMEWHAT CHARACTERISTIC		VERY CHARACTERISTIC	
A. Communicating Skills			1	2	3	4	5	6	7
Items 1. Communicates	Ch. 2								
	Ch. 19								
6. Listens	Ch. 2								
	Ch. 19								
11. Receives Feedback	Ch. 2								
	Ch. 19								
16. Gives Feedback	Ch. 2								
	Ch. 19								
21. Seeks Ideas	Ch. 2								
	Ch. 19								
26. Sells Ideas	Ch. 2								
	Ch. 19								
MEAN SCORE A	Ch. 2								
	Ch. 19								
B. Interpersonal Skills									
Items 2. Is Spontaneous	Ch. 2								
	Ch. 19								
7. Is Aware	Ch. 2								
	Ch. 19								
12. Deals with Conflict	Ch. 2								
	Ch. 19								
17. Experiments	Ch. 2								
	Ch. 19								
22. Seeks Close Relationships	Ch. 2								
	Ch. 19								
27. Is Dominant	Ch. 2								
	Ch. 19								
MEAN SCORE B	Ch. 2								
	Ch. 19								
C. Aspiration-Achievement Levels									
Items 3. Conforms	Ch. 2								
	Ch. 19								
8. Is Careful	Ch. 2								
	Ch. 19								
13. Is Organized	Ch. 2								
	Ch. 19								
18. Aspires	Ch. 2								
	Ch. 19								

Table 2.3 (Continued)

23. Is Dependable	Ch. 2									
	Ch. 19									
28. Is Committed to Ideas or Work	Ch. 2									
	Ch. 19									
MEAN SCORE C	Ch. 2									
	Ch. 19									
D. Problem-Solving Skills										
Items 4. Is Creative	Ch. 2									
	Ch. 19									
9. Is Resourceful	Ch. 2									
	Ch. 19									
14. Is Logical	Ch. 2									
	Ch. 19									
19. Analyzes	Ch. 2									
	Ch. 19									
24. Is Catalyst	Ch. 2									
	Ch. 19									
29. Evaluates	Ch. 2									
	Ch. 19									
MEAN SCORE D	Ch. 2									
	Ch. 19									
E. Leadership Skills										
Items 5. Is Competitive	Ch. 2									
	Ch. 19									
10. Is a Leader	Ch. 2									
	Ch. 19									
15. Is Confident	Ch. 2									
	Ch. 19									
20. Initiates	Ch. 2									
	Ch. 19									
25. Takes Responsibility	Ch. 2									
	Ch. 19									
30. Can Work in Unstructured Situations	Ch. 2									
	Ch. 19									

HRM PERFORMANCE INTERVIEW FORM

Interviewer _____   Interviewee _____

<u>GOALS:</u>

I. ATTENDANCE

What percentage of the class meetings will you attend?

100%–95%	94%–90%	89%–80%	79%–70%	69%–60%	59%–50%	49%–0%

II. PREPARATION

What percentage of the time will you come prepared?

Chapters read, HRM Skills Prepared, HRM Case Prepared	100%–95%	94%–90%	89%–80%	79%–70%	69%–60%	59%–50%	49%–0%

III. PROBLEM SOLVING

What percentage of the time will you:

	100%–95%	94%–90%	89%–80%	79%–70%	69%–60%	59%–50%	49%–0%
Understand key terms							
Prepare text assignments							
Develop correct answers							

IV. INVOLVEMENT

What percentage of the time will you contribute to team performance by:

	100%–95%	94%–90%	89%–80%	79%–70%	69%–60%	59%–50%	49%–0%
Showing interest in the meeting							
Initiating discussion							
Getting along with other team members							

PERFORMANCE OBJECTIVES FORM

Communicating Skills: Time Requirement

    1. _____

    2. _____

    3. _____

Interpersonal Skills:

    1. _____

    2. _____

    3. _____

Aspiration-Achievement Levels:

    1. _____

    2. _____

    3. _____

Problem-Solving Skills:

    1. _____

    2. _____

    3. _____

Leadership Skills:

    1. _____

    2. _____

    3. _____

Other:

    1. _____

    2. _____

    3. _____

OBSERVER RECORDING FORM

1. Level of involvement:
    Cautious   Low 1:2:3:4:5:6:7:8:9:10 High   Interested   _____

2. Level of communication:
    Doesn't listen   Low 1:2:3:4:5:6:7:8:9:10 High   Listens   _____

3. Level of openness, trust:
    Shy, uncertain   Low 1:2:3:4:5:6:7:8:9:10 High   Warm, friendly   _____

4. Level of collaboration:
    Authoritative   Low 1:2:3:4:5:6:7:8:9:10 High   Seeks agreement   _____

5. Level of influence:
    Gives in   Low 1:2:3:4:5:6:7:8:9:10 High   Convincing   _____

6. Level of supportiveness:
    Disagrees   Low 1:2:3:4:5:6:7:8:9:10 High   Supports   _____

7. Level of direction:
    Easygoing, agreeable   Low 1:2:3:4:5:6:7:8:9:10 High   Gives directions   _____

8. Level of competence:
    Unsure   Low 1:2:3:4:5:6:7:8:9:10 High   Competent   _____

9. Other: Low 1:2:3:4:5:6:7:8:9:10 High   _____

10. Overall style:
    Ineffective   Low 1:2:3:4:5:6:7:8:9:10 High   Effective   _____

A. PURPOSES

1. To examine several commonly held notions regarding women in management.
2. To understand the relationship between values and attitudes toward work situations.

B. PROCEDURES

Step 1. Before class, read the following statements. Place your ranked answer next to the statement.

Step 2. Form into groups and each group must reach consensus on each question. Fill in the following form by male-agreeing and female-agreeing. (1 = disagree, 2 = agree)

	Strongly disagree				Strongly agree
	1	2	3	4	5

1. A woman's place is in the home. ___
2. Most American women work just for pin money. ___
3. Women have a higher turnover rate and higher absentee rate than men. ___
4. The average woman doesn't want responsibility on her job. She does not want promotions or job changes which would increase her authority and responsibility. ___
5. The employment of mothers leads to delinquency. ___
6. Married women take jobs away from men. In fact, married women should quit the jobs they now hold. ___
7. Women don't work as long or as regularly as their male counterparts. ___
8. Women should stick to "women's jobs" and shouldn't compete for men's jobs. ___
9. Women are more satisfied than men with intellectually undemanding jobs. ___
10. Women are more concerned than men with the social and emotional aspects of their jobs. ___
11. Women would not work if they did not absolutely have to for economic reasons. ___
12. Women prefer not to take the initiative on the job. ___
13. Women are less concerned than men with getting ahead on the job. ___
14. Women are less concerned than men that their job be self-actualizing. ___

WOMEN IN MANAGEMENT FORM

Statements	Percent Males ____ Males Agree	Percent Females ____ Females Agree
1.		
2.		
3.		
4.		
5.		
6.		
7.		
8.		
9.		
10.		
11.		
12.		
13.		
14.		

A. PURPOSE

Sexual harassment is illegal as mandated by law. The lines between legal and illegal in the workplace are smudged. Some comments and acts are easily identified as illegal. There are other words, gestures, and acts that fall into the "shades of grey" area. This exercise is designed to help you decide where the line should be drawn in the workplace.

B. PROCEDURES

Step 1. Prior to class, read the information. Fill out the individual answer form.

Step 2. In class, form into groups. Each group is to reach consensus on the team response form.

Step 3. Fill in the individual rating (col. 1), the team rating (col. 2), correct rating (col. 3), individual score (col. 4), and team score (col. 5).

SEXUAL HARASSMENT IN THE WORKPLACE

From an article in *The Spokesman Review and Spokane Chronicle,* June 28, 1991:

> Seattle—The University of Washington has agreed to pay $125,000 plus attorney fees to a former student who claimed she was sexually harassed by a professor and that the school mishandled her complaint.

> The UW administration also agreed to seek changes in how it handles sexual harassment cases as part of a settlement of a civil lawsuit filed by Teri Ard in 1989.

> The school admitted no guilt in the settlement.

> Ard, now 23, alleged that forestry Professor Graham Allan had touched her sexually and made inappropriate sexual remarks between September 1987 and February 1989, when she was a forestry undergraduate.

From an article in *The San Diego Union-Tribune,* December 27, 1992:

> Even when the victims don't sue, sexual harassment costs the typical *Fortune* 500 company $6.7 million per year in employee turnover, absenteeism and reduced productivity, according to one 1988 survey by Klein Associates Inc., a Massachusetts consulting firm.

> *Working Woman* magazine, for example, surveyed 10,000 readers and interviewed personnel directors at 100 *Fortune* 500 companies. More than 60 percent of the readers said sexual harassment complaints were ignored in their companies; 82 percent of the personnel executives said complaints are investigated and offenders are punished justly.

Read the following quiz, and rank answers as follows: 1—Inappropriate/illegal, 2—Illegal, 3—Inappropriate/legal, and 4—No problem.

1. John, the project manager, enjoys talking about new assignments with team members in a more relaxed setting, away from the office. He asks Celeste, a new employee, to lunch. John asks Celeste how her work is progressing, and if she feels comfortable in her position. During the final half-hour the conversation changes to questions concerning her personal life. Is John guilty of any illegal harassment? ____

2. Jane tells Frank, her subordinate, that she has been invited to a very important work-related party. She wants him to be her date because of his good looks. Frank tells Jane that he will not be able to escort her. Jane responds with a remark about how important it is to always be a team player. Is Jane guilty of any illegal harassment? ____

3. Sue has been having an affair with her boss for several months. She willingly chose the relationship. She receives the next promotion in the department. Two coworkers, Betty and Donald, who have been on the job equally as long, are upset they were not chosen for promotion. They believe that the promotion was based on the affair, not job performance. Do Betty and Donald have grounds for legal action? ____

4. Mr. Smith likes early morning meetings with Rose, Bill, and Pete, members of his specialty team. Rose is always asked to perform the secretarial duties and to take care of coffee and doughnuts. Rose thinks she is being sexually harassed because the men are not asked to do this work. Is she correct? ____

5. The typing pool at a small company consists of two women and one man. The women, Connie and Sarah, have Chippendale calendars at their desks and continuously talk about male sexuality and their boyfriends. Kurt is the only male in the typing pool and he is offended by the nude calendars and sexual remarks. Does Kurt have justification for harassment charges? ____

HARASSMENT RATING FORM

Employee	Individual Rating Col. 1	Team Rating Col. 2	Correct Rating Col. 3	Individual Score Col. 4	Team Score Col. 5
1. JOHN					
2. JANE					
3. SUE					
4. MR. SMITH					
5. CONNIE					

TEAM COMPOSITION   # MALES _____
                     # FEMALES _____

HARASSMENT RATING FORM ANSWER SHEET

1. **3** A woman may feel she is being treated like everyone else and welcome lunch with the boss, but she may feel uncomfortable answering questions about her life outside the office. Women often perceive personal inquiries—and their intent—differently from men. Play it safe, John, stick to business.
2. **1** Jane is way out of line. This scenario has all the makings of the most severe sexual harassment. It seems Jane is making dating a part of Frank's employment.
3. **3** This has potential for a claim, but the issue is whether Sue got the promotion based on merit. That issue could end up in court. Any supervisor who dates or has an intimate relationship with a subordinate is asking for trouble. This boss is asking for trouble.
4. **2** This is sexual discrimination, not sexual harassment. Both are illegal. The problem should always be avoided by rotating the doughnut and secretarial duties evenly.
5. **1** It is offensive, it's inappropriate, and a good supervisor will always end this type of situation.

Case 2.1 Precision Products, Inc.

As Helen Brown, personnel manager, crossed the shop floor to get to the elevator that would whisk her up to her office, she noticed a group of 10 to 20 men in front of a tool cabinet laughing uproariously. Out of the middle of the group strode Jennifer White, clearly upset and angry.

As Jennifer disappeared into the women's restroom, Helen could hear the workers whistling and shouting after Jennifer, "What's the matter, Jenny?"

Quickly sensing foul play was afoot, Helen made tracks for the group of men. "What's going on here?" she demanded.

"Aw, we were just having a little fun with the new hire. Nothing serious, just a little joke," one of the men answered, pointing to the inside of the tool cabinet door.

Helen looked at the door and saw a poster of a generously endowed Playmate of the Month. Barely able to contain her anger, she seethed, "Do you have any idea what you've done?"

"Oh, it ain't no big deal," another man answered. "She'll get used to it. Besides, pretty soon she'll be playing up to the boss, and get promoted like some of the other women around here." By the way he was looking at her, Helen took this as a direct accusation.

After she had their supervisor take down the names and employee numbers of all the men and had calmed Jennifer, Helen headed up to her office. Helen rubbed her temples as she thought to herself, "If it wasn't for the union, I'd have each and every one of those men reprimanded on the spot."

Because she had been hired as personnel manager, Helen had worked hard to increase the number of women hired. However, with the rough and tumble environment that pervaded the shop floor, it was proving difficult to keep the newly hired women from leaving shortly after they were hired. It didn't help that the predominantly male ranks of lower management didn't see that there was any problem.

Leaving her office to get a cup of coffee, she looked up in time to see one of her female assistants playfully pat a male employee. He turned around and smiled, then went back to his filing.

Helen walked more slowly as she thought to herself, "How can I turn this thing around? What can I do about this attitude around here?" As she watched the machine dispense the coffee into the paper cup, Helen visualized the money that it could cost the company in possible legal actions. ∎

QUESTIONS

1. Was what the workers did to Jennifer White sexual harassment? Why? Why not?
2. What Helen's assistant did to the male employee—was it sexual harassment? Why? Why not?
3. You are Helen Brown. What could you do to "turn this around"?

ENDNOTES

1. Mary McElveen, "How to Avoid Discrimination Suits," *Nation's Business* (March 1992): 16.
2. The Associated Press, "Hyundai files to overturn sexual discrimination verdict suit," *The Oregonian*, 6 August 1999, p. B1.
3. See for example, "Ex-GM Worker Wins $1.25 Million in Suit, ADA," *Wall Street Journal*, 8 April 1987, p. 14; and Matt Chalker, "Tooling Up For ADA," *HRM Magazine* (December 1991): 61–65.
4. Robin Fields, "BP Amoco Taps Irvine Firm to Do Personnel Chores," *Los Angeles Times*, 10 December 1999, p. C1.
5. John Balz, "Young adults accept racial lines," *L.A. Times-Washington Post* Service, *The Oregonian*, 17 August 1999, p. A4.
6. Arne L. Kalleberg and Kevin T. Leicht, "Gender and Organizational Performance: Determinants of Small Business Survival and Success," *Academy of Management Journal* 34, no. 1 (March 1991): 136–61.
7. Mylene Mangalindan, "Women Still Battle to Get Venture Funds," *Los Angeles Times, Bloomberg News*, 5 January 2000, p. C6.
8. Linda E. Duxbury and Christopher A. Higgins, "Gender Differences in Work-Family Conflict," *Journal of Applied Psychology* 76, no. 1 (February 1991): 60–73.
9. Stephanie Overman, "Companies face child-labor, overtime violations despite DOL education drive," *HR News* 11, no. 9 (February 1993): section A.
10. David G. Savage, "Court Shields States in Suits on Age Bias," *Los Angeles Times*, 12 January 2000, A12.
11. Lean Nathans Spiro, "The Angry Voices at Kidder," *Business Week* (February 1, 1993): 60.
12. "Chevron Workers Win Bias Suit," *The Bakersfield Californian*, 4 May 1991, p. 1.
13. M. Zall, "What to Expect from the Civil Rights Act," *Personnel Journal* 7, no. 3 (1992): 40–44.

14. *Work Force 2000: Work and Workers for the 21st Century.* Executive Summary (U.S. Department of Labor: Washington DC, n.d.): 19.

15. "Suspect age bias? Try proving it." *Fortune* 139, no. 2 (February 1999): 58.

16. Rochelle Garner. "Golden oldies," *ComputerWorld* 33, no. 6 (February 8, 1999): 65–66.

17. Richard L. Brandt. "Here me," *Research-Technology-Management,* 42, no. 2 (March-April 1999): 9.

18. Terry Pristin, "Ex-Salesman, 65, Wins $4 Million in Age Bias Suit," *Los Angeles Times,* 12 October 1991, p. D1. See also Paul M. Barrett, "How One Man's Fight for a Raise Became a Major Age Case," *Wall Street Journal,* 7 January 1993, p. A1.

19. James A. Burns, Jr., "Should the ADEA protect persons under age 40?," *Employee Relations Law Journal* 24, no. 4 (Spring 1999): 135–38.

20. Donald F. Harvey and Richard A. Wald, "Age Discrimination, the EEOC and the Xerox Corporation," *Southern Business Journal* (Spring 1990): 1.

21. David G. Savage, "Court Shields States in Suits on Age Bias," *Los Angeles Times,* 12 January 2000, p. 1A.

22. Vineeta Anand, "Age discrimination issue raised by EEOC, others." *Pensions and Investments,* 27, no. 11 (May 31, 1999): 224.

23. Richard Pimental, James R. Redelen, and Jonathon Segal, "Avoiding ADA Related Liability," *Personnel* (August 1989): 46.

24. Jennifer Lach, "Disability (not equal) liability," *American Demographics* 21, no. 6 (June 1999): 21–22.

25. Alberta R. Karr, "Work Week, Overweight workers lose a discrimination suit, continuing a trend," *The Wall Street Journal,* 24 August 1999, p. A1.

26. Sandra E. O'Connell, "Information Management Issues and the ADA," *HRM Magazine* 37, no. 4 (1992): 31–32.

27. Michael A. Verespej, "ADA rulings help, but even with more guidance, much uncertainty remains," *IndustryWeek* 248, no. 13 (July 5, 1999): 56.

28. George W. Johnson, "Coping with AIDS: Today's Workplace Issue," *Labor Law Journal* 39, no. 3 (May 1989): 302. See also "Corporate AIDS Policies Found Lacking," *Los Angeles Times,* 11 November 1991, p. D1.

29. *Nassau County* v. *Arline,* U.S. 43 FEP 81 (1987).

30. George W. Johnson, "Corporate AIDS Policies Found Lacking," *Los Angeles Times,* 11 November 1991, p. D1.

31. Stephanie Overman, "Moving Labor into the 21st Century," *HRM Magazine* 36, no. 12 (December 1991): 36–39.

32. "The Disabilities Act," *Congressional Quarterly Researcher* 1, no. 32 (December 1991): 933–1016.

33. *Calif. Federal Savings and Loan* v. *Guerra,* 42 FEP Case 1073 (1987).

34. John P. Kohl and Paul S. Greenlaw, "The Pregnancy Discrimination Act: A Twenty Year Retrospect," *Labor Law Journal* 50, no. 1 (March 1999): 71–76.

35. "Family and Medical Leave Act of 1993," *Information Center,* and Occasional Fact Sheet published by The Society for Human Resource Management, February 1993.

36. *Wards Cove Packing Co.* v. *Antonio,* 109 US 2115 (1989).

37. G. Munchus III, "Check References for Safer Selection," *HR Magazine* 37, no. 6 (1992): 75–77.

38. Mary Reid, "Words That May Later Haunt You," *Wall Street Journal,* 20 December 1993, p. A12.

39. Stephanie Overman, "Companies face child-labor, overtime violations despite DOL education drive," *HR News* 11, no. 9 (February 1993): section A.

40. "Staff and wire reports, Nike says plant may have used child labor for counterfeit balls," *The Oregonian,* 28 August 1999, p. B1.

41. John Wilkens and Lorie Hearn, "Employers Action, Head FF Complaints," *San Diego Union,* 27 December 1991, p. C6.

42. Francis A. McMorris, "Employers Face Greater Liability in Race Cases," *The Wall Street Journal,* 1 July 1999, B1.

43. A. Meyer, "Getting to the Heart of Sexual Harassment," *HR Magazine* 37, no. 7 (1992): 82–84.

44. "EEOC spells out reasonable accommodation," *Business and Health* 17, no. 6 (June 1999): 9.

45. Ronni Sondroff, "Working Woman Survey Results: Sexual Harassment in the Fortune 500," *Working Woman* 13, no. 12 (December 1988): 69.

46. "Sexual Harassment: Men and Women in Workplace Power Struggles," *Congressional Quarterly* 1, no. 9 (August 1991): 539–59.

47. Arthur F. Silbergeld and Mark B. Tuvim, "Harris v. Forklift Systems: The Court Relaxes the Burden of Proving Sexual Harrassment Claims," *Employment Relations Today* 20 (Winter 1993–94): 465–74.

48. Sally Roberts, "Supreme Court rulings on unlawful harassment by company supervisors," *Business Insurance* 33, no. 26 (June 1999): 33.

49. "Bikini Team Lawsuit," *Wall Street Journal,* 11 November 1991, p. B4.

50. S. Caudron, "U.S. West Finds Strength in Diversity," *Personnel Journal* 7, no. 3 (1992): 40–44.

51. Albert R. Karr, "Work Week, Same-Sex Harassment," *The Wall Street Journal,* 24 August 1999, A1.

52. M. Zall, "What to Expect from the Civil Rights Act," *Personnel Journal* 7, no. 3 (1992): 46–50.

53. "Ideas and Trends in Personnel," *CCH Human Resources Management* (March 28, 1983): 48.

54. I. Asherman, "The Connective Discipline Process," *Personnel* (July 1982): 528.

55. John Hulpke, "Mexico's Border Problems," Working Paper, 1994. California State University, Bakersfield.

Chapter 3

The Success System: HRM Planning, Job Analysis, and Productivity

Objectives

Upon completing this chapter, you will be able to:

1. Define and discuss the concepts of quality of work life and job analysis.
2. Describe the steps in developing and implementing a job analysis program and understand its impact on the behavior of individuals in an organization.
3. Understand how to use the organization chart and job design techniques in an organization.
4. Identify and describe the major job analysis techniques and understand their importance.

Premeeting preparation

1. Read chapter 3.
2. Prepare for HRM Skills Simulation 3.1: Superior Products. Read and complete Step 1.
3. Read Case 3.1: Precision Products, Inc. Answer questions.

The factory is not just quiet—it seems almost deserted. The driveway, lined with thick pine forest, is a mile long and gives the place a muffled quality. The two main buildings are large enough to be airplane hangars—tall-shouldered, with blank metal walls so high that the doorways look puny. The inside of the far building is almost as still as the outside. There is plenty of equipment—tool carts, platforms for working around large items, racks of parts. But there is an air of work interrupted, and only a handful of people are visible.

It is, however, instantly clear what kind of work gets done here. Hanging from yellow overhead cranes are two of the largest jet engines in the world. It takes no great aeronautical expertise to appreciate these engines: Even unfinished, they look muscular. They're also huge: Each one is bigger than a Lincoln Navigator.

Although engines go out the door of this plant at a rate of more than one per day, the air of calm is hardly its most unusual aspect. The plant is General Electric's aircraft-engine assembly facility in Durham, North Carolina. Even within Jack Welch's widely admired empire, the Durham facility is in its own league—a quiet corner of a global giant, a place where the radical has become routine. GE-Durham has more than 170 employees but just one boss: the plant manager. Everyone in the place reports to her. Which means that on a day-to-day basis, the people who work here have no boss. They essentially run themselves.

The jet engines are produced by nine teams of people—teams that are given just one basic directive: the day that their next engine must be loaded onto a truck. All other decisions—who does what work; how to balance training, vacations, and overtime against work flow; how to make the manufacturing process more efficient; how to handle teammates who slack off—all of that stays within the team.[1]

A key issue facing organizations today is the way in which they respond to the changing environment of world class competition. HRM activities leading to improved productivity, efficiency, and quality have evolved to help organizations meet these challenges. For example, Boeing is in the process of reinventing itself to meet changing conditions. "We are dedicated to not doing what IBM, Sears, and General Motors have done—which is to get to the top, be the best, and then get fat and lazy," says Boeing President Dean D. Thornton. In the process of reinventing Boeing, the analysis is going all the way down to the level of the individual job.[2]

Changes in job design, such as those at Boeing, can result in increased productivity and employee satisfaction. The HR manager can help develop job analysis of line and staff employees and all levels of managers, so that every employee utilizes all his or her resources and capabilities. This job analysis is important in setting up work teams as well. Job analysis may be viewed as the hub of virtually all HR management activities.[3] In this chapter, we present the second stage of the Success System Model: designing a high-performing workplace. This chapter examines HRM planning, job analysis, job design, job enrichment, and self-managing work teams. The analysis of jobs is important in the team-based approach to determine how to divide and assign tasks.

CHANGE OR DIE

Business enterprises and nonprofit organizations are increasingly confronted with problems of stable or declining productivity, worker dissatisfaction and alienation, and increased domestic and foreign competition. Many federal regulations that once tended to protect inefficient operations are being removed and companies are now confronted with increased competition. Businesses no longer receive the degree of trade protection once afforded by their national government. As an example, for every $5 worth of goods or services a country produces, they may sell about $1 abroad.

The world is truly a global market and with it comes increased competition. Witness the rapid changes in the services and products offered by the telecommunications industry, the turbulent environment and mergers in the airline industry, the expansion of services offered by the once conservative banking industry, and the changes in the way health care is offered. Technological, economic, and regulatory shifts are forcing organizations in one industry after another "to change or die."[4]

It is common to read newspaper reports about the decline in U.S. competitiveness, another U.S. market being lost to foreign industry, or the continued deterioration in the quality of U.S. products. The United States is no longer leading the world in technological innovations. "In the 1950s, the U.S. initiated more than 80 percent of the world's major innovations; today it is close to 50 percent, and foreigners are acquiring a much larger share of U.S. patents (now over a third)."[5] But the problems are not only in the technology-based industries. Local, state, and federal governments are also trying to maintain or increase services despite budget reductions.

HUMAN RESOURCE PLANNING

Human resource planning, or manpower planning as it was originally called, had its start after World War II in the Industrial Training Boards in Great Britain whose mandate was to require effective manpower planning at the industrial level. It resulted from the influence of socialistic government policies in England to provide the correct number of skilled employees within certain age groups for their nationalized industries.

Although a few large companies have special departments to develop human resource plans and forecasts, most companies that employ up to a few thousand cannot afford to staff such specialists. In some large companies, the responsibility for human resource planning is assigned to the human resource manager. However, regardless where assigned, if a company is to grow and prosper, the functions of human resource planning must be carried out effectively.[6]

Human resource planning systems depend upon three key factors:

1. *Knowledge of the Human Resource Environment.* This provides information to answer the question, "What has been and is happening to our human resources?" The answer resides in the collection and analysis of such factors as labor turnover rates, recruiting effectiveness, and levels of training. These three factors comprise what is called the **human resource audit.** Other human resource environment factors that need to be considered in the human resource audit are technological and economic changes. These changes, while difficult to quantify, must be identified and evaluated.
2. *Knowledge of the Present Corporate Human Resources.* This is a prerequisite for planning for the future. The HRM manager must know what skills and potential are presently available before beginning to plan. This initial inventory is called the **human resource inventory.**
3. *Knowledge of the Present and Future Objectives of Corporate Planning.* This requires that business plans and objectives must be expressed in meaningful human resource terms. For example, consider the following: "The 5-year objective is to increase our market share to 30 percent at a rate of 6 percent per year resulting in the bottom line increase of $150,000 in sales volume." The

preceding statement needs to be changed to meet our criteria by reducing the expressed needs into an expression of human resource required for each *year* of the planning cycle and in terms of *type* and *level* of skill. This is essential, since such a statement of **human resource requirements** represents the central core of human resource planning.

These factors allow the corporation to develop short-term plans to cope with sudden changes in the environment and to anticipate future change. As a result, the corporation is prepared to handle expected changes arising from business plans as well as the unexpected changes resulting from rapid economic, political, and/or technical change. For example, Caterpillar's (the tractor company) use of information technology allows it to get twice as much production out of the same number of employees.[7]

It is important to recognize that corporate strategy will be determined, in part, by human resource planning. However, corporate strategy is first determined by *corporate vision* which is the reason for the existence and growth of the enterprise. It is the goal towards which all objectives of the divisions within the organization are directed.

Why does the organization need to implicitly define the corporate vision? It is not appropriate to state the corporate vision as profit or maximizing return on investment because neither provide a guide to optimizing scarce resources. Business success is determined by how management allocates scarce resources to alternative uses.

These resources are financial, physical, and human. There are countless alternatives for which the resources may be used. It becomes essential that prior to allocating these scarce resources management determines the limits within which they will operate. Without determining these limits, a company may prosper temporarily but will eventually squander their resources uneconomically in pursuit of diverse and conflicting objectives. The corporate purpose describes in explicit terms the arena in which the enterprise will operate.

Corporate Objectives

Once the corporate vision is determined, then precise objectives are stated. It is from these precise objectives that the corporate strategy emerges, of which human resource planning is but one component.

The corporate vision may simply state "to be a leader in the electrical appliance business." Or, "to be a leader in the electric appliance business in North America." Or, it could be more specific and narrow the product line to only kitchen appliances. The corporate vision becomes a reason for existing; the mission of the company, its guide to action.

However, before the corporate vision can be formulated, there is a prerequisite: Management must first be aware of the business in which it is presently engaged. For instance, a company selling photocopying machines could be in the copying business or business machines or, from a broader viewpoint, the communications business. Each business viewpoint represents important conceptual differences. Another example would be an airline that could be in the passenger transport business or the travel accommodation business. In one instance, we limit ourselves in allocating resources; in the other, we broaden the number of alternatives.

HRM Objectives

Once the corporate vision is developed, then the objectives of human resource planning can be stated as follows:

1. The optimum utilization of currently employed human resources.
2. The provision of future human resource needs in the areas of skills and numbers.

These two basic human resource planning objectives can also be stated in another way:

The right *number* of employees
with the right *level* of talent and skills
in the right *jobs* at the right *time*
performing the right *activities*
to achieve the right *objectives*
to fulfill the corporate vision.

Once the corporate vision has been determined, then a corporate strategy can be developed. There are four main components to corporate strategy: (1) internal resources, (2) environmental trends, (3) corporate values, and (4) levels of risk.

Internal resources are represented by capital, manpower, and financial factors. The proportion in which these internal resources are blended will result in the unique focus of the enterprise. Companies in the same business will often differ from others as a result of this utilization of resources.

Companies in the same industry may respond differently to identical *environmental trends* such as new inventions or changes in customer needs. Such changes in environmental trends offer opportunities for profit that are either exploited or missed. Those opportunities that are capitalized on will distinguish the successful company from the unsuccessful one. These successes identify the corporate values, the distinctive competence of the company: the things it does better than its competitors.

The final component of corporate strategy is the level of *risk taking*. While risk taking usually applies to finance, it can also extend to other areas such as human resources; for instance, decisions made in hiring, promotion or training, where one takes a risk because some personal quality is weak or skill levels are low.

At the heart of corporate strategy are human resources. The proper utilization of its human resources will be the final determination of company success.

From the company vision, a range of objectives will be identified, including standards of performance to obtain these objectives, resulting in a determination of skills and talent needed to sustain the performance. In other words, a *human resource plan*. (See Figure 3.1.)

SIMPLE STEPS TO IMPLEMENT THE HUMAN RESOURCE PLAN

Step One—The Human Resource Inventory

This involves a database with a headcount of all employees by organizational unit including such factors as pay, sex, age, training, education, length of service, and qualifications. A simple two-factor analysis may reveal some interesting trends. For example, age groups may be analyzed by sex, job classification, or length of service. Or, payroll costs may be analyzed by age, sex, or length of service.

The human resource inventory provides information as to the range of skills presently employed as well as those available for future company expansion. It also provides the basis for employee promotions, recruitment needs, personnel development, training, and an available resource base for company projects. This data can also give clues as to possible EEO problem areas (if, for example, certain job categories are filled exclusively with one sex or ethnic group or all younger workers).

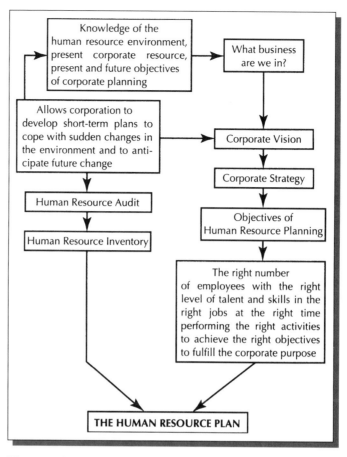

Figure 3.1
The structural process of human resource planning

The inventory can also help predict future needs. For example, if all employees in a specific shop are over 70 years of age, chances are good that it is time to plan for replacing future retiring workers. Since the human resource inventory is the census for manpower planning and forecasting, it needs to be updated on a regular basis. Fortunately, there are many computer programs available that enable these data to be put into a highly organized format that is readily available.

Step Two—The Human Resource Audit

The audit attempts to determine what has been and is happening to the company's manpower resources. While the human resource inventory collected data, the human resource audit analyzes the ratios and trends for both present and future explanations. For the human resource audit to make reliable forecasts, a database of from 3 to 5 years is required. Again, a two-factor analysis by age, sex, length of service, pay, or occupation could be made for employees leaving the company or for recruitment or absenteeism. For example, the company's increase in business volume will require an increase in manpower either through recruitment or by subcontracting. The result will be an increase in total costs. The human resource audit will be able to relate these costs to varying levels of production. If there is a reduction in the level of production or downsizing, the human resource audit will be valuable in determining termination costs and the effect of normal turnover or early retirement in reducing such costs.

Step Three—Developing Plans and Objectives of Required Human Resources

Assuming the company is on a 5-year plan, one uses the corporate projections of production and applies them to the individual work units or departments to determine the specific number of staff people, engineers, clerks, typists, electricians, welders, and other human resource categories that may be needed.

The cornerstone of human resource management planning is the proper execution of the job analysis function. When the organization collects significant information about the tasks performed in jobs, the working methods, the working conditions, and employee knowledge and skills, then it can begin the search for a profitable market niche. It is for this reason we begin our study of the functional areas of human resource management with job analysis.

Job Analysis

Job analysis is the process of gathering information about a job. It provides information in several areas including:

- How much time is taken to complete basic tasks?
- How are tasks grouped together into a job?
- How can a job be designed so that employee performance can be improved?
- What kinds of skills are needed to perform a given job?
- What kind of person is best suited for a certain type of job?
- What group of tasks can be handled by a team or small group?

This information provides a foundation for other HR activities.

The job analysis describes the major tasks of the job, the job duties and responsibilities, and the minimum required qualifications of skills, knowledge, and abilities. The result is the **job description.** If the job analysis is done correctly, the job description will accurately depict the job. The job description may then be used in recruitment efforts to develop advertisements, in interviewing to provide information to the recruitee to obtain the correct job/person match, in training to provide the knowledge and skills appropriate to the job, in job evaluation to ensure each job is fairly priced, in safety and health to prevent unnecessary injury, disease, or deaths, and in performance appraisals to provide a basis upon which to judge effectiveness. As noted in chapter 2, the Americans with Disabilities Act (ADA) requires that the essential elements of a job be specified in a job description. This enables the employer to consider reasonable accommodation for people to perform the job.

The usual format of a job description is to first state the identification, job title, location within the company, the supervisor, whether the job is salary (exempt) or wage (nonexempt), and the pay range. The second part of a job description is really the main section. It contains a general job summary using a couple of sentences and then follows with the job duties to be performed with an estimated time percentage each duty requires summating to 100 percent for the total job. This part also contains what the responsibilities of the job holder are and to whom they report. The final part is the job specifications, which states the qualifications required of all applicants. These are generally referred to as SKAs: skills, knowledge, and abilities. Although SKAs are generally measurable (such as requiring an MBA degree), others (such as working well with others and/or able to function as a team member) are more subjective and require judgements.

The Functional Job Analysis (FJA) technique provides a quantitative score for a particular job. This score can be compared with other job scores to form a basis from which to determine compensation. FJA resulted from efforts of the U.S. Training Service to classify jobs in the *Dictionary of Occupational Titles* (DOT).[8]

There are over 20,000 jobs defined in DOT. These jobs are classified by a nine-digit code. The first three digits refer to an occupation code, job title, and the type of industry. The next three digits indicate the degree to which the job exercises responsibility and judgement over data, people, and things.

The **Position Analysis Questionnaire (PAQ)** utilizes a structured checklist to identify 187 job instruments plus two items relating to pay.[9] The PAQ is concerned with six areas: information input, mental processes, work output, relationships with other people, job context, and other job characteristics.

This data is analyzed by a computer program to provide a job profile. This profile can be compared to other job profiles resulting in job families of similar profiles.

The Management Position Description Questionnaire (MPDQ) also utilizes a structured checklist although it is more quantitative than the PAQ.[10] The MPDQ analyzes the manager's concerns, demands, restrictions, and responsibilities. This is accomplished by 208 items which are classified into the following 15 factors: general information; decision making; planning and organizing; administering; controlling; supervising; consulting and innovation; contacts; coordinating; representing; monitoring business indicators; overall ratings; knowledge, skills, and abilities; organization chart; and comments and reactions. The result is data that facilitates placing new manager jobs in the right job family, determining training needs, evaluating the manager's job, providing accurate compensation, and devising appropriate selection techniques.

The Guidelines-Oriented Job Analysis form (GOJA) is completed by job incumbents and results in a job description, individual skills, knowledge and abilities required by the job, and a selection and performance appraisal procedure.[11] The procedure requires six steps to complete the form beginning with related job duties classified as a domain. This is similar to placing jobs into job families. Then, critical duties are listed and the frequency with which they occur. Skills and knowledge required to perform the critical duties is the next step, followed by the physical requirements to perform the job duties. The final step outlines other job requirements such as degrees, licenses, travel, and overtime. An interesting aspect of the GOJA is that there are three versions varying in the detail required. The amount of time required to complete the form varies from approximately 24 hours to 2 to 4 hours.

The Occupational Measurement System (OMS) is another computer-driven program using structured job analysis questionnaires developed by First Interstate Bancorp.[12] Questionnaire items are developed from an inventory of industry job tasks which are then applied to the using organization, and from job descriptions and inputs from the organization's job analysis staff. Several reports are generated by the computer program including a job function and task description, required job skill and knowledge levels, and an analysis of production costs.

The Interview

Although the techniques to obtain and analyze job information described above can be extremely helpful, in the final analysis someone has to "fill in the blanks." Whether a manager uses the PAQ, OMS, or any other system, there will be a need for interviews. As in any interviewing process, job analysis requires certain preparation before interviewing job incumbents. The interview site should be private with minimum interruption. Scheduling should permit ample time to avoid job incumbents waiting or hurrying for appointments. The interviewer should carefully study each job prior to the interview and take accurate notes.

Employees often bring their fears to the interview. Care should be taken to explain why certain employees have been selected. The interviewer should be aware of possible uncertainty of job abolishment, revealing poor work methods, and being subjected to an unannounced performance appraisal session. These anxieties and others need to be resolved in a thoughtful and sensitive manner before the actual job analysis process begins. Additional specific ideas on interviews are provided in a supplementary section near the end of this chapter.

THE JOB ANALYSIS PROCESS

Although all management activities have an impact upon the effective functioning and strategy of the organization, none are more important than job analysis. This is a key component of the Success System Model. For example, Microsoft (the most successful software company in the world) manages the work flow process for strategic advantage by using small product terms.[13]

Job analysis describes the major tasks of the job, the job duties and responsibilities, and the minimum required qualifications of skills, knowledge, and abilities. The outcome of job analysis is the job description including team manager roles. If the job analysis is done correctly, then the job description will accurately describe the position or the team assignments.

The job description may be used in recruiting efforts, developing advertisements, and interviewing applicants to provide information leading to the correct job and person match.[14] The job description also provides the knowledge and skills appropriate to the job for training purposes, for salary evaluation (to ensure each job is fairly paid), for safety and health to prevent unnecessary injury, and in performance appraisals to provide a basis for evaluating performance levels.

The following items are usually covered in a comprehensive job analysis:

1. *Job Activities:* This is the first step in job analysis. It is essential that data be gathered on the actual work done, such as accounting, painting, typing, or selling. Included in this section are why and when different elements of the job are performed. (See cartoon.)

Source: The Wizard of ID by Brant Parker and Johnny Hart, by permission of Creators Syndicate, Inc.

2. *Job Context:* This section of the job analysis includes data on the physical working conditions, the scheduled work hours, and both financial and non-financial work incentives. In addition, information about organizational and social interactions in the workplace would be covered in this section.
3. *Technical Skills:* Information concerning special tools, equipment, and machines utilized on the job would be included in this section.
4. *Job Standards:* This includes data on job standards to evaluate the employee's performance. Job standards usually include production times and production quality.
5. *Qualifications:* This includes data on any special skills, education, training, physical requirements, or job-related skills required for the position. Be careful here to keep in line with the letter and the spirit of legislation on disabled workers: Even folks with physical handicaps can often do a great job, with minor accommodation by the employer.

The compilation of job analysis data needs to be completed prior to other personnel activities. This job information assists the HR manager to complete several activities:[15]

1. *Recruitment:* The job analysis specifies the staffing required to complete the job duties.
2. *Selection:* The job analysis provides information used as the basis for selection of a job applicant.
3. *Education, Training, and Experience:* The information gathered in the job analysis will provide the level of education, training, and experience required for the job. These data may also be used in developing training programs.
4. *Compensation:* The job analysis and job description describe the job duties, education, skill requirements, possible hazardous conditions, or other factors in determining salary and other forms of compensation.
5. *Performance Management:* The job analysis provides data for performance appraisal so that an employee's actual performance may be compared to a standard level of job performance.
6. *Team Building:* Job analysis can help guide the HR manager in appropriately grouping tasks and people into effective working teams. The job analysis can be written so as to facilitate a team-oriented approach to work processes.

THE STEPS IN JOB ANALYSIS

The job analysis process involves a series of steps. Because job analysis data is critical for other activities, an accurate analysis process should be followed as described next.

HRM Planning

The first step in job analysis is to determine how the data will be used in HRM planning. HR managers should decide what data needs to be collected, the best method of collection, and the uses for the information in a comprehensive HRM strategy.

Organization Team-Power Needs

The second step requires studying organization charts, job descriptions, work process charts, and other organization information. HRM uses job analysis later in determining staffing needs, succession, levels of authority, and the flow of work process.

Job Analysis

A thorough job analysis is developed for each position or each cluster of positions. In a large organization, the HR manager may select a representative sample of job positions throughout the company for job analysis. In smaller organizations, such as a small business, it may still be a good idea to think through what needs to be done and by whom. However, you don't need paperwork just for the sake of paperwork.

Collect Job Data

After reviewing the historic data (and if necessary, selecting representative positions), HRM will start to gather job analysis data. This data includes education, training, experience requirements, working hours, equipment used, required job duties, and process work flow.[16] It is at this step when the techniques to evaluate job analysis data, described earlier, will be helpful.

Complete Analysis/Job Review

As the job analysis develops, the HR manager should review the data with the employee and/or the group as well as with the supervisor or the team leader. This review process will ensure the accuracy of the information developed. It also gives the employee or group an opportunity for input. This is especially important in self-managing work groups, which will be described later.

Prepare Job Description and Job Specifications

The final step in job analysis is usually to complete a written job description and a job specification for each position or group of positions. However, not everyone is an enthusiastic supporter of formalized job descriptions. Nevertheless, in most organizations, written job descriptions are seen as tools for better HRM. The job description lists the job duties and responsibilities, and the job specification lists the required education, training, skills, and experience requirements for a given position. Again, in keeping with the intent of the Americans with Disabilities Act, it is important to focus on work-related job specifications.

JOB ANALYSIS: INFORMATION

There are a variety of methods used in collecting job analysis information including the interview, questionnaire, observation, and job diaries and logs. The information about a specific job is then compared to the typical duties and tasks completed by an employee working on that job. This is termed a functional or job-oriented approach. A second approach involves analyzing the skills an employee needs to actually perform a job. This is usually termed a position, or skills-oriented, approach to job analysis. Either the functional or skills-oriented job analysis are acceptable under the Uniform Guidelines on Employee Selection Procedures, provided they identify critical tasks and behaviors involved in performing the job being analyzed.[17]

Regardless of the method used to collect data, job analysis must provide critical job information. Usually, job analysis involves interviews with both workers and supervisors, written information and records on the job, and observation of employees performing the job. (See Our Changing World of HRM.)

Nobody disagrees with the idea, at least not out loud. Women and men should both be paid fairly, and if the jobs are comparable, the pay should be expected to be the same. Now the problem: How in blue blazes can you tell which jobs are comparable? The question has been dismissed by some, saying "It can't be done, so I won't worry about it." This won't do, at least it won't do in Canada's most populous province, Ontario. Chances are the Ontario experience will impact everyone with human resources responsibilities before too long, and the first step has a lot to do with the subject of this chapter: Job Analysis.

The experience in Ontario gives some clues as to what the future may hold. In Ontario, all public (non-federal) and private sector employers having 100 or more jobs must have a "pay equity plan." The plan must begin with a job analysis. Jobs done mostly by women must be compared to jobs held mostly by men. If the skills, efforts, responsibilities, and working conditions are the same (or, we guess, comparable) then the pay levels for those female jobs must be boosted to the pay scale of the "lowest paid male job found to be of comparable value." This assumes (which will very often be the case) that females are being paid less than males before the pay equity comparability exercise begins.

Will such a **comparable worth** plan bankrupt the employers of the world once widely implemented? Not if Ontario is any indication. In fact, one study found that only 21 percent of the women in "female job classes" received any pay equity adjustments after the law took effect back in 1987. Most of the female private sector workers in "female job classes" were found to be getting "comparable" pay to men after the tricky job analysis was completed. Of course, 21 percent is significant, too. From what we hear, many employers griped and moaned for a while, but the word on the street is that the overall effects were positive.

Bottom line: Employees do value pay equity. Just because the employee happens to be a female does not give the employer the right to ignore this simple principle. And one important component of any organization's plan to ensure equitable pay is the topic of this chapter: a good solid job analysis. The Ontario law gives a reasonable place to start: skill, effort, responsibility, and working conditions. Then, apply specific criteria such as seniority or merit pay and see where you are. Do all this fairly and honestly, and chances are you are well on your way to a fair compensation plan. And, as a fringe benefit, you will be ready if and when a comparable worth law takes effect where you live. And it certainly may. After all, it's a changing world.

JOB ANALYSIS: DATA COLLECTION METHODS

Once an overall HRM strategy is developed and the jobs to be analyzed are identified, then the HR manager must collect the job analysis data. As noted, there are several methods or techniques that can be used to collect job data. These methods may be used individually or several approaches may be combined.

In order to comply with equal employment opportunity regulations and other federal and state regulations, an employer must complete a thorough job analysis process to establish job specifications, candidate selection methods, and job evaluation procedures. Therefore, the method of obtaining job analysis data must be appropriate to the process. (See Figure 3.2.)

THE ORGANIZATION CHART

An **organization chart** graphically portrays relationships between the operating units of an organization. In a good chart, the relationship between line functions (the individuals performing work duties) and staff functions (the advisers) are shown.

A typical organization chart contains both the vertical levels in an organization and also the horizontal or departmental relations. It gives the manager or the HR analyst an overall picture of how departments are related. The chart also illustrates

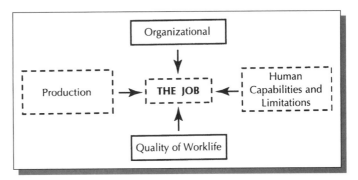

Figure 3.2
Job design factors

formal communication networks in the organization. An organization chart shows the way the organization works, at least in theory. Actual operation in the organization and the actual flow of communication may differ considerably from the "official" organization chart. However, even if inaccurate, the official chart can help managers develop an overall picture of the organization's task systems.

QUESTIONNAIRES

As mentioned several times earlier, questionnaires are used to gather a large number of quantitative responses. The questionnaire is particularly useful for studies of attitudes, values, and beliefs of respondents. Questionnaire data tend to be impersonal and anonymous and are often lacking in feeling and richness, but this method easily lends itself to quantitative analysis. Usually the employees who perform the job or their supervisors complete the questionnaires.

There are many problems involved in designing and administering an effective questionnaire. There are often problems of validity; that is: Does the questionnaire measure what it is intended to measure? There are also possible problems of the accuracy of information obtained: Did the person answer it realistically, or just to make a good impression? For example, one researcher found in a follow-up study that 29 percent of questionnaire respondents admitted answering falsely to some questions.[19] To deal with these problems, there are statistical techniques available that attempt to measure the reliability of the survey responses. There are also problems of nonresponse. Those who choose to respond may be those who have strong feelings (either positive or negative) about the content of the survey, but may represent only a small percentage of the total sample.

Questionnaires can be an inexpensive way to collect large amounts of information. It is an excellent way to collect a large amount of data in a short time frame. A structured questionnaire includes specific questions about job duties, job requirements, working conditions, tools used, and so on. A less structured approach would ask workers to "describe your daily job, in your own words." This open-ended format permits workers to use their own terms to describe a job.

The use of the questionnaire method depends upon the depth of information desired and the purpose of the information. In some organizations, survey follows survey without any effective results. This often leads to apathy and indifference in answering any subsequent surveys. Therefore, it is usually beneficial to inform the respondents beforehand about the purpose of the survey, how the information will be used, and how feedback of the results will be made available to them. The HR manager also has an obligation to the employee to (1) ensure confidentiality of all data; and (2) ensure that feedback of data will be made to all who participate. The HR manager should also

- Explain why the questionnaire is needed. Employees need to know why the questions are being asked and how the information will be used.
- Follow the "KISS" rule. "Keep It Simple, Stupid!" Use the simplest language to ask a question.
- Be as brief as possible—workers usually do not have time to complete long, complex surveys.
- Pretest the questionnaire before it is administered. Pretesting allows changes to be made in any questions before sending out large numbers of questionnaires in final form.

Questionnaires seem to achieve better job information in terms of quantity and validity if the questionnaire shows that the researchers are familiar with key issues on the job. Such event-based questionnaires, making clear that researchers are acquainted with important aspects of the job, are more likely to reveal information about the job than vague, theory-based questionnaires.

INTERVIEWS

Interviews are certainly one of the most common job analysis data collection techniques. Interviews allow the analyst to talk directly to the workers. The interview also gives an opportunity for the analyst to explain how the job analysis information will be used.

In one study of 245 firms, it was found that interviewing is one of the most widely used data-gathering techniques in many HRM programs.[20] It has the advantage of being more direct, personal, and flexible than a survey, and is particularly well-suited for studies of interaction and behavior. There are two advantages that set interviewing apart from other techniques. First, it's flexible and can be used for many different types of situations. For example, interviews can be used to determine motives, values, and attitudes. Second, it's the only technique that provides two-way communication. This permits the interviewer to learn more about the problems, challenges, and limitations of the organization. Interviewing usually begins with an initial meeting, and is best administered in a systematic manner by a trained interviewer. Data-gathering interviews usually last at least 1 hour. The purpose is to get the interviewee to talk freely about things that are important to him or her, and to share these perceptions in an honest and straightforward manner.

Interviews can be conducted with a single employee, a group of workers, or with a knowledgeable supervisor. When several employees do the same or similar work duties, a group interview is usually the fastest method to obtain job analysis data. Typically a structured form is used in interviews, so that answers from individuals and groups can be analyzed and compared.

It has been the authors' experience that people really want to talk about things that are important to them. If the HR manager can ask appropriate questions, then interviewing can yield important results.

DIRECT OBSERVATION

Another important source of data for job analysis is direct observation of worker behaviors and interactions. The analyst observes how people go about task performance and how they act or react in response to specific situations. The norms and attitudes expressed by members also present an important source of data. The observer looks for inconsistent or discordant behaviors: situations in which the observed actions are different from what has been previously described or expected.

Direct observation is often used for jobs, such as those requiring manual, standardized, and short-job-cycle tasks. Jobs performed by an assembly-line worker, a retail clerk, or a stockroom worker are examples of such jobs. The use of observation requires a trained observer and the ability to form varying tasks into structured format.

The HR analyst may use a diagram (i.e., a sociogram) to chart the communication process in team meetings; for example, to identify communications flows and patterns. Many analysts recommend that the observer be as inconspicuous as possible, should not use a stop watch (or other equipment), and should not take notes while observing. If the observer needs to make notes, he or she should leave the area. Often the observer may use indirect observation: that is, while seemingly observing one section, the observer may actually be observing another section across the room.

It is frequently valuable to visit work sites, field locations, or assembly-line operations to compare observed with reported behavior. This is obviously of greater value if the observer has a reasonably clear idea of what to look for. Observation varies from highly systematic, structured observations to nonsystematic, random observations. The more systematic the planning, recording, and observing, the greater the likelihood that observation will yield reliable and useful data. Too often, the observer's own biases influence what they see.

JOB DIARY OR LOG

The **job diary** or log is a written record of job tasks, the frequency of each task, and how the tasks are completed. In this technique, the employee keeps a diary or log on a daily or even hourly basis. Unfortunately, many workers are too busy to record accurate diary entries.

If a diary is accurate, it can provide information about the job tasks. The diary is useful when analyzing jobs that do not lend themselves to direct observation such as for a manager, an engineer, an outside salesperson, or a scientist.

JOB DESIGN

One of the most direct uses of Job Analysis is in **job design.** Job design has been a concern of managers for many years, but it was Frederick Taylor in 1911 who proposed the scientific design of a job.[21] The scientific management ideas that came from the industrial engineers tended to break a job down into its smallest and simplest task to reduce the human error, the training, and the skill required to do the task. Through time-and-motion studies, productivity was expected to increase. There was little regard for the human element other than to make sure that it was adequately controlled and supervised. More recently, organizations are discovering there is often a high price to pay in absenteeism, turnover, apathy, poor work quality, or even sabotage when the human element is not considered.

The current trend is to redesign jobs to improve worker satisfaction and productivity. Rather than focusing on an individual job, the tendency today is to look at a cluster of jobs, where possible. This is in keeping with the team approach to work, discussed throughout this book. There are still no easy solutions to redesigning jobs because there are many variables: the worker, the nature of the work, the organization climate, and the manager's style. Some successes in job design do provide guidelines to follow and the following is a discussion of two closely related theories of job design: *job enrichment theory* and *job characteristics theory*. Although these ideas have been around for years, they can be helpful to the manager responsible for designing a high-performing workplace, the second stage of the Success System Model.

JOB ENRICHMENT THEORY

Frederick Herzberg found, through interviews, that employees at all levels in the organization were interested in two facets about their work—the quality of the work itself and the benefits or rewards of the job (money, status, and so forth). Of the two, the quality of the work leads to job satisfaction. **Job satisfaction** occurs when employees experience work situations that entail increases in achievement, recognition, challenging work, responsibility, and advancement. **Job enrichment theory** holds that jobs should be redesigned to improve the motivators related to a job by permitting employees to attain increased levels of responsibility and achievement. Employees also can be given appropriate recognition and advancement in their careers for a job well done. And the work itself should be challenging, interesting, and meaningful. There are many techniques for improving these motivational factors and they must be tailored to fit specific situations. Several suggestions include:

- Give an employee or work group a natural and complete unit of work. This is in contrast to the practice of specialization of labor that has dominated the structure of most organizations in this century.
- Add more difficult assignments to an employee's job while providing appropriate training.
- Give an employee or a group additional authority. For example, an employee could be allowed to make increasingly more important or difficult decisions.
- Allow a peer in a work group or team to become an expert in a specialized area. Very likely, a work team could have several specialists that other employees could go to for information and help.
- Make information, including company reports, directly available to an employee instead of editing or censoring the information. This is particularly important where the information is related to the employee's work.
- Remove controls over an employee but still hold the employee accountable.

The job enrichment theory holds that extrinsic rewards such as money are important to accompany changes to the jobs. It also emphasizes that a system that only provides rewards will not improve worker performance. Improvements in both quality of the work and rewards are required to make a change in job design successful.

JOB CHARACTERISTICS THEORY

Another approach to job design is the **job characteristics** model conceived of by J. R. Hackman, G. R. Oldham, R. Janson, and K. Purdy[22] and based on the work of J. N. Turner and P. R. Lawrence.[23] The model attempts to develop objective meas-

Part II   The Success System: Attracting a High-Performing Workforce

ures of job characteristics that can directly affect employee attitudes and work behaviors. According to the model, five core job dimensions that affect work motivation and satisfaction are skill variety, task identity, task significance, autonomy, and feedback.

Skill variety is the degree to which a job requires a variety of activities and involves the use of different skills and talents. Employees usually see tasks that require the use of several different skills, especially challenging skills, as being meaningful.

Task identity refers to the degree to which the job requires completion of a whole and identifiable piece of work. It is doing a job from beginning to end with a visible outcome. An employee probably will find a task more meaningful if it entails producing the entire product rather than a small component.

Task significance is the degree to which the job has a substantial impact on the lives of other people, whether in the same organization or in the external environment. Work will likely be more meaningful when an employee perceives the results to have a substantial effect on other people.

Autonomy is the degree to which the job provides substantial freedom, independence, and discretion to the individual in scheduling the work and in determining the procedures to be used in carrying it out. Autonomy allows employees to take a larger part in planning and controlling their work. Generally, employees will have greater commitment to and ownership in their jobs when they have autonomy over their work. As discussed elsewhere, group dynamics are a critical aspect of any work situation, so the word "autonomy" here could be considered "autonomy for the work group" as easily as "autonomy for this individual."

Job feedback refers to the degree to which carrying out the work activities required by the job results in the individual obtaining direct and clear information about the effectiveness of his or her performance. Customers or other people internal to the organization who use the product or service can provide feedback if communication channels are provided to the employee. The feedback is directly based on how well the task was done and not on the evaluations of a peer or supervisor.

The five core job dimensions can be mathematically combined to derive a score which reflects the motivational potential of a job. As skill variety, task identity, and task significance jointly determine a job's meaningfulness, these three dimensions are treated as one dimension in the formula:

$$\text{Motivating Potential Score (MPS)} = \text{Job Meaningfulness} \times \text{Autonomy} \times \text{Job Feedback}$$

The first variable in the formula, job meaningfulness, is a function of skill variety, task identity, and task significance. So the formula can further be refined:

$$\text{Motivating Potential Score (MPS)} = \frac{\left[\frac{\text{Skill}}{\text{Variety}} + \frac{\text{Task}}{\text{Identity}} + \frac{\text{Task}}{\text{Significance}}\right] \times \text{Autonomy} \times \text{Job Feedback}}{3}$$

Based on the formula, a score of near zero on either the autonomy or job feedback dimensions will produce a motivating potential score (MPS) of near zero (any number multiplied by zero is always zero); whereas a number near zero on skill variety, task identity, or task significance will reduce the total MPS but will not completely undermine the motivational potential of a job.

When the core job dimensions are present in a job, the job characteristics model predicts certain positive effects in an employee's psychological state. High scores in skill variety, task identity, and task significance result in an employee experiencing meaningfulness in the job, such as believing the work to be important, valuable, and worthwhile. A high score in the autonomy dimension leads to an employee feeling personally responsible and accountable for the results of the work he or she does. And a high score in the job feedback dimension is an indication that the employee has an understanding of how he or she is performing the job.

There are several suggestions made by the authors of the model and other authorities. They suggest using research from the behavioral sciences to enrich jobs and produce a positive impact on the five core job dimensions. One approach is to take existing, fractionalized tasks and put them back together to form a new and larger module of work. This will increase the skill variety and task identity job dimensions of the work. General Motors has used this method for several years in their Saturn plant. Teams of workers are responsible for auto subassemblies such as doors or transmissions, resulting in higher productivity and increased morale.[24]

A second approach is to form natural work units by giving an employee a task that is an identifiable and meaningful whole. An employee will have greater ownership in and will more closely identify with the work and will understand the significance of the work done.

A third approach is to permit the employee to have direct contact with the people who use their product or service. This would mean directing complaints or questions from customers directly to the involved employee or employees.

A fourth approach is to load jobs vertically by giving employees controlling functions such as deciding work methods, when to take breaks, how to train new employees, formulating budgets, and managing crises. For an employee to undertake successfully these new responsibilities, which improve autonomy, it may be necessary to provide employee skill training in such areas as budgets, training techniques, and time management.

A fifth approach is to open or create feedback channels so employees can learn how well are performing their work. A specific approach that combines these approaches is self-managed work teams such as GM uses at its Saturn plant, which will be discussed later in this chapter.

RESULTS OF JOB DESIGN PROGRAMS

The results of job design programs suggest that they can be successful if they are managed correctly and have employee involvement. In a review of the literature on work-restructuring methods, William Pasmore[25] found that 90 percent of the reports of work-restructuring interventions cited improvements in productivity, costs, absenteeism, attitudes, or quality and that an increasing number of organizations are setting up such methods.

The results of job design efforts using Herzberg's job enrichment theory are not conclusive although there have been a number of studies. In a study conducted by R. N. Ford at AT&T, it was shown that 18 or 19 job enrichment projects resulted in improvements in productivity, quality, and job satisfaction.[26]

Several studies have confirmed the validity of the job characteristics theory. Studies by A. N. Turner and P. R. Lawrence,[27] M. R. Blood and C. L. Hulin,[28] and J. R. Hackman and E. E. Lawler,[29] provide evidence to support the general tenets of the theory. On the other hand, other studies by Y. Fried and G. Ferris,[30] P. C. Buttger and I. Chew,[31] E. Hogan and D. Martell,[32] and Wong and Campion,[33] question the validity of certain aspects of the model, but mostly support the model. Others, such as Roberts and Glick,[34] are more critical. Particularly questioned were the multiplication of the characteristics in the formula and the relevancy of several of the characteristics to improving the motivation of a job. Additional research into this theory is warranted, but until it is available, the basic ideas of the theory serve as a foundation for many changes in job design within organizations.

SELF-MANAGED WORK TEAMS

A **self-managed work team** is an autonomous group whose members decide how to handle their task. The task of the team is an identifiable task, service, or product. The groups may be permanent work teams or temporary teams brought together to solve a problem or develop a new product. Often teams are composed of people from different parts of the organization with different skills and backgrounds. Authority has been vested in them by upper management to manage their group processes, including production and personnel matters, in order to accomplish their objectives. A diversified background of members and the necessary authority gives the teams the ability to move around the bureaucratic organization and get the job done.[35]

Increased responsibility is placed on team members. Work teams are assigned a wide range of tasks such as budgeting, making job assignments, hiring and selecting team members, assessing job performance of fellow members, scheduling, purchasing equipment, and controlling quality. (See Our Changing World.)

OUR CHANGING WORLD OF HRM
THE TEAM APPROACH, SWEDISH STYLE[36]

Much is written about the emphasis on the work group in Japan. But there are numerous success stories involving worker participation from other parts of the globe, too.

WORKER INVOLVEMENT

Sweden provides a number of examples. The Kockems Shipyard in Malmo had what might have been the world's highest turnover rate in the past, partly due to the blue-collar revolt that seemed to sweep the United States and Europe and partly because of Sweden's liberal social security safety net: Nobody starved in Sweden, whether or not one worked. But these external factors were just part of the problem. Management pretty much had its head in the sand, too. Executives were far from the dust and noise; far from the areas where individuals had to cope with the day-to-day grind. Kockems turned itself totally around when management discovered the workers. Moving executives closer to the workforce led to improvements in lighting, ventilation, and most important, attitudes. Workers began to think management cared. Why? Management did care!

TEAM APPROACH AND CULTURE

In another example, Saab managed to take a tough industry—producing cars—and convince the Swedish workers that everyone counted. MIT professor Edgar Schein, one of the all-time greats when it comes to understanding organization change, credits Saab's au-

tonomous work teams. "Before, Saab had very high worker turnover. Now it has virtually none. A happy, motivated workforce not only saves a company retraining costs, but it makes it much more open to innovation," says Schein.

If the team approach can be used making automobiles in Sweden, one might think it could work anywhere. Unfortunately, "such systems work better in national cultures that are more team oriented, such as the Scandinavian and some Asian countries. In the United States, it's much harder to convince people that it's better to pull their resources together and operate as a group. I don't think we value groups and teams for their own sake as much as other cultures do."

Can the team approach work anywhere or only where the idea fits the national culture? Apparently the team approach is easier to pull off in some countries. But, this is no excuse to give up. This chapter suggests that it can be done. Organizational development is like most other valuable commodities: You have to work at it. Nothing worth having seems to come easily.

QUESTIONS

1. What do you think are the most important factors in increasing productivity?

2. Discuss the role of national cultures as they affect team relationships.

Though self-managed work teams are still controversial, Texas Instruments CEO Jerry Junkins says, "No matter what your business, these teams are the wave of the future."[37] Tom Peters (author and consultant) says as far as he can determine, there are no limits to the use of teams.[38] However, Edward Lawler, who has consulted and written extensively on the subject, is more reserved and says, "You have to ask, 'How complex is the work?' The more complex, the more suited it is for teams."[39]

Self-managed work teams also go by other names including self-regulating work groups, cross-functional teams, socio-technical systems, autonomous work groups, high-involvement work teams, and high-commitment work teams. Such companies as Digital Equipment Corporation, Aetna Life & Casualty, Procter & Gamble, Xerox, Boeing, DuPont, Texas Instruments, General Motors, the U.S. Navy's Naval Weapons Center, Cummins Engine Company, Dana Corporation, W. L. Gore, and TRW use them either throughout their companies or in specific facilities.

DuPont's plant in Towanda, Pennsylvania, is a good example of self-managed work teams. The plant lets employees find their own solutions to problems, set their own production schedules, and have a say in hiring. Managers call themselves "facilitators." Their main job is to coach workers and help them understand the external market forces which demand quality, teamwork, and speed. Says DuPont group vice president Mark Suwyn: "These people manage their lives well outside the factory. They sit on school boards or coach Little League. We have to create a culture where we can bring that creative energy into the workforce."[40]

Most companies (such as DuPont, Procter & Gamble, and Boeing) setting up the work teams, do not do so organization-wide, but typically choose specific sites. Some companies, like General Motors in its Saturn division, build new plants to house the teams. Though the teams are more common in production facilities than the service sector, they have been successfully applied in service-oriented organizations such as life insurance and government agencies.

A recent survey of 476 *Fortune* 1,000 companies published by the American Productivity and Quality Center shows that presently only 7 percent of their company's workforce is organized in self-managed work teams. The study also found that half the companies questioned say they will be relying significantly more on them in the years ahead. At the same time, it should be kept in mind that just announcing formation of teams will not ensure teamwork. If individuals are still given bonuses or rewards rated on performance of an individual, there may be a strong tendency to "hide" key resources. Teams are worth it, but they do require special effort by the HR manager.[41]

CHARACTERISTICS OF SELF-MANAGED WORK TEAMS

When self-managed work teams have been set up at a facility, there are several characteristics that are common to other self-managed work team sites.

- The structure of the organization is based on team concepts. There are few management levels in the plant or work site structure and few job descriptions.

- There is an egalitarian culture and a noticeable lack of status symbols. There are no management dining rooms, no assigned parking places, and no special furniture or decor for managers' offices. Managers may not have offices or, if they do, they often become team meeting rooms. There are no special dress codes so that if uniforms are required, such as at Honda's U.S. plant, everyone including the plant superintendent wears the uniform. At other sites, no one wears ties, special badges, or other signs of power.

- A work team has a physical site with boundaries within which members can identify.
- The number of people in a team is kept as small as possible. Typical sizes range from 3 to 15 members.
- Work teams order material and equipment. They set goals, profit targets, and decide their production schedule. They also help set rewards for their team members. They have a voice in whom is hired and fired in the work team and the hiring of managers. Says Robert Hershock, a group vice president at 3M, "You need to have a sense of who's not buying in, and let the teams kick people off who aren't carrying their weight."
- Team members have a sense of vision of their team and their organization. A vision provides direction and energizes team behavior to accomplish goals. Most companies have a simple, understandable creed that is well communicated to all employees.
- There is strong partnership between team members and management and, if there is a labor union, the union is also a member of the partnership.
- Team members are different enough in their backgrounds, cultural experiences, and training so that a variety of viewpoints will be represented and skills will be varied enough so that members can learn from one another.
- Information of all types is openly shared. The information system needs to be well developed and available to all members. Members are knowledgeable in accounting and statistical concepts so they can use the financial and production information to make decisions.
- Team members should be skilled and knowledgeable in their areas. Team members should have good interpersonal skills and a desire and ability to work with others.
- Training, and especially cross training, is a major requirement of self-managed work teams. A vice president of Tektronix says, "The growth and development of individual employees is the primary vehicle for advancing the company's long-term interests." The success of a team depends on members skilled and knowledgeable in a variety of areas including technical skills, finance and accounting, competition in the marketplace, and group process.
- Team members are knowledgeable of customers, competitors, and suppliers and the primary emphasis is to focus on customers. To the team, a customer may be someone within their organization who uses their product or someone external to the organization. Some organizations enter joint-training ventures with their suppliers. They recognize that the finished product is no better than components supplied by other companies.

QUALITY OF WORKLIFE

In the past, business and industry have placed employees, along with property, facilities, and capital, as a "factor of production;" however, their main emphasis has been on productivity, technological breakthroughs, and growth. **Quality of worklife (QWL)** is an attempt to improve an employee's worklife. The workforce in America has problems of alienation, and QWL tries to alleviate some of the problem-causing pressures on workers. Traditionally, QWL is focused on laborers and lower pay levels of an organization. However, QWL can impact the entire workforce of a business or industry.

What is the name of the company cited in *In Search of Excellence*, listed in *The 100 Best Companies to Work for in America*, listed among the top 10 companies for women to work for, and has a plant named by *Fortune* magazine as a top 10 plant in the United States? The company is the Dana Corporation. But who is Dana? And what are they doing to get all the accolades?

Dana is a diversified, $3.6 billion a year in sales, worldwide corporation employing 26,000 people with headquarters in Toledo, Ohio. It primarily makes transmissions, clutches, drive lines, and axles for vehicles. It also builds condos and is into banking, insurance, and real estate.

THE STRUCTURE

Dana has spent a good bit of effort building a flat, highly decentralized organization. It has only five levels of management. Dana's corporate office staff has decreased in number from 400 to 84. It pushed responsibilities down to lower levels of management. But just changing an organization chart is no guarantee that improvements will follow.

The Auburn plant, which manufactures clutches, is indicative of the programs at Dana. Though in 1981 they had a good reputation for quality, they also recognized they had many people problems. Maury Hagan, the plant manager, says, "There was a huge wall between the front office and the people working on the floor." They decided improvements in their communication system could help solve many of their problems. According to Mr. Hagan, "We want to be the best and largest clutch manufacturer worldwide, and that is our goal."

COMMUNICATIONS SYSTEM

The improvements in communications are directed at four areas: special events, mass communication, group communication, and individual communication. Special events are activities intended to communicate the importance of employees. These include an open house and a free physical examination for the employee and spouse every 6 months. Retirees are also included, as Dana believes that how you treat your retirees is an indication of what you really think of your active employees. The gain-sharing plan at the plant also communicates in a unique way how employees are performing.

Mass communication is formalized one-way communication coming from several managers to the employees. The supervisor has a minimum of one meeting each month to explain what is happening to the market, profits, deliveries, and quality. The area manager meets with all his or her people at least once a month. The plant manager meets at least four times a year with everyone in the plant in a mass meeting or in groups of 20 to 30. The next manager up, the division manager, has a meeting twice a year with everyone. The president or chairman of the board meets with everyone once a year. So the five levels of managers have a meeting with everyone in the plant, including line and staff employees, at least once a year.

Group communication consists of weekly staff meetings and **quality circles** for the 80 percent of employees who have chosen to participate in the circles. According to Mr. Hagan, "It is not the answer to everything, but is strictly a tool that opens avenues for your people." The decision to install the circles was left up to a vote of the people in the plant. The vote was 79 percent to try it. A line employee was promoted to a management position to be in charge of the circles and is also a full-time facilitator. The plant now has 26 circles and two full-time facilitators. Participation is completely voluntary. The facilitators give help and find information for the circles. The circles typically meet for 1 hour a week. Members have been given training in histograms, how to problem solve, how to brainstorm, and how to prioritize problems. The circle makes a formal proposal to the appropriate managers including the plant manager. The proposal is an oral presentation complete with cost data using slides and overheads. The presentations are videotaped for further review. A date is set when the circle will be told of management's decision on the proposal.

Individual communication occurs with the open-door policy that the managers have. Unless there is another meeting going on, someone coming to see even the plant manager, Maury Hagan, will not have to wait more than 5 minutes. The philosophy is that for the person coming to see a manager, that is the most important thing on the person's mind at the moment. If it means the manager has to work overtime in the evening to get their other work done, then that is the way it goes.

RESULTS AT THE AUBURN PLANT

Some significant changes in the plant are the changes in attitude. Before the communication program began, an hourly worker would sign up or apply for a management job. Mr. Hagan says, "They viewed management as an enemy, and they had no interest in joining management." Recently they had 47 hourly employees apply for a management position. Work habits have improved and productivity increased 16 percent in 2 years. They recognize they still have problems but they believe they are turning the corner. "Our competition is not within the plant anymore, it is on the outside and it is worldwide, and that is where we have to concentrate," says Mr. Hagan.

QUESTIONS

1. What type of productivity interventions does the communication program use? Is it quality circles, self-managed work teams, or something else?

2. What is the goal at the Auburn plant and how can it help direct their efforts?

3. Describe how the program at Dana's Auburn plant can be used at other organizations.

QWL's management philosophy and definition have been evolving and changing since the 1970s. There are many facets to QWL, including job design, participative management, organization development, quality work circles, job enhancement, the physical safety of employees, and the mental health of employees. Actually, QWL includes all these things and more. Today's managers consider QWL as a "philosophy of managing an organization in general, and human resources in particular."[43] Thus, QWL is not just a project to be completed within a specified time frame; it is, according to authors David Nadler and Edward Lawler, "a way of thinking about people, work, and organizations. Its distinctive elements are (1) a concern about the impact of work on people as well as on organizational effectiveness; and (2) the idea of participation in organizational problem solving and decision making."[44] There are no limitations on QWL: It ranges from improving each worker's self-respect to realignment of job descriptions to humanizing the environment of the workplace.

There are many descriptions of QWL. However, many businesses are still in the process of designing and developing QWL. In a presentation to the Conference on the Quality of Worklife, Richard E. Walton supplied one of the best descriptions of an ideal QWL.[45] In Walton's ideal QWL structure, there are eight major classifications:

1. *Adequate and Fair Compensation:* Does the income from full-time employment meet the standards of both society and the worker? Is the pay comparable and compatible with other types of employment?

2. *Safe and Healthy Working Conditions:* Are the work conditions physically safe? Are the working hours reasonable?

3. *Immediate Opportunity to Use and Develop Human Capacities:* Does the work allow the use of a wide range of skills? Does the work allow autonomy and self-control? Is relevant and meaningful information available? Is the work a complete or natural unit or is it a small part of a unit? Does the work allow for planning?

4. *Future Opportunity for Continued Growth and Security:* Does the work permit growth of a person's capacities? Are there advancement opportunities to use newly acquired skills or knowledge? What is the employment and income security?

5. *Social Integration in the Work Organization:* Is there freedom from prejudice? To what extent does the organization rely on status symbols and the hierarchy? Is there upward mobility? Is there interpersonal openness among members and support for each other?

6. *Constitutionalism in the Work Organization:* Do the members have the right to personal privacy? Can members speak out without fear of reprisal from higher authority? Is there equitable treatment of members? Is there due process for grievances and complaints?

7. *Work and the Total Life Space:* Does the work organization allow the members to have other life roles? What are the overtime requirements, travel demands, and geographical moves?
8. *The Social Relevance of Worklife:* How does the worker perceive the social responsibility of the organization: products, waste disposal, marketing and selling techniques, employment practices, relations to under-developed countries, participation in political campaigns, attitude to laws, and so on?

These eight classifications of QWL have a direct influence on human resource management. Today's managers are challenged to develop employment for meaningful job content in which each individual's abilities are utilized. In addition, job context should include enhancement or enrichment of work. In our opinion, when job enrichment and appropriate reward systems and leadership are used, the motivation, commitment, and involvement of all employees increase.

Summary

Job analysis is one of the most important tools of HR managers. The job analysis data is used in HRM planning, recruitment selection, training and career development programs, performance appraisal systems, and compensation. There are a variety of methods available to collect job analysis data. These include observation, interviews, worker diaries, and questionnaires. In this chapter, we have examined some productivity programs in work design that could be part of an HRM program. Some programs have been used over a period of several years with varying degrees of success; however, other methods are somewhat new.

Two views of job design include job enrichment and job characteristics. The results of both theories are mixed, but both can be useful to the manager.

Self-managed work teams represent a significantly new method of organizing and managing an organization. Most businesses that use this approach choose to apply it to specific plants or work sites instead of the entire organization. Self-managed work teams require a major commitment from the organization, both managers and workers. The long-term effectiveness of the teams has not been clearly established but many organizations and their members are enthusiastic about the approach. Self-managed work teams seem one of the most popular interventions and one that major corporations are hoping will make them competitive in the twenty-first century.

Quality of Worklife (QWL) is more of a management philosophy than a program; it is a way of viewing the organization life of workers. QWL is seen by some as incorporating work design, collective bargaining, industrial democracy, and organization development.

In the following simulation, you will have an opportunity to participate in using the ideas of job design and self-managed work teams. Though the experiment will be limited in size and time, you will be able to draw some conclusions of your own about the application of job design and self-managed work teams.

Productivity interventions are currently receiving much more attention and seem to be having some positive impact in improving organizations. There are several methods that will help HR managers in improving productivity, but there is a definite need for additional research into work design programs.

REVIEW QUESTIONS

1. Explain the job characteristics model and how it can be used to enrich jobs.
2. What are other names to describe self-managed work teams you could expect to encounter?
3. Contrast the similarities and differences in self-managed work teams and quality circles.
4. What are some problems that organizations have had when they implemented self-managed teams?
5. What are the major categories that can be used for analyzing the quality of worklife?

KEY WORDS AND CONCEPTS

Define and be able to use the following:

- Autonomy
- Comparable Worth
- Human Resource Audit
- Human Resource Inventory
- Human Resource Planning
- Human Resource Requirements
- Job Analysis

- Job Characteristics
- Job Description
- Job Design
- Job Diary
- Job Enrichment Theory
- Job Satisfaction
- Organization Chart

- Position Analysis Questionnaire (PAQ)
- Quality Circles
- Quality of Worklife (QWL)
- Self-Managed Work Teams

HRM SKILLS SIMULATION 3.1: SUPERIOR PRODUCTS COMPANY

Total time suggested: 1 hour

A. PURPOSE

This chapter discusses how people react to obtaining a high-performing workforce. In this simulation, you will have an opportunity to be involved in a small-group decision on change and begin to see how different individuals may perceive an evaluation situation in differing ways.

The purposes include:

1. To examine how you and others interpret guidelines and try to exert influence in an attempt to change another's position.
2. To understand the relationship between motivation and the acceptance or rejection of change.
3. To consider how employment situations are influenced by multiple criteria, and subjective versus objective considerations.

B. PROCEDURES

Step 1. Before coming to class, read the Company Situation. Each participant should then make an individual ranking of the employees from 1 (the first to be laid off) to 8 (the last to be laid off). Use the Superior Products Rating Form, recording your answers in column 1.

COMPANY SITUATION
SUPERIOR PRODUCTS COMPANY

The Superior Products Company is a medium-sized manufacturing company located in the suburbs of Fresno, California. The company is nonunionized, and attempted during the past 2 years to incorporate an objective performance review system that has been designed purposefully to provide feedback to employees. The system is designed to be objective, time-oriented, and representative.

The loss of a contract bid to a competitor has forced the Superior Products management to consider next week laying off one, two, or three of the poorest performers in the circuit board unit. This unit produces circuit boards that are sold to electronic firms. The layoff may be only temporary, but management wants to be sure that they have been fair in presenting an objectively based decision to the employees.

The people in the unit to be cut back are:

1. Albert Banks: White male, age 42; married; 3 children; 2 years of high school; 14 years with the company.
2. Bob Brown: Black male; age 37; widower; 2 children; high school graduate; 8 years with the company.
3. Chris Everet: White female; age 24; single; high school graduate; 2 years with the company.
4. Dave Fram: White male; age 50; single; finished junior college while working; 15 years with the company.
5. Pat Peters: White female; age 36; married; 4 children; high school graduate; 3 years with the company.
6. Ray Alfredo: Hispanic male; age 40; married; 1 child; high school graduate; 3 years with the company
7. Fred Green: White male; age 39; divorced; 2 children; 2 years of college; 7 years with the company.
8. George Jones: White male; age 42; married, no children; 1 year of college; 9 years with the company.

The company has evaluated these unit employees on a number of factors listed in Table 3.1. The ratings shown are an average of evaluations.

Step 2. Form groups of five members each, with additional members serving as observers. Each group is to reach a consensus on the ranking. Avoid voting, trading off, or bargaining. Try to reach a decision that all group members can support. Then record your team decision on the Superior Products Rating Form, column 2.

Time suggested for Step 2: 40 minutes.

Table 3.1
Superior products company supervisor evaluation

Employee	Average Weekly Output[a]	Rejects[b] (%)	Absences[c] (%)	Cooperating Attitude[d]	Loyalty[d]	Potential for Promotion[d]
Albert Banks	39.6	4.9	6.3	Good	Good	Fair
Bob Brown	43.4	5.3	7.9	Poor	Fair	Fair
Chris Everet	35.2	0.9	0.4	Excellent	Good	Good
Dave Fram	40.4	4.7	13.2	Excellent	Excellent	Fair
Pat Peters	40.2	9.6	9.3	Poor	Fair	Fair
Ray Alfredo	39.6	3.4	6.1	Good	Fair	Poor
Fred Green	36.2	4.8	5.0	Good	Good	Fair
George Jones	45.2	7.0	3.6	Fair	Fair	Good

[a]Higher score = more output.
[b]Lower score = fewer rejects.
[c]Lower score = fewer absences.
[d]Possible ratings: poor, fair, good, excellent.

Step 3. List each group's ranking on the blackboard, and compare and discuss differences in ranking. Also consider the following questions with the observers leading the discussion:

1. How did members differ in the criteria used to lay people off?
2. What were the reasons for the different criteria? Tangible and objective considerations, or subjective considerations?
3. Was there any resistance among team members to changing their positions?
4. What were the strategies used to influence and change team members' positions?
5. How were the differences resolved? To what extent was the group decision really based on consensus?

Time suggested for Step 3: 10 minutes.

Step 4. Score your individual and team answers. Where the actual and correct answers match, put +10 in columns (4) and (5) on the Superior Products Rating Form. If the actual and correct answers do not match, put 0 in columns (4) and (5). By totaling the points, an individual and team score can be calculated. Column (4) provides an indication of the individual participant's "correctness," and column (5) provides an equivalent measure of each group's performance.

Compare the individual and team scores. Individuals come to teams with varying degrees of preparation, and the final score may not reflect how decisions were made by the team. As a class, compare the scores of the teams.

Time suggested for Step 4: 10 minutes.

SUPERIOR PRODUCTS RATING FORM

Employee	Individual Rating Col. 1	Team Rating Col. 2	Correct Rating Col. 3	Individual Score Col. 4	Team Score Col. 5
1. A. Banks					
2. B. Brown					
3. C. Everet					
4. D. Fram					
5. P. Peters					
6. R. Alfredo					
7. F. Green					
8. G. Jones					
Total Scores					

Case 3.1 Precision Products, Inc.

Before Helen Brown got to the door of the conference room for the Monday morning meeting of the executive committee, she could hear Doc Spinks' voice raised in heated debate with Pete Newell.

"I don't give a damn what you think, Pete! There's only enough money in the budget for one administrative aide and I say we need him more in engineering than you do in marketing!" Doc shouted.

"Oh, yeah! Who says? I hear the same bull from you every time this comes up. You don't even know what you would do with him if you did get him! I'm telling you, if marketing doesn't get a warm body by yesterday, our operation will go to hell in a hand basket!" Pete shouted back.

Helen regretted her habit of showing up early for meetings as she pushed open the door to the conference room and saw Doc and Pete glaring at each other.

As Helen took a seat, both men turned briefly and said a terse "Good morning," to Helen and took up where they left off.

"Pete," Doc said, "we need a numbers man now; not tomorrow, not next week, but right now. We're trying to integrate that new software package into engineering and it's holding up the Santos Project."

"Jeez, Doc, how long will that take? A week, a month? It couldn't be anything longer than that. What are you go-ing to do with him after that? You're just trying to fatten up your head count to make your own life easier. We need a people guy in marketing to help smooze over those new accounts. If we don't get those new customers, you won't have any engineering to worry about."

"Now who's talking bull? If you did your job right, you wouldn't need anybody else to hold customers' hands. A numbers man, that's what we need!" Doc said, pointing his finger at Pete.

"No way! A people guy, *that's* what we need," said Pete, pointing back at Doc.

Doc turned toward Helen and said, "Well, you're personnel, what do you think?"

Wishing she had waited before entering the conference room, Helen took a deep breath as both angry men waited for her answer.

QUESTIONS

1. How would you define the conflict between Doc and Pete?
2. What role does human resources management play in this kind of conflict?
3. What suggestions should Helen make to diffuse the situation?

ENDNOTES

1. Charles Fishman, "Engines of Democracy," *Fast Company* (October 1999): 180.
2. F. Biddle and J. Helyan, "Behind Boeing's Woes," *The Wall Street Journal,* 24 April 1998, p. A1.
3. Dori Jones Yang and Andrea Rothman, "Reinventing Boeing: Radical Changes Amid Crisis," *Business Week* (March 1, 1993): 60.
4. Rosabeth Moss Kanter, "Innovation: The Only Hope For Times Ahead?" *Sloan Management Review* 25, no. 4 (Summer 1984): 51. See also Joe Smith, "Little Noticed High Tech Revival," *Wall Street Journal,* 10 January 1993, p. 1.
5. Heather A. Haverman, "Between A Rock and A Hard Place: Organizational Change and Performance Under Conditions of Fundamental Environmental Transformation," *Administrative Science Quarterly* 71, no. 3 (March 1992): 49.
6. D. W. Jannell, *Human Resources Planning* (Upper Saddle River, NJ: Prentice Hall, 1993).
7. D. Greising, "It's the Best of Times or Is It?" *Business Week* (January 12, 1999): 35.
8. U.S. Department of Labor, *Dictionary of Occupational Titles,* 4th ed. (Washington, DC: U.S. Government Printing Office, 1977).
9. Donald L. Caruth, Robert M. Noe III, and R. Wayne Mondy, *Staffing the Contemporary Organization* (New York: Praeger Publishers, 1990), 100.
10. Walter W. Tornow and Patrick R. Pinto, "The Development of a Managerial Job Taxonomy: A System for Describing, Classifying, and Evaluating Executive Positions," *Journal of Applied Psychology* 61, no. 8 (August 1976): 410–18.
11. Stephen E. Bennis, Ann Holt Belenky, and Dee Ann Soder, *Job Analysis: An Effective Management Tool* (Washington, DC: The Bureau of National Affairs, 1983), 42.
12. R. Wayne Mondy and Robert M. Noe III, *Human Resource Management,* 5th ed. (Needham Heights, MA: Allyn and Bacon, 1993), 128.
13. M. Fetwa, "Bill Gates' Next Challenge," *Fortune* (December 14, 1998): 30.
14. Phillip C. Grant, "What Use is a Job Description?" *Personnel Journal* 67, no. 2 (February 1988): 44–53.
15. Mary Tynes, "Job Descriptions That Get Good Applicants and Protect Your Company," *Recruiting and Hiring Handbook* (Bureau of Business Practice, 1990).
16. John G. Veres III, "Racial Differences in Job Analysis Questionnaires: An Empirical Study," *Public Personnel Management* 20 (Summer 1991): 135–44.

17. E. J. McCormick and P. R. Jeanneret, "Position analysis questionnaire," in S. Gael, ed., *The Job Analysis Handbook for Business, Industry, and Government,* vol. II (New York: John Wiley & Sons, 1988), 825–42.

18. John Hulpke, 1999. Comparable Worth: working paper. University of Technology, Hong Kong.

19. Michael A. Hitt and Robert L. Mathis, "Survey Results Shed Light Upon Important Developmental Tools," *Personal Administrator* 28, no. 2 (February 1983): 89–97.

20. Terry R. Armstrong and Walter J. Wheatley, "Identifying Client Needs: A Diagnostic Model for Consultants," paper presented at Academy of Management Meeting, 1989.

21. Frederick Herzberg, *Work and the Nature of Man* (Cleveland, Ohio: World Publishing Co., 1966); Frederick Herzberg, "One More Time: How Do You Motivate Employees?" *Harvard Business Review* 34, no. 1 (January-February 1966): 58–71.

22. J. R. Hackman, G. R. Oldham, R. Janson, and K. Purdy, "A New Strategy for Job Enrichment," *California Management Review* (Summer 1975): 57–71. See also J. Richard Hackman, Edward E. Lawler, and Lyman Porter, *Perspectives on Behavior in Organizations* (New York: McGraw-Hill, 1977); and Chi-Sum Wong and Michael A. Campion, "Development and Test of a Talk Level Model of Motivational Job Design," *Journal of Applied Psychology* 76, no. 6 (1991): 825–37.

23. A. N. Turner and P. R. Lawrence, *Industrial Jobs and the Worker* (Boston: Harvard Graduate School of Business, 1965).

24. Stephen E. Weiss, "Creating the GM-Toyota Joint Venture: A Case in Complex Negotiation," *Columbia Journal of World Business* (Summer 1987): 22–25; and Benjamin Gomes-Casseres, "Joint Ventures in the Fate of Global Competition," *Sloan Management Review* 30, no. 3 (Spring 1989): 17–26.

25. "Saturn Experiment is Deemed Successful," *The Wall Street Journal,* 18 April, 1995): B1.

26. R. N. Ford, *Motivation Through the Work Itself* (New York: American Management Association, 1969).

27. A. N. Turner and P. R. Lawrence, *Industrial Jobs and the Worker* (Boston: Harvard Graduate School of Business, 1965).

28. M. R. Blood and C. L. Hulin, "Alienation, Environmental Characteristics, and Worker Responses," *Journal of Applied Psychology* 51 (1967): 284–90. See also "Job Satisfaction and Subjective Well-Being as Determinants of Job Adaption," in *Best Papers Proceedings, Academy of Management* Annual Meeting, Las Vegas, Nevada, 1992, pp. 222–26; and Gerald V. Barrett, Ralph A. Alexander, and Dennis Doverspike, "The Implications for Personnel Selection of Apparent Declines in Predictive Validities Over Time," *Personnel Psychology* 72, no. 9 (Autumn 1992): 601–18.

29. J. R. Hackman and E. E. Lawler III, "Employee Relations to Job Characteristics," *Journal of Applied Psychology Monograph,* vol. JJ (1971): 259–86.

30. Y. Fried and G. Ferris, "The Validity of the Job Characteristics Model: A Review and Meta-Analysis," *Personnel Psychology* 40 (1987): 287–322.

31. P. Buttger and I. Chew, "The Job Characteristics Model and Growth Satisfaction: Main Effects on Assimilation of Work Experience and Context Satisfaction," *Human Relations* 39, no. 6 (1986): 575–94.

32. E. Hogan and D. Martell, "A Confirmation of Equation Analysis of the Job Characteristics Model," *Organizational Behavior and Human Decision Processes* 39 (1987): 242–63.

33. Chi-Sum Wong and Michael Campion, "Development and Test of a Task Level Model of Motivational Job Design," *Journal of Applied Psychology* 76, no. 6 (1991): 825–37.

34. Karlene H. Roberts and W. Glick, "The Job Characteristics Approach to Job Design: A Critical Review," *Journal of Applied Psychology* 66, no. 4 (April 1981): 193–217.

35. Brian Dumaine, "Who Needs A Boss?," *Fortune* (May 7, 1990): 52–60. See also K. Fisher, "Managing in the High Commitment Workforce," *Organizational Dynamics* (Winter 1989): 31–50.

36. John Hulpke. 1994. Working paper. Edgar H. Schein, "Corporate Culture is the Real Key to Creativity," *Business Month* (May 1989): 73–75.

37. Brian Dumaine, "Who Needs a Boss?," *Fortune* (May 7, 1990): 52.

38. Tom Peters, *Thriving on Chaos* (New York: Alfred A. Knopf, Inc., 1987), 303.

39. Brian Dumaine, "Who Needs a Boss?," *Fortune* (May 7, 1990): 53.

40. Brian Dumaine, "Creating A New Company Culture," *Fortune* (January 15, 1990): 130.

41. Stan Kossen, *The Human Side of Organizations,* 6th ed. (New York: Harper Wilkins, 1994), 259.

42. Movry Hagan and Dave Wordens, "Human Resources: Key to Excellence at Dana," in Y. K. Shetty and V. M. Buehler, eds., *Quality Productivity and Innovation* (New York: Elsevier Science Publisher Co., Inc., 1987), 111–20; John J. Kerwood, "Creating Work Cultivates with Competitive Advantage," *Organizational Dynamics* (Winter 1988): 5–27; and Edward Lawler III, *High Involvement Management* (San Francisco: Jossey-Bass Publishers, 1986), 156–59.

43. Shaker A. Zahra, "Building A Wholesome Quality of Working Life," *Management Quarterly* 28, no. 6 (Summer 1983): 12.

44. David A. Nadler and Edward E. Lawler III, 11, no. 5 "Quality of Work Life: Perspectives and Directions," *Organizational Dynamics* (Winter 1983): 26.

45. See James Thacker and Mitchell Fields, "Union Involvement in Quality-of-Worklife Efforts: A Conventional Investigation," *Personnel Psychology* 40 (1987): 97–111; Ricky Griffin, "Effects of Worker Redesign on Employee Perceptions, Attitudes and Behaviors: A Long-term Investigation," *Academy of Management Journal* 34 (1991): 425–35. See also William A. Kahn and Katy Krom, "Authority at Work: Internal Models and Their Organizational Consequences," *Academy of Management Review* 19 (1994): 17–50.

Chapter 4

The Success System: The Recruiting Process

Objectives

Upon completing this chapter, you will be able to:

1. Define and discuss the employee recruiting process.
2. Describe the steps in developing and implementing a recruiting program in an organization.
3. Understand and compare the advantages and disadvantages of external and internal sources of recruitment.
4. Identify and describe the major HR manager styles.

Premeeting preparation

1. Prepare for HRM Skills Simulation 4.1. Read Part A Objectives.
2. Prepare for HRM Skills Simulation 4.2. Read Part A Purpose.
3. Prepare for HRM Skills Simulation 4.3. Read Part A Purpose.
4. Read Case 4.1: Precision Products, Inc. Answer questions.

Background Information

One of the most important HR activities is **the recruiting process:** the attracting of a high-performing workforce. We exist in a society of large, medium, and smaller organizations. In these organizations, managers and employees work together to accomplish goals that are too complex to be achieved by any single individual. Before the organization can hire employees, it must locate and attract people who want the job. More and more it is recognized that the most significant factor in determining the success of any organization is the quality of its people.[1]

As Nation's Bank CEO Hugh McColl says, "Employees are our Number One priority at this stage. They will continue to be. If you look after employees, they look after customers. And that's good for shareholders." And as McColl also states, "Employees hold the key to future growth: When you stop growing, you start dying."[2]

HRM activities focusing on the recruitment of new employees are becoming a top priority in organizations. We exist in a global, competitive business environment where skilled people make the difference. One survey suggests that over half of the companies polled expect an inadequate supply of qualified workers in the years ahead.[3] Recruiting involves the set of activities used to attract job candidates who have the necessary abilities to be part of a high-performing organization.

During the 2000s, HRM activities in large and small organizations are taking on a new dimension of significance.[4] According to information compiled by the U.S. Bureau of Labor Statistics, workforce growth in the United States slowed from 2 percent a year for the 1976 to 1988 time period and will slow to 1.2 percent annually for the span between 1988 and the year 2000. Given the decreasing U.S. labor force growth and the increasing workforce diversity, managers will do well to heed the advice of Joel Dreyfuss, who comments, "Cast a wide net for workers—that's the only way you'll get through."[5]

In this chapter, the second stage of the Success System Model is presented: attracting high-performing individuals who can help the organization achieve its objectives. The HR manager uses the recruiting process and an effective HR style to improve the efficiency, effectiveness, and productivity of the organization. Several of the basic HRM recruiting activities and styles are presented including the recruitment process, the sources of job applicants, and the basic techniques involved in this function. The modern manager must not only be flexible and adaptive in a changing environment but must also be able to use recruiting to improve the organization. Teamwork is a big part of the Success System Model. Recruiting of new employees must be handled in such a way as to build a team-oriented workforce.

Recruiting

Emphasizing the essential nature of the recruiting function in today's business environment, Peter Drucker notes that "every organization is in competition for its most essential resource: qualified, knowledgeable people."[6]

An organization needs to hire the most qualified people it can at the most competitive price. Before an organization is able to hire an individual, it must locate qualified applicants who are looking for work. How does a company attract these qualified people to its premises? This is the recruiting process and it represents one of the major responsibilities of the HR manager. **Recruiting** may be defined as the process of seeking, attracting, and identifying a pool of qualified candidates in sufficient numbers to fill current and future workforce needs.

Merck, the pharmaceutical company, has been rated as the most admired company in a *Fortune Magazine* survey.[7] Richard Markham, head of worldwide marketing for the company, credits its success to attracting, developing, and keeping good people. Promotions and salary increases for executives are affected by how many people are recruited and trained. "We look at recruiting with the same kind of intensity as we do discovering new molecules in the lab." The Merck recruiting process is fully integrated with their team-building process.

Part of the Merck competitive advantage is their approach to recruiting. Their focus is on business and the need to hire the best people they can find. Diversity is not a separate program but is an integral part of business practices and strategy. Merck's success depends upon hiring committed and talented people with diverse perspectives. This requires a comprehensive search for the best recruits.[8]

HR MANAGER STYLES

The HR manager is the person who initiates and facilitates the HR recruiting process. One recent study suggests that HR managers are involved in and are using different skills and activities than in the past. In the past, much of HR was focused on individual development, but today there is greater emphasis on organization change and on building teams.

A number of **HRM styles** or approaches can be identified. Each style varies according to its underlying character, shaped by the kinds of skills and techniques the HR manager uses, the values they bring to their organization, and the manner in which they carry out their assignments. Other research has also examined the degree of emphasis the HR manager places upon two interrelated goals or dimensions of the HR recruiting process:

1. The degree of emphasis upon effectiveness or HR goal accomplishment.
2. The degree of emphasis upon relationships, morale, and participant satisfaction.

Based upon these two dimensions, five different types of HR styles may be identified. (See Figure 4.1).

Figure 4.1
HRM manager styles

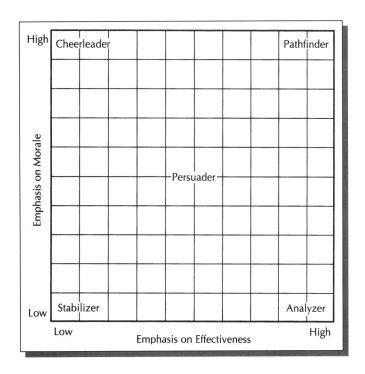

The Stabilizer HR Style

The goal of this HR style is neither effectiveness nor participant satisfaction. Rather, the HR manager is trying to keep from rocking the boat and to maintain a low profile. The underlying motivation is often survival, or merely following the directives of top management. Such a role is usually found in large organizations where HR programs may be a small part of the staff function and are not highly regarded by top management. This style is usually regarded as forced upon the individual by organization pressures, so that the individual has learned to conform and suppress internal motivations.

The Cheerleader HR Style

The cheerleader HR style places emphasis on the satisfaction of organization members and is chiefly concerned with employee motivation and morale. The cheerleader HR manager seeks warm working relationships, and, in general, is more comfortable in nonconfrontative situations. Effectiveness per se is not emphasized, the assumption being that if employee satisfaction is high, effectiveness will also be high. Unfortunately, there is a great deal of evidence that contradicts these assumptions. The cheerleader style strongly pushes for improved morale, and open conflict or locking horns is avoided by attempts to smooth over differences and maintain harmony.

The Analyzer HR Style

The analyzer HR style places greatest emphasis on efficiency, with little emphasis given to employee satisfaction. The analyzer feels most comfortable with a rational assessment of problems and assumes that the facts will lead to a solution. This type of HR manager may be quite confrontational, usually relying on authority to resolve conflict and on rational problem solving processes.

The analyzer HR manager usually has a background of specialized expertise, knowledge, and experience applicable to the solution of specific problems. The employee needs to have a problem solved, a service performed, or a study made—the analyzer takes responsibility for providing these functions. This type of HR style is based on the belief that the employee does not need to know or cannot learn the skills to solve his or her own problems.

The Persuader HR Style

The persuader HR style focuses on both dimensions—effectiveness and morale—yet optimizes neither. Such a style provides a relatively low-risk strategy, yet avoids direct confrontation with other forces. This approach may be used when the HR manager's power or leverage is low relative to other departments. This style is motivated primarily by a desire to satisfy; that is, to achieve something that is "good enough." A great deal of effort is applied in attempting to satisfy the differing forces, thus gaining a majority block of support for HR programs. The resulting HR program often may be watered down or weakened to the point where organization improvement is unlikely.

The Pathfinder HR Style

The pathfinder HR style seeks both a high degree of effectiveness and a high degree of employee satisfaction, believing that greater effectiveness is possible when all employees are involved and when problem solving is done through teamwork. There is an awareness that confrontation and conflict are often a means to a more effective organization and to more satisfied individual employees. The pathfinder approach uses collaborative problem solving and challenges the underlying patterns of member behavior.

Harold J. Leavitt uses this term to refer to developing a sense of value and vision. In this sense, the pathfinder HR manager is helping the organization to focus on its most critical issues and questions. The well-run smaller organization is also a good place to find managers using the pathfinder HR style. These managers know every person counts, because in the smaller organization there are so few people that everyone must pull their own weight.

We have identified five different HRM styles in this section. At the end of the chapter, you will have an opportunity to find out where your own style fits in this classification system. Most organization problems are complex situations, however, and may not neatly fit with any one particular HRM approach, but will depend upon the particular individual, the nature of the problem, and the type of organization climate that exists. Although the pathfinder approach fits well with the Success System Model, it is not the answer for every situation.

In summary, these five HR styles are not mutually exclusive. All HR styles can be effective and are interrelated. A HR manager may use different styles at various times to meet changing needs and deal with diverse situations. Frequently, some combination of the styles may be used.

One of the most important elements in the Success System Model is the HR manager style. As Douglas M. Reid, senior vice president of Xerox comments, "Indeed the essence of our Leadership Through Quality strategy is to satisfy the customer requirements." Reid said, "We're becoming much more sensitive to doing what's right by the customers, and listening and understanding their needs, versus what we may have done in the past—saying 'here's a product and we're going to convince you that you have to use it.'"

The emphasis on quality directly touches on many aspects of the human resource function, as Reid noted. It places a heavy reliance on the recruiting and training of quality personnel, and on communicating those quality objectives.[9]

THE RECRUITING PROCESS

The recruiting process is aimed at finding a pool of applicants with the abilities desired by the organization. The difficulty of recruiting depends upon a number of factors, as shown in Figure 4.2. The general economic conditions, of course, influence the labor market. In a time of recession, a job advertisement may generate hundreds of responses; in times of high demand, very few. The environment of the firm, the type of industry, and its location also influence recruiting. Finally, the labor supply and demand affect recruiting. If there is a surplus of certain job skills, it may be relatively easy to attract numerous applicants. On the other hand, if there is a scarcity of a certain type of skill, then prolonged and vigorous recruiting may be necessary.

The first part of the twenty-first century is seen by many economic forecasters to continue the conditions of a tight labor market and global competitive pressures experienced in the late 1990s. This scenario had already caused businesses to overhaul their hiring practices in the pursuit of a shrinking supply of job candidates.

The result is about 2,500 career web sites with large databases of job openings, resumes, and job-hunting tips. Job candidates can now apply instantly for a position and the HRM personnel need to contact them promptly. In some job categories and/or industries, the contact must be made within 72 hours or the prospective recruit will have a job.[10]

Successful recruiting involves attracting an adequate number of qualified candidates within a specified time frame. The recruiting process involves several steps. It begins with human resource planning and job analysis (as noted in chapter 3), and a determination of the organization's short- and long-term personnel needs. Based upon these needs and existing conditions, the firm then recruits from both internal

Figure 4.2
The recruiting process:
A key step of the
success system model

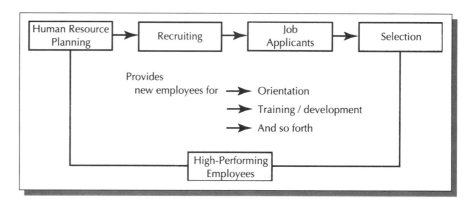

and external sources. This provides a pool of qualified job applicants, and the final step then is the selection from the applicant pool.

In general, recruiting is an expensive process, with the cost to recruit and relocate an employee in a professional position ranging from $40,000 to $80,000 a person. These costs can include **advertising,** interviews, travel, moving expenses, executive search fees, and real estate fees. Estimates of overall replacement expenses can run as high as one and a half times the employee's annual salary when orientation and training are included.[11] Obviously, in the smaller firm where the owner or manager makes hiring decisions independently, costs are not quite as much as when Microsoft recruits and selects an engineer. But make no mistake: The costs are still real and significant.

Recruiting Minorities and Women

Companies need to have a proactive recruiting program to attract qualified minorities and women. With the increased social awareness of employers to diversify their workforce, companies are experiencing increased competition in their efforts to maintain a pool of viable applicants.

Although a company's reputation as a good employer providing fair wages, benefits, and working conditions will attract applicants, more is needed to be done for the recruitment of minorities and women. To be successful, the human resource department needs to develop throughout the company a philosophy of openness and willingness to understand the special needs of these protected groups. (See cartoon.)

Source: B.C. by permission of Johnny Hart and Creators Syndicate, Inc.

The jobless rate continues to hover at all-time lows in the first part of the twenty-first century. In such an emerging economy, it might be expected the gender inequality of employing women as managers and professionals would disappear.

In an informative study, 114 multinational firms with headquarters in the United States and Japan, plus 40 domestic companies operating in Thailand produced some contrary results. The conclusion of this study was the organizational practice of gender inequality of employing women managers and professionals was the result of male employee's preferences.[12] Yet another challenge for HRM to overcome.

The HRM department, or whoever handles hiring in smaller organizations, needs to review sources of recruitment to determine whether the company's employment needs are known to minorities and women. Advertising notices in local newspapers and contacts with private employment agencies may not be adequate. Attention should be directed toward ethnic newspapers, social clubs, churches, barber and beauty shops, laundromats, and radio stations. The local United States Employment Office should also be notified. Because this is a competitive endeavor, other employers also are active in this search. More personal contact by HR managers with these sources may prove beneficial.

Associations of minority and women groups should be contacted. These include the National Urban League, National Association for the Advancement of Colored People, Ethnic Chambers of Commerce, League of United Latin American Citizens, Federation of Business and Professional Women's Talent Bank, National Council of Negro Women, and veterans groups such as the American Legion.

Once the minority and women applicants have been attracted to the company, the interviewing process needs to be flexible and adjust to their special needs. This may require moving the interview closer to prospective applicants' neighborhoods, providing temporary day care facilities, and possibly providing transportation.[13]

Company brochures and job placement ads should feature pictures of minorities and women. This helps convey the company's image as an equal opportunity employer.

RECRUITING THE OLDER WORKFORCE

As companies continue to downsize and offer early retirement, there is a growing pool of highly qualified people available for employment. The number of people in the labor pool over 50 years old is increasing dramatically. It has been estimated that almost one-third of all retired workers want to return to work either full- or part-time.[14] McDonald's, for example, has begun hiring older employees in their McMasters program to compensate for the loss of younger workers.

This older workforce group appears to be growing at least in part as a result of the 1986 amendment to the Age Discrimination in Employment Act of 1967. This amendment removed the upper age restriction of 70, allowing employees to work regardless of age as long as they can perform the job. Of course, changing social attitudes come into play, too. If older individuals want to work, why not? It can be a win-win situation, especially with removal of the social security earnings cap.

RECRUITING METHODS

Once the organization has become aware it needs additional employees, the HR manager is faced with the decision about how to generate the applicant pool necessary to satisfy labor needs. The organization can use internal sources and, if necessary, external sources for generating a sufficient number of applicants. Whenever there is a shortage of labor and skills inside the organization, it must effectively "reach out" to external candidates. It is here that the organization's choice of a particular method of recruitment can make a difference in the success of its recruiting program.[15]

With the economy experiencing a very low unemployment rate and a shortage of workers, many companies who believe the tight labor conditions will continue are adjusting their recruiting methods. These companies realize they must now sell themselves to candidates rather than expecting the candidates to do the selling. While this is the standard situation in the high-tech industries, other industries are joining the chase, including the fast-food industry. This requires HRM to be current on everything from salary trends and new and flexible benefits to the most effective stock option plans.[16]

Internal Recruiting Sources

Internal recruiting seeks applicants for positions from among those currently employed. Most organizations seek to fill positions with current employees. One study indicated that 96 percent of companies use internal recruiting beyond entry-level positions.[17]

Organizations can use job or skills inventories for identifying internal applicants for job openings. It is unlikely, however, that the HR manager is aware of all existing employees who are interested in a job opening. One method of solving this problem is called **job posting** or **job bidding:** Announcements of positions are made available to all current employees through bulletin boards, newsletters, and other company information sources.

HRM Job Posting

In the past, **job posting** often used bulletin boards and company publications for advertising job openings. Currently, job posting has become one of the more innovative recruiting approaches used by organizations. Many companies, such as Hewlett-Packard, now apply job posting as an integrated part of a comprehensive career development system.

Job postings are now frequently computerized and easily accessible to all employees. Computer posting systems allow the employee to match an available job opening with their own skills and experience. The posting presents information so the employee knows what needs to be done if they wish to apply for this position. Although computer job posting systems are not as complex as they may sound, they still may not make sense for smaller organizations. But in any size firm or agency, the principle still applies: To fill an opening, look at your current employees first. Do you need someone for marketing? Your hard-working clerk, already a member of your team, may be enthusiastic about making a move but still stay with your organization. One of the best sources of job candidates is the existing workforce. Recruiting internally has a number of advantages. First, there is the advantage of providing an opportunity for promoting an individual whose past performance is known. Past performance evaluations are usually available, and past managers will have a good idea of this individual's potential for promotion. The fit with your organization's culture has already been established. Because more information is available, the probability of making a good decision is greatly increased.

A second advantage is that a current employee also knows about the organization and how it operates. Therefore, the individual may contribute at a faster pace, and there is less likelihood of the employee being dissatisfied with the job or organization.

Another associated advantage of internal recruiting is the positive impact on employee motivation and morale. A policy of promotion from within where employees are considered for promotion provides a powerful incentive for good performance.

There are also disadvantages or problems with internal recruiting. One problem is that a promotion may leave several other internal candidates upset over not being selected, and infighting could occur with possible negative effects on morale.

A second problem is the possibility of conformity of ideas because people from within the system and culture are being promoted. Often some hiring from outside the organization is used to bring in fresh ideas or new cultural values. Many observers point out that the serious problems faced by General Motors in the 1990s were partly due to that corporation's long-standing policy of promoting from within. But when things finally got bad enough, even GM began to look outside for "new blood."[18]

A third problem is the danger of promoting internal candidates because of seniority rather than merit, which results in the "Peter Principle"—promoting people beyond their level of competence.

A fourth problem is the possibility of perpetuating a workforce built up over the years using discriminatory hiring practices. If your entire workforce is made up of individuals from one ethnic group, for example, promotions from within may limit opportunities to potential applicants from outside that ethnic group.

Referrals

Another internal source of recruitment is a **referral** system, in which present employees are asked to encourage friends or relatives to apply. You may be amazed at the connections your people have. Referrals are perhaps the most often used recruiting tool for many small organizations.

Some organizations even offer a "finder's fee" or monetary incentive for successful referrals. If they are used selectively, referrals of this kind can be a powerful recruiting technique. Organizations must be careful, however, not to unintentionally violate equal employment laws while they are using employee referrals. As an example, in *EEOC* v. *Detroit Edison* (1975), the U.S. Court of Appeals, Sixth Circuit, found problems of racial discrimination that are related to using referrals in recruitment. The court stated:[19]

> The practice of relying on referrals by a predominantly white workforce
> rather than seeking new employees in the marketplace for jobs was
> found to be discriminating.

This suggests that employee referrals should be used cautiously, especially if the workforce is already low in protected classes. It also suggests that it might not be wise to rely exclusively on referrals, but rather to use them as supplements to other kinds of recruiting activities.

In a tight labor market, many companies are paying their employees referral bonuses for new recruits who join their company. Some HRM departments are paying a commission to human resource employees for the information systems employees they recruit.

All of this increases recruiting costs, but it is still cheaper than using outside recruiting firms who charge 30 to 40 percent of the new employee's base salary. Most recruiters pay between $250 and $6,000 per referral.[20]

External Recruiting Sources

External recruiting is used when the organization is unable to fill its hiring needs from internal sources. The organization may be growing too rapidly, or may require highly specialized technical skills not available in the current workforce. The organization may want new ideas and new approaches. When an organization decides to recruit from outside the organization, the process becomes more involved and uncertain. There are both advantages and disadvantages to outside recruiting.

One advantage to external recruiting is that the new employees bring new ideas, different cultural values, and fresh approaches. Another advantage is that the size of the talent pool is usually larger and more diverse than the internal sources. It may also be less expensive to hire skilled workers than to train or develop them internally.

One major disadvantage to external recruiting is that it is usually more difficult, expensive, and takes longer. A second disadvantage is that outside hires usually require a longer training and orientation time in order to gain an understanding of organization processes and procedures. Finally, external recruiting may cause dissatisfaction and morale problems among the existing workforce.[21]

Signing Bonuses

In the past few years, signing bonuses are no longer the fruits of athletic stars, but have grown dramatically in the world of business. MBA's have been receiving them for years and now college graduates in business disciplines are the recipients. An example is accountants who graduate from quality institutions now expect signing bonuses.[22]

The Internet

Many company recruiters are now using the Internet as an easy and subtle method to contact employed job candidates. The traditional in-house HRM recruitment process is beginning to operate like a search or headhunter operation. This controversial turn is not restricted to the highly aggressive technology companies, but is now spreading to airlines, banks, oil, and biotechnology companies.

For the traditional HRM people, this new method presents ethical issues which cause them to avoid Internet recruiting. However, one consulting firm which offers seminars in Internet recruitment strategies points out that 30 to 40 percent of the attendees are in-house recruiters or HR managers. The attraction is that the Internet presents a largely untapped source of would-be job seekers waiting to be contacted.

One HR manager admitted her company recruiters were beginning to operate like search firms. She expects their recruiters to understand where to find possible recruits and to know who the competition is. Some search firms recruiters have loitered in companies' parking lots to offer job opportunities to employees entering and leaving their place of employment.

HR managers who would not cold call (making an unsolicited phone call) to a competitor's employees for job solicitations, do routinely cold e-mail them if they have posted an on-line resume. Usually such e-mail resumes include a link to the web site of any company they mention. They can then be located by searching for web sites linked to the company's homepage.

A form of computer hacking is "flipping," which uses the logic behind web site addresses to allow recruiters to locate employee lists or phone lists from a company site.

Recruiting is becoming an extremely competitive arena. The problem for HRM is that when managers share some of these methods, they may become part of the profession even after the labor crunch eventually eases.[23]

Boomerang Employees

Another sign of recruiting changes in the twenty-first century are the boomerang employees. These are former employees who have left the recruiting firm for better advancement opportunities. These departing workers are no longer classified as traitors but as possible future recruitable resources. Some former employers will hire these alumni to return as consultants or work on special projects.

These former employees will have become more valuable as a result of their experiences with other employers. They will have left their former employer with a positive exit interview. It is important they will have remembered to thank their former managers and peer groups for enjoyable work experiences. They will have expressed the value of these work experiences.[24]

USTES

The Wagner-Peyser Act of 1933 enables the United States Training and Employment Service (USTES) to partially fund state job placement agencies. This is not a "free" source. The state job employment agencies receive their funding from contributions to state unemployment insurance funds paid by employers. Also, part of employer's payments for unemployment insurance is returned by the federal government to the state employment agencies. These state job agencies are usually referred to as the Department of Labor, the Department of Human Resources, or other titles. They are located in most large cities.

Since unemployed persons receiving unemployment compensation checks must report to these agencies for work, these recruits may not be as motivated to accept work as those who have exhausted their unemployment benefits. Regardless, these state employment agencies are frequently contacted by companies as they provide a valuable resource pool. Although they maintain managerial and professional listings, they are primarily contacted for blue-collar and less skilled jobs. These jobs are listed on both a national and local computerized job bank that is available to both the company and the recruit. These state agencies have also been assigned responsibilities for controlling abuses in the public assistance programs designed for training the hard-core unemployed and the disadvantaged.

Other valuable services performed are testing services to measure skills in typing, spelling, and dictation. Aptitude tests are given to measure verbal, numerical, spatial, and clerical abilities; motor coordination; manual dexterity; and finger dexterity. The testing is performed free and saves the human resource office both time and money in gathering applicant data before the recruitment process begins.

Advertising

Media Advertisements   One survey found that 88 percent of surveyed companies use newspaper advertising, and this figure is higher for lower-level positions. Organizations use advertisements to attract recruits. Many types of media are used. The ones most commonly used are the daily newspaper help-wanted ads.[25] Organizations may also advertise in trade journals and professional publications. Other media which may be used are billboards, subway and bus posters, radio, and television.[26]

Help-wanted ads need to be carefully prepared. If the organization's name is not used and a post office box number is substituted (termed a "blind ad"), then ad response may not be as high. If the company name is used, too many people may respond, and screening procedures for a large number of applicants can be costly. This is one of the decisions in preparing a recruiting advertisement.

In addition, the firm must be careful not to violate EEO requirements by indicating preferences for a particular race, religion, national origin, or sex.

Employment Databases

In the mid 1980s, there were approximately 35 firms selling resume **databases.** Today, that number has risen to over 160.[27] The reason for such a dramatic increase is simple. Organizations can quickly and efficiently gain access to prospective applicants by using a database.

In general, databases can be classified into five categories depending on who owns the database and how much public access is allowed. These categories include

1. Databases maintained by executive search firms.
2. Databases maintained by university alumni groups.
3. Databases owned by private employment agencies.
4. Corporate databases.
5. Databases open to the general public.

Organizations can also gain access to a large pool of potential applicants by developing partnerships with government-affiliated job search services.

High Touch

Some companies are using high-tech recruitment; however, there is another approach called high touch. This approach is for potential candidates to remember a particular company.

These companies stand out because they make personal contacts and establish a presence in communities and educational institutions. It is the "act early and often" technique. Early means maintaining active corporate involvement with high schools and colleges to build solid foundations with promising students.[28]

Employment Agencies and Executive Search Firms

Employment agencies and **executive search firms** differ in many important ways. Executive search firms tend to focus recruiting efforts on higher-level managerial positions with salaries in excess of $100,000. Employment agencies tend to concentrate primarily on middle-level management or below. Many smaller firms find real advantages in working with employment agencies for openings at all levels. Larger firms often use both agencies and the more-specialized firms focusing on higher-level positions: the executive search organization. Most executive search firms are reimbursed on a retainer basis with the organization paying their fee.[29]

Employment agencies are usually paid only after they have actually placed the new recruit. For lower-level positions, all costs may be paid by the job applicant. Other employment agency arrangements include fee-sharing, where employer and employee both pay the agency, and the "employer-fee paid" system. Executive search firms also charge higher fees for their services.[30] One of the reasons that organizations are willing to pay higher fees is that executive search firms are able to accomplish the recruiting effort and still maintain the confidentiality of both the client organization and the applicant being recruited. IBM, for example, hired two executive search firms in its effort to replace former CEO John Akers.[31]

Special-Events Recruiting

When the supply of employees available is not large or when the organization is new or not well known, some organizations have successfully used special events to attract potential employees. They may stage employment fairs and open houses, provide literature, and advertise these events in appropriate media. To attract professionals, organizations often provide free hospitality suites at professional meetings. Executives also make speeches at association meetings or schools to gain visibility for the organization. Ford Motor Company, for example, conducts meetings on college campuses and sponsors cultural events to gain acceptance among college recruits.[32]

One interesting approach is to sponsor job fairs. A group of firms sponsor a meeting or exhibition at which each has a booth to publicize job openings. Many experts claim that recruiting costs have been reduced by using these methods. This technique is especially useful for smaller, less well-known employers, and is used more in some industries than in others. It appeals to job seekers who wish to locate in a particular area and those wanting to minimize travel and interview time. For example, a recent Los Angeles job fair was able to generate 4,000 job candidates in a little under 4 hours of operation.

Limited English—No Barrier

With the tight labor market, companies are recruiting workers who have very little English-speaking skills. One Oregon company manufacturing foam products has been very successful. The production supervisor is a native Vietnamese speaker with limited English. The production staff consists of 38 workers; four speak English, with the remainder speaking Spanish or Vietnamese.

A multilingual workplace could lead to chaos and miscommunication. However, with the unemployment rate low and the area's minority population growing, the company had no choice but to recruit those persons available to work in these low-paying jobs. Fortunately, the production supervisor learned enough Spanish so he could communicate. The result is a productive workforce with an unintended but welcome blending of languages to create a highly productive work group.[33]

The result was not the same in a Chicago manufacturing plant. The company recently instituted an English-only policy at the plant because of the need to improve communication in the assembly line. Workers were reprimanded for singing Spanish to themselves or just mumbling. Morale is low, production is down, and now employees are filing lawsuits.[34]

Summer Internships

Another approach to recruiting used by many organizations is to hire students during the summer as interns. This approach has been used by businesses, government agencies, and hospitals.

Summer internships provide benefits at several levels. Participating organizations can get extra help for specific projects without having to make the tough "decision to hire." Firms may be introduced to potential employees who may also act as goodwill ambassadors for the organization. In addition, an internship provides trial-run employment for an organization to look closely at prospective hires. The interns may also bring a high level of enthusiasm and new ideas to the job.[35]

An internship can provide numerous benefits to a high school or college student. An internship provides job experiences in the real world, leads for a possible future job, and a chance for personal growth as well as getting paid. In some cases, the intern can earn high school or college credit hours at the same time. The sponsoring organization usually provides supervision and a contract with the participatory organization.

There are also disadvantages to these programs. The interns may take up a lot of supervisory time, and the quality of work is not always the best. There are sometimes questions of legal liability: Who is responsible if an intern acts in a way that causes damage, loss, or injury? Internships have significant advantages to an organization and to the individual intern. However, internships require some planning and careful operation. Once again, the HR manager in a larger organization, or the manager in a smaller organization, must take a proactive role.

Recruiting the University Graduate

As previously mentioned, there are serious and growing gaps between the skills that organizations need and the skills in the pool of potential employees. Some estimates say that three-quarters of new entrants to the workforce will only be able to handle some 40 percent of newly developing jobs.[36] With the ever-increasing importance of technology, special skills, and college education, highly qualified employees will be increasingly tough to locate. Unfortunately, **college recruiting** can be tough, costly, and time consuming.[37] A continually changing world will force larger organizations to be highly visible and active in college recruiting, whether they like it or not. One survey reported that over 80 percent of all managers were hired through college recruiting.[38]

Recruiting for college-level employees is similar in some ways to other recruiting and different in other ways. In college recruiting, an organization typically sends an employee, called a recruiter, to visit specific campuses. The recruiter usually interviews candidates preselected by the college placement office. The recruiter also accomplishes a public relations function, describing the organization and providing brochures and other literature as well as providing the screening interview.

In larger universities, the placement office plays a key role. Students sign up for interview slots, and are often prescreened at this stage. The placement office is a way for students and employers to talk over placement possibilities. During the heaviest recruiting season, typically in early spring, the placement office will publicize upcoming visits in student newspapers, bulletin boards, and other information sources. After on-campus interviews, recruiters typically invite a few candidates to follow-up interviews, often at the place of potential employment.

Those students selected for second (or following) interviews are given more information on the job and on the organization. Typically a site visit involves potential supervisors, coworkers, and executives. The applicant will be shown around and evaluated as well. In most cases, the prospective employer covers all expenses, although this policy seems to weaken during economic hard times. If the organization and the recruitee both like what they see during the visit, the applicant may be given an offer at the end of the site visit or soon after.[39] There is usually some negotiation regarding salary and benefits, but this varies from organization to organization.

Given changing conditions, HR recruiters are finding it helpful to be creative in their college and university recruiting. New ideas are helping cut excessive recruiting costs, while still keeping a steady flow of new college graduates into the organization. One recent trend finds organizations working to build stronger relationships with potential employees while they are still in college. McDonald's does this by providing summer internships and restaurant management programs for potential future managers while they are still at college. The students get acquainted with McDonald's and they get valuable job experience too. Furthermore, McDonald's executives can look prospects over prior to making the crucial decision to hire.[40] Although many recruiters seek out the more prestigious schools, others such as PepsiCo prefer "second tier schools for people who aren't afraid to get their hands dirty."[41]

Brainstorming Sessions   With the intense recruiting competition between high-tech companies, one approach to developing a personal relationship with college graduates is having brainstorming sessions. This expensive approach is being used because the estimated turnover rate is 20 to 30 percent among entry level programmers and analysts.

One consulting firm holds brainstorming sessions for graduates eight times a year in their offices located in Massachusetts, Georgia, and California. The team exercise is designed to hire the right candidates and to make sure the graduates develop a favorable impression of the company.

Their program is very successful in matching the right people with the right environment. The company's staff has grown by 300 over the past year and they have one of the lowest industry turnover rates.[42]

Web Site Skinny

Although recruiters should take special notice, all HRM professionals need to be aware of ValutReports.com. This web site is the equivalent of the office water cooler where employees gather to exchange hushed gossip and learn the real "skinny" of what is going on in the company.

These are stories of withdrawn job offers, nasty bosses, unpaid expense accounts, what others are earning, who is receiving special perks, what it is like at a competitor, and other nonbulletin board material. However, most of the information is unsubstantiated, may be startling, and can contain raw language.

HRM types and students who are interviewing need to be aware of what is going on. One director of career services at a large university discovered a message board about a company about to interview on the campus. Her reaction was "Oh, my. Oh, my gosh." Since some of the information did not fit with her knowledge of the company, she wondered what effect it would have on the ability of the company to recruit.

Some companies will not allow its employees access to the web site. So, for whatever it is worth, awareness of even suspect information may have a value.[43]

On the Road: The Effective Recruiter

In a tight labor market, one would think recruiting would be a cinch. Not so. The college recruiter's job is never easy. When appropriately qualified applicants are scarce, the recruiter must use creativity and persuasion to obtain enough candidates. When applicants are plentiful, it is harder for the recruiter to screen through the numbers, to narrow the field to those most appropriate for consideration for this special job. Many people will influence the applicant during the recruiting effort: fellow students, friends, family, and sometimes university professors.

A key factor, of course, is the recruiter. The recruiter represents the organization to the student, and is seen as the kind of person the organization will likely hire. For this reason, good recruiters present an image that represents the organization well. A good recruiter is typically well informed, but also warm, caring, and personable. It takes more than a salesperson to recruit; therefore, the recruiter also has to assess numerous potential employees. The effective college recruiter relates well to college students, knows the organization and its culture, and is a good judge of human nature. With all these requirements, it is little wonder that good college recruiters are hard to find!

According to some studies, students want specific qualities in a recruiter: friendliness, sincerity, personal interest in the applicant, and honesty. In addition, students seem to prefer interviewers who are enthusiastic about their organization.[44]

What students do *not* like in college recruiters is exemplified by the following list:

- *Apathy toward the Applicant.* Students sometimes infer indifference if the recruiter's presentation is cold and formal. One student reported, "The company might just as well have sent a tape recorder."

- *No Enthusiasm.* If the recruiter seems disinterested, students may infer that he or she represents an uninteresting company.

- *Stress or Sarcasm.* Students dislike too many questions that convey a stressful or sarcastic interviewing style by the recruiter.

TEMPORARY EMPLOYMENT

In the early twenty-first century, over half of all working Americans joined the ranks of the temporary workforce.[45] This growing trend, perhaps related to the widespread downsizing and the selective labor shortages of recent years, reflects the rapid rise of temporary help agencies. In the 1980s, **temporary employment** agencies focused on providing clerical help during busy times. The image of "the Kelly Girl" (who incidentally were mostly female, but not always young) comes to mind. Times have changed, and Kelly Services provides professional men and women to thousands of employers. One survey by Western Temporary Services found that nine out of ten companies now use temporary services in one way or another.[46] Temporary agencies may be one potential solution to the specific skills labor shortages forecast during the twenty-first century. Approximately 80 percent of U.S. firms use temporary employees.

Temporary help agencies can provide relatively inexpensive labor, even with the overhead fees tacked on to the hourly rate the employee gets. Temps provide a quick source of experienced labor and also greater flexibility. It is easier to add or cut quickly. The cost advantage of using temporary agencies often is tied to such factors as not having to offer fringe benefits, training costs, and retirement plan costs.

Although temps are a growing part of the workforce, the temporary help movement is not without its detractors. For one thing, a disadvantage of hiring temporary help is that these individual temps may not know the organizational culture. The temp may need training, both about the job and about the organization. And, of course, there are the societal issues: Will temporaries be able to achieve career goals while working in jobs with little security and minimal or no benefits? Obviously, from the employee's perspective, temporary employment is not for everybody.

EMPLOYEE LEASING

A logical outgrowth of the temporary help industry is the "employee leasing" business. In **employee leasing,** a firm pays a fee to a company for handling all recruiting, hiring, training, compensating, and evaluating. The leasing firm provides a ready-made labor pool, and handles the paperwork that drives employers crazy. Smaller firms are particularly happy with employee leasing because this eliminates all kinds of HRM headaches and administrative burdens. Employee leasing is similar to the temporary help industry, but with employee leasing, the workers are usually hired for longer periods.

It seems that leasing employees is becoming more popular. When Ceramic Devices workers asked Chairman William Payne for a 401(k) savings plan in 1991, he fired them. A leasing group hired the 35-person workforce and leased it back, enabling Ceramic Devices to trim its accounting staff, while workers got their 401(k). Altel Sound Systems, Pleasantville, New York, and Dr. George Gruner, a Virginia neurosurgeon, save health costs by leasing employees, who get better benefits.

Texas Instruments leases up to 15 percent of its workers. Firms, mostly small ones, now lease more than a million workers, up from 850,000 in 1990, says the National Staff Leasing Association.[47]

Many leasing firms specialize in certain fields, such as computer-assisted design or engineering. Employee leasing is growing in importance for a number of reasons. Rising health care premiums and similar benefit costs are cited as one reason; government regulations are another. In an era where "employment at will" is becoming a thing of the past, it becomes more and more problematic to terminate any employee. The risk of a "wrongful discharge" lawsuit must always be considered. Leasing can relieve some of these fears: It is often easier to terminate a temporary employee than a regular member of the workforce.[48]

There are now more than 1,300 employee-leasing companies and roughly one million leased employees nationwide. The Aegis Group, a San Bernardino, California, consulting firm that specializes in employee leasing, forecasts that the industry will continue to expand at a rate of approximately 20 percent a year throughout the decade.[49]

COST BENEFITS AND RECRUITING

How can recruiting be evaluated? Several possibilities come to mind. Larger organizations can assign goals to individual recruiters by types of employees. One recruiter might be given a goal to hire 20 college graduates in a given year. The organization can compare results to objectives. If more than one recruiter is doing similar work, then their results can be compared. However, the strict use of hiring data can be misleading. Another significant factor would be how long new hires stay with the organization and how well they do. A reasonable approach would probably be to use both quantitative and qualitative information when evaluating the recruiting process (usually called a "turnover" report).

Sources of recruits can also be evaluated. In college recruiting, the organization can look at the number of employees hired from campus interviews to calculate the cost per campus visit. The colleges that result in fewer successful hires may not be worth visiting in the future.

Recruitment also takes place for jobs requiring little skill with short training requirements such as fast food or retailing. For the skilled trades and technical jobs, recruiters often visit vocational schools, including junior colleges. When supervisory, managerial, technical, and functional abilities such as accounting, finance, or marketing are required, recruitment usually takes place at the 4-year college or university.

Recruitment at this level has become very competitive as placement directors attempt to lure companies to recruit at their respective campuses. The process is reciprocal with colleges and universities desiring to present a past record of successful student placements, and companies examining their campus cost benefit ratios in regard to the quality and quantity of recruits who were hired. Since the recruitment "season" is generally October–November and February–March, the limited number of quality employers are eagerly sought after by a seemingly unlimited number of placement directors.

College Enrollments

The projection for college enrollment in the early years of the twenty-first century present some demographic challenges which will effect the recruiting process. Although the college population trend is for increased enrollment at least to the year 2007, more students will be younger with the majority of women continuing to increase.

During the period between 1995 and 2001, the college population was projected to increase at an annual rate of 1.3 percent. For the period 2001 to 2007, the projected increase is 1.1 percent.[50]

These projections will reflect both positive and negative changes within specific age groups. For instance, the 18-to-24-year-old group is expected to increase 16 percent by 2007. However, it is expected the 25-to-29-year-old group will decrease 10 percent by 2002, and then increase 10 percent by 2007.

The 30-to-34-year-old group is projected to decrease 19 percent by 2007. The same is projected for the 35-to-44-year-old group with an 8 percent decrease. The end result of these changes is projected enrollment increases for the younger age groups, which will more than offset the enrollment losses of the older groups.[51]

Women played a major role in the increase of enrollment between 1984 and 1997. Their share of total enrollment in 1997 was 56 percent compared to 52 percent in 1984. The projection for 2009: Their percentage will increase to 58 percent.[52]

The projected college enrollments are affecting how companies redesign their recruiting efforts to fulfill future employment needs. A common technique is to begin a prescreening of students as they start their junior year. This may be accomplished by using college professors as early identification sources of outstanding students. Professors may be asked to attend special one-day company programs to better understand the organization. They can then bring back to the campus their newly acquired knowledge about the company. Companies are taking the initiative by having their executives lecture or teach part-time on college campuses to identify and "sell" prospective recruits.

Since recruitment is a functional responsibility of the human resource manager, requests for human resources should be channeled there. These requests may come from the president's office if it is a planned change contained in the human resource plan, or from lower company levels in the form of a requisition for a specific job classification. In either case, the human resource manager will then implement **the recruitment plan.** (See Figure 4.3). Although smaller organizations

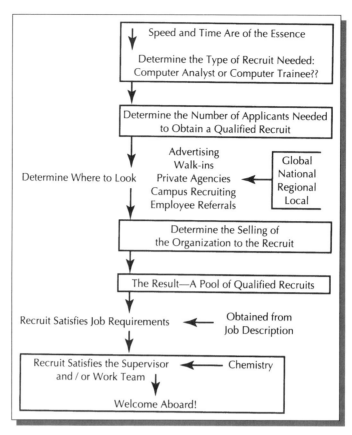

Figure 4.3
The recruitment plan sequence

may not have large human resources departments, the recruitment plan will fit any size organization.

LABOR CONDITIONS

Beneath the surface of all the company's recruiting techniques and efforts lies the prime qualifier for eventual success or failure. This prime qualifier is the labor market of the "real world" where the company exercises little control over existing forces. When there is high unemployment and an oversupply of qualified recruits, the recruitment process requires little effort, but the selection process becomes more difficult. It becomes more difficult in the sense of choosing a small number of hires from a multitude of highly qualified applicants.

In the reverse situation (low unemployment and short supply of qualified recruits), recruitment becomes more difficult and selection is reduced to choosing the few available. When a shortage of qualified recruits exists, one alternative is to expand the local labor geographical market to a regional, national, or global area. However, in such a scenario, the company's competitors will be doing likewise.

The challenge to the human resource manager, then, is to shift attention to broader labor markets when the need arises and to be able to adjust recruitment efforts. The ultimate success or failure of the company's recruiting techniques and efforts is related to the labor market; however, the changing demographics of the workforce becomes a dynamic factor in shaping this market.

THE RECRUITMENT PLAN

The request for additional personnel generally originates from two sources. One source results from the human resource plan. Other requests originate from the unscheduled and unexpected needs of supervisors. The human resource plan details the projected additions, promotions, transfers, and terminations. As in any plan, the unexpected often occurs, whether through economic circumstances, illness, or when a higher than planned rate of turnover occurs. Regardless of how a human resource need develops, there is a requirement for a recruitment plan.

The recruitment plan is an effort to quickly fill the human resource request with an individual who first, satisfies the job specifications and personal qualifications of the job description, and second, satisfies the supervisor or group where the individual may work. This latter stipulation centers around the subtle "personality factors" or "chemistry" that is so evident in the successful functioning of work groups.

The plan considers the number of potential recruits that must be contacted from which to obtain a number of qualified, interested applicants. (See Table 4.1.) Depending upon the job category, it is not unusual to contact, via advertising or other means, thousands of prospects in order to obtain a pool of several hundred applicants. Previous experience will offer an indication of how extensive the recruitment efforts will need to be. Then, based on knowledge of the job description, a determination is made on the types of people to be contacted. For instance, a computer programmer may be required with knowledge of certain computer programs, or one may need only limited computer experience with the company willing to provide additional training.

The next step is to decide where to look for the recruit. This refers to geographical area: global, national, regional, or local. The time available, the cost, and the availability of qualified recruitment personnel will be another important consideration.

Another step is to decide the media to be used to advertise the positions. As described earlier, this involves whether to depend in whole or part on advertising, walk-ins, private employment agencies, campus recruiting, and so forth.

The next step should be to consider how aggressively the company should target recruiting women, minorities, the handicapped, and older workers. This can successfully be done depending on where and what media is used.

The final step in the recruitment plan is how to "sell" the organization to the desired recruit. This will involve decisions as to number of trips, the company personnel with whom the recruit should talk, types of follow-ups, and company promotional material sent. The importance of the job to the company will determine how extensive the procedure will be. Once the plan is operational, the HR manager will do a more efficient job of developing a quality applicant pool.

The concept of recruitment in the twenty-first century requires companies to be proactive with recruiting a continual process. Many companies continue to treat

Table 4.1
The recruitment plan— drawing down the applicant pool

	Jan. 10	_____	Answered Ad:	200
	Jan. 20	_____	Interviews:	50
Time	Feb. 1	_____	Offers:	10
Span	Feb. 7	_____	Accepted:	6
	Feb. 15	_____	Reported to work:	5

recruitment as a reactive activity driven by personnel vacancies. The arrival of the Internet and e-mail allows companies to have continuous recruiting that can be decreased or increased as situations require.[53]

SUMMARY

Recruitment is the process of attracting applicants who are interested in and qualified for available positions. The organization is a system. The HR manager recruits employees for the system and develops processes, leadership, and controls for various purposes. The overriding HRM goal is to develop and maintain the dynamic fit between employees and the tasks which are necessary to yield organization effectiveness and human satisfaction. You have examined the various HR manager styles and possible approaches.

You have had the opportunity to gain insights into your own HR style, to assess your own strengths and areas of improvement as a potential HR manager, and to examine briefly the impact of a given style upon others. One important aspect of being a manager is to *know yourself*. Only by being aware of your own motives, reactions, and needs can you successfully hope to influence others.

The HR Style Matrix and HRM Skills Simulation 4.2 and 4.3 will provide an opportunity for you to gain some insights into how you approach problem situations. It is important to recognize that your answers to the survey may reflect more the way you wish to behave—an ideal—than the way you actually do behave. Your first objective is to get a clear reading on your actual HR style by getting feedback from your fellow participants. Their reports on how your actions affect them will enable you to move to a more effective style. You have begun this integration process here, but it should be a continuing process of feedback, reappraisal, and experimentation throughout this course and beyond.

Today we need organizations with flexibility and responsiveness, ever-faster innovations, and higher involvement among employees. The HR manager is the person who initiates, stimulates, or facilitates an HR program. In the next section, you will experience a situation where you can gain insights into your own HR style.

In summary, there are both advantages and disadvantages to internal or external recruiting. Several techniques have been discussed in this chapter. As a future HR manager, you must be sensitive to changes in markets, people, and competition, and be aware of the need for an adaptive and flexible organization.

You will have an opportunity to experience the need for HR recruiting skills in this class meeting. Students frequently complain about the lack of effectiveness and learning in the classroom. In HRM, we call this the awareness of a human resource problem. There is increasing evidence that the approaches to recruiting may result in different outcomes for the organization. The evaluation of recruiting programs in the future is more likely to focus on the quality dimension of the employees rather than the "body-count" criteria that have been used in the past.

REVIEW QUESTIONS

1. What role do job descriptions and job specifications play in an effective recruitment program?
2. What has led to an increased use of temporary employees in organizations? What are the major advantages of using temporary employees?
3. Name several problems associated with job posting and bidding and list your solutions.

Part II The Success System: Attracting High-Performing Workforce

4. What are some "free" and not-so-free sources that the company uses to locate qualified recruits?
5. Consider the relationship of college or university placement directors and company campus visits. Why is it reciprocal? Do you agree?
6. Discuss the steps of the recruitment plan and how they relate to success.
7. Reading a book or watching a video may help you identify examples of the recruiting process.

KEY WORDS AND CONCEPTS

Define and be able to use the following:

- Advertising
- College Recruiting
- Databases
- Employee Leasing
- Employment Agencies
- Executive Search Firms

- External Recruiting
- HRM Styles
- Internal Recruiting
- Job Bidding
- Job Posting
- Recruiting

- Referrals
- Summer Internships
- Temporary Employment
- The Recruiting Process
- The Recruitment Plan

HRM SKILLS SIMULATION 4.1: RECRUITING AN HRM ENTRY-LEVEL POSITION

A. OBJECTIVES

1. To better understand the relationship between the recruiter and the recruitee.
2. To experience and develop skills in interviewing.

B. PROCEDURES

Step 1. Members form into groups of threes: A) HRM recruiter/interviewer; B) HRM entry-level applicant; and C) observer. Then rotate so that each person does one interview. Review the Recruiting Interview Format and the Interviewer Tips.

INTERVIEWER TIPS

- Open the interview with brief general talk and establish rapport.
- Listen to the candidate's answers.
- Make sure the candidate understands the exact nature of the job.
- Take notes discreetly so as not to hinder discussion.
- Do not stereotype the candidate.
- Watch out for a halo-effect problem.
- Close the interview by giving some feedback as to when the candidate would know the decision.

RECRUITING INTERVIEW FORMAT

Name of Person Interviewed _____ Interviewer _____

1. Tell me about your scholastic and previous work experience that would qualify you for an entry-level position in HRM.

   a. _____
   b. _____
   c. _____

2. How would you describe the strengths you will bring to our HRM department?

   a. _____
   b. _____
   c. _____

3. What do you consider your past accomplishments or highlights as they would relate to a career in human resource management?

   a. _____
   b. _____
   c. _____

4. What is your philosophy about motivating your employees?

   _____
   _____
   _____

Step 2. Each HRM interviewer will interview the job applicant using the Recruiting Interview Format. The purpose is for you to gain enough information to determine whether this applicant would be a satisfactory candidate for the entry-level HRM position. The partners then rotate roles until each has had an interview.

Step 3. After all group members have experienced each of the three roles, decide the most effective and ineffective behaviors of the interviewer and the interviewee. Use the Interview Tips for evaluation.

Step 4. General Class Discussion. Each group of three will present their findings. The class will then discuss and attempt to agree upon the most effective and ineffective behaviors.

HRM SKILLS SIMULATION 4.2: HRM STYLE MATRIX

Total time suggested: 35 minutes.

A. PURPOSE

The role of the HR manager is both difficult and challenging. The HRM style matrix has been designed to give you information about your characteristic approaches to the HR relationship. This information may serve to reinforce existing strengths, or it may indicate areas of needed improvement. In either case, the data from the survey should prove helpful in learning more about your style.

At various times, there are many people trying to bring about change. They probably do not operate under the guise of an "HR specialist," but are more commonly referred to as managers, teachers, social workers, ministers, parents, and so on. You may now be, in some aspects of your life, using HRM skills, and at some time in the future you will most certainly be using HRM skills. That is, you now are or will be trying to initiate and implement HRM programs in an organization. This survey will help you gain some insights into ways you implement change.

B. PROCEDURES

Step 1. You will find in this survey 10 situations that call for your response. Each of the 10 situations presents five alternative ways of responding. Because you will be asked to rank-order these five responses to the situation, it is important that you read through all the responses before answering. Once you have read through all five responses, select the response that is most similar to the way you think you would actually behave or think in such a situation. Place the letter corresponding to that response (a, b, c, d, or e) somewhere on the "Most Similar" end of the 10-point scale appropriate to the intensity of your feeling. Next, select the response that is least similar to the way you would actually act or think. Again place the letter corresponding to that response somewhere on the "Least Similar" end of the scale. Complete the answers by placing the remaining three responses that reflect your actions or thoughts for those responses within range of previously selected most-least points.

As an example, the answer to a situation could be:

Most											Least
Similar	10	9	8	7	6	5	4	3	2	1	Similar

THE HRM STYLE MATRIX

In answering these questions, think of how you would actually act in or handle the situation, or how you think about change and the nature of change.

1. As a HRM relating to an employee, I will

   a. Support the client to work out their goals aiming at high morale.
   b. Generally set HR ground rules and then leave it up to the employee.
   c. Identify with the employee the goals of the HR program and then jointly work through the alternatives.
   d. Try to develop a friendly relationship, while suggesting HR goals.
   e. Provide expertise and use logic to convince the employee.

Most											Least
Similar	10	9	8	7	6	5	4	3	2	1	Similar

2. As an HRM manager, an HR program organization can best be initiated when

   a. I avoid involving too many people in the decision.
   b. The logic for the HR program is pointed out and results emphasized.
   c. The employee first has a good opinion of me and then I urge changes.
   d. I help the employee to gain self-confidence and satisfaction.
   e. The employee makes a choice of HR programs on the basis of mutual needs and goals.

Most											Least
Similar	10	9	8	7	6	5	4	3	2	1	Similar

3. If I am talking with an employee, I usually

   a. Try to be supportive by letting the employee do most of the talking.
   b. Try to let the employee talk and then slowly sell the employee on HR methods of change.
   c. Try to be sure the employee understands the logic of the decision.
   d. Share equally in the conversation and attempt to reach a shared conclusion.
   e. Say very little and only present my opinion when asked.

Most											Least
Similar	10	9	8	7	6	5	4	3	2	1	Similar

4. To achieve HR goals within an organization, I feel

   a. The employee has to be convinced that the plan for HR change has benefits as well as employee satisfaction.

b. The employee and the HR manager can mutually agree on alternatives.

c. The HR program and its implementation is left up to the employers.

d. The employee decides what HR programs are needed with support given by HRM.

e. The HR program is logically presented by the HRM.

Most											Least
Similar	10	9	8	7	6	5	4	3	2	1	Similar

5. When a HRM program is suggested and an employee reacts negatively to it, I am likely to

a. Accept the employee's position and search for mutual agreement.

b. Suggest the best course of action.

c. Go along with the employee's ideas.

d. Point out the requirements of the situation but avoid becoming involved in fruitless argument.

e. Search for a compromise position that satisfies both points of view.

Most											Least
Similar	10	9	8	7	6	5	4	3	2	1	Similar

6. The employee will probably be more accepting of the HR program if

a. The HRM emphasizes the rewards to the employee and downplays any problems.

b. The HR program will result in increased personal satisfaction and morale.

c. The employee is responsible for taking a course of action deemed appropriate.

d. It is made clear how HR programs will effect the bottom line.

e. The employee is an active participant along with the HRM in planning for the change.

Most											Least
Similar	10	9	8	7	6	5	4	3	2	1	Similar

7. A decision to change is most effective when the HRM

a. Tells the employee logically what is expected and how to best accomplish the HR program.

b. Gains the approval and friendship of the employee to get acceptable changes.

c. Actively participates with the employee in setting the HR goals.

d. Leaves the employee to make his or her own decision whether or not to change.

e. Allows the employee to take responsibility for the HR program while giving personal support.

Most											Least
Similar	10	9	8	7	6	5	4	3	2	1	Similar

8. In evaluating an HR program as an HRM, I usually use

a. The degree to which the employee complies with the HR program as well as the amount of pushing from me needed to gain conformance.

b. The employee's performance as measured by goals jointly set by both the employee and myself.

c. The employee's evaluation of his or her performance.

d. An adequate degree of satisfaction to ensure the employee's compliance in meeting HR requirements.

e. A high level of morale in the employee as well as a friendly relationship between the employee and myself.

Most											Least
Similar	10	9	8	7	6	5	4	3	2	1	Similar

9. In evaluating the employee's performance, the HRM should

a. Look at evaluation as a mutual responsibility.

b. Use a standard evaluation form to ensure objectivity and equal treatment among persons.

c. Present one's ideas, then allow questions, but casually push for specific improvement.
d. Compare performance with quantitative productivity standards.
e. Encourage the employee to make own evaluation with my moral support.

Most											Least
Similar	10	9	8	7	6	5	4	3	2	1	Similar

10. As an HRM, if there seems to be a personality conflict, I usually

 a. Try to ignore the conflict; avoid taking sides.
 b. Confront; use logic to gain acceptance of my position.
 c. Try to relieve tension; smooth over differences.
 d. Try to explore differences, resolve conflict, and reach mutual goals.
 e. Try to find areas of commonality, maintain morale, and seek compromise.

Most											Least
Similar	10	9	8	7	6	5	4	3	2	1	Similar

Step 2. Scoring Instructions for Table 4.2.

In Step 1, you wrote your answers (a, b, c, d, and e) above a number. Now transfer from each of the 10 situations your number values for each letter to Table 4.2. For each situation, look at the questionnaire to determine what number value you assigned to that letter, and then place that number in the columns. These computations will be made by the template if you are using the computer spreadsheet. The sum of each of the five columns is your score for each of the HRM styles. There is further explanation of the five change styles in Step 4.

Step 3. Scoring instructions for Table 4.3.

1. Transfer the numerical sums from the score sheet in Table 4.2 to Table 4.3, column 2, by rearranging them from highest to lowest score.
2. In column 1, write the appropriate word description or HR style beside the score.
3. Take the difference of the scores (column 2) for your 1st and 2nd choices, and record the difference on the first line of column 3. Then take the difference for your second and third choices, and record the difference on the second line of column 3. Continue taking the differences between the third and fourth choices, and the fourth and fifth choices. The difference between scores indicates the likelihood that a person will shift styles: A low score (1–10) suggests switching; a high score (over 20) suggests resistance to shifting.

Time suggested for Steps 2 and 3: 15 minutes.

Table 4.2

SITUATION	ANALYTICAL STYLE	CHEERLEADER STYLE	STABILIZER STYLE	PERSUADER STYLE	PATHFINDER STYLE
1.	e=_____	a=_____	b=_____	d=_____	c=_____
2.	b=_____	d=_____	a=_____	c=_____	e=_____
3.	c=_____	a=_____	e=_____	b=_____	d=_____
4.	e=_____	d=_____	c=_____	a=_____	b=_____
5.	b=_____	c=_____	d=_____	e=_____	a=_____
6.	d=_____	b=_____	c=_____	a=_____	e=_____
7.	e=_____	e=_____	d=_____	b=_____	c=_____
8.	a=_____	e=_____	c=_____	d=_____	b=_____
9.	d=_____	e=_____	b=_____	c=_____	a=_____
10.	b=_____	c=_____	a=_____	e=_____	d=_____
	_____	_____	_____	_____	_____
TOTAL POINTS	_____	_____	_____	_____	_____

Table 4.3

Your Choice	Word Description of HR Style (Col. 1)	Score (high to low) (Col. 2)	Difference between Scores (Col. 3)
1st Primary	_____	_____	_____
2nd Backup	_____	_____	_____
3rd Backup	_____	_____	_____
4th Backup	_____	_____	_____
5th Backup	_____	_____	_____

Step 4. HRM Styles of Implementing Programs.

You have just completed and scored your HRM survey. Following is a brief explanation of the five styles.

1. *The Pathfinder Style.* The person using this style constantly strives for achievement of the HR goals by other people in the HR program, and at the same time has maximum concern that the people involved in implementing the change are personally committed to the change and to the vision of the future.
2. *The Persuader Style.* This type of HR style has medium concern for achievement of the HR goals, and medium concern that the people implementing the change are committed to the HR goals. As a result, the HRM using this style is not consistent in behavior, and often changes the emphasis from concern for HR goals to concern for the people involved in the change program. The HRM believes too rapid a change will be disruptive and, therefore, attempts to implement change in small steps which allow people to become gradually accustomed to the changes and to avoid conflict.
3. *The Cheerleader Style.* The HRM using this style has minimum concern that the stated HR goals are accomplished, but does have maximum concern that the people involved in the HR program are personally committed to and happy with the change. There may be as many HR programs as there are people, because the cheerleader style consultant encourages members of a system to design and implement their own programs. The emphasis is on morale and friendly relationships.
4. *The Analyzer Style.* The HRM using this style has maximum concern for efficient accomplishment of the HR goals, and little concern that the people involved in implementing the program are personally committed to HR goals. The analyzer style sees people as a means to accomplish the change, and believes that people must be closely guided and directed because they lack the desire or capacity to change. A person using this style tends to use an expert-based style, and sets demanding performance standards as a method of implementing HR programs.
5. *The Stabilizer Style.* This HRM style has very minimum concern for goal accomplishment, and minimum concern for the people involved. The HRM does not care to get involved, and is only biding time until new orders come down. HR programs are viewed as a disruption of a well-ordered and secure environment.

You may now plot your average style scores on the graph in Table 4.4, HRM Styles. Complete the bar chart by shading in the score for each style (or the Lotus template will automatically plot it). This provides a profile of your scores.

A person does not operate using one style to the exclusion of others. The purpose of the scoring in Step 3 was to give you an indication of the importance you place on each of the five styles. The difference between your primary and backup styles indicates the strength of your preference and how quickly you will fall back on another style. Little difference between scores could indicate a tendency to vacillate between styles or vague thoughts about how to implement programs. A large difference could indicate a strong reliance on the predominant HR style.

This survey should be used as a point of departure for further reflection and observation concerning the way you attempt to work with other people. To obtain a better understand-

Table 4.4
HRM styles

	0	10	20	30	40	50	60	70	80	90	100
Pathfinder											
Persuader											
Cheerleader											
Analyzer											
Stabilizer											

ing of your HR style, try to become aware in your associations with friends, peers, and work associates of how you handle relations. It may also be helpful to observe other people when they try to influence your behavior, and to become aware of how you react to their methods.

Step 5. In plenary sessions, discuss the five consulting styles. Do your scores for your primary and backup HR styles seem congruent with the way you think you operate in change situations? Share your scores with class members with whom you have been working, and get their feedback. Does this feedback correlate with your scores on the matrix?

Time suggested for Steps 4 and 5: 20 minutes.

HRM SKILLS SIMULATION 4.3: CONFLICT STYLES

Total time suggested: 1 hour and 25 minutes.

A. PURPOSE

This simulation is designed to allow you the opportunity to influence and change other individuals, as well as to be influenced and changed by others. Although the story may seem minor, it describes a situation about which most of us have some rather strong feelings and ideas. Through diverse usage, we have found it to be a means to quickly get involvement and commitment to certain issues which you will select. This personal involvement is necessary so that in a later part of the simulation that requires you to change others' ideas and others to change your ideas, there will be a real and prior commitment to those ideas. The goals include (1) to identify ways of dealing with organizational or group conflict; (2) to discuss when and why different methods of resolving conflict are appropriate to different situations; and (3) to provide an experience in group decision making.

B. PROCEDURES

Step 1. Form groups of five members each. Any extra persons may join as the sixth member of a group, but no group should have more than six or fewer than four members.

Step 2. The following is a short story you are to read. Then *individually* answer the question that directly follows the story. Spaces are provided on Line A for your answer.

THE YOUNG WOMAN

In a house is a young woman married to a man who works very hard. She feels neglected. When her husband goes off on still another trip, the young wife meets an attractive man who invites her to his house. She spends the night and at dawn she leaves, knowing her husband is coming home. Alas! The bridge is blocked by a madman who kills everyone who comes near him. The young wife follows the river and meets the ferryman, but he demands 100 francs to take her to the other side. The young wife has no money. She runs back to her lover and asks for 100 francs; he refuses to help. The woman remembers that a platonic friend lives nearby. She runs to him and explains her plight. The friend refuses to help; she has disillusioned him by her conduct. Her only choice is to go by the bridge in spite of the danger, and the madman kills her. That is the story.

In what order do you hold the principals (woman, husband, lover, madman, ferryman, and friend) responsible for the tragedy?

Line A	1.	2.	3.	4.	5.	6.
Line B	1.	2.	3.	4.	5.	6.
Line C	1.	2.	3.	4.	5.	6.

Step 3. In your groups, you are to arrive at a group consensus for the answer to the question. Most members will not have the same answer, but it is important that your group make its decision in 15 minutes. Place the group's answer on Line B.

Time suggested for Steps 1–3: 20 minutes.

Step 4. Form a class group again, and focus your discussion on the following questions:

1. Was there much disagreement within your group?
2. If there was, to what could it be attributed?
3. How did your group reach its decision (consensus, voting, etc.)?
4. To what extent do you feel that other members of your group support the group's decision?

Time suggested for Step 4: 15 minutes.

Step 5. Go back to the story, and on Line C, answer the question again, but on an individual basis. Your answers may be the same as when you first responded to the story, or you may alter your original position based on the team discussion.

Step 6. Meet back in your groups to observe how individuals responded on Line C. Observe to see if Line C answers are the same as those on Line B and Line A, or perhaps different from any previous answers.

Time suggested for Steps 5 and 6: 5 minutes.

Step 7. Complete Table 4.5, Team Member Styles, by recording what you observed to be the primary and backup consulting styles (Pathfinder, Persuader, Cheerleader, Analyzer, or Stabilizer) of members in your group. Add any observations or comments about why that style seems to fit.

Time suggested for Step 7: 10 minutes.

Step 8. In Table 4.6, Individual Style Feedback, transfer the information from what the other team members recorded about you in their Table 4.5. From Table 4.6, try to draw some conclusion about your style of consulting. Discuss your conclusions with the other team members.

1. How did your survey style compare with the information received from your team?
2. Was there general agreement from your team on your consultant style? If there were differences, to what could they be attributed?

Time suggested for Step 8: 20 minutes.

Table 4.5
Team member styles

Group Member's Name	HRM Primary Style	Backup Style	Comments

Table 4.6
Individual style feedback

	INFORMATION RECEIVED FROM	PRIMARY STYLE	BACKUP STYLE	COMMENTS/ OBSERVATIONS
1				
2				
3				
4				
5				
6				
Consensus				

Step 9. Meeting with the entire class, discuss the following questions:

1. How congruent were your scores from Simulation 4.1 with the feedback from your group members?
2. If there was any difference, to what could it be attributed?
3. What consulting styles do you feel are most effective in an organizational development (OD) program to institute a new program or to revitalize a failing firm? Why?

Time suggested for Step 9: 15 minutes.

Case 4.1   Precision Products, Inc.

Helen knew this week would be hectic, so she pulled into the company parking lot at 6:30 A.M. Monday, about an hour earlier than usual. She parked at the far end of the lot ("my exercise quota for the day," she smiled) and walked briskly to her office.

Precision Products' president, H. J. Peterson, Jr., was fully committed to the expansion plans of the ambitious chairman of the board, so Helen knew she was going to have to produce or else. The immediate item on the early morning agenda was to prepare a recruitment plan on her ever-present yellow pad.

The phone buzzed, and Helen's secretary, Betty Moneypenny, announced the staff was assembled in the conference room ready to start on the recruitment plan. Walking into the conference room, Helen greeted her three-person staff: Curt Stump, who was responsible for Hiring and Safety; Viola Higgins, who handled Training, Health, and Cafeteria; and Mike Hudson, in charge of Affirmative Action and Labor Relations. Helen reached for her coffee cup, and said, "Gosh, do we have work to do!"

INCIDENT ONE

Curt Stump, Hiring and Safety, agreed with the other committee members that the recruitment plan sequence covered all the bases. As he said, "All we need is a human resource to start the ball rolling." However, his concern was that although hiring was a part of his job description, he felt uncomfortable with all the responsibility the recruitment plan placed upon him. The other members, Mike and Viola, agreed and offered to help out. Helen pointed out that they *all* would help out. The implementation of the recruitment plan would be a team effort. Because the human resource department was so small, they would all act as generalists and not specialists (with the exception of secretary Betty Moneypenny, who would be spared the combat zone experience). Everyone felt excited about the prospects of working for Precision Products in such a challenging environment. However, Curt began to fret again and asked the key question, "I am not concerned about presenting specific job information to the recruits because our job descriptions are in such good shape. But how am I supposed to *act?* Could my role behavior discourage an otherwise prime recruit?"

INCIDENT TWO

Viola Higgins, Training, Health, and Cafeteria, shared Curt Stump's concerns regarding the effect of her personality during interviews with recruits. However, she wondered if there weren't two sides to this personality situation, the other being the characteristics the recruit brings to the interview. Her question was, "What effects do the recruit's personality characteristics have upon the interview, and will that influence my behavior and response?"

INCIDENT THREE

Mike Hudson, Affirmative Action and Labor Relations, took a different tack and asked Helen about sources of recruitment and just getting recruits to report for that first day of work. Mike was disturbed about the few minorities the old recruiting procedure had attracted, which was compounded

by recruits accepting the company's job offer and then not reporting to work. Mike phrased his question, "How do we locate these minorities, and how do we get them and other recruits to report for work after we hire them?"

INCIDENT FOUR

Curt Stump found Helen's comments hit home regarding how the success of recruitment may depend upon the source from which recruits are obtained. "Helen," he asked, "would you go over those recruitment sources again as they might apply to Precision Products?" ∎

QUESTIONS

1. Help Curt Stump find an answer to his question from incident 1: "I am not concerned about presenting specific job information to the recruits because our job descriptions are in such good shape. But how am I supposed to *act*? Could my role behavior discourage a otherwise prime recruit?"

2. What suggestions can you make to help Viola Higgins with her question from incident 2: "What effects do the recruit's personality characteristics have upon the interview and will they influence my behavior and response?"

3. It appears Mike Hudson needs your help in incident 3 for the following question: "How do we locate these minorities, and how do we get them and other recruits to report to work after we hire them?"

4. How would you respond to Curt Stump's question from incident 4: "Helen," he asked, "would you go over those recruitment sources again as they might apply to Precision Products?"

ENDNOTES

1. J. Scott Lord, "External and Internal Recruitment," in Wayne Cascio, ed., *Human Resource Planning, Employment, and Placement* (Washington, DC: Bureau of National Affairs, 1989), 73–102.
2. Gary Hector, "Do Bank Mergers Make Sense," *Fortune* (August 12, 1991): 71.
3. "Labor Availability Results," *Nation's Business* (February 1991): 22.
4. Barbara W. Shimko, "All Managers are HR Managers," *HR Magazine* 35, no. 1 (January 1990): 67–70.
5. Joel Dreyfuss, "Get Ready for the New Workforce," *Fortune* (April 23, 1990): 167.
6. Peter F. Drucker, "The New Society of Organizations," *Harvard Business Review* (September-October 1992): 95–104.
7. K. Ballen, "America's Most Admired Corporations," *Fortune* (February 10, 1992): 43.
8. Raymond V. Gilmartin, "Diversity and Competitive Advantage at Merck," *Harvard Business Review* 77, no. 1, (January-February 1999): 146.
9. Stephenie Overman, "Leader Helps Improve Competitiveness," *HR Magazine* (May 1990): 58.
10. Joann S. Lublin, "In the race to fill job vacancies, speed demons win," *The Wall Street Journal*, Eastern Edition, 13 July 1999, p. B1.
11. David Sharp, "Getting the Jump on Job Hoppers," *Sourcebook* 3, no. 1 (Spring 1991): 62–65.
12. Stephen J. Appold, Sununta Siengthai, and John D. Kasorda, "The employment of women managers and pro-

fessionals in an emerging economy: gender inequity as an organizational practice," *Administrative Science Quarterly* 43, no. 3 (September 1998): 538–65.
13. Joan L. Kelly, "Employers Must Recognize That Older People Want to Work," *Personnel Journal* 69 (January 1990): 44.
14. Margaret Magnus, "Is Your Recruiting All It Can Be?" *Personnel Journal* 65, no. 2 (February 1987): 55–63.
15. P. L. Brocklyn, "Employer recruitment practices," *Personnel* 66, no. 2 (May 1988): 63–65.
16. Anita Lahey, "The most popular guys in the world," *Canadian-Business* 31 (June 16, 1997): 2.
17. Alex Taylor, "What's Ahead for GM's New Term?" *Fortune* (November 30, 1992): 58.
18. *EEOC v. Detroit Edison Company* (1975), U. S. Court of Appeals, Sixth Circuit (Cincinnati), 515 F. 2d. 301.
19. M. Meyers, "Is your recruitment all it can be?" *Personnel Journal* 66 (1987): 56.
20. Julie King, "Many earn big bucks referring IS pros," *Computerworld* 31 (June 16, 1997): 2.
21. S. Rubenfeld and M. Crino, "Are Employment Agencies Jeopardizing Your Selection Process?" *Personnel* 58 (1981): 71.
22. Edward Fleischman, "Signing bonuses: here to stay? Or not the only way?", *The CPA Journal* 69, no. 3 (March 1999): 13.
23. Sherry Kuczynski, "You've Got Job Offers!" *HR Magazine* 44, no. 3 (March 1999): 51–58.

24. Anita Bruzzese, "On The Job," *The Desert Sun,* Business section 15, January 2000, p. E1.

25. J. P. Bucalo, "Good Advertising Can Be More Effective Than Other Recruitment Tools," *Personnel Administrator* 28, no. 11 (November 1983): 73–79.

26. Rod Willis, "Playing the DataBase Game," *Personnel* 68, no. 5 (May 1990): 25–29.

27. Bill Montague, "CEO's Worries are Headhunters Gains," *USA Today,* 4 February 1993, p. 7B.

28. Beverly L. Little and Jerry Kinard, "Recruiting Employees for the health care industry," *American Business Review* 17, no. 2 (June 1999): 107–111.

29. W. Dee, "Evaluating a search firm," *Personnel Administrator* 28, no. 41–43 (1983): 99–100.

30. E. M. Fowler, "Recruiters Focusing Techniques," *New York Times,* 14 November 1989, p. Y35.

31. Natalie Engler, "We want you (please?!?)," *Computerworld* 32, no. 2 (March 23, 1998): 72–73.

32. V. R. Lindquist and F. S. Endicott, *Trends in the employment of college and university graduates in business and industry* (Evanston, IL: Northwestern University, 1989).

33. Emily Tsao, "Language barrier is no obstacle," *The Oregonian,* 24 August 1999, p. B1.

34. Martha Irvine, "More workers taking bosses to court over English-only policies." *The Associated Press* and *The Oregonian,* 3 September 1999, p. B3.

35. Robert E. Hite, "How To Hire Using College Internship Programs," *Personnel* 64, no. 2 (February 1986): 110.

36. Joan C. Szabo, "Finding the Right Workers," *Nation's Business* (February 1991): 16–22.

37. Sara L. Rynes and John Boudreau, "College Recruiting in Large Organizations," *Personnel Psychology* 39, no. 4 (Winter 1986): 739.

38. M. Hanigan, "Campus Recruiters Upgrade Their Pitch," *Personnel Administrator* 32, no. 11 (November 1987): 28–30.

39. Thomas J. Bergman and M. Susan Taylor, "College Recruitment: What Attracts Students to Organizations," *Personnel* (May-June 1984): 34–36.

40. Joel Dreyfuss, "Get Ready for the New Workforce," *Fortune* (April 23, 1990): 172.

41. Brian DuMaine, "Those High Flying PepsiCo Managers," *Fortune* (April 10, 1989): 82.

42. Carol J. Loomis, "The Hunt for Mr. X: Who Can Run IBM?," *Fortune* (February 22, 1993): 68.

43. L. M. Sixel, "Website contains the skinny on corporate culture," *New York Times* News Service, *The Oregonian,* 16 July 1999, p. B3.

44. J. E. Lubbock, "A Look at Centralized College Recruiting," *Personnel Administrator* 28, no. 9 (August 1983): 28–30.

45. Jaclyn Fierman, "The Contingency Work Force," *Fortune* (January 24, 1994): 30.

46. Rosalind Resnick, "Leasing Workers," *Nation's Business* (November 1992): 20. See also J. Scott Lord, "Contract Recruiting: Coming of Age," *Personnel Administrator* 32, no. 11 (November 1987): 49–53.

47. "Labor Letter," *Wall Street Journal,* 16 March 1993, p. 1.

48. Ibid.

49. "Temporary Services Offer Trials," *Bakersfield Californian,* 15 April 1991, p. D9.

50. U.S. Department of Education, National Center for Education Statistics, "Projections of Education Statistics to 2007," Chapter 2: Higher Education Enrollment, August 1996.

51. Opt. cit.

52. Debra E. Gerald and William J. Hussar, "Projections of Education Statistics to 2009," National Center for Education Statistics, Higher Education Enrollment, August 13, 1999.

53. Phillip Inman, "Recruiting drive: Putting your job right on the line," *The Guardian Manchester,* 16 January, 1999, p. 22.

Chapter 5

The Success System:
The Selection Process

Objectives

Upon completing this chapter, you will be able to:

1. Define and discuss the selection process.
2. Describe the stages in the selection process.
3. Understand and compare the advantages and disadvantages of various selection criteria.
4. Identify and describe the major employee testing techniques and understand their importance.
5. Define and be able to use the concepts of validity and reliability in selection.

Premeeting preparation

1. Read chapter 5.
2. Prepare for HRM Skills Simulation 5.1. Read Part A Purpose.
3. Read Case 5.1: Precision Products, Inc. Answer questions.

One of the lessons learned at Xerox, CEO Douglas Reid said, "is that it's important for the human resource people to understand the business strategy for new directions early so that we can start hiring people with the right skills and retraining people inside the company to be effective in the new business. That takes a lot of lead time."

"My experience has been there are more similarities than differences in managing human resources around the world. For those businesses like Xerox that are operating globally, there's going to be an increase in the interchange of people between the different countries," Reid believes.

Over the years he has seen that "as we've moved into this global economy, a technological advantage that any one firm has is short-lived. The company that's going to win in its particular business is the company that has a well-trained, highly motivated work force."[1]

The **selection process** is a critical one for any manager. One must take into account not only the fact that an incorrect decision can lead to a tremendous cost in terms of resources and opportunity, but also that many people will be affected by the decision. The right choice can mean growth and increased productivity for the entire work group associated with the new hire. The wrong selection can result in months of frustration, repetitive training, documentation, and low morale prior to the eventual termination of the recently hired person, after which the selection process begins all over again. Employee selection is a decision that needs to be made right the first time. Although this is true in organizations of any size, the impact of a wrong selection decision is magnified in a smaller firm. In a larger organization, one inappropriate placement can perhaps be reassigned or retrained. In the smaller organization, there may be no such luxury. Selection is critical.

The selection process begins when recruiting programs have developed a number of applicants for available job openings (as noted in chapter 4). In the twenty-first century, one of the most important issues is employee selection because of the costs involved and the legal implications.[2] Every day, managers are confronting complex employee selection problems, from top executives to the first line supervisor. Therefore, it is important that the HR manager develop procedures and policies which enable selecting the right person for the right job. This increased emphasis is due to new legal requirements, increasing scrutiny of employment practices, and the increasing cost of the selection process.[3]

In this chapter, we present the next stage of the Success System Model: selecting the Blue Chip performers. This includes a description of the employee selection process. We will discuss the advantages and disadvantages of various selection techniques and criteria, and discuss evaluating the quality of the selection process.

THE GOALS OF SELECTION

The basic goal of selection is to hire the employees most likely to attain high standards of performance. HR managers and all others involved in the selection process must concentrate on the most promising candidates, being as selective as possible. Identifying potential employees is a highly developed art, if not a science. In the past, this meant selecting candidates who had the skills the company needed today. Now it means selecting employees who can function at a high level in one job or with one work group today, and later be retrained or promoted as future needs dictate.[4] An effective selection process has several goals, including

- Developing a high-performance workforce, one which can implement organizational strategy and achieve bottom-line results, within legal constraints.

- Increasing the rate of return on recruiting costs (selection expense as an investment to reduce turnover, training, and benefits costs, and receive a good value for salary expenditures).

- Selecting top performers who will be able to attract others like themselves and continue a winning process.

FACTORS INFLUENCING SELECTION

There are a number of factors which influence selection. These include labor market conditions and organizational factors. If there is a surplus of applicants for a position, then selection can be very complex. When McDonald's opened their first restaurant in Moscow, they received over 27,000 applications for only 605 jobs. It was difficult to make the selection, but they had a highly qualified group of employees. They answered all 27,000 applicants with a letter.[5] On the other hand, if there is a shortage of applicants, then selection may appear easier, at least on the surface. There will be fewer applications to consider, but there may also be a shortage of applicants with the necessary skills to perform the duties needed in this organization at this time. All factors must be considered.

Organizational factors, including size, complexity, location, technology, working conditions, and the corporate culture, will also influence the selection process. Typically, large organizations use more sophisticated selection techniques. The complexity of tasks and degree of technology also must be considered. (See HRM in Action.)

HRM IN ACTION
THE SELECTION PROCESS AT WALT DISNEY[6]

What makes the Magic Kingdom magic? One of the authors went through the selection process at Disneyland, and there is something to be learned here. It's a selection process with unique Disney characteristics. Consider the difficulty of selecting the more than 33,000 people needed to fill over 1,000 different jobs that make the Magic Kingdom what it is. The Walt Disney Company has a reputation for creativity, innovative management, and unique and very effective approaches to selecting employees. One example of how HR management works at Disney is reflected in the approach to selecting new employees—or in Disney jargon, "casting for a role."

Everyone at Disney, managers and employees, uses the terminology of show business. This is evident in the language they use to describe themselves, their jobs, and the process of selecting new employees. In Disney jargon, a customer is a "guest," the uniform is a "costume," and when an employee is working, they are "on stage." New employees to Disney are "cast for a role," rather

than being "hired for a job." Applicants who are selected by Disney become a "cast member" in a show business production, rather than merely being "employees" doing a job. The HR person who interviews applicants is called a "casting director."

The selection (or "casting") process for jobs at Disney includes a number of effective HR management approaches. The casting director (or interviewer) typically spends 20–30 minutes with every applicant, even for an hourly job. During the interview, the casting director evaluates the applicant in terms of one's ability to fit into the Disney culture. This includes, for example, acceptance of grooming requirements (no facial hair for men, little makeup for women), a willingness to work on holidays (because the busiest dates are often holidays), and a courteous demeanor. After this initial "screening," the remaining applicants are then assessed in terms of interpersonal skills on how they interact with each other, and are rated on how well they would fit into the "show."

After people are hired, they become "cast members" whose inputs and talents are highly valued by The Walt Disney Company. Disney typically fills 60 to 80 percent of its managerial positions by promoting from within using its existing cast members. Every cast member attends an orientation and training program at "Disney University." Cast members first receive an overview of The Walt Disney Company and learn about the culture: its traditions, history, achievements, and philosophy. In addition, "cast members" learn about the key Disney "product"—a happy customer—and their roles in helping to create it. Next, each "cast member" learns about the benefits (health, social, recreational) of being part of the Disney "family," receives more information about their "role" in the production, and has a tour of the complex. The orientation has a goal of sharing the vision of Disney and developing a team, as well as communicating the core values of courtesy to "guests," safety of guests, and satisfying guests with an exciting "show."

QUESTIONS

1. Do you feel the cost of selection and training for this type of company pays off? Why?

2. Do you agree with using show business terminology?

SELECTION CRITERIA

As noted, The Walt Disney Company uses a set of characteristics to select its employees for effective performance. Before the selection process begins, a profile of characteristics required for successful performance should be developed for the job specification. There are several basic **selection criteria:**[7]

- **Technical Requirements**—These may include such criteria as education and work experience. Previous work experience is often a good predictor of future job performance. Any educational requirements should be documented as necessary to the successful performance of the job to avoid legal difficulties.

- **Interpersonal Requirements**—Depending on the position, this may include the requirement that an applicant be able to work in a team environment, speak before groups, or give and receive constructive feedback in a positive and appropriate manner. In some occupations, a leadership capability requirement may also be necessary for successful job performance and should be considered part of the selection criteria. (See cartoon.)

Source: CROCK by Bill Rechin and Don Wilder. © North America Syndicate, Inc.

- **Physical Requirements**—In certain occupations, specific physical characteristics may be a prerequisite for successful performance. Firefighting and working as a jockey both require physical attributes specific to that occupation. Business-based physical requirements can still be considered in the selection process, contrary to some generalizations about the Americans with Disabilities Act of 1990. Firms are obligated to make "appropriate reasonable accommodation" for disabled individuals in the applicant pool. But this does not imply that a professional football team must hire a quarterback who cannot throw.[8] Physical requirements may also include an absence of drugs or alcohol in the blood during a pre-employment examination.

Sometimes people participating in the interviewing process are unduly influenced by a candidate's personal appearance. It is something to be aware of, but it does occur. A recent article in *The Wall Street Journal* reports how we are impressed with a person's facial features. A group of researchers practice political psychology or biopolitics. They argue voters respond with primal instincts to the appearance and body language of political candidates. The process is similar to jungle animals who decide to flee, fight, or bond with unfamiliar animals.

The researchers have done some field studies with surprising results. When people had a quick glance at still photos and video clips, they knew the top vote-getters would include the eventual winner. According to the researchers, it is all based on the size of the lower jaw, the prominence of the cheekbones, and nonverbal behavior. Analysis of these characteristics in photographs of West Point cadets also successfully predicted which cadets would become generals.

While all of this seems a bit odd, one of the researchers has received a $140,000 grant from the National Institute of Mental Health for additional studies: our tax dollars at work. So if you are the interviewer, check your impressions; and if you are the interviewee, should you stick your chin out?[9]

THE SELECTION PROCESS

In many organizations, employee hiring is a continuous process. There are continuing vacancies due to retirement, turnover, and other normal attrition. Even an organization that is downsizing may well be hiring in specific areas. The selection process begins with the application blank and ends with a successful hiring decision. The purpose of the selection process is to differentiate among applicants to predict likely job performance. **Selection** may be defined as the process of choosing from a pool of applicants the individual or individuals who best fit the selection criteria for a given position. Changing employment legislation, changing lifestyles, emerging employee needs, and technological breakthroughs all act on the organization to cause a changing workforce. The degree of change may vary from one organization to another, but all face the need for adaptation to external forces.

Many of these changes involve increasing the costs of selection. It has been estimated that it costs approximately $50,000 to select a new professional-level employee or about 40 percent of an executives' annual salary in advertising, testing, and evaluating.[10] The smaller the organization, the less likely it is to follow the formal selection process, but almost all organizations follow a series of similar steps. (See Figure 5.1.)

The selection process must factor two important considerations into its procedural steps. The first consideration is to ensure there are no violations of EEO mandates as described in chapter 2. The other consideration is the use of job analysis and job evaluation as described in chapter 3 to develop accurate job descriptions and job specifications.

In the present tight labor market, some companies have introduced an informal step before the more formal recruiting process begins. The latest recruiting technique is known as the pal, handholder, or catcher. This is reserved for those scarce job candidates the company really wants to hire. It usually occurs after the candidates have successfully cleared their first round of interviews, but before any job offer or acceptance takes place.

Figure 5.1
The selection process

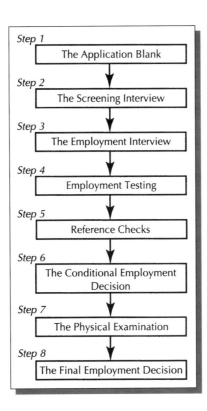

Step 1
> The Application Blank

Step 2
> The Screening Interview

Step 3
> The Employment Interview

Step 4
> Employment Testing

Step 5
> Reference Checks

Step 6
> The Conditional Employment Decision

Step 7
> The Physical Examination

Step 8
> The Final Employment Decision

The personal recruiter (pal, handholder, buddy, or catcher) is assigned a coveted promising candidate and then steers them through the company's recruiting process. They are usually from the candidate's alma mater and a young fast-track executive. They are employed by such companies as J. P. Morgan & Company, Chase Manhattan Corporation, Andersen Consulting, and Pricewaterhouse Coopers LLP.

The personal recruiter's shepherding includes visits, telephone calls, e-mail, and letter writing. The candidates are encouraged to ask any type of questions including dumb ones. They are assured anything that passes between them will not dim the candidate's chances of eventually joining the company.

At Duke University's Fuqua School of Business, 60 percent of the students find themselves paired with a potential employer's catcher while they consider the employment opportunities. That compares with fewer than 10 percent 5 years ago.[11]

Perhaps one of the most important factors underlying the selection process is the current global business environment which continues to change the world of work. The list of mergers and restructuring appears endless as companies struggle to cut costs. HRM is a key player in this drama as fewer employees are expected to produce more. A recent example is the French tire giant Michelin which is pursuing a new strategy to increase its productivity at least 20 percent. The result will be a loss of 7,500 jobs and the possible closing of some plants.[12]

Resumes continue to be an important tool in the selection process. Our high-tech business system continues to value resumes with techniques to scan them for key position words to increase their effectiveness. One issue of web-based recruiting is the increasing practice encouraged by some Internet security sources of resume sharing. This may be unfair to the job seeker who sends a resume to a company for a particular job and may not wish to be considered for jobs with companies that the initial company does business with. However, candidates who submit resumes to job fairs or an Internet resume bank want their resumes to be reviewed by as many companies as possible.[13]

The continuing problem with resumes is lying. A public relations firm reports applicants "stretch" their impact on past employment on a fairly regular basis. A recent survey by the Society for Human Resource Management reported that of 854 personnel offices, 53 percent reported job candidates sometimes falsify past salaries and criminal records.

The other side of this issue is omission. An executive assistant at the American Competitiveness Institute, Philadelphia, said she lied only "by omission" on her resume by not including computer and accounting experience. The reason: She did not want to use these skills on her present job.[14]

A final consideration of the selection process is to determine whether it meets the criteria of efficiency and effectiveness. These can be measured by determining various cost measures such as applicant interview cost and cost per accepted applicant. The effectiveness of the process is reflected in measures of absenteeism, turnover, retention, and promotion.

STEP 1. THE APPLICATION BLANK

The **application blank** provides an opportunity to gather certain basic selection data in a short time period. Several surveys suggest that all organizations, except the very smallest, have applicants complete an application form.[15]

The application blank is probably the best known form to most employees and is the most widely used. It can be verified for accuracy, it is easy to use, and it has face validity. Perhaps because of this general familiarity, its significance in human resource work is overlooked or taken for granted. The unfortunate result may be that the information collected is not fully utilized.

Evidence indicates that a properly validated application blank in the hands of a human resource specialist can increase the effectiveness of a company's selection process.[16] After all, the purpose of using the application blank in the first place is to assist in predicting the future success of the candidate.

The assumption underlying this technique is that performance in the future can be predicted by what was done in the past. Consequently, the application blank seeks information from applicants concerning their educational background, past employment history, work references, and personal data.

The application blank becomes a key link between recruiting and the final selection process for three reasons. First, it provides the usual recordkeeping information: date, name, social security number, home address, and telephone number, and who to contact in an emergency (name, address, phone number).

Second, it contains information to be used in evaluating the candidate: education, military experience, work history, and references.

Third, it contains the sign-off section, where the recruit agrees to certain conditions by signing their name and dating it. For blue collar jobs and possibly other positions, a common statement is: "In the event of termination, the employee will promptly return all company property."

Other affirmations include the truthfulness of statements, falsehoods which will lead to termination, and permission to contact references.[17] An important disclaimer that may be included (depending upon other laws) in this section concerns employment-at-will. That is, the company may terminate employment at any time, with or without good cause.

Further, the company may change human resource policies regarding pay, benefits, and employment unilaterally without the person's consent. Any oral statements causing a person to accept employment that are inconsistent with the employee handbook or company policy are to be considered invalid. Finally, the applicant, by signing the disclaimer, releases the company from any liability.

In most organizations, application blanks provide an initial screening process. Before making application forms too detailed, several factors should be considered. First, excessively long and complex forms may discourage potential applicants. Second, all items should be job-related. Finally, all questions must adhere to the guidelines set forth by equal employment opportunity laws. Basically, any application form question which could be construed as discriminating against a protected class must be demonstrably job-related, or it must be eliminated from the application blank.

The initial applicant screening usually takes place after potential candidates have completed an application form. In many cases, the determination of which candidates are screened in and out is accomplished without a systematic process.

The application blank can serve many purposes at once. The disclaimers such as the "employment at will" clause may help if it later becomes necessary to dismiss an employee. But the main purpose is to aid in the selection process. With this in mind, you can see why some application blanks are complex, such as the weighted application blank. Other application forms, however, are the utmost in simplicity. McDonald's restaurants, from time to time, print attractive application blanks on the place mats! The goal here is to get a pool of applicants quickly. What their application blank lacks in detail, it makes up in utility.

The Selection Process Requires Validation

To determine whether the selection processes used actually do work requires those selection techniques to be valid. The items or predictors used for such purposes as to hire and promote people must be shown to be accurate and job-related. Two general validation techniques used to help attain this information are criterion-related, which compares scores from the items used to make decisions, and content-based, which notes patterns between decision items.

Predictors and Criteria

The items used to make decisions may be contained in various tests, job interviews, or in role-playing-type assessments. These items are called predictors. The items for decision-making may be job performance, absenteeism, performance appraisals, or job tenure. These items are called criteria and are job-related. The predictors chosen to determine certain differences between persons must be consistent or reliable. The criteria chosen may represent a wide range of individual behavior such as teamwork, ability to learn quickly, maturity, or some specific job ability.

Validation: Predictive and Concurrent

Both techniques use job analysis to select the appropriate predictors and criteria. The predictive method uses samples of job applicants; however, concurrent uses samples of present employees. The predictive method hires applicants based on their predictor scores and then measures their criterion scores. The concurrent method scores present employees on their predictor items and measures their criterion scores at the same time.

The Weighted Application Blank (WAB)

One method of particular interest is the weighted application blank. The weighted application blank (WAB) has been around for decades, and ample research data indicates it works. Perhaps the simple nature of its design works against its general acceptance in a society of increasing high technology.

The WAB is a form designed to be scored as a systematic selection method. The purpose of the WAB is to relate characteristics to job performance.[18] Applicants are grouped into categories of high, middle, and low performers based on some performance criterion. Then the application blanks which the employees completed are retrieved, and the characteristics are compared to subsequent job performance. Those characteristics which show a positive relationship to job performance are given high weights; however, those items which demonstrate a low relationship to performance are given low weights.

The total score of each applicant is computed by summing the weights of the individual item scores. The resulting scores are then used in the selection decision. For example, education might be a good predictor for some jobs, but not for others. If the weights assigned are based on the job characteristics, then WABs have been found to be highly valid predictors of job success.[19]

In designing a WAB, the HR manager determines what specifically needs to be known. For instance, the WAB can be used to predict whether the responses of the applicant to items on the application blank are related to various criterion of job success. The more common usage of the WAB has been for predicting salary increases, creativity, absenteeism, job turnover, theft, and potential career success. It has been used in a wide variety of occupations, such as engineering and clerical work. All that is required is a specified time period, a specific job or personnel category, and the variable (turnover, absenteeism, etc.) to be investigated.

The Well-Designed Application Blank

A well-designed application blank will be legal. There will be nothing in it that violates federal or state antidiscrimination laws. The application blank needs to be as legally defensible as possible.

The application blank usually starts with instructions on how to complete the application and should include a statement that any applicant who provides unrequested information will automatically be rejected. Some applicants will include extraneous personal information so they can later claim their rejection was for unlawful reasons. An example would be a union organizer who lists this activity on the application even though it is not requested. If the union organizer is not hired, a claim can be filed that it was due to a union background.

It also would be wise to include how disabled applicants can request accommodations to help them complete the application. This helps the organization comply with the Americans with Disabilities Act (ADA) to provide reasonable accommodations during employment as well as each stage of the selection process.

Also, it is helpful to include an equal opportunity statement in the instructions section. This indicates to all applicants the company follows the principles of equal employment opportunity. Upon signing the application, applicants acknowledge this policy.

In the section of the application blank where information is asked of the person, any questions must be related to one's potential to perform the job. Only relevant, job-related questions should be asked.

Because the Equal Employment Opportunity Commission (EEOC) regards the application blank as a "test," it cannot have an adverse impact on protected applicants.

The application blank should not ask questions of race, religion, gender, age, national origin, citizenship, arrest records, financial status, military record, disability, or union affiliation.

The final section of the application blank usually asks the applicant to certify the accuracy of the provided information. A statement should specify that misstatements or omissions on the application blank could result in a refusal to hire. If discovered after hiring, it could be a reason for discharge.

In states which recognize the employee-at-will doctrine, the application blank could include disclaimers that employment does not result in an employment contract for any specific time period.

The preceding points will make a good legal application blank which should avoid employee lawsuits and EEOC problems. However, always double check with your company's attorney to cover all issues, including differences in state laws.[20]

STEP 2. THE SCREENING INTERVIEW

The screening interview is usually done after the applicant fills out the application. The interview is used to determine key information regarding job requirements and to get a general impression of the applicant.

When the screening interview process is complete, the result should be a satisfactory pool of candidates. Then the selection interview takes over. Although many in the company may participate in the interview process, it is still the responsibility of the HR manager to optimize the selection. Perhaps because so many untrained individuals participate in interviewing, several studies criticize the validity of the interview as an appropriate selection technique.[21]

The National Institute for Occupational Safety and Health has reported one-quarter of the American working population feels their job represents a highly stressful force in their lives. The screening interview could be the first attempt to discover how applicants are handling stress in their present environment. This early approach in the interviewing process would be very appropriate for jobs with high demand and little control over working conditions. This type of job presents the greatest health risk to employees.[22]

A historic study by W. D. Scott considered the reliability of interviewer's decisions.[23] Scott found that the interviewers for sales positions could not agree whether the candidates should be placed in the top or bottom ranking! This amazing result has unfortunately been replicated in other studies. Such critical studies have continued with Mayfield reviewing 20 years of interviewing,[24] and Arvey and Campion also finding wide variation among interviewers.[25]

However, despite criticism of the interview, its widespread use indicates the importance it is accorded in selection. This is due in part to the fact that in an interview, applicants can be asked questions about application blank information and test scores. Also, the interview permits going beyond the collected data to probe deeper in areas the company is interested in. This might include probing into the applicant's interpersonal skills, central life interests, and value system as they relate to the job. Will the applicant fit in well with the work team? An application blank will probably not help answer this key question. The screening interview effectively fills the gaps that are bound to occur within the time limits for obtaining accurate data. Of course, the more subjective the screening interview gets, the more exposure to liability for claims of discrimination.

STEP 3. THE EMPLOYMENT INTERVIEW

The **employment interview** is the most widely used selection technique.[26] Organizations incur tremendous annual expenses in interviewing applicants to fill even the lowest-level positions. Despite the costs and research suggesting that the selection interview is not as consistent or reliable as other techniques, it nevertheless plays a very important role in the selection process. Several studies suggest that it is one of the most important steps in selection.[27]

Depending upon the importance of the job, an applicant may be interviewed by one person or by several members of the organization. Although there is some doubt about the validity of the interview as a selection method, other researchers suggest several key features of the interview: (1) It is a fast and direct way to differentiate among a small number of applicants; (2) It serves several purposes—information gathering, public relations tool, and so forth; and (3) Skilled interviewers often provide reliable judgments. Some research has focused on the differences among interviewers rather than on the interview method. It is suggested that some interviewer evaluations may be more valid than others in the assessment of an applicant.[28]

The interview is often used to make assessments regarding the degree of fit between applicants and jobs. The interview is used to evaluate applicants and to predict which applicants are more likely to be successful in the organization.

With today's competitive world of work it is important that the most suitable job candidate is selected the first time around. An employee retention and development strategist in Chicago suggests the job candidate who seems perfectly suited for the position may not be.

Many jobs are continually changing and some just become obsolete. Perhaps employers should look for people who are comfortable adapting to change in their professional and personal lives. If this is correct, the qualities that should be looked for include

- A well-developed self-awareness, resulting from varied and emotionally demanding life experiences.
- A present need to be productive with a drive to do things differently.
- A different educational path, such as postponing one's education to work or raise a family.
- A short learning curve and a tendency toward boredom.

When interviewing such a job candidate, it should be challenging and confrontational, not comfortable and cozy. Values should match those of the organization. The interviewee may have responses that are not politically correct or not typically expected. This means the candidate is answering the questions honestly at the risk of not getting the job.[29]

Interviewing requires an awareness of developing trends affecting people. Years of prosperity appear to have bred a culture of risk takers. Various barometers of cockiness suggest a looser attitude toward career moves. A measure of those who voluntarily left their last jobs is called the quit rate. It is at the highest level since the boom of the late 1980s: 14.5 percent.

The glamour of job-hopping is at a record pace. The revenue of executive-search firms has doubled the level of 1993. The "let's go for it" attitude is apparent on the college campus. At the Harvard Business School, 30 percent of their recent graduates will join high-tech or venture capital outfits. This is up 12 percent from 1995.[30]

During the interview, the interviewer has certain "hard" data available to assist in the final decision to accept or reject. Such data may include the application blank, references, resume, psychological test scores of intelligence and personality, and perhaps background checks. While the mix of these data will vary, the one constant is that an interviewer or a group of interviewers will make the *initial* decision to accept or reject the candidate. Despite all attempts for objectivity, subjectivity will be present in varying degrees, contributing in large measure to the selection of effective performers.

One author refers to interviewing as a high-stakes game with hiring employees similar to going to Las Vegas. A professional job hire who is paid $48,000 per year but then leaves in a short period of time can cost the company more than $100,000 in advertising, travel, interview time, training, and other costs.

Few people fail in their new jobs because they cannot do them technically. It is the soft skills that do them in, yet these are the hard ones to determine. The best way to determine soft skills such as personality, motivation, and creativity is through face-to-face interviews.

Yet the interview is not perfect with corporate turnover averaging 16 percent (some high-tech companies are much higher). A study by Harvard University reports nearly 80 percent of turnover results from hiring mistakes.[31]

One must always bear in mind the implications of EEO laws during the interview process to avoid any discriminatory bias.[32] Also, the personal biases of the interviewer needs to be considered to eliminate as much as possible biased input in the decision-making process.

Various **interviewing methods** have been devised to eliminate a large measure of this subjective error. For instance, in the structured or patterned interview, interviewers ask a predetermined list of questions of all the applicants in the same order. This ensures that all important questions are asked and that the information base for each application is similar. A "true" structured interview would apply not only to the questions but to the answers as well. The answers would be structured similar to a multiple choice test. Under these conditions, there would be little or no interviewer bias. The more generally used structured interview applies only to the required questions with the applicant replies reflecting the attitudes and personality of the individual. Although this format also suffers from a lack of flexibility, it does improve the validity of interviewer judgments. (See Our Changing World.)

OUR CHANGING WORLD
THE JOB INTERVIEW—ASIAN STYLE: TAKE CHARGE![33]

An American executive had just returned from another frustrating trip abroad. This time she had been in Tokyo, trying to select the right person to head up the new office there. The office would oversee a joint venture, and the person in charge had to be able to do just that, "take charge!" Yet, no one on the finalist list seemed to have that "take charge" orientation, it seemed to her. Nobody seemed to be willing to even speak up in the interview.

The applicants looked great on paper, but they were almost shy in person. The language did not seem to be the problem either, because all of the applicants spoke English (so well that it was embarrassing to a typical, monolingual American). What, then, was the problem? Why didn't the Japanese speak up more? Why were the Japanese so reticent to speak, when surely they had much to say?

Although there is no single answer, a number of hints may help. For one thing, a non-U.S. observer to the whole situation thought this was asking the wrong question. To the neutral observer, the question was, "Why don't Americans shut up and listen once in a while?" Typically, American up-and-coming human resource executives pride themselves in aggressiveness and openness. More communication is naturally assumed to be better.

The Japanese, on the other hand, seem to realize that much can be learned by listening. This fits in with Japanese culture, where the most successful executive is more likely the one who listens best rather than the one who talks most.

With this in mind, who would blame the Japanese interviewees for appearing a bit on the quiet side to an American HRM specialist? It may be that there is another tool to be added to the HR manager's tool kit in addition to active listening. Maybe there is a role for passive listening too, especially when doing business anywhere outside the United States.

QUESTIONS

1. How would you resolve the "take charge" problem? In your answer, consider more than culture.

2. Would you agree the process of interviewing requires more listening than talking? Support either position.

Interviewing Methods

There are a number of types of interviews. The employment interview varies according to the method used to obtain information and the interviewer's approach to determine the applicant's attitudes.[34] The main difference arises from the amount of structure used by the interviewer. In the **structured employment interview,** the interviewer prepares a set of questions in advance and directs the course of the interview. In the unstructured interview, the applicant plays a larger role in determining the direction of the interview flow.

The Unstructured Interview

In **the unstructured interview,** the candidate controls the flow and topics discussed and the interviewer refrains from directing the applicant's remarks. The interviewer merely nods assent or repeats statements made by the applicant so as to encourage further discussion. The unstructured interview is highly subject to the interviewer's interpretations, which means it could be very biased. Because each interview is unique, it becomes difficult to evaluate the applicants as there is no common database from which to make decisions.

In this interview, the applicant is provided freedom in controlling the course of the discussion. The interviewer uses broad, open-ended questions, such as "Tell me more about your last job," then allows the applicant to talk freely without interruption. The focus of the unstructured interview is on bringing out any information, attitudes, or feelings that may be concealed by a more structured interview. However, because the applicant controls the direction of the interview and no set questions are used, the information from these interviews is difficult to compare with other interviews. Consequently, the reliability and validity of the unstructured interview may be minimal. This method is most likely to be used in interviewing candidates for higher-level positions and by highly skilled interviewers.

The Structured Interview

In **the structured interview,** the interviewer sticks closely to a prepared set of specific questions on forms. The questions are asked during the interview, and the answers are usually recorded later on a summary form. Because it is easier to train an interviewer to conduct the structured interview and the use of a standardized format, this method has relatively valid results.[35]

Advantages of the Structured Interview   The structured interview is used more frequently as a result of EEO requirements. There are a number of advantages to this interview, including the following:[36]

- The interview is based on job duties and requirements critical to job performance.
- The answers to each question may be determined and can be rated on a point scale defined in advance.
- Questions are consistent to ensure that each applicant has a fair chance.
- This provides documentation for future reference and in case of legal challenge.[37]

The structured interview is more likely to provide the basic information needed for making sound decisions. It also tends to reduce the possibility of charges of discrimination.

Computer-Assisted Interviewing

Technology is changing the way companies recruit and select personnel. Although still a relatively new technology, recruiters believe they will be able to reduce the hiring cycle by 90 percent. The technology will also anticipate in advance what skills will be in demand and respond by bringing up potential applicants on the computer screen.

A major clothing manufacturer, using computer-assisted interviewing to conduct the first round of interviews, saved $2.4 million during a 3-year period. Turnover was reduced from 87 to 51 percent. One of the Big Six accounting and consulting firms is using computer-assisted interviewing to find the "right" new college hires. The company recently used an Aspen Tree product to process 20,000 applications.[38]

Nike is another example of computer-assisted interviewing. The firm has used Apen Tree to hire trainees for Niketown, their retail stores selling Nike products. In response to ads to fill 250 positions, 6,000 people applied.

The applicants responded to eight questions over the telephone. Of the original 6,000, 3,500 applicants did not survive the first cut because they were not available when needed and/or did not have retail experience. Those remaining then had a group computer-assisted interview at a Niketown retail store. This was then followed by a personal interview. Nike's policy was to give everyone an interview who came to one of their stores, the rationale being "Applicants are customers as well as potential hires."

Experts agree the computer should not make the final decision to hire. What the computer does is help the interviewer to ask the right questions to gain additional information or check concerns flagged by the computer.[39]

In Great Britain, the electronic revolution in recruiting has so far failed to reach a majority of businesses. It is largely restricted to the computer and telecommunication industries. Most other industrial sectors and professions are far behind in computer-assisted recruiting.

The public section is notable by its absence. In middle Britain, the metal-related industries are still recruiting as they did 10 years ago. The British Data Protection Act presents more of a barrier than any lack of technology. The act prevents companies from the use of any software that screens candidates for qualifications because it may be used to discriminate against certain groups. However, the Yahoo! search engine is being used by applicants as well as the web site called Internet Cases.[40]

Other Interviewing Approaches

Most HR interviewers tend to use the approaches described earlier, or a hybrid of these approaches. Some interviewers prefer an interview devoted about half to carefully structured questions, leaving the remaining time for unstructured discussion. However, there are other types of interviews that may be used in certain situations. In order to overcome the restrictions of the structured interview and the complete lack of restrictions in the unstructured interview, other formats are used.

The Panel Interview   A panel or group of individuals may interview the applicant following either of the formats.[41] The results are subjected to the same advantages and disadvantages, with the exception that there are more interviewer opinions to evaluate and consolidate. Usually, the group tends to reduce more extreme positions and moves toward consensus. The use of **the panel interview** reduces single interviewer bias. Many team-based companies use panel interviews to select new members and to select team leaders.

The Situation Interview   The problem or situation interview is used where applicants "solve" a particular problem, or describe how they would behave on a job situation. Sometimes groups of applicants are interviewed at the same time to detect personality and attitude responses. For example, at GM prospective employees may be asked to describe a team project they have participated in.

The Stress Interview   Perhaps the most controversial is **the stress interview,** where the recruit is subjected to the stresses and strains supposedly encountered in the job situation. Although the intent is plausible, the result may be an applicant who turns down a job offer because the company environment appears hostile and nonsupportive. This type of interview, which focuses on interpersonal relationships, is often used in examining applicants where interpersonal skills are a primary job requirement.

So, different interview techniques offer differing advantages and disadvantages. However, central to all interview techniques are the errors that result from the inconsistency of interviewer judgments, inappropriate applicant responses to misunderstood questions, the accuracy of the interview information, and the accuracy of interviewer judgments.

The Just Relax Interview   A *Fortune* 500 company advertised a position for a van driver capable of doing light deliveries. The interviewer was surprised when one of the applicants arrived for the interview in a wheelchair.

During the interview, the interviewer excused herself and left the room to call the Disabled Businesspersons Association (DBA) of San Diego for advice on how to proceed.

The president of DBA points out the biggest battle recruiters face is with themselves, because they are uncomfortable in their relationship with the person who has the disability. Experts say the first thing to do is "just relax."

The reason interviewers need to relax is because they are nervous and unsure how they should act as well as what questions they can ask. Interviewers realize there are legal issues involved and there are certain rules of conduct which they probably are unaware of. Most people with disabilities realize the interviewer's position and will do what they can to make the interviewer more comfortable.

Interviewing people with disabilities is becoming more common. HR professionals report 82 percent more people with disabilities are returning to work, compared to 5 years ago. This means there will be more interviews with applicants who are in wheelchairs, or who are blind, deaf, or stutter.

The rules for interviewer behavior are complex and require assistance from local groups such as the DBA or EEO office. The HR professional will always treat all candidates with courtesy and respect. A visually impaired person is not a blind person, but a person who is blind. A person is not "bound" to a wheelchair, instead, the person "uses a wheelchair." That's a start, but there is much more.[42]

The Assessment Center

The **assessment center** is a technique which provides standardized evaluation of behavior on multiple inputs. Several trained observers and techniques are used. Observer judgments about applicant behaviors are made from specially developed assessment simulations. Participants are typically tested by using performance tests or work samples which simulate the work environment.

Pioneered in the 1960s by Douglas Bray at AT&T, assessment centers have expanded in use from just over 100 organizations to 2,000 organizations in the last decade.[43] Corporations, universities, and specialized consulting organizations establish these assessment centers where individuals are evaluated as they participate in a series of job-like real-life situations. The "assessment center" is not really a "center," but rather a *process*. The center uses in-basket exercises, role playing, group problem-solving, and other approaches to employee development.

These exercises are designed to simulate the type of work which the candidate will be expected to do. Performance in the situational exercises is observed and evaluated by a team of trained assessors. The assessors' judgments on each exercise are compiled and integrated to form a summary rating for each candidate being assessed. Assessment center activities provide examples of behavior that represent what is required for the position. At the end of the day's activities, assessors' evaluations are integrated to develop an overall picture of the strengths and weaknesses of the participants. A report is normally submitted to top management or to the HR manager, and feedback is then provided to all participants.

There is increasing study of the validity of assessment centers as a selection technique. Like other employment tests, the assessment outcomes must be validated. The exercises used in the center should be designed to reflect the job characteristics being evaluated. One study found a strong relationship between assessment center results and future performance on the job.[44]

Assessment centers have been used in identifying managerial talent and in helping with the development of individuals, but the method tends to favor those employees who are strong in interpersonal skills. The manner in which assessment center personnel conduct the exercises and provide feedback to the participants will play a major role in determining how individuals react to the experience.

STEP 4. EMPLOYMENT TESTING

Another step in the selection process is the employment test. An **employment test** is a method that attempts to measure certain characteristics of job applicants. These tests include aptitude tests, personality tests, achievement tests, job sample tests, graphology, and polygraph or honesty tests.

Personality Tests

Personality tests are based on the concept that certain people do better in certain jobs than other people, and personality characteristics are important in determining the correct match. In the 1960s and 1970s, personality tests were very popular in the selection process. With the advent of equal employment opportunity legislation, personality testing fell out of favor. In the 1990s, with its emphasis on worker participation and team development, personality testing is reemerging as a popular selection tool. This has resulted in part from new evidence of the validity of personality testing and the development of personality tests that do not cause adverse impact.[45]

The Polygraph or Honesty Test

The **polygraph** (sometimes called a lie detector) is an instrument that records changes in breathing, blood pressure, and pulse, of the person being questioned. It involves sensors that record the physiological changes in the applicant as the examiner asks questions that call for an answer of "yes" or "no." One pharmaceutical manufacturer reported some years ago that about one-quarter of its applicants who undergo polygraph tests are screened out. It has been estimated that at one point in time, nearly two million polygraph tests were being administered each year by employers in the United States.[46] However, polygraphs were never 100 percent accurate. Without a doubt, some dishonest applicants "passed" the polygraph tests. Equally troubling, some honest applicants were screened out because of questionable results from polygraph screening.

The growing concerns over the use of polygraphs in employment situations led to the passage of the Federal Employee Polygraph Protection Act of 1988. The act prohibits most private employers from using a polygraph as a selection device. Yet, in those situations involving cash or in the manufacture of controlled substances, the use of polygraph tests is sometimes permitted.[47]

Because of this law, organizations are using alternative tests such as paper and pencil tests of honesty and background checks of applicants.[48] The new federal law has stimulated use of honesty tests. These are often used by retail stores where employees have access to cash or merchandise. These tests ask questions regarding beliefs about frequency of theft in our society, punishment for theft, and perceived ease of theft. Some research studies suggest the weighted application blank is an appropriate instrument to determine honesty.[49]

Meanwhile, managers need to carefully use the results from such tests, but it seems likely that honesty tests will be of increased use in the future. Failure of the test should not result in immediate rejection or dismissal, but should serve as a red flag for further review.

Graphology/Handwriting Analysis

Graphology is a term that refers to **handwriting analysis,** and is being used in some organizations to make selection decisions. Graphologists are provided a sample of the applicant's handwriting, and then examine characteristics including the size and slant of letters, and so on, which they use to make inferences about the applicant's personality traits.[50] Although this sounds a bit like consulting a horoscope or fortune-teller to make employment decisions, some organizations swear that graphology input can help the HR manager make better selection decisions. On the negative side, research has found low reliability and little predictive power.[51]

Drug Testing

The use of drug tests to screen applicants and current employees for drug use is a controversial issue. Much of the controversy over **drug testing** arises from the technology and standards by which tests are conducted.[52]

When a company joins the war against drugs, it must make sure there is an understanding of the legal issues involved. This is extremely important if the decision to hire and fire is based on drug tests. A wrong move and the company is in court defending itself against negligence, violation of privacy, defamation, violating the Americans with Disabilities Act (ADA), or Title VII of the Civil Rights Act.

The issue of the right of employers to conduct drug tests has been approved by the courts. The ADA requires medical exams to be performed after the applicant has received a conditional offer of employment but excludes drug tests. Because recent litigation has focused not on whether an employer can test for drugs, but rather on how the test is done, caution is suggested.

After the conditional employment offer is made, the drug test should be administered immediately. This way, the applicant doesn't have ample time to eliminate the drugs from one's system.[53]

Among the firms that report using drug tests include Federal Express, General Electric, Kaiser Aluminum, Southern Pacific Railroad, and American Airlines. Employees who test positive are referred for treatment and counseling or may receive some form of disciplinary action.

The importance of drug testing should not be overlooked. A recent government report indicates that 70 percent of drug users hold full-time jobs. According to the report, this information should dispel the misconception that most Americans who use illegal drugs are poor and unemployed.[54]

The Drug-Free Workplace Act (1988) requires that all applicants and employees of federal contractors, Department of Defense contractors, and those under Department of Transportation regulations be subject to testing for illegal drug use. The usual procedure is to check references before hiring. If time is of the essence, then a partial check should be made with continuing employment contingent upon a more thorough check. Usually this should be completed within a "reasonable" amount of time.

Beyond those covered by the Drug-Free Workplace Act of 1988, drug testing as part of the selection process varies from state to state. For example, as of the mid-1990s, California courts seemed to be upholding the right of employers to test individuals selected for hiring. Testing of existing employees is a more complex issue, discussed later in chapter 14.

STEP 5. REFERENCE CHECKS

One of the final steps in the selection process is to check references. Generally, telephone checks are preferable because they save time and provide for greater candor. Usually the most reliable information comes from immediate supervisors who are able to report on an applicant's prior work attitudes and performance.

When contacting former employers, there may be a reluctance to disclose unfavorable information even when the applicant has signed permission to contact previous employers. The issue centers around invasion of privacy and legal interpretations of equal opportunity laws. A question the prospective employer needs to consider: Is the previous work experience comparable to the job being applied for? This will determine the type of questions asked and the amount of time allocated for questions.

The preferred method would be a telephone call, because unfavorable information may be more apt to be disclosed verbally rather than in a written format. Telephone calls should follow a standard procedure to increase objectivity and provide documentation of contact.

A potential source of background information that may be overlooked are part-time or temporary jobs. One should not contact a present employer before the applicant resigns, unless there is written permission to do so. Otherwise, if dismissal results, the job applicant may take legal action.

Other reference sources that may be examined include school and college records, military records, and special reference services such as credit agencies. However, if a negative decision is made based in whole or part on a credit report, the Fair Credit Reporting Act requires notification to the applicant of the name and address of the agency. In addition, in certain localities, use of credit reports in employment decisions is seen as violating the law. Before asking for a credit report or a driving record from the State Motor Vehicle Department, be sure there is an essential job-related purpose for this information.

The verification of applicant information is extremely important, because the information on the application blank (either by accident or design) may be false or misleading. Studies have found substantial differences between the responses on application blanks and information verified by previous employers. One study found that 15 percent of the sample applicants had never worked for the employer they listed. Also, application blank discrepancies were largest for duration of service and salary earned.

The problem of application misinformation is not limited to lower-level jobs. One survey of 223 companies found that one-third of the companies responded saying candidates for executive positions have increased the use of deceptive tactics to obtain employment. These companies suggest the best way to find applicant misinformation is through reference checking, although 82 percent of the survey companies indicated it has become more difficult to do so.[55]

Considering the unreliable nature of references, and the cost of determining accurate facts through phone calls or visits with references, the question is posed: Why make the effort? The reason the HR manager continues to use references to determine applicant qualifications is that it is one of the few sources of information available with data on the level of proficiency and behavior. However, the company's motivation in attempting to learn more about the applicant is to avoid the potential situation where the company negligently hires a person addicted to drugs, violence, and so forth who later harms an employee, customers, or the public.

The fact of life in today's legalistic society is that companies have been successfully sued (often for large amounts) when they failed to check the references of job applicants who, when hired, committed crimes or injuries to other employees. As imperfect as reference checking is, it is still the most prudent course to follow.

Resumes are sometimes required in lieu of the application blank, although eventually the application blank must be completed because of the protection offered the company through the disclaimers mentioned earlier. However, resumes must be approached with caution because they may contain exaggerations or misrepresentations. One survey of 501 executives found that 26 percent of the executives uncovered inaccurate information regarding job qualifications, education, and salary history. However, in another survey of 100 personnel directors at our largest companies, 91 percent stated that resumes continue to be instrumental in the hiring process.[56]

Since the enactment of the Family Educational Rights Privacy Act of 1974 (FERPA), which gives applicants the right to inspect personnel files, employers have been reluctant to provide anything other than general and often meaningless positive statements about past performance.[57] However, checking of references is still a highly advisable step in the selection process.

STEP 6. THE CONDITIONAL EMPLOYMENT DECISION

At this time, a preliminary decision to hire is made. However, final approval still is dependent upon the results of the physical examination.

STEP 7. THE PHYSICAL EXAMINATION

The physical examination is usually one of the last steps in the selection process because of costs. The use of preemployment medical examinations varies among industries, but it is estimated that about one-half of the companies surveyed by the Bureau of National Affairs used preemployment physical examinations to test prospective employees.[58]

A physical examination is generally used to ascertain that the applicant's physical condition is sufficient to fulfill job requirements. Professional football players (in the NFL, for example) are given intensive physical exams prior to hiring because physical performance is a critical part of the job.

In the past, some qualified job applicants were eliminated from employment consideration because of some physical exam result unrelated to the task to be performed. In the United States, this practice eliminated so many otherwise qualified workers that Congress passed the Americans with Disabilities Act of 1990. Employers can still require exams after a job offer has been made, but must be ready to accommodate applicants who could be helped to do the job.

STEP 8. THE FINAL EMPLOYMENT DECISION

The final step in the selection process is the decision to accept or reject the applicant based on the results of the physical examination. This is an important step because of the costs of recruiting and selecting, legal considerations, the relatively short probationary time in most organizations, and turnover of many new employees.

SUMMARY

This chapter has focused on several major selection issues. One is that organizations operate in a dynamic and changing environment and consequently must be selective in choosing new employees. You have been introduced to the selection process and the ways it is used to improve organizational effectiveness.

In order to match the individual's skills, knowledge, and abilities to organization needs, the HR manager must gather systematic information about job applicants. You, as a human resource manager, must be sensitive to changes in markets, people, and competition and be aware of the need for a continuing source of adaptive and flexible employees for the organization.

You will have an opportunity to experience the selection process and to develop skills in this class meeting. The selection process involves an assessment of an individual's predicted performance. The steps in the process are typical of most organizations.

In a changing environment, managing human resources effectively involves selecting and developing a high-performing workforce. In today's global world, learning how to select a multicultural workforce is an emerging challenge.

REVIEW QUESTIONS

1. How would you define "the selection process"?
2. Present examples of how selection techniques were used in organizations you have worked for.
3. Identify and demonstrate the use of the employment interview.
4. Contrast the difference between the various types of testing.
5. Discuss and explain the basic reference checks and how they are used.
6. Explain three basic issues in using a drug testing program.
7. Read a book or view a video movie, and identify an example of an organization selection process.

KEY WORDS AND CONCEPTS

Define and be able to use the following:

- Application Blank
- Assessment Center
- Drug Testing
- Employment Test
- Graphology/Handwriting Analysis
- Interpersonal Requirements
- Interviewing Methods

- Personality Tests
- Physical Requirements
- Polygraph
- Selection
- Selection Criteria
- Selection Process
- Structured Employment Interview
- Technical Requirements

- The Employment Interview
- The Honesty Test
- The Panel Interview
- The Physical Examination
- The Polygraph Test
- The Stress Interview
- The Structured Interview
- The Unstructured Interview

HRM SKILLS SIMULATION 5.1: EVALUATION OF JOB APPLICANTS

A. PURPOSE

The purpose of this simulation is to reach consensus within an organizational group setting.

B. PROCEDURES

Step 1. Form into groups of five. As a group, decide who is to play each role.

1. Corporate president
2. Vice president, personnel
3. Vice president, manufacturing
4. Vice president, marketing
5. Vice president, finance

Step 2. Before class, read the setting information, and then your role description (read your role only). Complete the individual portion of the form provided.

Step 3. In class, form into your groups again. Complete the entire form including committee column. Consensus must be reached on evaluation of each application by your committee.

ROLE DESCRIPTIONS (READ *ONLY* YOUR ROLE)

Role 1—Corporate president: You are responsible for overall decisions. You must answer to the board of directors (shareholders).

Role 2—Vice president, personnel: Recruitment and training are your major concerns.

Role 3—Vice president, manufacturing: Supply and productivity are your major concerns.

Role 4—Vice president, marketing: Advertising, sales, and consumers are your major concerns.

Role 5—Vice president, finance: Purchasing, corporate funding and contracts are your major concerns.

BACKGROUND

Your multinational corporation is interviewing prospective employees. The company will hire four new employees. Each department is in need of new staff members. The following resumes will give the information on each candidate. You must rank each candidate 1–8.

1 = First choice for employment
8 = Last choice for employment

Keep in mind that age, sex, and national origin cannot be factors in the employment decision. Use this exercise as a tool to help you see how easily discriminatory comments may come up in a discussion about selection.

CANDIDATES

Bill Smith

Bill majored in business administration with concentration in small business. He graduated 2 years ago.

Educational Record:	Cumulative G.P.A.: 2.3
	Rank in class: 340/551
Work Experience:	First Lieutenant (U.S. Army), summer work as construction laborer, salesperson; part-time employment as laborer, research assistant, sandwich sales business operator
Recommendations:	None provided
Personal Data:	Age: 23
	Married

Fred Jones

Fred will receive a B.S. degree in accounting this June.

Educational Record:	Cumulative G.P.A.: 2.2
	Rank in class: not available
Work Experience:	Summer employment at textile plant and as a junior auditor

Recommendations:	Two excellent; one average
Personal Data:	Age: 24
	Single

John Green

John will receive a B.A. degree in psychology with a minor in human resource management.

Educational Record:	Cumulative G.P.A.: 2.7
	Rank in class: not available
Work Experience:	Summer work on a farm, in a hospital, and as a student laborer
Recommendations:	One good; one average
Personal Data:	Age: 22
	Single

Chad Long

Chad graduated with a B.A. degree in political science with a minor in environmental science 2 years ago.

Educational Record:	Cumulative G.P.A.: 3.1
	Rank in class: 31/437
Work Experience:	Full-time work as an insurance salesperson; part-time employment as a salesclerk, restaurant worker, and legislative assistant for the General Assembly of California
Recommendations:	Two good
Personal Data:	Age: 25
	Single

Robert Anlt

Robert will receive a B.A. degree this year in liberal studies.

Educational Record:	Cumulative G.P.A.: 2.7
	Rank in class: not available
Work Experience:	Summer employment for a construction firm and management intern for a large corporation
Recommendations:	Two good
Personal Data:	Age: 22
	Single

Anthony Bono

Anthony majored in business administration and received a B.A. degree 1 year ago.

Educational Record:	Cumulative G.P.A.: 3.3
	Rank in class: 11/244
Work Experience:	Accountant (full-time); management intern (summer)
Personal Data:	Age: 22
	Married

Mary Post

Mary majored in electrical engineering and received a B.S.E.E. 1 year ago. She is presently in the army.

Educational Record:	Cumulative G.P.A. 2.3
	Rank in class: 1542/2117
Work Experience:	Second Lieutenant (U.S. Army); store worker (summer)
Recommendations:	One excellent; one good
Personal Data:	Age: 22
	Single

Sue Wing-Wa

Sue, a graduate of Cheng-Kung University, Republic of China, with a major in mathematics, received a B.A. degree 2 years ago.

Educational Record:	Cumulative G.P.A.: B (approximate)
	Rank in class: not available
Work Experience:	Assistant to professors (part-time)
Recommendations:	Two good
Personal Data:	Age: 22
	Single

EMPLOYMENT EVALUATION

Applicant	Corporate President	VP Human Resources	VP Manufacturing	VP Marketing	VP Finance	Observer
Bill Smith						
Fred Jones						
John Green						
Chad Long						
Robert Anlt						
Anthony Bono						
Mary Post						
Sue Wing-Wa						

Scale: 1–8
1 = Employ
8 = Last choice for employment

Case 5.1   Precision Products, Inc.

Helen had spent over 100 hours of the last month pouring over resumes, conducting first interviews, background checks, and conducting second interviews. By now, she had whittled down a list of 50 possibilities to an "A" list of four qualified people. As she stood at the end of the conference table in the president's office suite, she knew she was ready.

The serious faces of the president and the four vice presidents gazed at her as she distributed folders to each of the men.

"Gentlemen," Helen began, "here are the four most qualified applicants we have. I have personally interviewed each one of them at least twice, and each of them meets or exceeds the standards for the product manager position. If you'll open your folders, I can answer questions about the applicants."

"John Eagle!" Howard Peterson exclaimed, looking at the man's folder. "Is this guy an Indian?"

"Yes, sir. A Navajo Indian. He started a business on the reservation after finishing his master's at Stanford. He recently sold the business to the tribe. At the time of the sale, it was grossing $300,000 a year and employed 43 Navajo Indians. He speaks English, Spanish, and Navajo."

Howard mumbled something under his breath and flipped to the next applicant.

"Douglas Ironwood is next," Helen went on. "He holds a B.S. in business from California State Bakersfield, graduating 1 year ago. He's worked in his father's oil tool shop since he was a kid and wants to move on."

"Hey, Howard, look at this!" Carl Preston exclaimed. "It says here he was club champion at Blue Oak Country Club. A guy like this could do a lot for our golf team. Did you check this out, Helen?"

"Yes, it's true," Helen said. "The man can play golf."

"We might come back to him," Howard said. "Who's next, Helen?"

There was silence as the men looked at the list of Marcus Wright's activities in a local black college.

"Marcus is a disabled vet from the Vietnam conflict. He lost his arm in combat leading his platoon out of an ambush. He received the silver and bronze stars for saving his men. Using the GI Bill, he received his master's from George Washington University 5 years ago. He has been a supervisor for one of our rivals since then, but he is willing to come to us on a managerial level."

"I don't know, Helen," Howard said. "With all due respect for his record, a black man would have a lot of resistance to overcome trying to expand our sales through the new location. What else have you got?"

"Johnette Vasquez," Helen went on, "received her master's in business administration from USC 3 years ago. Since then, she has worked for IBM as a sales manager and district sales manager. She likes the idea of starting up our new location from scratch. She knows we wouldn't be able to match her current salary."

"How much does she make now?" Howard asked.

"Her paycheck stub shows she is making about $80,000 a year," Helen answered.

"You know, Howard, this one would be a double for us," Carl Preston said.

"You mean female and Hispanic? Yes, she would. That could deflect heat from the EEOC alright," Howard mused.

Howard said, "Schedule each one of these to have lunch with us next week. By the way, good work, Helen. You've done your bit for diversity." ■

QUESTIONS

1. Among the applicants represented, which would be your first choice for the job? Why?
2. Which applicant would be your last choice? Why?
3. Sexual harassment includes a hostile environment, according to the courts. What is your evaluation of the environment at Precision Products?

ENDNOTES

1. Stephanie Overman, "Leader Helps Improve Competitiveness," *HR Magazine* (May 1990): 60.
2. "New Employment Standards Needed as Meaning of Diploma Changes," *Personnel Journal* 71, no. 9 (September 1992): Supplement, 1–2.
3. Charles G. Tharp, "A Manager's Guide to Selection Interviewing," *Personnel Journal* 62, no. 8 (August 1983): 636–39; and A. Fleishman, "Some New Frontiers in Personnel Selection Research," *Personnel Psychology* 41, no. 4 (Winter 1988): 679–701.
4. Patricia Margin, "Jobs Must Be Marketed," *Personnel Journal* 70, no. 4 (April 1991): 87.
5. John Daly, "The 'Big Mac' Attack," *MacLeans* (June 19, 1992): 50.
6. John Hulpke, working paper 1994, source Michelle Martinez, "Disney Training Works Magic," *HR Magazine* (May 1992): 53.
7. Allen Wellins Consetins, "Choosing the Right People," *HR Magazine* (March 1990): 66–70.

8. Charlie C. Jones, "Determining Appropriate Reasonable Accommodations Under the Americans with Disabilities Act," Southwestern Federation of Administrative Disciplines Annual Meeting, New Orleans, Louisiana, 1993. Published in Southwestern Small Business Institute Association Proceedings.

9. John Hardwood, "Could a Candidate in a Presidential Race Win It by a Nose?," *The Wall Street Journal*, 24 June 1999, p. 1.

10. Michael Rozek, "Can You Spot A Peak Performer," *Personnel Journal* 70, no. 6 (June 1991): 77.

11. Joann S. Lublin, "Your Career Matters, For Hot Job Seekers, Personal Recruiters," *The Wall Street Journal*, 10 August 1999, p. B1.

12. Staff and Wire Reports. "Michelin's European restructuring will trim 7,500 jobs, Inside Briefcase," *The Oregonian*, 9 September 1999, p. B2.

13. Ruth E. Thaler-Cartier, "Recruiting Through the Web: Better Or Just Bigger?," *HR Magazine* (November 1998): 61–68.

14. Albert R. Karr, "Work Week, Prevarication Proliferates on Job Resumes, and That's No Lie," *The Wall Street Journal*, 24 August 1999, p. A1.

15. I. L. Goldstein, "The Application Blank: How Honest Are the Responses?" *Journal of Applied Psychology* 55 (1971): 491–92.

16. See Richard R. Reilly and Georgia T. Chao, "Validity and Fairness of Some Alternative Employee Selection Procedures," *Personnel Psychology* 25, no. 1 (Spring 1982): 1–62. See also Hannah R. Rothstein, Frank L. Schmidt, Frank W. Erwin, William A. Owens, and C. Paul Sparks, "Biographical Data in Employment Selection: Can Validities Be Made Generalizable?" *Journal of Applied Psychology* 75, no. 2 (1990): 175–84; Fleishman, "Some New Frontiers in Personnel Selection Research"; R. S. Lowell and J. A. DeLoach, "Equal Employment Opportunity: Are You Overlooking the Application Form?" *Personnel* 59 (1982): 49–55.

17. Robert P. Vecchio, "The Problem of Phony Resumes: How to Spot a Ringer Among the Applicants," *Personnel* 61, no. 2 (March-April 1984): 22–27.

18. Prentice Hall Information Services, "Policies and Practices," *Personnel Management* (1988): 2016.

19. Prentice Hall Information Services, "Policies and Practices," *Personnel Management* (1988): 2025.

20. Timothy Bland and Sue S. Stalcup, "Build a Legal Application," *HR Magazine* (March 1999): 129–133.

21. J. B. Miner and M. G. Miner, *Personnel and Industrial Relations* (New York: Macmillan Publishing, 1985).

22. Dolores Kong, *Boston Globe*, "Increasing evidence links job strain, ailments," *The Oregonian*, 8 September 1999, p. B10.

23. W. D. Scott, "The Scientific Selection of Salesmen," *Advertising and Selling* 25 (1915): 94–96.

24. E. C. Mayfield, "The Selection interview—A Re-evaluation of Published Research," *Personnel Psychology* 17 (1964): 239–60.

25. R. D. Arvey and J. E. Campion, "The Employment Interview: A Summary and Review of Recent Research," *Personnel Psychology* 35 (1982): 281–322. See also Robert C. Llden, Christopher Martin, and Charles K. Parsons, "Interviewer and Applicant Behaviors in Employment Interviews," *Academy of Management Journal* 36, no. 2 (April 1993): 372–86.

26. Barbara Felton and Sue Lamb, "A Model For Systematic Selection Interviewing," *Personnel* 59 (January-February 1982): 40–48.

27. R. L. Dipboye, *Selection interviews: Process Perspectives* (Cincinnati, OH: South-Western, 1992).

28. N. H. Anderson and V. J. Shackleton, "Decision Making in the Graduate Selection Interview," *Journal of Applied Psychology* 44, no. 6 (1990): 267–68.

29. Diane Sears Campbell, Knight Rider News Services, "Adaptability Can Set Job Candidates Apart, Expert Says," *The Oregonian*, 4 June 1999, p. E3.

30. Bernard Wysochi Jr., "How Life on the Edge Became Mainstream in Today's America," *The Wall Street Journal*, 3 August 1999, p. A1.

31. Carolyn Hirschman, "Playing the High Stakes Hiring Game," *HR Magazine* (March 1998): 80–86.

32. R. D. Arvey, "Unfair Discrimination in the Employment Interview: Legal and Psychometric Aspects," *Psychological Bulletin* (1979): 736–65. See also Charlene M. Solomon, "Testing Is Not At Odds with Diversity Efforts," *Personnel Journal* 72, no. 3 (March 1993): 100–04.

33. John Hulpke, 1994. Working paper, California State University, Bakersfield.

34. R. Forbes, "Improving the Reliability of the Selection Interview," *Personnel Management* 58, no. 7 (July 1979): 36–37.

35. Elliott D. Pursell, Michael A. Campion, and Sarah R. Gaylor, "Structured Interviewing: Avoiding Selection Problems," *Personnel Journal* 59, no. 11 (November 1980): 907–12. See also Sampo V. Paunonen and Douglas N. Jackson, "Accuracy of Interviewers and Students in Identifying the Personality Characteristics of Personnel Managers and Computer Programmers," *Journal of Vocational Behavior* 31 (1987): 26–36.

36. *Selection Interview Form (Revised)*, 1977, by Benjamin Balinsky, Ph.D. Published by Martin M. Bruce, Ph.D., Publishers, 50 Larchwood Road, Larchmont, NY 10538. Reproduced with permission.

37. Richard D. Arvey and James E. Campion, "The Employment Interview: A Summary and Review of Recent Research," *Personnel Psychology* 35, no. 2 (Summer 1982): 281–322. See also Robert N. McMurry, *Tested Techniques of Personnel Selection*, rev. ed. (Chicago: Dartnell, n.d.). See also Robert W. Eder and Gerald R. Ferris, eds., *The Employment Interview—Theory, Research, and Practice* (Newbury Park, CA: Sage Publications, 1989); and Sandy Sillup, "Applicant Screening Cuts Turnover Costs," *Personnel Journal* 17, no. 5 (1992): 115–16.

38. Beth Potter, "Recruiting, testing firm SHL group to open 50-person Boulder office," *Boulder County Business Report* 18, no. 1 (January 1, 1999): 10.

39. Linda Thornburg, "Computer-Assisted Interviewing Shortens Hiring Curve," *HR Magazine* (February 1999): 73–79.

40. Phillip Inman, "Recruiting drive: Putting your job right on the line," *The Guardian Manchester*, 16 January 1999, p. 22.

41. David J. Weston and Dennis L. Warmke, "Dispelling the Myths About Panel Interviews," *Personnel Administrator* 33, no. 5 (May 1988): 109–11.

42. Nancy Hatch Woodward, "Just Relax," experts advise HR Professionals; Interviewing People with Disabilities, *HR Magazine* (January 1999): 14.

43. Shari Caudron, "Are Self-Directed Teams Right for Your Company?" *Personnel Journal* (December 1993): 76–84. See also John Case, "What the Experts Forgot To Mention," *Inc. Magazine* (September 1993): 66–80.

44. J. R. Huck and D. W. Bray, "Management Assessment Center Evaluations," *Personnel Psychology* 29 (1976): 13.

45. G. C. Thornton III and W. C. Byham, *Assessment Centers and Managerial Performance* (New York: Academic Press, 1982).

46. "Answers For Your HR Regulatory Compliance Questions," *Products and Services for the Assessment and Development of Human Resources* (New York: Harcourt Brace Jovanovich, 1993), p. 2.

47. B. Kleinmutz, "Lie Detectors Fail the Truth Test," *Harvard Business Review* 63 (July-August 1985): 36–42.

48. Bureau of National Affairs, Inc., "Final Polygraph Rules Issued," *Bulletin to Management,* 7 March 1990, p. 65.

49. B. Lohman, "'Honest Test' is Lying in Wait for Jobseekers," *Honolulu Star Bulletin,* 29 June 1986, p. B4.

50. R. W. Rosenbaum, "Predictability of Employee Theft Using Weighted Application Blanks," *Journal of Applied Psychology* 61 (1976): 94–98.

51. L. Levy, "Handwriting and hiring," *Dun's Review* 113 (1979): 72–79.

52. G. Ben-Shakhar, M. Bar-Hillel, Y. Bilu, E. Ben-Abba, and A. Flug, "Can Graphology Predict Occupational Success? Two Empirical Studies and Some Methodological Ruminations," *Journal of Applied Psychology* 71 (1986): 645–53.

53. Jane Easter Bahls, "Dealing with Drugs: Keep It Legal," *HR Magazine* (March 1998): 104–16.

54. "What's News, World Wide," *The Wall Street Journal,* 9 September 1999, p. A1.

55. Dawn Gunsch, "Training Prepares Workers for Drug Testing," *Personnel Journal* 72, no. 5 (May 1993): 52–59.

56. Robert Vecchio, "The Problem of Phony Resources," *Personnel* (March-April 1984): 2–27. See also June P. Schafer, "The Resume," *Security Management* 62, no. 3 (1990): 21.

57. I. L. Goldstein, "The Application Blank: How Honest are Responses?" *Journal of Applied Psychology* (1971): 491–92.

58. John Hulpke. 1994. Impact of FERPA in Employment Decisions. Working paper.

III

The Success System: Developing a High-Performing Workforce

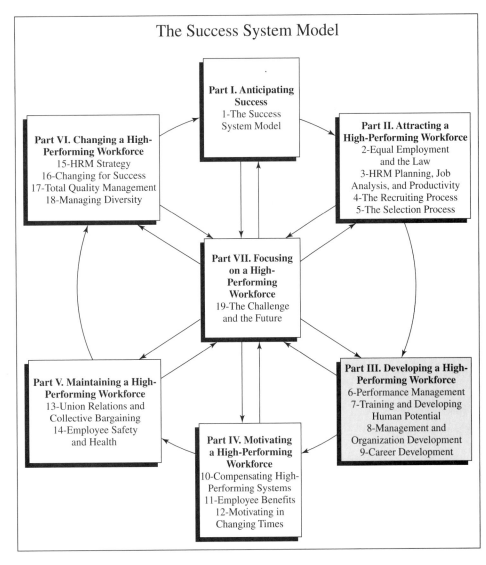

The Success System Model

Part I. Anticipating Success
1-The Success System Model

Part II. Attracting a High-Performing Workforce
2-Equal Employment and the Law
3-HRM Planning, Job Analysis, and Productivity
4-The Recruiting Process
5-The Selection Process

Part VI. Changing a High-Performing Workforce
15-HRM Strategy
16-Changing for Success
17-Total Quality Management
18-Managing Diversity

Part VII. Focusing on a High-Performing Workforce
19-The Challenge and the Future

Part III. Developing a High-Performing Workforce
6-Performance Management
7-Training and Developing Human Potential
8-Management and Organization Development
9-Career Development

Part V. Maintaining a High-Performing Workforce
13-Union Relations and Collective Bargaining
14-Employee Safety and Health

Part IV. Motivating a High-Performing Workforce
10-Compensating High-Performing Systems
11-Employee Benefits
12-Motivating in Changing Times

Chapter 6

The Success System: Performance Management

Objectives

Upon completing this chapter, you will be able to:

1. Define the concepts of performance management and appraisal and recognize how this can be applied in an organization.
2. Describe the steps in developing a performance management program and understand its impact on the behavior of individuals in an organization.
3. Understand the process and skills involved in an effective performance appraisal interview.
4. Identify and describe the major types of rating errors likely to be encountered in the appraisal process.

Premeeting preparation

1. Read chapter 6.
2. Prepare for HRM Skills Simulation 6.1. Read Parts A and B.
3. Read Case 6.1: Precision Products, Inc. Answer questions.

Background Information

"Do you genuinely believe that there are no limits to what the average individual can accomplish, if well trained, well supported and well rewarded for superior performance? If so, then you are aware of the major reason for our failure to keep up with world class competitors: an inability to tap our workforce's potential," says Tom Peters, leading author and consultant.[1]

One of the most important activities of an HR manager is maintaining and enhancing the workforce. After all the effort and costs involved in the recruiting and selection process, it is important to develop employees so that they are using their fullest capabilities, thus improving the effectiveness of the organization. Performance management is the ongoing process of evaluating and improving employee performance.[2] Therefore, it is important that the organization develop procedures and policies which comply with the process.[3]

The development of a standard performance appraisal process will help companies to improve their bottom-line performance, uplift motivational efforts, and resolve most morale problems. Today's performance appraisals should take the direction of coaching to capitalize on the opportunities to solve problems resulting from formal performance evaluations. This coaching emphasis will allow supervisors to develop insightful personnel records to form the basis for judgment on salary adjustments, improving performance plans, or termination.[4]

In the future, the only successful companies will be those that are able to increase productivity through improving the performance of their human resources. This is a critical problem because evidence suggests that most employees work at only 40 to 60 percent of their capabilities, with great variation between high and average performers. The cost advantages of using a comprehensive performance appraisal system has been estimated at $5.3 million for 1 year in one company.[5]

Over 95 percent of organizations have reported the use of performance appraisal systems, but the majority have expressed some dissatisfaction with the appraisal process. Several studies have reported widespread dissatisfaction with the process. One study reports numerous problems with appraisals.[6]

Preparing managers to cope with today's workforce diversity in the management and appraisal of performance is the central concern of this chapter. The modern manager must not only be flexible and adaptive in a changing environment but must also be able to recognize and comply with all legal requirements.

The purpose of this chapter is to provide an understanding of this stage of the Success System Model: a description of the performance management and appraisal process. This includes the major appraisal techniques, discussing various rating methods, and identifying several performance evaluation problems. Performance management is a key factor in enhancing the development of the organization's employees.

The Performance Management System

As an integral component of the Success System Model, the performance management system should provide benefits to both the employee and to the organization. For the individual, the appraisal should provide recognition and reinforcement essential to developing high performance. For the organization, performance appraisal should provide a management information system for making management decisions as well as a tool for improving performance. Today's organization can no longer afford to live with an ineffective appraisal system.

Practically all managers and many employees dislike the experience of performance appraisals. However, the pluses far outnumber the minuses with many good reasons for formally appraising performance. The appraisal is a more factual presentation to demonstrate an employee is failing within the functioning of a group or department. On the positive side, appraisals will identify individual's latent leadership skills and suggest ways to develop them. They will also provide valuable insights as to the future direction the department or work group will take.[7]

Performance may be defined as the accomplishment of an employee or manager's assigned duties and the outcomes produced on a specified job function or activity during a specified time period. **Performance appraisal,** review, or evaluation refers to a systematic description and review of an individual's job performance. **Performance management** refers to the total system of gathering information, the review and feedback to the individual, and storing information to improve organizational effectiveness. The primary goal of performance management appraisals is to improve organizational performance. The appraisals are used for a variety of purposes, including the following.

Compensation

One of the most common uses of performance management (reported by 75 percent of firms) concerns compensation, determining pay increases, bonuses, and other pay-related issues.

Performance Improvement

A number of companies, including Westinghouse, Amoco, Pratt and Whitney, and IBM, have installed appraisal systems which link performance improvement with pay. An effective appraisal system performance is necessary for these incentive systems to work. IBM's appraisal system identified high performers as "superstars" who then earn up to $50,000 bonuses for high performance.[8]

Internal Appraisal

Performance appraisal information is also used in performance decisions, to determine promotions, transfers, or, in the case of downsizing, to identify possible layoffs. Most organizations rely on performance appraisal information in deciding which employees to promote to fill openings and which employees to retain in a downsizing situation.

One problem with relying too heavily on performance appraisal information in making decisions about promotions is that the employee's performance concerns only his or her current job. If the promotion involves different skills from the employee's current job, it is often impossible to predict how the individual will perform at the new level. To deal with this, many organizations are using assessment centers in addition to normal appraisal data.[9]

Evaluation

Performance appraisal information may also be used to evaluate the effectiveness of the recruitment process, to validate selection criteria or other predictors of job performance. In these cases, the HR manager gathers on-the-job performance appraisals so that test scores or selection ratings can be correlated to job performance.

Internet Feedback

Otis Elevator Company uses a 360-degree feedback where employees send feedback to assist managers in assessing their leadership skills. The system is user-friendly and is seen by employees as worthwhile. The 360-degree feedback not only assesses managers' team leadership skills, but also helps them develop those skills.

The system uses two Internet technologies: Leading Empowered Active People Survey and Technical and Business Effectiveness Surveys. The advantages of the system include the reduction of paperwork, reducing employee's time, and maintaining employee's anonymity while providing prompt feedback. The result is informative feedback that promotes leadership development.[10]

Developmental Tool

Performance appraisals may also be used as a developmental tool for the individual employee, providing an opportunity for feedback, recognition, and reinforcement. This performance review also provides employees with career goals and direction for future performance.

The appraisal allows the organization to select those best qualified for promotion, suggest areas where training may be effective, and help improve individual performance, resulting in improved bottom-line productivity. Further, the performance appraisal information allows the organization to fulfill the requirements of equal employment opportunity laws (discussed in chapter 2) and to maintain accurate and objective performance records relative to promotions, compensation, training, and discharges.

From the individual's viewpoint, performance appraisals should provide recognition of one's contributions, a feeling of support from one's immediate supervisor, and the feeling of security from knowing one is performing satisfactorily.[11]

When giving feedback to an employee in an appraisal, the interviewer should have the necessary information to make the evaluation of job performance and present a summation of that information. At this point, the feedback session should turn to a discussion of developing strengths, thus shifting into a counseling session. It is suggested that supervisors keep a file on each worker, noting significant accomplishments or setbacks, and do appraisals as an ongoing process.

THE PERFORMANCE APPRAISAL REVIEW PROCESS

The performance appraisal review process provides a critical element in the development of the organization's most valuable resource: its employees.

Identifying Performance Standards

The appraisal attempts to identify the key skills, behaviors, results, and outputs to be reviewed, usually from job analysis data. Performance **standards** specify what is to be accomplished, and some measure of how well it is being accomplished. The clearer the performance standards are communicated to employees, the more accurate and fair the review process. In general, the greater the specificity of the standards, the more effective the system.

The Appraisers

The appraisal is usually performed by one's immediate supervisor. In fact, in 92 percent of organizations studied, appraisals were made by the employee's immediate supervisor.[12] The rationale is that this individual has the most opportunity to observe the employee, should have a better understanding of the job being performed, and is motivated to optimize the employee's performance appraisal because the supervisor's future is directly linked to the organizational unit's profitability.

The immediate supervisor should utilize techniques to minimize any appearance of giving criticism. This can be accomplished by focusing on results rather than individual personality. One should be aware how voice tone can change a person's interpretation of what is being said. The supervisor should regard the employee as a teammate and involve the person in the process.

The future should be stressed rather than the past. The emphasis should be on the positive benefits to be attained by adapting the suggested adjustments. At the same time, it should be pointed out if the adjustments are not made, there will be consequences.[13]

Self-Appraisal

Other performance appraisal sources include subordinate **self-appraisals** that are completed prior to the review session and then used as the agenda for that session.[14] The effectiveness of self-appraisals depends upon a trusting relationship between superior and subordinate. Also, not to be overlooked is the subordinate's expectation of one's peer group as to their honesty and accuracy in their own self-appraisals. (See cartoon.)

Peer Appraisal/Multiple Appraisal

Many organizations are finding that multiple raters add to the effectiveness of the appraisal system. Ratings collected from several sources tend to be more accurate and have fewer biases.[15] Still another form is **peer appraisal,** where one's fellow workers rate each other. Again, trust must prevail, along with accurate and frequent observation of each other's work behavior. Often peers (or customers) have better knowledge of certain aspects of the employee's work performance. This method often places greater emphasis on team performance and team rewards.[16]

Subordinate Rating

Yet another form is the reverse procedure of subordinates evaluating superiors. This may be placing an unfair burden upon the subordinates who, on top of being expected to perform their jobs satisfactorily, now are placed under the additional stress of evaluating the person who will soon be evaluating them. Also, this assumes the subordinate's criteria is similar to the goals and objectives of the organization. Many organizations use self, subordinate, peer, and supervisor ratings as a comprehensive appraisal. Although these sources of evaluation are innovative and thought-provoking, they are not generally accepted in most organizations.[17]

Source: CROCK by Bill Rechin and Don Wilder. © North America Syndicate, Inc.

Appraisal Devalued

A recent article discusses the devaluation of the performance review process over the last few years. Apparently this devaluation occurred when companies started to separate pay raises from the actual performance on the job. When the downsizing trend began and mass layoffs took place without documenting evidence of decreased performance, further devaluation took place. In today's tight labor market with its present high personnel turnover, performance appraisals became more infrequent and irrelevant. This is due to the fact there was not much of a historical record of performance to review for this highly mobile workforce.

This article continues that since 1995, there has been a trend of younger employees who demonstrated a less competitive effort with their peers. As a result, these younger employees became less interested in the performance appraisal process. However, regardless of criticism of the process, performance appraisal is like the employment application blank. They are both flawed but continue to be used today because they are extremely important to a productive business.[18]

PERFORMANCE APPRAISAL METHODS

The performance appraisal methods that appear to be in more general use include rating scales, ranking, checklists, forced distribution, paired comparison, essay, critical incidents, and management by objectives. The large number of performance appraisal methods listed is an indication of the importance placed on this process by management. Another factor is test validity.

Types of Validity

A test is said to be valid for selection purposes if there is a significant relationship between performance on the test and performance on the job. The better a test can distinguish between satisfactory and unsatisfactory performance of the job, the greater its validity. Applicants' scores on valid tests can be used to predict their probable job performance.

The four basic **types of validity** are (1) predictive validity, (2) concurrent validity, (3) content validity, and (4) construct validity. Each type is discussed as it relates to appraisal.

Predictive Validity

This method of validating employment practices is calculated by giving a test, and then comparing the test results with the job performance of those tested.

There are several problems with using predictive validity, even though it is considered sound in a statistical sense. For example, a relatively large number of people have to be hired at once, and the test scores cannot be considered. Obviously, the firm may initially hire both good and bad employees. Because of these and other problems, another type of validity is often used—concurrent validity.

Concurrent Validity

Concurrent essentially means "at the same time." Using concurrent validity, current employees (instead of those newly hired) are used to validate the test. The test is given to current employees, and then the scores are correlated with their performance ratings. A high correlation suggests that the test is able to differentiate between the better and the poorer employees.

Content Validity

This type of validity uses a logical and less statistical approach. In content validity, a person would perform a test which is an actual sample of the work done on the job. Thus, an arithmetic test for a cashier would contain some of the calculations that a cashier would have to make on the job. Content validity is especially useful if the workforce is not large enough to accommodate better statistical designs.

Construct Validity

This type of validity is somewhat more difficult to deal with than the others. In practice, construct validity describes some measure (such as a scale or index) of a variable that correlates with measures of other variables. These variables should agree with a theory as to how they are related.

For example, in studying racist attitudes, you as the researcher may believe that racism (the construct) is more evident in people of low self-esteem. To determine the construct validity of your belief, create an instrument (survey, questionnaire) to determine racism and an instrument to determine low and high self-esteem.

If there is correlation between your instruments (positive or negative), you may or may not have support for your racism belief (the construct). If you have support, it is construct validity. Construct validity is more likely to run into difficulties with measuring the person in abstract than the other three validities.

Rating Scales

Rating scales usually include graphic, weighted, and behaviorally anchored criteria. The **graphic rating** scale is the simplest and most commonly used. A list of performance variables is determined for the particular job, such as attendance, production, and cooperation. For each performance variable, there is a listing of levels of performance ranging from exceptional to below normal. The individual merely circles the performance level that is believed to have been achieved. Scoring is done by simply adding the number values assigned to each performance level, from exceptional to below normal.

The Graphic Rating

The graphic rating scale is the most widely used type of appraisal format. This method is easy to learn both from the standpoint of the rater and the ratee.[19] However, a serious problem is that it may not evaluate actual job performance. This results in raters tending to fall into the problems of central tendency and halo rating errors.

The Weighted Scale

The **weighted** graphic rating **scale** is the same as the graphic rating scale, with the exception that the performance variables receive different weights depending upon their importance in performing the job. The rating procedures is the same except that each variable has a box in which the rater indicates with a 1, 2, 3, and so on, the relevant importance of that variable. Scoring is achieved by multiplying these numbers times the value of the performance levels ranging from exceptional to below normal.

However, the weighted graphic rating scale, although emphasizing the more important performance variables, suffers the same problems as the graphic rating scale. Rater subjectivity is still present, as is the tendency to overrate present behavior and group people within a narrow range.

Behaviorally Anchored Rating Scales (BARS)

A more sophisticated form of rating is the **Behaviorally Anchored Rating Scales,** commonly referred to as **BARS.** BARS are graphic scales with the performance variables anchored in descriptions of actual job behavior. For instance, one of many BARS for a grocery clerk would range from "always placing heavy objects in the bottom of the bag" to the other extreme of "indiscriminately mixing heavy and light objects." BARS for a wage and salary administrator might range from "maintains a current data base" to "fails to coordinate with appropriate committees."

BARS are constructed for each individual job category, and not for individual positions within these job categories. The result are BARS that are broadly descriptive to cover the positions within job categories. The reasons for this are that constructing BARS is very time-consuming, very costly, and very often needs to be updated. It is often not practical to do this for each individual position.

This is evident when one considers the first step in constructing BARS requires a recent job analysis from which to prepare a comprehensive job description. Committees are often formed using the job description in determining job dimensions from which descriptive anchors are then developed within each job dimension. These job dimensions are really elements of the job, such as "budget planning" or "heat treating." The descriptive anchors then rate the job behaviors from good to bad in performing each job dimension. So, for a budget planner, one job dimension could be "preparation," with the descriptive anchors ranging from "uses all local and regional data bases" to "works alone and fails to utilize outside sources."

BARS appears to provide a workable system. It also has the advantage of using job categories which are closely reviewed for performance content. The anchors are job descriptive and should promote rater accuracy.

360 Degree or Multirater

This process allows employees to receive constructive and accurate rating feedback. The rating information is gathered from a questionnaire with approximately 100 items to obtain ratings. The questionnaire is usually completed by a work group of around ten people. This work group includes the person being rated, their boss, several peers, and subordinates.[20]

Ranking

Another appraisal method is ranking. Individuals are evaluated from best to worst on some single performance criteria. This procedure may be changed by alternatively ranking the best and worst, followed by the second best and second worst, until all individuals have been ranked. The result is a rather simplistic evaluation that may be difficult to defend—especially as one reaches the middle of the group, where the best and worst designation differences may be extremely difficult to decide.

Paired Comparison

Paired comparisons require the rater to compare pairs of ratees on performance, in which two individuals are compared at a time to determine which one is the better employee. Then, another two names are compared until every individual has been paired with every other individual. The final winning score would be the individual having been chosen most over the others.

The paired comparison method is simple, but cumbersome to use. However, when the number of employees to be ranked reaches 20, there would be 190 comparisons, the result of which would dilute one's ability to make distinctions. Yet, this method does seem to reduce the central tendency, leniency-strictness, and halo errors.

Behavioral Checklist

Checklist appraisals are another appraisal method and are either basic, weighted, or forced choice. The basic checklist development follows a procedure similar to BARS, in that a job analysis must be performed to come up with a job description.

Then, several performance categories are indicated from which a wide range of favorable and unfavorable behaviors are created. These are then randomly assigned to the checklist representing an accurate statement of favorable and unfavorable job performance. Randomness keeps the evaluator alert, because each behavior must be carefully read and helps control central tendency.

Although checklists are easy to use and score, they are time-consuming and costly to construct. Such checklists tend to be broad and to make them more job specific increases the cost. Also, basic checklists assign equal weight to each item, ignoring any contribution differences of performance variables. However, the weighted checklist overcomes this problem.

The procedure to determine weighting of the checklist is quite simple. A list of performance variables is drawn up, and knowledgeable persons assign varying weights depending upon their judgments as to the relative value of each variable for job performance. At times, organization policies, such as concern for safety, will be reflected in higher weights.

Forced Choice

The **forced-choice appraisal** technique is a rating method that requires the rater to make choices among descriptive sentences. The forced-choice checklist is a time-consuming method because it requires the development of a set of several sentences ranging from the high level of performance for a variable such as effort, to the lowest level of acceptable performance. If an accurate set of sentences is developed, then the result may be a reduction of rater error, particularly central tendency. One technique often used to keep the raters alert is using a combination of positive and negative sentences for each job variable. Raters are not given the screening format, so they are unable to intentionally give high or low ratings.

Forced Distribution

Another method of appraisal is forced distribution, which presents the rater with a limited number of categories and requires a designated portion of ratees for each category. This technique is relatively simple and inexpensive. Employees are divided into set categories, such as the highest-rated individuals for a particular variable (quality, attendance, etc.). This highest category must include 5 percent of all the employees being rated, the above average category must include the next 15 percent, the average category must include the next 60 percent, and so on.

One problem with forced distribution is that the group being evaluated may exceed or not meet the designated percentage category, thereby diluting the validity of the category. As with other forced techniques, rater errors such as central tendency tend to be reduced; however, the forced distribution may cause ill feelings among raters and ratees because the method is so subjective.

Managerial

The performance appraisal methods that appear to be most appropriate for managerial and top-level white-collar jobs would include essay, critical incident, and management by objectives.

Essay

The **essay appraisal** consists of several paragraphs of written narrative describing the individual's strengths and weaknesses relative to their job and recommendations for future development. This appraisal format permits commenting on the employee's unique characteristics. It is more effective when specific examples of employee behavior are cited, along with objective facts supported by any quantitative information. Some problems with the essay evaluation include that it can become time-consuming when describing all of the individual's characteristics, and that it may be unfair since the quality may depend upon the writing skills of different evaluators.

Critical Incidents

The **critical incidents** format is a narrative type of performance appraisal. The incidents that are discussed are both favorable and unfavorable. They must be observable, verifiable, and be reduced to a quantifiable basis. Individual employee files are maintained, and incidents should be documented as soon as they occur. Some companies send copies to employees so they may file a written response, especially if the incident is negative. Although the critical incident is unsurpassed for being timely and for documenting a chronological time sequence, it is subject to the usual rater errors in addition to creating unrelated incidents that become difficult to evaluate.

Management by Objectives

The final performance appraisal method is **management by objectives, or MBO.** This method is very popular, although there is some evidence that it is now in decline. A recent article on business fads states that management by objectives is a fad that is now out of favor. One company president indicated his company spent more time on the paperwork than the whole concept was worth.

The MBO approach is an appraisal system which uses a comparison of targeted goals to the actual results achieved. In the MBO system, company employees are viewed as members of a team, with the individual evaluation depending upon one's ability to achieve agreed-upon objectives. These objectives are usually measurable within a specific time frame, such as achieving a 10 percent scrap reduction within 90 days, or achieving a specific return within a designated period.

The MBO process begins at the top of the organization and works its way down. As a result, objectives set at a lower level are compatible with the objectives at higher levels. This avoids the dilemma of an employee who is successfully pursuing individual objectives that are not in agreement with company objectives.

Individual objectives are usually determined in a subordinate-supervisor meeting. Also, at this meeting, the supervisor and subordinate determine a plan of action and a timetable for accomplishing the agreed-upon objectives. The timetable will include additional meeting dates where progress toward the objectives is reviewed and any adjustments are made. The agreed-upon objectives are usually reviewed at the level of supervision above the supervisor to ensure the objectives are reasonable and compatible with the overall plan. The result is that the immediate supervisor is able to use MBO to motivate individuals to promote themselves, while at the same time they are promoting the objectives of the company. In this situation, the supervisor functions more in the role of a coach to the individual than as a judge or lecturer.

MBO is a costly process because the objectives are established in meetings which usually occur over several settings and may be lengthy. Differences in personalities may affect the sessions as there is a need for mutual trust and respect. Supervisory styles may cause problems as the supervisor needs to have a participative management style if MBO is to work. Although the concept appears logical and reasonable, its effectiveness, in practice, appears to break down.

Visual 360

A computer software program called Visual 360 automates multirater assessments from the 360-degree feedback process. This is a great time-saver because it tracks results from rating forms. It makes it easier for employees to intuitively apply the rating standards or competencies to the individual being evaluated. Visual 360 also simplifies rating a group of people in a meaningful manner.[21]

A business may have the latest performance management systems, but it will fail unless it is implemented or put into action correctly. Front-line supervisors may not understand the goal of the system and are confused by the objectives. Is the aim of the system to help employees meet the company's expectations which will further their job security? Or is the system designed to have a record that will inhibit employees from suing the company?

Actually, performance management is a mixture of both. It is not one or the other. The following suggests some aspects of implementing a performance management system.

- *Setting Expectations.* Employers must provide employees with clear instructions of what the company expects of them. It would be unfair not to do this and then terminate employees. Not only is it unfair, in adversarial proceedings (courts, arbitrators, or commissions) one of the first questions asked is " . . . did the employee fail to meet in terms of conduct, performance, or behavior?" Employers who reply the employee should have known will usually receive the reply, "You should have told them." Big trouble!

- *Notification of Not Making the Grade.* An employee discharge is unfair if the employee has not been told previously that one's job is on the line. This notifies employees they are not making the grade so they can make the suggested changes to preserve their job. When employees know their records reflect their shortcomings, they are less likely to sue, which would place their personnel records into the public record.

- *Nonpunitive Discipline.* Many supervisors are reluctant to punish their children, let alone adult employees. Most will not use discipline, even if the employer requires it. Nonpunitive discipline can be used and many believe it generates more effective results. Employees have the right to be treated like adults and should be counseled on their job shortcomings in a direct and nonpunitive manner.

- *Deficiencies, Not Causes.* When employers try to address the "real cause" of a workplace problem such as emotional, medical, or personal, there is a real risk of lawsuits under the Americans with Disabilities Act (ADA). The reason is when you do so you are actually considering the employee as having a disabling condition which is against the law. Focus only on what takes place at the workplace. Do not inquire nor speculate as to what may be the "real" underlying cause.

- *Avoid Intent.* When employees do not meet the company's expectations, it does not mean they are bad and do not care. Stay out of the trap of analyzing the employee's thoughts. You cannot prove an employee doesn't care, but you can prove missed deadlines and defective work. If you focus on subjective intent, you allow the employee to divert attention away from the real issue of objective deficient work behavior.

- *Avoid Delay.* If one must discipline employees, do not delay. The longer time elapses, the more rigid our view of the employee becomes. Employees should have a chance to improve, not be judged prematurely. By acting quickly, you reduce the possibility the employee will raise a protected complaint such as harassment or disability.

Other aspects of implementing performance management which requires attention is providing employees the opportunity to defend themselves. There are usually two sides to every work incident. Employees should have a reasonable opportunity to improve. Any discipline should be progressive with reasonable time between each step. The business should make good use of the introductory periods of 30 to 90 days at the beginning of employment to document employees' work problems. If the new employee will not work out, now is the time for discharge. It is only fair to the particular employee so they can invest their time and effort in a more suitable job. All discharges should be the same for similar situations. Double standards and favoritism will cause legal problems later as comparisons are made. Always provide an appeals procedure such as a peer review because although companies try to be fair, errors will occur.[22]

PERFORMANCE APPRAISAL PROBLEMS

Performance appraisals and merit rating plans sometimes fail. When this does occur, there are several possible explanations or problem areas. Sometimes these plans not only attempt to motivate individuals to increased effectiveness, but also directly link pay raises and promotions. When this takes place during the evaluation feedback session, employees are more interested in the final result: that is, will they receive increased pay or a promotion? The result is the ratee often pays little attention to the feedback portion of the session.

The feedback session should not include any pay raise or promotion decisions, if future employee motivation is one of the expected outcomes. Pay raises and promotion should be discussed at later sessions.

In a feedback session using employee self-ratings of their performance, there may be problems with the supervisor's ratings differing. Such issues usually go beyond just the differences in overall ratings and require additional discussion.[23]

One cause of appraisal problems may be the lack of top management support. The result is that both the rater and ratee realize little will result from the evaluation process, so they merely go through the motions, often wasting valuable time and energy. It is only when management supports appraisal and makes it known to the rater that their future with the company depends upon their effectiveness in evaluating ratees, will there be appropriate results. This also applies to the ratees, because they must be convinced their evaluations will eventually decide future career opportunities, pay raises, and possible promotions.

When the company is unionized, the major cause of evaluation problems is using seniority as the basis for pay increases, promotions, and other work-related issues such as vacations, shift preferences, and overtime. Although this is a contractual procedure, subject to negotiation, the company often does have other choices.

For instance, the company would prefer to keep the seniority unit as small as possible, permitting the seniority restriction to apply to the smallest number of people and thus allowing greater company discretion in appraisal. Of course, the union desires larger seniority units, because it hopes to maximize the number of people to whom the seniority rule applies. For example, in a layoff situation, the seniority person would bump the least senior person. When units are small, the effects of seniority are often minimized. Other approaches to the seniority issue would be a split merit and seniority system, with extra "performance" points given for years of service. Also, when merit measures favor a nonseniority person over a seniority person, a joint management-union committee could resolve the issue.

The seniority issue aside, performance management appraisal plans will continue to be a major factor in determining pay increases, promotions, and retention in business organizations. (See Our Changing World.)

THE APPRAISAL INTERVIEW

The **appraisal interview** gives a manager the opportunity to discuss a subordinate's performance record and to explore areas of possible improvement and growth. It also provides an opportunity to identify the subordinate's attitudes and feelings more thoroughly and thus to improve communication.[25] Usually the appraisals are conducted once or twice per year. In smaller organizations, appraisals may be few and far between, but they are important.

The format for the appraisal interview will be determined in large part by the purpose of the interview, the type of appraisal system used, and the organization of the interview form. Most appraisal interviews attempt to give feedback to employees on how well they are performing their jobs, and to make plans for their future development.[26] Interviews should be scheduled far enough in advance to allow the interviewee, as well as the interviewer, to prepare for the discussion. Usually 10 days to 2 weeks is a sufficient amount of lead time. Frequently, appraisal feedback is used as part of the self-managed team approach by an increasing number of organizations.[27]

Areas of Emphasis

A major purpose of the appraisal interview is to make plans for improvement; however, it is important to focus the interview's attention on the future rather than the past. The interviewer should observe the following points:

1. Emphasize strengths on which the employee can build rather than weaknesses to overcome.
2. Avoid suggestions about personal traits to change; instead, suggest more acceptable ways of performing.
3. Concentrate on opportunities for growth that exist within the framework of the employee's present position.
4. Limit plans for growth to a few important items that can be accomplished within a reasonable period of time.

Although the fairness issue is a major concern in all the working areas of HRM, it is very important in the appraisal interview. The principles of justice form the basis for HRM practices in hiring, performance appraisal, and rewards. There is ample evidence that fairness increases the company's employee loyalty. The result is satisfied, committed employees who are willing to demonstrate extra job effort. This leads to positive employee job behaviors even if they relate only to job descriptions, performance appraisals, or reward programs.[28]

The appraisal interview is perhaps the most important part of the entire performance appraisal process. Unfortunately, the interviewer can become overburdened by attempting to discuss too much, such as the employee's past performance and future development goals. Dividing the appraisal interview into two sessions, one for the performance review and the other for the employee's growth plans, can alleviate time pressures. Moreover, by separating the interview into two sessions, the interviewer can give each session the proper attention it deserves. It is difficult for a supervisor to perform the role of both evaluator and counselor in the same review period. Dividing the sessions also may improve communication between the parties, thereby reducing stress. A good, supportive feedback interview can result in greater employee satisfaction with the appraisal interview.[29]

Another source of ineffective performance is the normally happy employee who suddenly demonstrates negative behavior. Over a period of several weeks their behavior becomes aggressive and threatening. It could be caused by a medical condition, such as depression, or because the employee has stopped taking prescribed medication. Whatever is causing the behavior change must be unique to that person, although some people are naturally antagonistic or withdrawn. An important consideration is the disturbed employee may cause valuable employees to request a transfer or leave the company.[30]

Ineffective behavior may be caused by the work environment. The competitive world of work with its budget cuts, restructuring, and high-tech advances are extending the reach of the workplace, overloading many employees. Employees begin to burn out when the negative pressure, conflicts, and demands increasingly outweigh the positives of personal acknowledgement and successes. Exhausted workers report lower job satisfaction, lower commitment, and higher job turnover.

Because highly motivated and committed employees are more apt to burn out, the company is losing its best people. Companies must increase their acknowledgement and show appreciation to employees doing a good job. These rewards should be distributed fairly to employees because an unfair allocation increases negativism.[31]

Improving Performance

In many instances, the appraisal interview will provide the basis for noting deficiencies in employee performance and for making plans for improvement. Unless these deficiencies are brought to the employee's attention, they are likely to continue until they become quite serious. Sometimes, underperformers may not understand exactly what is expected of them. However, once their responsibilities are clarified, they are in a position to take the corrective action needed to improve their performance.

Sources of Ineffective Performance

There are many reasons why an employee's performance might not meet the standards. First, each individual has a unique pattern of strengths and weaknesses that play a part. In addition, other factors—such as the work environment; the external environment, including home and community; and personal problems—have an impact on job performance.

It is recommended that the appraisal of ineffective employee performance focus on three interactive elements: skill, effort, and external conditions. For example, if an employee's performance is not up to standards, the cause could be a skill problem (knowledge, abilities, technical competencies), an effort problem (motivation to get the job done), or some problem in the external conditions of work (poor working conditions, supply shortages, difficult sales territories). If any one of these three elements are unfavorable, performance will usually suffer.[32]

Improving Ineffective Performance

The first step in improving ineffective performance is to determine its cause. Once the cause is known, a course of action can be planned. This action may include providing training or improving the skills needed for effective performance. A transfer to another job or department could provide an employee with an opportunity to become a more effective member of the organization. In other situations, greater attention may have to be focused on incentives to motivate the employee.

If ineffective performance persists, it may be necessary to demote the employee, take disciplinary action, or discharge the person from the organization. Whatever action is taken, it should be done within legal limits, with fairness, and with a recognition of the feelings of the individual involved.

This should require a formal approach to a progressive discipline program. The most appropriate match of discipline to a specific offense should be governed by the severity of the offense, employee's past performance record, length of time employed, and past penalties for a similar offense. Appropriateness of discipline usually begins with the first step being a verbal warning, the second a written warning, and third, a final written warning indicating the disciplinary action.

The courts expect companies to fit the appropriate discipline to match the seriousness of the offense. So a minor form of discipline is not appropriate for a serious offense such as sexual harassment or discrimination. Usually these offenses, even for the first offense, are at step 2, written warning, or step 3, final written warning.[33]

Optimal Performance

The performance management process is designed to assist employees to develop their full potential; that is, to obtain their successful performance in the work environment. An interesting article in *HR Magazine* suggests that optimal performance may require more than performance appraisal feedback. With the flattening of company structure and the emphasis on quick response, more work is being done in task forces and project teams. Employees are placed in teams with members of varying skills and must move quickly to complete their assignment before moving on to a new team and a new project.

The management consultant believes this recurring redeployment of employees is not being accomplished in an efficient manner. They may be misassigned or mismatched. The situation may also be inappropriate for the employee to achieve optimal performance.

What is optimal performance? This occurs when employees produce outstanding or optimal results. For this to take place, the employee must be selected to perform in a particular work environment requiring that person's unique talents, which lead to their high-performance pattern.

Outstanding personal success is not random, accidental, or lucky. An employee does certain things when successful which are different when not successful. When successful, the person is in their high-performance pattern. Each person has a high-performance pattern which is unique to that person. No two people have the same high-performance pattern for successful performances.

To achieve successful performance, there must be a careful people-match between the job assignments and adjustments in how work is assigned to capitalize on the unique success patterns of the team members. Some companies have tried this approach and were highly successful. From the perspective of performance management, every performance review would become an original appraisal. This would appear to require a rethinking of the performance management process.[34]

SUMMARY

The performance appraisal process is becoming increasingly important for organizations in managing and improving the performance of employees, in making timely and equitable staffing decisions, and in developing the overall quality of the firm's services or products. The success of an organization depends largely on the performance of its human resources. To identify and optimize the contributions of each individual, it is necessary to have a formal appraisal program with clearly stated objectives. Carefully defined performance standards that are relevant and reliable are essential foundations for evaluation.

If appraisal interviews and any corrective actions are to be based on valid information, managers and supervisors should be thoroughly trained in the particular methods they will use in evaluating their subordinates. Participation in developing rating scales, such as a BARS, automatically provides such training. Whatever methods are used by the organization, they should meet both the objectives of the performance appraisal system and all EEO legal standards and interventions.

REVIEW QUESTIONS

1. How would you define "performance management"?
2. Present and discuss examples of how performance appraisal techniques are used in organizations you have worked for.
3. Do you feel managers should receive training in conducting performance evaluations? Why or why not?
4. Contrast and compare the difference between performance appraisal techniques. Which is better?
5. Discuss and explain the basic problems that can arise in performance appraisal.
6. How frequently should performance appraisals take place?
7. Read a book or view a video movie, and identify organization appraisal problems.

KEY WORDS AND CONCEPTS

Define and be able to use the following:

- Appraisal Interview
- Behaviorally Anchored Rating Scales (BARS)
- Checklist Appraisals
- Critical Incidents
- Essay Appraisal
- Forced-Choice Appraisal
- Graphic Rating
- Management by Objectives (MBO)
- Paired Comparisons
- Peer Appraisal
- Performance

- Performance Appraisal
- Performance Management
- Rating Scales
- Self-Appraisals
- Standards
- Types of Validity
- Weighted Scale

HRM SKILLS SIMULATION 6.1: HR MANAGER PERFORMANCE APPROVAL

Total time suggested: 1 hour.

A. PURPOSE

In most organizations, there is a lot of untapped human potential. In an excellent, renewing organization, this potential can be released, resulting in personal growth for the individual. Personal development and organization renewal involve changes in attitudes and behavior which are related to your self-concept, role, goals, and values. In interviewing, the HR manager learns to use good interviewing skills to improve employee performance.

B. OBJECTIVE

The goal of this exercise is to begin building trust with your employees through effective performance appraisals. You will have the opportunity to gain experience interviewing another person, which is a key skill for a potential HRM manager. Keep in mind that the primary goal of performance appraisal is to improve performance.

C. PROCEDURES

Step 1. Form into groups of three, with one person acting as the employee, a second as the supervisor, and the third as observer (see Observer Recording Form). Refer to the "Instructions for Developing Interviewing Skills." The supervisor will evaluate the employee using the HRM Performance Appraisal Rating Scale and the Instructions for Developing Performance Appraisal Skills. The supervisor will assess the employee appraisal based on an entry-level HRM position, such as a recruiter. The employee has been on the job 6 months and is generally performing at a satisfactory but not very satisfactory level. The supervisor role will require you to use your imagination in providing feedback.

The observer will observe the interview relationship using the Observer Recording Form and try to provide feedback on the interview style. At the end of each interview, the observer gives observations providing feedback to the supervisor using the Observer Recording Form. Then rotate roles so that every person is in each of the three roles. Continue the simulation by switching roles until all have played each of the roles.

Time suggested for Step 1: 15–20 minutes per person (in each of the rotating roles).

Step 2. Meeting with the entire class, discuss

1. How can we improve performance appraisals?
2. What appraisal style seemed to work best?
3. Whether we view evaluation as positive or negative.
4. The role of the observer. Was it helpful? How?
5. How effective was your team?

Time suggested for Step 2: 15 minutes.

OBSERVER RECORDING FORM

Your role during this part of the simulation is important because your goal is to give the supervisor feedback. Rate the supervisor by circling the appropriate number.

NOTES:
Words,
behaviors

1. Level of involvement:
   Cautious   Low 1:2:3:4:5:6:7:8:9:10 High   Interested   _____

2. Level of communication:
   Doesn't listen   Low 1:2:3:4:5:6:7:8:9:10 High   Listens   _____

3. Level of openness, trust:
   Shy, uncertain   Low 1:2:3:4:5:6:7:8:9:10 High   Warm,
                                                                                      friendly   _____

4. Level of suggesting corrective measures: Seeks
   Authoritative   Low 1:2:3:4:5:6:7:8:9:10 High   agreement   _____

5. Level of providing direction:
   Clear   Low 1:2:3:4:5:6:7:8:9:10 High   Convincing   _____

6. Level of supportiveness:
   Disagrees   Low 1:2:3:4:5:6:7:8:9:10 High   Supports   _____

7. Level of competence:
   Unsure   Low 1:2:3:4:5:6:7:8:9:10 High   Competent   _____

8. Overall style:
   Ineffective   Low 1:2:3:4:5:6:7:8:9:10 High   Effective   _____

EMPLOYEE PERFORMANCE APPRAISAL RATING SCALE

Evaluation of Team Member

A. Cooperation   Consider: Ability and willingness to work.

Unsatisfactory	Fair	Satisfactory	Satisfaction Plus	Excellent	Outstanding
☐	☐	☐	☐	☐	☐

B. Knowledge   Consider: Technical, know-how experience.

Unsatisfactory	Fair	Satisfactory	Satisfaction Plus	Excellent	Outstanding
☐	☐	☐	☐	☐	☐

C. Accomplishment   Consider: Check his or her work. Systems of work displays good judgement. Does he or she finish assigned work satisfactorily?

Unsatisfactory	Fair	Satisfactory	Satisfaction Plus	Excellent	Outstanding
☐	☐	☐	☐	☐	☐

D. Initiative   Consider: Ability to accomplish work assignments with available resources. Does he or she go out of his or her way to do a better job?

Unsatisfactory	Fair	Satisfactory	Satisfaction Plus	Excellent	Outstanding
☐	☐	☐	☐	☐	☐

E. Organization   Consider: Ability to plan and organize work in advance. Assumes responsibility.

Unsatisfactory	Fair	Satisfactory	Satisfaction Plus	Excellent	Outstanding
☐	☐	☐	☐	☐	☐

F. Overall Rating   Consider: Each of the above rating factors.

Unsatisfactory	Fair	Satisfactory	Satisfaction Plus	Excellent	Outstanding
☐	☐	☐	☐	☐	☐

COMMENTS OF APPRAISER

_____

_____

_____

_____

Signature of Supervisor _____   Date _____

Some characteristics of interviewing include

1. Two-way communication and influence.
2. Openness of expression of views, feelings, and emotions. Being able to tell it like it is!
3. Supportiveness. When you are in agreement, give your support. Learn to express differences without offending.
4. Awareness that conflict can be creative when differences are expressed appropriately.
5. Recognition of individual differences.
6. Confrontation with employee:
   a. The courage to express your own convictions.
   b. Can you give and take feedback?
   c. Are you worried about being shot down?
7. You may try to reflect the feelings of the employee. ("You seem to feel very strongly about this").
8. You may wish to disclose something about other employees. ("This is a problem for others, also.")
9. You may wish to use silence or nonresponse; just let the employee talk.
10. Indicate nonverbally that you hear what is said. (Example: eye contact, nod of head.)

Case 6.1   Precision Products, Inc.

Helen said, "Here is one of our appraisal problems. Sheryl Schoemaker came in to see me regarding her performance appraisal. She signed the form, but wasn't happy with the appraisal process. Her boss, William, called her into his office a few minutes before quitting time to give Sheryl her annual appraisal, even though it had been over a year since her last review. As she came in, William was on the phone talking to a customer. He indicated the appraisal form and said to her, 'Look it over and sign on the line. You'll notice I've given you good ratings.' Sheryl looked the form over, but she wanted William to spend some time discussing how she could get promoted. He said, 'Just sign the form. We have to get it in, so we'll talk about it later.'" ∎

QUESTIONS

1. Why do you think William did not take adequate time to explain the appraisal ratings to Sheryl?
2. What procedure should Helen follow in correcting this problem? Should she contact William directly?
3. How do you believe Sheryl will continue to perform on her job—more effective or less? Explain.

ENDNOTES

1. Tom Peters, *Thriving on Chaos* (New York: Alfred A. Knopf, Inc., 1987), 284–87.
2. D. Turacamo, "How am I doing," *HR Magazine* 37, no. 3 (1992): 110. See also Dennis Guessford et al., "Tracking Job Skills Improves Performance," *Personnel Journal* 72, no. 6 (June 1993): 109–14.
3. P. M. Podasakoff, M. L. Williams, and W. E. Scott, "Myths of Employee Selection," in R. S. Schuler, ed., *Readings on Personnel* (St. Paul: West, 1988), 178.
4. Lindo, David K., "Where's my raise?" *Supervision* 60, no. 4 (April 1999): 6–8.
5. Mary Ellen Duckett, "The Positive Side of Performance Reviews," *Sourcebook* (Spring 1991): 14; C. Hymowitz, "Bosses Don't Be Nasty and Other Tips for Reviewing Performance," *Wall Street Journal*, 17 January 1985, p. 28.
6. J. S. Kane and K. F. Kane, "A Survey of Performance Appraisal Effectiveness in Fortune 500 Firms: A Report of the Findings." Unpublished report, 1988.
7. Marilyn Moats Kennedy, "The Case for Performance Appraisals," *Across the Board* 36, no. 2 (February 1999): 51–52.
8. W. H. Wagel, "A Software Link Between Performance Appraisals and Merit Increases," *Personnel* 65, no. 3 (1988): 9–14. See also Laurie Hays, "IBM's Finance Chief Scours Empire for Costs to Cut," *Wall Street Jour-*

nal, 26 January 1994, p. 1; and Peter Eyes, "Realignment Ties Pay to Performance," *Personnel Journal* 72, no. 1 (January 1993): 74–77.

9. P. R. Sackett, S. Zedeck, and L. Fogli, "Relations Between Measures of Typical and Maximum Job Performance," *Journal of Applied Psychology* 73 (1988): 482–86.

10. Douglas G. Huet-Cox, Tjai M. Nielsen, and Eric Sundstrom, "Get the most from 360 degree feedback: put it on the Internet," *HRM Magazine* (May 1999): 92.

11. M. Duckett, "The Positive Side of Performance Reviews," *Sourcebook* (Spring 1991): 14–15. See also A. Haron, T. Ziner, Richard Kopelman, and Neomi Zivneh, "Effects of Performance Appraisal Format on Perceived Goal Characteristics Approval Process Satisfaction, and Changes in Ratio Job Performance," *Journal of Psychology* 127, no. 993, 281–91.

12. A. H. Locher and K. S. Teel, "Performance Appraisal: A Survey of Current Practices," *Personnel Journal* 56 (1977): 245–55.

13. Donald J. Klein, and Suzanne M. Crampton, "Helpful hints for sending criticism," *Workforce* 78, no. 3 (March 1999): 9.

14. H. Z. Levine, "Performance Appraisals at Work," *Personnel* 3, no. 6 (1986): 63–71.

15. M. R. Edwards, "Implementation Strategies for Multiple Rater Systems," *Personnel Journal* 69, no. 9 (1990): 130, 132, 134, 137, 139.

16. D. Waldman and R. Kenett, "Improve Performance by Appraisal," *HR Magazine* 35, no. 7 (July 1990): 66–69. See also Bradford A. Johnson and Harry H. Ray, "Employee-Developed Pay System Increases Productivity," *Personnel Journal* 72, no. 11 (November 1993): 112–18.

17. M. Levy, "Almost-Perfect Performance Appraisals," *Personnel Journal* 68, no. 4 (1989): 76, 77, 78, 80, 83.

18. Marilyn Moats Kennedy, "The case against performance appraisals," *Across the Board* 36, no. 1 (January 1999): 51–2.

19. P. W. Dorfman, W. G. Stephan, and J. Loveland, "Performance Appraisal Behaviors: Supervisor Perceptions and Subordinate Reactions," *Personnel Psychology* 39 (1986): 579–97.

20. Robert Bookman, "Tools for cultivating constructive feedback," *Association Management* 51, no. 2 (February 1999): 73–74.

21. Jim Mead, "Visual 360: a performance appraisal system that's fun," *HR Magazine* (July 1999): 118.

22. Jonathan H. Segal, "Performance Management For Jekyll and Hyde," *HR Magazine* (February 1999): 130–35.

23. Gordon W. Cheung, "Multifaceted conceptions of self-other ratings disagreement," *Personnel Psychology* 52, no. 1 (Spring 1999): 1–36.

24. John Hulpke. 1994. California State University.

25. S. J. Ashford and L. L. Cummings, "Feedback As An Individual Resource: Personal Strategies of Creating Information," *Organizational Behavior and Human Performance* 32 (1983): 370–98. See also John Watt, "The Impact and the Frequency of Information on the Performance Evaluation of Bank Personnel," *Journal of Psychology* 127 (1993): 171–77.

26. G. B. Northcraft and P. C. Earley, "Technology, Credibility, and Feedback Use," *Organizational Behavior and Human Decision Processes* 44 (1989): 83–96.

27. A. Gabor, "Take This Job and Love It," *New York Times,* 26 January 1992, pp. F1, F6.

28. David E. Bowen, Stephen W. Gilliland, and Robert Floger, "HRM and service fairness: how being fair with employees spills over to customers," *Organizational Dynamics* 27, no. 3 (Winter 1999): 6–23.

29. B. R. Mohrman, A. M. Mohrman Jr., and J. Milliman, "Interpersonal Relations As A Context for the Effects of Appraisal Interviews on Performance and Satisfaction: A Longitudinal Study," *Academy of Management Journal* 34 (1991): 352–69. See also J. Michael Crant and Thomas Bateman, "Assignment of Credit and Blame for Performance Outcomes," *Academy of Management Journal* 36 (1993): 7–27.

30. Dominc Bencivenga, "Dealing with the Dark Side," *HR Magazine* (January 1999): 50–58.

31. Jo Ellen Moore, "Are You Burning Out Valuable Resources," *HR Magazine* (January 1999): 93–97.

32. P. P. Schoderbek and Satish P. Deshpande, "Performance and Non-Performance Factors in Pay Allocations Made by Managers," *Journal of Psychology* 127 (1993): 391–98.

33. Paul Falcone, "Adopt a Formal Approach to Progressive Discipline," *HR Magazine* (November 1998): 55–59.

34. Jerry L. Fletcer, "Heading Toward Optimal Performance," *HR Magazine* (March 1998): 47–50.

Chapter 7

The Success System: Training and Developing Human Potential

Objectives

Upon completing this chapter, you will be able to:

1. Define the concept and major purposes of training in an organization.
2. Describe the steps in developing and implementing an effective orientation and training program.
3. Understand the uses of a systems approach to training in an organization.
4. Identify and describe the major types of training methods and techniques.

Premeeting preparation

1. Read chapter 7.
2. Prepare for HRM Skills Simulation 7.1. Complete Step 1.
3. Read Case 7.1: Precision Products, Inc.

Today's managers face greater challenges than ever to maintain their position among the top economic powers. American businesses are realizing that their place at the top is not guaranteed, and that they must find solutions to the declining productivity, competitiveness, motivation, and creativity of the workforce.[1] For example, the first 6 months after Rohr bought a new plant it spent $500,000 to $600,000 on training for a workforce of less than 500 people. Productivity didn't just improve at Rohr, it skyrocketed. By the end of the second year, "we were, and we still are, the shining star of Rohr Industries. We're the most productive, highest-quality facility," one Rohr supervisor said. "This workforce is basically a model for this type of participation."

Traditional management may be a lot easier, Rohr's General Manager Larry Stewart said, but it is much less rewarding. "Empowering people is a lot tougher, but it's a lot of fun. You enjoy it more." People want to be challenged, he said. "The workforce is completely changed; it's imperative that companies make the change" with them if they don't want to lose their best and brightest people. Instead, Rohr operates with a positive employee philosophy (PEP) that stresses service, commitment, teamwork, ownership, and ethical behavior. Rohr's Human Resource Director Michael Murray said, "If you want to be a world-class manufacturer, the greatest resource is the force working for you."[2]

During the 2000s, employee training will become increasingly important because of the pressures to reduce costs and increase productivity. The combination of increasing global competition, an expensive workforce, and cheap computers has severed the link between economic growth and job growth. American companies are learning that they can't compete in world markets unless they boost productivity and invest in a higher-trained and skilled workforce.[3] Employee training is a key factor in improving levels of organization productivity. Therefore, it is important that the organization enable employees to upgrade their skills and knowledge to meet these changing conditions.[4]

There is a growing body of evidence that suggests workplace training offers a significant return on the investment. A study reported that firms who spent an average of $900 per employee increased net sales $386,171 on average per employee from one year to the next. Firms who spent $275 per employee increased net sales $245,001. This represents a difference of net sales per employee of $141,170.[5]

In the future, the only winning companies will be those that respond quickly to changing conditions, increasing workforce diversity, and the critical issue of training-related problems. At one company, turnover has been reduced by better screening, preemployment requirements, a good benefits program, and a good training and communication program.[6] Preparing employees to function in a high-performing system is an important HR activity and is the focus of this chapter. The modern HR manager must not only be flexible and adaptive in a changing environment, but must also be able to develop a systems approach to training. Rapidly changing technology necessitates employees who have the skills, abilities, and knowledge to keep up with new, complex production processes and techniques.

Training is a process that begins with the orientation of the new employee and continues throughout an employee's career. Therefore, it is important that the HR manager develop training programs to improve employee skills and performance in a changing labor force. IBM reportedly spends over $1 billion yearly on the education of its employees.[7]

Training is critical because it provides the skills needed both now and in the future.[8] The underlying assumption is: If an individual employee becomes more productive and more involved, the total organization will also be improved.

An overlooked benefit of training is when it is a continuing process rather than occasional. It has been found that when companies train their employees continually, not only is there a high level of performance, but it also helps to eliminate a negative workplace.[9]

In this chapter, we present the next stage of the Success System Model: developing human potential. We discuss the purpose and importance of training and development programs. In the Success System, implementing a successful training program involves not only selecting appropriate techniques aimed at changing an organization's effectiveness, but also at enhancing the development of the organization's employees—its human resources.

WHAT ARE TRAINING AND DEVELOPMENT?

What makes one organization a winner when another fails to make use of the same opportunities? Too many Americans lack the skills needed to flourish in the laser-fast, high-performance, totally empowered, fully global world of the 2000s. Former Labor Secretary Robert Reich says: "American companies have got to be urged to treat their workers as assets to be developed, rather than as costs to be cut."

Smart businesses realize that they, not the government, must take responsibility for training workers. Nearly four in ten members of the National Association of Manufacturers say that deficiencies in math, reading, and technical skills are causing "serious problems" in upgrading factories and increasing productivity. Companies cannot wait for the schools to solve America's education crisis. The Bureau of Labor estimates that nearly two-thirds of the workers who will be in the labor force in the year 2005 are already on the job.[10]

Training

Although training and development are similar, and both are critical to the Success System Model, there are some important differences. **Training** may be defined as an attempt to improve performance by the attainment of specific skills such as typing, welding, running a computer, and so forth, to do the current job. The goal of training is to ensure that a number of job skills will be performed at prescribed quality levels by trained employees. In essence, training is investing in human resources. It tends to broaden the focus of the employee being trained.

Some of the best training in America takes place at Motorola. Its factory workers study the fundamentals of computer-aided design, robotics, and customized manufacturing, not just by reading manuals or attending lectures, but by inventing and building their own plastic knickknacks as well. The company runs its worldwide training programs from Motorola University, a collection of computer-equipped classrooms and laboratories at corporate headquarters in Schaumburg, Illinois.

Motorola calculates that for every dollar it spends on training, it receives $30 in productivity gains within 3 years. The company has cut costs by $3.3 billion—not by the normal expedient of firing workers, but by training them to simplify processes and reduce waste. Sales per employee have doubled in the past 5 years, and profits have increased 47 percent.[11]

Development

Development, however, is more general than training, and refers to learning opportunities designed to help employees grow. This provides employees with less detailed information, but provides broader learning which may be utilized in a variety of settings and for future jobs. Some examples would include learning computer programming so one could write programs, understanding human behavior as it relates to motivation, understanding TQM so it may be applied to quality control, and so on. The goal of development is to broaden the employee's comprehension of generalized situations that may overlap into specific events. In essence, development is macro, not micro. It results in comprehension of processes, and, through this understanding, results in better job performance.

An example of such a program is Six Sigma which is used by General Electric, Weyerhauser, Citicorp, Johnson and Johnson, Black and Decker, Motorola, and Allied Signal to develop new management talent. The challenge is to master the Six Sigma discipline that leads to black belts.

So what is a business black belt? Well, it is no relation to karate chops. Six Sigma was first started by Motorola Corporation with a rigorous training program to provide managers with specialized measurement and statistical tools to reduce costs in products and processes.

Candidates in training need to be grounded in math, statistics, data analysis, finance, and computer skills. Upon completion of the intensive training, which takes months, you become a green belt. You are now capable of reducing quality defects to the level of 3.4 per million products or processes and shrinking project costs. Complete more projects and you graduate to a black belt. Continuing on you will eventually reach the status of master black belt.

At Motorola's Advanced Technology Center, unlike some company's training, Motorola's focus is on interpersonal skills such as team building and consulting plus technical topics. Although interpersonal skills may be alien to some researchers, it allows graduates to tackle a wide range of problems.[12]

Combination Programs

Training programs may combine both training and development. In fact, development is becoming more of a factor in training programs as the business world begins to experience the serious deterioration of the education system in grades K through 12. As global competition increases, training programs for management are becoming more educational in scope, with instruction in such fields as ethnic and cultural development in the world marketplace.

An example of development is the problem of technical versus managerial expertise allowing for promotion of both and not creating dead-end jobs. One answer is to develop dual career paths allowing both groups promotional and development opportunities. Many industries have used this procedure and it is now quite common in information technology (IT) departments. By creating two career development paths—one by the traditional route of assuming management responsibilities and the other by moving up a technical ladder—this helps to cut turnover while building more efficient IT groups.[13]

PROBLEMS IN TRAINING

The size of the training problem becomes evident when one considers that some 95 percent of 21- to 25-year-olds in this country can only read at a fourth grade level. If we are to solve the training problem, it will require upgrading the skills of 50 million Americans by a factor of 40 percent in the twenty-first century. Even with a 100 percent success rate, it would take 5 years to succeed. Time is rapidly running out.[14]

What has caused this problem? Many members of the media, the public, and even some school administrators blame the educational system for bad habits. This would include using calculators instead of learning multiplication tables, and using computers for spell check rather than learning the basic spelling patterns. To some, it is the "dumbing down of America."

Although the above arguments have merit, we should not overlook the benefits that calculators and computers have brought us. Without them, we would not be enjoying the wide spread prosperity of the twenty-first century. However, the problem is real and as a human resource manager of a computer chip manufacturing corporation summed up, ". . . academically the job pool is certainly more shallow than it used to be."[15]

Another aspect of the training problem are the changes occurring in the demographics of entry-level persons entering the workforce. For the next several decades, entrants between the ages of 16 to 24 will decrease substantially. Within this group, the number of white males will also decline, and the proportion of minority groups will increase significantly. There will be more women, minorities, and older workers. The number of individuals in the age bracket between 45 and 65 will increase by at least 25 percent. However, even with the increased number of older workers, minorities, and women, the growth of the total workforce will be lower than in the past.[16]

Change in Technology

Many companies will have hundreds or thousands of employees in different jobs. Each job will have its own specific requirements and challenges. The HRM problem is to be able to match employees' skills with job requirements. Also, it is necessary to identify which important skills they do not have. Then, for the skills they lack, what type of training will provide those skills? Once all of this has been determined, how does HRM keep track of the training?

This is a large problem that is time-consuming, but must be accurate or the costs will be very large. Enter the computer with software to eliminate these problems. One such software is TRACCESS which will track each employee's training progress. It will also systematically measure employee competencies and then provide links to a variety of coursework to fulfill deficiencies. This is all structured so the employees complete the instruction at their own pace.[17]

In addition, the trend toward high technology in work processes requires programmable automation of robots and multifunctional machines and a more highly trained workforce. So the question becomes: How do we train these less skilled workers to become more effective performers? In the following sections, we will provide some possible solutions.

From the HRM viewpoint, it is important to recognize that technology does not take away jobs. What it does is create more demands on skills which require more training programs. In essence, work is an endless experience because people's expectations grow.

The issue for employees is not to worry about their present jobs continuing to exist, but rather whether they will have the new skills for future employment.[18] Studies indicate employees will have at least four major job changes in their lifetime.[19] Training and retraining programs will be their salvation.

THE TRAINING PROCESS

The present expenditure by business firms in the United States for training exceeds $100 billion.[20] Unfortunately, some of this money is wasted on unnecessary or obsolete training programs. To ensure that training dollars are invested wisely requires the same logic used in all management decisions. The manager must

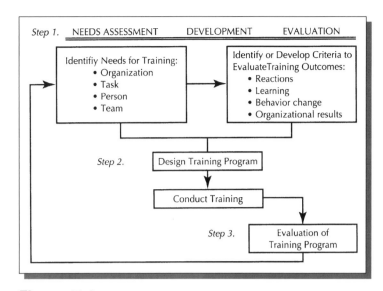

Figure 7.1
The success system model of training and development

(**1**) identify training needs and establish specific objectives and evaluation criteria, (**2**) design the appropriate training methods and conduct the training; and (**3**) evaluate the results of the training. (See Figure 7.1.)

STEP ONE: IDENTIFYING TRAINING NEEDS

The initial step in a training program is to identify training needs, often termed **needs assessment.** The needs assessment refers to a systematic, objective identification of training needs. Training needs can usually be determined by consulting with appropriate managerial personnel regarding the results of assessment centers, areas of need revealed through employee performance appraisals, and determining managers' concerns for specific training needs to improve bottom-line performance. If such needs can be pinpointed by hard data, survey information, and not by vague concerns of need, training improvements will result in increased employee efficiency. (See cartoon.)

Source: THE WIZARD OF ID by permission of Brant Parker and Johnny Hart and by Creators Syndicate, Inc.

The second step in a training program is developing **training objectives** and criteria. The instructional objectives and criteria describe the performance in terms of training. One example of an objective would be the attainment of a specific skill or performing a work task within a certain time frame. An example of a criteria would be a specified score on a test instrument or validation of performing a specific operation flawlessly a number of times.

There are two advantages to developing objectives. First, the objectives provide criteria for evaluating the training program. Second, the objectives provide trainers with the specific topics and content to focus on. This ensures that training programs are focusing on important topics and goals that have meaning to trainees.

Achieving the objectives and criteria can be accomplished through the selection of an appropriate training approach. The basic techniques include coaching, internship, on-the-job training, apprenticeship, job rotation, job instruction method, mentoring, case method, continuing education, college and correspondence courses, lectures, role-playing, simulation, programmed instruction, and vestibule training. These training methods can be used to achieve either one or a combination of learning objectives: cognitive, noncognitive, and psychomotor. Cognitive learning relates to job specifics. It is concerned with facts and method sequences. Noncognitive is concerned with behaviors: creating and responding to position requirements. Psychomotor involves performing tasks requiring the use of the hands, feet, and body.

These three learning types can be accomplished through the following training methods.

Orientation Training

Walt Disney Productions uses training to achieve their image of wholesome entertainment, cleanliness, and friendly employees.[21] This takes place in Traditions I, the initial orientation program for all new employees which stresses the four Disney disciplines of safety, courtesy, show, and efficiency. Once hired, employees are eligible for cross-utilization training such as teaching Traditions I. As a result of in-house training, some 70 percent of the promotions at Disney come from within.

Employee training and development has been defined as any attempt to improve current or future employee performance by increasing an employee's ability to perform.[22] Training usually consists of instructional programs aimed at improving performance of the individual, team, and organization. This implies that there will be some form of measurable change in output, knowledge, skills, motivation, or behavior. One of the key elements in a training program which sets the tone for the whole organization is the orientation of the new employee.

Orientation training may be defined as training that introduces new employees to the organization and learning the ropes, and familiarizes them with the rules, procedures, tasks, and values of the organization. In general, the orientation process accomplishes the socialization of the new employee.[23] Socialization (as noted earlier in chapter 1) refers to a new employee learning the norms, values, goals, work procedures, and patterns of behavior that are expected by the organization. (See Our Changing World.)

According to one study, 80 percent of U.S. organizations provide some form of orientation.[25] It is estimated the cost of hiring, orienting, and training an employee may run between $50 to thousands of dollars. This is a critical stage because it often takes a period of time before the new employee begins to fully contribute to the organization. Also, there is often a high rate of turnover among newer employees. Turnover often runs as high as 40 percent during the first year among new college recruits, representing a costly investment in recruiting to the organization. The initial period in an organization is also a critical point in determining whether a new employee will become a high performer, or simply perform at a minimum, mediocre level. This is why HR activities, through training and development, need to reinforce what is important to the organization.

In-House Coaching

Coaching requires a person who has the necessary knowledge to instruct other individuals on a one-to-one or small group basis. The coach most often is a supervisor, but may be a coworker. Coaching is most often associated with team sports, such as baseball and football, where individual and team skills are developed through practice and critique. Although knowledge of the task is important, an effective coach must also possess the ability to communicate the information to the individual in an efficient manner. The coach and the one being coached must develop a mutual trusting relationship, if this method is to be successful.

Coaching Consultants

A significant number of companies in the United States are recognizing the twenty-first century will witness the departure of 40 to 50 percent of their executives. This is particularly true of the larger, older companies. The continuing pace of early retirements, restructuring, mergers, and lean hierarchies have greatly reduced the once deep pool of middle managers. This is the very same group that was traditionally developed to become the next generation of executives.[26]

The problem is very common in workplaces around the country and is creating the soaring popularity of a management tool called executive coaching. These coaches are consultants who assist companies to prepare for succession by identifying and training the future top executives. They act as confidants to help and prod executives to enhance their performance on the job. Some executive consultants guide just-appointed managers to fulfill the expected role in their new jobs.

In our global world of work with an increasing fragmented workforce, the role of the executive consultant has found a special niche. Approximately 70 percent of the top 1,000 firms worldwide do some form of executive consultant coaching. A large number of mergers and acquisitions fail to achieve their projected bottom line because executives lack soft people skills to overcome cultural clashes.

Companies are finding that weeklong training programs fail to produce long-term results. However, when the executive consultant is added to the mix, employees are learning continually. Although training programs are usually general in nature, the executive consultant is more tailored to a manager's potential and skills.[27]

Internships

Interns usually follow a formalized training program. An internship program usually consists of a series of job assignments over specific time periods designed to prepare a person for greater job responsibilities. To ensure interns make the necessary progress in their job assignments, a daily log of their activities is kept and/or written reports are reviewed by appropriate supervisors. These jobs are usually channeled through the internship coordinator who oversees the progress and functions as the administrator of the internship program.

On-the-Job Training

On-the-job training is probably the most widely used method of training. One survey suggests that 90 percent of all industrial training is conducted at the work site.[28] In on-the-job training, the employee is placed in the work situation and the supervisor instructs the employee in how the job is done directly at the workstation. On-the-job training has several major advantages. First, it is cost efficient. Workers actually produce while they learn. Second, it builds motivation and involves a feedback situation.[29] Finally, it minimizes problems of **transfer of training.** When employees learn in the actual job situation, the skills learned are the ones needed.[30]

Although on-the-job training is usually low cost and practical, it does have some disadvantages. Because training is conducted at the normal production point, trainees may damage equipment, cause excessive waste materials, and involve significantly higher accident rates.[31]

Another major disadvantage of on-the-job training centers around the trainer. In the majority of cases, the instructors are either supervisors or experienced line workers. In either case, the trainer may not have the training skills, interest, or time necessary to properly train the new employee. These conditions could produce improperly trained employees who, through no fault of their own, are not performing the job at a high level of productivity and safety.

Apprenticeship Training

Among the oldest type of on-the-job training is **apprenticeship training.** This training is commonly used by industries including metalworking, construction, and auto repair, where the apprentices are trainees who spend a set period of time (usually 2 to 3 years) working with an experienced journeyman. When used properly, an apprenticeship program allows the worker to earn wages while learning in both on- and off-the-job situations.

The major disadvantage to apprenticeship training seems the set time period placed on all enrolled in the program. People have different abilities and learning rates, but all must serve the predetermined training period.

Apprenticeships are often used by unions, and are registered with the U.S. Department of Labor. The apprentice agrees to work at less than trade wages in exchange for training at a specific trade (i.e., plumber, electrician, etc.). On-the-job training is provided by fully qualified union personnel. Depending upon the trade, there are varying amounts of classroom training. Although the apprenticeship may run from 2 to 5 years, the programs are very comprehensive and may actually result in overtraining.

In the changing technological environment of the 2000s, apprenticeship programs also face new challenges. A trainee may spend several years learning a specific job skill, then find upon completion of the apprenticeship that these job skills are no longer needed.

Job Rotation

Job rotation training involves moving trainees around among different jobs within the organization. This system is often used for management-level training and self-managed work team programs. Job rotation allows the employee to learn several job skills and a wide range of operations within an organization. Cross-trained personnel also provide greater flexibility for organizations when unexpected transfers, absence, promotions, or other replacements may become necessary. Job rotation usually takes place at the same pay rate. It often occurs when the job is temporarily vacant due to a vacation, illness, or termination. The employee benefits from learning a variety of skills. The company benefits from having a group of experienced candidates from whom to choose when vacancies occur.

An example is the electronics company, Graphic Controls Corporation, that established a program to cross-train workers for highly skilled positions in its twenty-department manufacturing area. The program's goals were to produce a versatile, qualified workforce, willing to work in departments where there was a need.[32]

The Job Instruction Method

The **Job Instruction Method (JIM)** is a formalized on-the-job training method where the employee follows a series of written instructions to complete a procedure or to operate machinery. These written instructions may be provided by the manufacturer of the equipment or by skilled company employees. The JIM is effective for repetitive situations.

Programmed instruction (PI) provides the employee with short segments of information who then respond to selected questions. If the answer is correct, the employee moves on to newer, more complicated segments of information. If the answer is wrong, the employee returns to the previous short segment of information and tries again. Because this approach is self-correcting, it is fast, and, for some individuals, is a more effective learning tool.

Computer-Assisted Instruction

One popular method of training is **programmed instruction** or **computer-assisted instruction.** This involves a self-taught, self-paced learning system, usually using computers which eliminates the need for an instructor. Material is presented to trainees in written form, or by computer programs through a series of self-paced steps. Each step consists of factual material to be mastered, which is directly followed by a question. The trainees' responses are immediately verified after each question. If the replies are correct, the trainees proceed to the next item. If the responses are incorrect, the question is repeated. One survey suggests that 80 percent of *Fortune* 500 firms are using computers for training.[33] Computer-aided instruction offers the advantage of individualized training. Trainees progress at their own pace, receive immediate feedback, and are active, as opposed to passive, learners. The potential of computer-aided instruction is limited only by the amount of training needs, and is becoming one of the most popular training methods.

Vestibule Training

The vestibule is one of the earliest methods used in business training. It originally referred to a hallway where the employee learned to operate equipment correctly and then proceeded to the shop floor for the real thing. Today, it would be a room that duplicates the shop floor. It provides an environment where the employee can learn to produce a high-quality volume of goods with a minimal loss to the employer in defective goods and costly repair.

In **vestibule training,** the trainee learns the job in an off-site environment that simulates the actual workplace. Many companies have a small area within the plant set up for this type of training. Many larger organizations actually develop training schools. One example would be the flight simulators, which duplicate airplane cockpits, used by Boeing to train airline pilots.

There are several advantages to vestibule training. It provides on-the-job training in a controlled environment with a professionally trained staff. Motivation is usually high, the trainees receive individual attention, and training focuses on job skills. The disadvantage, however, is higher cost. Unless an organization is experiencing rapid growth or is continually hiring large numbers of new employees, the cost of vestibule programs may not be justified.

Strategic Partners

There is a new breed of HRM executives who take a broader, more strategic view of employee training. One of these is the supervisor for training and organizational development at the U.S. Steel group's Monongahela Valley plant in Pennsylvania.

In a 2-month training program, every member of the plant's 2,400 employees learned every aspect of the operation. They started with the mechanics of customer orders and on to the effect of market economics. The goal of the program is to have a partnership in which all partners have the same information so they can make quality decisions.

The reason for the program is the great competitive changes in the steel industry. In the Pittsburgh area over 40,000 steel worker jobs were lost due to uncompetitive pricing.

The plan is to move the partners and skills quickly within the different work areas. It will be a quick, agile, fast turnaround involving everyone. Both top-level management and the union approved the strategic program which was prepared in 18 months by an outside vendor.[34]

Mentoring

Mentoring establishes a formal relationship between junior and senior colleagues, or between a person with superior knowledge and a less experienced employee. It is similar to a parent-child relationship in that one provides guidance and tutorship in the ways of career success, including sponsorship, coaching, and protection of the colleague, exposure to important contacts, and assignment of challenging work.[35]

A mentor can be an important aid in the development of the junior person, and may also be valuable for improving the job involvement and satisfaction of the mentor. Several companies who offer formal mentoring programs include Federal Express, Xerox, Merrill Lynch, and The Jewel Companies.[36]

The mentor begins by determining the employee's job and the direction of the subsequent career path. Together, the mentor and the employee should develop career goals based on abilities and company promotional opportunities. One approach is for both parties to maintain a diary of events both as feedback and agreement of the progress attained.

An evaluation format should be established at the start of the mentoring program. This can be as simple as both parties discussing progress or evaluations by other managers of the employee, or more formal committee reviews at various points in the program.

The Case Method

The case method is a useful tool in classroom training sessions. Because the case is usually a generalized version of an actual job situation, it provides authentic data and the opportunity to suggest appropriate corrective action. Each trainee reads a case report which describes an organizational situation; then, in a team, they discuss problems, and present differing viewpoints and a plan of action.

Off-the-Job Training

Aside from initial orientation, on-the-job apprenticeship, and vestibule training programs, most other industry training probably occurs away from the actual job location. These programs may be taught by staff, professional trainers and consultants, or university faculty.

Off-the-job training provides a variety of training which would not otherwise be available to smaller companies. Programs can be designed to meet training needs without being restricted by the lack of organizational resources. Typically, off-the-job training creates an environment for learning.

Employers not only need to know the training needs of their employees, but also need to understand their learning preferences. This point is emphasized in a report done by Peggy Stuart, who found that many companies use a learning style inventory to determine employee preferences for learning.[37]

Once the training program is completed, if the employee can continue self-directed learning, then it becomes cost-effective to teach and demonstrate learning style theory. One approach to transfer of training is to provide a mentor in the workplace to reinforce what has been learned. This way, the learning experience continues in the workplace.

Continuing Education

Continuing education courses may be offered by colleges or professional organizations. They are usually of short duration and take place away from the organization. Topics range from self-improvement and learning particular skills to maintaining a desired level of professionalism (such as in nursing or accounting).

College and correspondence courses include educational, vocational, and technical. As a result of their broad range, they provide a valuable supplement to a company's training program. From the company's viewpoint, problems that occur include the course content may not satisfy the organization's specific needs and employee progress is difficult to monitor. (See HRM in Action.)

HRM IN ACTION
RETRAINING THROUGH COOPERATIVE EDUCATION

More and more Americans lack the kind of skills they need to get or keep high-paying jobs as employers react to foreign competition, labor-saving technologies, and other forces of rapid change. Cooperative education links job-related instruction in the classroom and paid work experience, usually in alternating terms for 2 to 4 years. Around the United States, many institutions offer such programs.

But the most successful training programs are overwhelmingly tilted toward the lower-paid factory and office workers. They identify a growing number of jobs that

require a couple of years of technical training, not advanced degrees, because the new breed of worker is often linked to a smart machine or computer. For instance, the 2-year chemical engineering technology program at Kansas State University/Salina College of Technology can't meet the demand for its yearly handful of graduates, who operate instruments that perform chemical analysis, mainly for environmental monitoring.

Ironically, the combination of such tools and technicians helps put higher-paid professional engineers out of work. What's worse, there are few retraining programs

---

for such professionals—or for the middle managers who once performed staff functions for big companies—mostly because generalized instruction is rarely relevant to their next jobs, says Anthony Carnevale, chief economist at American Society for Training and Development in Washington, D.C. The key thing a staff manager lacks is a deep understanding of his next employer's culture and industry, and that can be gained only through years of on-the-job experience.

Lecture formats allow the employer to present a large amount of material in a limited time frame. To overcome the problems of boredom and fatigue, the lecture may be supplemented with role-playing and simulations. Role-playing allows the employee to act out situations while applying the knowledge obtained from the lecture. The same can be said for simulations, which are a form of individual group exercises designed to solve business problems. One form of simulation is the in-basket exercise, where the individual learns to prioritize time and effective decision-making skills as one responds to memos, letters, telephone call slips, and reports within a limited time frame.

Following the establishment of the training needs and the developing of training objectives and criteria, the next step is the selection of the appropriate teaching method. The final step in the training procedure is the evaluation or appraisal of the effectiveness of the training methods.

QUESTIONS

1. Why is cooperative education directed to lower-paid factory and office workers? What are the advantages and disadvantages?

2. Cooperative education identifies jobs requiring a few years of technical training, not advanced degrees. How does this affect higher-paid professionals?

3. What are some of the more effective training formats? Discuss the ones you think most effective and least effective.

A twenty-first century solution to the problem presented in the previous paragraph is a program developed by Act Inc. of Iowa City, Iowa. The company's best known expertise is college-extrance exams but it is now expanding to testing and training networks.

Their new service includes testing for job needs profiles and providing a network of more than 200 centers at community colleges. These centers will evaluate the skills of job applicants and workers to determine their deficiencies. Then the centers will provide the required training per the employers' specific job requirements. In Texas, Austin Community College believes the low-cost software training library ACT provides will be an immediate success.[38]

STEP THREE: THE EVALUATION OF TRAINING

Evaluation involves gathering information on whether trainees were satisfied with and learned from the training. The evaluation considers several areas: Was the designated need or objective met and the specified criteria satisfied? Was the teaching method selected effective for the individual to learn? And finally, will the evaluation assist the instructor to be more effective in the teaching role?[39]

The answer to the first area of concern—whether the designated needs were met and the specific criteria satisfied—involves both the trainee and the trainee's supervisor. Some type of test will often measure the trainee's accumulation of knowledge. However, the key area is whether the training received by the employee translates back on the job to increased effectiveness. This knowledge is possessed by the supervisor who should be surveyed through some form of written appraisal after the trainee has returned to the job for an appropriate time period.

Whether the selected teaching method was effective will be the result of summating the trainee's test scores and the supervisor's rating of whether the employee is now more effective on the job. The final area of concern is the effectiveness of the instructor. The same evaluative data used in the previous appraisal can be used here also, although the analysis will be somewhat different. The student test scores and the supervisor's evaluation need to be reviewed for possible areas of course weakness and curriculum deficiencies. After determining these effects, the instructor can determine the appropriate changes at the teaching level to increase effectiveness.

A SYSTEMATIC APPROACH

A systematic approach is one reason that successful companies, like Walt Disney, are committed to training and developing their employees. Training is an investment in current and future employee performance. The purposes of training include

1. Orienting new employees.
2. Improving productivity.
3. Developing employee skill levels.
4. Enhancing job competency.
5. Solving organizational problems.
6. Developing promotable employees from within the organization.

In any organization, commitment to training must start at the top, as is the case with CEO Michael Eisner of The Walt Disney Company. At Disneyland, for example, customer service is the key to its success, and all employees are trained to focus on customer satisfaction. The true key to successful change is employee involvement and commitment. (See HRM in Action.)

HRM IN ACTION
COMMITMENT TO TRAINING AT TARGET STORES[40]

Even when a company is upsizing, training can be critical. Target Stores is a big company that is—believe it or not—hiring. A division of Dayton Hudson, the middle-market retail chain operates 506 stores in 32 states, and plans to open as many as 250 outlets and add up to 10,000 workers in the next 5 years. The Minneapolis company has used training to transform a hierarchical culture into one that invests employees (often young people earning low wages) with new powers to please customers. One of the first things they learn: to refer to shoppers as "guests." (As noted earlier, this originated at Disney.)

Whenever Target opens a new store, it sets up a Target University, a movable frolic of a course conducted by a veteran manager from one of the chain's other outlets. In a fast-paced, 4-hour session, sales clerks use role-playing to learn how to deal with Bad Mouth Betty, Hysterical Harold, and other "customers from hell." Target U. teaches the tenets of the chain's new "fast, fun, friendly" environment: Schmooze with your guests. Compliment them on their clothing. If they're buying pet food, talk to them about their dog, but never, never tell them to "have a nice day." (That phrase, says trainer Al Linner, is "the worst thing that California ever did to the rest of the country.") If a customer has a problem, don't bounce it upstairs. Deal with it. And never say: "Our policy is . . ."

Target U. also relies on novel methods to teach salesclerks the importance of helping one another. In one team-building exercise, employees linked in a human chain must each wriggle through two Hula-Hoops moving in opposite directions, without breaking the chain or letting the hoops touch the ground.

The new training has had a dramatic impact on employee turnover, which peaked at 89 percent among hourly workers in 1989—the year Target U. was born—and dropped to 59 percent in 1992. Customer service, as measured by the stores' semiannual surveys, has been on a steady upward trend. Says Senior Vice President Larry Gilpin: "Training was absolutely critical to bringing all this to life."

QUESTIONS

1. What is Target's training program investing in their employees? Is it effective?
2. How does Target train new employees? Discuss one aspect of the program you think is particularly important.
3. Do you approve or disapprove of the Hula-Hoops? Discuss.

TRAINING FOR WORKERS WITH DISABILITIES

When a company makes a commitment to hire persons with disabilities, the HRM department should consider special procedures for ensuring their job success. Such procedures may be a special budget requirement to fund the costs of identifying appropriate jobs and necessary workplace adjustments, reviewing their job process, training coworkers and supervisors in appropriate behavior and work expectations.

Management and coworkers need to know the disabled employee's qualifications and limitations. This may require a meeting of the interested parties including the disabled employee to make the job transition problem-free.

The effective manager will be ready to provide counseling. This process may be initiated by the employee or by the manager immediately upon identifying problems. Topics to be discussed would be any inappropriate job behavior by the person that causes them to be ineffective. This may be the person's first job, and they do not know what is appropriate behavior in a work group.

If problems occur within the work group, bring the parties together in an attempt to work out solutions. Fair treatment should be the rule, but where the problem persists after counseling and standards are not met, the employee must be informed of one's responsibilities. The responsibility does not end with the manager. All employees should be included in the training program to help make the disabled person become more productive.

INTERNET TRAINING

Interactive Web-Based Training

The problem is how to train a workforce with an industry average of 120 percent a year turnover. Add in 18,000 people at 1,800 locations worldwide with a budget limited to 11 trainers. The answer at Days Inn is interactive web-based training, including instructor-led training segments. Their program teaches reservation operations, housekeeping duties, supervision, and dealing with surly guests.

Because the web is interactive with people alert all the time, it is cost-effective. This translates to a 50 percent reduction in time and cost versus classroom training. One cost estimate finds interactive web-based training will save $350 per day per person in accommodation costs. A director of company education notes employees are not complaining about not being able to travel.[41]

Virtual University

The virtual university is alive and well in the twenty-first century. One in three U.S. colleges now offers accredited degrees online. This is twice as many colleges as in 1999 and the list is growing.

The latest entry is UNex.com, a startup of elite universities backed by former junk bond king, Michael Milken. These universities license their name to UNex.com and contribute business courses. The founding universities are Columbia, the University of Chicago, Carnegie Melon, Stanford, and the London School of Economics.

These universities will receive a cut of the revenue from UNex.com for the online classes. Their admission guidelines remain stringent. For example, at Stanford the online engineering students meet the same criteria as campus students and pay approximately $1,000 more per course.[42]

The HRM departments need to be aware of the diversity in learning styles of various groups. Although one cannot specify a particular learning style to a particular sex or race, there are factors which contribute to a singular learning style. These may include the person's age, their level of education, and cultural background. The result is that any group of trainees will have different learning styles.

To accommodate these learning styles, the trainer needs to determine individual training needs and attempt to build on them. This can be accomplished by allowing employees several different ways to learn, such as lectures, individual reading assignments, group discussions, and/or films or videos. By varying the educational approach, more effective learning will take place.

Computing the costs of a training program would include salaries for training personnel; training materials; expenses for travel, housing, and meals; facilities cost; the employee's salary; lost production time; and possible overhead costs (lights, heat, preparation, staff, etc.).

Computing the benefits of a training program would include production increases, reduced turnover, reduced absenteeism, reduced errors, and quality improvement. Less qualifiable benefits would include better attitude, better motivation, ability to do more than one job, promotability, and less supervision.

The training function requires a knowledge of **learning theory.** However, because training is a continuous process, it is important that supervisory management understand these concepts so as to be more effective in their roles of leader, teacher, coach, and motivator.

Global

The Philippines has many internal problems: a costly and unreliable electric system, bad roads, and an antique telephone system. Yet in the past 3 years, Intel Corp., Amkor Technology, Inc., Texas Instruments, Inc., and other chip companies have invested over $5 billion in the Philippines. Why would these corporations invest there? Answer: Low cost and highly trained labor.

Their school system is English language-based. Contrast training in China where all course material must be translated into Mandarin. In the Philippines, training is twice as fast. Add to that a high literacy rate with 30,000 to 40,000 engineers graduating each year and one can understand the $5 billion investment. Further, wages for a high-tech shopworker are at least 30 percent lower than Malaysia and other nearby countries.

With the increased global competitiveness, training becomes an important item. This places increased importance on effective training and development programs in the United States to preserve our high standard of living.[43]

Target Language

The global world of work requires communication which translates to foreign language training. This requirement extends beyond foreign countries to the United States which is no longer a homogeneous melting pot.

One learning approach is targeted language. The key here is not real fluency, which is a lifelong endeavor, but being able to function in a language. So how long does it take to reach a reasonable level of competence? The American Society for Testing and Materials (ASTM) has a guide book with industry standards.

The levels run from 0, no proficiency, to 5, educated native proficiency. At the minimal level of 1, a person can greet others, use basic etiquette and explain routine procedures. Depending upon the language, such as Spanish, level 1 will require at least 150 hours. For Japanese and Chinese, at least 350 hours.

Depending upon a company's goal, targeted language may be the best bargain in time and cost. For instance, employers doing surveys may have a list of straightforward questions requiring somewhat predictable answers. Targeted language can quickly teach them how to ask the questions and prepare them for various answers. Another part of targeting is to tailor the class to a person's needs. The class would be different for a nurse or someone in a toll booth.[44]

Learning Theory

One concept of learning theory addresses the problem of whether it is important to understand the whole process of the work flow or just the part the employee is concerned with. This is appropriately termed "whole versus part." The application of this concept may vary with the level of the job and the ability or interest of the employee. Generally, it is considered good learning theory to allow the employee to see the big picture and how the individual job contributes to it. This concept is similar to explaining to a draftsperson what the ultimate product will do and the environment in which it will operate, rather than just explaining the engineering specifications for a particular part within the product. There may be times when reference to the big picture will have a strong motivational effect upon the employee.

Another learning theory concept is whether it is more effective to learn the whole process at one time, or to split the process into more easily digestible segments. Again, the application of this concept will depend upon the complexity of the process, and the ability and interest level of the employee. Generally, it is considered good learning theory to separate material into logical and assumable segments.

Another learning theory concept is whether to delay the application of what is learned or to apply it immediately. Again, one needs to consider the complexity of the material and the practicality of application. Generally, the sooner the employee applies the material learned, the more likely there will be correct execution. It becomes a matter of facilitating immediate recall.

Practice and repetition is another learning theory concept. What is learned must be practiced and repeated over and over again. Some people may call this rote memory, but regardless, this is a very basic concept to the whole process of learning and cannot be underemphasized if effectiveness is to be achieved.

When an individual responds correctly to the training, the trainer should reinforce that individual's behavior through positively recognizing that behavior. This is called **positive reinforcement,** and consists of "well done," or what is generally referred to as the "pat on the back," or some other form of recognition.

Positive and Negative Reinforcement

The concept of both positive and negative reinforcement is based upon the law of effect. This law explains that people generally avoid acts that result in punishment and seek acts that reward.

Positive and **negative reinforcement** are feedback: that is, providing the individual with immediate results of their actions. People usually welcome positive feedback, but not negative feedback. The use of negative feedback is usually at the discretion of the supervisor, tempered by the gravity of the situation.

In any training situation, there is always the problem of transfer of training—Will the skills learned in training be applied back on the job? This question really has two parts. The first part applies to the training environment. What is learned must be the exact duplicate of the equipment layout, procedures, and tools used on the actual job. The second part applies to any change the training program plans to effect back on the work site. For change to be successful, a large number of employees need to be initially trained with the remaining group as quickly as possible. Also, management at the operating level must want these changes and be willing to implement them.

The Learning Curve

Another problem that occurs in the training process is **the learning curve.** Some employees learn quickly, others more slowly. Generally, more knowledge is accumulated early in the training program, but as time increases, units of further learning decrease. The amount of learning is large in the beginning, but as time goes on, the amount of further learning decreases as there is now a need to assimilate the material learned. Thus, the learning curve raises rapidly at the start, but diminishes at the end.

When the material becomes more complex, the opposite may occur. Initial learning may be slow at first due to the difficulty of the material, but as the employee develops basic understanding, the more time spent results in increasing learning.

In some learning situations, a combination of the previous situations may occur. Learning starts out slowly, and then suddenly increases, only to slow down at the later stages. This type of learning curve is generally most common. At first the training material is new and unfamiliar, so one learns slowly. Then, as one understands the fundamentals of the material, learning greatly increases. Now, as one attempts to apply and refine the learned material in application, the amount of learning slows down.

Sometimes the learning process slows down after the initial learning increases and plateaus. This may be the result of attempting to integrate or digest the learned information, or it may represent burnout or lack of motivation by the employee. The exact cause must be determined by the trainer, and corrective action taken. The cause may be as simple as forgetting what was learned, or a resistance to replacing old techniques with new.

The trainer must be alert to the appropriateness of the training material content, as well as the behavioral characteristics of the employees being trained. Both require constant reappraisal and review, if the training function is to be effective. (See HRM in Action.)

HRM IN ACTION
TRAINING AT RED LOBSTER[45]

The scene at a Red Lobster restaurant that opened recently here is a cross between a pep rally and a pop quiz. A large room is filled with raucous students learning the basics of their trade—waiting on tables. Their enthusiastic teacher raises his clenched fists over his head, fires off questions, and exhorts his students to answer as loudly as they can:

"What's the first thing we do at the table?"

"SMILE!" booms the class.

"And the second thing?"

"SAY SOMETHING PERSONAL!"

"And the third thing?"

"DESCRIBE THE SPECIAL FEATURES!"

"Very good! And what will be our vegetables of the month?"

"BROCCOLI AND CARROTS!" comes the roaring reply.

And so, in a burst of energy, begins a new Red Lobster restaurant, another eating house added to the world's largest—and still rapidly growing—seafood restaurant chain. It now includes 513 restaurants in this country, Canada, and Japan, with sales in North America of $1.13 billion last year. Red Lobster Canada maintains one of the most elaborate quality control programs in the food services industry.

Red Lobster's employee-driven retraining program is an employee-designed retraining initiative. Its goal? To help restaurant employees exceed guests' expectations.

The retraining will affect everybody from the president on down, and will help achieve unprecedented guest service at Red Lobster. Michael Andrews, a bartender with Red Lobster at the Sheppard Avenue location in Scarborough, was a member of the employee task force, and says this about Hospitality Plus: "The fact that the employees were given the responsibility to design a new training program is one of the reasons I have been an employee of Red Lobster for four years. This new program excites me, because it really gives us all the tools that can make our guests' experience a great one."

The hottest feature at Red Lobster is not a menu item, nor even the restaurant's reasonable prices (the average dinner check is around $11), their large selection (more than 100 seafood items on the menu), or the restaurant's clean, tasteful decor.

No, the big ticket item is simply good service—as in having your waiter greet you with a smile, ask you a friendly question, and tell you about the vegetables of the day. To ensure good service, the restaurant mounts a 4-day training course for servers before each restaurant opens, and thereafter requires its staff to attend monthly classes to polish skills and learn new trends in salad presentation, garnishing techniques, and the like.

Trainees are not let off easy. Every minute of every session is taken up in classes, trial runs, quizzes, and contests. On the first day, the students are given homework (to memorize the entire menu), and the next morning are given a written test on the material (the highest scorer won $100). There is a contest to see who could use the computer the fastest, and another to determine which server is best at describing desserts accurately, temptingly, and entertainingly.

Some of the seminars taught precisely the phrases to be used in such presentations. Judy Limbach, for instance, taught a class on entrée items. She circled a long table covered with every main dish on the menu, which she picked up, one by one, and described in detail.

When she put down the last dish, she walked back to the first one, picked it up, and commenced a surprise quiz. "Now that I've told you about the dishes, you can tell me about them," she began, smiling dryly at the worried faces that flashed through her class. "Chris, tell me about the popcorn shrimp."

"Popcorn shrimp," said Chris, stammering, blanching, "oh . . . it's shrimp . . . and it's, ahh, it's popcorn-sized, and . . ."

"It's bite-sized, lightly breaded, and golden fried," Judy corrected quickly. "You need to know this. . . . You need to describe it so it sounds really good."

Most crucially, all Red Lobster waiters and waitresses are encouraged during training to show a bit of their personality while meeting customers. The old Red Lobster uniform of shirts and slacks has been discarded in favor of a maroon apron, under which servers can wear clothing of their choice. And although stock descriptive phrases are taught in the seminars, the servers are encouraged to improvise their sales pitch.

"We try to remove the spiel and inject the personality," explained Jeff O'Hara, president of Red Lobster USA. "We're trying to bring it down to an intensely personal experience."

The company is also well known among waiters and waitresses, in most areas where it is found, as a good employer that offers solid benefits, a chance for advancement, and flexible hours. Most of all, it is known as a restaurant where the tipping is good. At the recent training course here, many students spoke of their hope to make more than $100 in tips on good nights.

QUESTIONS

1. What are the goals of such retraining?

2. Is this training better than on-the-job training?

3. How does Red Lobster's retraining program contribute to the company's effectiveness?

TRENDS IN TRAINING

There are several trends emerging. First, because of costs, the valuation of benefits directly related to training is important. In other words, training is increasingly being tied to dollar results. Second, there is a growing trend toward globalization of training because of the increase in worldwide operations. Organizations are having to develop global training programs, and to train expatriate managers for overseas assignments.

United Airlines has grown into an international airline in fierce competition with foreign international airlines.[46] However, United discovered most American workers were not properly trained to operate in this more demanding environment. So, an 18-month training program called "Best Airline—The Global Challenge" was designed to instill international awareness and a commitment to world class service. Eventually, 28,000 employees will have completed this program. Because employees will have varied backgrounds in international experience, United has prepared a 1,200-page pretraining manual to help equalize these differences before entering the training program. American companies are beginning to realize that individuals need to be better prepared for overseas assignments.

Another trend is training new workers to avoid sexual harassment. This is a result of recent Supreme Court decisions that emphasize the employer's responsibilities of training in this area. Some employers have begun to devote special attention to new employees, including interns and new college graduates. One New York City media company has added to its orientation course a 25-minute video on sexual harassment. The video covers potential harassers as well as their victims.[47]

The nonprofit board membership offers training and exposure for up-and-coming businesspeople. Although the practice of advancing one's career by joining a nonprofit board has been around for a long time, the emergence of a broker who charges a fee for placing clients on nonprofit boards is a new trend.

These brokers interview candidates to evaluate their interests and skills. Then they will broker their introduction to nonprofit organization board members. The fee can be $1,500 or more and is paid by the company the person works for. Clients include lawyers, CPAs, marketers, and other business executives.[48]

SUMMARY

In the past decade, training has become increasingly popular as an HR technique for improving employee and managerial performance in organizations. It has been suggested that most organizations provide some type of formal training and spend millions of dollars in this effort. An effective training program depends upon a systematic approach including a careful need assessment, program design, and evaluation of results.

In this chapter, we examined the major organization training and orientation programs. Rapidly changing technology and increasing competition are placing pressure on organizations to improve the workforce through training. Training and development includes the orientation of new employees, the training of employees to perform their jobs, and the retraining of employees as their job requirements change. Encouraging the development and growth of employees and managers is another aspect.

You will have the opportunity to assess a training problem and to develop a set of strategies and techniques for an organization training program. Clearly, a new employee's initial experience on the job can have a major affect on a later career, just as a student entering a new class. In evaluating learning in class, we measure changes in learning, skills, behavior, and results. The impact on the performance of the organization provides the bottom line.

REVIEW QUESTIONS

1. What are the major goals of an orientation program?
2. Present an example of your first day on the job. What orientation did you receive?
3. How important is motivation in employee training?
4. How do learning principles apply to training?
5. How would you determine training needs in an organization?
6. Do you feel training will become more or less important in the future? Why?
7. Read a book or view a video, and identify training needs or programs.

KEY WORDS AND CONCEPTS

Define and be able to use the following:

- Apprenticeship Training
- Coaching
- Computer-Assisted Instruction
- Continuing Education
- Development

- Internship
- Job Instruction Method (JIM)
- Job Rotation Training
- Learning Theory
- Mentoring

- Off-the-Job Training
- On-the-Job Training
- Orientation Training
- Positive and Negative Reinforcement

- Programmed Instruction
- The Case Method
- The Learning Curve

- Training
- Training Objectives

- Transfer of Training
- Vestibule Training

HRM SKILLS SIMULATION 7.1: THE EWING COMPANY

Total time suggested: 1 hour

A. PURPOSE

In this simulation, you will be able to plan training strategies in an organization. You will also critique and receive feedback on the effectiveness of your strategies. The goals include

1. To determine appropriate training strategy.
2. To experience diagnosing and contacting a client system.
3. To provide feedback on training approaches.

B. PROCEDURES

Step 1. Everyone reads the Ewing Company Background. Prior to class, divide the class into groups of five, as the Ewing Management Team consultants. (Roles are to be selected and read prior to the class meeting.) Each player reads only their role. Any additional class members can become observers. (See Figure 7.2.)

1. President
2. Vice president, human resource management
3. Vice president, manufacturing
4. Vice president, marketing
5. Vice president, finance

Step 2. The Ewing Management Team will meet to decide:

1. What are the major problems?
2. Should they continue training?
3. What strategies should be used to change?

Time suggested for Step 2: 40 minutes.

Step 3. The observer will provide feedback and guide the discussion using the Observer Form. All team members are encouraged to critique the Ewing team meeting and the role of the consultants.

Time suggested for Step 3: 10 minutes.

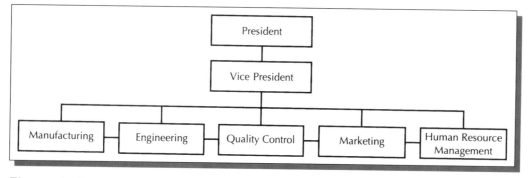

Figure 7.2
Ewing organizational chart

OBSERVER FORM

Low ____1 : 2 : 3 : 4 : 5 : 6 : 7 : 8 : 9 : 10____ High

1. Degree of cooperative teamwork: _____
2. Degree of team motivation: _____
3. Degree of member satisfaction: _____
4. Degree of information sharing (participation): _____
5. Degree of consensual decision making: _____
6. Degree of team conflict or competition (i.e., conflict directly faced and resolved): _____
7. Degree of quality of group decisions: _____
8. Degree of speed with which decision is made: _____
9. Degree of participating leadership: _____
10. Degree of clarity of goals: _____

Total ranking _____

BACKGROUND INFORMATION:
THE EWING COMPANY

Bob Jones is HR manager for the Ewing Company, a small manufacturer of oil field equipment located in Bakersfield, California. Ewing employs about 150 people. The industry is very competitive, and Ewing strives to keep costs at a minimum.

During the past year, the firm lost three major customers because of defective products. Further investigation found that rejects were running at 12 percent, compared to an overall plant standard of 4 percent. In discussion with the vice president, Bob decided that the problem was not in engineering, but in a lack of proper training in quality control for machine operators. Bob decided that a training program in quality control would reduce manufacturing rejects to acceptable levels.

Bob began designing the course. First, he assessed training needs and created training objectives from a nearby state university about conducting the project. He included factors affecting product quality, production standards, inspection techniques, and safety procedures.

Bob sent a memo to all first-line supervisors urging them to review their records, determine which employees had quality problems, and schedule these employees for the program. As a final design step, Bob wrote the following training objective for the program: "To reduce the current levels of product defects to standard plant levels of 4 percent within a 6-month period."

Because of a lack of space, the training sessions were held in the company's cafeteria. The training was scheduled to take place between breakfast and lunch, while cafeteria personnel were preparing the luncheon meal and washing breakfast dishes.

About 50 employees were expected to attend each session, but average attendance was closer to 30. Bob heard many supervisors say, "If I let everybody go who's supposed to attend, I won't make my quota this week. Then I'll really be in hot water. Sorry, but production comes first."

Bob also heard comments from some of the trainees that "the employees who really need to be here are still back in the shop."

The resulting chart of monthly trends for total product defects before and after the program was not encouraging. (See Figure 7.3).

Upon reviewing the data, Bob was dismayed and frustrated that the program had failed to achieve results. Six months after the program, defects were still running well above standard—almost as high as before the program was implemented. The pressure on Bob was really mounting as he prepared for a meeting with management to review the results of the training program. Bob felt a TQM program could be the answer.

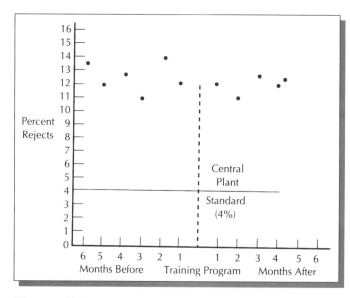

Figure 7.3
Product rejects before and after the training program

ROLE DESCRIPTIONS
(READ *ONLY* YOUR ROLE)

Role 1—President. You have been the president of Ewing for the past 14 years, and, in large part, its growth and success have been due to your own ability to select and motivate others. You are a college graduate, and have attended many executive seminars.

You still maintain close contact with day-to-day operations because you believe in "management by wandering around."

Over the past few years, growth has slowed, sales and earnings have declined, and turnover problems have emerged. You feel the rapid early growth may be the cause of current problems.

You are convinced that a TQM training process will improve coordination and communication.

You believe that the organization needs better morale and improved bottom-line results. Your vice president of HR has suggested that you try something new: a TQM program.

Role 2—Vice President, Human Resource Management. You have an MBA, and you were brought in 5 years ago to serve in your current position. You see the key problem as poor structure, a lack of coordination among departments, and lack of training at all levels.

All of the other vice presidents worked their way up to their present positions, and you consider their professional managerial training somewhat remiss (with the exception of the vice president of marketing, who has attended many of your training sessions). This is even more of a problem at the mid- and lower-level management ranks.

You feel that the answer to the problem is a decentralized operation, with increased integration and coordination between departments, and a participative, team style. You have read about TQM, and have talked to a colleague at another company who had high praise for their TQM program. You even discussed implementing a TQM program with the vice president of manufacturing, but there was little response. You feel a need to get conflicts out into the open where they can be resolved, rather than each unit seeking its own best interest. A unified team effort is needed.

You have attempted to initiate several training and change programs. These programs have been undercut by other managers. You got word that one vice president was openly attacking the programs, even though the president has been strongly supportive. You suggested some TQM training. Even though they might add to costs in the short run, you are sure that long-term effectiveness will be improved.

Role 3—Vice President, Manufacturing. You have been with the company for 22 years, working your way up through the ranks. You have a degree in engineering, and feel that you are competent, run a tight ship, and that your department is the main reason for past success. You believe that most problems are due to rapid growth that has resulted in loose structure, lack of coordination, and lack of control.

You feel that the company has too many meddling staff managers (particularly in marketing and personnel) who do not contribute to profits and only cause problems for the line manager. Several times, the HR vice president has tried to discuss with you management practices, such as leadership and some new kind of TQM program. You listened politely enough, but you got several good laughs out of it at your department meetings. The management training programs offered through the HR division have been a waste of time, and you have told your people you prefer they stay on the job instead of going to more meetings. The vice president of marketing continually wants a product modification, or comes up with some goofball idea for a new product. You have made it clear that you run manufacturing, and that includes R&D. You can't run a smooth operation and keep costs down if you are constantly making special modifications.

Role 4—Vice President, Marketing. You have been with the company for 10 years. You are a college graduate with a major in psychology, but you have gained your knowledge of marketing from experience. You feel that marketing is the major factor in the company's growth, and if your product managers were given greater authority, they could turn the profit picture around.

You see the major problem as the lack of communication among departments and the failure to utilize talented managers. You have tried to get the manufacturing division to make some special modifications in radar units, but they have been willing to comply only on very large orders—and then it generally took them so long that you almost lost several of the orders from your customers. Several of your product managers have met with representatives of manufacturing to discuss new quality ideas, but nothing comes of the meetings until your competitors come up with the identical product. Then it takes manufacturing a couple of years to design their own unit.

Your people are bringing back word from the field that the excellent reputation once enjoyed by Ewing is beginning to fade. It has been discouraging for you and your people to fight an uphill battle with manufacturing for new products, and the real kicker is to learn the competition comes out with your product idea.

Even though marketing has been accused of being run like a "country club," you feel your department performs well. The answer, you believe, is to develop a TQM program in product management by giving employees more authority over product quality.

Role 5—Vice President, Finance. You have an MBA from a major school. You instituted all financial systems and made it a smooth operation.

You feel the problems are the result of too many changes in too short a time. The company has too many bright young kids and too many wasteful practices. You suggest going back to the basics by instituting a tighter centralized system of financial control and cutting about 10 percent of the deadwood. With yourself as an executive vice president (and other vice presidents reporting to you), this job could be done. You would set up some basic company rules, then force the department heads to enforce them.

You avoid getting into conflicts over these issues. You like to let the facts and figures talk and deal mainly by memo. You realize that you are not as up-to-date on modern management systems as you might be.

You would like to avoid changes and keep things pretty much the way they are.

Case 7.1 *Precision Products, Inc.*

Helen Brown sat at her desk looking at the notes she'd scrawled on a yellow legal pad. Management and general employee training represented a new endeavor. "I'm really excited about starting up my own program," thought Helen. "It's nice not to be locked into someone else's system."

Helen's most pressing challenge at present was determining where to begin. "I've learned that effective training must have a purpose and should focus on real training needs," she thought. "What should my major objectives be? What are the most pressing needs?" On the legal pad in front of her, she began to write down some of the things she'd learned about.

There were significant differences of opinion. The director of marketing felt poor employee morale was due to poor interpersonal skills on the part of management. The product manager felt that the greatest problem was a lack of motivation and thinking on the part of productive employees. Helen had recently attended a seminar on the managerial grid and wanted these topics taught. The manufacturing manager wanted training on new automated robotics. The president had expressed concern that employees and supervisors were unfamiliar with TQM programs.

Helen began to wonder if she would be able to meet this diverse set of expectations, which should be addressed first. "Well, I've got to start somewhere," thought Helen. "The management committee is expecting my training recommendations in 4 days!"

QUESTIONS

1. What would you recommend for a training program for this company?
2. How can the difference of opinion be resolved into a comprehensive training program? Will there be winners and losers?
3. Discuss the problem of being locked into some other company's training program. List pros and cons.

ENDNOTES

1. Dori Jones Yang and Andrea Rothman, "Reinventing Boeing," *Business Week* (March 1, 1993): 67.
2. Stephanie Overman, "Workers, Management Unite," *HR Magazine* (May 1990): 40.
3. "Jobs, Jobs, Jobs," *Business Week* (February 22, 1993): 68.
4. R. R. Camp, P. N. Blanchard, and G. E. Huszczo, *Toward a More Organizationally Effective Training Strategy and Practice* (Upper Saddle River, NJ: Prentice Hall, 1986).
5. Shelly Reese, "Investment in people: getting your money's worth from training," *Business and Health* 17, no. 7 (July 1999): 26–29.

6. Linda Thornburg, "The Changing of the Guards," *Human Resource Magazine* 37, no. 7 (1992): 50–53.

7. D. Schaaf, "Lessons from the '100 best'," *Training* 27, no. 2 (1990): 18–20.

8. I. Goldstein and P. Gilliam, "Training Systems in the Year 2000," *American Psychologist* (February 1990): 134.

9. Tom Feltenstein, "How to avoid a negative workplace," Bridge News, *The Oregonian*, 27 August 1999, p. B3.

10. Ronald Henkoff, "Companies that Train Best," *Fortune* (March 22, 1993): 62.

11. Ibid., 73.

12. Hal Lancaster, "Managing Your Career, This Kind of Black Belt Can Help You Score Some Points at Work," *The Wall Street Journal*, 14 September 1999, p. B1.

13. Barb Cole-Gomolski, "Dual career paths reduce turnover," *Computerworld* 33, no. 8 (February 22, 1999): 24.

14. A. Packer, "America's New Learning Technology," *Personnel Administrator* (September 1988): 62.

15. John Snell, "Caught in the Spell," Tech NW, *The Oregonian*, 30 August 1999, p. C1.

16. I. Goldstein and P. Gilliam, "Training Systems in the Year 2000," *American Psychologist* 34, no. 2 (February 1990): 134.

17. Jim Meade, "A Solution for Comptency-Based Employee Development," *HR Magazine* (December 1998): 54–58.

18. Linda Campillo, "Hard-labor jobs available back in 1900 bear little resemblance to jobs of 2000," Career Marketplace, *The Oregonian*, 22 September 1999, 2.

19. Nancy McCarthy, "Former builder remodels career," Career Marketplace, *The Oregonian*, 22 September 1999, p. 4.

20. Morton E. Grossman and Margaret Magnus, "The $5.3 billion job for training," *Personnel Journal* (July 1989): 54–56.

21. Irwin L. Goldstein, *Training Organizations: Needs Assessment, Development, and Evaluation*, 2nd ed. (Monterey, CA: Brooks/Cole, 1986), 15.

22. Dana Gaines Robinson and James C. Robinson, *Training for Impact—How to Link Training to Business Needs and Measure the Results* (San Francisco: Jossey-Bass, 1989). See also Anthony R. Montebello and Maureen Hasa, "To Justify Training, Test, Test Again," *Personnel Journal* (January 1994): 83–86.

23. Michelle Martinez, "Disney Training Works Magic," *Human Resource Magazine* 37, no. 5 (1992): 53–57.

24. "Who gets Training?" *Training* (October 1990): 54.

25. Stephen B. Wehrenberg, "Skill and Motivation Divide Training vs. Orientation," *Personnel Journal* 68, no. 5 (May 1989): 111–113.

26. William C. Byham, "Grooming Next Millennium Leaders," *HRM Magazine* (February 1999): 46–50.

27. Mary Kane, "Consultants find niche in coaching," Newhouse News Service, *The Oregonian*, 12 September 1999, p. B1.

28. Leslie Helm, "The Rule of Work in Japan," *Los Angeles Times*, 17 March 1991, p. 1.

29. Bureau of National Affairs, "Training facts and figures," in *Bulletin to Management* (Washington: Bureau of National Affairs, 1990).

30. Robert F. Sullivan and Donald C. Miklas, "On-the-Job Training That Works," *Training and Development Journal* 39, no. 5 (May 1985): 118.

31. Darlene F. Russ-Eft and John H. Zenger, "Common Mistakes in Evaluating Training Effectiveness," *Personnel Administrator* 30, no. 4 (April 1985): 57–62.

32. R. B. McAfee and P. J. Champagne, "Employee Development: Discovering Who Needs What," *Personnel Administrator* 33, no. 2 (1988): 92–98.

33. R. D. Salinger, *Disincentives to effective employee training and development* (Washington: U.S. Civil Service Commission Bureau of Training, 1973).

34. Marc Adams, "Training Employees As Partners," *HR Magazine* (February 1999): 65.

35. Joyce E. Santora, "Keep Up Production Through Cross-Training," *Personnel Journal* 71, no. 6 (1992): 162–166.

36. N. Madlin, "Computer-based training comes of age," *Personnel* 64, no. 11 (1987): 64–65. See also William R. Tracey, "Customizing Off-the-Shelf Training Programs," *HR Magazine* (January 1993): 57–60; and Kelly Allan, "Computer Courses Ensure Uniform Training," *Personnel Journal* (June 1993): 65–71.

37. K. E. Kram and L. Isabella, "Mentoring alternatives: The role of peer relationships in career development," *Academy of Management Journal* 28 (1985): 110–32.

38. Albert R. Karr, Work Week "Expanded Testing," *Wall Street Journal*, 25 January 2000, p. A1.

39. Peggy Stuart, "New Directions in Training Individuals," *Personnel Journal* 71, no. 9 (1992): 92–94.

40. Ralph T. King Jr., "Job Retraining Linked Closely To Employers Works In Cincinnati," *Wall Street Journal*, 19 March 1993, p. A.

41. Bill Roberts, "Training via the desktop: 11." *HR Magazine* (August 1998): 99–104.

42. P. J. Huffstutter and Robin Fields, "A Virtual Revolution in Teaching," *Los Angeles Times*, 3 March 2000, p. 1.

43. Robert Frank, "U.S. and Philippine Companies Joined at the Chip," *The Wall Street Journal*, 2 September 1999, p. A9.

44. Kathryn Tyler, "Targeted Language Training is Best Bargain," *HR Magazine* (January 1998): 61–64.

45. J. Gordon, "Who is being trained to do what?" *Training* 25, no. 10 (1988): 51–60.

46. Ronald Henkoff, "Companies that Train Best," *Fortune* (March 22, 1993): 73.

47. D. McGill, "Why They Smile at Red Lobster," *New York Times*, 23 April 1993, pp. F1, F6; "Employee Drive Retraining Program."

48. Shari Caudron, "Training Helps United Go Global," *Personnel Journal* 71, no. 2 (1992): 103–05.

Chapter 8

The Success System: Management and Organization Development

Objectives

Upon completing this chapter, you will be able to:

1. Define and discuss the concepts of management and organization development.
2. Describe the stages in the organization development process.
3. Understand and compare the advantages and disadvantages of various organization development programs.
4. Identify and describe the major management development techniques and understand their importance.
5. Define and be able to use the OD approaches to change in an organization.

Premeeting preparation

1. Read chapter 8.
2. Prepare for HRM Skills Simulation 8.1. Read Parts A and B; complete Step 1.
3. Read Case 8.1: Precision Products, Inc. Answer questions.

Background Information

If anyone can shake up Ford Motor Company's stodgy corporate culture, it is Jacques Nasser. A few years ago, the Lebanese-born Australian rescued Ford of Australia by freshening the product lineup, restoring product quality, and trimming payroll by nearly 50 percent. "He took a company that was literally nonviable and left it viable," says John Ogden, who took the top Australian job after Nasser. And, Ogden adds, he maintained employee morale throughout this difficult transition.

Now Ford's CEO in Detroit, Nasser is transforming the automaker into a more nimble organization focused on shareholder value. Nasser has led the change effort by personally conducting information sessions to over 50,000 employees in offices and factories around the world. He explains about the need to cut costs, add shareholder value, and become a more entrepreneurial organization.

Nassar supports his vision of Ford's future through his actions. For example, he moved the heads of manufacturing, marketing, and finance to the same location so they can make quicker decisions about new product lines. His aggressive leadership style sets him apart from more cautiously bureaucratic executives typically found at Ford. "I have high personal standards, and I set the same standards for my team," he acknowledges.

Nasser shrugs off concerns that he is a tough taskmaster, stating that Ford needs a leader who can prepare the company for a more competitive future. "I am an agent of change," says Nasser. "I don't believe in stagnation." Even adversaries agree that Ford will benefit from Nasser's leadership talents. "Joe Nasser's a very charismatic leader with lots of ideas and energy," says the president of a rival automobile firm.[1]

The Challenge of Change

Change is the name of the game in organizations today. As the environment changes, organizations must adapt if they are to be successful. Managing change is a challenge facing every organization. How leaders manage change will often make the difference between success and survival in today's competitive environment.[2] "Technology changes so fast that we estimate 20 percent of an engineer's knowledge becomes obsolete every year. Training is an obligation we owe to our employees," says Solectron Chairman Winston Chen. Anthony Carnevale, the blunt-speaking chief economist at the American Society for Training and Development says: "If you want to build a high-tech, high-performance, flexible organization, then you have to train your managers and workers."[3]

One of the most critical elements in an organization's success is the quality of its managers. Without high-performing managers, the best an organization can hope for is mediocre performance. In a competitive world, however, that may mean the organization will not survive in the long term. American companies have come to see management development as an investment in future survival and success. As Howard Shultz, CEO of Starbucks Coffee, says, "Every dollar you invest in your employees shows up—and then some—on the bottom line."[4]

Management development is a systematic process of individual managers acquiring the skills, knowledge, and abilities to manage an organization to high-performance levels.[5] Many management theorists suggest that the team-based organization is the wave of the future. The self-managed team (discussed in chapter 17) should be one of the basic building blocks of the organization, and may well become the productivity breakthrough of the twenty-first century. Management consultant W. Edwards Deming (management guru to the Japanese, and responsible for much of Japanese post-war industrial success) said in a recent interview, "An example of a system well managed is an orchestra. The various players are not there as prima donnas—to play loud and attract the attention of the listener. They're there to support each other. In fact, sometimes you see a whole section doing nothing but counting and watching. Just sitting there doing nothing. They're there to support each other. That's how business should be."[6]

In this chapter, we present the next stage of the Success System Model: several proactive approaches to management and organization development. We examine some of the reasons for using management and organization development and discuss several approaches, including role playing, outdoor experiential training, and off-job techniques.

MANAGEMENT DEVELOPMENT APPROACHES

Management development is a critical factor in developing high-performing managers and then motivating them to move up in the organization. A comprehensive development program is important for a number of reasons.

High-Performing Managers at All Levels. In today's complex and rapidly changing organizations, managers need to continually acquire the techniques necessary to compete effectively.

Avoiding Obsolescence. Managerial obsolescence may be termed as not keeping current with new methods and processes that optimize employees performance. Rapidly changing technological, legal, and social environments impact the way managers perform their jobs.

Managerial Succession. A typical manager's career usually involves six promotions within the organization. Each promotion generally requires the development of new skills and techniques.

Personal Goals. In general, managers tend to be high achievers and need new challenges. Management development can provide training that results in greater organizational effectiveness and also increased personal development.

There are many differing management development approaches available. Unfortunately, few of the approaches have been empirically tested, and there is relatively little data to determine which approaches lead to more success than others.[7] In most organizations, there is some type of overall management training, with specific programs aimed at different levels of management. Perhaps the most frequently used methods are the case method, role-playing, and management game technique.[8]

Management development is becoming increasingly important in an environment of global competition. There are studies to suggest that U.S. corporations annually spend over $30 billion on management training.[9] There are many approaches which are used.

The Case Method

One of the most widely used approaches is the **case method.** A case is a written description of an organizational situation. Managers analyze the case to identify problems and propose solutions.

This case method involves the analysis and discussion of organizational problems. Participants are usually given written cases to analyze individually and later to discuss as a group. The managerial skills learned are directly related to the group discussion activity which focuses on the interpersonal skills used in problem solving. For the case study method to be effective, there must be open discussion and cases which relate to the organization's environment.

Role-Playing Techniques

Role playing involves the simulation of job situations, where trainees role play subordinate and supervisory positions. At the end of the role play, the trainees critique the behaviors and suggest improvement modifications.

Role playing is usually combined with other management training techniques. This method is often used to teach skills such as communication, leadership, and interpersonal skills.

Management Games

Management games are used to simulate organizational decision-making situations. In a typical game, managers form teams and are asked to make operating decisions in competition. The results can then be critiqued and compared.

Most management games require that groups of participants (each representing a separate enterprise) make a series of decisions affecting their business. These games usually involve business decisions and success requires a knowledge of general managerial principles. Typically, several teams compete while simulating an actual business situation, and the results are a function of the decisions made by each team.

Management games have several advantages. They compress several years of decisions into a short timespan, they are interesting, provide problem-solving feedback, and provide an understanding of the interrelationships among operational departments.

Executive Development Programs

There are also many management development programs offered outside the organization. For example, many management associations offer 3- to 5-day seminars, and many universities (including Harvard, Case, Cornell, Columbia, Michigan, Northwestern, Stanford, UCLA, and Wharton) offer advanced management or **executive development** programs.

For the thousands of managers who hope to join the next generation of CEOs and presidents, it's part country club, sure. But it's also part boot camp: study groups that meet into the early morning, classes that start at 8 A.M. sharp, and the throat-constricting challenge of making a presentation before a room of unfamiliar faces.

It's also expensive. Of the $12 billion spent annually on all executive development, slightly more than 25 percent goes to the business schools.[10]

Source: B.C. by permission of Johnny Hart and Creators Syndicate, Inc.

Over a short time span, an organization's management will undergo many significant changes. Some managers may be terminated; other managers will move to better opportunities with other firms. A large percentage of managers will remain at the same level, however, and a smaller percentage will move up the organizational ladder to executive management positions. For most, this move will be slow and deliberate; but for some managers, the move up will be fast and brilliant.

According to one management development specialist, if you want to qualify as a successful manager in the 2000s, you will have to pursue at least one of several unfamiliar paths. If you remain within the corporate world, you will have to transform yourself from an overseer into a doer, from a boss into a team leader, or maybe just a team player. You will be called on less to tell people what to do, and more to take responsibility for the success or failure of your business. Your skills will be measured on a global scale. You will need to be computer fluent.

"Our leadership challenge of the twenty-first century is to recalibrate people to global standards of play," says James Baughman, director of corporate management development for General Electric. "The people who will excel will be those who can build a team and integrate it with other teams. All other things being equal, the leader who is multilingual, multicultural, and fluent enough in information technology to maintain a proprietary edge will come out ahead."[11]

There is a probability of numerous management changes, particularly when the organization perceives rapid growth or decline. Organizational growth and change often create a demand for fresh managerial expertise. One example is IBM's selection of Lou Gerstner as its new chief executive officer. This culminates the most high stakes contest in corporate history with a controversial choice. IBM, suffering desperately from misreading breakneck changes in high technology, would be handing its future to an executive with superb management credentials but no computer industry experience.

Choosing Mr. Gerstner would amount to a decision that IBM's deep problems can be solved by better management, not a radical new vision for IBM's technology.[12] Consequently, management development should prepare managers to assume higher-level jobs and responsibilities. Few managers are able to move into increasingly challenging positions without some formal training programs.

Many organizations prepare a **management succession** plan. The succession plan indicates successors for each key position in the organization chart. This often combines current performance data with an assessment of promotion potential. The succession plan is valuable in determining promotions for the future.

Women Managers

Although all development programs are open to women managers, there are often opportunities to improve the equal employment situation by preparing women for possible top management openings. The lack of women in top management, often termed the "glass ceiling," results from a number of problems, including the need for more management development opportunities.[13]

Evaluation

Management development should be viewed as an investment in more effective management. Consequently, because management development can involve significant time and money, efforts should be made to evaluate the results of these programs. There is research to suggest that most organizations measure participant attitudes, but fail to evaluate changes in managerial performance. Unfortunately, if the organization fails to retain its employees after training, then they are basically providing training for someone else.[14]

ORGANIZATION DEVELOPMENT

What makes one organization a winner, yet another fails to make use of the same opportunities? The key to success often lies in developing the flexibility to meet changing conditions. The true key to successful change is employee involvement and commitment.

Change is a way of life in today's organization. But organizations are also faced with maintaining a stable identity and operations in order to accomplish their primary goals. Consequently, organizations involved in managing change have found that the way in which change is handled is critical. There is a need for a systematic approach, discriminating among those features that are healthy and effective and those that are not. Erratic, short-term, unplanned, or haphazard changes may well introduce problems that did not exist before, or allow side effects of the change that may be worse than the original problem. Managers should also be aware that stability or equilibrium can contribute to a healthy state. Change just for the sake of change is not necessarily effective; in fact, it may be dysfunctional.

A Definition of Organization Development

Organization development (OD) is defined as a long-range effort supported by top management to improve an organization's problem-solving and renewal processes through effective management of organizational culture. OD involves an attempt to achieve corporate excellence by integrating the desires of individuals for growth and development with organizational goals. According to Richard Beckhard, "Organization Development is an effort: (1) planned, (2) organization-wide, (3) managed from the top, (4) to increase organization effectiveness and health, through (5) planned interventions in the organization's processes using behavioral science knowledge."[15]

Why Organization Development?

Why has such a fast-growing field emerged? Organizations are designed to accomplish some purpose or function and to continue doing so for as long as possible. Because of this, organizations are not necessarily intended to change. Boeing is a good example. Boeing's top managers, faced with aggressive competition, were forced to radically reinvent the company.[16]

But change can affect all types of organizations, from giants like IBM to the smallest business. No one can escape change. This is why managers must be skilled in organization change and renewal techniques.

A study by Teresa Colvin and Ralph Kilmann examined why organizations initiate large-scale change programs. They found that the most cited reasons for beginning a change program were (1) the level of competition: 68 percent of respondents indicated that the organizations were experiencing a high or very high level of competition; (2) survival: some 15 percent indicated that the organization would cease to exist within the next few years without some type of change program; and (3) improved performance: 82 percent indicated that without a program, the organization would gradually suffer a decline in performance.[17]

Other goals cited included changing the corporate culture, becoming more adaptive, and increasing competitiveness. At Scandinavian Air Lines (SAS), for example, changing conditions are forcing the firm to become more effective in order to remain competitive. (See Our Changing World of HRM.)

OUR CHANGING WORLD OF HRM
A NEW CULTURE AT SAS[18]

When Scandinavian Air Lines (SAS) Chief Executive Jan Carlzon had to change planes in an SAS hub, Copenhagen, he noted with curiosity and a bit of anger that the plane he got off of had docked at gate A-1 (or the equivalent), but the connecting SAS flight was at gate Z-99. As Carlzon noted a large group of his fellow passengers trudging to connect to the same plane, Carlzon's fury grew. Gates, it turned out, were chosen to make life easy on the ground crew with little or no concern for the passengers. Something, Carlzon decided, had to change.

In a successful organizational development campaign, Carlzon managed to shift the entire airline towards a "customer first" attitude, and take SAS from an annual deficit of US$20 million to a profit of $54 million in 1 year. And, he got the gates changed.

Prior to the Carlzon-inspired shakeup, "SAS was very rigid and its employees could do little more than follow rules and regulations." In a comprehensive effort to turn around the business, SAS carried out both group and individual counseling. Employees at the customer service level were given more responsibility, and more authority. Even the canned script to be read before takeoff was no longer sacrosanct: Whoever read the safety and welcome message could improvise as long as the essentials got covered.

The end result was good not only for the employees, who felt and looked more responsive in their jobs, but was good for the traveling public as well. Ask someone who flew SAS then, and has flown SAS since the change. Ask if the new management has had an impact. The answers are easy to predict. Obviously, the customer service strategy, matched by a customer service culture, has made a world of difference.

QUESTIONS

1. Consider Carlzon's management style. How did he resolve the arrival gate problem? Do you agree or disagree?

2. What did Carlzon do to turn SAS around? Any other suggestions?

3. Compare the rigid environment at SAS before and after Carlzon's tenure. Will his efforts to change be short term or long term?

Managing organizational change is an important and complex action. In attempting to increase organizational and individual effectiveness, the HR manager must understand the nature of changes needed and the possible effects of various alternative change strategies.[19]

The starting point for setting in motion a change program is the definition of a total change strategy. As we have seen earlier, the HR manager's role and relationship with other departments and the organizational climate will influence the selection of specific intervention strategies aimed at improving organization effectiveness. A graphic illustration of the OD process is shown in Figure 8.1.

The diagnostic phase leads to the interventions, activities, and programs aimed at resolving problems and increasing organization effectiveness. At this point, the HR manager designs specific OD strategies to improve an organization's structure and processes. After diagnosing the problem areas associated with current performance, the opportunities for improvement are identified and a strategy to apply techniques and technologies for change are selected. Strategy involves the planning and direction of OD projects or programs; intervention techniques are the specific means by which change goals can be attained.

Before OD techniques can be implemented, the HR manager and the operating departments develop a set of strategies to guide future actions. OD is based primarily upon a collaborative change strategy: The operating manager is actively involved in defining problems and selecting the means for improvement. Within this basic approach to change, an OD change strategy is developed to meet the needs

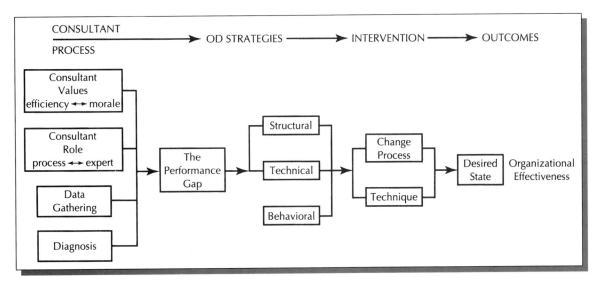

Figure 8.1
The OD process

of a specific client system. This next section describes several major OD strategies for setting up a program of change.

Basic Approaches

Three basic approaches to organization change are structural, technical, and behavioral. Organization structure is important, because it provides the framework that relates elements of the organization to one another. A poor structure may inhibit efficiency. Restructuring corporations to make them more competitive and less vulnerable to takeovers has been a major goal of corporations. Despite the restructuring of General Motors, it still has 21 layers between the chief executive and the plant line workers. Ford Motor company has 11 layers, and Toyota has 7 layers. In a statement about GM's overwhelming bureaucracy, John D. Rock, general manager of GMC Truck Division, says, "To take a company that has 800,000 people worldwide and try to change the culture, that's kind of like trying to parallel-park the Queen Mary."[20]

Technical processes also need to be given careful analysis. Often changes are required to bring them up to the state of the art in machinery, methods, automation, and job design. IBM's large investment in robotic-controlled production lines to build their personal computers has enabled IBM to bring new models on-line quickly and at prices competitive with imported personal computers.

The behavioral approach places emphasis on the use of human resources. In the past, managers placed emphasis upon fully analyzing an organizations' technical and mechanical capacities, but managers often neglected a vast untapped resource: its human assets. Furthermore, people generally have higher morale and are motivated toward organization goals when their personal resources and talents are being fully used. By increasing the levels of morale, motivation, and commitment of members, organization performance can also be improved.

Ford and General Motors illustrate the implementation of different change strategies. In the late 1980s, Ford was coming close to declaring bankruptcy. Lacking capital and facing a need to improve, Ford made structural and behavioral changes on the production line. Capital-rich GM, on the other hand, invested in expensive technological innovations such as new assembly lines and robotics. Ford's strategy paid off and its profits surpassed those of GM for the first time.[21] By the mid-1990s, both Ford and GM had learned expensive lessons. The Success System Model requires managers who understand the roles of people and organizational development.

One of the most critical elements in large-scale organization change is the individual. Excellence is going to be achieved by those organizations where risk taking and decision making are pushed down to the lowest possible level. This new culture is built upon the empowerment of the individual. The challenge is to empower the employee to take initiative and responsibility at all levels and functions of the organization. Organizations are designed to use the energy and ability of individuals to do work and realize goals. Members bring to the organization their values, assumptions, and behaviors. The success of future organizations, then, depends on how effectively the needs of individual members can be integrated with the vision and goals of the organization. People- or behavior-oriented changes are aimed at the psychosocial system functioning of the organization. These behavioral interventions may take various forms, but all are intended to improve the basic skills that enhance employee empowerment and thus underlie managerial effectiveness.[22]

In a survey of major firms, Barbara Block found that "firms that have transformed their culture claim to have increased productivity and number of clients, boosted employee camaraderie, made each employee feel a sense of ownership, and increased profits."[23] One essential factor in most OD programs is a greater openness of communication and improved conflict resolution, requiring the development of specialized skills among members.

There is a range of OD intervention activities aimed at enhancing the development and empowerment of the individual organization member. Essentially, the underlying assumption to these approaches is: If the individual becomes more effective, more involved, and more skilled, the total organization also will be improved. In a general sense, organization members attempt to improve their communication ability, interpersonal skill, and managerial performance. If managers can increase their interpersonal competence, the results should be improved organizational performance.[24]

Employee Involvement

Employee involvement (EI), empowerment, and buy-in management are new techniques for unleashing human potential in organizations. The central idea is to delegate power and decision making to lower levels and, by using concepts like shared visions of the future, to engage all employees so that people develop in themselves a sense of pride, self-respect, and responsibility.

Employee involvement attempts to move the organization from the traditional "I just work here, I don't make the rules" type of culture, to one of shared vision and goals. The idea is to have the individual's purpose and vision congruent with the organization's. The way it works at Ford Motor Company is that the employee involvement program is strictly voluntary. People form 6- to 10-person teams to tackle any problem that is important to the accomplishment of the organization and team goals. In a survey of employees at Ford, it was found that 82 percent felt they had a chance to accomplish something worthwhile, compared with only 27 percent before the EI program was initiated. The survey also reported a 50 percent increase in quality.[25]

The potential power to be unleashed under EI and buy-in management is enormous. Jack MacAllister, CEO of US West, describes his reaction to an empowered work team:

> I met with these people not too long ago. The energy in that room almost
> blew me out. I literally could not sit in that chair. These people were ex-

cited. One person said, "I'm doing things I didn't realize it was possible to do. I never thought I had it in me." Here was a group of people who had been empowered to think. The atmosphere alone was bringing out the very best they had in them. They were so highly energized . . . it was just remarkable to see.[26]

The following sections discuss some OD interventions used in developing employee involvement programs in organizations.

**OUR CHANGING WORLD OF HRM:
THE GOLD BADGE TEAM[27]**

As previously described, U.S. automobile companies have been working harder lately to instill a spirit of teamwork throughout their organizations. Team approaches can help develop the organizational culture needed to meet the global challenges of the twenty-first century. This is why the text says **team building** or **team development** are major OD techniques. The team, for one thing, can be a supportive change factor in an organization.

TEAM BUILDING IN JAPAN

Sharp is one of many Japanese organizations to realize and take advantage of this potential. Sharp pushes and encourages teams throughout the organization, but with a special twist. To help ensure an innovative corporate culture, something that is absolutely essential in the competitive and quick-changing consumer electronics industries, Sharp has created a special way to reward top innovators. Sharp puts them on "Gold Badge Project Teams" which report directly to the company president. According to *Fortune Magazine*, this special privilege instills pride in the elite Gold Badge Teams. Other workers set out scrambling for new ideas and new products hoping that they, too, might "make the team."

THE GOLD BADGE TEAM

How does the Gold Badge Team idea work? *Fortune* is upbeat. "Something as simple as a reward can help make a culture more innovative," they say. The Gold Badge Teams at Sharp are doing more than just improving the corporate culture. Specific results follow, too. "One result: the best-selling Wizard, an electronic organizer."

The Gold Badge Teams at Sharp offer one more perspective on the versatility and utility of the team approach. As the chapter points out, teams and teamwork can help management levels function better, can help communication and effectiveness between levels, and can work to mold a "Can Do" culture on the front lines. Sharp shows another role: encouraging an innovative culture through elite Gold Badge Teams. It's worth thinking about.

QUESTIONS

1. Do you agree with the Gold Badge Team approach? Why or why not?

2. Do you think the Gold Badge Team approach could backfire on Sharp? Support your position.

TEAM-DEVELOPMENT MEETINGS

The research on the effectiveness of team building is proving to be very effective, and it is currently a popular intervention being used in organizations. In an analysis of 126 studies that used OD interventions, interventions in general positively affected attitudes toward others, the job, and the organization. The analysis found team building to be the most effective OD intervention.[28] In a study of a team-building intervention in one major corporation, Donald F. Harvey and Neal Kneip found that team activities resulted in a greater clarification of problems and an awareness of a need for change in the organization.[29] For a different and high-tech approach to team development, see HRM in Action: Electronic Team Development.

Several companies are trying an unusual approach to meetings: one that encourages frank talk ("I've had enough—I'm looking for another job") and fast fingers. The approach calls for networking 20 to 50 personal computers around a horseshoe-shaped table. Participants sit at personal computers and type in their messages for all to read. There is no talking, as all communications are through the computers.

A computer program tracks and sorts topics typed in by participants. It then displays the messages on a central projection screen. The source of the message stays anonymous. To make up for lost nonverbal communications, the sender can add symbols to signify laughter, anger, boredom, and a smile. At the end of the meeting, everyone gets a printed synopsis.

ELECTRONIC MAIL

Digital Electronic Corporation (DEC) and a number of other companies have elaborate electronic mail systems which connect people around the world. At DEC, 75,000 people in 26 nations are linked together. DEC claims to be the best networked corporation in the world. It allows anyone on the system to "talk" to anyone else. This unrestricted approach differs from most organizations which restrict messages along organization lines. At DEC, a programmer sitting at a remote site on the Mojave desert near Death Valley can talk to another programmer in Australia or to the company president, Kenneth Olsen.

The electronic meeting, however, is different from DEC's approach in that the participants are in the same room, looking at each other over their computer screens. But no one knows who is typing what.

ROAR LIKE A LION

The approach can be brutally honest. One user says the anonymity of talking through a computer "turns even shy people powerful." Companies are finding they can get valuable, unfiltered information. Managers get feedback that can be threatening or insightful, depending on what the manager chooses to do with the information. Some managers have taken improvement courses as a result of the feedback.

Even managers who shrink at the process give the meetings high marks for efficiency. When you have to type in everything that is communicated, the process tends to cut down on chitchat.

USERS OF THE ELECTRONIC MEETINGS

A study by IBM and the University of Arizona found that the electronic meetings are as much as 55 percent faster than traditional meetings. Phelps Dodge Mining Company held its annual planning meeting electronically. Usually the planning session takes days, but it lasted only 12 hours when held electronically.

More companies like Greyhound, Dial Corporation, IBM, and Southwest Gas Corporation have tried the meetings. IBM is perhaps the biggest supporter of the idea. It has built 18 electronic meeting rooms and plans 22 more. Those taking part at IBM include the chairman and 7000 other IBM users. A project manager at IBM says the electronic meetings have "brought people together" who traditionally skirmished with one another.

THE DRAWBACKS

Though anonymity has its advantages, there are also some drawbacks. Those people who are computer-shy are reluctant to get heavily involved in the process. And the members find it helpful to be able to type. For those who come up with good ideas at the meetings, the system of anonymity makes it impossible to give credit to the person responsible.

One participant at a meeting typed in: "It's sad that we can't talk without sitting at terminals."

QUESTIONS

1. Do you think the electronic meeting could be used in an OD team building session? If so, how?

2. What do you see as the advantages and disadvantages of the approach?

3. Do you think the electronic meeting could get people to talk verbally, face to face? Why or why not?

4. What is your opinion of the electronic meeting?

OUTDOOR EXPERIENTIAL LABORATORY TRAINING

Within the last few years, **outdoor experiential laboratory training** (sometimes called outdoor labs, wilderness labs, adventure learning, or the corporate boot-camp) has become a common technique used for team building and leadership training.[31] The idea is to take a group of people who normally work with one another and place them in an outdoor setting where they participate in experiential learning exercises. The outdoor setting provides a different setting than the normal work environment, and the learning exercises are typically foreign and varied enough to most participants' background that no one has a distinct advantage. Thus, the outdoor lab puts most participants on an equal footing. This seems to hasten discussions surrounding leadership styles, teamwork, and interpersonal relationships.

The Outdoor Lab Process

Outdoor labs are typically offered by training companies that specialize in them. Some organizations that use the labs extensively, such as Federal Express, operate their labs through the OD or human resource development divisions. To be something more than a company retreat that has only short-term gains, the outdoor lab needs to fit into a larger program that builds the groundwork for the lab and follows through after the lab has ended. Many who have been active in outdoor labs say that the success of a lab is directly proportional to the amount of preplanning and follow-up.

The HR manager decides the type of outdoor lab experiences that would be appropriate to fit the desired goals and the physical abilities of the work group. Assuming the lab will be offered by another company specializing in this type of training, a training program is arranged. Many providers of outdoor labs will design a training program to a team's specific objectives. Some providers will send their trainers to a company ahead of time to research the needs of the work team. The team's HR consultant also may accompany them at the outdoor lab.

Before returning to the workplace, participants spend time summarizing what they have learned and how it applies to work. Team members draw up goals for what they hope to do back at work, and they make a plan for how they can accomplish the goals. Back at work, the team holds meetings to define the goals and develop more detailed plans. The trainer will often make a follow-up visit to the work site after several weeks to reinforce the learning of the outdoor lab. The HR consultant also helps the team continue to work on their goals.

Cautions in Using Outdoor Labs

Outdoor labs are not without their risks to both the organization and to the individual. But by taking some modest precautions, most problems can be minimized.

It is beyond the scope of this discussion to present the legal consequences of outdoor labs, but like any work activity, the employer is liable for the health and safety of its employees.[32] Safety should be a major concern, and the safety record of the provider and safety training of the trainers should be investigated. Recently, a participant of a youth-oriented outdoor lab died of dehydration and heat exposure when the trainers and their group got lost in a remote area north of the Grand Canyon. The group consisted of troubled youths, and the trainers had designed the program to help them gain self-esteem and self-control. Although there has not been a known death in a corporate outdoor lab, safety should be a major concern. For both liability and OD philosophical reasons, participants must be free to participate and there should be no coercive pressure to do so. Participants should also feel absolutely free to decline to participate in specific exercises.

Results of Outdoor Labs

Outdoor labs have become highly popular within the last few years as a team-building and leadership-development technique. Major corporations, such as AT&T, Times Mirror, General Motors, IBM, Frito Lay, and Citicorp have outdoor labs, and hundreds of smaller profit and not-for profit organizations have sent their employees to the labs. DuPont recently contracted with one provider for the training of 20,000 managers.

One study at Martin Marietta conducted by a private consulting firm compared two work groups who had similar characteristics except that one participated in outdoor labs and the other did not. The group that participated had an annual turnover rate of 1 percent, and the other group had turnover of 11 percent, the company average. The study also found that those who participated had increased promotions and greater employee commitment.[33] Though these studies are not proof of the effectiveness of outdoor labs, they show encouragement for use of the labs.

SUMMARY

Management development and organization development. OD is a long-term effort to introduce planned change in an organization. Therefore, the selection of specific strategies and techniques is an important action step.

The OD strategy involves the planning and direction of the intervention activities. A comprehensive approach involves the way the organization is managed, the way jobs are designed, and the way people are motivated. The consultant and the client determine the appropriate strategy to best attain change objectives. There are also a number of OD techniques. Based upon the change strategy, specific action interventions that will best resolve problem conditions and increase organization effectiveness are then set in motion.

Three basic approaches to change were identified: structural, technical, and behavioral. Structure provides the framework that relates elements of the organization. These units are engaged in some task or technical accomplishment, and are also bound together in an interrelated network of social and behavioral relationships.

There are a variety of intervention techniques which may be used in organization development. Although these techniques differ, they aim at the same basic goals: (1) to improve the functioning of the client system; (2) to increase the organization's adaptive capability toward a more anticipative system; and (3) to enhance the development and potential of the individual members of the organization.

You will have an opportunity to diagnose a problem, and to develop a specific set of strategies and techniques for executing an organization change program. You will probably find differing departmental objectives which must be reconciled with organization goals. You may also experience differing approaches to change among different individuals. One person may view the problem as calling for a structural change, although another person may view it as requiring behavioral or technical change strategies. After a change strategy has been agreed upon, specific techniques for achieving change must then be designed and carried out.

All the major variables are interrelated, and often a change in structure; for example, they may have consequences on technical and behavioral elements. Therefore, a systems approach or integrative approach involves analyzing the way work is designed, the way the organization is managed, and the way people are motivated.

One important notion regarding behavior change is the idea of choice. Before becoming aware of the consequences of certain behaviors, we often are behaving in certain ways because it has been somewhat effective. Yet this has been largely by habit, and not by choice. As you begin receiving feedback on your "blind spots" and on the impact of your behavior on others, this opens up a choice. You can choose to continue behaving as you have and accept the consequences. Or you can choose to alter your patterns of behavior in hope of changing the consequences to more effective modes. Either way, once you have recognized the choices and take responsibility for your actions, more authentic and effective behavior is possible.

REVIEW QUESTIONS

1. How would you describe "organization development?"
2. Present examples of how management development techniques are used in organizations you have worked for.
3. Identify and describe the possible consequences of not being involved in management development training.
4. Contrast the difference between attitude change and interpersonal skills training programs.
5. Discuss and explain the basic HR management development and organization functions and the Success System Model.
6. Read a book or view a video movie, and identify examples of organization development or management development.

KEY WORDS AND CONCEPTS

Define and be able to use the following:

- Case Method
- Employee Involvement (EI)
- Executive Development
- Management Development

- Management Games
- Organization Development (OD)
- Outdoor Experiential Laboratory Training

- Role Playing
- Team Building
- Team Development

HRM SKILLS SIMULATION 8.1:
THE FRANKLIN COMPANY

Total time suggested: 1 hour and 45 minutes.

A. PURPOSE

In this simulation, you will be able to plan and implement structural, technical, and behavioral strategies in an organization. You will also critique and receive feedback on the effectiveness of your strategies. The goals include

1. To determine appropriate intervention strategy.
2. To experience diagnosing and contacting a client system.
3. To provide feedback on consulting approaches.

B. PROCEDURES

Step 1. Everyone reads the Franklin Company background. Prior to class, divide the class into groups of six. Five people will serve as the Franklin management team, one as the HR consultant, and extras as observer(s). (Roles are to be selected and read prior to the class meeting.) Each player reads only his or her own role. Any additional class members can become observers. The consultants become familiar with the OD Consulting Guidelines and the Diagnostic Form located after the role descriptions. The roles are

1. President
2. Vice president of human resource management
3. Vice president of manufacturing
4. Vice president of marketing
5. Vice president of finance
6. HR consultants

Step 2. The Franklin management team will meet with the HR consultant to decide

1. What are the major problems?
2. Should they use an HR consultant?
3. What strategies should be used to change?

The HR consultant will assist the committee in arriving at a decision. The observer will not take part in the committee decision.

Time suggested for Step 2: 45 minutes.

Step 3. The observer will provide feedback and guide the discussion using the Observer Form. All team members are encouraged to critique the Franklin team meeting and the role of the consultants. Discuss the following questions:

1. How was a decision reached? (By consensus, vote, and so forth.)
2. What type of process skills did the consultants use? (Try to give examples.)
3. What did the consultants do or say that was helpful?
4. What did the consultant do or say that was dysfunctional?
5. Any suggestions of improvement for the Franklin team and the consultants?

Time suggested for Step 3: 10 minutes.

BACKGROUND:
THE FRANKLIN COMPANY

The Franklin Company, a medium-size company with about 1,800 employees, manufactures radar units for use in small aircraft and in police cars. The company is actually over 90 years old and initially manufactured wind vanes and lightning rods, but since World War II, it has manufactured only radar units. During the last 4 years, growth in sales has been stable and profits have decreased slightly, as contrasted to the previous 20 years of steady growth in sales and profits. Industry sales continue to show a steady growth, but new competitors have entered the field with new products and features, cutting into the firm's market share. Franklin has 12 distinct products with an average of three different models per product. New products have been brought on line, but usually several years after the younger competitors. To make matters worse, several Franklin key managers, researchers, and salespeople have joined the competition.

The current abbreviated organization chart is shown in Figure 8.2. All of the company's operations are conducted from the one site. Salespeople are also physically based at the plant, but they make calls throughout the United States.

The president has called in an HRM consulting team to diagnose and propose solutions to the current problems.

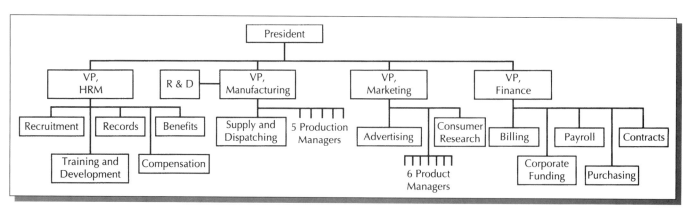

Figure 8.2
Franklin organizational chart

Part III The Success System: Developing a High-Performing Workforce

Role 1—President. You have been the president of the Franklin Company for the past 14 years, and, in large part, its growth and success have been due to your own ability to select and motivate others. You are a college graduate and have attended many executive seminars. You have tried to apply these concepts to Franklin.

You still maintain close contact with day-to-day operations because you believe in "management by wandering around."

Over the past few years, growth has slowed, sales and earnings have declined, and turnover problems have emerged. You feel the rapid early growth may be the cause of current problems.

You are convinced that the lack of coordination between the four operating groups is the major problem, and that a more decentralized operation will help resolve this. You also think a management information system (MIS) will improve coordination and communication. You have asked the vice president of finance to look into MIS.

You believe that the organization needs better morale and improved bottom-line results. Your vice president of HRM has suggested that you try something new: an organization development program. The vice president has invited a team of consultants to meet with your executive committee. You believe in modern techniques, so perhaps these consultants can get the various members to find an agreeable compromise to solve the problem.

Role 2—Vice president of human resource management. You have an MBA, and you were brought in 5 years ago to serve in your current position. You see the key problem as poor structure, a lack of coordination among departments, and weak managerial competence and training at all levels.

All of the other vice presidents worked their way up to their present position, and you consider their professional managerial training somewhat remiss (with the exception of the vice president of marketing, who has attended many of your training sessions). This is even more of a problem at the mid- and lower-level management ranks.

You feel that the answer to the problem is a decentralized operation with increased integration and coordination between departments, and a participative, team style. You have read about OD and have talked to a colleague at another company who had high praise for their OD program. You even discussed implementing an OD program with the vice president of manufacturing, but there was little response. You feel a need to get conflicts out into the open where they can be resolved, rather than each unit seeking its own best interest. A unified team effort is needed.

You have attempted to initiate several training and change programs. These programs have been undercut by other managers. You got word that one vice president was openly attacking the programs, even though the president has been strongly supportive. You suggested bringing in some HRM consultants in hopes of initiating some badly needed changes. Even though they might add to costs in the short run, you are sure that long-term effectiveness will be improved.

Role 3—Vice president of manufacturing. You have been with the company for 22 years, working your way up through the ranks. You have a degree in engineering, and feel that you are competent, run a tight ship, and that your department is the main reason for past success. You believe that most problems are due to rapid growth that has resulted in loose structure, lack of coordination, and lack of control.

You feel that the company has too many meddling staff managers (particularly in marketing and personnel) who do not contribute to profits and only cause problems for the line manager. Several times the vice president of HRM has tried to discuss with you management practices, such as leadership and some new kind of OD program. You listened politely enough, but you got several good laughs out of it at your department meetings. The management training programs offered through the personnel division have been a waste of time, and you have told your people you prefer they stay on the job instead of going to more meetings. The vice president of marketing continually wants a product modification or comes up with some goofball idea for a new product. You have made it clear that you run manufacturing and that includes R&D. You can't run a smooth operation and keep costs down if you are constantly making special modifications. You believe you manufacture enough models to allow a customer to find a suitable product with minor modifications.

You feel the solution is to move into a more highly centralized structure and to appoint an executive vice president to centralize cost control (like yourself, for example) and lay off some of the deadwood.

You hear that the president has invited some HRM consultants in, against your advice. You do not know much about this, but it sounds like pouring money down a rat hole to you. Besides, this HRM business is a bunch of "touchie-feelie" nonsense anyway, which is the last thing you need.

Role 4—Vice president of marketing. You have been with the company for 10 years, and are a college graduate with a major in psychology, but you have gained your knowledge of marketing from experience. You feel that marketing is the major factor in the company's growth, and if your product managers were given greater authority, they could turn the profit picture around.

You see the major problem as the lack of communication among departments and the failure to utilize talented managers. You have tried to get the manufacturing division to make some special modifications in radar units, but they have been willing to comply only on very large orders—and then it generally took them so long that you almost lost several of the orders from your customers. Several of your product managers have met with representatives of manufacturing to discuss new product ideas, but nothing comes of the meetings until your competitors come up with the identical product. Then it takes manufacturing a couple of years to design their own unit.

Your people are bringing back word from the field that the excellent reputation once enjoyed by Franklin is beginning to fade. It has been discouraging for you and your people to fight an uphill battle with manufacturing for new products, and the real kicker is to learn the competition comes out with your product idea.

Despite the problems with the manufacturing division, you find that if you treat your people well, they will perform for you. You have attended most of the management training sessions and have encouraged, though not mandated, your managers to attend. Your department meetings even have follow-up discussions of the training sessions.

Even though marketing has been accused of being run like a "country club," you feel your department performs well. The answer, you believe, is to decentralize the firm into major independent groups and utilize more of the "whiz kids" (the young MBA types) in product management by giving them more authority over product operations. You would like to see yourself as executive vice president over the product managers.

You understand that some HRM consultants are coming in, and see this as a great opportunity to implement your ideas.

Role 5—Vice president of finance. You have an MBA from a major school. This and prior banking experience led to your successful 17 years at Franklin. You instituted all financial systems and made it a smooth operation.

You feel the problems are the result of too many changes in too short a time. The company has too many bright young kids and too many wasteful practices. You suggest going back to the basics by instituting a tighter centralized system of financial control and by cutting about 10 percent of the deadwood. With yourself as an executive vice president (with other vice presidents reporting to you), this job could be done. You would set up some basic company rules, then force the department heads to enforce them.

You would like to see people be required to follow the chain of command. You have heard too many stories of people at lower levels cutting across the formal structure and meeting with their counterparts in another division. This may sound good on the surface, but it usually fouls up the operation later on. You would like to see all communications go up through their appropriate vice president and then back down the chain of command. This type of centralized control is necessary to coordinate everything. You believe there are too many committees throughout the company, and you find it amazing that anything gets accomplished. Further, with all these committees making decisions, it's hard to figure out who to blame when something goes wrong. As far as you are concerned, a camel is a horse designed by a committee.

You avoid getting into conflicts over these issues. You like to let the facts and figures talk, and deal mainly by memo. You realize that you are not as up-to-date on modern computerized systems as you might be, and though the president has asked you to look into a management information system (MIS), you consider it to be a waste of time and money. An MIS would call for a newer computer, and you have heard horror stories about computers and believe your current data processing system to be excellent.

You would like to avoid changes and keep things pretty much the way they are. You hear that some HRM consultants are coming, and your reaction is: Why do we need them? They represent just the kind of wasteful practice you oppose.

Role 6—HRM consultant guidelines: You hope to accomplish several things at this meeting:

1. To develop a consultant/client relationship with all the committee members.
2. To make a preliminary diagnosis of possible problems.
3. To gain support for a possible OD project and convince them of the advantages.
4. To introduce them to some of the goals of OD by doing some process consultation during the meeting.

Observer Guidelines. You are not to take a part in the Franklin meeting, but you are there as an observer so you can provide them information. Use the Observer Form at the end of the simulation and the questions to record your observations.

DIAGNOSTIC FORM

1. Who is the client?
   A. Who has the most influence in the client system? _____
   _____
   _____

   B. Who do you feel is the client? Why? _____
   _____
   _____
   _____

2. Identify major formal and informal problems of the organization.
   A. _____
   B. _____
   C. _____
   D. _____

3. What strategy(s) might you select?
   A. Structural: _____
   _____
   _____

   B. Behavioral: _____
   _____
   _____

   C. Technical: _____
   _____
   _____

   D. Integrated: _____
   _____
   _____

OBSERVER FORM

Instructions: For each item, place a number in the blank to the right representing your reaction to how your group performed based on the following scale.

Low _____ 1 : 2 : 3 : 4 : 5 : 6 : 7 : 8 : 9 : 10 _____ High

1. Degree of cooperative teamwork: _____
2. Degree of team motivation: _____
3. Degree of member satisfaction: _____
4. Degree of information sharing (participation): _____
5. Degree of consensual decision making: _____
6. Degree of team conflict or competition (i.e., conflict directly faced and resolved): _____
7. Degree of quality of group decisions: _____
8. Degree of speed with which decision is made: _____
9. Degree of participating leadership: _____
10. Degree of clarity of goals: _____

Total ranking _____

Case 8.1   Precision Products, Inc.

Situation: Management and Organization Development Meeting

Helen buzzed her loyal secretary, Betty Moneypenny, and together they walked into the conference room. The group was already assembled and eager to start. Everyone knew the topic was management and organization development, so they were hoping to obtain some inside information on the secrets of promotion.

Opening her famous green binder, Helen began to write on the board the accumulated wisdom of Professor Bovineless's classes. All hands were active as the notebooks began to fill up with valuable information—the wisdom of the ages!

Curt Stump, Hiring and Safety, questioned whether Precision Products was ready to commit the necessary financial resources to develop a management development program. He wondered who would be assigned this responsibility because it appeared to be so specialized. Did this mean present staff members would be selected for additional training? Would an outside specialist be hired? Would the responsibility be turned over to an outside consultant?

Viola Romano, Training, Health, and Cafeteria, shared some of the same concerns as Curt Stump did. However, her main concern was that although she was knowledgeable in management development training techniques, her present workload would prevent her from assuming additional duties. Viola wondered how Helen expected to resolve this issue. Did she have a specific plan to present to the group?

Mike Hudson, Affirmative Action and Labor Relations, took a different tack and asked Helen about team development. He felt Precision Products was far from accepting this concept. Mike suggested a job evaluation study resulting in all job descriptions be rewritten to reflect the new teamwork relationships. His question to Helen: "What is top management's position on team development, and is there a timetable?"

Curt Stump pondered whether the wilderness training program was too progressive for Precision Products management. Curt wondered if they all would have to participate. He felt his bad heart should exclude him from such a program.

QUESTIONS

1. How do you recommend Precision Products should proceed with implementing a management development program? Would you use a consulting firm?

2. Viola's concerns about additional workload seems justified. How do you suggest Helen approach her concerns?

3. Based on your knowledge of Precision Products, how do you think the team development concept be approached? Is a job evaluation study appropriate?

4. Consider Curt Stump's concern regarding the wilderness training program. How would you present these issues positively to Precision Products management?

ENDNOTES

1. Kathleen Kerwin (with Keith Naughton), "Remaking Ford," *Business Week* (October 11, 1999): 132.

2. D. Bottoms, "Facing Change or Changing Face?" *Industry Week* (May 1, 1995): 12.

3. Ronald Henkcoff, "Companies That Train Best," *Fortune* (March 22, 1993): 73.

4. Matt Rothman, "Into the Black," *Inc.* (January 1993): 59.

5. Jay Lorsch, ed., *Handbook of Organizational Behavior* (Upper Saddle River, NJ: Prentice Hall, 1987); and Alan Mumford, ed., *Handbook of Management Development* (Brookfield, VT: Gower, 1986).

6. "Deming's Demons," *Wall Street Journal,* 4 June 1990, R41.

7. H. Bernhard and C. Ingolls, "Six Lessons from the Corporate Classroom," *Harvard Business Review* (September-October 1988): 40.

8. R. Fulmer, "Corporate Management Development: The State of the Art," *Journal of Management Development* 7, no. 2 (1988): 57.

9. Albert A. Vicere and Virginia T. Freeman, "Executive Education in Major Corporations: An International Survey," *Journal of Management Development* (1990): 5–16.

10. Special report, "Back to School: The B-Schools That are Best in Executive Education," *Business Week* (October 28, 1991): 102.

11. John Huey, "Where Managers Will Go," *Fortune* (January 27, 1992): 50.

12. E. RanaDall, "IBM's Grass Roots Revival," *Fast Company* (April-May 1997): 64–75.

13. Brian O'Reilly, "Your New Global Work Force," *Fortune* (December 14, 1992): 52.

14. K. Kim Fisher, "Managing in the High-Commitment Workplace," *Organizational Dynamics* (Winter 1989): 38.

15. Richard Beckhard, *Organizational Development: Strategies and Models* (Reading, MA: Addison-Wesley Publishing Co., Inc., 1969), 9.

16. D. Vangard and A. Rothman, "Reinventing Boeing," *Business Week* (March 1, 1993): 60.

17. Teresa J. Colvin and Ralph H. Kilmann, "A Profile of Large Scale Change Programs," Proceedings, Southern Management Association, 1989, 202.

18. John F. Hulpke, Working Paper, California State University, Bakersfield, Bakersfield, CA, 1994.

19. For additional information, see W. Warner Burke, *Organization Development, A Normative View* (Reading, MA: Addison-Wesley Publishing Company, 1987); and Eric H. Neilsen, *Becoming an OD Practitioner* (Upper Saddle River, NJ: Prentice Hall, 1984).

20. Jay Lorsch, ed., *Handbook of Organizational Behavior* (Upper Saddle River, NJ: Prentice Hall, 1987).

21. James B. Treece, "Will GM Learn From Its Own Role Models?" *Business Week* (April 9, 1990): 62.

22. James B. Treece and Judith H. Dodrzynski, "Can GM's Big Investors Get It to Change Lanes," *Business Week* (January 22, 1990): 31.

23. Barbara Block, "Creating a Culture All Employees Can Accept," *Management Review* (July 1989): 41.

24. See, for example, Rosabeth Moss Kanter, *When Giants Learn to Dance: Mastering the Challenge of Strategy, Management, and Careers in the 1990s* (New York: Simon & Schuster, 1989); and W. Warner Burke, *Organization Development: A Normative View* (Reading, MA: Addison-Wesley Publishing Company, 1987).

25. Philip Caldwell, "Cultivating Human Potential At Work," *Journal of Business Strategy* 20, no. 1 (Spring 1984): 75.

26. Robert Waterman, *The Renewal Factor*, p. 98.

27. John Hulpke. Working paper. 1984.

28. G. A. Neuman, J. E. Edwards, and N. S. Raju, "Organizational Development Interventions: A Meta-Analysis of Their Effects on Satisfaction and Other Attitudes," *Personnel Psychology* 42 (1989): 461–89; and R. A. Guzzo, R. D. Jette, and R. A. Katzell, "The Effects of Psychologically Based Intervention Programs On Worker Productivity: A Meta-Analysis," *Personnel Psychology* 38 (1985): 275–91.

29. Donald F. Harvey and Neal Kneip, "The Results of an Integrated OD Program for Training and Team Building" (paper presented at Western Academy of Management, San Diego, CA. 1990).

30. Jim Bartimo, "At These Shouting Matches, No One Says a Word," *Business Week* (June 11, 1990): 78; and Leslie Helm, "How the Leader in Networking Practices What It Preaches," *Business Week* (May 16, 1988): 96.

31. For a more complete description of outdoor labs, see Alex Prud'homme, "Management Training No Longer Means Seminars in Self-discovery," *Business Month* (March 1990): 61–66; Harvey Chipkin, "A Team Builder's Guide to the Galaxy," *Business Month* (March 1990) 66–69; Adrienne Gall, "You Can Take the Manager Out of the Woods, but . . ." *Training and Development Journal* (March 1987): 54–58; Janet Long, "The Wilderness Lab Comes of Age," *Training and Development Journal* (March 1987): 30–39; Richard Polley and Jarle Eid, "Leadership Training on the Bergen Ford," *Group and Organization Studies* 15, no. 2 (June 1990): 192–211.

32. For a more detailed discussion of legal risks, see Susan Chesteen, Lee Caldwell, and Larry Prochazka, "Taking Legal Risks Out of Adventure Training," *Training and Development Journal* vol 33, no. 7 (July 1988): 42–46.

33. Adriene Gall, "You Can Take the Manager Out of the Woods, but . . . ," *Training and Development Journal* (March 1987): 58.

Chapter 9

The Success System: Career Development

Objectives

Upon completing this chapter, you will be able to:

1. Define and discuss the career development process.
2. Describe the stages in the career process.
3. Understand and compare the advantages and disadvantages of various career planning approaches.
4. Identify and describe the major career development programs.
5. Define and be able to use the concepts of downsizing and job layoffs in career planning.

Premeeting preparation

1. Read chapter 9.
2. Prepare for HRM Skills Simulation 9.1. Read Parts A and B, Step 1.
3. Read Case 9.1: Tucker Knox Corporation Answer questions.

Sometimes the best way to get ahead is to "boomerang"—to go back to your former company as a new, improved version of your old self. Martin Cox left his job at Lotus Development Corp. in 1994 to chase a dream that he couldn't realize there: to ship of piece of software that had his name on it. After years of working on a tool kit that supported other developers, Cox, now 38, longed to be a developer himself. So he jumped ship and went to Individual Inc., where he helped build First! in Brief, a customized news-delivery program that ran on the Lotus platform.

Fast-forward 2 years. First! in Brief shipped successfully, and Cox was hungry for new challenges. He had become a topflight software programmer, and now he wanted to deepen his understanding of how companies use software to reach their business goals.

Cox decided that consulting to other companies would give him the knowledge he craved. He believed that his gold-star resume would make him a shoo-in at companies like Andersen Consulting. But, after a year of soul-searching, he decided to consult for Lotus, the company that he'd left not so long ago. He figured that his work with Lotus software, which he knew cold, would give him an invaluable head start there.

Today Cox is back at Lotus—and he's not the only Lotus vet to reenlist. At companies large and small, people are choosing to return to where they once belonged. Call it boomeranging, the next logical step in the evolution of corporate free agency: People are getting ahead by leaving their companies, acquiring critical experience elsewhere, and returning to their former employers with deeper skills and know-how.

As it turns out, you *can* go home again. But going back is not risk-free. Realizing why you really left your old company takes extreme self-awareness. Convincing your ex-employer to take you back takes considerable negotiating skills. And walking back into your old office and facing down people who may think of you as a deserter takes more than a little courage.[1]

Change continues to be the tenor of the twenty-first century. As a result, companies need development of employees to meet competitive challenges, and employees need a broader range of skills—as in the following example.

Tom Brown, 44, had been working as New York regional comptroller for McKesson, the big wholesale drug distributor, when he got the news that he no longer had a job. He knew that layoffs were inevitable, but he still thinks he should have been treated better after 13 years with the company. "Management didn't want to talk to me after my position had been eliminated," he says. "They basically didn't want to know that I existed."

Terry Cantine, 49, was product marketing manager for a Sun Valley, California, company called AVX Filters when she got the ax last September. She's been brushing up on her computer skills, and she tells prospective employers she's willing to take a big pay cut, but nothing has turned up yet. Says Cantine: "My life was my job, but now I'm finding out how wrong that is."

James Kmetz, 46, was laid off last April after 4 years as a trust specialist at Norwest Corp. in Minneapolis. He received a 1-minute outplacement interview and no severance, and he has grown weary of hearing that his education and experience make him overqualified for the menial jobs he applies for. Says Kmetz: "I have no career aspirations. I don't want to move up. At my age, I'm not very hopeful about finding another good job. For me, the American Dream is dead."[2]

These cases illustrate the fact that the workplace has changed, and that individuals need to reassess their attitudes toward careers. In the twenty-first century, companies and individuals will need to take a more active, systematic approach to career development. In an environment of increasing competition, continuous innovation in technology, corporate downsizing and restructuring, and increasing pressure for promotions, career development becomes even more important.

More and more, organizations are realizing that they must use the energy and ability of individuals if they are to be successful. A key feature of this new approach is empowerment: The company, managers, and their employees are partners in developing career paths. Employee involvement in career development attempts to move the organization from the traditional "I just work here" type of culture, to one of shared vision and goals.[3]

In these changing times, it seems that individuals should develop new and better personal skills in self-assessment and career planning. Organizations are becoming more active in developing career development programs. Many organizations are designing career programs in an attempt to increase employee productivity, prevent job "burnout," and improve the quality of employee worklife.[4] One approach is termed the proteam career. A proteam career is a career that is frequently changing based on both changing interests and values of the individual and changes in the work environment.[5]

In this chapter, we will examine stage three of the Success System Model: developing human potential in career development. Organizations must become more proactive in developing career concepts and approaches, the stages of career paths, and the impact of downsizing on career planning. The modern workplace has changed, and the Success System approach reflects new career-related attitudes and behaviors. For example, Generation X employees are often unimpressed with the status symbols, but want job flexibility and meaning from work.[6]

CAREER MANAGEMENT

A **career** may be defined as the individually perceived sequence of positions occupied by an individual during the course of one's lifetime. This includes the attitudes and behaviors associated with work-related activities and experiences.[7] This suggests that "career" implies neither success nor failure, except in the judgment of the individual. The term "career" refers both to the way an individual views his or her work experiences, and the way an organization views the series of job positions held by the individual.

Employers are evaluating workers more thoroughly than in the past, and the terms of the unwritten contract between employees and their company, changing for the past decade, have grown almost indecipherable. According to Robert L. Swain, a New York City consultant and outplacement specialist: "Long range is now the end of the quarter. I am seeing a lot of very talented executives, with great skills and broad experience, who simply failed to recognize how impatient their bosses had become." The emphasis on continuous learning is changing the direction and frequency of movement within careers.

Jeffrey A. Sonnenfeld, an Emory University management professor, found startling results in a study he recently conducted of 300 mid-career executives in the financial services field. About 20 percent believed they lacked the skills to meet the expectations of their bosses, and another 75 percent replied they would probably be behind the curve within 5 years.[8]

The first step in taking hold of your career is to stand back and take a hard look at yourself. Your performance appraisal from the company probably doesn't tell you enough about how you are doing. Arrange to get some more feedback, formal or informal, from associates, subordinates, and peers. If you try to assess yourself honestly, with sufficient input from others, you may be surprised at the results.

In today's fast changing world, perhaps the most appropriate way of looking at your career is that it is "boundary-less," including several employers and possibly different occupations.[9]

Career development, the ways in which career decisions and choices are made, is important both to the employee and the organization. **Career planning** refers to the efforts by an individual to become more aware of one's own skills, interests, values, and opportunities. This involves identifying career-related goals and developing plans for achieving those goals.[10] (See Figure 9.1.)

Career development can contribute to the high-performing organization by utilizing the individual differences among employees through motivating them and also influencing their job satisfaction and productivity. Career development also involves employees in planning their own career needs. One of the HR manager's responsibilities involves helping employees to develop and realize their individual potential. Unfortunately, in this age of restructuring, there is a growing group of so-called "discouraged" workers—those who have simply given up after looking months or years for work. This suggests one important way career planning is changing.

The big problem, say human-resources experts who counsel older workers, is that many of these employees are financially and psychologically unprepared for retirement. Michael C. Barth (senior vice president at ICF Inc., a Washington, D.C., human resources consulting firm) says: "Somewhere about 18 to 24 months down

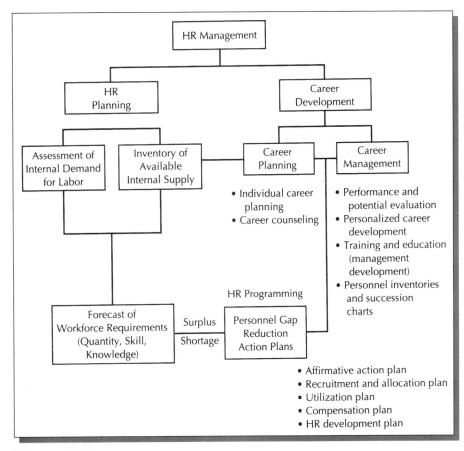

Figure 9.1
Relationship between career development and HR planning

Source: T. G. Gutteridge, "Organizational Career Development Systems: The State of the Practice," in D. T. Hall and associates, *Career Development in Organizations* (San Francisco: Jossey-Bass, 1986), p. 57. Courtesy of Jossey-Bass.

the line, they often discover two things. First, they need money. Second, they are bored out of their skulls."[11] One example of the career planning process takes place at Goldman, Sachs & Co. (See HRM in Action.)

HRM IN ACTION
MAKING PARTNER AT GOLDMAN[12]

Goldman, Sachs & Co. is one of the last of Wall Street's major private partnerships. Each year the firm picks a small number of new partners from among its hundreds of young executives. Winners are set for life, and they typically retire as multimillionaires after only a decade or so. But it's getting harder to decide who gets the prize.

Exactly what goes on behind the scenes of the 2-month-long competition is a closely held secret. Current partners describe it, of course, as a rigorous but fair process in which politics are unimportant. The process certainly is rigorous. It starts with a winnowing down of the worldwide workforce of 6600 to a list of 50 to 60 serious candidates. Each potential new partner must then be nominated by a current partner.

What do partners look for? In addition to keen business judgment and a proven track record of success, partners look for team players and "culture carriers." Such people fit Goldman's conservative style and its customer-oriented tradition that dates back to the 1860s, when Marcus Goldman began hawking commercial paper on the streets of New York.

Partners, who are expected to back their nominees' causes throughout the process, then file mountains of endorsement letters. For the next several weeks, an eight-member management committee reviews these materials and checks out the nominees. Members of the committee who are not in a candidate's division grill department heads and other partners about the candidate's qualifications, and then report back. Candidates themselves are never interviewed. In fact, they're not even supposed to know that they are candidates. But of course they do.

After a dizzying round of management-committee summit meetings, a final "town meeting" of all current partners is held, at which the management committee presents its final list for discussion and debate—even though it's pretty clear that the committee's list is final. Following the "town meeting," the partners announce the list of newly minted millionaires. In 1 year, Goldman added 32 members to its exclusive club, which now numbers 148.

QUESTIONS

1. What appears to be the process for choosing new partners? Is it fair? Is it effective?

2. Discuss the role of culture in choosing new partners. How important is culture in the decision-making process?

3. Where do the candidates themselves fit into the selection process? What are the pros and cons of the process?

CAREER STAGES

In career planning, HRM managers need to understand the complex issues employees face as they move forward in their careers. As the Success System Model shows, the organization cannot function at its fullest unless a way is found to develop the human potential of organization members.

Researchers have found that individuals progress through several career stages which follow life patterns.[13] Each career stage is distinguished by differing needs, motives, and tasks. Most people begin career choice in their education and training. They then take a first job and go through organizational entry, career stabilization, and eventually retirement. Each stage presents distinct developmental challenges for the individual. In addition to these typical career stages, there are also circumstances which interrupt or postpone the career cycle. As an example, many women interrupt their careers in order to raise families, and then may resume their career pursuits later in life. In addition, many individuals change careers in mid-life. In either situation, a conflict between career and life needs often occurs.

Individuals pass through a series of typical **career stages,** as described in the following sections. (See Figure 9.2.)

Stage One: Organizational Entry

The new employee enters the job market, joins an organization, and begins to establish a career. Often the employee usually expects to have a long-term career. Two factors in this stage appear to be (1) the initial job assignment; and (2) the characteristics of the first supervisor, or mentor. A mentor is an experienced senior employee who helps develop less-experienced employees. Many organizations today actively promote mentor relationships.[14]

When a new employee makes a smooth transition from this preparatory work stage into the mainstream of organizational life, he or she has the potential to become a productive and satisfied worker. However, the initial job experience may be frustrating and disappointing for some new employees. It is not unusual for the new employee to encounter conflict between career expectations and the organization's job demands.

The organization, as well, may be disappointed by the performance of the employee. It is suggested that the unrealistic expectations of both employee and organization may often contribute to this "career shock" syndrome. Unfortunately for both the employee and employer, the consequences of these unmet expectations often lead to ineffective use of human resource potential, dissatisfaction, and high turnover among new employees.[15]

Minimizing Early Career Problems

In order to lessen the possibility of unrealistic expectations, it is important for the new employee to receive an accurate job preview and orientation. In addition, during the early entry stage, new employees need frequent feedback on how they are doing in order to reinforce learning and encourage self-improvement. New employees must adapt to the job, establish work patterns, and develop work relationships. During this stage, individuals need to maintain effective performance levels and develop support from key members of the organization. At this early career stage, the individual should also develop a career orientation, set career goals, and understand the possible career paths for goal accomplishments.[16]

Figure 9.2
Career stages

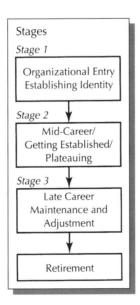

Stage Two: Mid-Career

This usually occurs after a few years on the job, when the productive employee begins to experience a loss of challenge in their career. The individual's career becomes a major consideration during this stage. At this point, the individual may have had several promotions. The major tasks in the mid-career stage are to examine and reappraise the early career results, make changes in goals, and remain productive on the job.[17] If the employee has been in the same position for several years, then one must recognize the possibility of changing job requirements, lateral job movement, corporate politics, lessening of promotional opportunity, and even possible job loss or layoff.

At this stage, the individual may need to cope with becoming "plateaued." A **plateau** refers to the point in a career at which the chance of future promotions appears to be very low. At mid-career, individuals may also discover that their knowledge and skills are no longer current enough to enable them to perform their jobs at a satisfactory level. In fact, they may be in danger of losing their jobs and confronting the economic and emotional impact of being laid off.[18]

Many organizations are **restructuring** their management, thus closing off promotion opportunities. The number of people who are unlikely to receive promotions has increased dramatically, highlighting the need to better understand reactions to career plateaus. According to Georgia Chao, early perceptions of a career plateau may be viewed negatively and may motivate the individual to avoid the plateau.[19] Mid-career employees in this position may suffer from depression, poor health, fatigue, and hostility toward coworkers, which may result in lowered job performance.

During this period in one's career, there may be a slowing down of physical and mental processes. Many employees fear that they will be replaced by brighter and younger employees, and that they will become obsolete and be put out to pasture. This perspective may influence both employee satisfaction and productivity levels. The HR manager needs to develop training programs to promote career planning and minimize the consequences of these problems. Some companies, like General Electric, rotate their middle managers into different positions to improve their performance by giving them new perspectives on their work.[20] One example of dealing with a career plateau is discussed in the following HRM in Action.

Stage Three: Late Career

The extension of mandatory retirement to age 70 has given rise to the "graying of the workforce." Many organizations now have preretirement planning programs to assist workers in making this transition. The Conference Board study found that companies continue to lay off or early retire senior workers, even though they are

Source: B.C. by permission of Johnny Hart and Creators Syndicate, Inc.

In Chicago, Continental Bank is encouraging employees to move across departmental lines on a horizontal basis, because vertical promotions are less frequent. Someone from auditing might switch to commercial training; someone from systems research and development might move into international development. The inflexible HRM policies of the past are rapidly fading to accommodate present and future problems. Another strategy used by Continental Bank is to create dual technical and management ladders. New "technical executive" positions are equal to management jobs in title and dollars. For example, the bank has created senior lending positions and positions for accounting and systems specialists that are equivalent to senior managerial posts in those departments.

An alternative way to placate people who do not move up is to pay them more for jobs well done. For years, companies that rely heavily for growth on creative people—including scientists, engineers, writers, and artists—have provided incentives for them to stay on. Companies are now offering such incentives to a broader spectrum. For example, at Monsanto, favored scientists can now climb a university-like track of associate fellow, fellow, senior fellow, to distinguished fellow. The company has 130 fellows, and they earn from $65,000 a year to well over $100,000.

At General Electric, "plateaued" employees (either organizationally, through a lack of available promotions; or personally, through lack of ability or desire) are sometimes assigned to task forces or study teams. These employees have not been promoted in a technical sense, but at least they have gotten a new assignment, a fresh perspective, and a change in their daily work.

Finally, Prudential Life Insurance Company rotates managers to improve their performance. Rockwell International uses task forces, where possible, to "recharge" managers so they do not feel a loss of self-worth if they do not move up as fast as they think they should.

QUESTIONS

1. Discuss some new policies that have replaced the inflexible HRM policies of the past. Do you agree or disagree?

2. How do you placate people who are not promoted? Are these techniques successful?

3. What is causing the change from vertical to horizontal "promotions"? Do you think this will satisfy employees?

---

more reliable than younger employees, have better work attitudes, have better job skills, are absent less often, and are less likely to quit. About 70 percent of the companies surveyed also said older workers were at least as cost-effective as their younger colleagues. The Conference Board concludes: "The effect of current practices and trends may be eroding a valued resource to a degree that is unintended and imprudent."[22] For the majority of employees, the late-career period is a time to remain productive and to prepare for retirement. During late career, many individuals have to deal with the consequences of mid-career obsolescence or "plateauing."

In order to adjust successfully to late careers, individuals should maintain positive, forward-thinking attitudes and receive support from colleagues and spouses. Late-career employees should engage in long-term planning of their finances and leisure pursuits with their spouses, and should plan their retirements with care and attention.

Individuals may respond differently to retirement for a number of reasons. Often the individual looks forward to this stage as a time of lessening of the stress and regimentation of the job. These individuals view retirement as an opportunity to take part in interests and hobbies their job had not permitted. Some people begin new educational and career paths at this point. For others, retirement is a threatening experience accompanied by negative feelings. The loss of a job identity leaves many individuals with feelings of emptiness and lack of direction. In addition to this identity crisis, many individuals face adjustments to home and family life as well. HR managers are faced with the challenge of understanding this career stage in the best interests of both the employee and the organization.

For example, IBM and other companies have innovative programs for early retirement and part-time work for older employees. These programs have not only been beneficial for improving the outlook of the older workers and retirees, but have also saved the companies considerable money.[23]

CAREER PLANNING AND PATHING

Currently, many organizations have developed career planning programs, which involve integrating the individual's career aspirations with the realities of organizational opportunities. **Career path** refers to the sequencing of specific job positions to lead to a desired career goal. For example, a manager who wishes to move into top management may need line management or international management experience. (See Figure 9.3.)

Determining Individual and Organizational Needs

A career development program should be viewed as a dynamic process aimed at matching the needs of employees to the organization. The individual employee must identify their aspirations, abilities, and interests; recognize what career options exist; and develop a career plan. HR managers should encourage employees to take responsibility for their own careers, offering assistance by providing information on career opportunities that might be available. Career development programs benefit the employee by giving them increased opportunity for managing their own careers and benefit the organization by increasing motivation and communication.

Fast-Track Employees

Organizations often identify individuals with high career potential, and place them on a **fast track** for promotion in the company. AT&T, for example, uses assessment centers for the early identification of managerial talent. These employees are given rapid and intensive developmental opportunities in the company.[24] The development of fast-track employees require organizations to put forth specialized recruitment and continuous monitoring of the employees' career. Southland Corporation,

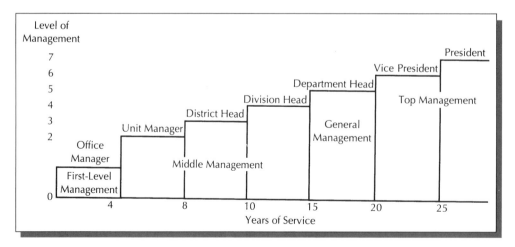

Figure 9.3
Career path

for example, uses a computerized career development program for its fast-track employees to plan and monitor their career paths.[25]

Mentoring

The relationship between individuals with others at higher levels in the organization who share knowledge and support them in the development of their careers is termed **mentoring.** Managers who coach, advise, and encourage employees are termed mentors.

Informal mentoring goes on within many organizations. Although most mentoring relationships develop over time on an informal basis, there has been a rapid growth of formal mentoring plans calling for the assignment of a mentor to all employees considered for upward movement in the organization. The mentor provides guidance on goals, opportunities, expectations, standards, and support in fulfilling the individual's potential.[26]

Career Development for Women

One of the current trends is the employment of women in jobs that until recently were held predominantly by men. Organizations are currently under considerable pressure (as a result of EEO/affirmative action requirements) to increase the proportion of women they employ at upper management levels.

Many organizations are developing programs to help women managers fit into the existing culture. Women in management have often been handicapped by not being part of the so-called "old boy network," the informal network of interpersonal relationships that has traditionally provided a way for senior (male) members of the organization to act as mentors in providing opportunities and career coaching to junior (male) employees. Women have often lacked role models to serve as mentors because not many women have yet reached the upper ranks of management, and often males may hesitate to act as mentors for female protégées because of possible sexual harassment charges.

The advancement of women in management has been hindered by a series of sex-role stereotypes that have shaped attitudes toward working women. Fortunately, there is substantial evidence that stereotyped attitudes toward women are changing. As women pursue career goals assertively and attitudes continue to change, the climate for women in management will be even more favorable.

The Glass Ceiling

The **glass ceiling** is a term used to describe why women are not being promoted to upper levels of management: A recent study found less than 7 percent of *Fortune* 500 companies' top management positions were held by women. It has been estimated that in the twenty-first century, only 20 percent of *Fortune* 500 companies' top management positions will be held by women.[27]

Although progress has been slow, opportunities for women to move into management positions are definitely improving. In addition to breaking down the barriers to advancement, the development of women managers demands a better understanding of women's needs and the requirements of the management world.

Managing Dual Careers

As more women pursue careers, one of the major problems facing women is having both a managerial career and a family. Women managers with younger children often experience conflict between their responsibility to the children and their jobs.

One career strategy for reducing job/family conflict for women managers has been called the "mommy track." It has been suggested that women managers who primarily want careers should be differentiated in organizations from women managers who want both careers and families. It has also been suggested that career-primary women (i.e., women who are willing to set aside family considerations) should be treated like their male counterparts. As managerial candidates, they should be identified early and provided with developmental opportunities to help them advance into the highest levels in the organization. Career-and-family or career-secondary women, on the other hand, should receive different types of career planning so that they can eventually work toward long-term management positions.

In recent years, many organizations, including IBM, Digital Equipment Corporation, and Pacific Telesis, have inaugurated programs to assist the career-oriented woman. These programs, including alternative career paths, extended leave, flextime, job sharing, and telecommuting, provide alternative approaches to balancing career and family needs.[28]

DOWNSIZING

Many companies are rushing to downsize in an attempt to increase productivity and profitability in a highly competitive global economy. Unless there is careful planning, the end result may be lower morale, loss of key people, and increased costs.

A recent survey by the American Management Association found less than one-half of downsized companies reporting an increase in profits. The survey also disclosed lower morale for the surviving employees and increased overtime costs, with 22 percent of the companies revealing they had released the wrong people.[29] A similar situation occurred at NYNEX Corporation after separating from AT&T. The company used a voluntary program to downsize and was successful in obtaining the desired number of employees to downsize. Later on, it was discovered some divisions had too many employees; other divisions were short. The end result was the expenditure of millions of dollars to rehire for 4,000 positions.

The successful company downsizing requires a strategic human resource plan in place at the beginning of the process. Such a plan will identify the company's core businesses and provide a human resources planning and allocation program. The result will be a company vision of the future, a demonstration of top management leadership, and an action plan ensuring employees are treated with equity and fairness.[30]

BURNOUT

As HRM continues to participate in the development of wellness programs, the approach is becoming more holistic in protecting employee health. Part of this approach is a growing concern over employee **burnout.** This may result from downsizing as employees find their job responsibilities and demands increasing.

Burnout may occur when the employee has the perception he or she is not receiving the expected satisfactions from doing their job. The employee probably has unrealistic expectations of achieving unrealistic goals. Such individuals often become error-prone, irritable, and cynical.[31] When this takes place, other employees may become copycats, causing it to spread within the organization.

The burnout phenomenon is a common stress among managers, with some suggesting as many as half of all employees are affected.[32] This can result from a corporate culture with active organizational politics, misunderstood expected job content, and work overload. Managers need to be alert for these symptoms of burnout, and intercede quickly to prevent its growth and spread within the organization.

The world now knows about places like Japan. Even smaller economies, such as South Korea, Singapore, Hong Kong, and Taiwan, have caught the attention of the West. But there are many other things happening in this changing world too, and we had better take note now. For example, countries such as India and Indonesia, with over a billion people between them, are undergoing rapid change and rapid economic growth. This may mean many human resource managers from the rest of the world will be involved in businesses in these parts sooner than you think. But will the same principles and practices learned in the United States or Europe apply in places like Indonesia? Yes, and no.

Management, as a technical art, is probably pretty much the same in Djakarta as in Des Moines. Production, finance, and accounting look at least somewhat similar across the seas in Indonesia. Not so human resource management. There's a world of difference.

It should be obvious that organizations, the products of human thinking, will be a result of the combined thinking patterns and cultural values in the countries where the organizations exist.

In Indonesian society, "follow the leader" and "paternalism" are strongly valued cultural norms. Elders are expected to take important roles in any organization. Because most Indonesian organizations started as family businesses, and because in the family the patriarch makes all decisions, this becomes the expected pattern in organizations nationwide.

Hiring decisions reflect these beliefs and values. All hiring decisions are the job of the top person—the patriarch. If not made directly by him (and it is almost always "him," not "her," at this stage in Indonesia's history), employees are at least hired with his consent. In the hiring process, trustworthiness is more important than job skills, knowledge, or experience.

The Western negative attitudes contained in the term "nepotism" would make no sense in Indonesia. Only family members are expected to be in the inner circle in any organization. Those outside the family are allowed to have jobs family members don't want or cannot do. About the only way for a total outsider to get into a position of power in an Indonesian firm is to marry the boss's daughter.

Can these principles really hold in the very large "sogo sosha" conglomerates in Indonesia? Not totally, but the ideas still linger in the background. For sure, don't expect anyone in Indonesia to object if a key job somewhere goes to a family member. That's not only the way things have always been done, it is the way things *should* be, at least in Indonesia.

QUESTIONS

1. How are the economic growth and rapid people changes taking place in such countries as India and Indonesia going to affect human resource management techniques as practiced in the United States?

2. Discuss some specific culture norms and how they impact HRM. Who should change—them or us?

3. What are some approaches HRM should develop in providing leadership to their companies planning to open plants or form partnerships in other countries?

SUMMARY

We have focused on several major career issues. In the past few years, organizations have been operating in a dynamic and changing environment, and consequently have begun to take a more active approach to the career development of their employees. You have been introduced to the emerging techniques of career management and the ways career development can be used to improve organizational effectiveness.

You, as an HRM manager, must be sensitive to changes in markets, people, and competition and become aware of the need for an adaptive and flexible career program. Today, because of changing conditions, many companies are unable to deliver on the implicit career promises made to their employees.

You will have an opportunity to experience and practice career planning skills in this class meeting. A career is the sequence of organization positions occupied by a person during one's worklife. Career planning, at this stage, is important because the consequences of career success or failure are very important. Career planning allows you to reassess your career goals and redirect your efforts toward new goals.

REVIEW QUESTIONS

1. How would you define "career path"?
2. Present examples of how outplacement techniques are used in organizations you have worked for.
3. Identify and demonstrate the uses of career planning in an organization.
4. Contrast the difference between single and dual career conflict. Is this discussed in-depth enough in the chapter?
5. Discuss and explain the basic career planning functions and the Success System Model.
6. Explain three basic responses an individual has to a career plateau.
7. Read a book or view a video movie, and identify a career path or dual career issue.

KEY WORDS AND CONCEPTS

Define and be able to use the following:

- Burnout
- Career
- Career Development
- Career Path

- Career Planning
- Career Stages
- Dual Careers
- Fast Track

- Glass Ceiling
- Mentoring
- Plateau
- Restructuring

HRM SKILLS SIMULATION 9.1: CAREER LIFE PLANNING

Total time suggested: 1 hour.

A. PURPOSE

The purpose of this simulation is to examine the interdependence among team members and to provide insights into the concept of culture. To study culture, we may examine the culture of a group which shares certain cultural traits. The goals include:

1. To compare decisions made by individuals with those made by the group.
2. To practice effective consensus-seeking techniques.
3. To gain insights into the concept of cultural values.

B. PROCEDURES

Step 1. Prior to class, form into groups of five members, each group constituting an executive committee. Assign each member of your group as one of the committee members. (Extras act as observers.) Use the Career Values Worksheet. Observers may use the Observer Form located at the end of this simulation to gather data on group process.

1. Executive vice president, marketing
2. Executive vice president, finance
3. Executive vice president, manufacturing
4. Executive vice president, personnel
5. Executive vice president, research and development

Before class, individually read the employee profiles that follow and rank-order the 10 employees on the work sheet from "1" for least likely to "10" for most likely to be expendable. Participants are to enter their ranking in column 1 on the Career Values Worksheet.

Step 2. **Executive Committee Meeting.** Through group discussion, exploration, and examination, try to reach a *consensus decision* reflecting the integrated thinking and consensus of all members. Remember, a consensus decision involves reaching mutual agreement by discussion until all agree on the final decision.

Follow these instructions for reaching consensus:

1. Try to reach the best possible decision, but at the same time defend the importance of your department.
2. Avoid changing your mind simply to reach agreement and to avoid conflict, but support solutions with which you are able to agree.
3. Avoid "conflict-reducing" techniques, such as majority vote, averaging, or trading in reaching your decision.
4. View differences of opinion as a help rather than a hindrance in decision making.

At this point, meet together as the executive committee, and enter your results in column 2 on the Executive Committee Decision Work Sheet.

Time suggested for Step 2: 40 minutes.

Step 3. Each team lists its results on the blackboard, and the instructor posts the actual performance ranking. Enter the performance ranking in column 3.

Time suggested for Step 3: 5 minutes.

Step 4. The instructor leads a discussion of the activity, letting each team explain its scores on the Career Value Worksheet. Consider the following points and compare results for each team:

1. What were the similarities and differences?
2. The extent to which efficiency, effectiveness, and member satisfaction were emphasized in the values.
3. What kind of culture would you see fitting with your own career values?

Time suggested for Step 4: 15 minutes.

CAREER VALUES WORKSHEET

Instructions: Rank-order the values which you hold most strongly by placing the number 1 beside your preeminent value, 2 by the second most strongly held, and so on.

Individual Role

____ Get ahead

____ Be honest

____ Work hard

____ Pursue happiness

____ Accrue goods and wealth

____ Become educated

____ Know the right people

____ Be productive

Team Role

____ Help others

____ Win

____ Look out for yourself

____ Find a better way

____ Adjust to the prevailing social norms

____ Stand up for what you think is right

OBSERVER RECORDING FORM

Your role during this part of the simulation is important because your goal is to give individuals feedback on their counseling style. Following are listed eight criteria of helping relationships. Rate the consultant by circling the appropriate number.

1. Level of involvement:
   Cautious   Low 1:2:3:4:5:6:7:8:9:10 High   Interested   _____

2. Level of communication:
   Doesn't listen   Low 1:2:3:4:5:6:7:8:9:10 High   Listens   _____

3. Level of openness, trust:
   Shy, uncertain   Low 1:2:3:4:5:6:7:8:9:10 High   Warm, friendly   _____

4. Level of suggesting corrective measures:
   Authoritative   Low 1:2:3:4:5:6:7:8:9:10 High   Seeks agreement   _____

5. Level of providing direction:
   Clear   Low 1:2:3:4:5:6:7:8:9:10 High   Convincing   _____

6. Level of supportiveness:
   Disagrees   Low 1:2:3:4:5:6:7:8:9:10 High   Supports   _____

7. Level of competence:
   Unsure   Low 1:2:3:4:5:6:7:8:9:10 High   Competent   _____

8. Overall style:
   Ineffective   Low 1:2:3:4:5:6:7:8:9:10 High   Effective   _____

Total time suggested: 1 hour, 10 minutes.

A. PURPOSE

This simulation will give you experience in preparing career and life plans, and in acting as a helper for someone else formulating career life plans.

B. PROCEDURES

Step 1. Individually prepare a set of career life goals. The list could include career, professional, personal, and relational goals (List 1).

Step 2. Divide into dyads, with one person acting as a consultant. The consultant then goes through the list reality testing, determining priorities, and looking for conflicting goals. Revise the list as necessary. When one person has completed, trade roles.

Time suggested for Step 2: 20 minutes.

Step 3. Individually make a list of important past accomplishments or happenings, including peak experiences, accomplishments, things that have made you feel happy or satisfied, or times when you felt most alive or real (List 2).

Step 4. With each person taking a turn at being a consultant, work through a comparison of the individual's goals (List 1) with the list of past achievements (List 2); look for conflicts or incongruencies between the two lists.

Time suggested for Step 4: 20 minutes.

Step 5. The outcome of Step 4 is a set of firm goals with relative priorities. Each person now prepares a detailed plan of action specifying how to get from where he or she is to where the goal indicates he or she should be.

Time suggested for Step 5: 15 minutes.

Step 6. As a class, critique the usefulness of a career life planning session. Additional questions include:

- What things did the consultants say or do that were helpful?
- What things did the consultants think they did that were helpful?
- What things did the consultants think they did that were not helpful?
- What things would the consultants not do again?

Time suggested for Step 6: 15 minutes.

CAREER PLANNING

Career Goals

Begin by listing your career goals. What do you want to be? How much money do you want to make? What kind of an organization would you like to work for?

Job

What specifically would you like to be doing in 5 years?

Salary

How much money would you like to be making? $_____ per year.

What size company would you like to work for?

1. Small (less than 300 employees)
2. Medium (300 to 1,000 employees)
3. Large (1,000 employees or more)

What industry would you prefer to work in?

Case 9.1   Tucker Knox Corporation

INTRODUCTION

Ed Leonard sat slumped behind his desk at Tucker Knox Corporation. It was 6:00 P.M., and everyone else had left for the day. Ed recalled the progress he had made over the last 4 years. He had joined the TKC to help the company develop a new automation design department. In the first 2 years, he had designed and developed the new department, and had helped to automate the production process to the point where new products were very competitive and profitable. The final year had been filled with political turmoil due to changes in top management.

A new challenge and a new set of goals was what Ed needed. He sat there at his desk staring at a phone call message from another company. Ed had been pursuing his personal goals with Tucker Knox, but felt that the phone message was the moment he had been waiting for. Ed had been planning a move away from Tucker Knox, and this was his chance. Where did it all go wrong?, he wondered.

COMPANY BACKGROUND

Tucker Knox Corporation is a world leader in keyboard design and manufacturing, supplying keyboards to computer system producers. Since 1981, TKC held the number one position in the market share (sales volume) of the capacitive switch keyboard design for private manufacturers. However, Tucker Knox is not just in competition with private keyboard manufacturers; it is also in competition with the captive keyboard manufacturing divisions of such system giants as IBM, Sperry, and Honeywell. The number one position was not easy to come by for a company that was founded by a retired corporate executive in a rented garage in 1969.

Larry Henderson, a strong-willed entrepreneur, pledged his personal assets, mortgaged his home, and called on five of his closest friends and business associates to build and grow the company into a world market leader with sales over $110,000,000. Larry, president and CEO, had always clearly been the father figure for TKC and for all of those whom he had personally selected to join him at the senior management level. Like sons answering to their father, each of the senior vice presidents would always look to Larry for his "nod of the head" of approval or disapproval.

TUCKER KNOX GOALS

During an executive board meeting, the major topic of discussion was once again focused on a continual challenge to retain its market share in an aggressive price-competitive market. "Our current challenge is (1) to compete in the world market with private and captive manufacturers; (2) to have efficient manufacturing facilities in locations in the United States and overseas as required to meet price and cost demands; and (3) to retain our corporate headquarters in the United States while the other manufacturers are moving their entire operations overseas." Larry started the meeting as he always had, by setting the issues directly on the table.

"These challenges mean that besides the usual corporate functions of marketing, sales, finance, and engineering, we will also have to provide those functions required to support our unique product design," Larry said. In the keyboard business, the major areas of product uniqueness is the design of the "piece parts" comprising the physical and mechanical portion of the keyboard. The unique features in each manufacturer's part design leads to very high labor costs for assembly. These unique designs lead to no readily available automated assembly machines on the market that will aid in reducing the high cost of assembly labor. "I've waited patiently for you boys to provide a solution to this world competition issue, and I trust that the solution will be presented today," continued Larry.

Much to Larry's pleasure, the skilled fatherly coaching would pay off once again as the decision was announced by Howard Watson that, "beginning next year, I will develop a corporate automation engineering department. The new department will be responsible for the concept, design, manufacture, installation, and maintenance of all custom automation for TKC's five manufacturing facilities: three in the United States, one in Ireland, and one in Taiwan." Larry was pleased, not only with the decision, but because Howard had been the one to announce it. With this new advanced technology department, Larry Henderson envisioned keeping his company ranked number one in world keyboard sales.

DEVELOPMENT OF THE DEPARTMENT

Howard Watson, director of manufacturing engineering, worked closely with Larry in developing the automation engineering department. Howard not only knew of Larry's fondness for equipment, but Howard was also eager to move up in TKC. Howard was a very aggressive manager with a positive attitude toward his job, traits which Larry liked in his management staff. Although his responsibilities were many, and growing, he had not yet selected a manager to develop and run the new department.

In fact, Howard had not filled either of the two vacant manager positions in his division. Howard was not a distrusting manager, but a great deal of convincing was always required before he would delegate control. Howard knew that for the automation engineering department to be successful, he would need a manager with a strong technical background as well as a good understanding of the business.

The manager he hired would be very visible to the corporate staff, including Larry. The manager would eventually have to develop and "sell" his own cost savings automation programs to the vice presidents. There were several people within the manufacturing engineering department who had the qualifications to manage the new department, but none with the technical background and none with the desire to have such a visible position.

Through a friend of his at Tucker Knox, Ed Leonard learned of the decision to develop an automation engineering department. In June, Ed began discussing with Howard the need to build the new department and the potential of joining the TKC team. Ed was a mechanical engineer with an MBA and both management and manufacturing experience who was seeking a new career challenge. Ed's engineering degree and experience easily satisfied the technical requirements of the position. However, his management skills were mainly in the project management area with some personnel management. Ed's managerial style was not as aggressive as Howard's, but his highly motivated, hard-work ethic and commitment to the project appeared to be the balance that Howard was looking for. In November, Ed joined the Tucker Knox team, not as the automation engineering department manager, but as a machine design engineer.

Howard wanted Ed to first prove his technical abilities in the seven-person machine design department that Howard had created as a beginning for the automation department. Ed would then progress through the step of department supervisor before moving to manager and further developing the department. This progression was important to Howard for two reasons. "The performance and success of this department is very important to the future of TKC. The employees in the department must function as a closely knit team. It is essential that each team member accept and be accepted by every other member. Therefore," Howard continued, "each person functions in their new position for a period of time to demonstrate their ability and to become accepted by the team."

The second reason for this slow progression (which Howard did not discuss) was his nature of being very slow to delegate and relinquish authority. This play, being agreed upon by both Ed and Howard, was the beginning of a very strong management team that was about to develop within Tucker Knox. Within a year, Ed has proven his abilities and was promoted to supervisor of machine design.

Soon after Ed Leonard's arrival at Tucker Knox, the machine design team was divided in two by Howard's boss, Jack Donaldson. Jack was a relatively new member of the Tucker Knox team that Larry Henderson had brought in as the vice president of technology. Larry Henderson was planning on retiring in a few years, and had tried to groom several candidates for taking over his position. Jack Donaldson was the latest of these candidates. In attempting to establish his "signature" on the Tucker Knox organization, Jack decided to reduce some of the power that Howard possessed within TKC by splitting the machine design team.

The multiple copy manufacturing group was split off from the R&D group and assigned to Matt Jackson, plastics engineering director. Matt was not only one of Howard's peers, but also his strongest rival.

Howard was not the type to take such change lightly. Howard disagreed with the decision not just because some of his organization was given to his strongest rival, but because the decision was not founded, in his opinion, on sound financial information. Howard and Ed worked closely, developing cost savings justifications which Ed used to convince Larry Henderson and Jack Donaldson to recombine the multiple copy manufacturing group with the R&D group. By allowing Ed Leonard to present the data and plan to Jack, Howard once again demonstrated his ability to achieve his own goals through his skillful managing of people at all levels within the organization. He also put Ed Leonard in the middle of an internal political conflict.

GROWTH OF THE DEPARTMENT

Ed continued to build the machine design department into a 23-person automation engineering department through corporate organization streamlining. The test equipment department, responsible for designing and building custom test equipment, was merged with the automation group in January of year 3. The plastics engineering department, part of Matt's division, was merged into the automation department 6 months later. The plastics automation department, also part of Matt's division, was merged into the automation department in December of the following year. This rapid growth of the automation engineering department was due to the efforts of both Ed and Howard. Ed provided the technical expertise for the department growth. He also presented the justifications for cost reduction, increased output, and increased response to the ever-changing customer demands in the market place for new keyboard designs.

New keyboard designs resulted in demands from the vice presidents that the production facilities have the automation in place at the same time the new keyboard design arrived in production. The automation was viewed to be essential to provide the low production costs necessary to stay ahead of the competition. Howard's contribution to the team was not only his position as director, but more so his natural ability to understand people almost better than they understand themselves and his ability to use internal politics to achieve his goals.

Howard had the ability to know how to deal with each of his peers and superiors in a way that bordered on manipulation. His intent was to influence decisions by communicating with each person in a unique way, so that each person was comfortable with the decisions. Howard used his position and communication skills to present the development steps to Larry Henderson and Jack Donaldson for their approvals. He often presented the idea to Larry Henderson first, and then to Jack Donaldson, as a "fait accompli!"

CHANGE IN SENIOR MANAGEMENT

In June of year 2, a change took place in the vice president assignments. Jack Donaldson was promoted to a newly created position of senior vice president. But as the corporate staff members were expecting Howard and Ed to also be promoted, trouble arose in the Ireland plant.

The managing director of the Ireland plant was unexpectedly forced to retire for health reasons with no time to groom a replacement. The Ireland plant played a major role in the European market. Howard possessed the most in-depth knowledge of the manufacturing part of the plant because he was responsible for having set it up. Jack Donaldson, being a relatively new member of the Tucker Knox top management team (and possibly being displeased with Howard for his political maneuvers in the machine design department) decided to assign Howard to the Ireland plant.

Howard moved to Ireland in August of the second year. Jack Donaldson filled his own vacated position of vice president of technology with Sam Martin. Jack handpicked Sam from outside TKC so that he could begin building his own loyal management team. Sam came from a high-tech firm in California with the experience of high-volume manufacturing of custom products comprised of "standard piece parts." Sam also brought several years of experience in worldwide competition, including the creation of two foreign production facilities.

During his first couple of months at TKC, Sam Martin made no changes, no promotions, and no attempts of any kind to fill the personnel vacancies. After acquainting himself with his new departments, Sam Martin recommended promoting Ed Leonard to the position left vacant by Howard, but was overruled by Jack Donaldson. There was much discussion between Jack and Sam over Ed Leonard's record of continued cost reductions and excellent performance of timely installations of new equipment in the critical manufacturing facilities. However, without giving any explanation for his decision, Jack Donaldson overruled Sam. Sam Martin was ordered to fill the vacancy from outside the company.

CONCLUSION

Within the next few weeks, it became apparent that Jack was trying to fill the vacant positions in the senior management staff with people who would be loyal to him. Another newcomer, Art Hodges, would be brought in to fill Howard Watson's position. Although Jack was hand-selecting his own team, he made sure that Sam Martin actually did the hiring so that it would appear that the "team" was selecting its own members. Art had been the manager of a packaging design department for a scientific instruments company in Portland, Oregon, where he had worked since graduating from college 10 years previously. He did not have the years of management experience that Sam had, and would therefore be easily manipulated by Jack.

Three weeks after arriving at TKC, Art Hodges (at the direction of Jack Donaldson) reassigned Ed Leonard to the company's largest manufacturing facility to set up a maintenance department. Ed was told by Jack and Art that, after successfully completing the assignment, he would be able to return to his department. With virtually no experience at TKC, Art followed Jack's direction without question, and 4 weeks later assigned Ed's automation engineering department to Matt Jackson. Within 3 months, Jack Donaldson had managed to rearrange the manufacturing engineering department and surround himself with managers that he had hand-selected and who he felt would be loyal to him. Six months after being given the assignment to set up the maintenance department, Ed was brought back to the corporate facility and given 6 weeks to find another job within the company or be laid off.

Ed Leonard sat slumped behind his desk at the keyboard manufacturing company. It was late in the day and everyone had gone home. Ed recalled the progress he had made over the last few years, as well as the lessons in management that he had so painfully been taught. Routine was not what Ed wanted, and routine is certainly not what he got.

QUESTIONS

1. What role does the HRM department at Tucker Knox play in the promotion and retention of personnel? Is it reactive or proactive? What HRM changes would you suggest?
2. How does management development and training fit into the planning at Tucker Knox? What steps should the HRM department take?
3. Discuss how the HRM department could have avoided the problem at the Ireland plant when the managing director was forced to retire be-

cause of poor health. What HRM policies and programs would have served to reduce the resignation problem?
4. What can the HRM department do to minimize the apparent political problems occurring between Senior Vice President Jack Donaldson and Howard Watson, director of manufacturing engineering? Suggest some specific policies and programs to reduce this issue while promoting the long-range future of Tucker Knox Corporation.

1. Ron Lieber, "Want to Get Ahead? Get Back," *Fast Company* (July-August 1999): 217.

2. R. Deigh, J. Rachlin, and A. Saltzman, "How To Keep From Getting Mired," *U.S. News and World Report* (April 25, 1988): 76–77.

3. D. T. Hall, "Proteam Careers of the 21st Century," *Academy of Executive Management* (1996): 8–16.

4. M. A. Von Glinow, M. J. Driver, K. Brousseau, and J. B. Prince, "The Design of a Career Oriented Human Resource System," *Academy of Management Journal* 8 (1983): 23–32

5. D. M. Raisson, "Changing the Deal," *Academy of Management Trends* 11 (1996): 50–61.

6. P. Sellers, "Don't Call Me a Slacker," *Fortune* (December 12, 1998): 181.

7. Douglas Hall, *Careers in Organizations* (Goodyear, 1976), 4.

8. Kenneth Labich, "Take Control of Your Career," *Fortune* (November 18, 1991): 87.

9. M. B. Arthur, "The Boundaryless Career," *Journal of Organizational Behaviors* 15 (1994): 295.

10. D. T. Hall, "Dilemmas in Linking Succession Planning to Individual Executive Learning," *Human Resource Management* 25 (1986): 235–65.

11. Labich, "The New Unemployed," p. 43.

12. W. Power and M. Siconolfi, "Who will be Rich? How Goldman Sachs Chooses New Partners: With a lot of angst," *Wall Street Journal,* 19 October 1990, pp. A1, A8.

13. J. H. Greenhaus, *Career Management* (New York: Dryden Press, 1987). See also J. L. Brooks and A. Seers, "Predictors of organizational commitment: Variations across career stages," *Journal of Vocational Behavior* 38 (1991): 53–64.

14. D. Turban, "Role of Protégé Personality in Mentoring," *Academy of Management Journal* 7 (1989): 688–702.

15. C. Bachler, "Workers Take Less of Job Stress," *Personnel Journal* (January 1995): 38.

16. G. J. Gooding, "Career Moves—for the Employee, for the Organization," *Personnel* 65, no. 4 (1988): 112, 114, 116.

17. J. H. Greenhaus, *Career Management* (New York: Dryden Press, 1987).

18. Daniel C. Feldman and Barton A. Weitz, "Career Plateaus Reconsidered," *Journal of Management* 14 (March 1988): 69–80.

19. Georgia Chao, "Exploration of the Conceptualization and Measurement of Career Plateau: A Comparative Analysis," *Journal of Management* 16, no. 1 (March 1990): 181–93.

20. E. C. Gottschalk, Jr., "Blocked Paths: Promotions Grow Few as "baby boom" Group Eyes Managers' Jobs," *Wall Street Journal,* 22 October 1981, pp. 1, 16.

21. P. T. Kilborn, "Companies That Temper Ambition," *New York Times,* 27 February 1990, pp. D1, D6.

22. *Fortune* (March 8, 1993): 43. See also Cathy Ventrell-Monsees, "Downsizing and Age Discrimination," *Textbook Authors Presentations* (Washington, DC: American Association of Retired Persons, October 1993), 40–48.

23. A. R. Herzog, J. S. House, and J. N. Morgan, "Relations of Work and Retirement to Health and Well-Being in Older Age," *Psychology and Aging* 6, no. 2 (1991): 202–11.

24. See also P. Thompson, K. Kirkham, and J. Dixon, "Warning: The Fast Track May Be Hazardous to Organizational Health," *Organizational Dynamics* 13 (1985): 21–33.

25. H. Ferlandand S. Harving, "Entry Level Fast Track Development," *Human Resource Planning* 27 (1998): 290.

26. A. Geiger, "Managers for Mentors," *Training and Developers Journal* (February 1992): 65.

27. Roy Adler, "Cracks in the Glass Ceiling," *New Woman* (February 1993): 42.

28. JoAnn S. Lubin, "Rights Law," *Wall Street Journal,* 30 December 1991, p. B1. See also Sally Dunnaway, "Americans with Disabilities Act and Older Workers," *Textbook Authors Presentations* (Washington, DC: American Association of Retired Persons, October 1993), 54–57.

29. K. Cameras, "Organizational Downsizing," *Human Resource Management* 38 (1994): 183.

30. S. Greengard, "Don't Rush Downsizing: Plan, Plan, Plan," *Personnel Journal* 73, no. 11 (November 1993): 64–76.

31. Patti Watts, "Are Your Employees Burn-out Proof?" *Personnel* 67 (September 1990): 12–20.

32. "Half of Managers Suffer Work Stress," *Supervision* 51 (July 1990): 10.

33. John Hulpke, working paper, 1994. *Sources:* Bob Widyahartono, "A Note on the Indonesian Style of Management," [University of Michigan] *Southeast Asia Business Newsletter* (Spring 1992): 5–6.

Part IV

The Success System: Motivating a High-Performing Workforce

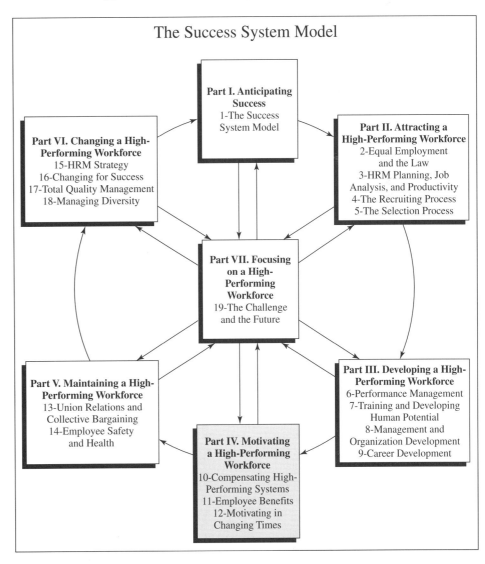

The Success System Model

Part I. Anticipating Success
1-The Success System Model

Part II. Attracting a High-Performing Workforce
2-Equal Employment and the Law
3-HRM Planning, Job Analysis, and Productivity
4-The Recruiting Process
5-The Selection Process

Part III. Developing a High-Performing Workforce
6-Performance Management
7-Training and Developing Human Potential
8-Management and Organization Development
9-Career Development

Part IV. Motivating a High-Performing Workforce
10-Compensating High-Performing Systems
11-Employee Benefits
12-Motivating in Changing Times

Part V. Maintaining a High-Performing Workforce
13-Union Relations and Collective Bargaining
14-Employee Safety and Health

Part VI. Changing a High-Performing Workforce
15-HRM Strategy
16-Changing for Success
17-Total Quality Management
18-Managing Diversity

Part VII. Focusing on a High-Performing Workforce
19-The Challenge and the Future

Chapter 10

The Success System: Compensating High-Performing Systems

Objectives

Upon completing this chapter, you will be able to:

1. Define and discuss the compensation process.
2. Describe the methods and objectives of a compensation system.
3. Understand the relationship of compensation to goals of employee satisfaction and productivity.
4. Identify and describe the major job evaluation programs.
5. Define and discuss the external and internal factors which impact compensation.

Premeeting preparation

1. Read chapter 10.
2. Prepare for HRM Skills Simulation 10.1: Invest in Bonds. Complete Step 1, Part B, and assign roles.
3. Read Case 10.1: Precision Products, Inc. Answer questions.

If you could have one wish, what would it be? To attain fabulous wealth? If you can't have that—sorry, we've got to be real—would you accept working for the rich? Would you be willing to watch over their money, say $100 million, for a 1 percent management fee, year in, year out? Well, the market exists and the job's available. In fact, says one high-end money manager, "it's wide open, the most undeveloped part of the financial marketplace." It's a nice, steady, recession-proof business. Good work, if you can get it.[1]

Let's face it, there is still lots of room at the top of the money list and more join each payday. For instance, back in the 1980s, you could make the *Forbes* 400 list of the most wealthy in the United States for a mere $150,000 million. Today, to be the poorest of the very rich, the four hundredth place person needs to be worth $1.2 billion. Each year it is common for CEO salaries to raise 36 percent, white-collar incomes to increase 3.9 percent, and blue-collar incomes to increase 2.7 percent.[2]

Compensation is one of the most important HRM functions because it impacts so many areas of the organization. Compensation covers all types of rewards that individuals receive for performing organizational tasks, including challenging work, interesting jobs, equitable rewards, competent managers, and a rewarding career. Earlier it was noted that employees are more concerned than their predecessors with the quality of worklife and with the psychological rewards attained from their job. But most of them would also admit that the money they earn is an important element too.

An effective compensation system is one that provides fair and equitable rewards to meet employee skills and expectations. Compensation, therefore, is a major HRM function in every organization because it provides employees with a tangible reward for performance, as well as providing recognition and motivation. In addition, compensation has an impact on employee recruiting, productivity, and turnover.

Although compensation is very important in recruiting, productivity, and turnover, other factors may be more important. Consider in today's multi-ethnic work environment that turnover for multicultural professionals can be three times greater than for Caucasian males and twice that of Caucasian females. Could it be money? It could be, but it might also result from a feeling of not "fitting in" due to a lack of mentors, sponsors, or other peer buddies. Maybe supervisors have not been trained to manage diverse people, or they may be assigned to safe, nonstretching, nonchallenging projects.[3]

Compensation is also important because it represents a significant operating cost. In many manufacturing firms, compensation may represent 50 percent of total expenditures, and in service enterprises, it often exceeds 70 percent. An effective compensation system, therefore, is essential in order to motivate employees who can achieve high levels of productivity.

In the 2000s, with its wide variety of pay systems, incentive programs, and benefit packages, the compensation system becomes even more complex. Compensation is important to organizations because it represents over half of the operating expenses of most firms and affects the recruitment and retention of key employees. Improved compensation approaches are recognized as an effective way to reduce costs and increase productivity. Therefore, it is important that the organization develop procedures and policies which provide an attractive and equitable pay system. Although there is no exact method of determining individual salaries, there are continually increasing pressures to reduce labor costs.

Stock options appear to offer a unique lure for today's mobile and fluid workforce. They offer the perfume of princely sums of money in a relatively short period of time. It is the twenty-first-century version of the California gold rush of

1849. They beckon seasoned executives who already have cutting-edge technology, growth-potential jobs to take pay cuts and perform temporary menial tasks. Recent and not so recent college graduates also covet the stock option lure.[4]

Like all things in the category of "too good to be true," the Council of Individual Investors, an organization of mutual funds and large pension funds, has become concerned with the flood of stock options being offered to broader and broader employee groups.

Employees who are granted stock options share only the upside of the market, not the downside. Unlike shareholders, they are not exposed to risk. Also, a study showed that companies using stock options engaged in more mergers and acquisitions and spent less on research and development.[5]

However, in today's new-economy companies, the amount of compensation required to retain executives has reached new heights. An example is Nick MacPhee who welcomed the twenty-first century by quitting his job as vice president of operations at Microsoft after nine years of employment.

His career at Microsoft was a routine of 80-hour work weeks. Finally tiring of the hectic pace, he quit at age 43 with several million dollars in savings. He points out his situation is not unusual with many companies who are trying to keep executives to stay by offering more money, ". . . but most won't do it for $5 million or $10 million more."[6]

In this chapter, we present the fourth stage of the Success System Model: motivating for performance, the compensation process. We will discuss the advantages and disadvantages of various compensation techniques and criteria, and discuss evaluating the quality of the total compensation process. As you will see, compensation decisions are very complex, but they are one of the key elements in developing a high-performance system.

WHAT IS COMPENSATION?

For most employees, pay is a necessity of life. Compensation level determines one's lifestyle, status, and feelings toward one's employer. The compensation received from working provides for individual and family needs and is one of the major reasons why employees perform a job. The compensation system may be defined as the system of rewards that an individual receives in return for organizational performance. Compensation not only satisfies one's basic needs, but pay and the things it buys are also recognition of achievement, providing signs of power and status in society. Compensation also represents the recognition of the individual's worth to the organization, thereby providing self-esteem to the employee.

If compensation is inequitable or pay levels are too low, then it may be difficult to attract and retain highly qualified employees. If pay levels are high, then firms may attract and retain high-performing workers, but costs may be too high. If compensation does not match performance levels, then high-performing individuals may leave the organization. For all of these reasons, an effective compensation system is an important factor in a high-performing organization. This is often termed expectancy theory.

When an individual values the offered reward, then high performance will result. To motivate high performance, the attractiveness of any monetary reward should be sufficient to be valued by the employee. Employees must believe that good performance is important to their employer and will result in an expected reward. (See Figure 10.1.)

Compensation is built around the concepts of exempt and nonexempt personnel. Exempt employees are executive, administrative, or professional "white

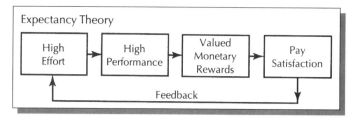

Figure 10.1
Relationship between pay-for-performance and expectancy theory

collar" workers who are paid a salary and are not paid overtime. However, non-exempt "blue-collar" employees are paid an hourly wage and do receive overtime pay.

These distinctions result from the Fair Labor Standards Act (chapter 2) which establishes three requirements before an employee is exempt from the overtime provision of the act: (1) The employee must be "white-collar," 2) paid on a salary basis, and 3) meet a duties test. The salary basis test is very difficult for employers because an innocent mistake, such as deducting an exempt employee's pay for an absence of less than a day, can result in 2 or more years worth of back pay.

Like most government regulations, the provisions are difficult to interpret. Although the salary test has been around for decades, the exempt status, overtime, and other issues still remain unclear to this day. These are reasonable accommodation issues of leave and schedules, modifying workplace policy, reassignment, and medication issues that are complex enough to require legal assistance.[7]

A specific, limited compensation issue can sometimes backfire and become an expensive general issue. For instance, the referred bonuses discussed in Chapter 4 can have a double meaning. Many companies, particularly in the hi-tech field, are paying present employees a referral bonus if they refer a new employee. The rationale is that such a bonus is cheaper than paying for the services of a headhunter or professional recruiter. However, a publishing firm recently tripled the bonus it pays for information services (IS) types. When word got out, the firm was forced to provide the same bonus plan across all of its business departments.[8]

Within the competitive global world of business, another compensation issue is how companies use money to encourage their employees to volunteer for jobs in foreign countries. A good example is how Daimler Chrysler uses compensation to convince employees that moving around the globe will be worth it. One of the most contentious issues is how generous the compensation will have to be to encourage employees to volunteer for jobs abroad.

Because Chrysler was less global-oriented than Daimler, it put less value on international assignments as stepping stones for promotions. Also, going abroad is not so much part of the American culture as it is in European culture. To overcome these problems, Chrysler has a compensation plan referred to as "goodies": moving expenses (which also includes hotel and meals); a lump sum worth 3 months' salary to cover any miscellaneous expenses for setting up house overseas; a salary bonus if the cost of living increases; upkeep of the employee's existing home, including snow removal and lawn care; 25 days of paid vacation and one plane trip home each year, including families; $5,000 per year for "activities" to help the spouse enter the new job market; tuition and related school expenses abroad for the children; and discounted employee rates for Mercedes vehicles. Now that is one really huge relocation compensation package.[9]

There is an old saying—"equal work for equal pay, unequal work for unequal pay." That is, if employees regard pay as fair for the work they perform, the company will receive its money's worth. However, if workers perceive they are underpaid in relationship to other employees' pay, they will slack off and the company will not receive its money's worth. This also applies to workers who are being overpaid, because they rarely increase their productivity to match the overpayment.

Although compensation offers economic benefits, it also functions as a social status symbol of how well we are doing in our society. We may not directly ask an individual how much they earn; however, we do use an indirect means to obtain such information. Hence, the age-old phenomena of "keeping up with the Jones's." In an increasingly consumption-oriented society, most individuals are aware of who is making more and those who are making less.

The level of compensation also has important psychological consequences. Employees will perform to the extent that the performance itself or the organizational rewards fulfill important needs. Many individuals regard salary as a measure of self-worth; of their importance; of their whole meaning in life. Although most surveys of workers' preferences show pay as either second or third, this may only reflect a satisfaction with pay and not the other preference. However, some surveys do show pay as being the workers' number one concern, not job satisfaction or job security.

In this twenty-first century, HRM personnel are recognizing that over the past few years, college graduates have become more savvy and self-assured than their predecessors. The result is higher cost-compensation packages. This new group of graduates are not afraid to ask for their wants—even when they are unreasonable. Their expectations include sign-on bonuses, relocation expenses, and paid trips home.

One way to avoid some of these problems is to make sure job requirements are reasonable and not overstated. Looking for someone who can walk on water will demand a higher compensation package, which can disrupt the logic of a company's pay plan. Such a person surfaced at one company when the individual wanted a $15,000 sign-on bonus for accepting a $40,000 salary position.[10]

In this battle of compensation packages, both the companies and the job candidates have an interesting source of information on the web site *VaultReports.com*. Although the information is mostly unsubstantiated, there are tales of companies' withdrawals of job offers and cheap expense account practices. There are also comments about compensation and what jobs are currently earning at different companies. The site is a valuable source of the latest perks and who is offering them. For the really curious, the web site of Dilbert, the cartoon character, lists a "pointy-haired boss index" of many companies.[11]

Source: CROCK by Rechin and Wilder © North America Syndicate, Inc.

An accurate source to determine how to compare salary offers that are fair and competitive in your career field is to refer to the Bureau of Labor Statistics. You will be able to determine whether you should be paid more working in San Diego, California, or Atlanta, Georgia. The recently released study compares average salaries in approximately 770 categories on the Internet at *http://www.bls.gov/ols/ols*. Another Internet salary source is the Employee Benefits Research Institute at *http://www.ebri.org*.[12]

COMPENSATION PROGRAM RATIONALES

There appear to be two key factors that influence pay. First, one concern is the fairness or equity of pay. Second, a standard for comparison is needed so the fairness of one's salary can be evaluated. This allows the organization to use compensation levels as a standard relative to some other level to evaluate its fairness.

One often sees newspaper stories about pop star Madonna earning over $60 million a year, or baseball player Ryne Sandberg of the Chicago Cubs receiving over $7 million per year. In general, these salaries may cause us to question the fairness behind such levels of compensation.

One HR manager might suggest, "Let's just pay what our competitors do," because this information can be readily obtained through local wage and salary studies or through more general government data. In fact, most organizations do make a decision (either formally or informally) whether to pay above the average, at the average, or below average salary levels. Organizations such as IBM or Procter & Gamble may decide, as a company compensation policy, to be at the high end of the local, regional, or national wage scale. This policy is not the result of charitable interests, but rather emerges from a corporate culture which implies they are the best. This culture requires hiring only the best and most highly qualified employees.

If you, as an employee, feel you are the best, you will not accept an average level of pay, but rather you will attempt to get the highest pay and best deal for yourself that you can. Because there is a limited number of highly qualified individuals, many companies will try to outbid their competitors to obtain these employees. One major consulting company (BCG) used to claim that they always hired the "top gun" (the top graduate) of the Harvard MBA program. In theory, the only companies that can outbid others for the limited top of the line are those companies profitable enough to afford the high costs of wages, benefits, and working conditions. Other companies, who are not so profitable, cannot afford the highest level so they settle for second, third, fourth, and so on.[13] (See Our Changing World of HRM.)

**OUR CHANGING WORLD OF HRM:
WHAT TO PAY IN BARRANQUILLA?[14]**

Although it isn't easy, at least you know some places to start. You could try to find a salary survey, or see what your competitors are paying. Then you have some idea how much to pay your workers. But what if you are starting up a brand new venture in a totally new country?

This sort of dilemma is facing more and more firms as the world continues to shrink on a daily basis. And,

if the lessons learned many years ago by Del Monte are any indication, it won't be easy. Del Monte had a brilliant "all-win" idea. The San Francisco-based food products company could not competitively ship California-grown products to Europe, but it thought there might still be a way. The idea developed: reclaim worthless scrub land near Barranquilla, Colombia. Clear the land and grow tomatoes. Build a processing

---

plant nearby, thereby employing some of the thousands and thousands of unem-ployed. Make Del Monte Tomato Sauce at the plant and ship it to Italy, where consumers would benefit from the lower prices brought about by the mass production and large scale growing of tomatoes. It was an all-win deal, right? But first, how much to pay the agricultural workers? How much to pay the processing plant workers?

The end result proved once and for all it is not easy making it in international business. The firm decided to be a good corporate citizen and offered workers about 50 percent above the typical wage for Northern Colombia (and of course, with so many unemployed, even the "typical" wage was hard to come by). This should please everybody, right? No way!

The local Barranquilla business community, which was not exactly booming, screamed! All their workers heard about the Del Monte high wages and now wanted big raises too (raises which would probably bankrupt some of the firms). Meanwhile, back in California, the Farm Workers advocates claimed "foul!" The wages paid in Colombia, as high as they were by Columbian stan-

dards, were considerably below what farm workers were paid in California. Obviously, the move to Barran-quilla was a plot to export jobs and to put the poor California farm workers deeper into poverty. As if that was not enough, the Italian tomato growers and processors complained loudly too. The "cheap" tomato sauces from Colombia were ruining the centuries-old agricultural efforts of many small Italian villages. Obviously, the farm workers in Colombia were being paid too low.

QUESTIONS

1. Why did Del Monte open up an operation in Colombia? What type of compensation survey do you think was taken? How would you approach this compensation problem?

2. In any global operation, what are some important compensation considerations that must be investigated during the planning process?

3. What has Del Monte learned about compensation issues from their Barranquilla operations? Do you think it has been costly?

The first area of comparison for compensation level is the evaluation of market equity. In making market comparisons, employees compare the pay they receive to pay in other organizations. One typical type of external comparison is that made by a new college graduate receiving several job offers. The jobs may look similar, but each company is offering a different compensation package.

Each organization sets starting salary levels based on their ability to pay and their perceptions of the labor market for a specific job. If there are a large number of potential employees available and demand for these employees is weak, companies will usually offer lower salaries. If, on the other hand, the labor supply is low and demand is high, higher salaries will be offered to attract quality applicants. The point is that attracting employees in the market involves competition among many organizations.

The second type of comparison made by employees is termed internal equity, or pay equity within the organization. Employees evaluate the pay for their job relative to the pay for other jobs within their company.

A continuing compensation problem is that nearly everyone entering the world of work in the twenty-first century claims some form of computer proficiency. Before a company spends scarce valuable resources, how can the HRM professional determine the accuracy of skills presented in the resume?

This is important because computers have become an accepted and integrated tool in most companies. The result is a company focus on computer competency. A tool to validate candidates claims of their level of computer skills to efficiently perform the job is the Microsoft User Specialist (MOUS) program.

The program validates a person's competency in any of Microsoft Office applications. This requires a complete hands-on exam to validate their skills. If one passes the exam, the person will receive a certificate verifying their qualifications. The certificate is proof to the HRM professional the person can fulfill specific job requirements.[15]

The process of collecting job information is usually done through a job evaluation program. The most important goal is obtaining the appropriate facts about the jobs under consideration. The job facts obtained in such a comprehensive analysis will be those compensable factors indicating why each job is paid a certain amount. Other job facts will indicate what workers do and how it is accomplished, work objectives, job demands, relationships with other jobs, and other work conditions. This is all accomplished through the process of job analysis (as described in chapter 3).

Compensable Factors

Compensable factors are those task components that apply to most jobs and represent what the company is willing to pay for them. Many jobs contain compensable factors in varying amounts including such factors as mental, physical, and skill requirements, responsibility, and working conditions. The total of what the company is willing to pay for these individual factors determines the hourly scale or monthly salary for these jobs. Because all jobs are ranked in some hierarchy, the compensable factors are actually yardsticks to compare the equity of payment between jobs.

The method of determining compensable factors requires them to be present in varying amounts in jobs; they must be distinct and not overlap with one another; there must be consensus (employer, employee, union) in their selection; and be generally present in all or most jobs under study.

Whether the compensable factors are present in all the jobs under study or present in most jobs is easily resolved. When the compensable factors are not present in all jobs, jobs are placed in similar clusters responding to their same compensable factors.

Key Jobs

An important consideration in the job evaluation process is determining the number of **key jobs,** sometimes called benchmark jobs. The number of key jobs are selected to represent the complete range of jobs in the job evaluation process. They should be well-analyzed jobs, with pay rates that are generally acceptable as are their pay rate differentials. In this step, it is decided what factors the organization is paying for.

These compensable factors are the benchmarks used to determine relative job pay. The process is usually quite straightforward. A committee is formed of management, employee, and union representatives who are highly experienced and know the key jobs very well. They review the job descriptions and then list the job characteristics, requirements, and conditions that need to be considered in determining the pay level of each job. The initial list is reduced until the final list of five or six compensable factors is reached.

Studies indicate that if pay is related to performance, employees produce higher quantity and quality of output. **Pay for performance** refers to a range of compensation systems designed to differentiate between average and high performers, including commissions, bonuses, profit sharing, and stock options.[16]

Job Evaluation Systems

As noted earlier, one important component of the compensation system is the worth of the job. Organizations usually determine the value of jobs through the process of job evaluation. **Job evaluation** may be defined as the systematic process of determining the relative worth of jobs in order to establish which jobs should be paid more than others within the organization. Job evaluation tries to establish an internal equity basis between the various jobs. The relative worth of a job is usually determined by comparing it to others in the organization.

The next step is to select a particular job evaluation method. Four basic methods of comparison are used in the principal systems of job evaluation. Regardless of the techniques being used, it is important to remember that all job evaluation methods require some input of managerial judgment.

The Factor Comparison Method

Factor comparison compares jobs based on compensable factors using benchmark jobs, one factor at a time. The factor comparison system permits the job evaluation process to be accomplished on a factor-by-factor basis. The compensable factors to be evaluated are compared against the list of selected tentative key jobs within the organization that serve as the job evaluation scale. It is a variation of the **ranking method,** although a more sophisticated method, because the job factors are compared to the benchmark jobs.

There are four basic steps in developing and using a factor comparison scale: (1) selecting and ranking key jobs, (2) allocating wage rates for key jobs across compensable factors, (3) setting up the factor comparison scale, and (4) evaluating non-key jobs.

The five steps to follow in the basic factor comparison method are as follows:

1. *Job Descriptions and Specifications.* The factor comparison method, as with all other job evaluation methods, begins with the collection of information by the job analysts. Once the job information has been obtained, the job descriptions and job specifications can be written. The job descriptions methodically detail the duties of each job. The job specifications are written using the standard five compensable factors for the factor comparison method: mental, physical, and skill requirements, responsibilities, and working conditions.

2. *Tentative Key Jobs Selected.* Once the job descriptions and job specifications have been rewritten, they are analyzed to ensure the five compensable factors are present in the selected tentative key jobs. This means the five compensable factors are present in varying amounts in all jobs; the compensable factors must be distinct and not overlap each other; there must be agreement by all parties (management, employees, union) in the selection of the tentative key jobs; and the tentative key jobs selected are regarded as being correctly paid. This last step is a requirement for the factor comparison method, but not for the other methods. Further, the selection of the tentative key jobs must be done correctly, because it is the entire foundation for the factor comparison method. Depending upon the size and complexity of the organization, the number of tentative key jobs selected may range from less than 15 to 25 or more.

3. *Ranking of Tentative Key Jobs.* Although this ranking is based upon the subjective judgment of individual committee members, it is solidly established by the rewritten job descriptions and job specifications. Any method of consensus may be used, such as averaging individual tallies; whatever is used, those jobs failing to meet the key job test are discarded, with only the "tentative" true key jobs remaining.

4. *Distribution of Wages and Salaries.* This step is also highly subjective, although once again it is based upon the rewritten job descriptions and job specifications. Using the present wage or salary for the tentative key job, an amount is allocated to each of the five compensable factors to represent how much of the total wage or salary is being paid for the contribution of that compensable factor. For example, let us assume the job of staff-assistant is paid at

the rate of $13.75 per hour ($2,210 per month salary, divided by 160 hours worked for 1 month: 4 weeks or 20 days times 8 hours per day equals 160 hours worked per month).

Mental requirements	$5.50
Physical requirements	.98
Skill requirements	3.73
Responsibility	2.75
Working conditions	.79
	$13.75 per hour

This illustrated distribution is made for all the company tentative key jobs. The usual procedure for the distribution of the hourly rate per hour is for the committee members to do so independently. Then, the whole committee meets and a consensus is obtained.

5. *Comparison of Money Allocation Judgments.* The main purpose here is to ensure the jobs that have been selected are truly key jobs. This is accomplished by comparing the rankings for each compensable factor in Step 3 and those in Step 4. When a tentative key job receives the same ranking in both tables for all five compensable factors, it became a "true" key job.

Those tentative key jobs not receiving equal ranking are not key jobs. They are eliminated from future consideration, unless the committee decides there is a problem of inaccurate judgments and decides to reconsider the rankings based on a reexamination of the data.

Job Ranking System

The simplest and oldest system of job evaluation is the **job ranking system,** which arrays jobs on the basis of their relative worth.

Job ranking requires the organization's jobs to be ranked on the compensable factors from highest to lowest. Totals are then obtained to indicate respective ratings. One problem with ranking is that it requires personnel who are very familiar with all the jobs being ranked. At the department level, this is often not too difficult, but in a large organization it can become almost impossible to find such people.

The job-classification method defines classifications or grades of jobs and then fits the jobs into these categories. One problem with this method is the use of broad definitions that fail to properly distinguish between the different contributions of the compensable factors within jobs.

The Point Rating System

The **point system** is a quantitative job evaluation procedure determining each job's relative value by calculating the total points assigned to it. It has been successfully used by many public and private organizations, both large and small.

Point rating is a more involved method, and is used by most of the wage and salary companies, such as the Hay Company, who perform wage and salary surveys for private companies. It uses compensable factors that vary for various levels of complexity. Points are assigned these factors; they are then totaled, and using various predetermined tables, compensation values are assigned to the jobs. The principal advantages of the point system are that it provides a more qualitative basis for making job comparisons than either the ranking or classification systems, and can produce results that are more valid and less easy to manipulate.

The point system evaluates jobs quantitatively on the basis of factors—commonly called compensable factors—that constitute the job. The education, experience, skills, efforts, responsibilities, and working conditions of a job are the more common major compensable factors. These major compensable factors are then further subdivided into subfactors and degrees. The number of compensable factors an organization uses depends on the type of organization and the type of jobs to be evaluated.

The point system usually uses a point manual: a handbook that contains a description of the factors and the degrees to which these factors may exist within the jobs. A manual also will indicate the number of points allocated to each factor and to each of the degrees into which these factors are divided. The point value assigned to a job represents the sum of the numerical degree values of each compensable factor that the job possesses.

Point plans have often been criticized by some for the amount of time and effort required in designing them and for their tendency to support a bureaucratic management. One advantage of this method is that the system may be used over a long period of time. As new jobs are created or old jobs are substantially changed, then the job evaluation committee reevaluates the jobs and updates the manual. Only when compensable factors change, or for some reason the weightings become inappropriate, does the plan become obsolete.

The Hay Guide Chart-Profile Method

One of the most widely used versions of the point method is the **Hay guide chart-profile method.** The Hay plan uses three compensable factors: know-how, problem solving, and accountability. Point values are assigned to these factors to determine the final point profile for any job.

Know-how is the sum total of all knowledge and skills needed for satisfactory job performance. It has three dimensions: the amount of practical, specialized, or scientific knowledge required; the ability to coordinate many functions; and the ability to effectively deal with and motivate people.

Problem solving is the degree of original thinking required by the job for analyzing, evaluating, creating, reasoning, and making conclusions. Problem solving has two dimensions: the thinking environment in which problems are solved (from strict routine to abstractly defined); and the type of mental activity presented by the problems (from repetitive to uncharted). Problem solving is expressed as a percentage of know-how because people use what they know to think and make decisions.

Accountability is the responsibility for action and accompanying consequences. The three dimensions of accountability are the degree of freedom the job incumbent has to act, the job impact on end results, and the extent of the monetary impact of the job.

The Hay plan is an extremely popular approach to determining compensation. It is used by thousands of employers worldwide. The popularity of the Hay plan provides an important advantage: Hay can provide job comparisons between firms worldwide. Thus, the method serves to determine both internal and external equity. Another advantage is that the Hay system has been legally challenged and upheld by the courts. One disadvantage is the cost, which makes it less likely to be used by smaller firms.

THE UNDERPAID EMPLOYEE

When **underpaid employees** (called **green circle**) are considered to be good employees and if the company desires to keep them, an upward adjustment will be made. Otherwise, the employee will learn of the discrepancy (if they don't already know), and will quit or become less productive. So, two courses of action are available: Either the company raises the employee's pay, or, if the employee is not a productive employee, a transfer may occur to a job where skill and wages are equal.

THE OVERPAID EMPLOYEE

The **overpaid employee** is a more difficult problem. No one welcomes being paid less for performing the same job. This is not an unusual event, as evidenced by the common terminology that has grown up over its occurrence. Such terms used to refer to this problem are usually called **red circle,** red allowances, flagged, and ringed.

The solutions are to freeze the present rate and allow future increases to bring the underpay up to standard, to transfer or promote the individual to a higher pay job equal to the individual's ability, or to allow only part of future increases to occur until parity is obtained. This approach suggests that any discrepancy between where an employee is in the pay range and where he or she could be—based on performance—should be corrected within a reasonable amount of time. This approach usually means larger pay increases for outstanding performers who are being paid at or near the bottom of their pay ranges.

RATE RANGES AND WAGE STRUCTURES

The final step in setting up a wage structure is to determine the appropriate rate ranges into which each job should be placed on the basis of its evaluated worth. Usually this evaluation is determined on the basis of job requirements, without regard to the performance of the person in that job. Under the wage range system, the performance of those who exceed the requirements of a job may be acknowledged by merit increases within the class range or by promotion to a job in the next-higher wage class.

Rate ranges generally are divided into a series of steps that permit employees to receive increases up to the maximum rate for the range on the basis of merit, seniority, or a combination of the two. Most wage structures provide for the ranges of adjoining wage groups to overlap. The purpose of such an overlap is to permit an employee with experience to earn as much as or more than a person with less experience in the next-higher job classification. (See Figure 10.2.)

The Final Step

Rate ranges help to eliminate the problem of underpay or overpay. These ranges occur within a job classification and allow the company to reward superior performance. Most organizations claim that there is a wide range of pay in the merit progression system, but studies show that up to 80 percent of employees are at the top of their rate range. So most increases may be the result of seniority.

Companies justify the use of rate ranges because of the wide differences between employees in individual productivity. Of course, some jobs—such as assembly line work—do not allow for differences in productivity, so rate ranges are not appropriate.

The rate ranges vary within organizations with hourly jobs demonstrating a spread from 10 to 25 percent, 25 to 35 percent for office jobs, and 30 to 100 percent for management. Within each job classification, a minimum and maximum are established with an overlap. This permits individuals within a particular pay grade

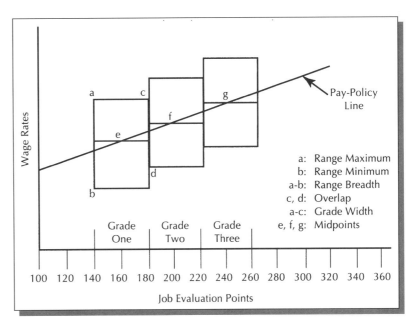

Figure 10.2
Job hierarchy—pay grades overlap

or classification to eventually earn more than a beginning person in a higher pay grade or classification.

Such an arrangement removes the sting for an employee who cannot advance to the higher pay grade or classification due to no fault of the employee. This may occur because the company does not have a training program, or because there is no present vacancy for the employee to move into.

This type of system often fails to reward employees for the skills or knowledge they possess or to encourage them to learn new job-related skills. One way to correct these problems is the use of skill-based pay plans used by many organizations. Skill-based pay plans try to compensate the employee for the skills and knowledge they possess, rather than for the wage category.

Employees point to the marketplace as the explanation for the compensation differences between the sexes. Others suggest it is the old-boy network.

One study by two sociologists who analyzed four landmark pay discrimination cases concluded that paycheck size often reflects inequities within the organization. They point out men (the old-boy network) tend to dominate debates of job evaluations and wage surveys. Their opinion is that what the courts and/or policy-makers need to understand is the source of these inequities and make appropriate changes.[17]

Whatever the real cause of the wage inequity, although it continues to narrow, it is still a significant difference. For example, depending upon the source of your information, women make between 74 percent and 76 percent of what men make in the United States. Even at levels where highly educated men and women hold the same or similar jobs, the women on average make less.

Although women hold almost half of the executive administrative or managerial positions, they still only make 66 percent of what men in the same category earn. As one women's advocacy group points out, the wage gap really exists at all levels. Hopefully, this compensation gap will end in the early part of the twenty-first century through the efforts of HRM professionals and not the courts.[18]

Part of the total compensation picture is the pay cycle or how personnel are paid. Any attempt to change the existing pattern should proceed with caution. HRM needs to be aware that any change which effects this cycle of employees' paychecks is likely to cause fear, be disruptive, and have a negative effect on morale.

These pay cycles are usually weekly, biweekly, semimonthly, or monthly. The weekly pay cycle can be a result of the union contract or a tradition. It helps lower-paid employees to maintain an adequate cash flow. The biweekly cycle works well for exempt and nonexempt employees because expenses can be divided into middle and end-of-month billings. It is cheaper for the company to cut 26 paychecks a year than 52. During the 2 months that contain three pay periods, employees "find" two extra paychecks a year.

The semimonthly pay cycle also saves the company money because only 24 checks are cut each year per employee. However, each pay period becomes 2.16 weeks which creates problems computing overtime pay. The monthly pay cycle is cheapest for the company, although for some months employees will be waiting longer to be paid. Another problem is some states may require that non-exempt employees be paid more often than once a month.[19]

THE ISSUE OF EQUAL PAY OR COMPARABLE WORTH

One of the most important compensation issues of the twenty-first century is equal pay for comparable work. The issue stems from the fact that jobs performed predominantly by women were sometimes paid less than those performed by men.[20] This practice results in what is often termed institutionalized pay discrimination, with women receiving less pay for jobs that are different from, but comparable in worth to, those performed by men.

The issue of **comparable worth** goes beyond providing equal pay for jobs that involve the same duties for women as for men. It is not only concerned with whether a female secretary should receive the same pay as a male secretary. Rather, the argument for comparable worth is that jobs held by women should be compensated the same as those held by men, if both job types contribute equally to organizational success.[21] However, this is a continuing problem, and will continue to be an active issue as the percentage of women in the workforce continues to climb.

Part of the aftershock of the Supreme Court 5-4 decision regarding age discrimination affects this equal pay issue. The Supreme Court has now ordered lower courts to review any decisions they may have made under the 1963 federal law involving comparable worth.

The justices want cases to be reconsidered based on their ruling state employees cannot use federal law in age bias suits. So, the Supreme Court has set aside lower court rulings to allow employees at state universities in New York and Illinois to proceed with lawsuits by female faculty members claiming the universities violated the 1963 Equal Pay Act. The issue is state employees cannot use federal law to sue their employers for age discrimination issues. The states must use state laws which may or may not exist.[22]

TWO-TIER PAY

Two-tier pay rates are a recent innovation as businesses attempt to cut their labor costs. There are actually two different pay systems for the employees. Some plans continue this difference for long time periods and others set a time limit—such as 90 days or longer before they become equal.

FAIR AND SQUARE

What can HRM professionals do to make their compensation program achieve wage parity while avoiding federal scrutiny for a defective gender-neutral system? Although employees use different techniques to keep salaries fair and square, equitable compensations have several common features such as salaries based primarily on the industry market pay rates, not on some employee's value to the firm based on an arbitrary evaluation system.

Another common feature is a system in which skills, performance, and tenure are objectively evaluated and measured. This allows HRM to monitor the process and control adherence to the approved procedures. The results should be accepted as not deviating from the process.

The last common feature of a gender-neutral compensation system is a regular review for any irregularities caused by cutbacks, transfers, mergers, or sudden increases in recruiting. When irregularities are uncovered, they are immediately corrected.

The cornerstone of all companies' fair and square compensation system requires continuous adjustments. The gender-neutral system goal is to be able to highlight any unfair treatment for all employees, even between two white male employees.[23]

VARIABLE PAY

The twenty-first century is witnessing the hottest trends in HRM. It is the redesign of compensation packages to support organizational goals and objectives. This is the result of helter-skelter compensation plans with no coherent policies.

The answer to these problems is the total compensation plan. In such a plan, employees receive a base pay for core duties, individual and small group achievement pay, and variable pay that is based on the company's success.

Total compensation plans are not uniformly successful. The reason is poor implementation of the variable pay segment of the plan. The correct implementation requires careful attainable performance goals and techniques to objectively measure those goals. This requires knowledge of the company's recent performance results in key areas and comparative industry data.

The variable pay program success requires establishing employees' trust. If employees do not trust their management to tell them the truth or fairly consider their suggestions without ridicule or punishment, variable pay programs will not work.

To make variable pay work, companies should do the following:

- *Do not make the program complicated.* Goals must be clear and straightforward. One way to accomplish this is to follow the example of a major national food manufacturer. Employees were asked to set specific variable pay goals for each plant. A representative group developed very specific goals for manufacturing output, safety, and waste control. Although management would have the final approval, employees were told the implementation would be immediate.

- *Never underestimate the ability of employees to understand.* They are at least as sharp as the managers who created the original compensation program. When the subject is pay-related, they listen carefully and are aware of inequities which they will then share with other employees.

- *Avoid compensation legal terms and unnecessary details.* All employee communications containing excessive financial and legal terms are very ineffective. A more effective method is quarterly posters to update employees on the two main goals of variable pay: operating margins and customer satisfaction. An effective poster tells what is needed and is understood in seconds.

• *Management must acknowledge present deficiencies in the current compensation plan.* The current deficiencies are the reason for implementing the variable pay plan. The real success is whether margins and customer satisfaction improve as a result of employees recommending improvement strategies.

The success of a variable pay program is whether the employees perceive it as being fair and equitable. The employees must buy-in that the variable pay plan is in their and the company's best interest.[24]

SUMMARY

Compensation is one of the most critical and difficult functions in the HRM Success System Model. Developing a compensation system is a complex activity because of the multiple factors which influence pay. Several compensation objectives and approaches have been described.

Organizations are developing strategic compensation plans to meet a cost-conscious, competitive business environment that requires high quality and continuous innovation. The compensation program must be acceptable to the organization's culture and still meet strategic objectives. In addition, compensation decisions must meet the Fair Labor Standards and Equal Pay Act. The controversy over comparable worth is also causing organizations to consider how rates of pay are computed for male and female positions.

In the HRM Skills, you will have a chance to experience using information and making a compensation decision. You may find that compensation is not a simple process, because it involves both the employees' needs and organizational constraints. Because of its motivational importance, individuals are very concerned with the equity of their pay relative to others both within and outside their organization. Organizations are also very concerned with pay, not only because of its importance as a cost, but because it motivates the decisions of key employees about continuing on a job, or leaving the organization. In this chapter, the important elements of a compensation process have been described, and now you will have an opportunity to practice and apply these concepts and skills. Compensation provides one approach to motivating employees to continued organizational membership and higher levels of performance.

REVIEW QUESTIONS

1. How would you define "compensation management"?
2. Present examples of comparable worth in organizations you have worked for.
3. Identify and demonstrate the impact of compensation on employee satisfaction and performance.
4. Discuss the rationale entering into a company deciding upon a compensation policy that advocates setting wage scales at the top of the market.
5. What are the compensable factors? Why are they called yardsticks? How are they determined? Where are they found? Discuss.
6. Explain three basic responses a manager has to correct an overrated job.
7. Read a book or view a video movie, and identify organization compensation issues.

KEY WORDS AND CONCEPTS

Define and be able to use the following:

- Accountability
- Comparable Worth
- Compensable Factors
- Expectancy Theory
- Factor Comparison
- Green Circle

- Hay Guide Chart-Profile Method
- Job Evaluation
- Job Ranking System
- Key Jobs
- Know-How
- Overpaid Employee

- Pay for Performance
- Point System
- Problem Solving
- Ranking Method
- Red Circle
- Underpaid Employee

HRM SKILLS SIMULATION 10.1: INVEST IN BONDS

A. PURPOSE

This simulation is intended to allow participants the opportunity to set compensation within an organizational setting. The purpose is to experience and develop interpersonal and group skills that enhance effective organization functioning. Specifically, it is to experience interdependence and to observe

1. How compensation information is shared among team members.
2. How various compensation strategies influence results.
3. How collaboration and competition affect team problem solving.

B. PROCEDURES

Step 1. Prior to class, form into five member Executive Committee teams. (Roles should be selected prior to the class meeting.) Additional class members will serve as observers and should be divided equally between the Executive Committee teams. They will then observe their individual teams and rate them on the Team Profile/Observer Form. At the conclusion of their Executive Committee team meeting, the observers will meet and attempt to reach a consensus rating.

Step 2. Executive Committee Meeting.
The Executive Committee teams will use the information in the Background Information: San Francisco Giants to arrive at a decision whether to approve the Barry Bonds contract. The observers use the Team Profile/Observation Form, but do not participate.

Time suggested for Step 2: 40 minutes

Step 3: The observers will complete the Team Profile/Observer Form. The teams will discuss the results with their Executive Committee teams.

Time suggested for Step 3: 10 minutes.

Step 4: As a class, the teams will discuss the Team Profile/Observer Form results.

Time suggested for Step 4: 5 minutes.

BACKGROUND INFORMATION: SAN FRANCISCO GIANTS

Barry Bonds signed a contract with the San Francisco Giants baseball team. He could be worth as much as $47.75 million if MVP incentives are met during the 6-year agreement.

In the same year, Terry Steinbach signed a 4-year contract for $14 million and Bob Melvin signed a 2-year deal for $2.35 million.

Several major-league owners were shocked and angered by the size and length of Bonds's contract. Small market teams such as the Padres and Pirates attempted to reverse the sport's salary spiral.

But look at Bonds's contract this way: Once he starts earning $8 million a year, the Giants will need to sell about 1,432,000 $8.00 tickets a season just to pay his salary. About 31 percent of the team's gate receipts go to the visiting teams, the league office, and for stadium rent. The season prior to Bonds's contract, the Giants' home attendance was only 1,561,987.

The general manager has called a meeting of the compensation committee to decide whether or not it will be wise to approve this contract.

ROLE DESCRIPTIONS (READ *ONLY* YOUR ROLE)

Role 1—General manager. You are the team's general manager. Your principal interests are your team and the winning morale. You have been with the team for 8 years. Although you started fast, things have slowed down for the past 2 years. Your goal is to turn things around right now and show a winning team. You basically would like to hold the line on salaries, because the real question is value—which your team has always provided. But, in this instance, you'd rather pay the price than lose this player because other teams are involved. You feel the way to keep people coming to the games is to appeal to their loyalty to the San Francisco Giants' winning tradition.

Role 2—Director 1. You have been a director for 4 years. You feel strongly that what the organization needs to solve its problems is an increased marketing and promotional effort. You recognize that the established wage rate is important, but also that a firm must be innovative and adapt to changing markets with new players and promotions. You have been selected as a member of the compensation committee because you are an expert on the *ranking* method of job evaluation. You will use this method to determine your recommendation for pay.

Role 3—Director 2. You have been a director for over 10 years. You worked your way up through the ranks. You see increased efficiency as the major goal, because excessive spending in marketing is needlessly raising costs. You are convinced that costs can be reduced drastically by limiting new players, limiting the cost of contracts, and by slowing down the introduction of new players (which marketing always wants). This will allow a more stable and efficient team operation, rather than the hectic, constantly changing situation you have now. You have been selected as a member because of your skill in using the *factor comparison method.*

Role 4—Director 3. You have been a director for 5 years. You feel strongly that the most important resource in the organization is people. Morale and the satisfaction of individuals are the primary goals, as you see it. You have been selected for expertise in using the *point rating method.*

Role 5—Director 4. You have been a director for 3 years. You see long-term effectiveness as the most important goal. Both profit and market share depend on the ability to remain competitive on the field. You feel that the team must become more innovative and improve marketability to survive. You have been selected because of your knowledge of the *Hay Guide Point Profile method.*

Role 6—Observers. Use the Team Profile/Observer Form to analyze group processes.

TEAM PROFILE/OBSERVER FORM

Below are several value orientations. Based on the following scale, individually rate your Executive Committee team values in the SF Giants problem.

	1 NOT AT ALL CHARACTERISTIC	4 SOMEWHAT CHARACTERISTIC	7 VERY CHARACTERISTIC

VALUES	INDIVIDUAL RATING	TEAM RATING
1. High Productivity		
2. Effective Relationships		
3. High Quality		
4. High Achievement		
5. Seniority (Age)		
6. Time Consciousness		
7. Dress/Neatness		
8. Amount of Education		
9. Positive Attitudes		
10. High Professionalism		

Case 10.1 Precision Products, Inc.

Helen was working late again. Precision Products was continuing the steady growth pattern of previous years, and the personnel department was feeling the pressure. The personnel staff was responding well to the demands, but Helen knew there eventually would be a breaking point. She knew her staff training program was important, so there was no turning back. Turning the last page of Professor Bovineless's notes on compensation, she was now prepared and ready for tomorrow's staff meeting.

Betty Moneypenny quietly announced to Helen the staff meeting was ready to begin. They both walked into the conference room to find everyone alert and still full of enthusiasm. "Thank goodness for that," she thought. "Let's hope it lasts."

After about 50 minutes of presentation and discussion, Helen looked about the room and the questions began.

QUESTIONS

1. Curt Stump wondered how the expectancy theory could work on different employees if their respective value systems differed. Are there any suggestions you can make to Curt?
2. Viola Higgins thought the Hay guide chart-profile appeared to be the most effective method. Can you suggest to Viola how the factor comparison method might be a simpler yet viable alternative?

3. Mike Hudson wanted to know how the top management of Precision Products regarded the issue of equal pay or comparable worth. In particular, he wondered if they were ready to remedy some of the obvious present inequities. What approach would you suggest to the top management of Precision Products?

ENDNOTES

1. William E. Sheeline, "Selling Advice to the Super-Rich," *Fortune* (June 29, 1991): 56.
2. Arianna Huffington, "Wealth carries big obligations," *The Oregonian,* 5 July 1999, p. B11.
3. Vanessa J. Weaver, "If Your Organization Values Diversity, Why Are They Leaving?" *Mosaics* 5, no. 3 (1999): 1–5.
4. Elisa Williams, "As Options Go, It's Worth the Trade," *The Oregonian,* 29 August 1999, p. B1.
5. Paul L. Gilles, "Alternatives for Stock Options," *HR Magazine* (January 1999): 40.
6. Carol Hymouritz, "In the Lead, the New Fast Trackers Work Like Maniacs and Then Take a Walk," *The Wall Street Journal,* 22 February 2000, p. B1.
7. Timothy J. Bartl, "The Salary Basis Test: A Trap for the Unwary," *Legal Report* (May-June 1999): 1–5.
8. Julia King, "Many Earn Big Bucks Referring IS Pros," *Computerworld* 31 (June 16, 1997): 1.
9. Jeffrey Bell, "Daimler Chrysler's Transfer Woes," *The Wall Street Journal,* 24 August 1999, p. B1.
10. Angela Hullah, "Talking Dollars: How To Negotiate Salaries with New Hires?" *HR Magazine* (July 1998): 73–78.
11. L. M. Sixel, "Website Contains the Skinny on Corporate Culture," *New York Times* News Service, *The Oregonian,* 16 July 1999, p. B3.
12. L. M. Sixel, op. cit.
13. B. Gerhart and G. T. Milkovich, "Organizational Differences in Managerial Compensation and Financial Performance," *Academy of Management Journal* 33 (1990): 663–91.
14. E. E. Lawler, "Paying the Person: A Better Approach to Management," *Human Resources Management Review* 1 (1991): 145–54.
15. "How to Spot an Office Expert," *HR Magazine* 44, no. 2 (February 1999). Microsoft Office MOUS User Supplement.
16. R. Bradley Hill, "A Two-Component Approach to Compensation," 72, no. 5 *Personnel Journal* (May 1993): 154–61.
17. Richard Gibson, "Who Decides Pay, The Marketplace or The Old Boy Network?" Work Week, *The Wall Street Journal,* 14 September 1999, p. A1.
18. Celia Colista, "Male-Female Wage Gap Narrows, But at 25 Percent, It's Still Significant," Copley News Service, *The Oregonian,* 22 September 1999, p. 24.
19. Carla Joinson, "Pay Attention to Pay Cycles," *HR Magazine* (November 1998): 71.
20. T. A. Mahoney, "Job Evaluation: Endangered Species or Anachronism?" *Human Resources Management Review* 1 (1991): 155–60.
21. E. E. Lawler, "Paying the Person: A Better Approach to Management," *Human Resources Management Review* 1 (1991): 145–54.

22. Robert S. Greenberger, "Supreme Court Declines to Review Case Challenging Fee for Internet Addresses," *Wall Street Journal*, 19 January 2000, p. B9.

23. Marc Adams, "Fair and Square," *HR Magazine* (May 1999): 39–44.

24. Don Barksdale, "Leading Employees Through the Variable Pay Jungle," *HR Magazine* (July 1998): 110–12.

Chapter 11

The Success System: Employee Benefits

Objectives

Upon completing this chapter, you will be able to:

1. Define and discuss the concept of employee benefit programs.
2. Describe the "hot issues" of employee benefit systems.
3. Understand the relationship of employee benefits to goals of employee satisfaction and productivity.
4. Identify and describe the major types of benefit programs.
5. Define and discuss the external and internal factors which lead to flexible benefit programs.

Premeeting preparation

1. Read chapter 11.
2. Prepare for HRM Skills Simulation 11.1. Complete Step 1, Part B.
3. Read Case 11.1: Precision Products, Inc., Answer questions.

Background Information

For more than 60 years, Social Security has been a good investment for U.S. workers. Millions of Americans have received far more in benefits than they paid in Social Security taxes. No wonder Social Security became one of the most popular government programs.

Now that era has come to an end. For the first time, some Americans who are retiring will be getting less in benefits than the accumulated value of what they and their employers paid in taxes. And it appears this is not the end. Although everyone knows the program transfers money from young to old, few realize its biggest impact these days is to redistribute income from rich and middle-class retirees to poor ones.

What's more, with the baby boomer generation edging closer to retirement, they are going to find their retirement benefits will be squeezed even further. A lot of the taxes boomers are paying today, although they are Social Security trust funds, are being used for current government expenses. The trust funds are in surplus, but what they actually contain are IOUs, which will eventually have to be redeemed—either by borrowing or by boosting income taxes on the younger population. The retirement age will probably have to be raised again, perhaps to 69 or 70, and cost-of-living increases limited.

Employee benefit programs have become an increasing part of the overall compensation package. Because of the growing costs of benefits, it is becoming one of the most important HRM issues. In the past, employee benefits were termed fringe benefits, but recently it is estimated that from 35 to 42 percent of total payroll costs are included in the employee benefit package.

Employee benefits may be defined as the indirect compensation concerned with enhancing the quality of worklife. These include group life and health insurance programs, retirement programs, paid vacations and holidays, and other options including vision care, dental, and tuition reimbursement plans.

Although the number of employee benefits continues to increase, there appears to be no end to their variety. Their effect is not only financial but also influences the social life of our country. An example is how the flexible job benefits at John Hancock's Information Technology department in Boston allowed a systems analyst to adopt a child and still return to her original job.[1]

Employees are also having more input as to the benefits they receive. Capital One Financial Corporation, one of the nation's largest issuers of Visa and Mastercard credit cards, asked employee focus groups what benefits they would enjoy the most. Their answers: time off from work and the ability to save money. As a result, Capital One now offers 3 weeks of vacation in the first year of employment, 3 family-care days, and a 9 percent company contribution to their 401(k) plan.[2]

Benefits have become common in smaller organizations such as restaurants where many low-paying jobs are concentrated. With a tight labor market resulting in a shortage of low-skilled workers, smart restauranteurs are becoming more aggressive and creative in attracting employees. The result is higher wages and benefit packages including improved medical insurance, 401(k) plans, stock-purchase options, retirement plans, discount cards, transportation allowance, and tuition refunds.[3]

Restaurants with HRM departments are attempting to recruit new employees and retain them by offering some unusual perks. These include home entertainment centers, trips to Paris and Italy, expensive gift certificates, and even new cars.[4]

In this chapter, we focus on the next stage of the Success System Model: the various types of benefit programs used in the recruitment and retention of high-performing employees and the changing trends in this area. In the past few years, the trend has been to offer an increasing amount and array of benefit packages. The benefits package is generally believed to increase the organization's ability to attract and retain a high-quality labor force.[5]

EMPLOYEE BENEFITS PROGRAMS

Almost all organizations provide a benefit package to supplement the wages or salaries paid to their employees. These benefits (many required by law) are usually considered to be a part of the total labor costs. As with direct labor payments, employee benefits are a growing cost of doing business. Many organizations are now using the term **total compensation package** to emphasize the fact that employee benefits are a major portion of an employee's total income. In the following sections, we present the characteristics of **employee benefit programs,** the major types of benefits offered, the types of services provided, and the various retirement programs being used.

Employee benefits provide indirect compensation intended to enhance the quality of worklife for the organization's employees. Because employees have become accustomed to an increasing level of benefits, the motivational value of these benefits may be lessened. Although benefits were previously thought of as a gift from the employer, now benefits are often considered employee rights. Consequently, this has become one of the fastest-growing areas of employment law and litigation. This trend has required the HR manager to develop and manage a wide range of benefits and services.

Employee benefits were initially introduced by employers to reward employee loyalty and discourage unionization. As unions emerged during the 1930s and 1940s, their bargaining included additional benefits as well as higher wages. During World War II, the War Labor Board exempted employee benefits from wage stabilization controls, and the war-time wage freeze resulted in the growth of employee benefits. At that time, benefits comprised less than 5 percent of total pay. According to figures from the U.S. Chamber of Commerce, benefits now add about 38 percent to total compensation costs.[6] During World War II, employers provided special inducements in the form of pensions, paid vacations, sick leave, and health and life insurance. After the war, employers found themselves obligated to continue the benefits because employees were reluctant to give them up.

At that time, employee benefit programs were quite standardized, but now there are a variety of benefits offered by organizations. Many companies, including IBM and Procter & Gamble, for example, provide many family options including family-care leave, child- and elder-care support, dependent care, alternative work schedules, and on-site day care. In general, larger companies provide a wider range of benefit options.

Benefits as a percentage of total pay have risen 20 percent in the past decade. There are a number of reasons for this dramatic increase.[7] First, the Social Security Act was expanded to cover more employees and included a variety of benefits (survivor, disability, and health benefits). Second, the federal tax policy favors the use of pension programs for both employees and employers. Third, employee benefits became a favored bargaining goal of labor unions in their labor negotiations.

Fourth, federal legislation has also influenced benefits, including the Age Discrimination in Employment Act (ADEA) which established benefit protection for older workers. The Retirement Equity Act extended the coverage of previous legislation for the workforce. In general, this type of legislation made employees more aware of and increased demand for many benefit programs.

The final reason for the increase in benefits has been a greater emphasis by employers. Although many programs answer the needs of employees (such as long-term disability and child-care), other programs were developed to have a positive impact on the "bottom line." Many companies adopting the family benefit packages (such as IBM) believe there is a relationship between family concerns and the recruitment and retention of high-performing employees. Other similar benefit programs include employee stock ownership programs (ESOPs), suggestion systems, and educational programs.

BENEFITS VERSUS RIGHTS

The increase in employee benefits is causing a change in the concept of what is meant by a benefit. Benefits now include a range of items (including food services, parking, and employee counseling) which are often seen as an integral part of the total compensation package. In fact, employees no longer perceive benefits as a fringe element, but rather as a part of total compensation. However, as benefits have grown into a larger percentage of an employee's total compensation, they are becoming less attractive to employers. Among newer benefits being offered are corporate-sponsored diet programs, health clubs, child-care, pre-retirement, personal financial counseling, and others.[8]

EMPLOYEE BENEFITS PROGRAM PLANNING

It's difficult for HR managers to take a proactive approach to benefits management when so much time is spent reacting to changes in today's business world. New regulations are continually emerging at both state and federal levels. Top management is deciding to restructure or downsize to keep the business competitive, and health-care costs continue to escalate faster than company profits.

Benefits management certainly is becoming more difficult in today's business climate, but human resource professionals are finding ways to gain an improving return on human resource expenditure. One method is termed strategic benefits planning, which may be defined as a long-term evaluative approach to the planning and cost of present and future benefits.

"Strategic benefits planning is emerging as one approach for companies that want to remain focused on future objectives," said Victor S. Barocas (HRM consultant). Although more of an art form than an exact science, strategic benefits planning provides executives with an improved focus and sense of perspective about their organization's benefits programs.[9]

The basic objectives of the strategic benefits program are to improve employee morale, recruit and motivate high-performing employees, reduce turnover, prevent unions, and gain a favorable competitive position. One key objective is focusing on cost containment—a major issue in today's competitive global marketplace.

Strategic benefits planning involves an examination of the various tradeoffs among benefits that can be offered, the relative preference of employees for each type of benefit, and the estimated cost of those benefits. Because employees are the key customers, their input in designing the benefits program is essential and opens communication channels for any problems associated with the benefits.[10]

American companies are now using outsourcing—the transfer of routine and repetitive tasks to an outside supplier—to allow management to concentrate on tasks that are more critical to business, and at the same time, get routine functions done more efficiently. Outsourcing has been an accepted practice in payroll administration, but is often overlooked in benefits administration.[11]

However, when Coca-Cola entered the twenty-first century, they announced about 21 perent of their global workforce would lose their jobs as a result of outsourcing. At their Atlanta headquarters, about 40 percent of the jobs would be outsourced. The jobs to be outsourced included maintenance, compensation, and benefits.[12]

Due to the costs involved and the financial commitment needed for the future, benefits planning is becoming one of the most critical elements in HRM planning. For example, American automotive companies believe expansive benefits programs are a major factor in U.S. companies becoming less competitive. Benefits planning typically begins with several factors within a 3- to 5-year strategic plan. The factors to be considered include costs, the compensation strategy, employee preferences, union agreements, legal implications, and the HRM strategy of the organization. Of course, the benefits plan needs to be coordinated into the total compensation program.

Many HRM professionals suggest that benefits are important in the recruitment process. Studies suggest that women prefer working for a company which has a strong family benefits package. However, employees often underestimate the cost of benefits to the organization. One study found, for example, that employees estimated the cost of benefits to the organization to be about 12 percent, but the actual cost was 31 percent of total pay.[13]

MAJOR TYPES OF BENEFITS PROGRAMS

According to the U.S. Chamber of Commerce, benefits are typically classified into three basic categories: required benefits, payment for time not worked, and employee services. In the following sections, we will discuss the basic options.

Required Health and Pension Benefits

Employers are legally required to provide certain benefit programs for all employees. Probably the benefit of most importance to both employees and employers today, because of the increasing costs, is health care insurance. This category includes unemployment compensation, social security plans, and worker's compensation.

Unemployment Compensation

Employees who are covered by the Social Security Act and who are laid off may be eligible for **unemployment compensation** up to 26 weeks. In 1991, a bill extended these benefits for an additional 20 weeks. Employees who meet requirements must apply for unemployment and register for suitable work through the state employment agency, which attempts to find them suitable work. To be eligible for unemployment compensation, the worker must have been employed previously in an occupation covered by the insurance, have been dismissed by the organization, be available for and actively seeking employment, and not be unemployed because of a labor dispute.

The amount of compensation that workers are eligible to receive varies by state, and is determined by the employee's previous wage rate up to a maximum amount. The average is about $175 per week. An unemployed worker's benefits are derived from a federal payroll tax that is paid by the organization, with the insurance rates for companies varying as a function of the amount which is charged to each organization.

In some industries, typically negotiated through collective bargaining, **supplemental unemployment benefits (SUBs)** augment unemployment compensation and provide weekly benefits in the event that employees' work weeks are reduced or they are permanently laid off. In the automobile industry, union employees who are laid off often receive up to 90 percent of their pay through unemployment insurance and supplemental programs.

Workers' Compensation Insurance

Both state and federal **workers' compensation insurance** are to compensate employees or their families for the cost of work-related accidents and illnesses.

In most states, workers' compensation insurance is compulsory. Workers' compensation laws typically stipulate that insured employees will be paid a disability benefit that is usually based on a percentage of their wages. Each state also specifies the length of the period of payment and usually indicates a maximum amount that may be paid. Benefits, which vary from state to state, are generally provided for four types of disability: (1) permanent partial disability, (2) permanent total disability, (3) temporary partial disability, and (4) temporary total disability. Disabilities may result from injuries or accidents, as well as from occupational diseases such as "black lung," radiation illness, and asbestosis. Before any workers' compensation claim will be allowed, the work-relatedness of the disability must be established. Also, the evaluation of a claimant by an occupational physician is an essential part of the claim process.

Health Insurance

The majority of organizations in the United States provide **health insurance** for employees. Approximately 75 to 80 percent of employees are provided with some form of health insurance. These plans generally provide hospitalization (room, board, and services), surgery, and major medical expenses. Most organizations provide a basic coverage for all employees, with additional coverage for salaried employees. Disability allowances are often more generous for professional and managerial employees. The typical health insurance plan requires employees to pay a deductible for the first $100 or $200 of expenses before they are eligible for group coverage. Health care benefits are usually provided through private insurance companies, such as a Blue Cross/Blue Shield Association or Health Maintenance Organizations (HMO).

The cost of health care benefits spending in the United States in 1998 was $1.1 trillion. This represented a 5.6 percent increase from the previous year. The average cost of health care benefits was $4,094 per person. The increase was due to the rising costs of drugs and health insurance.[14] Employers report their health care costs will rise 9.7% in 2000. At least 70% of employers will pass some of the costs on to employees. A main contributor to the increase is the high cost of drugs.[15]

One factor contributing to the high cost of health insurance is "entitlement mentality." In our global super-fast economy, everyone seems to be working all the

Source: CROCK by Rechin and Wilder © North America Syndicate, Inc.

time so employees feel entitled to take a day off. According to CCH, Inc., a Chicago publishing and research firm, most employees who are away from the job on short notice are not sick. They are staying home because of stress, family issues, or personal needs because they believe they deserve a day off. Unscheduled absences cost employers an average of $602 a year per employee.

Some employers are attempting to correct this problem by using workplace flexibility working hours and stress management benefits. Mid-size businesses with 1,000 to 2,400 employees have suffered a 51 percent increase in unscheduled absences. However, small employers have made the most progress controlling the problem with a 76 percent decrease. The industries suffering the most from this problem are health care with the highest number of days off, followed by universities, and then government.

General Motors (GM), for example, has estimated that the cost of health insurance adds $370 to the cost of every auto they produce; Chrysler figures the cost at $700. Ford Motor Company has estimated that it pays over $15 million in unnecessary hospital bills each year. The high cost of health insurance for an aging workforce and retirees is one of the biggest factors in making autos more expensive to produce in this country.

The most common approaches to controlling health costs include (1) reduction in coverages; (2) increases in the deductible and employee copayment for medical care; (3) mandatory second opinions from physicians; (4) incentives for outpatient surgery and testing, and (5) the use of health maintenance organizations.

Health Maintenance Organizations (HMOs)

Health maintenance organizations provide health care professionals who provide services on a prepaid basis. Many organizations have reported sizeable savings after implementing HMO programs.

There has been an increase in coverage for other forms of health insurance in addition to the basic medical coverage. Dental care, mental health, drug-abuse treatment, home health care, and vision care are the most common forms of the extended coverage. Over 77 percent of organizations reported providing some form of dental and vision coverage.

Because of corporate downsizing, one of the biggest fears of employees is to be laid off without health insurance. One study reported that 84 percent of companies provide medical coverage to retirees. However, over half also indicated that they are reducing these benefits. Many organizations are eliminating retiree health care coverage for new hires.[16]

Abandoning Health Care Plans

The Xerox Company is considering scrapping its employee health insurance program by replacing it with a worker-paid plan. The company is frustrated by the cost and administrative hassle connected with their present plan. Their alternative is to pay employees a sum of money and let them buy the insurance they desire.

The company has been formulating change over plans which could take place in 5 years. Because Xerox has long been an innovator in health benefits, many large and small companies are closely evaluating their plans.

Many companies are studying ways to overhaul their present plans. This is the result of rising health care costs, increased federal and state regulation, mounting legal exposure, and worker dissatisfaction with present plans.

The present thinking at Xerox is to provide all employees with $5,000 to $6,000 a year to buy health insurance on the open market. Some cities believe this would be devastating on less healthy and older workers. Others claim it would destroy American health care.

Although the Xerox plan is at the far extreme of present health care, it does have support among many companies. Because other companies are serious about the need to reform the present health care system, it seems certain there will be changes occurring.[17]

FEHB

The Federal Employees Health Benefits Program (FEHB) has been in operation for 40 years. FEHB is pronounced as "feeb" and has provided health care to millions of government workers and families.

The operation of FEHB is similar to the Xerox idea in that members are given a voucher to purchase the health plan they decide upon. The program screens over 300 plans nationwide, and in most parts of the country, there are at least 10 plans to choose from.

This changes the health care coverage into a customer buyer's market, which promotes a consumer-friendly competition not present in the private-sector. If members are hassled or they experience poor service, all one does is to switch to another company.

Advocates of FEHB claim it provides better prices, service, and benefits. Opponents say it won't work.[18]

Eliminating the Middleman

Two State of California pension funds are considering dropping the managed care plans that provide their members with health care. The pension funds' alternative is to contract directly with doctors and hospitals and eliminate the middleman—the managed care plans.

The two pension funds are the California State Teachers Retirement System and the California Public Employees Retirement System (CalPers), representing approximately 1.5 million people. The teachers fund, which represents about 500,000 members, is expected to establish a pilot program the first part of the twenty-first century.

CalPers is the second largest buyer of health insurance—after the federal government—and has been studying the switch for almost a year. The state treasurer, who sits on the boards of both pension funds, believes the switch should absolutely be considered and be pursued very seriously. If approved, this end-run around health maintenance organizations could change the face of health care across the nation.

The two California pension funds believe that by eliminating the managed care plans, they will be able to save millions of dollars. This will result in better local control over administration and costs.[19]

Life Insurance

One of the most common forms of employee benefits is group **life insurance,** which provides death benefits to beneficiaries. Many organizations offer group life insurance, providing coverage to all employees without physical examinations and with premiums based on the group's characteristics. Many plans call for the employer to pay the entire premium, although this is changing and more organizations are now requiring the employee to pay part of the premium. Some companies also offer optional additional life insurance along with other survivor benefits.

Social Security Insurance

Today, virtually all employees are covered by **Social Security.** The Social Security Act (1935) provides insurance designed to cover individuals against the loss of earnings resulting from various causes. These causes include retirement, unemployment, disability, or, in the case of dependents, the death of the person supporting them. Like other types of casualty insurance, social security does not pay off until a loss of income is actually incurred from loss of employment.

To be eligible for old-age and survivors' insurance (OASI), as well as disability and unemployment insurance under the Social Security Act, an individual must have been engaged in employment covered by the act. Most employment in private enterprise, self-employment, active military service, and employment in governmental agencies are subject to coverage under the act. Railroad workers and civil service employees are covered by their own systems and exempted from the act.

The social security program is supported by means of a tax levied against an employee's earnings which must be matched by the employer in each pay period. Social security taxes collected from employers and employees are used to pay three major types of benefits: (1) old-age insurance benefits, (2) disability benefits, and (3) survivors' insurance benefits. The program transfers money from younger workers to the older workers. In the future, however, retirees will be getting less benefits.[20]

Pension Plans

Pension plans have been around since the late 1800s, when the first-known plan was initiated by the American Express Company. A few years later, the railroads followed by developing pension plans for their employees. Personnel in the civil and military services of the federal government were also among the earliest to receive pension benefits.

These early pensions were based on a reward system, viewing pensions as a way to retain employees by rewarding them for staying with the organization. New pensions are based on an earnings system, regarding a pension as deferred income that employees accumulate during their working lives and that belongs to them after a specified number of years of service.

A pension refers to a payment to a retired employee based on the time and level of employment with the organization. There are about half a million private employer pension plans which cover about 75 percent of nonfarm American workers. Larger, older organizations are more likely to offer pensions than smaller, newer ones. Public employees are almost always covered by pension plans.

The pension plan usually requires employees to pay into the pension (usually a deduction from the paycheck), but some are provided by the employer. The employer sets aside a pension fund managed by a trustee (usually an insurance company). Income taxes on employer contributions are deferred, and retirees pay no taxes on the pension income until after retirement. All pension plans must conform to the requirements established in the Internal Revenue Code.

Private pension plans are subject to federal regulations in the **Employment Retirement Income Security Act (ERISA).** ERISA requires that all persons participating in retirement plans be notified about the plans in writing and in understandable language.

There are two main types of pension plans. The first type, the **defined-benefit plan,** specifies the payment based on a percentage of preretirement pay. The amount is based on years of service, average earnings during a specified period of time (usually 3 to 5 years), and age at time of retirement. When combined with social security benefits, retirement income averages about half of final average income. A growing percentage of pension plans (about 5 percent) are indexed to adjust pension rates for inflation. Because of the predictability of benefits, older employees generally prefer this plan.

The second type of pension plan, the **defined-contribution plan** (sometimes called "cash balance"), establishes a fixed rate of contribution and has been growing in popularity in recent years because it can be linked to organizational performance. Stock bonuses, savings plans, profit sharing, and ESOPs are examples of defined-contribution plans. The level of employee benefits depend on the growth of the benefit fund. Thus, if the organization prospers, the fund will be larger and the employee will have an increased pension. Employers often prefer this approach to benefits, because they do not owe more than the money which has been contributed. Everything beyond this amount is a direct function of the investment of the money which was contributed. Younger workers generally prefer this type of pension plan.

When International Business Machines Corp. (IBM) tried to change their pension plan from a defined-benefit to a defined-contribution or "cash balance," management was met with an angry backlash from older employees. These employees cried age discrimination and Congress held a hearing to investigate.

The cash balance pension plan was criticized for benefiting younger workers at the expense of older ones. The traditional defined benefit pension plans are structured so employees earn half as much of their retirement pay in their last 5 to 10 years of employment.[21]

Many older workers have discovered if they switch from a defined benefit to a cash balance, they may lose anywhere from 20 to 50 percent of their pension value. This means some older workers who are switched to the cash balance pension plan would have to work for 5 or more years to earn their way back to their old benefit levels. This phenomenon is called "pension plateau" or "wearaway."[22]

As a result of the media coverage from the Congressional hearing and the creation of a web site full of angry postings, IBM altered their plans. The company's new response is that any employee aged 40 or older with at least 10 years of service has the option of remaining in the old plan. The reason IBM chose the cutoff point at age 40 is because the Age Discrimination Act of 1967 protects workers aged 40 and older. IBM believes this will protect them from age-discrimination complaints. However, the Communications Workers of America has used the controversy to launch organizing drives at IBM.[23]

Northern States Power also made the switch to a cash balance pension plan but avoided the problems at IBM. Northern States did not encounter any controversy because they allowed all employees the choice of staying in their traditional plan or switching to the new cash balance plan. The result was nearly two-thirds of the 3,700 workers selected the new plan. These workers were younger with an average of 4 years on the job. The 36 percent who chose the traditional plan were mostly within 15 years of retirement.[24]

Pension cutbacks continue to remain a fact across corporate America. These pension reductions commonly occur in mergers, acquisitions, and divestitures. They affect managers and employees both. When one large insurance company decided to sell its health care unit to another company, managers led the charge when they determined 17,000 employees, many of them longer-service employees, would have their pensions cut as much as 40 percent. They complained vehemently to the chief executive's office and the company backed down. They agreed to allow departing employees to receive an early retirement subsidy that was not available when units were spun off to new owners.[25]

Individual Retirement Accounts (IRAs)

Another popular form of retirement fund is the **individual retirement account (IRA).** IRAs are funded entirely by the employee, but they are widely used because the money contributed, up to $2,000 per year, is not subject to taxes under certain total income limitations. Also, the interest earned on the amount set aside is not taxed, regardless of total income.

Money can be set aside until age 70½, and money can be withdrawn without penalty beginning at age 59½. Funds drawn prior to that date are subject to income tax plus a 10 percent penalty. The major advantages of an IRA are that the employee can decide where to invest the extra retirement income, and a tax shelter is created because income tax is deferred until retirement.

Salary Reduction 401(K) Plans

The **401(k) plan** (after the section of the IRS code defining them) works much like an IRA. This plan serves as a tax shelter for a portion of income until retirement. The payment is a salary deduction and the money can be invested only in a limited set of employer-approved funds. A larger amount can be set aside in these plans— $7,000 per year or up to $9,000 for educators. These plans are popular with higher-paid managers and executives but can be used by any employee.

The aging of the U.S. workforce is causing problems for many organizations because of pension obligations to retirees. At GM, for example, the ratio of active to retired workers is about 2:1. At Ford, the ratio is about 1.5:1. At the Nissan plant in Tennessee, by contrast, only 1 in over 3,000 workers was eligible to retire. This is a result of a younger workforce, so Nissan had no other retirement obligations to worry about.

A continuing problem with companies is how to provide information to their employees about investing their money without providing personalized investment advice. If a company does provide such advice, there is a strong possibility it may have an unacceptable fiduciary liability or violate federal law. A fiduciary liability means the employer has been empowered by employees to perform in their interests. If investments are not wisely made, the employer could be liable for the results.

This has become a huge issue because 401(k) assets now exceed those of traditional pension plans that are managed by professionals. So, who will provide the advice employees need? The answer appears to be a new industry of high-tech vendors offering investment advice through the Internet.

There are now dozens of high-tech vendors. Two examples are Financial Engines and 401k Forum. Both provide professional advice with participants able to log on 24-hours-a-day wherever there is Internet access. Because this becomes a fiduciary arrangement, the responsibilities and disclaimers should be in writing and employees need to understand them.[26]

Payment for Time Not Worked

The **payment for time not worked** includes paid vacations, holidays, sick leave, personal days, and days to perform civic responsibilities such as jury duty, military obligations, and so forth. The cost of paid time off is another of the costliest benefit expenses for employers today. According to the U.S. Department of Labor, payments for time not worked average about 13 percent of total payroll costs.[27]

Paid Vacations

After employees have worked for a specified period of time, they become eligible for a **paid vacation.** The amount of paid vacation time typically is based upon the employee's length of service. One survey found that employees with 10 years of experience in larger companies average about 16 days of paid vacation, and employees with 15 years of experience average about 18.5 days. Another survey reported that over one-fourth of surveyed organizations offer 5- to-6-week vacations for employees with 25 years of service.[28] In general, hourly employees must work for longer time periods than salaried employees in order to qualify for the same amount of vacation time. Union employees typically receive more vacation time than do nonunion employees.

Paid Holidays

Both hourly and salaried employees average about 10 **paid holidays** per year. Some organizations now offer 2 or more personal days off per year for a variety of personal reasons (death or illness in the family, legal matters, or special events).

Sick Leave

Almost every type of organization offers **sick leave** for their employees, with an average of about 10 days per year. Where permitted, employees can often accumulate unused sick leave days, in case of a prolonged illness or injury in the future. A recent trend for organizations is the sick leave bank. A sick leave bank allows employees to borrow sick leave from a common fund in an emergency. Some organizations are now offering "well pay" incentives: In this case, employees receive a bonus if they are not absent or tardy over a specified period of time.

Employee Services

There are a number of employee benefits in the category of **employee services** (as shown in Table 11.1). These services also represent a cost to the employer. The typical employee services include educational assistance, financial services such as credit unions and sports and health programs, employee assistance programs (EAPs), housing and relocation services, employee recognition programs, and child-care.

Employee services are seeing an increase in family-focused programs. Work-friendly programs are mostly common in corporate office towers and the suburban campuses of big cities. As a result of a tight labor market and increasing attention to workers' values, these programs are now spreading across the United States in a variety of geographical locations.

The Round Mountain Gold Corp. in Round Mountain, Nevada, is 250 miles of desert roads from Las Vegas and very remote. However, the company offers one of the most family-friendly programs around. Their program offers a child-care center and a general store. The company helped start a medical clinic for its 670 employees. Recognizing the needs of families for dual earnings, the company recently began offering jobs to recruits' spouses.[29]

In Georgia, Greene County is one of the state's poorest counties with one-third of the population below the poverty line. Most employers offered few benefits and there was a labor shortage.

This was the environment in which Chipman-Union, a growing soy manufacturer, found itself. With a labor shortage and 22 percent employee turnover, they needed to attract and retain workers. So they began a family-friendly program. They noticed many workers left their children home alone or brought them to work. The company responded by helping to raise money and donated land for a subsidized child-care and family-resource center.

Chipman helps agencies train welfare-to-work mothers and noncustodial fathers. The company also lets production workers swap shifts when a family needs time off. This allows the workers to maintain their earnings and the company does not dock their checks for the time off the job. Family-friendly programs will continue to be part of HRM during the twenty-first century.[30]

Table 11.1
Major employee services

Child care	Merchandise discounts
Company car	Recreational programs
Educational assistance	Relocation expenses
Elder care	Stock programs
Employee recognition programs	Suggestion systems
Financial assistance	Transportation programs
Food service	Wellness programs

Educational Assistance Programs

One of the most common programs provided are educational assistance programs for employees, which range from tuition refunds for college to literacy training. Many organizations, such as Aluminum Co. of America, also provide college scholarships for employees' children. According to one report, over 85 percent of full-time employees of medium to large U.S. firms are covered by some form of educational-aid plan. The basic purpose of such programs is to keep employees current in their fields of expertise and prepare employees for potential opportunities within the organization. Motorola is providing a program focusing on "lifelong learning," providing 40 hours of educational programs for each employee per year.[31]

Employee Assistance Programs

When supervising personnel make an employee referral to an employee assistance program (EAP), there is a need to be cautious. When an employee's work is failing for reasons that appear to be personal, guiding the employee into an EAP requires some finesse. If the indication is the company believes the failure is due to alcoholism, mental illness, or other sensitive areas and then later there is a termination, there could be trouble. The company may be open to a lawsuit under the Americans with Disabilities Act (ADA). The reason? ADA protects not only people with disabilities, but also those perceived to have disabilities.

Although the company needs to be careful, it also cannot ignore erratic behavior. If the erratic behavior leads to consequences, the company could be held liable for negligence for not correcting the situation. The solution is to make suggestions to seek out the EAP, not recommending the person do so. At no time express any conclusions about the employee's mental or physical health.[32]

Financial Services

Many organizations also provide financial assistance to employees. Payroll savings plans, credit unions, and various thrift plans are the most common. Payroll savings plans sometimes provide matching funds for employee savings. Credit unions provide affordable savings and usually provide low-cost loans to employees. There are over 17,000 credit unions, holding assets in excess of $125 billion, with over 52 million members.[33] Some organizations also offer financial planning services.

Shift Workers

With 17 percent of workers on shifts other than daytime and another 27 percent on flexible work hours, HRM is no longer an 8 A.M. to 5 P.M. schedule. Today's competitive workplace requires adjusting to all employee needs.

Shift workers' concerns are a closed cafeteria with leftovers in the vending machines, meetings held during the day, poor parking lot lighting, falling asleep while driving home, and plant security issues. These concerns lead to problems of alertness, social isolation, and physical distress. This requires HRM to create or modify policies and training to neutralize physiological and other related problems.

Some solutions are relatively low cost. Because shift workers have two to three times as many digestive problems as the day shift, one solution is to provide fruit trays or other light snacks. Providing microwaves and refrigerators allows employees to bring their own food. Companies can contract with a caterer to provide meals or pizzas. Day care can become a problem, so Saturn Corp. contracted a provider to run a subsidized center to remain open 22 hours a day, 6 days a week. For employees who want to continue their education requirements, classes can be duplicated for day and night shifts. Video-based programs and distance learning are other alternatives.[34]

Transportation can be a problem, but one company contracted with a taxi service, agreeing to splitting the cost with the employee. Because the body's circulation rhythms interfere with sound sleep during the daytime, this may cause shift workers to be deprived of sleep. To overcome this problem, some companies provide exercise rooms and nap rooms, increase lighting levels, and play upbeat music.

Education programs may be introduced to help shift workers cope with physical and social distress, sleep more soundly, and understand the most effective use of caffeine. Other accommodations for shift workers are to have rotating HRM shifts two or three times a week and an automated phone access menu to access 401(k) accounts or to request change forms.[35]

Sports and Health Programs

Organized sports, recreational, and health or "wellness" programs for employees are increasing in popularity. At least some 75 percent of organizations are sponsoring some type of recreational programs. The most common wellness programs include aerobic exercise activities and antismoking programs. Several companies (including Kimberly-Clark and Prudential Life Insurance) support the effectiveness of "wellness" programs. (See HRM in Action.)

HRM IN ACTION
LIVE FOR LIFE[36]

Johnson & Johnson's "Live for Life" (LIF) program is a pioneer in health promotion. It is a "total immersion" approach, including fitness, smoking cessation, moderation of drinking, nutrition, weight control, blood pressure control, and stress management. J&J also has altered the work environment by establishing a smoke-free corporate headquarters and regional offices, improving nutritional value in company cafeterias, and providing messages about the importance of a healthy lifestyle. The goals of the program are basic: stop smoking, eat more fruit and fewer fatty foods, exercise regularly, and buckle up your seat belt.

THE LIF PROGRAM

The LIF program includes several levels of services. The first level is a confidential health screening program consisting of a 19-page questionnaire that becomes part of a health-risk profile. A nurse practitioner goes over the results with the employees, takes their blood pressure, and tests their pulse while they exercise. The second level of the programs, if an employee decides to continue with the program, consists of exercise, diet and weight control, and smoking cessation.

J&J's headquarters has a gym on-site. At other company locations, facilities are provided on-site or at a local organization such as at a YMCA.

THE RESULTS

J&J has kept comprehensive records of the costs and benefits of the LIF program. Last year the program cost $200 per employee and saved $378 per employee by lowering absenteeism and by slowing the rise in health care expenses.

In a study that lasted 3 years and involved 8,000 employees, J&J carefully tracked the program from its introduction. In the first year, the program cost more than it saved. In the second year, it broke even. In the third year, it saved enough to pay back losses incurred in the first year.

The LIF program has been so successful that J&J sells the program to other companies. To date, over 60 companies with 850,000 employees participate in some form of the service.

THE CREDO

The LIF program at J&J is compatible with their corporate credo and culture. The Credo (a 44-year-old, 309-word statement created by Robert Johnson, son of the founder) stresses honesty, integrity, and putting people before profits.

As a consequence, J&J was named in *Fortune* as the most community and environmentally responsible company. J&J's current CEO Ralph Larsen says, "The Credo shouldn't be viewed as some kind of social welfare program. It's just plain good business."

QUESTIONS

1. What advantages do you see to J&J's LIF program?
2. Must a company's culture be similar to J&J's to implement a successful wellness program?

Long-Term Care

One of the fastest growing employee benefits is long-term care (LTC) insurance. Sales have been increasing 25 percent a year, doubling that of life insurance. LTC insurance usually pays the cost of nursing care. They are reimbursement contracts that pay a benefit amount for actual expenses. Another type of contract policy pays a specific amount each day regardless of expenses.

The majority of employers offering LTC insurance have voluntary plans with either some or none of the premiums paid by the employer. The employer-sponsored LTC has little control over the insurance company once the policy is issued. Employees must then rely on the insurance company to treat them fairly in the future.

This means the company and the benefits officer have the responsibility to select the best insurance company to provide the best coverage and service for the employees. Because there are more than 100 writers of LTC insurance with mergers occurring frequently, it is a difficult situation. It becomes even more difficult because rates are easily increased because it is not difficult for the insurance companies to obtain state regulators' approval.

The final responsibility falls upon the company's benefits manager, who performs a due-care analysis in conjunction with a broker who has particular knowledge of the LTC market. These two individuals can then act as the advocate for the employer and the employee.[37]

Housing and Relocation Services

It has been estimated that American companies are spending over $14 billion per year in relocation of employees. One study reported an average cost of an in-country relocation of over $40,000, with the cost of international relocation being significantly higher. Companies may also offer special assistance in selling homes in case of company relocation and pay the expenses for finding a new home. There may be special loan programs for the purchase of the new home. Many companies also provide job placement services for the spouse, in case of a dual-career family.

The traditional transferee is male, around 38 years old with dependent children, and earns approximately $60,000. However, the population of transferees is becoming more diverse with changing demographics which now include more female transferees representing 17 percent of those transferring. Now there are more spouse and partner issues such as child care, assisting the transferee's aging parent, and the increasing influence of quality-of-life issues on the final decision.[38]

Most companies regard employee mobility as being essential to an effective workforce. The result is that relocations are less discretionary and much more strategic. Companies report only 53 percent of relocations as being related to promotions versus 67 percent in 1988.

Many companies are recognizing the benefits of employees arriving at the new location comfortable and in a productive frame of mind. Employers that provide additional benefits such as counseling and spouse's job placement have better morale and productivity. The days of "pack 'em and move 'em" are over.[39]

Atlas Van Lines reports about three-fourths of the companies responding to their annual relocation survey cited family ties as the reason employees most often gave for declining a transfer. A close second was concern over the spouse's career. A clear emerging issue is elder care.[40]

The uprooting of families and severing social ties to relocate has created relocation counseling to meet employee's changing needs. Today private relocation agencies are being used by companies to handle this problem. These relocation agencies are now doing a great deal of counseling face-to-face rather than over the telephone.

The counseling continues long after the move. One relocation agency provides a lot of follow-up support for the whole family. They have counselors with PhD's or master's degrees calling the family for a whole year. Families tend to be the most vulnerable in the 9th to 18th months after the move.[41]

Employee Recognition Programs

Organizations often offer awards to employees to recognize work-related achievements or suggestions for improving organizational effectiveness. These awards are usually presented in the form of gifts and travel rather than cash. Suggestion systems offer incentives to employees who submit ideas which result in measurable improvements in efficiency or profitability for the organization. It has been reported that employees were awarded almost $125 million for suggestions in 1 year by U.S. firms.

Child Care

The increased employment of women has created a need for child care. There is evidence to suggest that company-sponsored child-care programs tend to reduce employee absences, improve recruitment, and help to retain employees.[42] Several organizations have reported an increase in job applications as a result of starting a child-care program. Many companies offer on-site child care, including Campbell Soup Company, Marriott, and Wang Laboratories. (See HRM in Action.)

HRM IN ACTION
MARRIOTT'S FAMILY MATTERS[43]

Little 2-year-old Rachel Kane toddles down the hallway of Marriott Corporation's main building, her blond curly hair twirling as she picks up speed. A strange and wonderful entourage accompanies her: other toddlers in colorful cotton overalls, and day care teachers pushing small children in strollers.

Laughing, babbling, and chattering away, these little people regularly tour the halls of the company offices on their way from the 5,600-square-foot on-site child development center to the playground.

Later, Rachel's mom, Jane, a Marriott administrator, will visit her for lunch. They'll dine at pint-size tables and chairs amid preschool art work, brightly colored toys, and wooden cubbyholes that overflow with sweaters and stuffed animals (helpmates for children's naptime). Her mom will peek in through the window or grab a quick hug if work permits. At other times during the day, the children may visit offices upon request, often from departments that don't even have children in the center.

The child development center is only one small component of Bethesda, Maryland-based Marriott's extensive array of programs that are a part of its Department of Work and Family Life. Started in 1989, the department is illustrative of the company's determination to address family concerns in the workplace and to increase the quality of life of employees and their children, such as Jane and Rachel.

"It's made me feel much better about my job," says Jane Kane. "My job is extremely stressful, and if I hadn't had the chance to have Rachel here, I would have felt more split. I want to be with her, but I also have a responsibility here at my work."

A survey of employees regarding the child-care program revealed some interesting comments:

- Personal life demands directly affect job performance.
- Time is the crucial issue to balancing work and family.
- Male and female employees reported *in equal numbers* the difficulties of managing work and family roles.
- Problems with child-care arrangement increase the employees' level of stress and limit their ability to work certain schedules or overtime.
- Elder-care issues are growing in importance.
- A manager supportive of personal concerns is central to a good work situation.

To address these issues, the company developed a 3-year work and family life strategic plan. It consists of several core programs with the idea that the department would sign and implement division-specific programs after the core programs were in place.

QUESTIONS

1. How do you feel about Marriott's child development center and the contribution to productivity? Are you for or against it?

2. Would you consider a similar program for elder care? Why?

3. Who should administer Marriott's child development center: HRM or outside sources?

Since the introduction of the Marriott's Child Care Center (see the previous HRM in Action) in Atlanta, the company has been forced to scale back the operation due to weak demand. Originally, the center was designed to be open 24 hours a day, 7 days a week.

As of the first quarter of 2000, the hours have been changed to 5:30 AM to midnight on week days and until 7 PM on Saturdays. It is closed on Sundays.

Only about a third of the 200 children enrolled come from families working in the hotel industry. Most of the other children are from low income families in the area. Some problems at the center include the fact that families are uncomfortable going outside their extended families and neighborhoods and the center is regarded as custodial care.[44]

The California State Department of Transportation and the Department of Motor Vehicles have also set up child-care centers in Sacramento. The Pentagon has elaborate facilities to care for over 200 children. Although there are approximately 800 employers that have developed on- or near-site centers, a high percentage of them prefer other options, such as promoting community centers and helping employees find suitable facilities.

Already plagued by labor shortages, many employers are using child-care benefits in an attempt to retain their female employees. The benefits may also help recruitment, because a large percentage of those entering the labor force in the next decade will be women. Although it is a costly service, one employer whose child-care center accounted for $60,000 in red ink in a year remarked, "On paper it looks like a real loser, but the benefits—reduced turnover, absenteeism, and retraining costs—are not quantifiable."[45]

A major concern of parents is how their child's development is affected by placing them in child care or what is commonly called day care. In a long-term study of 1,300 children by the University of California, Irvine, children who were placed in high-quality day care facilities have higher social and language skills than those who were not. In general, enrollment in day care did not affect the parent relationships.[46]

The key to this study is that most of the development occurred in a high-quality day care center, not a lesser quality one. The 3-year-old children who attended a high-quality day care were 10 percentile points higher on language and comprehension tests than children who stayed at home or who were enrolled in lesser-quality centers.

Although the higher-quality day care centers scored higher, there are other factors which influenced the children's increased language and comprehension tests. These other higher influence factors were the parents' income, psychological well-being, and parents' personal behavior.

When parents have no other options than day care, they must focus on the high-quality issue because about only 11 percent of day care centers are ranked excellent. The rest are ranked 31 percent good, with 6 percent considered poor.[47]

An alternative to full-time day care centers is a backup center. These centers are a place where children can go if a sitter is ill, their center has a snow day, or the youngster is sick and can't go to day care. It also provides a temporary stop gap while the parent shops for a new or replacement day care center.

Many companies in New York City such as JP Morgan and Sony Music utilize backup day care. A Boston-based company runs 18 backup centers nationwide. Chase Manhattan Bank saved $820,000 one year in reduced absenteeism by offering backup child-care for their New York employees.

The companies pay for these services. A company with 300 or fewer employees generally pays $28,000 per year or more to buy one space at a care center. Because building an on-site child-care facility can cost millions, which would exclude small companies, many client companies say the service pays for itself.[48]

Workplace Lactation

A recent development in the workplace that is gaining widespread company acceptance and support is a woman's right to breastfeed or express milk during the workday. The minimum criteria for a space is privacy, an electrical outlet, a table, and a chair. At Amway Corporation in Ada, Michigan, their lactation rooms are secured and mothers have their own access code.

Companies providing these programs find they reduced health care costs and employee absenteeism caused by infant illness. According to the American Academy of Pediatrics (AAP), breast-fed infants have fewer allergies, respiratory infections, ear infections, and serious diseases such as diabetes.[49]

The workplace lactation programs at the Los Angeles Department of Water and Power (LADWP) reduced health care claims by 35 percent and absenteeism by 27 percent. Aetna Incorporated, a health insurance company in Kensington, Connecticut, had a similar experience. The company had a 2.7 to 1 return on their investment. However, this was not the only reason for the program; their workforce is 76 percent female and it was a big return-to-work initiative.[50]

Elder Care

Responsibility for the care of aging parents and other relatives is another fact of life for increasing numbers of employees. The term **elder care,** as used in the context of employment, refers to the circumstance where an employee provides volunteer care to an elderly relative or friend while remaining actively at work.

Because the topic of elder care is relatively new to employers, many are focusing on information gathering and distribution. Elder-care counseling, educational fairs or seminars, and distribution of printed resource materials are types of employee assistance offered by such firms as Marriott Corporation, American Security Bank, Pepsi Company, Pitney Bowes, Florida Power & Light, and Mobil Corporation.

There are over 4,000 U.S. companies offering some form of child-care support, such as referrals or financing. A smaller number of companies also provide on-site centers. With increased government financial support now available, it seems that child-care may be included as a standard employee benefit in the future.

The situation is rapidly changing due to the dynamics of demographic changes in the United States. In 1995, there were 33.6 million people over age 65. By 2005 this number will increase to more than 40 million, and by 2025 there will be 62.2 million people over age 65. Demographers predict the fastest growth will be among the "old old," those over age 85 who typically require daily care.[51]

The National Partnership for Women and Families conducted a poll in which 54 percent of Americans believe they will be caretakers of elderly parents or a relative within the next 10 years. The National Council on Aging reports that caretakers spend an average of 15.1 hours per week for caregiving. Fifty percent of caregivers take time off from work, go in late, or work fewer hours. They also are more unlikely to relocate. All of these events have a negative effect on productivity.[52]

The 1999 SHRM Benefits Survey indicates how little has been done to resolve this problem. Of the respondents, only 14 percent indicated their organizations provide elder-care referral services. Organizations offering a company-supported elder-care center—one percent! Even more startling is that few respondents indicated their company planned to introduce either referral services or an elder-care center within the next year.[53]

CAFETERIA-STYLE BENEFIT PLANS

In order to limit costs and to be responsive to the individual needs of employees, there is a growing trend toward **flexible benefit plans,** also known as **cafeteria plans.** These plans enable the employee to select the benefits that are best suited to their particular needs.

More than one-quarter of U.S. companies offer flexible, or cafeteria-style, benefit plans. Because of the increasing diversity of the workforce, employees seem to prefer a more flexible plan, and employers can realize cost savings through their use. The HR department typically assesses employee preferences for the various benefit options by using a benefits survey. Cafeteria plans are probably most useful to the two-wage earner family, because any redundant coverage can be eliminated.

One way out of the medical cost quagmire is the use of cafeteria plans. They're not a new idea—PepsiCo's pioneering plan is 11 years old—but pressure to contain costs is causing more companies to adopt them. A survey of 1,000 large companies last year by Foster Higgins, a benefits consulting company, reported that 27 percent had such flexible plans and another 11 percent intended to introduce them in the future.

Unions don't like cafeteria plans, seeing them as an effort to limit benefits. "They really boil down to cost shifting from employers to individuals," says Karen Ignagni, director of benefits for the AFL-CIO. "They limit corporate liability but leave the employee holding the bag." Cafeteria plans are usually confined to management or nonunion employees because sometimes unions won't go along with them.[54]

American Can Company uses a sophisticated flexible benefits program that provides its employees with a greater degree of choice than any workforce in the country. In a survey, the satisfaction with employee benefits at American Can was found to be 50 to 100 percent higher than that of a national sample of employers using a traditional benefits plan.

COMMUNICATING THE BENEFIT PROGRAM

One measure of a successful benefit program is the degree of appreciation by employees. Despite the increasing cost of benefits, employees often have little understanding of the costs involved in these programs. According to one report, employee communication is the "keystone of the program . . . without effective communication, the benefit program remains incomplete and the considerable effort and expense consumed in planning, designing, and administering plans becomes largely unproductive."[55]

SUMMARY

In this chapter, we have focused on several major employee benefit programs. This is important because employees receive a sizable portion of their total compensation in the form of benefits. For organizations, benefits represent a significant expenditure and cost of doing business. There is a great deal of evidence to support an increasing review of costs and demands. HR managers are operating in a dynamic and changing environment, and consequently need to be developing adaptive benefit programs.

You have been introduced to the emerging field of employee benefits management and the ways it can be used to improve organizational effectiveness. You, as a human resource manager, must be sensitive to changes in markets, people, and competition and be aware of the need for an adaptive and flexible organization.

Because employees now prefer a choice of benefits, the use of flexible benefits or cafeteria plans is increasing so employees are able to select the benefits they want. Many organizations are beginning to introduce flexible benefit plans as a way to meet employee needs and reduce costs.

The rapidly increasing costs of health care benefits are posing a major challenge to organizations. Several alternatives to traditional health care programs are being examined. A number of organizations are attempting to reduce the costs of benefits by changing the type of pension plans.

Changes in mandatory retirement are having a definite impact on HR planning. Many organizations are offering preretirement programs to help employees prepare for the social, emotional, and financial aspects of retirement.

You will have an opportunity to experience the need for human resource skills in this class meeting. The rising costs of health care and other benefits are posing a major challenge to HR managers.

In the HRM Skills, you will have a chance to practice developing a benefits program. You may find that an equitable program is not a simple process, because it includes trade-offs between costs to the organization and employee needs. Because of the costs involved, the legal complexity, and changing employee needs, the benefits plan will continue to be a problem area in the foreseeable future.

REVIEW QUESTIONS

1. In your opinion, what is the single most important benefit?
2. Present examples of how employee benefits are used in organizations you have worked for.
3. Do you feel employee benefits are important in choosing an employer?
4. Why are the costs of health care benefits rising so rapidly and what can an organization do?
5. Discuss and explain the basic cafeteria and flexible benefits programs? Do you agree with these programs?
6. Read a book or view a video movie, and identify some element of employee benefits in an organization.

KEY WORDS AND CONCEPTS

Define and be able to use the following:

- 401(k) Plan
- Cafeteria Plans
- Defined-Benefit Plan
- Defined-Contribution Plan
- Elder care
- Employee Benefit Programs
- Employee Services
- Employment Retirement Income Security Act (ERISA)

- Flexible Benefit Plans
- Health Insurance
- Health Maintenance Organizations
- Individual Retirement Account (IRA)
- Life Insurance
- Paid Holidays
- Paid Vacation
- Payment for Time Not Worked

- Pension Plans
- Sick Leave
- Social Security
- Supplemental Unemployment Benefits (SUBs)
- Total Compensation Package
- Unemployment Compensation
- Workers' Compensation Insurance

HRM SKILLS SIMULATION 11.1: THE SLICKLINE COMPANY

A. PURPOSE

The purpose of this exercise is to experience and observe how employee benefits impact effective organization functioning and how goals can be in conflict. You will experience how conflicting benefit goals can sometimes be resolved.

B. PROCEDURES

Step 1. Prior to class, form groups of five (extras act as observers), select roles, and read the Slickline Company Background Information and your role description. Read *all* the roles, and make your individual decision. The roles are:

1. HR manager
2. Accounting representative
3. Information systems representative
4. Employee representative (1)
5. Employee representative (2)
6. Observer

Step 2. Meet with your team members and the HR manager, who conducts the meeting. Your task is to select a benefit plan from the options.

Time suggested for Step 2: 30 minutes.

Step 3. Critique your team meeting and the quality of the meeting. The observers will provide feedback. Also consider the following:

1. Share at this point any information not previously disclosed in the team meeting.
2. Were both individual and organization benefit goals adequately met?

Time suggested for Step 3: 15 minutes.

Step 4. Meet with the other teams to compare decisions.

1. Each team presents their decision and the factors most important in arriving at the decision.
2. To what extent was there member support for the final decision? How could support have been increased?
3. How closely did differing teams achieve goal agreement? If there were differences, to what could the differences be attributed, considering all teams had the same base of information?

Step 5. The class should discuss the process of benefit planning and conflict resolution.

Time suggested for Steps 4 and 5: 10 minutes.

BACKGROUND INFORMATION: SLICKLINE CORPORATION

Slickline is a medium-size company offering software services for health care systems. The headquarters of Slickline is a new facility located in a planned suburban community, almost a rural setting, with the most up-to-date facilities. The company has a complete health facility (which is part of its "wellness" program), company-provided van pools, bicycle paths connected to the communities' extensive bicycle paths, free covered parking lots, and a company-subsidized restaurant and cafeteria. Because of cost overruns, you must cut the benefits program.

ROLE DESCRIPTIONS
(READ *ONLY* YOUR ROLE)

Role 1—HR manager. The four representatives will report directly to you and your job will be to coordinate their activities.

One of the first tasks facing you and your team is to select a benefit plan. Although you have reserved the right to make the final decision, you have called a meeting of those on the benefit committee to receive their input so that you can make a more informed decision. You are also interested in getting off to a good start with the employees, as your success is largely determined by how well they do their job. Therefore, you would like to have them agree upon a decision which best meets both the individual and company goals.

You have drawn up a summary of the available options (see the Benefits Alternative List).

You have been informed that the maximum the company is willing to spend is $12,000 a month, though you would like to reserve $1,000 for last-minute changes. The benefits have a group of options available. Most of the options have specific costs and you will have to select options that will not exceed $12,000 less the $1,000 reserve. Also, you would like to keep costs to a minimum.

Roles 2 through 5—All Representatives. You have been chosen as the representative from your division to select benefits plans.

The HR manager has called a meeting of representatives to help select the plan. The HR manager has reserved the right to make the final decision, but he or she would like to get your input. The manager has given you a summary of the options with pertinent information. (See the Benefits Alternative List.)

The HR manager has informed you that the maximum the company is willing to spend on the benefit program is $12,000 a month. You will also need to build support for your choices with the other representatives, and most certainly try to convince the HR manager of your choices. You may say anything in order to build this support. You should place a rating on the Slickline Benefit Rating Form of each benefit in column 1, and your estimated costs in column 2.

Role 6—Observer. You will only observe during the role play session so that you can help the team critique their meeting in Steps 3 and 4. The Observer Form may assist you in providing feedback.

OBSERVER FORM

Instructions: For each item, place a number in the blank to the right representing your reaction to how your group performed based on the following scale.

Low ____ 1 : 2 : 3 : 4 : 5 : 6 : 7 : 8 : 9 : 10 ____ High

1. Degree of cooperative teamwork: _____
2. Degree of team motivation: _____
3. Degree of member satisfaction: _____
4. Degree of information sharing (participation): _____
5. Degree of consensual decision making: _____
6. Degree of team conflict or competition (i.e., conflict directly faced and resolved): _____
7. Degree of quality of group decisions: _____
8. Degree of speed with which decision is made: _____
9. Degree of participating leadership: _____
10. Degree of clarity of goals: _____

Total ranking _____

SLICKLINE BENEFIT RATING FORM

BENEFIT	INDIVIDUAL RATING COL. 1	INDIVIDUAL COST COL. 2	TEAM RATING COL. 3	TEAM COST COL. 4	TOTAL COST COL.5
1.					
2.					
3.					
4.					
5.					
6.					
7.					
8.					
9.					
10.					

Total
Costs

BENEFITS ALTERNATIVE LIST

BENEFIT	ESTIMATED MONTHLY COST
1. Educational assistance	4,000
2. Financial assistance	1,250
3. Transportation programs	2,500
4. Wellness programs	2,000
5. Recreational programs	3,000
6. Child care	4,000
7. Relocation expenses	2,000
8. Stock programs	5,000
9. Elder care	2,000
10. Employee recognition programs	1,500

Case 11.1 Precision Products, Inc.

Helen Brown, personnel manager for Precision Products, returned to her office deep in thought. She'd just spent the last hour and a half in a heated discussion with Curt Stump regarding the latest turnover crisis among assembly employees. Shrugging her shoulders, Helen wondered if Curt was right. Maybe the current turnover problem was her fault—well, the fault of the personnel department. According to Curt, if she'd done a better job in selecting employees in the first place, Precision Products would not be in the current mess. "You hired losers," he argued, pointing to the high turnover among temporary and permanent full-time employees.

Precision had a core workforce of 150 employees. Depending on the level of business, as many as 50 temporary employees must also be hired. The temporary workers were paid higher base salaries than regular employees ($10.50 an hour). However, they were not eligible for any benefits, including vacation leave, day care, and sick leave. If they were sick, they had to take time off without pay. They also could not participate in Precision's highly successful profit-sharing program and matching pension fund. (See Exhibit 11.1.)

Full-time, regular assembly workers were paid $9.50 an hour. Although Precision's hourly rate was below the industry average of $10.00 an hour, employees more than made up this amount in performance bonuses.

Last year, regular employees received bonuses of approximately $2,000 each. This amount was lower than usual due to the recession. Since the program was implemented in 1990, bonuses had averaged $4,000 per employee. This year bonuses were expected to be back on target. Helen anticipated handing out bonuses in the range of $4,500 per employee. Employees had the option of taking the money in one lump sum, in quarterly installments, or in even distri-

butions throughout the next year. According to HR policy, employee bonuses would be announced at the semi-annual employees' meeting.

Helen was proud of her benefits program as well. Employee benefits as a percentage of payroll averaged 30 percent in the industry. Precision's percentage was 42 percent. All full-time employees with 1 year's seniority were eligible to participate in the extensive benefit program, which included such innovations as an on-site day care center (Helen's brain child, which took her 2 years to get approved), and an employee-assistance program, including free legal assistance. The company also matched dollar-for-dollar employee contributions to a retirement fund, and offered two college scholarships annually to employees' children. Helen was particularly proud of Precision's fitness center, which could be used by any "regular" employee and their families. Swimming lessons were provided free of charge to all family members.

Precision's vacation days were also higher than the industry average. Employees with 2 years of seniority earned one-half day of paid vacation per month, three-fourths day per month with 3 to 5 years seniority, and one day per month with more than 5 years of service. Personal days accrued at the same rate for regular employees. To prevent abuse, employees calling in absent before or after a holiday or after a payday are charged with an absence of 1.5 days. Employees with less than 1 year's service and temporary employees are not reimbursed for absences. The failure of any employee to call in to report an absence at least 4 hours before his or her shift starts is grounds for disciplinary procedures.

By having the core of regular employees, Precision is assured of having enough employees to meet normal

Exhibit 11.1
Precision Products turnover

Reason	Higher Pay	Better Benefits	Supervision	Moving	Better Job	Job Security	Fired
Group Permanent							
<1 Year	40	22	1	2	3	1	2
1–2 Years	10	0	3	3	2	4	1
<2 Years	1	0	5	4	4	2	0
Temporary							
<6 Months	10	45	4	3	10	17	3
6–12 Months	12	23	1	0	2	32	2
>1 Year	5	15	2	3	15	19	0

production demands. By paying temporary employees base salaries above the labor market average, Precision's bottom line was improving 9 percent each year.

Helen wondered where things had gone wrong. Maybe Curt was right—she just hadn't picked the right kind of employees. Shaking her head in bewilderment, she had her assistant, Margo Woods, interview some employees to see what was going on. Additionally, she prepared a report on causes of turnover. (See Exhibit 11.1.)

According to Margo, the following comments are representative of the feelings of full-time permanent employees:

- "Sure, it's a great place to work, but I'm tired of those young kids walking in off the street and making more than I do."

- "I know, I know, we're eligible to get bonuses, but they just can't make up for a weekly salary—at least not when you have three kids to support."

- "I worry that things are going to be the same as last year. I hung in there and look what I got, a lousy $2,500. The bottom line is that I still made less than temporary employees. I don't like it one bit."

The following comments are typical of the views of workers with less than 2 years seniority:

- "I got really steamed last month when they docked my pay for being sick. I mean, I was really sick. I hadn't gone out with the girls or anything. I was down flat in bed with the flu. Why should I work hard here if I can't even get a lousy day off when I'm sick?"

- "I've worked here 7 months already, and I'm pulling my own weight around here. Know what I mean? Well, it doesn't seem right that I should be paid less than those part-timers."

Among temporary workers, the view was:

- "Yeah, we make a good rate of pay, but that's not everything. My wife had to have a C-section last month. Without insurance, it cost me a bundle."

- "I work just as hard as everyone else, so why shouldn't I have the same benefits? I'm getting up there in years. It'd be nice to have a little bit set aside."

In reading these comments, it seemed to Helen that she couldn't win for losing. Maybe the most current employee attitude survey (see Exhibit 11.2) would be of help. At least it was worth a try. All she knew was that if they didn't come up with a strategy soon, the turnover would be a serious problem.

QUESTIONS

1. What should Helen do to resolve the current crisis?
2. Can you support Curt Stump's comment about "hiring losers"?
3. Of what value are Margo Woods' charts to help resolve the problem?

Exhibit 11.2
Results of the employee attitude survey

	PERMANENT			
	<1 YEAR	1–2 YEARS	>2 YEARS	TEMPORARY
Satisfaction with				
1. Pay level	2.1	2.3	2.4	3.4
2. Pay system	1.5	2.4	3.2	3.3
3. Benefits	1.0	3.2	4.1	1.1
4. Supervision	3.4	4.1	3.7	3.3
5. Job	2.4	2.7	3.1	2.3
6. Coworkers	3.3	4.0	4.7	2.3
7. Work environment	3.4	4.1	3.6	2.7

ENDNOTES

1. Jill Vitiello, "Unmarried with Children," *Computerworld* 32, no. 13 (March 30, 1998): 71.

2. Scott Hays, "Capital One is Renowned for Innovative Recruiting Strategies," *Workforce Costa Mesa* 78, no. 4 (April 1999): 92–94.

3. Margaret Sheridan, "Head Count," *Restaurants and Institutions* 108 (January 1, 1998): 59–60.

4. Robert Karla, "The Gimme Effect," *Restaurant Business* 98, no. 9 (May 1, 1999): 48–50.

5. Nancy Rivera Brooks, "Stress, Feeling of Entitlement Rise," *LA Times-Washington Post* Services, *The Oregonian,* 1 October 1999, p. B3.

6. Ibid.

7. Jonathan Zach and Mark Cohen, "Managing Health Costs," *Personnel Journal* (March 1993): 107.

8. Jennifer Haupt, "Employee Action Plans Management," *Personnel Journal* (February 1993): 96.

9. Karen Matthes, "Strategic Planning: Define Your Mission," *Benefits Management* (February 1993): 11.

10. Jennifer Haupt, "Employee Action," *Personnel Journal* (February 1993): 107.

11. Virginia M. Gibson, "Outsourcing Can Save Money and Increase Efficiency," *Benefits Administration* (March 1993): 19.

12. Justin Bachman, "Coke to Lay Off Work Force," *The Desert Sun,* Business Section, 27 January 2000, p. E2.

13. A. E. Barber, R. B. Dunham, and R. A. Formisano, "The Impact of Flexible Benefits on Employee Satisfaction: A Field Study," *Personnel Psychology* 45 (1992): 55–76.

14. What's News—World-Wide," *The Wall Street Journal,* 10 January 2000, p. A1.

15. Pamela Sebastian Ridge, "Business Bulletin," *The Wall Street Journal,* 9 March 2000, p. A1.

16. Lenore Schiff, "Is Health Care a Job Killer," *Fortune* (April 6, 1992): 30.

17. Alissa J. Rubin, "Xerox Weights Worker-Paid Insurance Plan," *Los Angeles Times,* 4 December 1999, p. A1.

18. Shailagh Murray, "Why Health Insurance That Works Still Fails to Catch on Broadly," *The Wall Street Journal,* 18 January 2000, p. A1.

19. Sharon Bernstein, "Pension Funds May Bypass Health Insurers," *Los Angeles Times,* 14 December 1999, p, A1.

20. "From New Deal to Raw Deal," *Business Week* (April 5, 1993): 66.

21. Boomer, "Backlash, Controversy Besetting New Pension Plan," *The Wall Street Journal,* 20 September 1999, p. A1.

22. Ibid.

23. Ibid.

24. Ellen E. Schultz and Rhonda L. Rundle, "Utility's Pension Plan Allowing Choice," *The Wall Street Journal,* 23 September 1999, p. C1.

25. Ellen E. Schultz, "Managers, Like Other Staffers, Are Fighting Pension Controls," *The Wall Street Journal,* 1 July 1999, p. C1.

26. Leon Rubis, "Retirement Plans Take the Next Step," *HR Magazine* (May 1999): 46–56.

27. U.S. Department of Labor, *Employee Benefits in Medium to Large Firms* (Washington, DC: Department of Labor, 1992), p. 3.

28. *Salaried Employee Benefits Provided by Major U.S. Employers* (Lincolnshire, IL: Hewitt Associates, 1990).

29. Sue Shellenbarger, "Work and Family," *The Wall Street Journal,* 21 July 1999, p. B1.

30. Ibid.

31. "Motorola: Training for the Millennium," *Business Week* (March 28, 1994): 158.

32. Jane Easter Bahls, "Handle With Care," *HR Magazine* (March 1999): 61–66.

33. Credit Union National Association, *Economic Report* (Madison, WI: Credit Union National Association, March 1992).

34. Carla Joinson, "Don't Forget Your Shift Workers," *HR Magazine* (February 1999): 81–84. Workplace Visions, "Good News on Day Care?" no. 2 (1999): 3–4.

35. Carla Joinson, "Don't Forget Your Shift Workers," *HR Magazine* (February 1999): 81–84.

36. Neal Templin, "Johnson & Johnson Wellness Program for Workers Shows Healthy Bottom Line," *The Wall Street Journal,* 21 May 1990, p. B1.

37. Christopher Hotze, "Selecting Long Term Care Coverage," *HR Magazine* (February 1999): 95–100.

38. H. Cris Collie, "The Changing Face of Corporate Relocation," *HR Magazine* (March 1998): 97–102.

39. Howard R. Mitchell III, "When a Company Moves: How To Help Employees Adjust," *HR Magazine* (January 1999): 61–65.

40. Carla Joinson, "Relocation Counseling Meets Employees' Changing Needs," *HR Magazine* (February 1998): 63–70.

41. Ibid.

42. Charlene Alhrmer Solomar, "Marriott's Family Matters," *Personnel Journal* (October 1991): 40.

43. Ibid.

44. Ellen Graham, "Work and Family," *The Wall Street Journal,* 2 February 2000, p. B1.

45. Jennifer Haupt, "Employee Action," *Personnel Journal* (February 1993): 98.

46. "Good News on Day Care?," *Workplace Visions* no. 2 (1999): 3–4.

47. Ibid.

48. Maggie Jackson, "Backup Daycare Pays Double Dividend," The Associated Press, *The Oregonian,* 23 September 1999, p. B2.

49. Tyler, Kathryn. "Got Milk?" *HR Magazine* (March 1999): 68–73.

50. Ibid.

51. "The Growing Need for Eldercare," *Workplace Visions* no. 2 (1999): 2–3.

52. Ibid.

53. Ibid.

54. Jeremy Main, "The Battle Over Benefits," *Fortune* (December 16, 1991): 94.

55. Bill Leonard, "Communication is Key to Employee Benefit Programs," *HR Magazine* (January 1994): 58.

Chapter 12

The Success System: Motivating in Changing Times: Pay for Performance

Objectives

Upon completing this chapter, you will be able to:

1. Define and discuss the concept of employee incentive programs.
2. Describe the growth and objectives of major employee incentive systems.
3. Understand the relationship of employee stock ownership plans (ESOP) to goals of employee satisfaction and productivity.
4. Identify and describe the major types of incentive programs.
5. Define and discuss the external and internal factors which lead to flexible incentive programs.

Premeeting preparation

1. Read chapter 12.
2. Prepare for HRM Skills Simulation 12.1. Complete Step 1, Part B.
3. Read Case 12.1: Precision Products, Inc. Answer questions.

BACKGROUND INFORMATION

In the mid-1990s, Pete Cruz, a local market manager for KFC Corp., persuaded the Universidad Metropolitana in San Juan, Puerto Rico, to let KFC manage their cafeteria. Now students enjoy Kentucky Fried Chicken, Pizza Hut pizzas, Taco Bell tacos, and Frito-Lay snacks. And PepsiCo Inc., which owns all those brands, is happily selling twice as much food there as it expected.

Cruz's efforts were motivated by more than taste buds. PepsiCo points to Pete Cruz's enterprise as the product of SharePower, an incentive plan that rewards Cruz and 120,000 other workers with a piece of the PepsiCo pie. For 4 years, Cruz has received options on company stock worth 10 percent of his previous year's compensation. The result? Cruz thinks like an owner of the company and is very wealthy. His stock options have more than doubled their original value.[1]

The International Labour Organization, funded by the United Nations, recently issued a report indicating American workers spent an average of 2,000 hours per year on the job. This is almost 2 working weeks more than our nearest competitors, the Japanese. The situation of long working hours on the job does not seem to be decreasing and is probably increasing.[2]

With growing emphasis on balancing the demands of the worklife environment and the stressful competitive global world of work, companies are searching for solutions. The need is to motivate employees to increase their productivity of quality products. One solution that is increasing in popularity is the pay for performance concept.

Although pay for performance is not new, companies are rediscovering that carefully designed pay practices can have advantageous effects on making their organization a place in which high-performing employees will want to work. In taking the pay for performance approach to pay design practices, the company offers the employees the context of ownership. The employees will know their efforts are central to the success of the company. By performing their job in a productive and quality orientation, they will share in the success they helped to create.[3]

Incentive programs have become an increasing part of the overall compensation package. Because of the growing costs of labor, incentives are now one of the most important HRM activities. In the past, employee incentive plans were usually based upon individual incentives, such as **commissions.** However, commissions no longer top the list of incentives as more bonuses and other variable compensations are now being paid to a growing number of middle managers, production workers, and support staff.[4]

The reason for performance-based systems is an attempt to motivate employees to perform at a higher capacity. Poorly motivated employees are unlikely to meet the high performance standards needed in today's organization. In addition, increased concerns over productivity and satisfying customers have prompted new interest in motivating employees. Federal Express, for example, is noted for having a direct relationship between worker pay and customer satisfaction. Most organizations are attempting to get more motivational 'bang' out of the employee compensation dollar by linking it more directly to performance.

One study found a difference in earnings between companies who adopted bonus plans or performance incentive plans. The *Journal of Accounting, Auditing, and Finance* reported in a sample of 53 firms there were distinct differences. The 32 firms with bonus plans showed no decline in a measure of earnings. However, the 21 firms who adopted performance incentive plans showed a significant increase in a measure of earnings. This sample suggests better earnings resulted from the performance incentive plans.[5]

Many companies are also trying to develop a stronger relation between pay and key output standards by trying some form of incentive system. A survey of

Fortune 1000 companies found that over 50 percent have some form of incentive systems covering all employees in the organization. These organizations include Blockbuster Video, Burger King, United Parcel Service, Federal Express, General Motors, Grumman, Merrill Lynch, and Reebok. Performance incentives may add an average of 29 percent to the base compensation of executives earning $100,000 or more.

In attempting to increase productivity, HR managers are trying to identify variables that determine the effectiveness of pay as a motivating factor. Compensation incentives and other recognition are often a powerful motivator of performance. Some incentive plans can improve performance by as much as 30 percent, and team incentives have reportedly boosted productivity from 18 to 200 percent.

A more cautious approach finds it is extremely unrealistic to assume all incentive programs will work or that removing individual rewards will double and triple employee's productivity. This cautious approach believes whether incentive rewards are good for the company or bad for morale really depends upon what the rewards support. For instance, if the rewards support company goals of increased profit and customer loyalty, then this is good. However, if the rewards create an environment of unhealthy competitiveness and back stabbing among employees, then there are big problems.

A company must have talented personnel with courage to create the appropriate workplace to achieve the desired results. In such a workplace, employees must feel they are important, feel their work is important to themselves, and care about each other. This workplace environment must exist with or without an incentive program.[6]

Employee incentives may be defined as that part of a compensation system related to motivating employee performance and productivity. These incentives, also called variable pay systems, include individual, team, and organizational incentives, including both pay for performance and other forms of recognition. The current trend is to offer an increasing amount and variety of pay for performance incentives (with an emphasis on "self-managed" work teams) to increase organizational performance.

THE GLOBAL CHASE

The United States is not alone in the world of work in applying the pay for performance concept. Countries around the world are using variable pay techniques to promote flexibility. This is the result of foreign employers attempting to avoid the growing problem of rising wage costs by rewarding merit, not tenure.[7]

For instance, the U.S. model for executive pay being dependent upon performance has been used previously in Great Britain and is now taking hold elsewhere in Europe. However, rather than awarding bonuses for performance pay as is done in the United States, European executives are receiving long-term incentives such as the right to buy stock at a later date at a fixed price.[8]

The popularity of pay for performance is also growing in Asia as more firms are linking bonuses to performance. This is the result of a search to reduce costs by making wages more flexible and the need to retain the best employees by rewarding them.

A recent survey of Hong Kong firms reveals 86 percent are offering variable bonuses. In Singapore, authorities have been persuading firms to use flexible-wage systems, and now 98 percent are offering a discretionary bonus. With the recession of 1999, Asian managers have increased their use of pay for performance to reward staff based on individual performance instead of across-the-board pay increases.[9]

A Japanese company, Matsushita, is responding to global competitive pressures and is changing the way it pays its employees. This is a groundbreaking event for companies in Japan and many other Japanese firms are following suit. The approach by Matsushita is a change from the traditional attitudes of seniority-based pay and lifetime employment. The new plan is a performance-related model complete with an appraisal process which results in individual scores.[10]

The largest food company in Taiwan, President Enterprises, is revising its wage system to reward performance over seniority. The company will now link pay and promotion to the employee's performance and responsibilities. This change has resulted from a slowing economy and increasing foreign competition.

The change by President Enterprises is a radical departure for a Taiwanese company. There is a strong negative culture in Taiwan's Japanese-style conglomerates regarding the idea of pay for performance. If President Enterprises succeeds with their new compensation plans and increases profits, it is expected the other conglomerates will switch to pay for performance techniques.[11]

The pay for performance concept is also being applied to the vendors of companies. An example is the recent contract between Nissan Motor Company and their advertising agency, TBWA/Chiat/Day. The new contract is no longer based on an exclusively fee-based arrangement, but now includes performance bonus incentives.[12]

The recent change in the relationships between customers and advertising agencies in the United States has been referred to as "sea change" as corporate America turns its back on the old 15 percent commission arrangement. Two of the top U.S. advertisers, Procter & Gamble and General Motors Corporation, are moving away from the 15 percent commission and adapting pay for performance plans. Also, two of the advertising giants, Young and Rubican and DDB Needham Worldwide, are now favoring the pay for performance formulas.[13]

A recent survey of advertising agencies confirms this growing trend with 30 percent of the Association of National Advertisers members using incentive compensation agreements. The prediction is that by the year 2004, at least three-quarters of their client agreements will include incentives. The rationale is that clients achieve superior results through the use of incentives which align agencies' interests with those of the clients.[14]

In this chapter, we present stage four of the Success System Model: motivating for performance. We will focus on the major types of pay for performance incentive programs that are being used at the individual, team, and organization levels, and examine trends and problems in this area. A motivational pay for performance program needs to be developed to support a high-performing organization. This also reinforces team contributions as well as individual efforts.

MOTIVATION

As global competition causes our businesses to restructure, the empowerment of employees to work faster and smarter has become increasingly important. However, the success of employee empowerment depends upon our ability to motivate this extra effort. Motivation may be defined in terms of some performance behavior. Motivation is an emotive state causing persons to want or need something intensely enough to put forth the necessary effort to achieve it. This drive to achieve is usually goal-directed, and becomes more complex when dealing with groups or teams. What drives us as individuals to achieve is often difficult to decipher, as our needs and desires will vary over time.

There are many theories of motivation. The human relations school believes employees want to do a good job. Although their individual behavior may differ, they would be motivated to achieve their potential. One of the early human behaviorists was Abraham Maslow, known for his hierarchy of needs theory. These needs

Figure 12.1
The motivation process

exist in a hierarchial order starting with the most basic physiological needs, followed by safety needs, belongingness, and love needs, and ending with self-actualization needs. The ability to satisfy these needs should be present at work and in the job, resulting in a motivated employee.

Another behavioral theory is Frederick Herzberg's two-factor theory of hygiene factors and motivators. Hygiene factors include working conditions, pay, company policies, and interpersonal relations. When hygiene factors are the only factors present in the job, they do not motivate employees, they only satisfy them. However, if they are not present, the work then becomes dissatisfying. To create motivation, the employee needs the presence of the hygiene factors plus the motivators. The motivators are higher-level employee needs of achievement, recognition, responsibility, and opportunity. According to Herzberg, motivation is achieved by removing the dissatisfiers and increasing the motivators.[15]

Expectancy theory is generally associated with the work of Victor Vroom and suggests people act to obtain specific goals. However, before individuals act to obtain these goals, they must believe their behavior will lead to their attainment. A crucial element is how valuable the goal is to the individual. The more value the individual attaches to the goal, the more effort the individual will expend to achieve the goal.[16]

The acquired needs theory of David McClelland proposes people are not born with needs, but rather acquire them through early life experiences. The three basic needs are achievement, affiliation, and power. The need for power is defined as controlling others, assuming responsibility for others, and having authority over others. McClelland often found the need for power associated with successful top level management.[17]

The previous discussion of some of the many motivation theories suggests the complexity of the field. Motivation is still an art form and not a science, and successful application still depends upon managerial skills. Pay for performance is one method used to apply motivational theory, as shown in HRM in Action.

HRM IN ACTION
FIRST BOSTON SEES DEFECTIONS TIED TO PAY[18]

Angered by compensation they say is sharply below that paid by competitors, dozens of traders and investment bankers have defected from First Boston Group in the past. Publicly, First Boston downplays the defections. "I don't think it's that overwhelming," says Archibald Cox, Jr., First Boston's chief executive officer and president. "We've lost some people we're sorry to lose, some we're less sorry to lose, and some we wanted to lose." He adds, "Our competitors are trying to make the most of our people leaving."

Yet privately, many First Boston executives say the exodus has cost the firm some of its most talented in-

vestment bankers and traders, and has hobbled its ability to recruit new ones. Although Mr. Cox denies the departures are affecting First Boston's ability to recruit bankers, he acknowledges that the investment bank hasn't hired a single managing director in any of the affected areas since the beginning of the year.

"Clearly, First Boston has had a significant number of defections that will cause it to begin addressing management issues and compensation," says Joan Zimmerman, an executive recruiter with G. Z. Stephens. Harvard Business School Professor Samuel Hayes says: "First Boston is having to do some fancy footwork to hold people right now."

The anger over pay erupted at a dinner last month for First Boston senior managing directors, called by top executives days after the energy team defected. At the dinner at Manhattan's Exclusive Links Club, some directors yelled at Mr. Cox and at Jack Hennessey, First Boston's chairman, amid complaints that promises by Messrs. Cox and Hennessey to raise their compensation last year never materialized.

According to some who attended the dinner, many First Boston managing directors griped that they were paid more than 25 percent less than their peers at other Wall Street firms. (Managing directors in First Boston's merger-and-acquisition department earn a yearly average of $800,000 according to a person familiar with the firm.)

QUESTIONS

1. Discuss Archibald Cox's comments regarding the loss of personnel at First Boston. Is he realistic? What is the real purpose behind his comments?

2. What factors should First Boston consider in reviewing their compensation structure?

REASONS FOR PAY FOR PERFORMANCE PLANS

Many organizations have implemented incentive plans for a variety of reasons: increasing labor costs, more global competitive markets, faster technological advances, and greater needs for production quality. In the twenty-first century, incentive plans are focusing on pay-for-performance, improved quality, and productivity. By using pay for performance, managers are finding employees improve their job performance.

Incentive plans may not always lead to organizational improvement, for two main reasons. First, some companies feel that incentive plans are in conflict with a team-oriented approach. Second, management may have given insufficient attention to the design and implementation of incentive programs.

A survey of 738 companies across the United States found 69 percent offered short-term incentives. Over two-thirds of these companies used short-term incentives and found them effective in improving performance. The companies, 95 percent of them, offered cash as the short-term incentive. Deferred cash, stock options and combinations of both, were mainly used at the executive level.[19]

The success of a pay for performance system mainly depends on the organization. If the organization has a strong corporate culture, high morale, and employees trust the management, then there is a stronger probability of success.

Team incentives should not be used in situations where a few individuals are likely to maximize their output at the expense of their coworkers. Group incentives should reduce rivalry and promote cooperation and concern for all members in the unit's overall performance. Many companies, including Boeing, Procter & Gamble, and United Technologies, are using incentive systems based on team and company-wide performance measures.(See cartoon.)

Source: CROCK by Rechin and Wilder © North America Syndicate, Inc.

There are three important points related to the effective administration of incentive plans:

1. *Incentive.* Incentive systems are effective only when management is willing to pay incentives based on differences in individual or team performance.
2. *Motivation.* Incentives must be large enough to motivate and reinforce exceptional performance.
3. *Standards.* Incentive systems must be based on clearly defined and accepted performance standards effectively communicated to employees.

There are a number of types of incentive programs, which are described in the following sections.

Individual Incentives

Many factors are involved in the design of an **individual incentives** plan. For example, most incentive plans are designed to set production rates according to the technology used. Incentive payments for hourly employees are based upon the number of units produced, by the achievement of specific performance goals, or by productivity improvements in the organization.

Who should be included in incentives? The incentive system should be designed with a focus on specific employees in mind—such as production, middle managers, salespeople, engineers, or senior executives. Most organizations use different incentive systems for different levels. McDonald's, for example, uses eight different incentive systems for differing levels of employees, and IBM uses a system of six different levels.

How will performance be measured? The decision whether to use an individual, team, or organization-wide incentive is critical. The major factor is the extent to which results can be measured at the individual or team level, whether the individuals' contribution is measured, and the effect on teamwork among unit members.

The GM Saturn plant in Tennessee, for example, found individual measurement was possible on a number of important production measures, but an individual incentive system was considered to conflict with the company's team-oriented approach to production. The Saturn's incentive system is based on team and companywide measures of performance. The critical issues in selecting the performance measures (individual, group, organization) include defining and measuring performance criteria related to the organization's strategic plan and then linking those measurements to pay.

Piecework

One of the oldest, most commonly used incentive plans is piecework. In a **straight piecework plan,** the employee receives a certain amount of pay for each unit produced. Compensation is then determined by the number of units produced during a specific time period (e.g., hour, day). Employees often earn as much as 55 percent more than their base pay in a piecework system. The **differential piece rate plan** enables employees whose production exceeds the standard output to receive a higher rate for *all* of their work than the rate paid to those who perform below the standard.

The piecework system is more likely to succeed in repetitive jobs where units of output can be reliably measured, when quality is less critical, and with a continuous flow of work. Unfortunately, it is not effective in jobs that do not have reliable standards of performance.

One of the weaknesses of piecework is that it may not always be an effective motivator. If workers find that increases in output bring disapproval from their fellow workers, then the need for friendship and approval may outweigh the incentive to produce more. Secondly, the standards for piece rates often tend to change, because employees discover ways to do the work in less than standard time.

Individual Bonuses

An **individual bonus** is an incentive payment that supplements the basic wage. It has the advantage of rewarding workers with more pay for higher performance effort, yet still providing a basic paycheck. At GM's Saturn plant, for example, UAW members work for a salary with approximately 20 percent of the amount fluctuating up or down because it is tied to assessments of car quality, productivity, and profits.[20]

Team Bonuses

Team bonuses are usually used when the contributions of an individual employee is either not measurable or when performance depends on team cooperation. With work processes requiring more teamwork and coordination among workers, team bonuses are very popular. Most team bonus plans are tied to such measurable outputs as company profits, improvements in quality, or cost reductions. Team bonuses, like individual incentive plans, often improve employee motivation. This allows the organization to

1. Reward team productivity.
2. Compensate team members for new skills.
3. Increase overall performance.

Incentives for Management Employees

Merit raises represent one of the most commonly used incentive systems for managerial level employees. They are used to motivate managerial, sales, and professional employees where raises can be directly related to performance. Merit increases are usually separate from the person's base pay.

Beginning with the first payout in early 2001, the Boeing company initiated a new annual cash bonus program for managers that could be worth as much as 2 weeks salary.

The new incentive is based on Boeing's economic profit. This is found by subtracting from net earnings a charge for inventory, plant, and equipment costs. The concept is that managers will regroup their factory-floor operations by shutting down unprofitable businesses. This frees cash to be used for profitable operations. Although Boeing has had a traditional engineering culture, the cash bonuses program increases emphasis on finances.[21]

Sales Incentives

Sales incentive plans are often based on the same factors as individual incentive programs. The drive needed in selling demands highly motivated sales personnel. The competitive nature of selling underlies the widespread use of sales incentives.

Sales incentive plans often share many of the characteristics of individual incentives, but there are also unique requirements. Sales output measures can usually be established as the level of sales (in dollars or units), but salespeople are not paid just on sales volume. They often provide other services, such as customer training, product development, consultation, and new accounts which involve complex measures of performance. A critical first step for a sales incentive program, then, is to determine the most important performance factors. In general, sales performance may be measured by the total sales volume and by their ability to generate new accounts. If measures are used, such as promoting new products and providing customer service, then more complex measures may be used.

Setting performance standards for sales personnel are not without problems because sales performance is often affected by external factors beyond the control of the salesperson. There are economic and seasonal fluctuations, differing levels of competition, changes in demand, and more lucrative sales territories which can all affect an individual's sales level. Because sales volume alone may not be an accurate indicator of the effort salespeople have expended, many organizations set quotas based on sales potential. In designing an incentive plan for salespeople, there are also the problems of rewarding extra sales effort and compensating for promotional activities that may not impact directly on sales.

Types of Sales Incentive Plans

Many variations of sales incentive plans exist. One commonly used approach is the commission plan—approximately 75 percent of all salespeople are on some form of commission plan. Compensation plans for sales personnel include a straight salary plan, a commission only plan, or a combination salary and commission plan. A **straight salary plan** pays salespeople for performing duties not directly related to sales volume—such as providing services and satisfying customer needs—without penalizing their income. The major disadvantage of the straight salary plan is that it does not provide the motivating force for salespeople to maximize their sales.

The **straight commission plan,** on the other hand, bases payment on a percentage of sales. It provides maximum motivation and is straightforward to compute and understand. The straight commission plan, however, has some disadvantages:

1. Major emphasis is placed on sales volume rather than on long-term or repeat sales.
2. Customer service, unless directly related on a sale, is likely to be minimal, often resulting in dissatisfied customers.
3. Commission pay tends to fluctuate widely between high and low seasonal periods, resulting in high turnover of trained salespeople.

Another common sales incentive uses a **combination salary and commission plan.** The base salary provides a basic monthly wage with a percentage of compensation paid out in commissions. Under this plan, a salesperson working under a 70/30 combination plan would receive total compensation of 70 percent base salary and 30 percent commission. The advantages of combination salary and commission plan is a salesforce that is motivated to achieve organizational sales targets, in addition to long-term customer satisfactions.

Managerial and Executive Incentives

There is research to support the use of incentive systems for executives, which are usually related to the strategic goals of the organization. Incentives for managers and executives are believed to have an impact upon organizational performance although there is little data to support this belief. In most cases, executive incentive plans are linked to net income, return on investment, stock price, or total dividends paid. These incentives are usually paid in the form of bonuses and stock options. CEOs often receive over half of their compensation from incentives resulting in criticism of what they actually contributed to the corporation.

Executives at major U.S. companies have been earning "staggeringly high" paychecks. This is the result of a pay structure in which most executive compensation is directly connected to the stock market through high stock-option grants. This becomes apparent with the average paycheck of U.S. executives having increased some 442 percent since 1990.

The proponents of this compensation system point out the amazing performance of American companies is not by chance and the payment of huge salaries is the price of guaranteeing that CEOs will make moves which benefit all investors. However, the link between executive pay and performance is not a proven fact.[22]

A study by Chicago-based SCA Consulting LLC found the majority of Chicago area firms did not get their money's worth from their stock option-rich CEOs. The records of 97 CEOs were examined in 1998, and those firms who saw shareholder value fall outnumbered gains 63 to 44. Although a 3-year track record is generally recorded as a more comprehensive picture of pay for performance, the study does indicate the persistent controversy of whether CEOs are worth their compensation packages.[23]

Adding to this controversy is that declining profits do have an adverse effect as witnessed by the fate of some senior chemical executives' compensation. According to recent proxy statements filed with the Securities and Exchange Commission, six CEOs at chemical companies failed to receive bonuses in 1998. For around 75 percent of all companies that filed proxy statements, overall compensation—excluding long-term benefits—fell for their CEOs. With a lack of comprehensive data, the pay for performance system appears to be working, rewarding some and not others.[24]

Some question whether stock options actually fulfill their original purpose of motivating and rewarding superior executive performance. This group suggests the design and implementation of stock options is flawed. They believe within the next few years, there may be a return to greater use of cash long-term plans.[25]

The National Bureau of Economic Research presents a more positive view of the effect of executive stock options upon performance. In a recent study of the CEOs of 478 large publicly traded corporations over a period of 15 years, the study investigated what would happen if their stock holdings were replaced with a similar number of stock options. The results found the sensitivity of the normal CEO to the positive effect on their pay in improving corporate performance would approximately double. The CEOs became very aware of how much their pay would increase if the corporation's performance increased.[26]

Organizations sometimes use **career salary curves** as a method of calculating salary increases for professional personnel. The salary curve provides for an annual salary rate based on experience and performance. Salary curves are then established to reflect different levels of performance (outstanding, average, below average), and to provide for salary increases. The salary curve for high performers rises to a higher level at a faster rate than the salary curve for lower performance levels. (See Figure 12.2.)

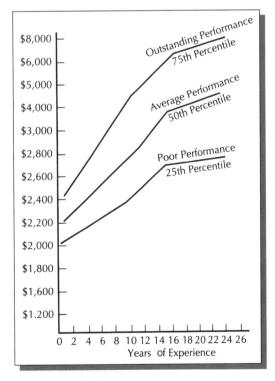

Figure 12.2
Salary curves for professionals

Organizations typically use several types of compensation for executives in order to meet different organizational goals and executive needs. Chief executive officers (CEOs), for example, often have compensation packages which are heavily weighted toward long-term incentives. CEOs should be more focused on the long-term impact of their decisions rather than short-term implications. Group vice presidents, on the other hand, may require more short-term incentives, because their decisions are measured on short-term results.

One example of executive incentives is the plan at Salomon Brothers, Inc. Under the plan (see Figure 12.3), the chief executive officer will be paid an annual performance bonus that could total as much as $24 million, if the firm's return on equity hits 30 percent and is 10 percentage points higher than its five major rivals. (See HRM in Action.)

HRM IN ACTION
CAMPBELL LINKS EXECUTIVE PAY TO SHARE STAKE[27]

Campbell Soup has a stock ownership plan for its chief executive and about 70 other senior executives that would link management income with shareholder returns.

Under the plan, David Johnson, president and CEO of the Camden, New Jersey-based soup and packaged-food company, is required to hold three times his 1992 base salary of $757,500 in shares for a period of 2 years. He must maintain the three-times-earnings stake every year until he leaves the company.

"Campbell's new executive stock ownership standards emphasize that management and shareowner thinking are as one," Johnson said. Institutional investors have been pushing for companies to introduce plans like Campbell's, and a growing number of firms (including Eastman Kodak Co., Xerox Corp., and Chrysler Corp.) now require or ask executives to own large stakes in the companies they run.

QUESTIONS

1. Will linking management income with shareholder returns actually improve the financial return of both parties?

2. What are the advantages and disadvantages of executive stock option plans?

The main difference between managerial and executive incentives is the time frame of performance measures. Lower-level managers' incentives are usually based on short-term measures. Top executives, on the other hand, usually have longer-term performance incentives. Managers usually receive bonuses based upon profits. The bonus amount is typically based on a percentage of their salary, although there is a trend toward awarding bonuses not related to the base pay. As higher profitability is attained, the manager receives bigger bonuses. The bonus structure for any given manager often depends on the relative contributions of all managers, with the assessment of relative contribution made at a higher level. This method suffers from the disadvantages noted earlier regarding individual incentives.

Often managers feel that they have little impact on organization profits. As the link between performance and pay becomes weaker, the reward loses its incentive value. This relationship can be more clearly defined by basing the amount of the bonus on corporate profitability.

Long-term rewards usually relate to future profitability. The most commonly used approach is based on the appreciation of stock value using various stock purchase plans. About 90 percent of the 500 largest U.S. corporations now provide stock option plans, up from 52 percent in 1974. A **stock option** plan gives an executive the right to purchase a stated number of shares of stock, at a future date, at a relatively low fixed price. If the stock price increases, the executive exercises the stock option at the lower fixed price, receiving as a bonus the difference between the lower option price and the higher market value. Congress periodically revises legislation controlling the awarding of these stock options.

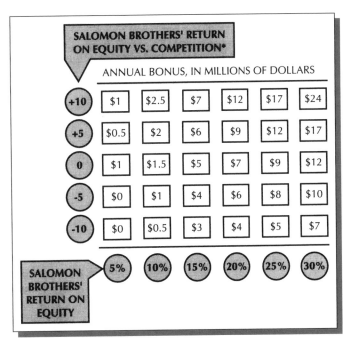

Figure 12.3
Executive officer performance bonus plan
*Percentage point differential from average ROE of Morgan Stanley, Merrill Lynch, Bear Stearns, J. P. Morgan, and Bankers Trust. *Source:* Salomon Brothers, Inc.

Pros and Cons of Executive Bonuses

Are top executives really worth the exorbitant salaries and bonuses they receive? The answer usually depends on whom you ask. Corporate compensation committees feel that big bonuses are necessary as a way to reward superior performance as a "fact of business life" reflecting market trends for CEO compensation.

However, as previously noted, strong criticism is being voiced regarding the high salaries and bonuses being paid to senior executives. Others point out that some critics often find executives may receive record bonuses even though their organizations are performing poorly and employees are being asked to take wage and salary cuts or layoffs.

Executive Perquisites

In order to recruit and attract top people, executives usually receive special benefits termed perquisites. **Perquisites,** or "perks," are recognized as an executives' importance in the organization, the extras used to supplement basic compensation. Perks also serve as a status symbol to both insiders and outsiders. Perquisites also provide tax savings to executives, because most perks are not taxable as income (although this is constantly changing). The more common perks range from company car, special parking, expense accounts, plush offices, chauffeurs, country club memberships, special vacations, physical exams, an executive dining room, and liability insurance. Perks are an entrenched feature of executive compensation.

Team Profit-Sharing Plans

There has been an increase in the number and type of team or group incentive plans. **Team incentive plans** are becoming preferable to individual incentives as a result of the increasing use of team-based approaches. An effective team incentive plan is based on the same factors as individual plans. The measures differ in that a team plan is based on some measure of team productivity. Team plans are particularly effective when teamwork is essential, and when the incentive system is trying to involve the level of participation. Team plans are used when jobs are so interrelated that it is difficult (or impossible) to identify individual output measures. The size of a "team" usually ranges from 5 to 20 people, depending upon the task and the required coordination between team members. The smaller the team, the higher the identification on team performance. There is increasing evidence that team incentives increase productivity.

Many companies also use profit sharing as a tool to reduce employee turnover. At Johnson & Johnson, the allocation is distributed in equal increments over a period of years, but the employee loses any remaining distributions if they leave the firm early. In general, profit sharing works best as an incentive when the team size is small enough that employees believe they have some impact on profitability.

Gainsharing Plans

Gainsharing plans try to reduce the amount of labor required for a given level of output (cost saving) or increase the output for a given amount of labor (productivity increase). The method for determining the standard production rate and the incentive rate must be clearly defined. Gainsharing plans are based on the assumption that better cooperation among workers and between workers and managers will result in greater effectiveness.

These plans, which bear the names of their originators, Joe Scanlon and Alan Rucker, are similar. Both plans emphasize participative management and encourage cost reduction by sharing with employees the resulting savings.

The Scanlon Plan

The philosophy underlying the **Scanlon plan** is that employees should be involved in ideas and suggestions for improving productivity and be rewarded for these efforts. If the plan is properly implemented, then the Scanlon plan can result in improved efficiency and profitability for the organization.

The Rucker Plan

The **Rucker plan** is another successful group incentive system. The Rucker plan normally covers only production workers but sometimes covers all employees. Like the Scanlon plan, worker committees are formed to evaluate and use employee suggestions. The Rucker plan, however, uses a less complex structure.

Profit-Sharing Plans

One of the most popular incentive plans in use is profit sharing. **Profit sharing** is a method where the employer makes cash disbursements or pays bonuses based on the organization's profits.

Profit sharing is designed to provide employees the opportunity to increase their earnings by increasing the growth of the organization's profits. These incentives are usually directed toward improving product quality, reducing operating costs, improving work processes, or increasing morale rather than merely increasing productivity. The basic idea of profit sharing is to have employees feel like partners in the organization. Profit sharing seeks to motivate increased involvement from employees, rather than have them just doing a job.

One example of a successful profit-sharing plan is the one used for several decades at Lincoln Electric Company, a manufacturer of arc welding equipment and supplies. The company annually distributes a percentage of its profits to employees based upon their salary level and merit ratings. In the past, the annual bonus often ranged from a low of 55 percent to a high of 115 percent of annual wages.

The Worker Capitalists

The final stages of the last century witnessed the rapid rise of business start ups and the wildfire spread of stockownership. This trend is now continuing into the twenty-first century with practically one in every two households in the United States owning stocks or mutual funds.

According to a financial study, this is more than twice that of 15 years ago. This is such a drastic change, one think-tank spokesperson proclaimed it was history's first class of "worker capitalists." This change is taking place from Silicon Valley to the factory floor as more Americans bypass the tradition of paycheck and pension. In its place entrepreneurial employees are choosing riskier incentives for more money.

An economist with the Federal Reserve Bank of Boston points out it is the employees, not the employers, who are the real capitalists. They have made the big investments in their skills and take the big risks. This is taking place in a compensation environment of profit sharing in the form of bonuses and incentives. Those who are most familiar with this trend call it goal sharing. It is occurring in almost two-thirds of 2,800 companies surveyed annually by the American Compensation Association.

Some examples of the new goal sharing include Cummins Engine Company of Columbus, Indiana, an 80-year-old firm more representative of the "old" economy than that of the twenty-first century. There, $30,000-a-year assembly workers are paid 10 percent or more depending on how they perform as individuals, how "their" plant performs, and how the whole company performs.

At Northwest Natural Gas Company, a Portland, Oregon, natural gas distributor, even the lowest-paid hourly workers have 5 percent of their pay dependent on how the employees and the company performs. For middle management the percent climbs to 25 percent.

The Unilever's plant at Cartersville, Georgia, occupies 100 acres of rural land and makes soap powder. Recently production workers discovered air compressors were consuming too much costly electricity. They solved the problem and the resulting savings went into the quarterly "goal sharing" payments. Similar savings across the plant resulted in more than 12 percent of workers' pay. Last year that was almost $5,000 per employee.

Of particular interest to human resource professionals is that the new risks employees are taking have changed the old social contracts with employers. They have exchanged a worklife of comfortable living for new, risky entrepreneurial arrangements.[28]

Improshare

The last type of gainsharing is called **Improshare,** which stands for "improved productivity through sharing." Improshare is similar to Scanlon, except that the Improshare ratio uses standard hours rather than labor costs. Engineering studies or past performance data are used to specify the standard number of hours required to produce a base production level, and savings in hours result in reward allocation to workers.

Improshare bonuses are based on the overall productivity of the work team. Improshare output is measured by the number of finished products that a work group produces in a given period. Both production (direct) employees and nonproduction (indirect) employees are included in the determination of the bonus. Improshare is intended to increase the interaction and support between employees and management.

The success of these gainsharing plans depends on the level of involvement and support by top management, employee participation, and realistic employee expectations. Companies which do not involve unions in strategic goals will also experience problems in applying gainsharing programs.

Employee Stock Ownership Plans

Employee stock ownership plans (ESOPs) are becoming a more common method of incentives for productivity, warding off corporate raiders, or reducing taxes.

Employee stock ownership plans have been used in organizations for many years. These programs are sometimes implemented as part of an employee benefit plan. Organizations that offer stock ownership programs to employees usually believe that it provides an incentive. By allowing employees to purchase stock, the organization is hoping to increase productivity with a resulting rise in the stock price.

The use of stock options (previously discussed) used to be offered only to CEOs and executive management is becoming commonplace for employees. The stock options phenomena is now spreading to retail stores as a benefit for temporary help. The Borders Group, Inc., a chain of bookstores, is now allowing temporary employees to become eligible for stock options after 1 month on the job. If the temps stay on, they will be eligible for merit-pay increases after 6 months.[29]

However, a recent article in *The Wall Street Journal* reveals stock ownership is not widely distributed. The most recent year for which data is available indicates although 43.3 percent of households owned stock, nearly 90 percent of all shares were held by the wealthiest 10 percent of households. Another way of looking at the data is the top 10 percent held 73.2 percent of the country's network in 1997, which is up from 68.2 percent in 1983. Although the popularity of pay for performance grows, it will be well into the twenty-first century before it becomes a major factor in the stock market.[30]

Pay for Performance Trend

One of the reasons pay for performance will continue to grow is reflected in a comprehensive survey sponsored by the American Compensation Association (ACA). The survey found that the pay for performance techniques produced a 134 percent net return. For every dollar payment, a gain of $2.34 was obtained. In another survey of 400 British and 100 American firms, additional positive information was obtained. The firms using pay for performance produced on average over twice the shareholder returns compared to those firms with low variable pay.[31]

The trend toward pay for performance plans is another plus for HRM with increased responsibilities and input at the highest level of companies. To ease the HRM workload, a Maryland software provider, IncenSoft, has developed the IncentPower program to provide the technology to devise and operate a broad based pay for performance system.

HRM uses a series of linked menus to calculate and store the performance pay rewards. A data base of financial and employee data is established and a formula determines final distribution. The software provides a comprehensive manual of pay for performance systems, including procedural steps to begin and implementation of the system.[32]

SUMMARY

In this chapter, we have presented several major employee incentive programs, including individual incentives, team incentives, and organization incentives, using both nonpay recognition and pay for performance programs. This is important because employee incentive programs represent a sizable expenditure to the organization. There is every indication that increasing costs and demands will continue.

HR managers will have to operate in a dynamic and changing environment, and consequently must develop new, more adaptive incentive programs. You have been introduced to the emerging field of employee motivation and pay for performance, and to the ways it is used to improve organizational effectiveness. You, as a human resource manager, must be sensitive to changes in markets, people, and competition, and be aware of the need for an adaptive and flexible organization.

You will have the opportunity to experience the need for human resource skills in this class meeting. The rising costs of production and services are posing a major challenge to HR managers. In the HRM Skills, you will have a chance to practice developing an incentive program. You may find an equitable program is not a simple process, because it includes both costs to the organization and employee needs. Because of the costs involved, the legal complexity, and employee demands, this will likely be a continuing problem.

The bottom line remains that for any incentive system to work, rewards valued by the employee must be directly linked to performance.

REVIEW QUESTIONS

1. In your opinion, what is the single most important motivating factor?
2. Present examples of how employee incentives are used in organizations you have worked for.
3. Do you feel employee pay for performance programs are important in choosing an employer?
4. Why is the lack of motivation among employees rising so rapidly, and what can an organization do?
5. Discuss and explain the basic individual incentive program. Do you agree?
6. How do you motivate a work team? Explain the basic factors that affect an individual's motivation in a work group.
7. Read a book or view a video movie, and identify some element of employee motivation in an organization.

KEY WORDS AND CONCEPTS

Define and be able to use the following:

- Bonus
- Career Salary Curves
- Combination Salary and Commission Plan
- Commissions
- Differential Piece Rate Plan
- Employee Incentives
- Employee Stock Ownership Plans (ESOPs)

- Gainsharing Plans
- Improshare
- Individual and Team Bonuses
- Individual Incentives
- Perquisites
- Profit Sharing
- Rucker Plan
- Sales Incentive Plans
- Scanlon Plan

- Stock Options
- Straight Commission Plan
- Straight Piecework Plan
- Straight Salary Plan
- Team Incentive Plans

HRM SKILLS SIMULATION 12.1: THE MAINLINE COMPANY

A. PURPOSE

The purpose of this exercise is to experience and observe how employee incentives impact organization functioning by

1. Examining the effects of collaboration and competition in intergroup relationships.
2. Demonstrating the effects of win-win and win-lose approaches to compensation planning.
3. Practicing using pay incentives and problem solving.

B. PROCEDURES

Step 1. Prior to class, form into groups of five members, each group constituting an executive committee. Assign each member of your group as one of the committee members. (Extras act as observers.)

1. Executive vice president
2. Compensation manager
2. Employee representative
4. Manager of human resources
5. Union representative
6. Observers

Before class, individually rate the employee incentive systems, and rank-order on the worksheet from "1" for least likely to "10" for most likely to improve performance. Note the employee pay survey responses, Table 12.1. Participants are to enter their ranking in column (1) on the Mainline Rating Form.

Step 2. Executive Committee Meeting. Through group discussion, exploration, and examination, try to reach a *consensus decision* reflecting the integrated thinking and consensus of all members. Remember, a consensus decision involves reaching mutual agreement by discussion until all agree on the final decision.

Follow these instructions for reaching consensus:

1. Try to reach the best possible decision, but at the same time defending the importance of long-term goals.
2. Avoid changing your mind simply to reach agreement and to avoid conflict, but support solutions with which you are able to agree.
3. Avoid "conflict-reducing" techniques, such as majority vote, averaging, or trading, in reaching your decision.
4. View differences of opinion as a help rather than a hindrance in decision making.

At this point, meet together as the executive committee and enter your results in column (2) on the Mainline Rating Form.

Time suggested for Step 2: 10 minutes.

Step 3. Score your individual and team answers by subtracting the Individual Rating (column 1) from the Team Rating (column 2). By totaling the points, an individual and a team score can be calculated. Individuals and teams can be compared based on these scores.

Time suggested for Step 3: 10 minutes.

Table 12.1
Pay method survey responses

Pay Method/Incentive	Very Important	Somewhat Important	Not Too Important	Not at All Important
1. Employee stock ownership plans (ESOPs)	6%	31%	42%	21%
2. Team incentive plans	20%	43%	24%	13%
3. Individual performance bonus for nonmanagement personnel	21%	46%	22%	11%
4. Management or executive performance bonuses	16%	35%	37%	22%
5. Piecework (e.g., production incentive plans)	28%	34%	17%	21%
6. Profit sharing plans	16%	44%	24%	16%
7. Stock options	15%	50%	27%	8%

Step 4. The instructor leads a discussion of the activity, letting each team explain its scores on the Mainline Rating Form. Consider the following points and compare results for each team.

1. The consensus process within each group: Things that went well and difficulties, and the dynamics behind the posted scores.
2. The extent to which efficiency, effectiveness, and member satisfaction was emphasized in the meeting.
3. The culture that will likely develop as a result of the decisions made in the meeting.

Time suggested for Step 4: 20 minutes.

OBSERVER FORM

Instructions: For each item, place a number in the blank to the right representing your reaction to how your group performed based on the following scale..

Low ____ 1 : 2 : 3 : 4 : 5 : 6 : 7 : 8 : 9 : 10 ____ High

1. Degree of cooperative teamwork: ____
2. Degree of team motivation: ____
3. Degree of member satisfaction: ____
4. Degree of information sharing (participation): ____
5. Degree of consensual decision making: ____
6. Degree of team conflict or competition (i.e., conflict directly faced and resolved): ____
7. Degree of quality of group decisions: ____
8. Degree of speed with which decision is made: ____
9. Degree of participating leadership: ____
10. Degree of clarity of goals: ____

Total ranking ____

Background Information: The Mainline Company

Mainline, Inc., founded in 1985, is a small, family-owned petroleum industry manufacturer. The company got off to a fast start, mostly because of its creative and innovative approaches to designing and solving the production problems of oil field operations that was new to the industry. Both managers and workers have put in many long hours, often sacrificing their personal time to get the company off the ground and keep it competitive.

A significant downturn in the national and local oil industry and economies has been experienced recently and is expected by most experts to last for another 3 to 5 years. At Mainline, it is becoming increasingly obvious that some adjustments will have to be made if the company is to survive.

Given the current economic conditions, management is about to conduct an analysis of the entire situation. However, having recently attended an executive seminar on motivation at a nearby university, the president is asking employees of the company to consider the situation and to meet with management to present any ideas they have as to how to deal with the company's current difficulty. It appears that unless the company can achieve performance improvement, it will not be able to continue operating.

The preliminary analysis conducted by the company's management indicates that the company has no choice but to increase productivity if its workforce is to survive. The analysis has been a careful one, with other alternatives explored thoroughly. Accordingly, the problem facing management is to decide which pay incentive plan to adopt.

There has been general recognition among Mainline's employees for the last few months that the company is in trouble and something will be done. A particular concern is that management will decide to reduce the size of the workforce.

Role Descriptions (Read *Only* Your Role)

Role 1—Executive vice president. Your goal is to be promoted to group vice president, and to do this, you need to turn things around immediately and show a good profit picture. To accomplish this, you want to institute the employee stock ownership plan. You operate best in a directive, structured, and centralized situation, and feel that the current problems stem from a lack of control and coordination among departments. Your goal now is to increase short-run profits at any cost.

You basically would like to improve pay system policy because the real question is value, which your company has always provided. You feel the way to keep people from leaving is to increase their ownership of stock.

Role 2—Compensation manager. You feel strongly that what the organization needs to solve its problems is an increased team incentive plan. You recognize that the reasons why are important, but also that employees must be motivated to adapt to changing markets with new products and competition.

You feel that competitors are forcing you to change your pay policies; therefore, you must change or lose profits. You feel that team incentives are the best way to retain people.

Role 3—Employee representative. You have been with the company for over 20 years. You see piecework incentive plans as the major goal. You are convinced that profits can be increased by a piecework system which will allow a more stable and efficient production-line operation.

Role 4—Manager of human resources. You favor a profit sharing plan and a type of leadership that is concerned with human needs. You feel strongly that the most important resource in the organization is people. Morale and the satisfaction of individuals are the primary goals as you see it.

You see a real problem in the competitive marketplace, and feel that profit sharing may need to be instituted. You wish to retain key people, and think more profit sharing for its employees will retain and attract good people.

Role 5—Union representative. You feel that a system built on security, solidarity, and seniority increases total productivity. You feel that the company must become more cohesive and improve product marketability to survive.

You feel that the key to sustained performance is the relationship between management and its employees.

In the meeting, you wish to argue against any pay incentive plan. You feel that the current problems are due to stagnant, low-risk management, low-risk strategies, and front-office interference. The production department is old and obsolete, both in methods and equipment. You believe that incentive pay systems may favor only the younger, more ambitious employees, and actually depress earnings.

Role 6—Observer. Observe the meeting to find out how your rating on the Mainline Rating Form compares to the final team Rating.

MAINLINE RATING FORM

Pay Method	Individual Rating Col. 1	Team Rating Col. 2
1. ESOP		
2. Team Bonus		
3. Individual Bonus		
4. Management Bonus		
5. Piecework		
6. Profit Sharing		
7. Stock Options		

Total Scores

Case 12.1   Precision Products, Inc.

Donna Robbins was anxious to get back to work Monday morning. She was excited about her chance of getting a large bonus. Donna was a machine operator with Precision Products, Inc. She operated a PC board-soldering machine, soldering components onto PC boards. Precision paid assemblers on a piece-rate basis: Each operator got a certain amount for each part made, plus a bonus for producing above standard. A worker who produced 10 percent above standard for a certain month received a 10 percent bonus. For 20 percent above standard, the bonus was 20 percent. Donna realized that she had a good chance of earning a 20 percent bonus that month. That would be $287.

Donna had a special use for the extra money. Her daughter's birthday was just 3 weeks away. She was hoping to get her a used car. She had already saved over $800, but the car she wanted cost $1100. The bonus would enable her to buy the car.

Donna arrived at work at 7:00 that morning, although her shift did not begin until 8:00. She went to her soldering machine and checked the supply of blank PC boards and electronic components. Finding that only one rack of boards was on hand, she asked the fork-lift driver to bring another. Then she asked the operator who was working the graveyard shift, "Sarah, do you mind if I sort my components while you work?"

"No," Sarah said, "that won't bother me a bit."

After this, Donna thought of ways to simplify the motions involved in loading, soldering, and unloading the PC boards. As Donna took over the soldering after the 8:00 whistle, she thought: "I hope I pull this off. I know the car will make her happy. She won't be stuck at home while I'm at work."

QUESTIONS

1. What are the advantages and disadvantages of a piece-rate pay system?
2. How would you advise Donna?

ENDNOTES

1. "More Workers are Getting A Stake—For Now," *Business Week* (April 12, 1993): 30.
2. Nancy Rivera Brooks, "Stress, Feeling of Entitlement Rise," *LA Times-Washington Post* Service, *The Oregonian*, 1 October 1999, p. B3.
3. Valerie L. Williams and Jennifer E. Sunderland, "New Pay Programs Boost Retention," *Workforce* 78, no. 5 (May 1999): 36–38.
4. Michelle Cottle, "What to do with the Bonus Check?" *New York Times Late Edition*, 31 January 1999, p. 12, sec. 3.
5. Alka Arora and Pervaiz Alam, "The Effect of Adopting Accounting Based Bonus and Performance Incentive Plans on the Earnings Response Coefficient," *NS* 14, no. 1 (Winter 1999): 1–28.
6. Scott Hays, "Pros and Cons of Pay for Performance," *Workforce* 78, no. 2 (February 1999): 68–70.
7. Frances Cauncross, "A Fair Day's Pay," *The Economist* 351, no. 8118 (May 8, 1999): 12–14.
8. Kamalakshi Melta, *Work-Link* 12, no. 1 (January-February 1999): 72–73.
9. Chan Sze-Wei, "More Firms in the Region Link Bonuses to Performance," *Asian Wall Street Journal Weekly* 20, no. 21 (May 24–30, 1999): 6.
10. "Putting the Bounce Back Into Matsushita," *The Economist* 351, no. 8120 (May 22, 1999): 67–68.
11. Russell Fleming, "President Enterprises Tries to Create a New Wage Policy," *Asian Wall Street Journal Weekly* 21, no. 7 (February 15–21, 1999): 11.
12. Aice Z. Cuneo, "Nissan Ties TBWA's Pay to New Car Sales," *Advertising Age* 70, no. 24 (June 7, 1999): 1.
13. Patricia Winters Lauro, "New Methods of Agency Payments Drive a Stake Through the Heart of the Old 15% Commission," *New York Times Late Edition*, 2 April 1999, p. C2.
14. John Emmerling, "Incentive Compensation: a Trend or a Tsunami?" *Advertising Age* 70, no. 9 (March 1, 1996): 6.
15. Frederick Herzberg, "One More Time: How Do You Motivate Employees?" *Harvard Business Review* (January-February 1968): 53–62.
16. Victor H. Vroom, *Work and Motivation* (New York: Wiley, 1964).
17. David C. McClelland, *Human Motivation* (Glenview, IL: Scott, Foresman, 1985).
18. Laurie P. Cohen and Sara Calian, "First Boston Sees Defections Tied to Pay," *Wall Street Journal*, (April 8, 1993): C1.
19. "Short-term incentives considered ineffective, survey reveals," *HR News*, January 2000, Vol. 19, No. 1, p. 5.
20. Phil Frame, "Saturn Workers Get Bonuses," *Automotive News*, 24 January 1994): 2.
21. "Aerospace." *The Wall Street Journal*, 11 January 2000), p. C4.
22. "Executive Pay," *Business Week* no. 3625 (April 19, 1999): 6.
23. Kevin Knapp, "Majority of Chicago-area Firms Did Not Get Their Money's Worth," *Gain's Chicago Business*, 22, no. 17 (April 26, 1999): 3.

24. Karol Nielson, "Falling Profits Hit CEOs in the Wallet," *Chemical Week* 161, no. 13 (April 7, 1999): 8.

25. Allan Johnson, "Should Options Reward Absolute or Relative Shareholder Returns?" *Compensation and Benefits Review* 31, no. 1 (January-February 1999): 38–43.

26. "The Better Option," *Electric Perspectives* 24, no. 3 (May-June 1999): 6.

27. "Campbell Links Executive Pay to Share Stake," *Los Angeles Times,* 5 May 1993, p. D2.

28. Peter G. Gosselin, "Workers Rolling the Dice," *Los Angeles Times,* 14 December 1999), p. A1.

29. Albert R. Karr, "Work Week, Retailers Staff Up Early and Generously for the Holidays," *The Wall Street Journal,* 19 October 1999, p. A1.

30. Jacob M. Schlesinger, "The Outlook, Wealth Gap Grows; Why Does It Matter?" *The Wall Street Journal,* 13 September 1999, p. A1.

31. Fred Luthans and Stajkovic, "Reinforce for Performance: The Need to Go Beyond Pay and Even Rewards," *The Academy of Management Executive* 13, no. 2 (May 1999): 51.

32. David Shair, "IncentPower Provides Dependable Structure for Incentive Pay," *HR Magazine* (November 1998): 48–51.

Part

V

The Success System: Maintaining a High-Performing Workforce

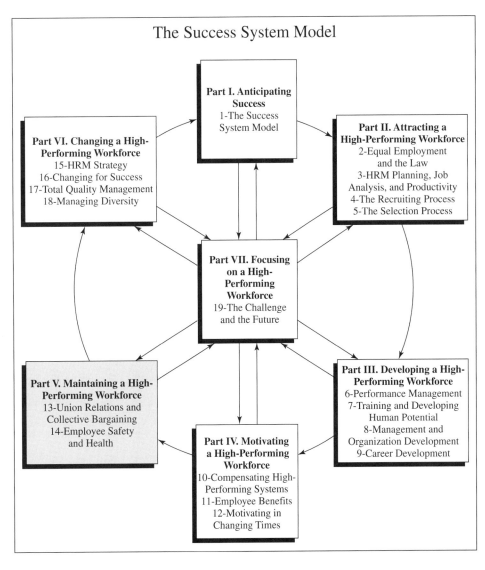

The Success System Model

Part I. Anticipating Success
1-The Success System Model

Part II. Attracting a High-Performing Workforce
2-Equal Employment and the Law
3-HRM Planning, Job Analysis, and Productivity
4-The Recruiting Process
5-The Selection Process

Part VI. Changing a High-Performing Workforce
15-HRM Strategy
16-Changing for Success
17-Total Quality Management
18-Managing Diversity

Part VII. Focusing on a High-Performing Workforce
19-The Challenge and the Future

Part III. Developing a High-Performing Workforce
6-Performance Management
7-Training and Developing Human Potential
8-Management and Organization Development
9-Career Development

Part V. Maintaining a High-Performing Workforce
13-Union Relations and Collective Bargaining
14-Employee Safety and Health

Part IV. Motivating a High-Performing Workforce
10-Compensating High-Performing Systems
11-Employee Benefits
12-Motivating in Changing Times

Chapter 13

The Success System: Union Relations and Collective Bargaining

Objectives

Upon completing this chapter, you will be able to:

1. Define and discuss the concept of labor union programs.
2. Describe the growth and objectives of labor legislation systems.
3. Understand the relationship of labor unions to goals of employee satisfaction and productivity.
4. Identify and describe the process of collective bargaining.
5. Define and discuss the external and internal factors which lead to labor-management programs.

Premeeting preparation

1. Read chapter 13.
2. Prepare for HRM Skills Simulation 13.1: United Electrical Motors. Read Parts A and B, Step 1.
3. Read Case 13.1: The Northwest Freight Line. Answer questions.

The arrival of the twenty-first century presents the labor unions of the United States with a different environment. The turn of the century presents a highly competitive global economy featuring free trade. The result is a global search for efficient low-cost labor, larger mergers, deregulation, and privatization.

In the United States the economy is rapidly moving from a manufacturing to a service orientation. Some examples of this turbulent shifting scene is General Electric Company's decision to cut 44 percent of their employees at their refrigerator plant in Bloomington, Indiana, and move the remaining jobs to Mexico.[1] AT&T Corporation announces another slash of $2 billion in costs with a hiring freeze to maintain maximum flexibility to meet fierce price competition in their industry.[2]

Boeing Company's chairman realized his company did not want a union strike to halt airline production so at the eleventh hour he personally entered negotiations with the Machinists Union, offering them a "cushy contract," that was overwhelmingly accepted. The generous gains the Boeing machinists won is part of an emerging pattern of labor unions suddenly displaying new clout after years of losing ground.[3]

During the past decade, union membership has decreased substantially to approximately 13.9 percent of the nonfarm U.S. workforce. An example is the Mon Valley area of Pennsylvania. It once was the home of 400,000 steelworkers. Now in the twenty-first century, there are 2,500 left to work. These remaining union members of the United Steelworkers of America (USWA) who fought the companies "tooth and nail" have now joined them in a partnership agreement written in the contract to ensure their joint survival.[4]

Unions are still an important influence upon organizations, and their influence is also important outside of the United States, particularly in Europe. In the United States, there are still some 70,000 local unions and 173 national unions. Of these, 110 belong to the influential AFL-CIO, representing about 80 percent of all unionized employees in the United States. Unionized firms tend to be more constrained because many basic management decisions (such as compensation, promotion, employee appraisal, job redesign, and termination) necessitate union involvement.

In general, management must negotiate personnel matters with union representatives rather than with each individual employee. Unions also have a great deal of influence on the compensation and appraisal system. Nonunion firms are also concerned with union activities because they frequently want to maintain their nonunion status. The working conditions, wages, and terms of employment in a unionized firm have an effect upon the way in which nonunion employers manage their employees in order to avoid union status. For example, the Nissan automobile plant in Smyrna, Tennessee, has provided favorable benefits to its employees, and despite efforts by union organizers, the employees have continued to vote to remain nonunion.

Many business students appear to have a negative attitude toward the American labor movement. They may see unions as antimanagement, working to maintain or even reduce productivity while striking for higher wages and job security for workers.

An employee union may be defined as an organization of employees united to act as a single unit when dealing with management work issues. In this chapter, we present stage five of the Success System Model: the process of unionization, the collective bargaining process, and current trends. With approximately only 13.9 percent of the American workforce belonging to unions, is this topic really relevant for managers of the twenty-first century? Perhaps the information presented in this chapter will assist in helping you finalize your decision. Whether or not managers approve of labor organizations, they will not become unimportant in the United States. Even if they did, labor organizations are still very important in many nations around the world in which we do business. Today's manager, whether in a unionized or nonunionized environment, will always need to consider good employer-employee relations as a top priority.

Unions are one of the forces in shaping organizational practices, legislation, and political thought. They continue to be important because of their influence on productivity, competitiveness, and HRM policies. However, unions are undergoing changes in both operation and philosophy. Labor-management cooperative programs, union-company buyouts, and union representation on an organization's board of directors are some examples of labor's adjustment to the realities of the world of work.

The continuing importance of unions and the complexities of union relations present HRM problems. In the following sections, we will describe the labor relations process, the reasons for unions, and contemporary trends in labor organizations.

LABOR'S "NEW FACE"

The AFL-CIO entered the twenty-first century prepared to be a more sophisticated, relevant, and open organization with a vision of what the workplace of America should become. They believe workplaces should be for the good of workers, consumers, owners, and managers.

This vision will be accomplished through "workplace democracy." The AFL-CIO sees this as a process by which workers help to influence decisions at work throughout the organization. These decisions include worker education and training programs, employment needs, how work is organized, technology in the workplace, definition of quality, and investments needed to remain productive. They believed these worker influenced decisions will result in a basic business strategy required for companies to remain successful.

Although their vision represents a challenge of thinking for the business community, it also presents a challenge to the HRM profession. Our challenge is that the AFL-CIO will be taking a more active role in HRM functions as they attempt to implement their vision in smoothing relations between employers and unions.

As Nancy Milk, director of the AFL-CIO's Center for Workplace Democracy at the union's headquarters building points out, HRM is part of the real strategic business planning process and that it is also their interest. Director Milk believes HRM's input for planning strategies for recruitment, education, and training is critical for job creation. These issues are the twenty-first century interest and focus of organized labor. She believes organized labor will now be working with HRM professionals to achieve these mutual goals.[5]

Whether this union's "new face" will be effective remains to be seen. However, the Bureau of Labor Statistics reported in the first month of the twenty-first century that U.S. labor unions gained more members in 1999 for the first time in 20 years.

Although some states such as New-Jersey lost union members, California led the nation gaining 132,000 with 74,000 of the total being home care workers. The highest rate of union membership is the government with 37 percent which compares to the private-sector rate of 9.4 percent. This results in the overall national unionization rate of 13.9 percent.[6]

THE MANAGEMENT-UNION RELATIONSHIP

Most managers feel strongly about not having their employees represented by a union. Why? The major reason is a reducing of management control and adding a factor to the management-employee relationship. Further, the union often stands between the management and the employee as the protector of employee rights.

Employee Rights

What are employee rights? Employees have the right to band together to increase their pay, benefits, and working conditions. Further, they have the right to unionize and to strike.

Employee rights, or more accurately called labor rights, apply only to employees covered by Section 7 of the National Labor Relations Act, or other state labor relations laws. These rights, as defined by the NLRA, are usually enjoyed by employees in the larger businesses and some nonprofit organizations. Unless there are state laws, most employees in smaller businesses do not have these rights. Most agricultural employees do not have them. Most employees in businesses located within a local economy, whose goods, people, or money do not cross state lines, do not have them.

Where did employee rights come from? At one time, they simply belonged to management. What Congress and state legislatures in the 1930s did was to take these rights from the employer and give them to the employee. In essence, some of the old master and servant obligations in the employment exchange were eliminated. The intent was to replace them with employees trading their labor and skills for employer's providing pay and benefits. (See cartoon.)

Union Classification

Unions are usually classified as either craft or industrial. The distinction depends upon whether the membership skills are mainly in a single job skill, such as carpentry or electricians, resulting in the term "craft unions." If the membership includes a certain industry, such as automobile or steel, they are referred to as "industrial unions."

The original American Federation of Labor (AFL) is a craft union organized in 1886 from a group of autonomous national craft labor unions. The first president was Samuel Gompers, a cigarmaker from London, who served until his death in 1924. He declared the AFL would be organized along craft lines, union activities would promote economic, not political issues, and the individual national craft unions would have autonomy in running their internal affairs.

In 1938, approximately 30 unions were expelled from the AFL over craft versus industrial unionism. The expelled group wanted single unions composed of all workers within a particular industry, regardless of the craft. The AFL continued as a craft union with machinists, electricians, plumbers, and so forth, all maintaining their individual unions within a particular industry, but under the leadership of the AFL.

The expelled group became the Congress of Industrial Organizations (CIO), and continued as a union for about 20 years. Their organizing efforts were very suc-

Source: THE WIZARD OF ID. © 1995 Creators Syndicate.

cessful, and membership grew very rapidly. However, in 1955, the AFL and CIO ended their rivalry, and merged into one union known as the American Federation of Labor and Congress of Industrial Organizations (AFL-CIO). The feud ended with consensus that craft and industrial workers were both appropriate. The result was the elimination of competitive membership organizing among themselves, and a much stronger union as to membership and industrial coverage. Although there are about 70,000 local unions in the United States with charters from national unions, approximately 55,000 local unions are affiliated with AFL-CIO.

There are approximately 175 national unions who are not members of the AFL-CIO. These include large unions (such as the International Brotherhood of Teamsters, Chauffeurs, Warehousemen and Helpers of America, the United Mine Workers, and the International Brotherhood of Longshoremen) and smaller unions (such as the American Radio Association and the National Rural Letter Carriers Association).

The Union Movement

However, the union movement is far from becoming an unimportant factor in the world of work. In some manufacturing industries, such as steel and automobile, union membership is still close to 45 percent. Even in the nonmanufacturing segment of the economy, union membership is approximately 15 percent. Union ability in organizing the growing number of service industries and white-collar workers is further indication that the union movement continues to be a significant factor in future management-employee relations.

The labor movement became a significant force in the economy as a result of federal and state legislation forcing employers to recognize and bargain with groups representing their employees and protecting employees from retaliation by employers. The first major federal legislation was the Railroad Labor Act of 1926, allowing railroad and airline employees to determine by election whether they wished to be represented by a union. Further, the law provided that employees could legally engage in union activity without fear of retaliation.

The next major federal legislation was the Norris-La Guardia Act of 1932. This law had little effect in promoting union growth in the private sector; it did not require employers to bargain with groups representing their employees, nor did it prevent employers from retaliating against those employees who were involved in promoting union membership. However, it did prevent employers from coercing employees to sign "yellow-dog contracts" specifying employees would not join unions or they would be fired.

Labor Legislation

It was not until the passage of the Wagner Act of 1936 (National Labor Relations Act) that union membership began its phenomenal growth and its influence upon the national economy. The importance of the Wagner Act was that it became legal for workers to organize and to be free of employer harassment. The act also defined several employer unfair labor practices, such as coercing employees, interfering with organizing activity, firing or discouraging employment because of union activity, and refusing to bargain. Another part of the legislation was the establishment of the National Labor Relations Board to conduct union selection elections and to investigate unfair labor practices.

Taft-Hartley

In an attempt to correct both management and union practices that abused employees, the 1947 Labor-Management Relations Act (known as the Taft-Hartley Amendments) was passed to amend the Wagner Act. Management had formed its own unions to avoid outside unions, and then entered into wage contracts (sweetheart contracts) favoring the company. This practice was now prohibited by the Taft-Hartley Amendments. The amendments also required that unions represent all employees in the **bargaining unit** whether or not the employees were union members. It said that employees outside of a **union shop** (one in which all employees must join the union) cannot be discriminated against because of nonmembership in the union. The Taft-Hartley Amendments recognized that employees had the right not to organize, and unions were now required to bargain in good faith. The amendments also recognized state right-to-work laws had preference over collective bargaining agreements requiring union membership for employment. Further, the amendments established the Federal Mediation and Conciliation Service to assist in resolving labor disputes by providing **arbitrators** who act as neutrals who attempt to bring the parties in the dispute to agreement.

Landrum-Griffin

The Labor-Management Reporting and Disclosure Act of 1959 (known as the Landrum-Griffin Act) resulted from labor racketeering and established certain rights for union members who had been denied them by their union leadership, including nominating candidates, voting for candidates, and attending and participating in union meetings. The act said unions must submit an annual financial statement to the Secretary of Labor, and union officials must be bonded. Employers and labor consultants must report any funds spent to influence employees on their bargaining rights.

The legislation just cited provided a positive environment for unionization, but the basic process starts with either a group of employees or a particular union. Once the union organizing campaign begins, at least 30 percent of the employees must be persuaded to sign authorization cards before a representative election can be called. If the necessary percentage of signed cards has been obtained, the National Labor Relations Board (NLRB) is petitioned, and an examiner is appointed. The examiner decides whether the signatures are valid, and if a bargaining unit has been determined, the NLRB schedules the election. When the balloting is over, the board counts the ballots and certifies the election results. If the union has won the election by a simple majority, the union officials are authorized to negotiate a bargaining agreement with the company.

During this process, both management and the union are subject to certain restrictions mandated by the National Labor Relations Act to ensure fairness. These restrictions are called employer unfair labor practices and union unfair labor practices.

Good Faith Bargaining—Unfair Labor Practices

For instance, the employer cannot interfere with employees as they attempt to organize or engage in collective bargaining. This includes any restraining or coercing of employees. The National Labor Relations Board regards such employer actions very seriously—so much so it is not necessary to prove the employer intended to produce such acts, or an employee was actually coerced, but rather the acts would tend to coerce a reasonable employee. Such acts would be threats of discharge or shutting down the plant, or promising benefits to employees voting against unionization.

Unfair Practices

Employers cannot dominate the labor union, nor interfere with its organization and administration, nor contribute financial support. The employer is considered guilty if it is reasonable to infer the employer's actions caused the union not to represent the employees in a dispute.

Employers cannot encourage or discourage employee membership in any union. This prohibits firing, withholding benefits, promotions, discipline, refusal to hire, denying bonuses, or insurance benefits, if such actions are designed to discriminate against union employees.

Employers cannot take action against employees who are subpoenaed by the National Labor Relations Board. Both employees and supervisory personnel are protected by the NLRA. This protection also included the filing of charges against the employer with the NLRB.

Employers have the duty to collectively bargain with the union, and must confer with the authorized union representatives. This is referred to as good faith bargaining. Past NLRB decisions have indicated several situations in which the employer was found guilty of bad faith bargaining. These include delaying tactics, maintaining the same position (take it or leave it), shifting positions just when agreement is imminent, unilateral action, rejecting previous terms, pattern of undermining the union, not furnishing appropriate information, not bargaining on the issue of racial discrimination, and offering proposals more unfavorable than previous proposals.

The final unfair employer labor practice is entering into hot cargo agreements. This provision applies to both the employer and the union, prohibiting an agreement between the two parties where the employer agrees to stop doing business with another company because of coercion by the union.

Collective Bargaining

The National Labor Relations Act also restricts the activities of unions with unfair labor practices. For instance, unions or their agents cannot coerce employees and employers by threats or other means regarding the employees' rights guaranteed them by the NLRA or when employers select their collective bargaining representatives.

The union cannot discriminate against an employee to whom membership has been denied or terminated, except where required fees have not been paid as a condition for membership. Also, the union cannot coerce the employer to discriminate against an employee.

The union cannot refuse to bargain collectively with the employer when the union does, in fact, represent the employer's employees. The union is prohibited from coercion to force an employer to accept a noncertified union over a union certified by the NLRB, or to make particular work assignments. Unions are also prohibited from using secondary boycotts in practically every situation. A secondary boycott includes activities to cause a secondary employer to take some type of action upon the primary employer to make that employer submit to union demands. For instance, it is illegal to stop a subcontractor from crossing a picket line if the subcontractor's work is not part of the struck employer's day-to-day operation.

Other Unfair Practices

When there is a compulsory union agreement permitted by the law, the union cannot charge excessive or discriminatory initiation fees. However, fees may vary between reasonable classification of employees. It is unfair labor practice for the union to charge the employer to pay for labor services not actually performed. This is called "featherbedding." An example would be the union demanding the employer hire employees for whom there is no work to perform, such as a fireman on a diesel locomotive. The union is prohibited from organizational or recognitional picketing for an uncertified union unless an election petition is filed with the NLRB within 30 days.

The union is prohibited from entering into agreements with the employer where the union has coerced the employer or caused work stoppages so as to prevent doing business with another employer. This is called a "hot cargo" agreement. However, there are certain exceptions for the construction and garment industries, based on prior practices.

The final labor unfair practice applies to strikes or picketing at health care institutions. The union must provide the employer with 10 days notice. This includes all types of strikes. However, an exception would be where there is a serious employer unfair labor practice.

Although the employer and union unfair labor practices protect the union employee, what protection does the nonunion employee have? Nonunion employees are given the right to organize and select a person to speak for them per the Taft-Hartley Amendments. The NLRH gives employees the right of concerted activities for the purpose of protection.

For a nonunion employee's activities to be concerted requires that the employee does not act as an individual, but in concert with at least one other employee. However, an individual may act over matters that affect the common concerns of other employees. If the nonunion employee is to be protected from employer reprisal, activities must not only be concerted but also protected by the NLRA. An employee activity may be concerted, but it does not necessarily follow it is protected.

For an activity to be protected, it must be related to the job. An example of not job-related would be a slowdown by employees to pressure an employer to agree to their demands. Although this is a joint effort and thus concerted, it is not protected because the employees are receiving pay, but are not providing the company with the usual full amount of work for the earned wages.

The Union Relations Process

Many organizations are required to deal with a formal organization of their employees. Because individually, the employees may not be able to exercise much power with employers, unionization provides a way to organize and bargain with the employer collectively. The **union relations process** consists of a series of four steps: (1) Workers must vote for collective representation, (2) the union organizing campaign, (3) collective negotiations, and (4) contract administration. (See Figure 13.1.) Legislation influences each step by granting special privileges to or imposing defined constraints on employees, management, and union officials.

Why Employees Unionize

The research on why employees unionize generally include (1) economic needs, (2) job dissatisfaction, and (3) to fulfill social and status needs. Employees see a union as the way to gain satisfaction they cannot gain by acting individually. Unionized firms usually have higher layoff rates as nonunionized firms.

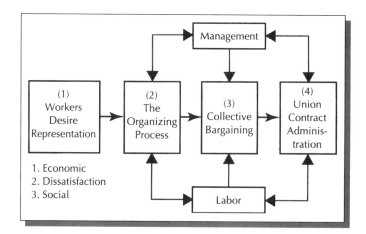

Figure 13.1
The union relations process

Economic Reasons

Dissatisfaction with wages, benefits, or working conditions seems to be one of the major reasons why employees join a union. Both union members and nonmembers usually have high expectations of union membership about wages in collective bargaining. Wages are one of the basic issues on which unions were built.

Job Dissatisfaction Reasons

Employees may also join a union when managerial practices regarding promotions, job transfers, shift assignments, or other job-related policies are perceived as unfair. Employees often cite supervisors' favoritism as a major reason for joining unions. This is particularly true in the areas of discipline, promotion, and wage increases.

The failure of some organizations to allow employees an opportunity to participate in workplace decisions may also encourage union membership.

Social Reasons

Often employees have social needs for status and recognition that are not being satisfied, and find that joining unions provides an outlet for satisfying these needs. In a union, workers are often able to socialize with others who share similar problems and complaints.

Some studies on employee unionization in the public sector have found public employees' reasons for unionizing are similar to those in the private-sector. One study, for example, reported that extrinsic factors—wages, benefits, job security, and protection against arbitrary and unfair management treatment—were among the primary motives for unionization. Other studies suggest if employees are dissatisfied with these factors, then they often perceive the benefits of joining a union to outweigh the costs of membership.

UNION ORGANIZING

Once employees express a desire to unionize, an organizing campaign will typically be started either by a union organizer or by employees. Larger unions like the AFL-CIO, the United Auto Workers, and the Teamsters have organizing departments whose function is to identify organizing opportunities and initiate organizing campaigns.

A form of union organizing that the National Labor Relations Board (NLRB) has attempted to clarify is the practice of "salting." This occurs when union organizers apply for jobs with the intent to unionize the present employees.

When the salts are not hired, they complain to the NLRB and are usually awarded the jobs with back pay. However, in some cases they are not awarded the jobs causing confusion.

To clarify the issue, the NLRB has now ruled their general counsel (when representing the salts) must prove the salts were qualified but not hired because of "antiunion animus" (hostility/antagonism) toward the union. If proven, the employers must prove the salts were not as qualified as other applicants and should not have been hired.

Unions regard the NLRB ruling as providing a consistent foundation for future cases. Employers find the ruling to be "a mixed bag."[7]

Because organizing campaigns are expensive, union leaders generally try to evaluate their chances of success as noted in the Federal Express example. Union organizers also must consider the overall strength of their union within the geographical area. The organizing process typically includes the following steps.

Step 1. The first step involves employees and union officials exploring the possibility of unionization. During these contacts, employees will investigate the advantages of a union, and union organizers begin gathering information about employee needs, problems, and complaints. Union organizers will also try to get detailed information about the organization's financial state, supervisory methods, and human resource policies and practices. To gain employee support, the union organizers need to find reasons *for* having a union.

Step 2. The organizing campaign usually begins with an initial union meeting to attract more supporters. The organizer uses the information gathered to identify employee problems and how the union can solve these problems. Other purposes of having an organizational meeting include (1) to identify key employees to help the organizer and (2) to open communications with all employees.

Step 3. The third step in the organizing drive is forming an employee organizing committee to provide internal leadership for the campaign. The committee's role is to solicit other employees to join the union. The most important task of the committee is to have all employees sign an **authorization card** indicating their willingness to be represented by a union. The number of signed authorization cards demonstrates the potential strength of the labor union, and over 30 percent of the employees must sign authorization cards before the NLRB will hold a representation election.

Step 4. If the required percentage of employees support the union drive, the organizer will file a petition with the NLRB requesting an election.

EMPLOYER CAMPAIGN TACTICS

In general, management usually resists unionization for fear of losing a competitive edge. Once a union campaign starts, the employer cannot threaten employees with the loss of their jobs or with other repercussions should they vote for a union. As noted earlier, under the Taft-Hartley Amendments, employers are able to express their position on possible disadvantages of being represented by a union. Employers can also emphasize the advantages of the nonunion employer-employee relationship. Employers may also emphasize the advantages in wages, benefits, or working conditions the employees have, in comparison with organizations that are already unionized.

Employers may also publicize any unfavorable factors about the union concerning corruption or the abuse of members' rights. Employers often use government statistics to show that unions commit numerous unfair labor practices. Often the union has engaged in a number of strikes, and employers can emphasize this as a warning to employees about possible strikes. Employers are likely to stress the cost to employees of union dues.

TYPES OF NLRB ELECTIONS

The NLRB offers two types of elections. The first is called a **consent election.** This is used when the petition to hold a representation election is not contested. In this case, there are no disagreements between the union and the employer; therefore, no preelection hearing is called for. The NLRB sets a date for the union election, and voting is conducted by secret ballot.

When the request for representation is contested by the employer, then preelection hearings must be held. This second type of election is called a **stipulation election.** At preelection hearings, several important issues are presented, including the NLRB's jurisdiction to conduct the election, the determination of a bargaining unit (if contested), and the voting choice(s) to appear on the ballot. Because more than one union may be seeking election, the ballot contains the names of the unions that are seeking representation and also provides for the choice of "no union."

After the election, the winning choice will be determined based on the number of actual votes, *not* on the number of members of the bargaining unit. As an example, suppose the bargaining unit of a company numbered 1,000 employees, but only 800 employees voted in the election. The union receiving over 400 "yes" votes among the 800 voting (a majority) would be declared the winner, and the union would then be the bargaining agent for all 1,000 employees.

If none of the unions receives a majority, then a runoff election is held between the two top choices. Unless the majority votes "no union," the union that receives a majority of the votes in the run-off election is the one certified by the NLRB as the bargaining agent for a period of at least a year, or for the duration of the labor contract. Once the union is certified, the employer must begin negotiations toward a labor contract.

One important factor in union elections is the past record of unions in certification elections. This ratio is usually regarded as an indication of the overall power of the unions. In recent years, unions won less than 45 percent of elections held by the NLRB. This compares with the union win rate of 74.5 percent in 1950 and 60.2 percent in 1965. However, in 1998, unions won 51.2 percent of elections (see endnote 6). Although 1 year does not indicate a trend, it may represent a change.

COLLECTIVE BARGAINING

Collective bargaining is the process of union representatives meeting with management representatives to reach agreement on employees' wages and benefits, work rules, and the resolution of disputes or violations of the union contract. As noted earlier, the general trend for union membership has been declining in the last few years, but for some 17 million workers, collective bargaining still represents the major process for negotiating their wages, benefits, and working conditions.

It is highly improbable that unions or collective bargaining will disappear. But to survive in the future, the union tactics and the unions themselves will need to change. Unions are currently trying to expand into white-collar workers, women, and minorities, as an increasing part of the labor force.

For the HR manager, a knowledge of union relations and collective bargaining is important. Recruiting and selection, for example, are covered by the union contract. In a union shop, everyone hired must eventually join the union. Finally, a knowledge of collective bargaining is probably most necessary in compensation and benefits, because wages and benefits are typically open to negotiation.

Collective bargaining needs to be viewed as a two-way communication channel. This suggests that the contractual interests of management should be protected just as much as the rights of employees.

Part of the collective bargaining process is how it takes place. Sometimes it occurs with an individual company, groups of companies, or pattern bargaining. When pattern bargaining occurs, the entire industry and the union bargain to achieve the same contract (excluding local issues). An example is U.S. Steel and Bethlehem Steel bargaining with the United Steelworkers of America (USWA).

The steelmakers are interested in joint bargaining because they believe the early negotiations will help each reach a quicker agreement. If correct, this will ensure them of a steady supply of steel to their customers and of signing them up to long term contracts. The UAW is interested in the joint bargaining process because they believe it will significantly improve their chances of restoring pattern bargaining. If the union achieves their goal of pattern bargaining, they believe this will allow them to obtain greater employee job security.[8]

THE LABOR CONTRACT

The labor contract is a formal agreement between a union and management which sets forth the conditions of employment and the union-management framework over an agreed-upon period of time (usually 2 to 5 years). The negotiating process involved prior to signing this contract is a complex and difficult task, requiring both sides to be willing to compromise on some issues.

Union Contract Negotiations

Bargaining strategies can take many approaches, depending upon the relations among the union's negotiating units (i.e., industrywide, national, regional) and the type of employer negotiating unit (i.e., multiemployer, companywide, plant). Both parties may decide that a larger negotiating unit would be advantageous. (See HRM in Action.)

HRM IN ACTION
CATERPILLAR AND UAW AGREE TO MEDIATION[9]

The United Auto Workers strike against Caterpillar, Inc., was like "a little Cuban missile crisis," and the union blinked, according to labor relations educator, Edward J. Kelly.

Hiring permanent replacement workers "is a terrible weapon," said the labor relations czar. "It's a little like nuclear war."

"It's a terrible thing, but the worse thing is not to have a Caterpillar plant at all because they couldn't get an equitable contract. This may have been the only way to settle it."

The UAW had called for continuation of **pattern bargaining** at Caterpillar, the construction equipment company based in Peoria, Illinois. The union sought a contract patterned on one the union had reached with John Deere & Co.

But Caterpillar saw contract bargaining as outmoded in a time of global competition, and threatened to fill the jobs of striking employees with permanent replacement workers.

After a 5-month-long strike, Caterpillar set a deadline for about 12,600 striking employees to return to work. About 400 workers returned that day. The following day, the company began advertising for replacement workers.

Although some may see the Caterpillar situation as an indication that the power of unions had been broken, "I don't think it's a death rattle for labor," Kelly said, "but it's a real wake-up call." He does see it as "a clear message" that pattern bargaining has been broken.

QUESTIONS

1. Why does the union consider hiring permanent replacement workers "a terrible weapon"? Present the pros and cons.

2. How does pattern bargaining fit in a world of global competition? Will it survive?

Step 1: Preparing for Negotiations

Preparing for negotiations involves planning a strategy and gathering data to support bargaining positions. In order to prepare for negotiations, a strategy is needed. Preparation includes reviewing and diagnosing the mistakes and weaknesses of prior negotiations, and gathering data on recent contract settlements in the local area and industrywide (e.g., comparative industry and occupational wage rates and fringe benefits). Negotiators often prepare a bargaining handbook, including data on economic conditions, consumer price indices, cost-of-living trends, and projections of the short- and long-term economic outlook. This also includes company data on minimum and maximum pay for each job classification, number of grievances, and levels of overtime.

In preparing for negotiations, the negotiating team must review other contract agreements in similar industries. They must also recognize the prevailing patterns relating to wages, benefits, and working conditions. The union typically tries to negotiate wage and benefit increases which are better than other agreements in their industry. Management, on the other hand, presents data supporting lower wages and fewer benefits.

Step 2: Contract Negotiations

Contract negotiations may take a few days, a few weeks, or sometimes several months. One of the most important objectives in the early negotiating meetings is to establish a climate for negotiations. Certain issues are mandatory bargaining issues, and others are permissive. At this time, it will be determined whether the climate of the negotiations is going to be characterized by mutual trust or by adversaries. These initial meetings are used to develop the bargaining rules and procedures to be used throughout the process. This stage of negotiations is like a high-stakes poker game, with each party trying to guess the value of the opponent's hand, without revealing their own. Each party tries to conceal the relative importance they attach to key issues so as not to disclose possible strategies. Each party tries to guess what concessions the other party is willing to make, and the minimum levels they are willing to accept.

Successful negotiations are contingent upon reaching an end result between the maximum and minimum levels acceptable to each of the parties. The **bargaining zone** (as shown in Figure 13.2) is that area within the limits which both the

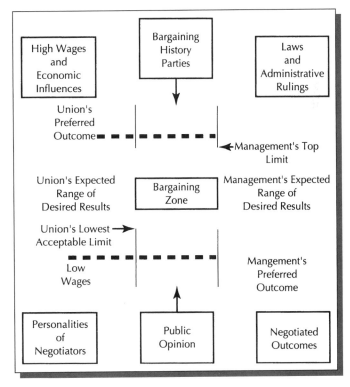

Figure 13.2
The bargaining factors

union and the employer are willing to accept.[10] If either party is unwilling to change their demand levels to bring them within the bargaining zone, then negotiations may reach an impasse.

The management negotiating team then presents the management proposal, which typically includes counterproposals and data to support its position. In these initial meetings, the two parties are often far apart in their demands; however, as negotiations proceed, there is generally a movement toward a compromise agreement. As proposals are presented, concessions are offered by each side, counterproposals are made, and finally an agreement is reached.

After contract agreement is reached, it is voted on by the union members. If approved, the contract is signed; if not, the negotiating process continues. The final step is the signing of the agreement by union and management.

Step 3: Bargaining Tactics

The objective of each negotiating team during contract negotiations is to get its key bargaining points into the contract. To achieve their objectives, the negotiating team may use several bargaining tactics. Three commonly used tactics include the trading point tactic, the use of counterproposals, and the use of strike threats.

The trading point tactic involves evaluating the demands of the other party to determine which key elements they are most interested in achieving. As an example, management may determine that a wage increase is a key point for the union. If the employer can live with this, then management may agree to the wage increase. But in return for this increase, management may insist that the union agree to one of its key demands, such as less job security or benefits coverage.

Counterproposals are another frequently used bargaining tactic. Management, for example, might counter a union demand for a $1.25 increase in hourly wages by offering a $0.95 increase. The union then proposes an increase of $1.20, countered by a management offer of $1.05. This pattern of counterproposals continues until an agreement is reached.

During good economic times, unions generally make more significant contract gains during labor negotiations. This is because management's defense against union wage demands is less viable in a more profitable economic situation. Similarly, during economic recession when profits are down, unions tend to ask and accept less. One example of this occurred during the recessions of the 1990s. At this time, economic concessions were often made by unions. Due to the downsizing and layoffs in the recessions, job security became more important than wages for the unions.

Strike threats are another tactic used to put pressure on the employer. The UAW, for example, usually picks one of the big three automobile companies to negotiate with, threatening a strike against that company if its demands are not met. When a satisfactory agreement is reached with one, the UAW then approaches the remaining two automobile companies using the new contract as the model for them to accept.

A variation of this tactic occurred in late 1999 when the UAW first negotiated with General Motors and Daimler Chrysler. With the deal with GM and Daimler Chrysler in their pocket, the UAW then approached Ford Motor Company.

After months of negotiations, a new 4-year contract was approved by 85 percent of the union membership. As one would expect, the Ford contract mirrors many of the similar terms agreed to by GM and Daimler Chrysler with exceptions being local issues. So the big three auto manufacturers contracts contain 3 percent yearly raises, a $1,350 signing bonus, and improvements in pensions. The average union member pay will increase more than $29,000 over the 4 years of the contract.[11]

A tactic recently used by Boeing before contract negotiations had even started resulted in psychological affect upon the Society of Professional Engineering Employees in the Aerospace union. Boeing announced several days prior to negotiations they were extending health care benefits to the same-sex domestic partners of salaried nonunion employees. Although the executive director of the union responded that his union would like the benefits, his view was Boeing's announcement seemed designed to sabotage his union's contract negotiations.[12]

Bargaining Deadlocks

Successful contract negotiations are dependent upon both sides remaining flexible and open to compromise. If neither is willing to compromise, then negotiations may reach a deadlock or impasse. In such a case, a strike on the part of the union, or a **lockout** on the part of management, may be the result.

How can these deadlocks in negotiations be avoided? One method is to delay consideration of the hotter issues to the later stages of negotiations. The easier issues can be negotiated in the early stages, providing both parties with a feeling of agreement. Another method of avoiding deadlock is for each party to be prepared to compromise and accept alternative solutions on the more controversial points.

In some instances, government intervention has been necessary to resolve deadlocks. This occurs when a strike threatens the national security or the public welfare. One of the provisions of the Taft-Hartley Amendments is a national emergency strike provision which gives the president of the United States the power to stop a strike if it imperils national health or safety.

The Strike

One common tactic of unions is to call a strike. A **strike** occurs when employees refuse to perform their jobs. Strikes usually occur when a union is unsuccessful in negotiating an acceptable offer from management. It has been estimated that about 15 percent of all contract negotiations actually end up in a strike. Although strikes tend to make headlines in the media, strikes represent less than 1 percent of total lost workdays. Before a union calls a strike, it is important to assess the members' willingness to make the sacrifices and endure the hardships (e.g., lost pay) that are part of a strike, as was the case in the Caterpillar strike. This assessment also involves determining the extent to which the employer can continue operating by using supervisory and nonstriking employees. Highly automated firms often have contingency plans which enable the companies to operate at near 100 percent capacity. There are a number of risks involved in calling a strike. The main one is that replacement employees can vote the union out in an NLRB-conducted **decertification election,** as happened at Caterpillar.

The strike is becoming less used as a tactic. Increasing automation, favorable court rulings, and the increasing number of unemployed workers willing to serve as replacement workers have provided more power for management. The strike by the UAW against Caterpillar in the mid-1990s was unsuccessful because Caterpillar hired replacement workers. This was the first time a large industrial company (Caterpillar is the world's largest manufacturer of construction equipment) replaced thousands of union workers. Many former Caterpillar workers who went on strike found that their jobs were not waiting for them when the strike ended.

In some cases, unions will call for a strike vote simply to strengthen the union position. In fact, the union wants to avoid a strike, but it may use the strike vote as a threat to gain concessions. This tactic forces both parties to reexamine their contract demands, and, in some cases, increases the likelihood of compromise.

Sometimes the threat or management's fear of a strike can be a very persuasive union communication tool. An example is why United Airlines Incorporated (UAL) adopted a new performance-based pay system for their top executives. The reason? The UAL unions insisted the top executives pay system be tied to workers' satisfaction, customer satisfaction, and on-time performance. These newly adopted criteria which the union insisted upon will account for over half of the executives' evaluations.

Why did UAL make the change? The airlines could not afford a strike. However, it did not hurt the union's cause that the union owns 60 percent of the company's shares.[13]

Even a series of 1-day strikes can be an effective union weapon. Barclays Bank in London experienced a series of 1-day strikes extending over a 1-year period because of a very unpopular employee performance pay system. The bank gave in and introduced a new employee pay system and a partnership agreement which will be phased in over a 3-year period. This move by Barclays Bank won praise by the trade unions.[14]

The Reluctant "S" Word   Union leaders and members are reluctant to use labor's ultimate weapon, the strike. The president of the United Automobile Workers Union, Stephen Yokich, points out the world is different today. Mr. Yokich believes once the union begins to rattle their strike sword then they have to be prepared to use it. He prefers a more professional approach to negotiations.

This approach recognizes that using the sword can hurt many people, including union members. Today's structure of labor relations has changed. Workers have become stockholders. The spread of technology and globalization has put union members' jobs at risk.

As Ron Blackwell, AFL-CIO's director of corporate affairs, points out the threat of replacement workers is driving the decline of strikes. After President Ronald Reagan in 1982 fired the striking air-traffic controllers, yearly major strikes dropped below 100 for the first time and have never recovered.

With strikes becoming more risky, unions have looked for other options to pressure management. The more likely approach is to launch a public relations campaign against the employer. Another tactic is to lobby the big money-management firms investing union pension funds.

Unions also recognize that strikes are bad for recruiting new members. Although the United Automobile Workers Union membership began rising in 1998 for the first time in 10 years to about 780,000 members, it is less than half the 1970 level of 1.6 million. Many of the people the UAW wants to recruit as new members are turned off by strikes.

The former president of the UAW, Douglas Fraser, thinks globalization has caused workers to realize their well being is tied to the survival of their employer. Mr. Fraser finds strikes are very negative for unorganized workers and it is their fear of strikes which contributes to their not joining unions.[15]

Picketing

Another union tactic is picketing. In picketing, the employees on strike advertise their position by discouraging others from entering the plant. Picketing usually takes place at the plant or company entrances, and makes for good media coverage. Pickets can result in financial losses for a firm, and may cause a plant shutdown if a majority of employees refuse to cross the picket line. During the machinists' strike of Eastern Airlines, the pilots and flight attendants honored the picket lines of the machinists, causing the airline severe financial losses.

Sickout

When the union and management are negotiating and the discussions drag on with no immediate agreement in sight, union members may suddenly call in sick and do not report for work. The employer is caught off guard as production and/or services slow to a crawl and customers' complaints soar.

The union leadership claims they have no part in this event. In due time, good health returns and so do the stricken employees with the point made as negotiations continue.

An example of this tactic recently took place between Northwest Airlines and the union representing the flight attendants. With their contract negotiations stalled, the flight attendants suddenly became ill and did not report for work. The result was many cancelled flights and very upset customers. This increase in illness was much higher than normal, prompting a Northwest Airlines spokesperson to call it "guerrilla warfare."

The local union officials protested stating their members had been advised not to participate in any illegal job actions such as not reporting to work or a slow down. However, a federal judge was not convinced and issued a temporary restraining order requiring the union to stop the flight attendants from staging a "sickout."[16]

Boycotting

Boycotting involves union members actively refusing to patronize the company—refusing to purchase the employer's products or services. The union tries to get public support for the boycott, placing economic pressure on the company. For example, the farm workers used media pressure to get consumers to stop buying fruits and vegetables.

Collective Bargaining Issues

The major factors covered in collective bargaining include the following:

1. *Wages.* These include basic wage rates, cost-of-living adjustments (COLAs), wage differentials, overtime pay rates, and two-tier wage systems.
2. *Economic benefits.* These include pension plans, paid vacations, paid holidays, and health insurance plans.
3. *Institutional.* These include the rights and duties of employers, employees, and unions, including union security (i.e., union membership as a condition of employment).
4. *Administrative.* These include seniority issues, employee discipline and discharge procedures, and employee health and safety.

Although the last two issues are important, wages and benefits are usually the most critical during contract negotiations.

GRIEVANCE PROCEDURE

If an employee believes that the labor contract has been violated, then the employee files a **grievance.** A grievance is a formal complaint regarding the event, action, or practice which violated the contract. The primary purpose of the grievance is to determine whether the labor contract has been violated.

Grievance procedures include (1) how the grievance is to be filed, (2) the steps in the process, (3) identifying representatives from each side, and (4) a specified time within which the grievance must be resolved or taken to the next level. Any failure to comply with time limits or due process may result in loss of the grievance.

TWENTY-FIRST CENTURY TRENDS

There are continual changes to the management-union relations environment. The restructuring trend, caused by economic recession and foreign competition, forced unions and management to change their old relationships. As a result, there has been a move away from the traditional adversarial bargaining relationship toward a more collaborative, problem-solving relationship.

The cooperation and collaboration trends of the mid-1990s issues continue to describe union-management relations in the twenty-first century. This collaboration includes employee representation on the board of directors, committees with employee representation, shop committees, department committees, or quality circles. However, there are still some problems. For instance, a ruling by the National Labor Relations Board imposed limits on worker-management teams. The NLRB ordered DuPont to disband seven safety and fitness committees, ruling they were illegal labor organizations because their decisions required management approval and undermined the authorized bargaining union.[17]

Worker-management committees are not of recent origin, forming almost a century ago. They reappeared about 20 years ago as American businesses attempted to respond to the threat of Japanese imports. Today some 80 percent of *Fortune* 1,000 companies use work-management committees.[18]

Physicians Unite!

The labor movement is gaining popularity in several sectors of the growing service section of our economy. The twenty-first century may witness some amazing union growth patterns.

"Physicians Unite!" may become the slogan of the next group of trade unionists. The Hippocratic Oath, which reads "With purity and with holiness I will pass my life and practice my Art," may not have the significance today as in yesteryear. The established HMOs, PPOs, case management reviews, and fresh MBAs concentrating on the bottom line have created doctors who are militant and feel they are being victimized.

In mid-1999, the American Medical Association (AMA) at its annual convention, voted to sponsor a doctor's union.[19] The AMA also approved measures that will provide physicians with collective bargaining rights. AMA members voted to end their long-standing opposition to unionization and to establish a labor organization for physician employees (presently physicians in private practice are subject to antitrust laws and cannot form unions) and medical residents. They also voted to lobby for new laws that would allow private practice physicians to set up local "joint negotiating units."

Texas Governor George W. Bush signed a bill in mid-1999 to give doctors the right to become members of joint negotiating units in communities where a health plan has enough market power to increase the cost or reduce patient care availability.[20]

Joining the AMA in their endorsement of unions is the American Nurses Association (ANA), which is expected to witness a "surge" of nurses beginning organizational efforts. A new union was formed, the United American Nurses (UAN), with voluntary membership for all the state nurses associations. The plan for UAN is to resolve internal problems between nurses with and without collective bargaining differences.[21]

American Union Growth

For unions in the United States, the big question for the twenty-first century is whether union growth will continue. The National Labor Relations reports that unions won more representative elections in 1998 than the previous year and official data indicates this trend continuing.

The AFL-CIO contributes the increase to success in particular industries such as health care. Apparently as a reaction to managed care, hospital workers are joining unions at an "unprecedented rate."[22]

This optimistic union view results from several factors. For instance, a victory by the International Union of Electronic, Electrical, Salaried, Machine and Furniture Workers (IUE) over Osram Sylvania of Massachusetts after a 3-year legal battle. The IUE's victory is one of their biggest membership increases in years and adds to its recent number of successes.[23]

Unions expect to win big with the arrival of gambling in Detroit, Michigan. There are four unions involved in the casino council: United Auto Workers, International Brotherhood of Teamsters, International Union of Operating Engineers, and the Hotel Employees and Restaurant Employees International Union. These four unions expect to gain 8,000 to 13,000 members in Detroit's new casino industry.[24]

Delta Airlines is largely nonunion. The Transport Workers Union (TWU) is attempting to unionize the ramp workers, mechanics, ticket agents, and flight attendants. The TWU is receiving support for the very first time from a powerful group which has previously remained aloof from the organizing campaign: the Airline Pilots Association which represents Delta's 9,000 unionized pilots.[25]

At the eight campuses of the University of California, there are 10,200 graduate student employees. They have voted to affiliate with the United Auto Workers. There are similar organizing campaigns at approximately 26 other college campuses in the United States. If they all join, that would triple the number of campuses with graduate school union members.[26]

Even the employees at the Securities and Exchange Commission (SEC) are attempting to organize. The employees have approached the National Treasury Employees Union (NTE) to represent them. The NTE already represents 150,000 employees at the Internal Revenue Service, Federal Communications Commission, and the Federal Deposit Insurance Corporation.

The SEC is not the usual place for union activity. Approximately 80 percent of the employees are professionals, mostly lawyers.[27]

The future face of the American union movement growth in the twenty-first century may be in WashTech, the high-tech equivalent of a labor union. WashTech was started by three contingent (temporary workers) about 2 years ago at Microsoft. They were concerned about pay and benefits for the large number of temporary employees, about 30 percent of the workforce. The idea has spread to several parts of the country.[28]

WashTech has now become the Washington Alliance of Technology Workers and is actively trying to persuade temporary workers to form a union.

They are accusing Microsoft of violating a State of Washington law requiring employers to make personnel files available to employees. Microsoft states they are not the temp's employers, the employers are the contingent staffing agencies who supply them with the temps. Many of the temps have worked for Microsoft for years and are known as "permatemps."[29]

Microsoft has lost a number of important court decisions and the final resolution is proceeding through the federal court system, a process that is expected to continue into the mid-twenty-first century. If the court decisions do continue to favor the Washington Alliance of Technology Workers Union, it may be the membership comeback unions have been looking for and it will be via the hi-tech route.[30]

A recent article in *HR Magazine* suggests unions in the United States could be staging a comeback. This position is the result of many recent union organizing victories, labor's renewed emphasis on recruiting and unlikely coalitions with religious groups.

Further support is provided in a poll by a research organization conducted in the spring of 1999, which found 43 percent of employees surveyed would vote for a union where they worked. This represents an increase from 39 percent in the mid-1990s and 30 percent in 1984.

The article concludes HR professionals should keep current with these union activities. They will need to ensure their companies keep and maintain working environments which will eliminate employees' need for union representation.[31]

German Union Memberships Decline

The world's last powerful labor unions in Germany are in decline. This is the result of high wages, rigid labor rules, global competition, new technology, and free markets. For years Germany's trade unions maintained their clout as United States and British unions weakened.

However, German unions still remain powerful with half the workers in Western Germany and a quarter in the old East covered by union contracts. Yet the decline is apparent with a loss of 3.5 million union members since 1991. This has cut the proportion to one in four workers in unions from one in three. In the United States the proportion is one in seven workers are union members.

A contributing reason for this decline is the goals and methods of the unions are out of touch with the businesses their union members work for. Unlike unions in the United States that are adjusting to changing conditions, Germany unions are stuck on such issues of politics and class struggle. The question is whether the German unions will change and remain powerful.[32]

UNIONS AND QUALITY-OF-WORKLIFE ISSUES

As discussed earlier, quality-of-worklife (QWL) issues continue to be an important element in union-management relationship (see Figure 13.3). Some QWL programs—such as job redesign efforts, self-managed work teams, and quality circles (QCs)—

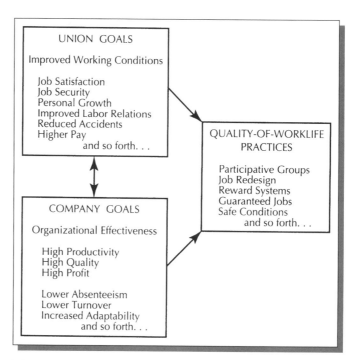

Figure 13.3
Union/management quality-of-worklife issues
Source: Adapted from C. C. Hain and W. O. Eistein, "Quality of Work Life (QWL): What Can Unions DO?" *SAM Advanced Management Journal,* Spring 1990, p. 19.

have elicited negative union responses. Often union membership opposes any negotiated worker involvement programs. The union members often fear that management will use these programs to reduce employment, increase workloads, and to minimize the union. Management neglect in not inviting union participation is a contributing factor in the failure of many QWL programs. In general, in a union firm, management needs to proceed more cautiously when implementing the QWL programs than in nonunion firms.

Living Wage Movement

The City of Tucson, Arizona, has become the thirty-ninth city to join the living wage movement. This requires local companies within the Tucson city limits to pay workers a minimum wage of at least $8.00 an hour versus the federal minimum wage (as of November 1999) of $5.15 an hour.

Unions, churches, and community groups are the spirit behind the movement. They say these laws are needed because workers can't live on the minimum wage. Campaigns are under way in 50 municipalities across the country. An economics professor at the University of Massachusetts-Amherst reports the movement has a "pretty strong momentum."[33]

SUMMARY

This chapter has focused on stage five of the Success System Model: maintenance of a high-performing system, discussing several key employee relations issues. This is important, because employees are usually attracted to form unions because of dissatisfaction with conditions, pay, or a perceived feeling of being powerless to change. In general, the goal of unions is to improve economic and working conditions of employees.

Historically, unions and organizations have formed an adversarial relationship because their goals are usually in conflict. There is every indication that unions and management have begun to cooperate to achieve mutually agreed-upon goals. Union and management relationships are reaching a critical point. Increasing costs and global competition have resulted in a greater emphasis upon strategic goals of survival.

The direction union relations will take is not clear. Workers continue to express dissatisfaction about their jobs and job security. The question remains whether employees believe unions can bring about changes. Certainly, unions will continue to represent workers' economic concerns; however, the future impact of unions is uncertain.

The general perception is that unions have been responsible for many of the labor problems in the auto and steel industries. The union problems emerge at a time of increasing competitive pressures requiring a more flexible organization. Long-term union contracts often restrict an employer's ability to downsize workforce levels, use part-time employment, change work rules, close inefficient plants, and other options.

As an HR manager, you will have to operate in a dynamic and changing environment, and consequently must develop proactive employee relations programs. You have been introduced to the emerging field of employee unions and management, and how collective bargaining is used to improve organizational effectiveness. As a human resource manager, you need to be sensitive to changes in markets, people, and competition, as well as being aware of the need for an adaptive and flexible organization. You will have an opportunity to experience the need for human resource skills in this class meeting. The rising costs of labor, union conflict, and other employee issues are posing a major challenge to the HR manager. In the HRM Skills Simulation, you will have a chance to practice developing a bargaining situation. You may find that an equitable program is not a simple process, because it includes both costs to the organization and employee needs. Because of the costs involved, the legal complexity, and employee demands, this will likely be an area of continuing problems.

REVIEW QUESTIONS

1. In your opinion, what is the single most important factor in making unions attractive? Has this changed?
2. Present examples of how employee unions are used in organizations you have worked for.
3. Do you feel employee unionization is an important factor in choosing an employer?
4. Why are the costs of union management conflict rising so rapidly, and what can an organization do?
5. Discuss and explain the basic collective bargaining approaches or program. Do you agree with this approach?
6. Read a book or view a video movie, and identify some element of union-management relations in an organization.

KEY WORDS AND CONCEPTS

Define and be able to use the following:

- Arbitrators
- Authorization Card
- Bargaining Unit
- Bargaining Zone
- Boycotting

- Collective Bargaining
- Consent Election
- Decertification Election
- Grievance
- Lockout

- Pattern Bargaining
- Stipulation Election
- Strike
- Union Relations Process
- Union Shop

HRM SKILLS SIMULATION 13.1: UNITED ELECTRICAL MOTORS

A. PURPOSES

The purpose of this HRM Skills Simulation is to experience and observe how union management relations affect individuals' response to dramatic change by

1. Increasing awareness of the dynamics of competition and collaboration in union negotiations.
2. Experiencing the effects of the use of influence in union-management situations.
3. Exploring the effects of role expectations on behavior and reactions in win-lose situations.

B. PROCEDURES

Step 1. Prior to class, form groups of five. Select one role from the following:

1. CEO/President
2. Vice president, human resource management
3. Vice president, manufacturing

4. Business agent of local union
5. Shop steward
6. Observer

Any extras act as observers.

Group size: Groups of five members each.

Time required: 1 hour

ROLE DESCRIPTIONS
(READ *ONLY* YOUR ROLE. READ PRIOR TO CLASS)

Role 1—CEO/President. You want to move to the Newtown facility as soon as possible so your company can begin manufacturing electric motors with the least disruption. The Newtown site has an industrial park with several excellent manufacturing facilities available for immediate lease. The manufacturing VP has made a detailed report to you indicating the advantages of moving to Newtown. These advantages include a nonunion environment, significantly lower manufacturing costs, closer to prime customers, closer to major suppliers, closer to recreation areas, lower utility costs, ample skilled low-cost labor pool, cheaper housing, lower taxes, and an almost zero crime rate. You support the manufacturing VP's report, and believe United Electrical Motors should develop a strategic plan to make the move as soon as possible. You consider any problems to be minor and can be resolved quickly.

Role 2—Vice president, human resource management. You support the move to Newtown for sound economic reasons, but believe the company needs to consider some unexplored costs. Although the manufacturing VP briefly included you in his plan, there were many of your concerns which were not considered. The union contract includes severance costs and early retirement pension costs. The company needs to know how many employees will move and how many will elect not to. There is also a need for a skills inventory to determine the number of employees who will be replaced and whether there are similar skills in Newtown. Will the company have a two-tier pay schedule to reflect lower labor costs in Newtown? If Newtown cannot supply certain labor skills, the company may have to offer present employees inducements to move. This could include guaranteeing the sale of their present homes, moving allowances, full or partial temporary housing costs, and planning the move during their school's summer vacation schedule.

A hidden agenda is the reaction of the union. You know they have not been consulted on this and the grapevine will certainly pick it up within a few days. Suppose the union views this as a union busting attempt. The resulting legal problems could completely stall what will be very delicate negotiations. You are also concerned about child-care facilities in Newtown and the quality of their schools. At present, United Electrical Motors meets all EEO requirements. But the move to Newtown may complicate this situation. You need to make clear to all concerned the necessity of including the human resource management department in all future company planning, including the proposed move to Newtown.

Role 3—Manufacturing vice president. You have been working closely with the CEO on his plan. Your staff group has researched the proposed move, and you presented the data to the CEO. You have touched base with the human resource management vice president, but have had no contact with the business agent of the local union. Because you were under a strict time constraint and it is only a proposal, you have limited your communication channels.

Role 4—Business agent of the local union. You have just received a memo from the CEO of United Electrical Motors, asking you to be present at a meeting in his office tomorrow. Not only is it short notice, but it is one of the few memos you have ever received from him. You notice the memo was also sent to some of the company's vice presidents, so it must be very important. Your first thought is downsizing, yet business has been good. Perhaps the company is being merged. You really have no idea what is going on.

Role 5—Shop steward. The business agent just called and notified you that you are to be present at the CEO meeting and wants your input. You know nothing. The grapevine has rumors of a proposed move. If so, you want to fight for higher pay, moving costs, and job security. However, many employees enjoy living in the present community, and have deep roots in the area. You feel something major is in the works.

Role 6—Role of observer. Observers indicate their reaction to the group performance.

OBSERVER FORM

Instructions: For each item, place a number in the blank to the right representing your reaction to how your group performed based on the following scale.

Low   1 : 2 : 3 : 4 : 5 : 6 : 7 : 8 : 9 : 10   High

1. Degree of cooperative teamwork: _____
2. Degree of team motivation: _____
3. Degree of member satisfaction: _____
4. Degree of information sharing (participation):   _____
5. Degree of consensual decision making: _____
6. Degree of team conflict or competition (i.e., conflict directly faced and resolved):   _____
7. Degree of quality of group decisions: _____
8. Degree of speed with which decision is made: _____
9. Degree of participating leadership   _____
10. Degree of clarity of goals: _____

                                         Total ranking   _____

Step 2. Meeting. The purpose of this planning period is to determine the strategic plan for United Electric Motors' proposed move to Newtown. The CEO and president will open the meeting with an overview of the proposed change, and then ask for input. You will need to develop a strategy to attempt to achieve your interests as indicated your role. Three possible strategies include collaboration (mutual support), bargaining (making deals), and coercion (threats of punishment), or combinations of these strategies. (See Table 13.1.)

In this step, complete the following tasks:

1. Discuss your reactions to the company's proposed move. What are your self-interests?
2. Now agree on the team's self-interests. What are the team's priorities?

Employ your chosen tactics to achieve your strategy. Finally, reach a team consensus on the proposed move.

3. Observers report their reaction to their group's performance using the Observer Form.

Time suggested for Step 2: 40 minutes

Step 3. Individual Team Presentations and Agreement

1. Each team will present their strategic plan for United Electric Motors' proposed move to Newtown.
2. After each team has presented its strategic plan, compare similarities and differences between plans.
3. Attempt to obtain the team's agreement for a single strategic plan.

Time suggested for Step 3: 50 minutes.

Table 13.1
Negotiation strategies

Collaborative Strategy (Win-Win):

To build a cohesive, united force (coalition) out of two or more individual team members, you will need to develop and use such skills as:

1. Risk-taking, trust-building, establishing credibility

2. Sharing and using member resources, consensus-seeking

3. Sharing self-interests, openness

4. Listening and communicating skills

5. Joint goal-setting, planning, organizing

6. Value clarification

Bargaining Strategy:

If you are to be successful in negotiating, you will need to develop and use such skills as:

1. Bargaining without selling out

2. Making the first demand as high as the facts will justify

3. Seeking opportunities to turn a trade-off into a win-win situation

Coercive Strategy:

If you are to be successful in using coercion, you will need to develop optimum skills consistent with your self-interest. These may include:

1. Overwhelming opponents with superior force and greater speed

2. Exploiting the weaknesses of other groups

3. Using good timing to shock or surprise

4. Making convincing threats

Case 13.1: The Northwest Freight Line

INTRODUCTION

Allen Yates, the division manager of the Northwest Freight Line, hired Dave Keller to be human resource manager for the Medford Freight Terminal. (See Figure 13.3.) Dave Keller is a recent graduate of State University, and his human resource management experience was limited to only 3 years as an HRM intern at a regional truck freight company. Yates believed Dave demonstrated he has the ability to act intelligently, rationally, and quickly in a crisis. Dave was advised that his selection was based on his being single, being willing to accept a temporary position, and able to make independent decisions.

BACKGROUND

Dave was hired as HR manager due in part to his youth and his physical condition needed to stand the stress of the position. The previous HR manager had a heart attack on the job and was unable to return to work.

HUMAN RESOURCE MANAGEMENT DEPARTMENT

Dave's responsibility included supervising a staff of four performing the HRM functions of recruiting, selecting, performance appraisals, and local training. The headquarters HRM staff had overall responsibility, but concentrated on wage and salary, EEO compliance, manpower planning, labor relations, and benefits.

As Dave studied the operation of the Medford Freight Terminal, he noticed countless instances of overstaffing. There seemed to be many people sitting around, waiting for something to happen. Although terminal staffing requirements were not his prime responsibility, he wondered what action, if any, he should take?

In talking with supervisors, he found a lack of understanding of EEO requirements. No one had even heard of the EEO Compliance Guidelines. As far as he could determine, there were very few women and minority employees. Those he did see appeared to be in the lowest paid positions.

Another area of concern was the lack of adequate job descriptions. They all appeared to be written 30 years ago. When he questioned the supervisors and employees, the general response was they always performed the job and were all too busy to update paperwork. Dave wondered how they could hire qualified new employees, how they would write the annual performance appraisals, and how they would promote the best people into jobs which were overpaid or underpaid. After checking the pay ratings, it appeared there were no underpaid jobs—only overpaid jobs. No wonder everyone seemed happy with the system. Now he understood why those job satisfaction surveys originating from the headquarters HRM department were so high for the Medford Freight Terminal.

Dave sat at his desk, wondering what he should do to correct the HRM problems he had encountered. Because apparently the status quo had been going on for years, maybe he should leave well enough alone. However, there is scheduled next month a meeting for all the freight terminal HR managers at the company's headquarters. Perhaps he should wait and determine the headquarters' environment before proceeding. However, before making a final decision, Dave decided to gather more information and have an action plan ready for next month's meeting.

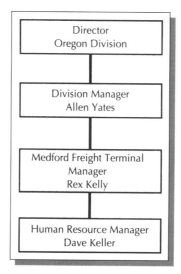

Figure 13.4
Organizational chart: Northwest Freight Line

QUESTIONS

1. What should Dave do—act or wait?
2. Regarding Dave's action plan, to what extent should he involve the branch personnel?
3. What should Dave do regarding his division manager? Confide in Allen Yates his concerns, or proceed on his own initiative?
4. What should Dave do about the problems he saw regarding overstaffing, EEO, job descriptions, performance appraisals, and promotions? Act now, or wait until next month's meeting?

ENDNOTES

1. Wire Reports. "GE Plans to Cut Indiana Jobs, Move Some Work to Mexico," Inside Briefcase, *The Oregonian*, 10 September 1999, p. B2.
2. Rebecca Blumenstein, "AT&T Freezes New Hiring; Layoffs May Follow," *The Wall Street Journal*, 15 September 1999, p. A3.
3. Pailthorp Bellamy, "Safe Landing for Boeing," *U.S. News and World Report* (September 13, 1999): 43.
4. David G. Epstein and Miles Z. Epstein, "Hand in Hand," *HR Magazine* (July 1998): 103–08.
5. Bill Leonard, "The New Face of Organized Labor," *HRM Magazine* (July 1999): 55–65.
6. Nancy Cleeland, "Union Ranks Up in '99, Led by California," *Los Angeles Times*, 20 January 2000, p. A1.
7. Carlos Tejada, "Employers and Unions Chew on New Salting Rules," Work Week, *The Wall Street Journal*, 6 June 2000, p. A1.
8. Adam Ritt, "This Year's Bargaining Pattern," *New Steel* 15, no. 6 (June 1999): 2.
9. Stephanie Overman, "Caterpillar and UAW Agree to Mediation," *HR News* 11, no. 5 (May 1992).
10. Ross Stagner and Hjalmar Rosen, *Psychology of Union-Management Relations* (Belmont, CA: Wadsworth, 1965): 95–97.
11. From Staff and Wire Reports, "UAW workers at Ford Motor Company overwhelmingly approve contract," Briefcase, *The Oregonian*, 27 October 1999, p. B1.
12. The Associated Press, "Boeing Will Grant Benefits to Same-Sex Partners," *The Sunday Oregonian*, 24 October 1999, p. C6.
13. David Leonhardt, Aaron Bernstein, and Wendy Zellner, *Business Week*, no. 318 (March 1, 1999): 38.
14. Jennie Walsh, "Barclays Unveils Landmark Pay and Partnership Deal," *People Management* no. 4 (February 25, 1999): 13.
15. Jeffrey, Ball, Glenn Burkins, and Gregory L. White, "Why Labor Unions Have Grown Reluctant to Use the 'S' Word," *The Wall Street Journal*, 16 December 1999, p. A1.
16. Associated Press, "Northwest Union Ordered to Halt 'Sickout,'" *Los Angeles Times*, Briefly, January 6, 2000, p. C4.
17. J. Shiver, Jr., "NLRB Orders DuPont to Deal Directly With Union," *Los Angeles Times*, 8 June 1993, p. D1.
18. Ibid. p. D11.
19. Josh Fischman, "Physicians Unite!" *U.S. News and World Report* (July 5, 1999): 51.
20. Allison Bell, "National Underwriter," *Life and Health Financial Services Edition* 103, no. 26 (June 28, 1999): 1.
21. J. Moore and I. Duncan, "ANA to Form a Collective Bargaining Unit," *Modern Healthcare* 29, no. 26 (June 28, 1999): 3.
22. "Unions See More Election Victories in 1998," Knight Rider News Service, *The Oregonian*, 10 August 1999, p. A1.
23. Glenn Burkins, "Light Bulb Maker Agrees to Recognize Union After Three-Year Fight," Work Week, *The Wall Street Journal*, 5 October 1999, p. A1.
24. Glenn Burkins, "Labor Unions Win Big as Gambling Arrives in Detroit," Work Week, *The Wall Street Journal*, 10 August 1999, p. A1.
25. Martha Brannigan, "Delta's Pilots Union is Supporting Drive to Organize Many of the Other Workers," *The Wall Street Journal*, 11 August 1999, p. A2.
26. Albert R. Kan, "Graduate-Student," Work Week, *The Wall Street Journal*, 29 June 1999, p. A1.
27. Michael Schroeder, "SEC Immersed in Testy Effort by Employees to Unionize," *The Wall Street Journal*, 10 August 1999, p. C1.
28. Mark Boardman, "Unions Go Hi-Tech," *HR Magazine* (May 1999): 160.
29. Rachel Zimmerman, "Permatemps Seek Access to Reviews," *The Wall Street Journal*, 27 October 1999, p. NW1.
30. Wire Reports, "Microsoft Records on Temps Show Evasion of Laws, Alliance Says," *The Wall Street Journal*, 28 October 1999, p. B1.
31. Sharon Leonard, "Unions Could Be Staging a Comeback," *HR Magazine* (December 1999): 207.
32. Cecilie Rohwedder, "Once the Big Muscle of German Industry, Unions See It all Sag," *The Wall Street Journal*, 29 November 1999, p. A1.
33. James P. Miller, Tucson Becomes the 39th City to Join the Living Wage Movement, Work Week, *The Wall Street Journal*, 12 October 1999, p. A1.

Chapter 14

The Success System: Employee Safety and Health

Objectives

Upon completing this chapter, you will be able to:

1. Define and discuss the concepts of safety, health, and stress in the workplace.
2. Describe the stages and objectives of a health and safety program.
3. Understand the relationship of wellness programs to goals of employee satisfaction and productivity.
4. Identify and describe job stress warning signs and techniques to develop stress relief programs.
5. Define and discuss the requirements of OSHA and its impact on the organization.

Premeeting preparation

1. Read chapter 14.
2. Prepare for HRM Skills Simulation 14.1. Read Parts A and B, Step 1 and Step 2.
3. Read Case 14.1: Precision Products, Inc. Answer questions.

One of the industry trends continuing in the twenty-first century is the interest in safety, health, and well-being. More Americans (as well as in other countries) are participating in sports, jogging, aerobics, and joining health clubs. Many organizations see benefits in having a safe workplace and a healthier workforce.

The number of American workers who died from injuries received at work in 1998 was the lowest since the Labor Department started keeping records in 1992. According to the agency's Bureau of Labor Statistics, job-related deaths in American industries were down from 6,238 in 1997 to 6,026 in 1998. However, this still represents about 17 fatal injuries each day of the year.

The second leading cause of on-the-job deaths after injuries is homicide. This category also decreased and accounted for much of the overall decline. In 1997 there were 860 people murdered at work, compared to 709 in 1988.[1]

There are usually 6.8 million incidents of occupational injury or illness per year. Approximately 25 percent of Americans with disabilities are injured each year because of a work-related accident or illness. Over 400,000 people per year contract diseases or illnesses considered as related to their occupations.

Consequently, an increasing number of firms are realizing that they can improve the workplace by offering effective employee health and safety programs. Every year, over $25 billion in costs are expended because of employee illness and injury. Employee safety and health programs are becoming more important due to the costs, the increasing legal requirements, and the increased employee moral and productivity that result from a healthier workforce.

In this chapter, we present stage five of the Success System: workplace safety and health. An unsafe work will have a negative effect on the employee's ability and motivation to be productive. This chapter will cover the current issues related to employee safety and health and discuss some of the innovative steps organizations are taking to improve their employee safety and health performance records.

THE CHALLENGE OF SAFETY MANAGEMENT

The challenge of safety management presents the human resource professional with the opportunity to achieve humanitarian goals, while obtaining significant cost reductions for the organization. The suffering and trauma resulting from job-related accidents and deaths is probably impossible for the average person to comprehend. Although these human costs are incalculable, the dollar costs of occupational accidents and disease in the United States are estimated by the National Safety Council to average $25 billion annually. It is also estimated occupational accidents result in 10,000 deaths a year and 6 million injuries. Not included in these estimates is the toll from the resulting stress and lowering of the quality of life in the workplace.

The high number of accidents is not due to a lack of effort by many organizations and concerned companies: the National Safety Council, insurance companies' accident prevention programs, state safety inspectors, the American Society of Safety Engineers, the Industrial Medical Association, and the American Industrial Hygiene Association all work for greater safety. Yet, despite the activities of these groups, the high accident rate in manufacturing continues, as does the number of occupational diseases.

Occupational Safety and Health Act

These conditions prompted Congress to pass the **Occupational Safety and Health Act (OSHA)** authorizing the federal government, through the Department of Labor, to establish and enforce occupational safety and health standards as they apply to private business. OSHA functions as an agency within the Department of Labor and covers more than 4 million private business firms that affect interstate commerce. The law also established the National Institute for Occupational Safety and Health (NIOSH) in the Department of Health, Education, and Welfare. NIOSH carries out safety experiments, sets criteria standards, and researches hazardous substances. It is interesting to note that after more than a decade of OSHA, the results are mixed: The number of nonfatal cases without lost workdays has decreased, but the number of lost workdays has increased.

OSHA has been active in inspecting work sites to make the workplace safer. In 1998, a total of $79 million in penalties was levied. With 2 months left in fiscal year 1999, penalties already totaled $75 million with a total of 34,000 inspections scheduled. The most frequently found serious violations were scaffolding fall protection and hazard communication.[2]

Occupational Disease

The incidence of occupational disease is a large problem, and some experts predict it will become even more significant in the future. About 13,000 known toxic chemicals are now in general use, and approximately 500 new substances are being introduced each year. Unfortunately, OSHA has been slow to establish standards on these substances, owing to a lack of funding. It has been estimated that, based on the present progress of OSHA, it will take another 100 years to establish standards on existing chemicals, and progress in standards on the continuing growth of new chemicals is nonexistent. The range of health hazards includes physical, such as heat and noise; chemical, such as gases or dust; biological, such as bacteria; and psychological, such as stress.

Human resource managers may not be doctors, electricians, plumbers, or safety engineers, but as the person responsible for the safety and health of company employees, they must interact with these groups. Even in larger firms, where human resource professionals do not directly supervise the safety and health functions, the ultimate responsibility is still theirs. This is particularly true when it comes to ensuring compliance with new laws and regulations.

The importance of safety, health, and working conditions for the employer and employee is receiving even more emphasis. This is the result of continuing government regulations and a greater awareness by management of how safety costs can adversely affect a company's competitiveness in a global economy. One example would be Weyerhaeuser Company, where the company's philosophy on preventing on-the-job injuries changed from a treatment to a preventative approach, resulting in an annual savings of approximately $20 million, not counting the additional savings of reducing time-loss accidents and lost workdays.

Safety Costs

There is an increasing awareness of top management for the health and safety of their employees. As noted, safety violations can result in criminal charges and financial losses for unsafe companies. Thousands of deaths, injuries, and illnesses occur because of safety violations, poor equipment design, or negligence.

The death and accident figures vary among industries. The most dangerous jobs include mining, construction, firefighting, and positions working at the flour mill, in sheet metal, lumber, and forestry, and manufacturing or petrochemicals. According to OSHA records, the most hazardous major industry in the United

States is meatpacking: Meatpacking employees have four times more injuries than the national average. The American workplace is safer today than it was a half century ago, but there is still a need for improvement. There are over 50,000 different chemicals in common workplace use today. The majority of these have not been tested for toxicity, and no regulatory restraints control their use. Many new materials are being introduced into the workplace at an alarming rate, with little or no knowledge of possible effects on worker health.

Another increasing health problem is referred to as **repetitive trauma disorder.** One Labor Department study reported that repetitive trauma disorder accounted for over 60 percent of the 6.8 million job-related injuries. Another study concluded that workplace stress is reaching epidemic proportions because of company restructuring, increasing work demands, layoffs, job conflicts with family obligations, and so forth.

In the next section, we will review the major legislation related to health and safety, basic programs which organizations are using to reduce accidents and injuries, and the current employee health and safety programs.

Workers' Compensation

As noted earlier (see chapter 11), workers' compensation is a federally mandated insurance program based on the concept of "liability without fault," which provides that workers who are victims of work-related injury or illness are granted benefits regardless of who is responsible for the accident. This means that if an organization participates in the workers' compensation system, a worker may not sue the employer for negligence, even if the injury was clearly the employer's fault. On the other hand, even careless or accident-prone workers are generally covered by workers' compensation, and injuries that are the result of coworkers' negligence are also covered. Some state laws, however, deny benefits if the worker was under the influence of alcohol or controlled substances (illegal drugs) when the injury occurred.

Although workers' compensation laws have encouraged efforts to improve health and safety records, the outcomes of such efforts have not been very impressive. Many states took matters into their own hands in an effort to do more in this area, creating a myriad of rules and regulations. The result was a lack of uniformity in policies and regulations across the states, a situation which prompted political pressure from numerous constituencies (particularly unions) for a federal law aimed primarily at the reduction and prevention of occupational fatalities, injuries, and illnesses. The result of the pressure was the passage of OSHA.

The Occupational Safety and Health Administration Act

The safety and health standards that are to be met originate with federal, state, and local authorities. Perhaps the most important of these is the federal law, the Williams-Steiger Occupational Safety and Health Act of 1970, sometimes called the Job Safety Act. The provisions of the Job Safety Act are administered by the Occupational Safety and Health Administration (OSHA) in the United States Department of Labor. Practically all employers must obey OSHA regulations or similar rules established by state law. The Job Safety Act establishes three types of standards: initial standards, permanent standards, and a standard interestingly called "emerging temporary."

The initial standards apply to general industry and include national consensus standards set by various industrial institutes representing different producing organizations and those standards already established by federal agencies prior to the Job Safety Act.

The permanent standards are established by a rulemaking committee after input by interested parties presented at open hearings, with the final result published in the *Federal Register.*

The emergency temporary standard results when OSHA believes a new hazard exists or there is grave danger from toxic substances and is effective immediately upon publication in the *Federal Register*. OSHA then has 6 months to make the standard permanent following the procedure in the paragraph above.

The Job Safety Act has a general duty clause. Although employers must comply with OSHA regulations, in the absence of such regulations, they are still under the obligation to provide a safe and healthful workplace free from recognized hazards liable to cause death or serious harm. Coverage of OSHA, which extends to virtually all employers and their employees in the United States, is provided either directly by federal OSHA or through an OSHA-approved state program (21 states have their own programs).

Standards

OSHA is responsible for developing enforceable safety standards. It is the employer's responsibility to become familiar with the standards applicable to their establishments and to ensure that employees have and use personal protective gear and equipment when required for safety. Where OSHA has not promulgated specific standards, employers are responsible for following the act's general duty clause. What is a recognized hazard? OSHA defines such hazards as commonly known in the particular industry and can be determined through accepted tests. This is a rather wide-open definition and places the employer at risk.

The OSHA definition of causing death or serious harm also creates employer concern, as these are gray areas. Further, the definition states "likely to cause death or serious harm" but with no time frame. When is an injury serious or not? What about toxic substances that may cause harm after exposure over many years? Congress has debated this general duty issue with little concrete clarification. Violations of the general duty clause are considered by OSHA to be as serious as if one were violating a specific standard. If the state's safety and health plan is approved by OSHA, then the employer must abide by state standards, not federal standards. However, the employer must allow OSHA inspections and continue to submit certain reports to OSHA. OSHA has greatly expanded its role in protecting workers from hazardous materials. Maximum exposure limits were set for 164 substances for the first time, and limits were tightened for 212 others. The limits cover the maximum amount a worker can be exposed to during an 8-hour workday. Among the substances regulated for the first time were wood dust, grain dust, gasoline, acrylic acid, tungsten, and welding fumes. OSHA also cut maximum exposure limits for, among other substances, carbon monoxide, chloroform, and hydrogen.

Recordkeeping and Reporting

Before OSHA, no centralized and systematic reporting system existed for monitoring occupational safety and health problems. Statistics on job injuries and illnesses were collected by some states and by private organizations. With OSHA came the first basis for consistent, nationwide procedures—a vital requirement for gauging safety problems and solving them.

What is considered to be an occupational injury or illness? An occupational injury is any injury, such as a cut, fracture, sprain, or amputation, which results from a work-related accident or from exposure involving a single incident in the work environment. An occupational illness is any abnormal condition or disorder, other than one resulting from an occupational injury, caused by exposure to environmental factors associated with employment. Included are acute and chronic illnesses or diseases which may be caused by inhalation, absorption, or ingestion of or direct contact with toxic substances of harmful agents. Alcoholism has even been considered an occupational illness in a case involving an employee who developed an alcohol-related problem as a result of the socializing responsibilities associated with one's job.

All occupational illnesses must be recorded, regardless of severity, if they result in

- Death (must be recorded, regardless of the length of time between the injury and death)
- One or more lost workdays
- Restriction of work or motion
- Loss of consciousness
- Transfer to another job
- Medical treatment (other than first aid)

OSHA Enforcement

Authority to Inspect To enforce its standards, OSHA is authorized to conduct workplace inspections. Every establishment covered by the act is subject to inspection by OSHA compliance safety and health officers (COSHOs), who are chosen for their knowledge and experience in the occupational safety and health field, and trained in OSHA standards and in recognition of safety and health hazards.

OSHA has the right to make unannounced inspections, providing they are at reasonable times and conducted in a reasonable manner. However, the U.S. Supreme Court has ruled, in *Marshall* v. *Barlow's, Inc., 98 SCT 1816* (1978), that employers can deny OSHA inspectors access to the workplace if they do not have search warrants. The OSHA inspection has three parts: the initial conference, where credentials are presented with an explanation about the purpose of the inspection and what it will cover; the actual inspection; and the closing conference.

The actual inspection is called the walkaround. During the walkaround, the inspector may be accompanied by one representative selected by the employees and one from management. Samples may be taken of toxic materials, noise levels recorded, and photographs made of apparent safety hazards. During the inspection, the OSHA inspector may talk to employees about safety practices in private, if necessary, because the law requires employee consultation.

In the closing conference, the inspector will explain any violations or suspect conditions. If a situation of imminent danger exists, the inspector will explain this to the employer and affected employees. Corrective steps will be discussed, which could include civil action in the courts to shut down the dangerous condition. The inspection and enforcement powers of OSHA are very extensive. As a result, employer compliance becomes a matter of survival. With very few exceptions, inspections are conducted without advance notice. In fact, alerting an employer in advance of an OSHA inspection can bring a fine of up to $1000 and/or a 6-month jail term.

If an employer refuses to admit the inspection team, or if an employer attempts to interfere with the inspection, the act permits appropriate legal action. Based on a 1978 U.S. Supreme Court ruling in *Marshall* v. *Barlow's Inc.*, OSHA may not conduct warrantless inspections without an employer's consent. It may, however, inspect after acquiring a judicially authorized search warrant based upon administrative probable cause or upon evidence of a violation. If employees are represented by a recognized bargaining representative, the union ordinarily will designate an employee representative to accompany the compliance officer. Similarly, if there is a plant safety committee, the employee members of that committee will designate the employee representative.

A ready tool available to HRM is the use of job analysis. The usual application of job analysis is considered to be job placement, performance evaluation, and wage/salary compensation. However, it can be used to determine safety requirements for particular jobs. Once determined, these can become part of the job description. Whether a company uses a full-time safety director or depends upon a human resource professional, the usual organizational structure is to use safety committees. These committees may be centralized at the top of the organization, but are usually more decentralized, with many department level committees consisting of employees and their supervisors.

Voluntary Protection Programs

The **Voluntary Protection Programs (VPPs)** are one part of OSHA's effort to extend worker protection beyond the minimum OSHA standards. Such programs are cooperative approaches to help meet the goals of OSHA.

Two VPPs—Star and Merit—are designed to

- Recognize outstanding comprehensive safety and health programs.
- Motivate other companies to achieve excellent safety and health results.
- Establish a cooperative relationship between employers, employees, and OSHA.

The Star program is the most difficult and the most prestigious. It is open to employers in any industry who have successfully managed a comprehensive safety and health program to reduce injury rates below the national average for the industry. The requirements for the Star program include systems for management commitment and responsibility; hazard assessment and control; and safety planning, rules, work procedures, and training. The companies who earned a Star rating include Occidental Chemical, Mobil, Motorola, and Texaco USA.

The Merit program provides entry to Star program participation. Any employer with a basic safety and health program, but who is committed to improving the company's program within a specified period of time, may work with OSHA to develop Star Qualifications. The Merit winning companies include Georgia-Pacific, Rohm-Haas, and Midas International.

When new jobs are created or when new tools or new equipment are purchased, safety becomes a concern at higher management levels and for each department safety committee. Appropriate accident policies and safe work procedures must already be in place before work can begin.

Regular and thorough inspection of the work environment and equipment needs to take place. This can be effectively performed at the department level with supervisors and employees joining together on teams to do the inspecting. There will be a need for keeping checklists and maintaining records. The reason for this is obvious when one considers that OSHA has 250 pages of occupational safety and health standards. Keep in mind that although plant and machine safety equipment as well as personal protective equipment is an engineering and production responsibility, the human resource management department will probably be assigned responsibility for the supply and proper use of such equipment. When OSHA finds an employee not wearing the correct protective equipment, it is the employer who receives the citation and/or fine, not the employee.

Somehow the company has to motivate the employee to work safely and wear the correct protective items. The company cannot afford to be constantly policing their employees for compliance. Employee motivation can be accomplished by including the aspect of safe performance in the training for each and every job, establishing the employee's responsibility for performing that job safely, developing a "safety watch" where each employee looks out for the safety of other employees, including safety as an important part of the employee's performance appraisal records, and involving employees in determining safety procedures—and once safety rules and procedures have been agreed upon, everyone will be expected to conform. Finally, there are no exceptions to the rules, including management.

This all requires constant communication. Safety meetings need to be held weekly to maintain the necessary emphasis on the topic. During safety meetings, employees must be part of the input to identify and correct hazardous conditions. Those "near-miss" accidents should be part of the agenda. The employee membership on the department safety meetings needs to be rotated among the group to maintain the widest indoctrination and input. Employees should be involved in not only the selection of protective clothing, but also in the purchase of equipment with proper safety equipment. Another avenue of employee involvement is a safety suggestion system with incentive awards such as jackets, gloves, and so forth, for usable ideas. Safety and accident prevention also requires a baseline measurement from which to determine the extent of the problem and the progress or lack of progress towards eliminating it.

Injury Rate

The company first needs to determine the actual injury rate down to the department level. The number of injuries and illnesses that have occurred for each year can be determined from the department records. The next step is to determine the number of hours worked by employees for the period being investigated. Exclude hours for vacations, holidays, or time off for illness, even if they have been paid. The base used is 100 full-time employees working 40 hours per week for 50 weeks per year. The base rate is computed as 100 times 40 times 50 equals 200,000. The formula for determining the incidence rate is:

$$\frac{\text{Number of injuries and illnesses} \times 200,000 \text{ (base rate)}}{\text{employee hours worked}} = \text{incidence rate}$$

Two other formulas used in establishing an injury baseline are the injury-frequency rate and the injury-severity rate. The injury-frequency rate is number of injuries per million work hours and is calculated as follows:

$$\frac{\text{Number of injuries during the year} \times 1,000,000 \text{ work hrs}}{100 \text{ workers} \times 40 \text{ hours} \times 52 \text{ weeks}} = \text{injury-severity rate or I.S.R.}$$

The injury-severity rate is the number of days lost per million work hours and is calculated as follows:

$$\frac{\text{Number of workdays lost by injured workers} \times 1,000,000}{100 \text{ workers} \times 40 \text{ hours} \times 52 \text{ weeks}} = \text{injury-severity rate or I.S.R.}$$

These three formulas provide the company with comprehensive information about their employees' illness and injury rate. Once this data has been compiled, it must be analyzed for trouble areas and trends. Finally, and most important, corrective action must be taken.

Every injury will require the completion of an accident report. Such a report includes data about the person injured, the time and place of the accident, witnesses, description of the injury, and cause of the injury as to the work environment and/or the actions of the employee. There should also be a medical report detailing the extent of the injury, probable cause, and recommended steps to prevent reoccurrence. Some companies also require employees to report off-the-job injuries. These are analyzed for frequency and possible disruptive behavior (such as alcohol or drugs) that could later impact on the workplace.

The on- and off-the-job accident reports assist in identifying those individuals who appear to be "accident prone." Although "accident prone" is a misnomer, because people generally do not go through their whole life having accidents, some people do go through certain parts of their lives when they do have more accidents.

This can be due to lack of maturity, inattention, job dissatisfaction, or emotional problems. In any event, these individuals need to be identified for special training, job transfer, or more careful supervision.

Safety training is no different than other forms of training. The prerequisite requirements are: qualified instructors, motivated employees, active participation by the employee during training sessions, and a scheduled program of follow-up and rehiring. Because a new job requires many individual adjustments, Day One is a good time to begin safety training when the new employee is eager and receptive. Older employees may be more difficult to reach and not be as receptive to changing old habits, having developed their own "shortcuts." This situation may only change through more observant supervision and involvement of safety committee workmates.

Safety Discipline

Once the safety rules and regulations have been determined through employee involvement and cooperation and the safety training programs have been implemented, then the final deterrent is safety discipline. The resort to discipline represents a breakdown of employee participation and training. However, it is all that prevents a complete breakdown of safety practices and the resultant human suffering.

The usual sequence of events in safety discipline is similar to other areas of discipline. The level of discipline will depend upon accident frequency and severity. The first step is usually a verbal reprimand, the second step is a written warning with copies to the employee and human resource file, the third step would be written notice of being penalized with time off without pay, and the final step (although rare) would be discharge.

Part of a company's safety program is providing on-site health facilities to treat accidents and to provide any needed rehabilitation. Small companies may only have an unstaffed facility with first aid supplies, though larger companies often have comprehensive medical facilities. Services that are provided may include periodic health examinations, health education, providing a healthy work environment through industrial hygiene and company sanitation, and diagnostic screening.

Federal law requires employers to provide first-aid care for their employees, maintaining a facility with proper equipment to treat accidents likely to occur. Many states have similar laws. OSHA requires someone trained in first-aid to be available if no other medical treatment is available nearby. Larger employers usually maintain a staff of registered nurses, trained first-aid persons, and full-time doctors. Depending upon the number of employees, there will be several first-aid stations located throughout the plant facilities. These stations will include many pieces of medical equipment, such as X-ray machines and sterilizers. Although OSHA does not cite employees for violations of their responsibilities, each employee "shall comply with all occupational safety and health standards and rules, regulations, and orders issued under the Act" that are applicable.

Back on the Job Disability Programs

Aetna, Inc., a large insurance company, is introducing a program to get employees out on disability injuries back on the job sooner. This is an attempt to control disability costs which can amount to 6 percent of a company's payroll, plus an additional cost of nearly 6 percent for overtime and replacement workers.[3]

The program is called HealthWorks and combines elements of managed health care plans with those of disability insurance lines. Aetna believes their program will reduce employers' disability costs up to 20 percent by speeding up the return to work of disabled workers. The plan will also cut costs by identifying potential cases that may require surgery early in the process.[4]

Disability now becomes another disease management program which follows patients through their period of need and back to work. Although health care costs have been steady for 5 years, they are now rising in the twenty-first century.

EMPLOYEES' RIGHTS

Employees have a right to seek safety and health on the job without fear of punishment. That right is spelled out in Section 11(c) of the act.

The law says employers shall not punish or discriminate against workers for exercising rights such as

- Complaining to an employer, union, OSHA, or any other government agency about job safety and health hazards.
- Filing safety or health grievances.
- Participating in a workplace safety and health committee or in union activities concerning job safety and health.
- Participating in OSHA inspections, conferences, or hearings, or other OSHA-related activities.

If an employee is within these OSHA rights, the employer is not allowed to discriminate against that worker in any way, such as by termination, demotion, taking away seniority or other earned benefits, transferring the worker to an undesirable job or shift, or threatening or harassing the worker.

In *Whirlpool* v. *Marshall,* the U.S. Supreme Court ruled in 1981 that, although there is no specific language in the law about walking off a job, employees who have a reasonable apprehension of death or serious injury may refuse to work until that safety hazard is corrected. The employer may not discipline or discharge a worker who exercises this right, although the employer need not pay the worker for the hours not worked.

Employees who find that they have been discriminated against for exercising safety and health rights have to contact the nearest OSHA office within 30 days of the time they learn of the alleged discrimination. The employee does not have to complete any form because OSHA staff members will complete the necessary forms, reporting what happened and who was involved.

After a complaint has been filed, OSHA investigates. If an employee has been illegally reprimanded for exercising safety and health rights, OSHA requests restoration of the worker's job earnings and benefits. If necessary, and if it can prove discrimination, OSHA will take the case to court. One major question, however, is whether the enactment of OSHA has reduced deaths, accidents, or injuries. The data on this question is unclear. It appears that there have been no significant reductions in work-related deaths, illnesses, or injuries since the law took effect. In fact, there has been an increase in injuries and illnesses every year since 1984.

OSHA focuses almost exclusively on unsafe working conditions and managerial responsibility. There is little attention given to employee behavior and responsibility. Because of this lack of attention, most experts agree that the impact of OSHA on accident rates will be fairly small. GM, for example, reported it was spending $15 per car to comply with OSHA regulations, but there had been no positive impact on accident rates as a function of the regulations. Other safety experts maintain that the long-term impact of OSHA regulations will be positive because of the increased knowledge of hazardous substances discovered through OSHA investigations. OSHA research has unearthed, for example, critical information about a number of possible carcinogens, including asbestos, cotton dust, PCBs, and vinyl chloride.

The Health Company Cafeteria

The company cafeteria may be the last place you would expect to find fresh, low-fat food, but more businesses are discovering healthy foods promote good health which results in profits. The healthy food trend started over a decade ago in a few employee-oriented businesses and has greatly expanded in recent years.

Companies across the country are recognizing that eating right is the key to well-being, resulting in happier employees and reduced health costs. There are fewer sick days from conditions linked to diet such as diabetes, heart disease, and high cholesterol.

One investment firm in New York City has two company dining rooms. In one room there is standard food and prices. The other dining room offers mostly vegetarian meals for free. In addition, each floor has a pantry with fresh fruit, fat-free yogurt, and bottled water, all for free.

Xerox Corporation has a team of health experts who attempt to encourage their employees nationwide to make health choices in their diets. The company's liaison with their contract food services provider quotes studies which find healthy employees are more productive.

One computer specialist for Xerox in El Segundo, California, eats in the company cafeteria about four times a week, ordering mainly vegetarian meals. The cafeteria also offers rotisserie turkey and water-packed tuna.

In San Antonio, Texas, at the United Services Automobile Association, the food service contractor provides an alternative to shopping at the local grocery store. After work employees stop by the fruit and vegetable stand to order a healthy dinner to go which can be deducted from the shopper's paycheck.

At Amgen Inc., a biotechnology company in Thousand Oaks, California, the cafeteria's evening takeout menu includes healthy family dinners for $3.95 to $5.25. If the employee doesn't like the menu, they can talk to the chef and special order.

Employees appreciate having the opportunity to enjoy healthy food. There is a feeling the company is taking care of their people, which helps develop loyalty.[5]

Daimler Chrysler: Cost Cutters

Daimler Chrysler officials organized a 5-day workshop at St. Joseph Oakland Hospital in Pontiac, Michigan. The goal was to streamline its emergency room operating procedures.

They were able to change inefficient, redundant, and expensive operating practices. The workshop was a success because the emergency room effectively cut wait time, improved patient care speed, and increased patient volume by 7 percent.

The end result for Daimler Chrysler was their employees received quality care at a lower cost. The company has held more than 60 workshops for health providers cutting costs and improving service.

This is important to the company because the most expensive part of a Chrysler vehicle is not steel nor plastic but health care.[6]

Communicable Diseases

Although the courts usually have considered communicable diseases as disabilities under the Americans with Disabilities Act and applicable state laws provide significant protections for affected employees, employees have the right under OSHA and state laws to have a workplace free from communicable diseases.

This issue becomes a problem in certain work areas as food preparation and health care. However, other work areas which have a low risk of disease being transmitted may not justify the expense or the inconvenience of methods to reduce the risk of disease spreading.[7]

In assessing what steps to take regarding the infected person, the disease must debilitate the employee to the point they are not otherwise qualified to do their job. For instance, a common cold may not affect a person's ability to perform their job functions.

The employer should not make a decision which places other employees at significant risk of catching a disease. Yet, the employer must be careful not to violate federal and state laws affecting the person's legal and privacy rights.[8]

AIDS and the Workplace

AIDS is now the leading cause of death for persons between the ages of 25 and 44. According to the Center for Disease Control (CDC), over 275,000 Americans had died of this disease by the end of 1993. Consequently, AIDS had become a critical health care issue for both employers and employees.

As noted in chapter 2, AIDS is a handicap protected by federal and local laws which prohibit discrimination against persons with disabilities. AIDS has been defined legally as a disability under the Rehabilitation Act of 1973 (which prohibits discrimination against the disabled by federal contractors), and is also covered by the 1990 Americans with Disabilities Act (ADA). Although there is still no evidence that AIDS can be spread through casual workplace contact, there have been a number of lawsuits related to AIDS.

OSHA issued new standards regarding AIDS and other viruses in 1991. Employers must provide gloves, masks, mouth guards, and smocks for workers who might come in contact with blood. Many states even require boxing and sports trainers to use these safeguards. Most major companies have developed specific policies for dealing with AIDS-related issues at work. The standard position is that an AIDS-afflicted employee should be treated the same as other employees as long as they are able to do their jobs. The CDC takes the position that AIDS-afflicted employees do not have to be isolated or restricted from any work area.

Levi Strauss, IBM, and Wells Fargo have been at the forefront in the development of a comprehensive AIDS-awareness program. These programs include informative brochures, a manager's guide to treating AIDS-afflicted employees, a policy manual, and a guidebook. The company also provides an opportunity for employees to meet with medical professionals to discuss the issues in more detail. Levi Strauss is very satisfied with its program because it has had no lawsuits, no employees refusing to work with AIDS-afflicted employees, and no requests for reassignments. IBM sent out a brochure on AIDS (developed by the CDC) to all 240,000 of its employees. The IBM policy is to encourage AIDS-afflicted employees to work as long as they are capable and to ensure their privacy.

Retiree Health Care

Retirees are finding their health care is undergoing some difficult times. The U.S. General Accounting Office (GAO) reports the number of companies offering health care to their retired employees has shrunk from about 65 percent in the 1980s to less than 40 percent in the twenty-first century.

In the past few years, the per capita personal health care spending by the elderly has increased from $4,040 to $7,016. This means companies are evaluating their retiree health care. The result is a change from companies maintaining pay-as-you-go systems and moving into managed care and requiring retirees to contribute to the premium plus paying deductibles.[9]

These company changes are only temporary as any savings resulting from these changes about equals increased costs. A government report projects health care spending will double to $2.1 trillion by the year 2007. Some companies are increasing the eligibility standards to require 35 years of service to qualify for employer contribution of 75 percent. Those retirees with 19 years of service usually qualify for 30 percent.

Companies offering retiree health care are careful to include in their plans language that will allow them to change or eliminate benefits. GM had been paying all health care costs for retirees and spouses, even after the death of the company retiree. GM changed the plan so retirees would pay up to $750 per year. It took GM 10 years for the courts to approve the new plan. Both General Electric and 3M have language in their health care plans allowing them to change, modify, or eliminate their plans.[10]

Flu Shot Productivity

Every year, an average of 75 million workdays are lost in the United States as a direct result of the flu. The total of direct and indirect costs of influenza is more than $12 billion per year. Even in the twenty-first century, flu results in 150,000 hospitalizations and more than 20,000 deaths annually in the United States.

With numbers like these, it is no wonder employers are touting the value of flu shots. It has been estimated that for every $1,000 spent on flu shots for working adults, medical bills were reduced, on average, by $1,600. When the cost of lost work time is added, the net savings average increased to $4,685. This represents a $47 savings per person receiving a flu shot which is covered in most health care plans.[11]

Employers offering flu shots on company property face a number of regulations that vary between states. An example is Indiana which may require employees to sign as many as five waivers. In addition, the company would need to have a hazardous waste needle plan that would satisfy federal and state regulations. One company in Indiana also decided it was cheaper for their coverage plan to include doctor office visits for flu shots.[12]

Drugs in the Workplace

The drug problem in American organizations is no longer just a company concern. The Federal Drug-Free Workplace Act requires companies who do business with the U.S. government to ensure that their employees do not use drugs. This law now requires contractors awarded federal contracts over $25,000 must produce a policy stating the workplace will be drug-free and outline the actions that will take place against violators; train supervisory staff through the use of drug awareness programs to learn how to identify drug users; and establish a drug-awareness program to educate employees of the dangers of abuse and the availability of counseling, rehabilitation, and assistance programs. Each employee must receive a copy of this policy and be notified it is a condition of employment.

The *Association of Management* indicates a full-service program for drug abuse will save companies $17 for every dollar spent. Approximately 80 percent of the *Fortune* 500 companies have employee assistance programs. The Drug-Free Workplace Act of 1988 requires federal contractors to provide a drug-free workplace. Organizations must have specific policies on substance abuse, establish awareness programs, and notify employees and applicants that a drug-free state is a condition of employment.

Data by drug agencies and institutes show the use of marijuana in the workplace is increasing. According to the SmithKline Beecham Clinical Laboratories, 59 percent of all positive test results revealed use of marijuana, which was up from 52 percent the previous year.

The use of prescription drugs is also increasing in the workplace. Drug enforcement agencies indicate at least 5 to 30 percent of drug abuse involves prescription drugs. These drugs are not always detected by standard tests, although a new 10-panel drug screening test is more effective. Prescription drugs are as addictive, impairing, and destructive as the common street drugs.[13]

Low unemployment and the need to fill job openings may unknowingly cause companies to relax their drug policies just to keep production rolling. In this type of a situation, a wiser course might be to officially change from a zero-tolerance policy to a two strikes and you are out.

Drug sales have moved from the street to the company. This tends to make a myth that drug users are street people. The workplace is an excellent place to sell drugs with dealers who sell on credit to their coworkers on Monday and then collect on Friday's payday. Employees who are users become the middlemen and resell to coworkers so they can pay off their dealer. The result is many companies now cooperate with local police to establish video surveillance and allow undercover drug stings to operate on company property.

There is data to indicate drug use by women is on the increase. Women become addicted sooner than men and also develop drug-related diseases sooner. Today's girls when compared to their mothers are 15 times more likely to start using drugs by the age of 15. Teenage boys and girls are equally as likely to drink or use illegal drugs.[14]

There are many questions regarding drugs in the workplace. One of them is just how many companies in the United States are actually testing employees for drugs? The percentage of companies testing for drugs will vary depending upon the data you choose to rely on. For instance, the Labor Department data shows 40 percent of U.S. workers are employed by companies with drug testing programs.

The American Management Association survey of its corporate members found more than 80 percent (primarily large companies) were testing for drug use. However, the effectiveness of testing is questioned by the National Institute of Sciences. They found little or no data to indicate the effectiveness of drug-free programs in the workplace to reduce drug use.[15]

Before initiating any form of a drug testing program, companies need to consider the answers to several important questions:

- Why do we want this program?
- Do we have a problem with drugs in our company?
- Can our current discipline policy handle violations of this policy?
- How much will the program cost?
- Should it be a punitive or rehabilitative program?

Only upon completely answering these questions should a company begin to consider whether they should proceed with the implementation of a drug testing program. If the final decision is to proceed, then there are five basic approaches to a drug testing program:

1. Preemployment screening
2. Random testing of current employees
3. "Reasonable cause" testing in response to performance problems
4. Return-to-duty testing after drug treatment
5. Post-accident testing

Once the decision has been made to proceed with a drug testing program, the type of test must be chosen. Of companies using drug testing, according to the American Management Association survey, 92 percent used urine sampling, 15 percent used blood sampling, 2 percent used hair sampling, and 2 percent used nonmedical performance testing. For the math-oriented students, the totals exceed 100 percent because some companies use multiple testing methods.[16]

One of the more recent testing methods is hair analysis. It has its share of controversy as do all drug testing methods. Although urine and blood testing can only detect the current drug user, the hair strand proponents claim their test can detect drug use from 3 to 90 days after consumption. However, the U.S. Food and Drug Administration has not approved any drug testing using hair analysis.

Steelcase, Inc., in Grand Rapids, Michigan, uses hair testing because it is cost efficient and it works. The company has found hair analysis yields an 18 percent positive rate, compared to a 2.7 percent rate using urine analysis. If the company used only urine analysis, the company would have hired in error 15 drug users for every 100 employees hired.

Because it costs the company $7,000 per year to hire a drug user, the company would save $105,000 for not hiring the 15 drug users. Even though the hair tests cost $50, compared to $30 for urine, the cost would still be $800 less per positive test.[17]

Although the urine and blood tests are only effective at detecting current drug use and the hair test is effective from 3 to 90 days after drug use, marijuana shows up better in urine than in hair. Therefore, some companies like American Toxicology Institute, Inc., of Las Vegas, run both tests because it gives them a 90-day "window" of drug usage and it is effective on a broader range of drugs. In deciding the type of drug tests to use, one should remember there are presently two states that prohibit hair testing: Oklahoma and Hawaii.[18]

Drug Testing Issues

There are two basic questions related to drug testing: (1) Exactly how much of each specific controlled substance must an individual ingest in order to be impaired? and (2) What specifically defines "impaired?" Most states, for example, have set a 0.10 percent blood alcohol level to establish impairment by alcohol, but no similar standard exists for controlled substances.

Although some employers use a positive drug test result (showing *any* amount of a controlled substance) as grounds for rejecting an applicant or discharging a worker, others have set a threshold level for an assumption of impairment. Computerized tests are now available to help employers determine whether workers in safety-related jobs are impaired. These tests operate like a video game and require less than a minute to determine eye-hand coordination and reaction time. Known as "fitness-for-duty" tests or "performance testing," these gauges measure whether an employee can safely perform a job. They are being touted by civil libertarians and some safety analysts as less intrusive and more effective than the urinalysis used in current tests, which also frequently raise questions about individual rights and privacy.

Employment Decisions

Many employment decisions made on the basis of positive drug test results have been legally challenged. Some experts maintain that hair analysis (a reliable but more costly alternative to urinalysis) is a less invasive technique which may not be as legally troublesome. Although there are no federal laws regulating drug testing, drug testing programs have been challenged using a number of legal theories. Private-sector employers have generally been able to successfully defend their drug testing programs in court; however, there are exceptions. In California, for example, the state court ruled that Southern Pacific wrongfully fired a computer programmer when she refused to provide a random-test urine specimen. However, other court decisions have supported drug testing.

Although public employers are bound by the Fourth Amendment of the U.S. Constitution (which forbids "unreasonable" searches and seizures), even characterizing a urine test as either a search (of the urine) or a seizure (of body fluids) has not led irrevocably to judicial declarations that drug testing by public employers is unconstitutional. U.S. Supreme Court decisions have permitted public employers to use drug testing for employees engaged in jobs in which public safety is an issue, such as railroad engineers, U.S. Customs agents, and nuclear power plant workers. Private-sector employers, however, are not bound by the Fourth Amendment, and challenges must be based on contract claims or public policy grounds.

Drug Testing Policy

In developing a drug testing policy, a company must determine what, if any, substances are permissible (e.g., will a positive reading for marijuana be treated the same way as a positive reading for heroin?). It must also determine whether, if testing is done on current employees, testing will be done only "for cause" (for example, after an accident, or if a supervisor determines that an employee appears impaired), or randomly, without cause.

Potential legal claims in regard to drug testing in the public sector include Fourth Amendment challenges to the testing (if there was no reasonable cause to conclude that the employee had ingested controlled substances) or a violation of an employee's constitutional due process rights (if the employee is discharged without being given an opportunity to challenge the test results). All employers may face charges of defamation (if test results become known to anyone but those who need the information), contract claims (for currently employed workers), and perhaps claims of discrimination against workers with disabilities (for example, if the employee is a recovering drug abuser). Human resource managers should consult with legal counsel before developing a drug testing program. A number of programs that have successfully met legal challenge are available.

Depression Malady

The cost of depression for U.S. businesses is staggering. Depression is a malady (disorder or disease) affecting 19 million Americans each year. This costs businesses $44 billion annually in absenteeism, direct treatment costs, mortality, and production loss. The personal loss is immeasurable with a negative effect upon career paths and lifetime earnings power.

One company in a cost-cutting move eliminated mental health coverage for their employees. The resulting business costs were staggering. When the company totaled the cost for increased absenteeism from employees who no longer had mental health treatment, they realized the loss. For the $54 the company saved per person by eliminating mental health coverage, they lost $355 per person denied treatment. The point is: Treatment saves money.[19]

A study in the *Journal of Clinical Psychiatry* put the cost of a depressed worker at $600. One-third of the $600 is for treatment costs with two-thirds resulting from absenteeism and lost production. It is estimated employee depression amounts to an annual loss of 200 million workdays. These losses are hard to justify when approximately 75 percent of depression can be treated.[20]

Smoking in the Workplace

One of the most controversial issues for human resource management today is that of workplace smoking. There is a growing body of evidence suggesting that health care costs are more for smokers than nonsmokers. This is causing many companies to develop antismoking programs.

The Environmental Protection Agency (EPA) has released a report classifying environmental tobacco smoke (ETS) as a Group A carcinogen. This is the classification for only the most dangerous cancer-causing agents in humans. The EPA also estimates that in addition to the cancer risk, between 35,000 and 40,000 excess heart disease deaths are caused by ETS among nonsmokers. ETS also aggravates the health of people with asthma, chronic bronchitis, and allergic conditions. Even people who are not allergic to ETS may suffer eye irritation, sore throat, nausea, and hoarseness.[21]

According to public health reports, the cost of smoking in the workplace in the United States is $72 billion per year. An additional $4 billion costs annually result from property losses due to fires, work productivity losses, and costs of maintenance cleanup.[22]

The EPA "Guide to Workplace Smoking Policies" recommends that employers create separate ventilated smoking lounges. Although the majority of organizations still allow smoking in most areas with very few constraints, a growing number have developed restrictive policies which range from the use of designated smoking areas to the banning of all smoking in the workplace, and for some, nonsmoking as a condition of employment. Insurance premiums and unnecessary health care costs are major reasons for employers' interest in issues related to smoking; however, pressure by nonsmokers for a smoke-free work environment has also certainly contributed to the development of smoking policies at most large organizations.

In developing workplace smoking policies, it is important to recognize some problems. The only consistency in laws relating to workplace smoking is inconsistency. There is no federal monitoring in this area and state and local municipalities are left to deal with the problem. Add to this mix the fact that there are more than 560 local jurisdictions which have enacted nonsmoker's rights ordinances.[23]

If a company already has a policy or is thinking they should have a policy, consider the following points:

- Review state, local, and other business regulations. Obtain legal counsel to determine what regulations apply in your area. Check other local businesses to see how they are addressing the problem.
- Know your employees and what they want. Do not ignore or discount any workers. Be sure to involve smokers, nonsmokers, and former smokers in policy discussions.
- Focus on the job, not the smoking. Are smokers abusing smoke breaks and being away from their desks too long making other workers angry? Is productivity being harmed?
- Review hiring policies. There are no current laws preventing discrimination against smokers.
- Modify policies as needed. Over time smoking restrictions have become stricter in the United States. However, the reverse is happening in Britain—strict laws are coming full circle with a reintroduction of designated smoking and nonsmoking areas.[24]

Video Display Terminals

The growing use of computers in the workplace has generated controversy over possible health hazards with some 30 million workers now using video display terminals (VDTs). Computer operators are complaining of eyestrain, blurred vision, various muscular and wrist problems, and miscarriages or failed pregnancies. Pregnant women who work at VDTs may have a higher risk of miscarriage than other clerical workers. Some companies, such as IBM, are now reassigning pregnant women to jobs not involving VDTs.

A number of states have issued guidelines regarding work with VDTs in order to reduce repetitive trauma disorder. New Jersey and other states now require 15-minute breaks every 2 hours and eye exams every 5 years for all state employees who work with VDTs.

Of interest to HRM professionals is that these health problems may not be the result of just work-related duties. A survey by Vault.com., a job-search Web site, found 90.3 percent of employees acknowledge they surf nonwork-related sites during working hours. This practice has been called "the millennium cigarette break."

Even with software available to monitor employee computer activity and employee dismissals rising for unauthorized use, 55 percent of those surveyed do not believe they are being monitored. Companies need computer usage policy guidelines in their employee handbooks to reduce health-related problems and to prevent lawsuits from employees who may be offended by what coworkers are downloading.[25]

Health Care Coalitions

Health care coalitions are local area employers joining with a system of hospitals as partners. These partners want to provide generous health benefits rather than cutting benefits, while at the same time trying to improve their health care system.

An example is the Central Florida Health Care Coalition which includes Disney World and similar local large employers in the Orlando area. Because Orlando's labor market is tight, the idea is to attract new employees and keep present employees through a health program of generous benefits and quality services.

Disney believes quality is high and excessive use of many medical procedures have dramatically dropped. The results of these partnerships have been very rewarding. Disney's turnover is one-third that of the service sector average of 100 percent. Their turnover is far below that of competitors.

Disney finds its employees are healthier and more satisfied workers. This is reflected in their higher morale. The result is the key ingredients of workers providing customers with Disney's high standards of service and caring.[26]

THE MANAGEMENT OF STRESS

Many occupations require employees to adapt to work conditions that place stringent pressure on them. Over time, these pressures create stresses that can affect the health of employees, as well as their productivity and satisfaction.

Stress Management and Burnout

Stress occurs with the interaction between an individual and the environment which produces emotional strain affecting a person's physical and mental condition. Stress is caused by **stressors,** which are events that create a state of disequilibrium within an individual. The responses an individual has to the stress may be positive (as when it causes someone to be challenged in the performance of tasks), or they may be negative (as when someone worries so much about doing a good job that a heart attack results).

The cost of too much stress to individuals, organizations, and society is high. Many employees may suffer from anxiety disorders or a stress-related illness. In terms of days lost on the job, it is estimated that each affected employee loses about 16 workdays a year because of stress, anxiety, or depression.

Researchers now link job stress to higher rates of heart disease and other physical ailments. They have explored the effects of working long hours or being disenchanted with their job. Workers with the most job strain had significantly higher blood pressure than those with the least job strain.

Because the stress issue is global, European and Japanese scientists have looked at the influence of job strain on a variety of factors. These include heart disease, gastrointestinal illness, immune system function, back and joint pain, and absenteeism. They have found a relationship to workplace stress.[27]

Other sources of individual stress include conflicts between job obligations and family obligations. Women in particular tend to experience this conflict as family responsibilities can place tremendous pressure on women. When both husband and wife have careers, the wife is often expected to keep her housekeeping role in addition to her work role.

Many corporations are becoming aware of these extra pressures on women and are providing employment options designed to reduce this source of stress. Companies such as DuPont, Merck, and General Mills offer family leave, flexible work schedules, and on-site day care. For example, this workplace benefit may help reduce turnover and absenteeism and increase productivity in companies which help employees balance work with family obligations.

Sources of Job-Related Stress

Stress can be traced to on-the-job activities and to events occurring away from work. But because people cannot completely separate their work and personal lives, the way people react and handle stress at work is a complex issue. Until recently, scientists had known with certainty that stressful events could raise blood pressure temporarily, but the long-term effects on heart disease was not definite.

A study published in the *Journal of the American Medical Association* concludes "that job strain may be a risk factor for both hypertension and structural changes of the heart in working men."[28] The study was the first time job characteristics have been related to both hypertension and structural changes in the heart. According to the report, jobs causing the most problems were *not* those with a great deal of pressure to work hard and fast, such as high-powered executive jobs which are often associated with heart attacks. Instead, the types of jobs causing increases in blood pressure were lower-level jobs. These were jobs where there was high psychological demands coupled with little control over the workplace and little use of skills.

Some jobs are more likely to cause stress than others. Air traffic controllers, for example, report higher than average rates of ulcers, chest pain, and headaches, but only after 3 years of work. Police work is also very stressful. Although high-level executives lament their highly stressful responsibilities, the evidence regarding stress-related illnesses does not support the belief that higher-level management jobs are more stressful than other jobs. In fact, one large-scale study found that rates of coronary heart disease were greater at lower management levels.

For "high strain" jobs, researchers found workers were 3.09 times as likely to have chronic high blood pressure as the control group. But where a high-stress job included ways to control the situation, there was no increase in blood pressure. What appears to matter is coming to a job every day where the demands are high and the control is down and having to biologically turn on to manage these threats. "The implications is the need to start thinking about job design, enhancement of skills, better job training and increasing worker participation in decision making."[29] Many HRM programs now try to solve these types of problems.

To summarize, factors in potentially stressful work activities include

- Little control of the work environment.
- Lack of participation in decision making.
- Uncontrolled changes in policy.
- Sudden reorganizations and unexpected changes in work schedules (overtime).
- Conflicts with other people (subordinates, superiors, and peers) and other departments.
- Lack of feedback.
- Not enough time to do expected duties.
- Ambiguity in duties expected to be achieved.

Stressful events occurring away from work are extensive, but often include problems related to marriage, children, serious illness, death of a family member or friend, finances, change in social activities, impending retirement, life and career goals, and environmental pollution (noise, traffic, and air quality).

Job Burnout

Although stress is normal and may even be helpful, **job burnout** occurs when people lose interest in what they are doing on the job and there is no longer any feeling of fulfillment in one's work. People tend to lose the picture of what they are and focus on the cares of the world, not on themselves as individuals with real purpose.

People need to feed their brains and do things they value. To avoid burnout, people need to be clear on their own values for values are a source of one's energy. It is important to have a mission statement to guide our activities. This mission statement can be as simple as what one wants to do with their life and what one wants to accomplish with their life.

Job burnout has become recognized as a major work stress problem. Burnout seems most common among professionals who must deal extensively with other people—clients, subordinates, and customers on the job. The professionals who seem most vulnerable to job burnout include managers, accountants, lawyers, nurses, police officers, and social workers.

Those persons who experience job burnout seem to show few common personality characteristics, but they do show many significant and consistent job, work setting, and organization characteristics. They tend to

- Experience much stress because of job-related stressors.

- Be perfectionists or self-motivating achievers.

- Seek unrealistic or unattainable goals.

Under burnout, the individual can no longer cope with the demands of the job, and his willingness to try drops dramatically. The costs of job burnout, both to the organization member suffering from this syndrome and the organization, can be high.

Stress Management Programs

Many organizations have developed stress-management programs to teach employees how to determine negative effects of job-related stress. These programs involve relaxation techniques, coping skills, listening skills, methods of dealing with difficult people, time management, and assertiveness. All of these programs are aimed at breaking the tension that goes with job-stress situations. They also help employees achieve greater control of their lives. Other techniques such as clarifying the employee's work role, redesigning and enriching jobs, correcting physical factors in the environment, and effectively handling interpersonal factors are also included. (See cartoon.)

A **stress management** program is any activity or program that attempts to reduce the cause of work-related stresses, or to help individuals to cope with the negative outcomes of exposure to the stress. The HRM program itself is a stress management intervention, as HRM tries to create an organization that reduces the conditions that lead to harmful types of stressors being placed on its members. These HR programs have been successful in reducing stress.

Stress management and reduction programs are common in industry today. At Motorola, for example, programs emphasize exercise, nutrition, relaxation techniques, time management, and self-awareness. Other organizations have attempted to reduce physical stressors by redesigning the workplace. Role ambiguity and role conflict can often be reduced by interventions following a job analysis and survey research. Immediate supervisors may be a primary source of stress among workers. Survey data is helpful in pinpointing unit-level problems before they result in serious organizational difficulties, such as termination, absences, and disabilities.

Source: THE WIZARD OF ID by permission of Brant Parker and Johnny Hart and by Creators Syndicate, Inc.

The disadvantage of having individuals learn to cope with stress is that it does not reduce the source of the stress. Sometimes stress reduction programs are used as substitutes for dealing with legitimate workplace issues that are creating stress. The burden of adjustment should not be put on the worker when the real source needs to be determined.

With this caution in mind, there are things that can help individuals buffer the long-term effect of living with stress. Several methods used for stress management include wellness programs, biofeedback, meditation, career life, planning, stress management training, and job burnout seminars.

Although stress at work is a continuing topic, the recent comments by Peter Drucker, Professor at Claremont College's Peter F. Drucker School of Management, are of interest to HRM professionals. Dr. Drucker points out some people find stress to be bad; however, others find they thrive in a stressful environment. Although the proportion of those who strive is not known, he believes it is a large proportion. Dr. Drucker has written 28 books and is an active professor at Claremont College. In November 1999 he turned 90 years old.[30]

Wellness Programs **Wellness programs** were initially associated with only physical fitness, but recently wellness has come to include nutrition counseling and smoking cessation. Johnson & Johnson Company's "Live for Life" program is probably the best-known wellness program, and has become so popular with other companies that J&J has made its program commercially available. One company with a smoking cessation program, U-Haul, deducts $5 every other week from the paychecks of employees who smoke, or are either overweight or underweight.

Relaxation Techniques Two commonly used relaxation techniques are biofeedback and meditation. A **biofeedback** course will usually take from several weeks to 3 or 4 months. The course takes place in a clinic with a trained technician and will normally begin with an analysis of the person's stress points: work, family, and so on. Instruments that can measure brain waves, heart activity temperature, and muscle activity are connected to a person to measure physical reaction to stress. By receiving biological feedback from the monitoring machines, the person learns to control consciously his or her autonomic nervous system through decreasing pulse rate and blood pressure. With practice, the person no longer needs the feedback from the monitoring devices and can practice biofeedback out of a clinic and in a work or personal activity that is stressful.

Meditation has reported outcomes similar to biofeedback, except that instruments are not used to relax. People using meditation repeat in their mind a specific sound called a mantra during two 20-minute sessions a day—one in the morning and another in the late afternoon. Meditators often report higher energy and productivity levels, ability to get along better with others, lowered metabolic rates such as heart rate, and increased creativity.

Career Life Planning Some cases of stress in people may need to be treated with career life planning. The planning may be one-to-one or in group sessions.

SUMMARY

In this chapter, we have examined stage five of the Success System Model: health and safety factors in the workplace. Some programs have been used over a period of several years with varying degrees of success, and other approaches are somewhat new. Top management is now taking a more active role in improving the health and safety of employees. A more aggressive OSHA, new regulations, the threat of heavy fines and possible criminal prosecution, staggering health insurance costs, and research which shows that healthy employees are more productive employees have all contributed to the renewed attention to health and safety issues. More companies are developing formal health and safety policies, because management is now more likely to be held accountable for accident rates and other health-related incidents. The twenty-first century will see even greater interest in safety and health. In particular, more emphasis will be placed on programs focusing on employee behavior, including drug testing, antismoking programs, EAPs, and wellness programs. These new techniques are contributing to a more productive and healthier workforce.

Managers are now being held accountable for the health and safety of their employees. In the present legal environment, managers are generally responsible for the actions of their employees. Prevention and training on health and safety issues should be major organizational concerns. Wellness or health management is more of a management philosophy than a program: It is a way of viewing the organization life of workers.

In the HRM Skills Simulation, you will have an opportunity to participate in an organization using the ideas of health and safety. Though the experiment is limited in size and time, you perhaps will draw some conclusions of your own about the application of job wellness programs. In the last several years, health-safety programs have received much more attention and seem to be having some positive impact in improving organizations. There are several approaches that will help HR managers improve safety levels, but there is a definite need for additional research into health and safety programs.

REVIEW QUESTIONS

1. Why are accident rates reliably higher for younger workers even after controlling for years on the job?
2. How could you as a manager develop a strategy for increasing employees' motivation to work more safely?
3. Do you think that managers should be held criminally liable for health and safety violations?
4. Do you support a policy of random drug testing for all employees? Why or why not?
5. Should a company be allowed to prohibit smoking on or off the job for its employees? Why?
6. Review book or movie for safety. (For example, *China Syndrome.*)

KEY WORDS AND CONCEPTS

Define and be able to use the following:

- AIDS
- Biofeedback
- Burnout
- Occupational Health and Safety Act (OSHA)

- Repetitive Trauma Disorder
- Stress Management
- Stressors

- Voluntary Protection Programs (VPPs)
- Wellness Programs

HRM SKILLS SIMULATION 14.1: THE UNION MEDIA COMPANY

Total time suggested: 2 hours, 10 minutes

A. PURPOSE

The purpose of this simulation is to appreciate the complexity of implementing a new HRM program within an organization. During this simulation, you will experience the emotions associated with the acceptance and rejection of an action plan within an HRM environment.

Your goals will include

- Sponsoring the most effective HRM wellness program.
- Shaping different viewpoints for common agreement.
- Attaining consensus in a mutual concession situation.

B. PROCEDURES

Step 1. Prior to class, form an HRM team of five. Each team member will assume one of the following six roles:

1. Vice president, human resource management department
2. Manager, HRM labor relations section
3. Business agent for the local union
4. OSHA consultant
5. Employee safety representative
6. Observers

Step 2. Read the costs of different wellness programs in Table 14.1 and the following role background information and assume a role. Extras act as observers and will complete the Observer Form for their team.

Time suggested for Step 2: 10 minutes.

Step 3. The HRM manager will chair the meeting for each team and be responsible for developing an action plan to be presented to the president. One objective will be a realistic yet comprehensive plan. The other objective, if possible, will be team consensus.

Time suggested for Step 3: 60 minutes.

Table 14.1
Cost of different wellness programs

	PLAN 1 HEALTH EDUCATION	PLAN 2 PHYSICAL FITNESS	PLAN 3 HEALTH EDUCATION WITH FOLLOW-UP OFF-SITE	PLAN 4 HEALTH EDUCATION WITH FOLLOW-UP ON-SITE
1. Screening costs ($15/employee every 5 years; $10/employee over the 3-year study period. Required only under Plans 3 and 4)			$ 32,910	$ 19,950
2. Health educator services (number hours, at $30/hour)	$ 22,500 (750)		$ 11,250 (375)	$ 10,650 (355)
3. Follow-up counseling (number hours, at $25/hour)	$ 27,500 (1100)	$ 16,250 (650)	$171,875 (6895)	$161,500 (6460)
4. Health improvement program	$ 52,870	$ 22,300	$ 37,175	$ 12,486
5. Physical fitness equipment and supplies		$ 96,500		$ 2,570
6. Physical fitness attendant services (number months of attendant services)		$421,500 (32 mos)		
Total direct costs for 3 years	$102,870	$556,550	$253,210	$207,156
Average number employees in workforce	1,851	4,021	2,633	1,785
Average cost for 3 years per employee	$55.58	$138.40	$96.17	$116.05

Step 4.

1. All HRM teams will present their action plans to the class. Similarities and dissimilarities will be noted.
2. Observers present their team rankings.
3. The class will then attempt to develop consensus for a single action plan to present to the president.

Time suggested for Step 4: 60 minutes.

ROLE DESCRIPTIONS
(READ *ONLY* YOUR ROLE)

Role 1—Vice president, human resource management. You have received a memorandum from the company president regarding your feedback for an employee wellness program. Specifically, you are charged with developing an action plan as soon as possible so the company may consider a comprehensive health and safety program.

Role 2—Manager, HRM labor relations. You have read the president's memo and are very enthusiastic about this new program. Some of the approaches you favor include a comprehensive wellness program of physiological tests, individual health profiles, and education classes for lifestyle change (including smoking, stress, fitness, nutrition, child care, and weight control). You do not know the budgetary amount involved in the program, but you believe the company should develop a solid program. After all, you have read countless reports indicating employee health programs have an impact on the bottom line.

Role 3—Business agent of the local union. You received a short telephone briefing from the HRM manager regarding the president's memorandum. Apparently this is a hot issue, because you have been asked to join the discussions regarding a comprehensive program. Your initial concerns are whether this is another company attempt to upstage the union. Also, whether the company will use the cost of such a program to offset future union wage and benefits demands.

Role 4—OSHA consultant. The President has asked you to be a member of this team. You have performed various consulting assignments with Union Media previously and understand the culture. Your past experience with other companies regarding wellness programs is that they drastically underestimate initial and long-term costs. You are determined not to let this happen with Union Media Company.

Role 5—Employee safety representative. You have been the employee safety representative for a long time, and believe the company fails to provide enough resources and top management support for programs. This wellness program has all the aspects of more promo, but no dollars. You favor a reduced program, but with adequate funding.

OBSERVER FORM

Instructions: For each item, place a number in the blank to the right representing your reaction to how your group performed based on the following scale.

Low _____ 1 : 2 : 3 : 4 : 5 : 6 : 7 : 8 : 9 : 10 _____ High

1. Degree of cooperative teamwork: _____
2. Degree of team motivation: _____
3. Degree of member satisfaction: _____
4. Degree of information sharing (participation): _____
5. Degree of consensual decision making: _____
6. Degree of team conflict or competition (i.e., conflict directly faced and resolved): _____
7. Degree of quality of group decisions: _____
8. Degree of speed with which decision is made: _____
9. Degree of participating leadership: _____
10. Degree of clarity of goals: _____

Total ranking _____

Case 14.1   Precision Products, Inc.

Helen Brown, personnel manager of Precision Products, had just returned from the fabrication department where another serious employee accident had occurred when the telephone rang. It was Hank Freeman from the budget and accounting office, inquiring about the recent increase in the company's worker compensation rates with their private insurance company. His last comment was, "CEO Peterson won't like this."

Helen knew she would be on the carpet again, so experience taught her it was better to be proactive than reactive. She telephoned Dick Still, head of labor relations, and inquired what progress he had made since last month's discussion on a company-wide safety program. Dick replied "zero progress," so they decided on an emergency meeting tomorrow at 8 A.M.

QUESTIONS

1. Suggest some reasons why companies like Precision Products are slow to establish accident prevention programs.

2. What are some reasons accidents occur? Consider reasons for accidents from the perspective of the employer and of the employee.

3. Assume Helen and Dick ask you for your input. What would you suggest regarding the organization of a company-wide safety program? Be sure to include involvement, responsibility, and training considerations.

ENDNOTES

1. "Number of U.S. Job-Related Deaths Drops to Lowest Level Since 1992," Wire Report, Briefcase, *The Oregonian*, 5 August 1999, p. D1.
2. William Atkinson, "When OSHA Comes Knocking," *HR Magazine* (October 1999): 35–38.
3. Ron Winslow, "Aetna Program Aims to Get Workers on Disability Back on Job More Quickly," *The Wall Street Journal*, 9 September 1999, p. A3.
4. Ibid.
5. Renee Tawa, "Fare Labour Practices," *Los Angeles Times*, 27 December 1999, Section E, p. 1.
6. Susan J. Wells, "Avoiding the Health Care Squeeze," *HR Magazine* (April 2000): 47–48.
7. Brent M. Giddens and Weston A. Edwards, "Communicable Diseases in the Workplace," Legal Report, *SHRM* (March-April 1999): 1–4.
8. Ibid.
9. Stephanie Overman, "Keeping Retiree Health Benefits Afloat," *HR Magazine* (December 1998): 115–19.
10. Ibid.
11. Ronald D. Hawkins, "Flu Vaccination is Shot in Arm for Productivity," *HR News* 18, no. 10 (October 1999): 1.
12. Ibid.
13. Jane Easter Bahls, "Drugs in the Workplace," *HR Magazine* (February 1998): 81–87.
14. Ibid.
15. Ibid.
16. Ibid.
17. Stephanie Overman, "Splitting Hairs," *HR Magazine* (August 1999): 43–48.
18. Ibid.
19. Robert LaGrow, "Cost of Depression for American Businesses Called Staggering," *HR News* 18, no. 10 (October 1999): 4.
20. Ibid.
21. Lin Grensing-Pophal, "Smokin' in the Workplace," *HR Magazine* (May 1999): 58–66.
22. Ibid.
23. Ibid.
24. Ibid.
25. Frederic Biddle, "Personal Internet Use," Work Week, *The Wall Street Journal*, 21 December 1999, p. A1.
26. Forrest Briscoe and James Maxwell, "Hands-On Health Care Benefits," *HR Magazine* (March 1999): 73–78.
27. Dolores Kong, "Increasing Evidence Links Job Strain, Ailments," *Boston Globe, The Oregonian*, 8 September 1999, p. B10.
28. Schnall et al. "The Relationship Between 'Job Strain,' Workplace Diastolic Blood Pressure, and Left Ventricular Mass Index," *Journal of the American Medical Association* 263, no. 14 (April 11, 1990): 1929–35.
29. Ibid.
30. Thomas Petzinger, Jr., "Talking About Tomorrow," *The Wall Street Journal*, 1 January 2000, p. R34.

Part VI

The Success System: Changing a High-Performing Workforce

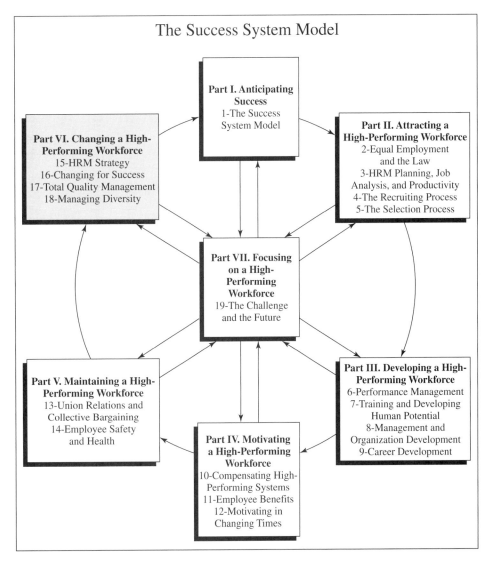

The Success System Model

Part I. Anticipating Success
1-The Success System Model

Part II. Attracting a High-Performing Workforce
2-Equal Employment and the Law
3-HRM Planning, Job Analysis, and Productivity
4-The Recruiting Process
5-The Selection Process

Part VI. Changing a High-Performing Workforce
15-HRM Strategy
16-Changing for Success
17-Total Quality Management
18-Managing Diversity

Part VII. Focusing on a High-Performing Workforce
19-The Challenge and the Future

Part III. Developing a High-Performing Workforce
6-Performance Management
7-Training and Developing Human Potential
8-Management and Organization Development
9-Career Development

Part V. Maintaining a High-Performing Workforce
13-Union Relations and Collective Bargaining
14-Employee Safety and Health

Part IV. Motivating a High-Performing Workforce
10-Compensating High-Performing Systems
11-Employee Benefits
12-Motivating in Changing Times

Chapter 15

The Success System: HRM Strategy

Objectives

Upon completing this chapter, you will be able to:

1. Define the concept of strategy and explain the basics of the HR strategy formulation process.
2. Understand the relationship between human resource strategy and overall organizational strategy.
3. Recognize the importance of corporate culture and its relation to strategy.
4. Experience these concepts in a management simulation.

Premeeting preparation

1. Read chapter 15.
2. Prepare for HRM Skills Simulation 15.1, The Genteck Company. Read Parts A and B, Step 1.
3. Read Case 15.1: The Space Electronics Corporation. Answer questions.

In the boardroom of the futuristic corporate headquarters of Hewlett-Packard (not far from the campus of Stanford University in Palo Alto), the executive committee, led by chief executive Carly Fiorina, examines future strategic plans for this corporation. The strategic plan sets forth a map of targets and timetables projected 5 years into the future. These meetings provide a constant interplay between Hewlett-Packard's corporate goals and the ever-changing competitive conditions in which they exist. The meetings emphasize consensual-style decision making, with managers asking probing questions leading to agreement on future strategy.

The best defense is preemptive self-destruction and renewal: "We have to be willing to cannibalize what we're doing today in order to ensure our leadership in the future. It's counter to human nature, but you have to kill your business while it is still working." Or as they say in Silicon Valley, it's better to eat your lunch before some else eats it for you.

Jump-starting HP's innovation machine is tops on CEO Fiorina's list, too. HP hasn't had a mega-breakthrough product since the inkjet printer was introduced in 1984. Until recently, even its record on shipping new versions of its computer servers has trailed rivals. Then there's the problem of HP's staid brand. Although synonymous with quality, Fiorina says, "we have to make sure it represents the next century rather than the last one," she says.

And, unlike her predecessors, CEO Fiorina must recalibrate HP's vaunted culture, dubbed the "HP Way." Founders Bill Hewlitt and David Packard were renowned for emphasizing teamwork and respect for coworkers. But in recent years, that has translated into a bureaucratic, consensus-style culture that is at a sharp disadvantage in the Net-speed era. "They have this ready, aim-aim-aim, fire culture," says Bain & Co. consultant Vernon E. Altman, who has worked with HP. "These days, it has to be aim, fire, reaim, refire." Disposing of the bad habits while retaining the good shouldn't be a problem, says CEO Fiorina, who plans to use a scalpel and not a machete. "Our people are very proud and smart. So, first, you reinforce the things that work," she says, "and then appeal to their brains to address what doesn't."

Can CEO Fiorina, a medieval-history and philosophy major, succeed at this storied engineering company? HP's search committee members say there isn't a better fit. The committee members—Ginn, Hackborn, and retiring CEO Lewis E. Platt—came by their decision after each one detailed 20 qualities they would like to see in the new CEO. Then they boiled it down to four essential criteria that played to CEO Fiorina's strengths: the ability to conceptualize and communicate sweeping strategies, the operations savvy to deliver on quarterly financial goals, the power to bring urgency to an organization, and the management skills to drive a nascent Net vision throughout the company.

CEO Fiorina builds consensus decisions by asking penetrating questions and listening closely to the answers; she is committed to "hands off" management and to coaching others in solving problems.[1]

Entrepreneurship is a dominant value at Hewlett-Packard. CEO Carly Fiorina is reorganizing the company to remain competitive in the rapidly changing Internet environment while seeking to maintain the risk-taking spirit that has made it an exceptional company.

There is a lot of risk-taking and continual innovation in product line. For example, 70 percent of Hewlett-Packard's total revenues result from products developed in the past 2 years. Consequently, the focus of strategic management is to identify key product and market trends and to develop future competitive position. This low-key, informal style is known at Hewlett-Packard as "management by wandering around" (MBWA), and this HR style has kept HP a leader in the competitive high-tech electronics field. A vital organization, Hewlett-Packard is constantly recruiting new employees and changing strategy to meet the needs of its stakeholders. CEO Fiorina is reorganizing Hewlett-Packard into a company capable of meshing people and values into an Internet leader.

HRM Strategy

In a world of unpredictability and rapid change, what makes one organization a winner, yet another fails to adjust to the same opportunities? How do some smaller companies move forward and seize new product and market opportunities, yet other larger companies fail to take advantage of their size and situation? How did Bill Gates and others lead Microsoft from virtual obscurity to the *Fortune* Top 500, while at the same time Gulf Oil (once the ninth largest U.S. corporation) was taken over by another company? The answer lies in the firm's ability to change its strategy to meet a changing competitive environment.

A strategy is a way of getting things done. It provides a game plan for action. Strategy includes the formulation of goals and action plans for their accomplishment. Strategy considers the competitive forces at work in managing an organization and the impact of the outside environment on organization actions.[2] Good management does not mean trying harder by using old, out-of-date methods. It involves developing strategies for coming up with new products, making sure they are what the customer wants, and recruiting skilled employees to provide a competitive advantage.

Accelerating changes in technology, shorter product life cycles, and new unexpected competition contribute to make succeeding in business harder than ever. The evidence indicates that people play a major role in whether or not an organization performs. Managers make strategy and strategy determines business success or failure.[3] The excellent companies must be able to transform the way they operate and recognize the importance of corporate culture in devising and executing new strategies. In fact, we suggest the biggest stumbling block in the path of strategic change is usually an old and inflexible corporate culture.

A culture that prevents a company from meeting competitive threats or from adapting to changing economic or social environments can lead to the company's stagnation and ultimate failure unless it makes a conscious effort to change. These HRM cultural change efforts include activities which are designed to improve the skills, abilities, structure, and motivational levels of organization members. The goals are improved technical skills and improved interpersonal competence and communications. Such HRM efforts may also be directed toward improved leadership, decision making, and problem solving among organization members. The assumption underlying such efforts is that by developing an improved culture, a more effective organization will result.

In meetings similar to those at Hewlett-Packard, organizations around the world hammer out strategic goals and plans. In this arena, strategic management takes place, and strategic decisions are made. Former CEO Stanley Gault of Rubbermaid was one of the key leaders who developed the strategic management system, enabling his company to plan its competitive position into the future and making it one of America's most admired companies.[4] At monthly meetings like those described, managers examine financial reports of sales, profits, return on investment, and the status of their competitors. These managers try to analyze and anticipate virtually every existing or potential problem Rubbermaid is likely to face. The emphasis of these meetings is on problem solving for potential new products and markets in an uncertain economic environment. The purpose of strategic management is to develop an anticipative plan for future management actions and HR needs.

The need for strategic management has increasingly become a fact of organizational life. The strategic plan, or lack of one, is often the starting point for the evaluation of the actions of management personnel and their organizations. Strategic management provides the basic direction and framework within which all organization activities take place. An understanding of strategic management, potentially the most advanced and sophisticated type, makes it easier for managers to develop a vision of the future for their organization.

In this chapter, we examine stage six of the Success System Model: changing for success. An overview of the strategic management process will be presented in order to help clarify what strategic HR management is, why it is used, and how it fits into the strategic management process. If you gain a thorough understanding of this process, you are more likely to become an effective HR manager.

ORGANIZATIONAL STRATEGY

Accelerating changes in technology, shorter product life cycles, and unexpected competition contribute to make succeeding in business harder than ever. The evidence indicates that managers play a major role in determining how well an organization performs.[5]

Management consultants Thomas J. Peters and Robert H. Waterman examined the qualities of 43 "excellently managed" U.S. companies, including Hewlett-Packard, IBM, 3M, Boeing, Bechtel, Procter & Gamble, and McDonald's. These firms were not only consistently profitable over a 20-year period, they were all unusually successful in responding to customer needs, providing a challenging working environment for their employees and being good corporate citizens. In their book, Peters and Waterman concluded that these companies were successful because of an emphasis on the people part of management.[6]

Although many company presidents agree with these findings, the book is not without its critics. Daniel T. Carroll, Peter Drucker, and others have criticized the methodological and conceptual problems in Peters and Waterman's work, including use of a small, nonrepresentative sample and the lack of a group of unsuccessful companies for comparison. There is also a lack of a detailed description of how the key characteristics were derived.[7] From their research, Peters and Waterman derived eight attributes and characteristics representing the management style of these excellent companies. The attributes emphasize the critical role of management in stressing the values and practices that lead to excellence. These excellent companies exhibit four core characteristics which suggest how these best-run organizations are managed (see Figure 15.1).

1. *Managing into the Future.* The first characteristic is the necessity to think constantly about new products and then to allocate resources and get them to the marketplace fast. Well-managed companies provide a clear sense of direction and strategic vision of the future. There is a bias toward action, rapid problem solving, and innovation.
2. *A Strategic Action Plan.* The managers of best-run companies tend to develop a strategic game plan for achieving competitive advantage. Successful companies do their marketing homework. Staying close to the customer is a characteristic of successful firms: They seek what the customer wants. A related factor is staying close to what the competition is doing.
3. *The Corporate Culture.* In well-run organizations, people make things happen. There is a commitment to corporate values and objectives and a willingness to take risks. There is a sense of autonomy in entrepreneurship and a belief in the importance of HRM values and services. The key factor in today's competitive world seems to lie in developing strategic entrepreneurship within the large corporation and managing creativity. IBM, for example, has devel-

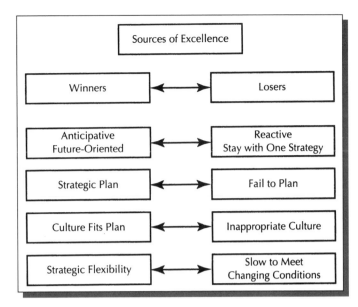

Figure 15.1
Strategic characteristics of best-run companies

oped new business groups that operate as autonomous units with complete responsibility for new product development.

4. *Strategic Flexibility.* The companies that cope best with the rapidly changing environment try to anticipate changes, even if this means reformulating strategy or altering the corporate culture. These companies are results-oriented and market-driven. There is a belief in productivity through people that encourages change and supports risk-taking in order to gain success in both current and new product markets.

The answer, then, to the excellent firm lies in the strategic decisions made by top management of these organizations. Successful companies are effective in developing a strategic HR plan for achieving future objectives. Although many firms simply let their organizations drift toward uncertain goals, effective managers are able to design results-oriented systems for coordinating a diverse set of product and market endeavors. Some executives are unable to focus the resources of their organization, and the result is ineffective performance. Sears Roebuck, for example, had some poor financial results, and developed a new strategy to involve employees in their vision and values.[8]

In a dynamic, competitive environment, an organization must either move forward with purpose and direction or fall back. There is no standing still. The difference between success and failure depends on how well a manager is able to perform the strategic management function: developing an effective, winning organization.

INTEGRATION OF STRATEGIC HRM WITH CORPORATE STRATEGY

The human resource strategy of an organization should be integrated with the corporate strategy (see Table 15.1). In other words, corporate strategy should drive the human resource strategy. Tom Kelley (chairman of the Society of Human Resource Management) once remarked that, "Human resource managers need to be

Table 15.1
Major characteristics
of strategic human
resource management

HUMAN RESOURCE STRATEGY
• Recognizes the impact of the competitive environment
• Recognizes the dynamics of the labor market
• Focuses on long-range goals (3–5 years)
• Integrates people concerns with corporate strategy

involved in the strategic planning of global issues, rather than the day-to-day personnel transactions of the previous personnel administrators . . . [and] along with that strategic planning process, it is imperative that the human resource professionals establish goals and objectives that support the corporate goals."[9] The HR manager needs to develop recruitment, training, and development strategies to achieve the goals set forth in the corporate strategy.

For example, if an organization is going to grow and dominate a market, such as Apple Computer's strategy in the past, then its human resource strategy would be aiming at the rapid recruiting of employees. If retrenchment is the strategy, such as at IBM, then a hiring freeze with downsizing and termination of employees is the typical HR strategy.

The strategic HRM approach differs from the traditional functional approach. As Leonard Schlesinger states, human resource management needs to get out of the "people business" and into the business of people.[10] In a competitive environment, human resource managers need to be major role players on the strategic management team.

CORPORATE STRATEGY

In a general sense, HRM strategies represent more gradual approaches to strategic change, focusing on developmental and participative change processes. Corporate strategy changes, on the other hand, may involve drastic, abrupt change to organization structures, management processes, downsizing the workforce, and reengineering the corporate cultures.[11] It is important to note that because strategy aims for organizational survival in a competitive environment, the strategic changes may or may not be developmental in nature and, in many instances, are not accomplished by using participative processes. Strategic changes often include such techniques as takeovers, mergers, and plant closures which often involve large-scale downsizing, layoff of employees, and massive restructuring.

Strategic changes, then, are large-scale transitions which fundamentally alter the way an organization relates to its environment, its people, the way it does business, its product mix, and other strategic factors. Secondly, such changes arise from discontinuities in the environment (such as deregulation, takeovers, new competition, and the like) which force managers into a reactive, rather than a proactive, mode so that strategic change must be done rapidly. In a time of crisis, the choice is often between rapid change or organizational extinction.

STRATEGIC HRM CHOICES

The basic strategic human resource management choices involve several key factors. These human factors impact organizational planning and the people choices the organization must make when deciding on an HRM strategy. First, the organization must decide whether to be *proactive* or *reactive* in its human resource planning. The HR manager, then, either anticipates future needs and systematically plans for them far in advance, or simply reacts to changes as they arise. Obviously, strategic HRM planning aims to ensure that the organization will obtain an adequate number of employees with the qualifications, skills, and abilities that are needed. At Hewlett-Packard, for example, the strategic plan contains only four numbers—projected revenues, projected costs, projected profits, and projected manpower needs (how many engineers, scientists, and technicians will be needed in future years).

Second, the organization can decide upon a narrow strategic focus by planning in only one or two human resource areas, such as recruitment or selection, or it can choose a broad focus by planning in all human resource areas including training and compensation.

A third element involves the degree to which the human resource strategy is integrated with the strategic plan. The HR strategy may have only a minor input to the overall corporate strategy, or (as is the case at Hewlett-Packard) it may be integrated into the strategic plan. The HR strategy works best by integrating it into the strategic plan.

Finally, there must be flexibility—the ability of the HR strategy to anticipate and adapt to changing competitive moves. At Apple Computer, for example, rapid early growth took place without a human resource strategy. Later, however, an HR strategy was developed and integrated with Apple's overall strategy.

Human resource strategy involves making decisions about the recruiting and performance of the workforce. The human resource strategy focuses on the organization's strategic objectives and a plan for developing the resources to meet those objectives.

When a company grows rapidly, such as Apple Computer, its employment needs will increase. Growth objectives are often a key part of an organization's overall strategic plan, because growth usually involves changes in the future size of the company. Jack Welch, CEO of General Electric, for example, decided he wants to be either number one or two in every industry GE is in or else GE will get out of that market. This is a key element of GE's strategy.[12] Growth objectives are often expressed in terms of revenues, market share, return on investment, development of new products, and development of new markets.

Human resource managers need to integrate the strategic human resource plan with the organization strategy. A growth strategy will require aggressive recruiting, hiring, and training. Many high-tech companies, including Apple, Hewlett Packard, and Microsoft, were not prepared for their rapid growth, and either had difficulty finding qualified employees or paid premium prices for specialized skills.

Source: CROCK by Rechin, Parker, and Wilder. © North America Syndicate, Inc.

In times of economic recession, many organizations are facing restructuring and downsizing. In this case, human resource managers are often dealing with tough and unpleasant decisions. It is important to have a strategic HR plan to deal with these problems in order to minimize damage and make the best out of a crisis situation. During the 1990s, many companies in the farm equipment business (including John Deere and Company), faced massive layoffs. John Deere and Company was relatively successful in protecting its public image and critical human resources by using strategic HR planning and carrying out the layoffs in a professional way. After the company had returned to high levels of profitability with a downsized, but efficient workforce, some employees were rehired. Divestitures and mergers also provide a challenge for the human resource department. Merging two or more firms often involves layoffs, transfers, and reassignments.

Downsizing

Organizations with declining sales, market share, or profits soon realize their workforce is too expensive. To increase their competitiveness, top management typically makes a strategic decision to cut their payroll. The first step is usually to use attrition; that is, not replacing employees who retire or quit. This is one way to reduce overall HRM costs. Under a budget cutting scenario, organizations such as IBM are decreasing their labor costs by 10 to 25 percent and laying off 25,000 employees.[13]

HRM IN ACTION
DOWNSIZING: LAYOFFS, AND ALTERNATIVES TO LAYOFFS[14]

The most painful aspect of **downsizing** is deciding what to do with the managers and professionals whose jobs are declared "surplus." Companies vary widely in the ways they deal with these surpluses. Consider, for example, Tenneco in Houston, Texas, where 1,200 employees were laid off over a 6-week period. According to eyewitness accounts, many of them first found out they were no longer employed when armed guards appeared on their office floors early in the morning with boxes for them to use in clearing out their desks. The stunned workers were given 20 minutes to leave the building, and were watched by the guards as they packed up their belongings and emptied their lockers at the company gym. Those managers who had come to work in company cars or van pools were given coupons for taxi rides home.

Said one angry ex-employee to the *Houston Business Journal:* "This was at best an outrageous and unnecessary slaughter of human self-respect and dignity. . . . Tenneco obviously planned the day well in advance. More than 250 boxes were ordered and stockpiled for use by laid-off employees. The cab coupons also were purchased in advance. A line of cabs formed with amazing quickness around Tenneco's downtown headquarters to cart all the terminated employees away."

Contrast the situations of these employees—and those of their "more fortunate" coworkers who remained employed—with those of Hewlett-Packard's workforce as that company recently went through some hard times. At that time, the entire electronics industry suffered a drop in orders and most companies were laying off people in significant numbers. At Hewlett-Packard, estimates indicated that it was necessary to cut back 10 percent in both output and payroll to match the decline in orders. The obvious solution would have been to follow its competitors and lay off 10 percent of the workforce. Top management, however, was committed to avoiding layoffs. After considerable discussion, a novel solution surfaced. Management decided to require everyone from the president to the lowest-paid employee to take a 10 percent cut in pay and to stay home every other Friday. By distributing the "pain" across organizational levels, Hewlett-Packard avoided both the human resources loss and the human costs associated with layoffs.

Credit for the company's committed workforce in a Silicon Valley of job hoppers has to be attributed partly to practices such as these. A key part of Hewlett-Packard's business strategy is based on maintaining a strong corporate culture. Culture is something lived by people; high turnover makes it almost impossible to keep a clear set of values within all members of the organization. A 10 percent layoff would have severely injured the HP culture; the increased voluntary turnover that most likely would have damaged the firm for years after the layoff would have impeded growth plans and

---

added to overall personnel costs. It is unlikely that Tenneco will, several years away from its sudden cutbacks, come out with a workforce as committed to serving the company as Hewlett-Packard's.

QUESTIONS

1. What do you think of the downsizing plan of Tenneco in Houston? Considering HRM, would you change anything? Was it planned in advance?

2. How did Hewlett-Packard achieve a 10 percent cutback in pay? What were the results?

3. What is the key part of Hewlett-Packard's business strategy that contributed to the pay cutback plan?

Some companies, like Hewlett-Packard, try to keep the morale of the employees up even during a downsizing. Organizations that communicate the changes early and provide the employees to be released with outplacement, retraining, or a chance to develop new skills before termination, increase the employee morale. Additionally, the remaining workers are usually asked to take on more responsibility and work. Often special training, equipment, and more control over the job are provided as a means of keeping the remaining workers satisfied. However, in many situations, the quality of the product or service often drops drastically due to downsizing, and morale is usually extremely low. Downsizing requires a carefully planned HR strategy for two reasons: (1) The organization wants to retain its key employees; and (2) Litigation—layoffs often increase situations of possible legal action.

HRM Strategies of Change

There are several possible approaches to large-scale change programs depending upon the existing conditions. One approach, which may be termed the incremental approach, refers to long-term planned change which relies upon collaboration and participation from organization members. The second approach, transformative change, usually refers to immediate, drastic change accomplished by directive methods.

Dunphy and Stace have identified a model of large scale change strategies based upon three key dimensions: the time frame of the change, long or short; the level of support of the organization culture; and the degree of discontinuity with the environment.[15] From these three dimensions, four HRM change strategies can be identified (as shown in Figure 15.2).

1. *Participative Evolution.* This incremental strategy is used to keep an organization in fit with its environment in anticipation of changes, when minor adjustments are needed, and when sufficient time is available. Such change is achieved by collaborative means with the support and participation of organization members.

2. *Charismatic Transformation.* This transformative strategy is used to accomplish radical change in a short time frame, with support from the organization culture. Fred Smith of Federal Express and Steve Jobs, founder of Apple Computer, are two examples of leaders who used such strategies to accomplish change.

3. *Forced Evolution.* This strategy is used to make minor adjustments over longer time frames, but without the support of the organization culture. The change programs of David Roderick, former chairman at USX, Donald Peterson at Ford Motor Co., and Charles Parry, former chairman at Alcoa, would typify such changes. The organization culture did not support the changes and, in

	INCREMENTAL CHANGE STRATEGIES	TRANSFORMATIVE CHANGE STRATEGIES
Collab-orative Modes	1. Participative Evolution Use when organization is in "fit" but needs minor adjust-ment, or is out of fit but time is available and key interest groups favor change.	2. Charismatic Transformation Use when organization is out of "fit," there is little time for extensive participation, but there is support for radical change within the organization.
Coercive Modes	3. Forced Evolution Use when organization is in "fit" but needs minor adjust-ment, or is out of fit but time is available and key interest groups oppose change.	4. Dictatorial Transformation Use when organization is out of "fit," there is not time for extensive participation, and no support within the organization for radical change, but radical change is vital to organizational survival and fulfillment of basic mission.

Long ←——————————————→ Time

Figure 15.2
Strategies for planned organizational change
Source: Adapted from Dexter C. Dunphy and Doug A. Stace, "Trans-formational and Coercive Strategies for Planned Organizational Change Beyond the OD Model," *Organizational Studies* 9, no. 3 (1988), 317–34.

fact, Charles Parry was replaced by a CEO who returned Alcoa to its basic businesses.

4. *Dictatorial Transformation.* This change strategy is used in times of crisis, when a major restructuring is needed which may run counter to the en-trenched interests of the corporate culture. In these conditions, authoritative direction may be the only option to ensure organizational survival. When Jack Welch, Jr., became CEO of General Electric, he wanted to make GE into a world class competitor. To accomplish this, Welch set goals for each of GE's products to become number one or two in its markets or be a candidate for divestiture.

The key point for HR managers is recognizing that the selection of appropri-ate HRM strategies depends on an analysis of the situation. However, just as im-portant is the fact that large-scale changes in times of crisis can be more effectively implemented, if it is combined with the behavioral skills of the HRM approaches. (See Our Changing World.)

OUR CHANGING WORLD OF HRM
A NEW CULTURE AT SAS[16]

In chapter 8, we discussed how when Jan Carlzon, newly-named Scandinavian Airlines (SAS) Chief Execu-tive Officer, had to change planes in Copenhagen (an SAS hub), he noted the problem with the gate connection and decided upon a change strategy.

Carlzon started HR management-type programs that trained employees at the customer service level to take more responsibility and authority. The customer service strategy, matched by a change to a customer serv-ice culture, was the successful difference at SAS.

In another recent and less successful strategy change, CEO Carlzon led a rigorous movement to merge SAS with KLM, Swissair, and Austrian airlines. He was the original architect of this merger program (called "Alcazar"). The Alcazar concept required an immense amount of Carlzon's time, resulting in a neglect of SAS's attempt to achieve financial success. The European airline industry was startled by the surprise resignation of Carlzon. Carlzon's Deputy President also resigned. These events have led to the rumors Carlzon was pushed to resign. Apparently, the merger strategy failed to achieve Carlzon's objectives.

QUESTIONS

1. What do you think of Carlzon's merger strategy? Did it contribute to his resignation?

2. Recall the earlier successful strategy and the present unsuccessful strategy. What do you think were the important differences?

THE CORPORATE CULTURE

The concept of **corporate culture** has become increasingly important as a factor in large-scale changes. Each organization forms its own culture. An organization's culture includes the shared values, beliefs, and behaviors formed by the members of an organization over time. The leadership style of top management and the norms, values, and beliefs of the organization's members combine to form the corporate culture. Organization effectiveness can be increased by creating a culture that achieves organizational goals and at the same time satisfies member needs. The CEO's words alone do not produce culture; rather the actions of managers do, as noted by *Business Week:*

> A corporation's culture can be its major strength when it is consistent with its strategies. Some of the most successful companies have clearly demonstrated that fact, including: International Business Machines Corp. where marketing drives a service philosophy that is almost unparalleled. The company keeps a hot-line open 24 hours a day, seven days a week to service IBM products.[17]

The corporate culture reflects the organization's past, and is often deeply rooted in the firm's history and mythology. Many cultures were started by the firm's founder, such as Fred Smith of Federal Express, and have been reinforced by successful operations and strategies. The corporate culture influences how managers approach problems, react to competition, and implement new strategies.

The Strategy-Culture Fit

Corporate culture is important because of its relationship to organizational effectiveness. There is increasing evidence that firms with effective corporate cultures claim to have increased productivity, boosted employee camaraderie, increased employee's sense of ownership, and increased profits.[18]

Strategy refers to a course of action used to achieve major objectives. This includes all the activities leading to the identification of the objectives and plans of the organization and is concerned with relating the resources of the organization to opportunities in the larger environment. Organizations are finding it increasingly necessary to change business strategy to meet emerging discontinuities in the environment.

Culture provides a set of values for setting priorities on what is important, and "the way things are done around here." Because of this, culture is a critical factor in the implementation of a new strategy. An organization's culture can be a major strength when there is a fit with the strategy and can be a driving force in implementing a successful change. This is the strategy-culture fit.

Recognizing the importance of culture in his strategy to revitalize IBM, CEO Louis Gerstner of IBM said, "One of the key issues is culture. We have to free up the culture from the enormous, bureaucratic, overstuffed organization it became over the last few years, one that never talked about its problems."[19]

Each organization evolves a unique culture. But this culture must also change to meet changing conditions. A number of studies have indicated that corporate strategy alone cannot produce winning results. Management consultants have suggested that only one company in 10 can successfully carry out a complex change in strategy. But the need for devising and executing strategic changes is rapidly increasing.

Culture: A Definition

There is widespread agreement that organizational culture refers to a system of shared values held by members that distinguishes one organization from another. **Characteristics** that describe an organization's culture include

- *Individual Autonomy*—the degree of responsibility, independence, and the opportunities for exercising initiative for members of the organization.
- *Structure*—the degree of rules and regulations and amount of direct supervision used to control member behavior.
- *Performance Incentives*—the degree to which incentives in the organization (i.e., salary increases, promotions) are based on member performance.
- *Risk Behavior*—the degree to which members are encouraged to be aggressive, innovative, and risk seeking.[20]

By combining each of these characteristics, then, a composite picture of the organization's culture is formed. The culture becomes the basis for the shared understanding that members have about the organization, how things are done, and the way members are supposed to behave.

A company's success rests on its ability to change strategy in order to meet rapidly changing market conditions. Under these conditions, the culture must be adjusted so the firm can confront and deal with factors that may contribute to its failure, stagnation, or success. The culture influences each member's adjustment to these changes. Productive corporate changes increase the company's capacity to meet new challenges. To be effective, managers must be able to motivate their employees and help them adapt to changing conditions. Success depends on management's skills and strategy, and the communication of change to the organization members.

Organizations operating in different environments with differing competitive situations may need to develop different cultures, each one focused upon the goals of its strategy and competitive arena. Similarly, organizations existing in several markets may need to have differing subcultures to meet the unique strategies of each specific business environment. A corporate culture reinforcing innovation, entrepreneurship, and participation, for example, may be necessary for a high-tech firm competing in a highly dynamic and complex industry. On the other hand, a more traditional firm in a mature, smokestack industry may develop a culture focusing on stability, quality, and productivity.

Sharing the Vision

One important element in organizational and culture change is the development of a **vision.** Many management theorists feel that vision is the very essence of leadership. Any attempt at cultural change should begin with a clear vision of the new strategy and what it will take to make it work. Organizations are driven by a vision, not by directives from the chain of command.

A widely used definition of vision is "a mental image of a possible and desirable future state of the organization . . . (which) articulates a view of a realistic credible, attractive future for the organization, a condition that is better in some important ways that what now exists."[21] The vision provides a sense of identity, purpose, and direction for organization members. An effective vision should be challenging, inspiring, and aimed at empowering people at all levels.

In a study of one organization, Shelley R. Robbins suggests that sharing the vision—that is making certain that all levels of the organization are involved and communicated with—is critical.[22] The fact of the matter is that the McDonald's employee flipping burgers and waiting on the customer is the one who will ultimately carry out the vision, not owner Joan Kroc and her management team at McDonald's corporate headquarters. One example of how a shared vision can impact an organization would be the vision of Steve Jobs, founder of Apple Computer. Jobs galvanized his whole organization into revolutionizing the way people processed information by sharing the dream that personal computing—and what *they* were doing—could change the world.

Developing a shared vision involves several stages, as shown in Figure 15.3:[23]

- *Share the Vision.* People will buy into a clear challenging vision that has meaning for them and will improve society.
- *Empower the Individual.* People need to feel they have a stake in the outcome and that they have participated in defining the vision. The idea is to have individual purpose congruent with the organization's vision.
- *Acknowledge Performance.* An effective vision must set goals for challenging performance, but must allow people to "buy in" to the vision and provide feedback on performance.
- *Reward Performance.* An effective vision also rewards the achievement of outstanding performance. At Apple Computer, for example, along with financial awards, Macintosh team members were included and recognized at product launch meetings and other award ceremonies. This element also includes support for taking risks, providing the freedom to fail, and pushing decision-making information downward to the lower levels.

A shared vision provides a starting point for a cultural and organizational HR strategy.

Cultural Strength

Every organization has a culture, but some cultures are stronger than others. IBM, for instance, has a more tightly held culture than does a conglomerate of newly acquired companies, or a very young firm. Harvard University has a more cohesive

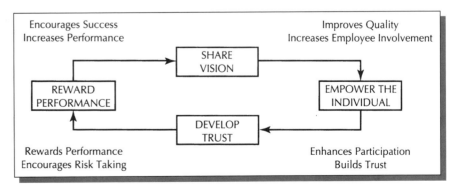

Figure 15.3
Sharing the vision

culture than many newer competitors. In strong cultures, the behavior of members is constrained by mutual accord, rather than by command or rule.

It has become increasingly popular to differentiate between strong and weak cultures. The evidence suggests that strong cultures have a greater impact on employee behavior and are more directly related to reduced turnover.[24]

A strong culture is characterized by the organization's basic values being both intensely held and widely shared, as shown in Figure 15.3. Each dimension can be envisioned as existing along a continuum from low to high. The more members sharing these basic values and the greater their commitment to those values, the stronger the culture.

By this definition, IBM and AT&T would have strong cultures, whereas relatively young companies or ones which have had a high turnover of executives and employees would be considered to have weaker cultures. It should also be noted that once an organization develops a "strong" culture, there is a high resistance to changes which affect the culture. (See Figure 15.4.) The organization can survive high turnover at lower ranks because new members can be strongly socialized into the organization.[25]

It is important to recognize that cultural strength does not necessarily guarantee corporate effectiveness. Though many current writers argue that strength is desirable, the fact remains that the relationship between culture and effectiveness is not simple. The definition of the culture and the degree to which its solutions fit the problems posed by the environment seem to be the critical variables here, not strength alone.

Managers often have a difficult time in recognizing the relationship between culture and the critical performance factors on which excellence depends. There are several key components of the organization—structure, systems, people, style—which influence the way key managerial tasks are performed. Culture is the product of these components. Strategic change is largely concerned with adjustments in these components to accommodate the perceived needs of a new strategy. So, managing the strategy-culture relationship requires sensitivity to the interaction between the changes necessary to implement strategy and the compatibility or "fit" between those changes and the organization's culture. Johnson & Johnson, an organization undergoing cultural change, is described in HRM in Action.

The Strategy-Culture Matrix

Strategic changes can more effectively be implemented when the culture of the organization is considered. In an effort to minimize the risks inherent in a proposed change, the extent of the need for change and the degree to which the change is

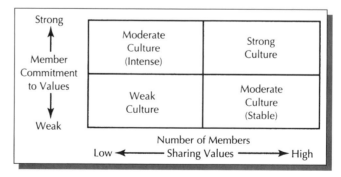

Figure 15.4
Relative strength of corporate cultures

Johnson & Johnson is a leading manufacturer of health-care products and has been rated as a well-managed company under current chief executive officer Ralph S. Larsen and former chairman James E. Burke, a Harvard MBA. Larsen is now attempting to change the strategy of the organization and move from a consumer goods firm into an advanced technology leader—"from band-aids to high tech." J&J is also attempting to develop an innovative and risk-taking corporate culture to continue the flow of new products, thus creating new markets.

The company has been known for its unique decentralized operating structure, with each of its 170 businesses operated as autonomous profit-center units. However, the number of old, maturing products were slowing future growth. Therefore, Larsen is focusing more resources in high-growth, high-margin businesses (such as pharmaceuticals) by consistently increasing Research and Development expenditures in these areas to well over the industry average. In the past, J&J has also used an acquisition strategy to move into new high-tech areas, including biotechnology, nuclear magnetic resonance (NMR), and surgical lasers.

Former chairman Jim Burke felt that innovation is built into decentralization by creating smaller, more entrepreneurial groups. These subsidiary groups let managers focus their energies and imagination on a small group of related products, while the parent company provides the resources and funding for production and marketing to turn good ideas into blockbuster products.

CHANGING THE CULTURE

But J&J initially failed to adapt to these changes. The type of cooperation and communication between units needed by the new strategy has not been completely accepted by the old culture. In the old culture, managers operated as independent profit centers and were evaluated on their own results. Under the new plan, managers need to share marketing and R&D resources—which requires collaborative teamwork versus the old independent operation.

J&J has boosted earnings by 16 percent per year and is likely to keep growing at this rate for several years. In fact, new products now account for 22 percent of sales. This compares favorably with 3M, which is regarded as one of the most innovative of companies.

CULTURE SHOCK

Many managers, however, failed to adapt to these changes. Managing high-tech products required differ-ent managerial skills and styles than the older consumer product lines. The new kind of communication and sharing of resources required was in direct conflict with existing cultural values.

J&J is trying to regain its share in traditional markets and to exploit new strategies in biotechnology and magnetic resonance. The change in strategy and culture has caused many problems and posed big risks for an old line company.

The company encourages people to take risks by creating a corporate culture where even a research failure may be a badge of honor. Mistakes are the inevitable byproduct of innovation. But even the failures have not dulled former CEO Jim Burke's passion for urging his managers to keep taking risks and to be daring.

TAKING CHANCES

This emphasis on innovation and risk taking comes from Jim Burke's own experience early in his career. One of his attempts at product innovation failed dismally. Then-chairman General Robert Wood called Burke into his office, and asked, "Are you the one who just cost us all that money?" Burke nodded, thinking this could be the end of his career, but Wood said, "Well, I just want to congratulate you. If you are making mistakes, that means you are making decisions and taking risks. And we won't grow unless you take risks."

Jim Burke believed that innovation can be nurtured through creative conflict. He says, "Any successful growth company is riddled with failures, and there's just not any other way to do it. We love to win, but we also have to lose in order to grow."

New CEO Ralph Larsen is aware that he must keep up the flow of innovation, both in new areas like biotechnology and in older product lines as well, if J&J is to remain competitive in the future.

QUESTIONS

1. Corporate executives have been quoted as saying that the greatest challenge J&J faces is to change its culture. Do you agree?

2. In the Burke-Wood meeting, if you were Burke, would you have nodded or gave an explanation? Why?

compatible with the culture should be viewed together as each impacts upon the other. Four basic alternatives in determining strategy changes are:[27]

1. Manage the change (manageable risk).
2. Reinforce the culture (negligible risk).
3. Manage around the culture (manageable risk).
4. Change the strategy to fit the culture (unacceptable risk).

The need for strategic change and the compatibility of the change, viewed together as a strategy-culture matrix, will largely influence the method used to manage the strategic change (see Figure 15.5).

Manage the Change (Manageable Risk)   An organization in quadrant 1 is implementing a strategy change that is important to the firm, where the changes are compatible with existing corporate culture. Therefore, the company can pursue a strategy requiring major changes, and the HRM should manage the change by using the power of cultural acceptance and reinforcement. The change strategies should emphasize these basic elements:

• Share the vision. The changes must be related to the overall goals and mission of the organization. This builds on existing strengths and makes any changes legitimate to members.

• Reshuffle power to raise key people to positions important in implementing the new strategy. Key people make visible the shared values and norms that lead to cultural compatibility.

• Reinforce the new value system. If the new strategic direction requires changes in marketing, production, and so forth, the changes should be reinforced by the organization's reward structure.

Reinforce the Culture (Negligible Risk)   An organization in quadrant 2 needs relatively little strategic change, and the changes are highly compatible with the existing culture. Here the HR manager should emphasize several factors:

• Forge a vision of the new strategy that emphasizes the shared values to make it work.

• Reinforce and solidify the existing culture.

At Apple Computer, CEO John Sculley made changes to the firm's competitive position, but he was also determined to reinforce the existing culture in carrying out the new strategy.

Manage around the Culture (Manageable Risk)   Organizations in quadrant 3 need to make some strategic changes, but these changes are potentially incompat-

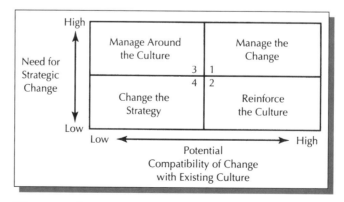

Figure 15.5
The strategy-culture matrix

ible with the corporate culture. Here the critical point is whether these changes can be implemented with a reasonable probability of success. The key element for the HR manager is to manage around the culture, without confronting direct cultural resistance (see B.C. cartoon). The approaches include

- Reinforcing the value system.
- Reshuffling power to raise key people.
- Using any available levers of change such as the budgeting process and reorganization.

Source: CROCK by Rechin, Parker, and Wilder. © North America Syndicate, Inc.

H. Ross Perot, a former vice president and member of the board of directors at General Motors, commenting on GM's inability to alter its culture said, "I come from an environment where, if you see a snake, you kill it. At GM, if you see a snake, the first thing you do is organize a committee on snakes. Then you go hire a consultant who knows a lot about snakes. Then you talk about it for a year."[28]

Change the Strategy (Unacceptable Risk)   An organization in quadrant 4 faces a different challenge, because the strategic change is important to the company, but the changes are incompatible with the entrenched corporate culture.

First Chicago Bank, for example, illustrates the dilemma faced by an organization under these conditions. The company faced the challenge of attempting to change its culture from an "aversion for risk," to an "aggressive risk-taking style." The challenge of changing the culture is an expensive long-term undertaking that is practically impossible to achieve.

When an organization is in this situation—facing large-scale change with a high probability of cultural resistance—the HR manager must determine whether strategic change is really a viable alternative. The key question is: Can the strategic change be made with any possibility of success? If the answer is no, the organization should modify its strategy to fit more closely with the existing culture.

Strategic Change Management

Noel Tichy proposed the strategic change management model which provides an important integration of the strategic interventions discussed earlier.[29] Tichy's model seeks an alignment among an organization's strategy, structure, and human resource systems, and a fit between them and the organization's environment. Strategic change is a function of how well an organization manages these alignments.

Tichy proposes that organizations are composed of three **systems: technical, political,** and **cultural.** Three basic management tools, including organizational strategy, structure, and human resource management, may be used to align the three systems with each other and with the larger environment (see Figure 15.6).

Changing the Culture

There is a general agreement that an effective corporate culture can result in superior performance. There is also considerable agreement that organizations facing discontinuity—out of fit with the environment—may need large-scale cultural change. However, changing the corporate culture is often very difficult because the culture is based upon past successes.[30] Therefore, organization members may hold deeply entranced beliefs and strong personal investments in the existing culture. There is research by J. B. Barney which suggests that a firm's culture can be a source of sustainable competitive advantage if it is difficult to imitate, thus making it difficult for less successful organizations to imitate a more successful culture.[31]

The organization culture may inhibit the implementation of a strategy and prevent a firm from meeting competitive threats or from adapting to changing economic conditions. This can lead to the firm's decline, stagnation, or even ultimate demise, unless the culture is changed. One company that has systematically changed its cultural emphasis is PepsiCo., Inc. under former chairman Donald M. Kendell.

At one time, the company was content in its number two position, offering Pepsi as a cheaper alternative to Coca-Cola. But today, a new employee at PepsiCo quickly learns that beating the competition, whether outside or inside the company, is the surest path to success. In its soft-drink operation, for example, Pepsi's marketers now take on Coke directly, asking consumers to compare the taste of the two colas. That direct confrontation is reflected inside the company as well. Managers are pitted against each other to grab more market share, to work harder, and to wring more profits out of their businesses.

Because winning is the key value at Pepsi, losing has its penalties. Consistent runners-up find their jobs gone. Employees know they must win merely to stay in place—and must devastate the competition to get ahead.[32]

Terrence Deal and Allan Kennedy suggest that there are only five reasons to justify large-scale cultural changes:[33]

1. When the company has strong values that do not fit a changing environment.
2. When the industry is very competitive and changes with lightning speed.
3. When the company is mediocre or worse.
4. When the firm is about to join the ranks of the very largest.
5. When the firm is small but growing rapidly.

HR managers facing these situations may need to change their culture in order to adapt a changing environment or to perform at higher levels of effectiveness.

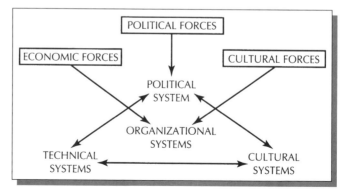

Figure 15.6
Environmental forces and organizational systems

Implementing cultural change can be extremely difficult and time consuming. Given the problems associated with culture change, many HR managers suggest that major changes to the culture should be attempted only after less difficult and costly solutions have been ruled out.

There are also problems of meshing different cultures or subcultures within the same organization. Pillsbury Co. had problems of internal conflict between subcultures. At Pillsbury's high-rise corporate headquarters in Minneapolis, managers tend to be very formal and traditional—dark three-piece suits are the uniform. (Note: Since then, Pillsbury has been acquired by a British conglomerate.) At the Burger King subsidiary's tropical headquarters on Biscayne Bay in Miami, however, pink is the exterior color: They favor flashier cars, more colorful clothes, and no ties, forming a low-key, laid-back, informal culture. These cultural differences have led to the factional nicknames "Minneapolis Ice" and "Miami Vice."[34]

This cultural clash becomes even more evident in the case of mergers or takeovers when two differing cultures must be integrated. In one case in the author's experience, one high-tech firm, Company B, with a very innovative, participative culture, was acquired by Company A, a larger competing firm with a very formal, traditional, top-down culture.

At the time the acquisition was announced, Company A stated that no major changes were planned, and that Company B would continue operating as a separate company. But within 6 months, 80 percent of the Company B management team was replaced, large-scale layoffs were instituted, and the Company A corporate culture was imposed on Company B. The results included loss of key people, loss of sales (including one $60 million customer), a decrease in morale and productivity, an increase in turnover, and a lack of trust among remaining employees. The integration of differing corporate cultures during merger situations appears to provide a very cost-effective area for the use of HRM cultural change programs in the future.[35]

For many businesses, changing the culture is not in the best long-term interests of the firm. For example, Apple Computer management recognizes that its most important challenge will be to retain its small-company culture even though it has grown into a top *Fortune* 500 firm.

In summary, leadership in today's fast changing world involves developing an innovative corporate culture—a culture which recognizes employee needs, the firm's history, the marketplace, and the company' products and services. Top managers invariably try to develop a framework for transmitting the corporate culture and for adapting to change. Unfortunately, often a strong culture may prove to be a liability if it fails to respond to changing market forces. When the corporate culture is resistant to change, then HRM strategies may be used to move the culture in a more innovative direction.[36]

SUMMARY

This chapter has presented stage six of the Success System Model: HRM programs for helping organizations transform to meet new strategic directions. Such large-scale change programs typically occur in response to, or in anticipation of, fundamental environmental or technological changes. Environmental discontinuities often require dramatic shifts in organizational strategy, which in turn necessitate changes to organization processes, corporate culture, and human resources. These HR strategy interventions are aimed at relating the organization to its broader environment and achieving a higher level of corporate excellence.

Corporate culture includes the shared values and beliefs of organization members and determines how members perform. Corporate culture is a key determinant of how an organization implements strategic change and what strategies and techniques the HR manager may bring to such programs. Changing the corporate culture starts with developing a shared vision, the **empowerment** of members, and the development of a trust relationship at all levels.

The strategy-culture matrix provides one tool that the HR manager can use in implementing strategic changes. Changing the corporate culture can be an extremely challenging task. Such change requires clear strategic vision, reinforcement of new values, and reshuffling the power-reward systems to fit the new strategy. Strategic change management presents another systems view of the organization as technical, political, and cultural systems and involves aligning these systems with the environment.

In the simulation, you will have the chance to experience the meshing of different values and risk values in forming a strategy. One important point is the difficulty and complexity of strategic HRM programs and the need for HRM skills in implementing new programs in organizations.

Organizational excellence in a rapidly changing world requires an innovative and adaptive corporate culture. Strategic change has become increasingly important in recent years and often influences the very survival of an organization in a volatile environment. The corporate culture can be a force in reinforcing or resisting strategic changes. Therefore, when the culture is resistant to innovations, HRM programs may be used to enhance successful strategic changes.

REVIEW QUESTIONS

1. Define and discuss an organization's HRM strategy.
2. What forces might contribute to making a culture strong?
3. How does the culture affect an organization's ability to change?
4. Can you identify the characteristics that describe your organization's culture?
5. Review a novel or video movie for examples of strategy.

KEY WORDS AND CONCEPTS

Define and be able to use the following:

- Downsizing
- Empowerment
- Strategy

- Strategy-Culture Fit
- Technical, Political, and Culture Systems

- Vision

HRM SKILLS SIMULATION 15.1: THE GENTECH COMPANY

Total time suggested: 2 hours, 10 minutes

A. PURPOSE

The purpose of this simulation is to experience and observe how information affects strategic decision making. In this simulation, you will be able to develop strategy and culture in an organization. You will receive feedback on your risk-taking level. The goals include:

- Comparing strategic decisions made by individuals with those of the team.
- Learning how task information is shared among group members.
- Identifying how individual risk-taking levels influence results.
- Learning how collaboration and competition affect team problem solving.

B. PROCEDURES

Step 1. Prior to class, form GenTech teams of five. Additional members may serve a consultants. Each member selects one role and reads the company and strategy information. Extra members act as Observers. The roles include

1. Executive vice president, corporate strategy
2. Vice president, human resource management
3. Vice president, manufacturing
4. Vice president, marketing
5. Vice president, engineering

Individually, read the GenTech Company Background, Terminology, and Strategy Descriptions that follow. There are four basic strategies. Within each strategy, there are two implementation alternatives. For the four strategies, allocate a percentage of investment to each strategy that reflects the degree of emphasis you want to place on that strategy. Record your choices on Form 1: My Individual Strategic Decision, Column 1, Individual Strategy. The four strategies should add vertically to 100 percent.

Then for each of the four basic strategies, allocate a percentage of resources between Implementation Alternatives A, B, and C. Record your percentages in Column 2, Implementation Alternatives A & B & C. The sum of the percentages for Alternatives A and B and C within each of the four strategies will total 100 percent. (As an example, you may give "Market Penetration" 30 percentage points. Within this strategy, you may give Alternative A 50 percentage points, Alternative B 20 percentage points, and Alternative C 30 percentage points. You would then go through the other three strategies and allocate percentage points in a similar manner.)

Step 2. The Executive Committee Meeting. The committee meets to select a strategy. Through team discussion, exploration, and examination, try to reach a *consensus decision* reflecting the integrated thinking and consensus of all members. The two parameters of team effectiveness include (1) the determination of an optimal strategy; and (2) the completion of the task in the least amount of time.

Follow these instructions for reaching consensus:

1. Try to identify the best long-term strategy.
2. Avoid changing your mind simply to reach agreement and to avoid conflict, but support solutions with which you are able to agree.
3. Avoid "conflict-reducing" techniques such as majority vote, averaging, or trading in reaching your decision.
4. View differences of opinion as a help rather than a hindrance in decision making.

At this point, meet together as the executive committee and enter your committee's decision on Form 2, Executive Committee Strategic Decisions.

Time suggested for Step 2: 45 minutes.

Step 3. Each team lists its results on the blackboard and discusses the team decision rankings as they reflect HRM input.

Time suggested for Step 3: 10 minutes.

BACKGROUND: THE GENTECH COMPANY BACKGROUND

The GenTech Company is a medium-sized high-tech firm selling computers, computer components, software, and information systems. Until the past 5 years, GenTech has had a strong and steady growth record, and its products have traditionally been highly rated by customers. Their employees have been highly motivated and committed to the company. GenTech has a sound financial position, but during the last 5 years, it has been losing its market share because of new competitors entering the field with more advanced products at lower prices. Further, employee turnover and absenteeism have been gradually increasing. Supervisors have been complaining new hires were difficult to train.

In the past, GenTech has been particularly noted for its fast growth. People always know where they stand around GenTech. However, recently several of the newer and more promising managers and engineers have quit to join competitors. Exit interviews indicated pay and benefits were not the reason. As a relative newcomer to the computer industry (GenTech was founded 11 years ago), GenTech is still a medium-sized company in its industry, but it has been modestly successful in competing with big firms like DEC and IBM. GenTech is a fast-moving company, and employee behavior is somewhat unorthodox in that it is highly flexible. GenTech has always operated on the concept of "Let's get it done now, and we'll worry about rules and regulations tomorrow."

The executive vice president has called a meeting of key managers to form a new corporate strategy based upon the goals of the company. One key factor is how to allocate the investment funds into a total company strategy.

TERMINOLOGY

1. A *market penetration* strategy involves an attempt to increase market share in an existing market niche, one in which the firm already offers a product or service.
2. *Market development* introduces an existing product or service into new market areas, often by expansion into new market segments or geographic areas.
3. *Diversification* involves the development of new products and services and entry into new markets. The degree of change often makes this a high-risk strategy.
4. *Product development* is a technology-based strategy that involves developing new or advanced products for existing markets.

STRATEGY DESCRIPTIONS

Inclusive in all of these strategies was the need to include HRM programs in recruitment, training, appraisal, team management, employee empowerment, and motivation. Top management believed the future of GenTech required highly selective employees, capable of technical training, intensely motivated, and adaptive to team management.

The board of directors has suggested four basic strategies, with two implementation alternatives within each basic strategy, as follows.

Strategy 1. Market penetration
A. Increase advertising expenditures, number of sales reps, and promotional activities, and possibly cut prices. This strategy will focus on the products with greatest profit margin (printers, keyboards). There is an 80 percent estimated probability that this strategy will increase demand for currently profitable products, with a need to recruit new production employees.

B. Increase advertising and introduce new high-end "cadillac" products into existing lines. This new, improved company image may lead to customer acceptance of these higher margin products in existing and increased market niches with an estimated 75 percent probability of success, but no recruitment.

C. This strategy requires the recruitment of high quality sales representation to sell the product line in market penetration strategies A and B. Incentive and benefits programs need to be reviewed to attract the high quality people to achieve this strategy. Training programs also need to be reviewed to update new product development.

Strategy 2. Market development
A. Identify and develop new markets for existing products by promoting products in markets not currently served, new demographic, or geographic markets. Market research estimates a 75 percent probability that increasing demand in new markets would add to sales growth, profits about the same (possibly slightly lower), but with increased volume of sales, and hiring of new employees.

B. Identify and develop new markets by differentiating our existing products to tailor them to new geographic markets, or new market niches. The profit margins are likely to be high on this strategy, even with relatively low volume of sales with an estimated 70 percent probability of success, because uncertainty in the industry could result in low sales. This could lead to a downsizing of production levels.

C. Increased staffing will involve HRM in recruitment, training, incentives, appraisals, and team management in market development strategies A and B. Present HRM progress must be reviewed to reflect the new strategy requirements.

Strategy 3. Product development

A. The production group has proposed new product development aimed at designing a new low-cost, low-price keyboard and disk drive to meet competition. In the past, the firm has been a high-quality product with an investment in manufacturing efficiency. A low-cost product could be developed resulting in increased sales to the low-end market, estimated at a 70 percent probability of success and increased hiring.

B. A second new product would involve the development of a new high-performance keyboard and laser printer. This would provide an increase in market share at the high-end market against foreign competition. This requires up-front design investment, but has a 65 percent probability of considerably higher profit margins and increased market.

C. Any new products in product development strategies A and B will require the HRM to reassess present skill levels. Recruitment sources may need to be changed to acquire more technically oriented new hires. Any product production change will probably need new training programs, particularly in the area of team worker effectiveness. Wage and benefit programs will require change to adjust to changing labor and economic conditions.

Strategy 4. Diversification

A. There is an opportunity to acquire a competing firm making color monitors which would fit with our line of products. This would allow a complete line of peripherals and would increase volume, but involves an industry in which we have little expertise; the estimate of success is rated at about 65 percent, but could increase total sales volume and profitability. HR would be involved in the merger.

B. The company has a chance to develop a new laptop or notebook-size computer by acquiring a small company in this field. This would move the company into entirely new markets and increase its potential return and profitability. This builds on existing expertise, although much of the technology comes from the acquired company; thus, its estimated probability of success is only 60 percent, but it has become a very attractive, high-growth industry (representing the fastest growing segment of the market), and offers high rewards if successful. Our risk is that of alienating some current customers. This involves hiring new workers.

C. The HRM concerns expressed for the other strategies are also important considerations in diversification strategies A and B. Although considerations of corporate culture are a high priority in the other strategies, it becomes of primary importance in any acquisition. HRM will need to determine the compatibility of other firms with GenTech's culture. Specific HRM training programs may be required to insure GenTech's culture is readily accepted and perpetuated.

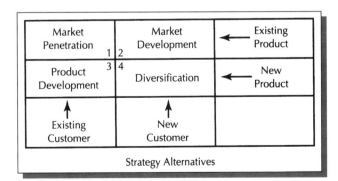

Exhibit 15.1
Strategy matrix

FORM 1

MY INDIVIDUAL STRATEGIC DECISION

Strategy	Individual Strategy (Column 1)	Implementation Alternatives A & B & C (Column 2)
1. Market Penetration	_____ %	A. _____ % B. _____ % C. _____ % 100%
2. Market Development	_____ %	A. _____ % B. _____ % C. _____ % 100%
3. Product Development	_____ %	A. _____ % B. _____ % C. _____ % 100%
4. Diversification	_____ %	A. _____ % B. _____ % C. _____ % 100%
Total	100%	

FORM 2

EXECUTIVE COMMITTEE STRATEGIC DECISIONS

STRATEGY	TEAM STRATEGY (COLUMN 1)	ALTERNATIVES A & B & C (COLUMN 2)
1. Market Penetration	_____%	A. _____% B. _____% C. _____% 100%
2. Market Development	_____%	A. _____% B. _____% C. _____% 100%
3. Product Development	_____%	A. _____% B. _____% C. _____% 100%
4. Diversification	_____%	A. _____% B. _____% C. _____% 100%
Total	100%	

OBSERVER FORM

Instructions: For each item, place a number in the blank to the right representing your reaction to how your group performed based on the following scale.

Low   1 : 2 : 3 : 4 : 5 : 6 : 7 : 8 : 9 : 10   High

1. Degree of cooperative teamwork: _____
2. Degree of team motivation: _____
3. Degree of member satisfaction: _____
4. Degree of information sharing (participation):   _____
5. Degree of consensual decision making: _____
6. Degree of team conflict or competition (i.e., conflict directly faced and resolved):   _____
7. Degree of quality of group decisions: _____
8. Degree of speed with which decision is made: _____
9. Degree of participating leadership: _____
10. Degree of clarity of goals: _____

                                   Total ranking   _____

Case 15.1   The Space Electronics Corporation

The Space Electronics Corporation is a subsidiary of a major firm with sales in excess of $200 million. The company held substantial positions in commercial and military electronic system markets; however, profitability and market position have been declining. A recent employee survey found employee morale and job satisfaction in a drastic decline. This was substantiated by a recent increase in absenteeism and job turnover. About a year ago it became apparent that two R&D projects were coming up: the stealth bomber and the Star Wars proposals. Both programs will require new technical skills and increased teamwork. It is apparent a crash training program will be needed if employees' skill and motivational commitment are to meet these challenges. These appeared to be the only two major projects coming up in the next few years. The executive committee was to decide whether or not they should pursue these two projects. This would involve taking a radically new course of action in developing a more responsive human resource strategy.

THE EXECUTIVE COMMITTEE MEETING

In mid-September, *Reade Exton, the president,* opened the meeting. "As you all know, our profitability and market position have been declining. We have landed only one new proposal during this period, and there is great pressure from headquarters to go after these major projects. However, there are some real concerns whether our present employees are sufficiently trained and committed to meet our new technical challenges. We have all had an opportunity to review a copy of the proposals, and I'll let Glenn start the discussion."

Glenn Overton, vice president, engineering: "About a year ago it became obvious that our engineering activity was going to decline. The decision was made that a joint effort with marketing would be undertaken and after a series of meetings, it was decided that our best course of action was to aggressively pursue these two large contracts."

Oliver Whittier, vice president, finance: "Frankly, Glenn, I have reservations about such a major departure from our past policies and by the magnitude of these projects. I'm worried about the increased overhead and the drain on our current profits. In particular, I am concerned with the training costs plus what appears to be needless expenditures on some so-called people programs."

Ted Byron, vice president, marketing: "These contracts will put us on the map. My best 'guesstimate' is that our chances are closer to 75 percent than 60 percent. I believe our employees are up to the task. These employee surveys are never that accurate."

Paul Brown, vice president, human resource management: "I am worried about our ability to produce the new high technology that these projects require. We have not been attentive to a human resource strategy regarding futuristic electronic development. We need to conduct a skills survey and compare what level our employees are versus the new required skill levels. If we are talking empowering work teams, it is a long-term financial commitment."

Mort Jensen, vice president, manufacturing: "Let's face it, if we pull these two proposals out of the hat, they will love us at headquarters. We'll be superstars! But on the other hand, we could take a real beating if these projects fizzle out. I think we have to consider the risk factor and what might happen to the company if we fail. Are we prepared to take on this challenge?"

Glenn Overton: "Listen, fellows, there are no lead-pipe cinches in this business. But don't you think Ted and I have a better feel for our problems, both present and future, than people in the human resource management department? If a downturn were to occur, our company will be hard pressed anyway. Frankly, I'm not quite as optimistic as Ted here, but I still think our chances are in the 60 percent range. Our company will benefit greatly, and our R&D will stand to gain a heck of a lot by being involved in the state of the art. We'll be able to attract new talent."

Mort Jensen: "One of our past problems was the isolation of R&D from the rest of the organization. I feel that we should seek to achieve more interdepartmental cooperation. What we need is more open communication between departments. There seems to be a growing distrust between management and our employees. So I think it is important to get all the differing viewpoints out on the table."

Reade Exton: "I think we have had a good discussion, but now what is our decision? As you know, there is a lot of pressure from headquarters to go after these projects, but it has to be a group decision. Frankly, we are between a rock and a hard place. There will have to be a significant expenditure just to pursue these major contracts."

QUESTIONS

1. What do you see as the major advantages to a new strategy?

2. What is the "downside?"

3. What strategy would you support and why?

ENDNOTES

1. Peter Burham, "The Boss," *Business Week* (August 2, 1999): 76.
2. Don Harvey, *Strategic Management* (Westerville, OH: Merrill, 1988), 6.
3. Andrew D. Szilagyi, Jr. and David M. Schweiger, "Matching Managers to Strategy," *Academy of Management Review* 9, no. 4 (1984): 626–37; and LaRue T. Hosmer, "The Importance of Strategic Leadership," *Journal of Business Strategy* 3, no. 2 (Fall 1982): 58.
4. Alan Farnham, "America's Most Admired Corporations," *Fortune* (February 7, 1994): 50.
5. "Did He Jump? Or Was He Pushed?" *Air Transport World* 38, no. 11 (November 1993): 9.
6. Thomas J. Peters and Robert H. Waterman, Jr., *In Search of Excellence: Lessons from America's Best-Run Companies* (New York: Harper & Row, 1982), 285.
7. Daniel T. Carroll, "A Disappointing Search for Excellence," *Harvard Business Review* (November-December 1983), 78–88. See also *Wall Street Journal,* 6 June 1985; *Business Week* (June 3, 1985).
8. A. Rucci, S. Kirn, and R. Quinn, "The Employee-Customer Profit Chain at Sears," *Harvard Business Review* (January-February 1998): 82.
9. K. Martelbald and S. Carrol, "How Strategic is HRM?" *Human Resource Management* 34 (1995): 253.
10. Leonard A. Schlesinger, "The Normative Underpinnings of Human Resource Strategy," *Human Resource Management* 22 (Spring/Summer 1983): 8396.
11. P. Wright, G. McMahn, and A. MacMillan, "Human Resources and Competitive Advantages," *Human Resource Management* 5 (1994): 301.
12. Robert Berra, "What It Takes to Succeed at the Top," *HR Magazine* (October 1991): 34–37.
13. Laurie Hays, "IBM's Finance Chief Cuts Costs," *Wall Street Journal,* 26 January 1994, p. 1.
14. Robert M. Tomasko, "Downsizing: Layoffs and Alternatives to Layoffs," *Compensation and Benefits Review* 23 (July-August 1991): 19–32.
15. Dexter C. Dunphy and Doug A. Stace, "Transformational and Coercive Strategies for Planned Organizational Change Beyond the OD Model," *Organizational Studies* 9, no. 3 (1988): 317–334.
16. John F. Hulpke, Working Paper, University of Technology Hong Kong, 1999.
17. "Corporate Culture," *Business Week* (October 27, 1980): 148.
18. See Barbara Block, "Creating a Culture all Employees Can Accept," *Management Review* (July 1989), 41.
19. Judith Dobrzynski, "Running the Biggest LBO," *Business Week* (October 2, 1989): 79.
20. Adapted and modified from J. P. Campbell, M. D. Dunnette, E. E. Lawler III, and K. E. Weick, *Managerial Behavior, Performance, and Effectiveness* (New York: McGraw-Hill, 1970), 393.
21. Warren Bennis and B. Nanus, *Leaders: The Strategies for Taking Charge* (New York: Harper & Row, 1985).
22. See Shelley R. Robbins, "The CEO as Change Agent: The Vision of the Leader." Paper presented at The Academy of Management, August 1989.
23. John W. Alexander, "Sharing the Vision," *Business Horizons* (May-June 1989): 57–59.
24. E. H. Schein, "The Role of the Founder in Creating Organizational Culture," *Organizational Dynamics* (Summer 1983): 13–28.
25. Ibid.
26. Ibid.
27. Howard Schwartz and Stanley M. Davis, "Matching Corporate Culture and Business Strategy," *Organizational Dynamics* (Summer 1981): 43.
28. Maryann Keller, *Rude Awakening: The Rise, Fall, and Struggle for Recovery of General Motors* (New York: William Morrow and Company, 1989), 181.
29. Noel Tichy, *Managing Strategic Change* (New York: John Wiley & Sons, Inc., 1983).
30. Donald F. Harvey and R. Wald, "Changing the Organizational Culture." Paper presented at San Diego, CA, 1998.
31. Jay B. Barney, "Organizational Culture: Can It be a Source of Competitive Advantage?" *Academy of Management Review* 11, no. 3 (1986): 656–65.
32. "Corporate Culture," *Business Week* (October 27, 1980): 148.
33. T. E. Deal and A. A. Kennedy, *Corporate Cultures: The Rites and Rituals of Corporate Life* (Reading, MA: Addison-Wesley, 1982), 65–66.
34. "Cultural Clash at Pillsbury," *Wall Street Journal,* 23 October 1986, p. 1.
35. Donald F. Harvey and Gayle Ogden, "The Impact of Corporate Culture in an Acquisition Situation." Working Paper, 1990.
36. Paul Myerson and Robert D. Hamilton III, "Matching Corporate Culture and Technology," *Advanced Management Journal* 51 (Winter 1986): 8.

Chapter 16

The Success System: Changing for Success

Objectives

Upon completing this chapter, you will be able to:

1. Recognize the importance of corporate culture to organizational success.
2. Identify the key factors used in assessing the corporate culture.
3. Describe the cultural and organizational factors which lead to effective organizations.

Premeeting preparation

1. Read chapter 16.
2. Prepare for HRM Skills Simulation 16.1. Read Parts A and B, Step 1.
3. Read Case 16.1: The Dim Lighting Company. Answer questions.

The General Electric Corporation has a 115-year history of business success. When John F. Welch, Jr., became GE's chief executive officer, the corporation was considered to be among the bluest of the blue chips. Yet, Jack Welch saw weakness where others saw strength and began a culture change program to completely change the corporate structure and the way business was conducted.

The weakness of GE was evident in the corporation's net income, steadily declining at a 2 percent annual rate. As a result, GE's stock lost about 25 percent of its investment value while the Dow Jones industrial average declined 15 percent.

When Jack Welch became CEO, he said, "I want a revolution." One of Welch's rules was "Change before you have to." By downsizing, Welch eliminated 35,000 employees or about 9 percent of GE's total. Welch also divested 117 business units and reduced the workforce by another 37,000 employees. Welch's goal for management and employees is to implant the values of self-confidence, candor, and facing reality, even if it's painful. He wants GE employees to share their employer's goals, and thus eliminate much of management's supervision. Welch believes the intellectual and creative capital of the workforce is more important than the financial capital.

Welch's revolution appears to be working. The recent value of the company's stock was $94 per share or seven times more than when Welch became CEO.[1]

The Challenge of Change

Change, massive change, is impacting on all facets of society, creating new dimensions and great uncertainty. The issue facing us today is how to manage such change. The HR manager provides a renewal process enabling managers to adapt their style and goals to meet the changing demands of the environment. These changes—improving quality, increasing innovation, and adopting a customer orientation—are so fundamental that it usually means changing the organization's culture.[2]

Change is inevitable. Executives are adapting to changing market conditions and at the same time facing the need for creating a "renewing" rather than a "reactive" managerial system. They are searching for ways to manage an increasingly complex technology and a more sophisticated workforce. To accomplish these diverse goals, HR managers need more than short-term HRM programs dealing only with current crises. They need long-term efforts to prepare for future organization manpower requirements. In the new millennium, changes will be faster and more unpredictable.

In such a chaotic world, the only excellent managers will be those who are constantly leading change—those not only able to deal proactively with shifting forces, but those able to take advantage of opportunities.[3]

An effective organizational climate and a realistic vision of the future are both essential to future success. At Citicorp, for example, "We're in the business of managing change. That requires a combination of vision and execution," says CEO John S. Reed. Managing change is a challenge for every organization. How well organizations manage change will determine their success or failure.[4]

As R. H. Kilmann has noted:

> The organization itself has an invisible quality—a certain style, a character, a way of doing things—that may be more powerful than the dictates of any one person or any formal system. To understand the soul of the organization requires that we travel below the charts, rule books, machines, and buildings into the underground world of corporate culture.[5]

The lessons of management seem to point out companies with outstanding financial performance often have powerful corporate cultures, suggesting that "culture" is the key to an organization's success. **Cultural change** does not just happen in an organization: Rather, it is usually the result of a complex change strategy implemented by the company's management.

Given an environment of rapid change, a rigid, inflexible organization culture is no longer workable. HR managers need to be able to recognize when changes are needed and possess the necessary skills and competence to implement such changes. The organization must try to adapt itself to a dynamic environment by introducing internal changes which will allow the organization to grow or downsize into a more effective system.

In this chapter, we present stage six of the Success System Model: changing for success. We will discuss (1) the concept of corporate culture; (2) the impact of key cultural factors; and (3) the goals and values of an HRM program. This stage presents an opportunity for the HR manager to assume a more dynamic role in assuring a successful organization.

THE CORPORATE CULTURE

Every organization has a culture. At IBM, for example, service to the customer is a dominant value that forms a basis for action from top management down through all levels of the company.

Pepsi Cola also has its own culture. "Pepsi's values reflect the desire to overtake Coke. Managers engage in fierce competition against each other to acquire market share, to squeeze more profits out of their business, and to work harder. Employees who do not succeed are terminated. They must win to get ahead. A career can be made or broken on one-tenth of a point of market share. Everyone knows the Pepsi corporate culture thrives on the creative tension generated. The internal structure is lean and adaptable. Company picnics are characterized by intensively competitive team sports. Pepsi managers frequently change jobs and are motivated to excel. Their culture is characterized by a "go-go" atmosphere and success at all costs."[6] (See Our Changing World.)

OUR CHANGING WORLD
PEPSI, COKE, AND "GO-GO" CULTURES[7]—THE COLA WARS

The news clips were impressive. Most of the Berlin Wall was still standing, but everywhere big gaps were opening, with the tacit approval of the soon-to-be eliminated East German government. Hustling through those gaps in the wall were Coca-Cola trucks, loaded with Coke for thirsty East Berliners. Coke gave away thousands of free Cokes, demonstrating that Cola Wars are not confined to any one country.

Coke is now entering an new era with a pretty significant amount of cash on hand, including the $1.1 billion it got from selling Coke's 49 percent interest in Columbia Pictures to Sony. Coca-Cola's president, Robert Goizueta, plans to spend some of the cash on new international bottling joint ventures. Why go overseas? Goizueta responds: "Why did Willie Sutton rob banks? That's where the money is."

THE PEPSI CHALLENGE

In years to come, look for aggressive moves from Pepsi on the international front, too. As a *Forbes* article puts

it, "Pepsi wants to go international in the worst way." However, they have not really arrived yet, in spite of Pizza Hut franchises in Russia, Kentucky Fried Chicken outlets in Beijing and elsewhere, and Pepsi just about everywhere. The truth is that Pepsi is not turning those overseas ventures into the kinds of profits Coke earns. Coke earns 66 percent of its soft drink revenues and 80 percent of its soft drink profits outside the United States. Pepsi, by contrast, earns 50 percent of its soft drink revenues and only 15 percent of its soft drink profits from foreign operations. The Pepsi Challenge is going global. As PepsiCo chairman, D. Wayne Calloway, put it: "We are still basically an American company with offshore interests. As the '90s progress, that's going to change. We'll be a truly global consumer products company."

---

in point is India. Coca-Cola was forced out of India in a political move, where one faction attempted to embarrass the faction that had allowed Coca-Cola access to India. Coke was ordered to give the locals the secret Coke formula as a condition of staying in business. To no one's surprise, Coke shut down its operation and left.

Meanwhile, PepsiCo has had its eyes on the Indian market. Indians don't drink much cola now, but Pepsi figured aggressive marketing might pay off. For instance, in neighboring Pakistan, soft drink consumption is 13 bottles per person per year, compared to only three bottles per person per year in India. By comparison, Egypt boosted consumption to 80 bottles per capita per year after a cola war broke out there.

"GO-GO" AT ANY COST

The details of the Pepsi deal allowing it to go into India are complex, but at least Pepsi is there. Were risks involved? You bet. But they are just part of the Pepsi "Go-Go-win-at-any-cost culture. Under the new Pepsi culture, there was no option. Given even a slim chance at such a large potential market, there was simply no choice: Pepsi had to go ahead and give it a try.

QUESTIONS

1. Identify differences between the Pepsi and Coca-Cola cultures.

2. Why does Coca-Cola continue to plan to spend cash on international bottling joint ventures? Do you agree with his philosophy? Why?

WHAT IS CORPORATE CULTURE?

A **corporate culture** is a system of shared values and beliefs which interact with an organization's people, structure, and systems to produce behavioral norms (the way things are done around here.)[8] (See Figure 16.1.) (See cartoon.)

We shall use the term corporate culture to refer to all types of organizations: Thus, a university or a city government has a corporate culture, even though they

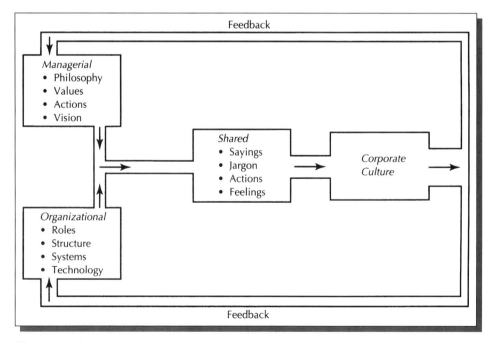

Figure 16.1
Culture formation

Source: B.C. by permission of Johnny Hart and Creators Syndicate, Inc.

are not corporations. An organization may also have subcultures with differing or even conflicting corporate cultures.

Management style and corporate culture are central factors in the success of a company. "One of the most critical factors in organizational strategy is management style and culture. This sets the tone for the whole organization and influences the communication, decision making, and leadership patterns of the entire system."[9] There is no one basic culture that works best for all organizations. The management style and the set of norms, values, and beliefs of the organization's members combine to form the corporate culture. According to Terrence Deal and Allan Kennedy, "A shared history between members builds a distinct corporate identity or character."[10]

A corporate culture must achieve goals as well as satisfy the needs of members in order for the organization to be effective. Culture influences how managers and employees approach problems, serve customers, react to competitors, and carry out activities. In comparing the style of Japanese and American automakers, Robert Waterman suggested the importance of culture:

> It has not been just strategy that led to big Japanese wins in the American auto market. It is a culture that inspires workers to excel at fits and finishes, to produce moldings that match and doors that won't sag, and to change processes that allow continuous improvement.[11]

A strong, widely internalized corporate culture is frequently cited as a reason for the success of such companies as 3M and Procter & Gamble. In these organizations, the rewards, ceremonies, and other symbolic forms of communications maintain a culture that guides the actions of its members.[12] Similarly, in a study of 24 organizations, Henry Migliore has identified a set of 20 cultural factors termed the corporate culture index which may be used to measure the organizational culture.[13] These factors include managerial style, communications, and decision making.

The Corporate Culture and Success

A corporate culture gives the organization's employees a sense of how to behave, what to do, and where to place priorities in getting the job done. Culture helps members fill in the blanks between formal directives and how the work actually gets done. As a result, culture is of critical importance in the implementation of strategy.

A great majority of outstanding companies trace their culture back to an influential founder who personified a value system and relentlessly hammered on a few basic values which became the cultural core of the company.[14] However, with today's rapidly changing environment, many corporate cultures fail to adapt to change and therefore fail as economic entities.

One example of clashing corporate cultures occurred when General Motors acquired Electronic Data Systems (EDS). CEO Roger Smith (now retired) allowed EDS to keep their corporate culture. He then transferred 10,000 employees from GM to EDS. The GM employees had a difficult time dealing with EDS' corporate culture, which was radically different from GM's culture. In fact, there was a near revolt. The GM employees couldn't deal with the strict rules and regulations of EDS—such as no tassels on shoes and no alcoholic drinks at lunch. Over 600 of the transferred employees quit. A similar situation occurred when GM acquired Hughes Aircraft. Once again, Roger Smith allowed Hughes to retain their corporate culture. Some GM managers were brought over and they had problems adjusting to Hughes' corporate culture, but Smith protected them by forming independent subsidiaries.[15]

CREATING A WINNING CULTURE

What makes for **excellence** in the management of an organization? In recent books and videos on the management of corporations, Tom Peters and Robert Waterman have provided some insight into developing an effective organization.[16] Today's key words are flexibility and innovation. Organizations are being forced to make dramatic changes just to remain competitive. These changes, such as improving product quality, increasing speed of responsiveness, and expanding customer orientation, are so basic and fundamental managers must alter the corporate culture. However, cultural change implies a change in the basic values in the hearts and minds of the individual employee.

In their earlier book, *In Search of Excellence,* Peters and Waterman studied the practices of 43 companies that are often used as examples of well-managed organizations, including IBM, McDonald's, and Hewlett-Packard. The book's basic message was that U.S. organizations can regain their competitive edge by paying more attention to the culture and to people—customers and employees—and by developing those core skills and values that employees know how to do best.

In Search of Excellence was a response to management's emphasis on traditional structures and values and on "number crunching" as an answer to all problems. Perhaps the most important message is that the excellent companies of today will not necessarily be the well-run companies of tomorrow. An excellent company must develop a core culture which leads to innovation and adaptation to the changing environment. At 3M, McDonald's, and Hewlett-Packard, for example, the culture and values that drive the behavior of employees are harmonious with the market-driven strategies of the companies. In their later books, both Tom Peters and Bob Waterman suggest the only excellent firms are those that are rapidly changing.

The Impact of Key Factors

In order to create a **winning culture,** managers need to adapt their managerial style, values, and goals to fit the changing demands of the environment. The focus of HRM is to improve an organization's self-renewal process so managers can quickly initiate changes to the corporate culture to meet new problems which are emerging. Tomorrow's leaders will be those who are most flexible and innovative.

There are several key factors which organizations need to be aware of to improve the level of effectiveness:

- **Create a Vision for the Future** A shared vision provides direction, focus, and commitment. Harold Leavett has termed this action "pathfinding," and it involves the dreamer, the innovator, the creator, and the entrepreneur.[17] Some very successful organizations began with a vision. Steve Jobs at Apple Computer, for example, dreamed of a computer for everyone—"one person, one computer"—as a way toward a better world. Fred Smith at Federal Express bet his personal fortune on overnight delivery and on the need for faster information processing in a high-speed world. These visions are compelling and involve all members in striving toward goals: vision provides meaning.

- **Develop a Model for Change**   Total organization change often starts in one unit or subculture of the organization. When Steve Jobs started to develop the Macintosh computer system at Apple, he started with a handpicked team of young dedicated designers, whom he termed the "pirates," working under the black skull and crossbones flag. Similarly, at a large utility, one department manager instituted an MBO program even though most corporate managers said it would never work. This change led to increased performance of this department, and ultimately the whole organization was motivated to use this system. Though it may be coincidental, this manager is now the president of his company.

- **Reward Changes**   One of the most basic underlying concepts of motivation is that people tend to behave in ways that provide rewards or reinforcement for them. If the system still rewards the old culture, then it won't make sense for people to change. This, of course, includes pay and promotion, but other incentives as well. For example, in Japan, Sharp Corporation rewards top performers by putting them on an elite "gold badge" project team. At Apple, awards and recognition were used to gain employee involvement and people were willing to work incredible hours to bring out products. They wore t-shirts that celebrated their dedication with sayings like: "Working ninety-hours a week and loving it."[18]

There is considerable debate over whether changing these deeply held values is possible. In the next sections, we examine **cultural resistance** to change and some power tools suggested to use in HRM change programs.

Cultural Resistance to Change

Changing a corporate culture is not easy. Culture emerges out of the shared behaviors of organization members and working relationships which have developed over time. Consequently, it takes time for a cultural transformation to take effect.

A culture can also prevent a company from remaining competitive or adapting to a changing environment. People Express, Inc., built its early success on an unusual and highly decentralized form of management in which every employee was an owner-manager. Employees were encouraged and even required to perform different functions, such as a pilot also working as a ticket agent. The result was that employees tended not to get bored and learned other aspects of the business. This type of happy disorganization worked well when the company was small, but it became chaos and created substantial problems for a billion-dollar-a-year company. When People Express was warned about their management practices being inappropriate, the company would respond with the statement, "This philosophy is what made us great. We're not going to change." The company president, Donald C. Burr, still held on to this culture up to the point that People Express, suffering from heavy losses, was forced to sell out to its arch rival, Texas Air.[19]

People Express demonstrates the importance of culture in managing a company's strategy. As a result, changing the culture to successfully implement a strategy is critical. "HRM in Action" illustrates this difficulty at Procter & Gamble.

The need for developing and executing better strategies is becoming readily apparent. Recession, deregulation, technological upheavals, social factors, foreign competition, and markets that seem to emerge and vanish as quickly as they come, have increased the pressure on companies to be flexible and adaptable. "The fashionable view holds that the biggest stumbling block on the path to adaptation is often an inappropriate culture."[21] Dennis Nowlin, manager of executive development

Procter & Gamble, once considered very slow and cumbersome, is pushing authority down, speeding up decisions, and becoming more responsive to its customers. P&G is reinventing its corporate culture and undergoing a radical restructuring under new chairman, Edwin Artzt. In the process, P&G is reinventing the packaged goods industry of the future. But can a large and bureaucratic organization make these radical changes without totally destroying the culture that made it great?

TRADITIONAL VALUES

P&G has been known as a corporation with traditional, old-fashioned values. The organization man in the gray flannel suit feels right at home and hierarchy and tradition reign—drinking at lunch or wearing light colored socks or red suspenders is discouraged. Middle managers rarely made key decisions, and the decision process often traveled through several management layers. But as John G. Smale, former CEO, commented, "You can't be old fashioned and be successful in the markets in which we compete."

At a time when sales of Pert Plus, the combined shampoo and conditioner, took off in the United States, Mr. Artzt grilled managers about why the product wasn't being sold in Europe and Asia. People present say that Mr. Artzt, when told that P&G lacked manufacturing capability, exploded, "You mean all you need is four walls. Why don't you pitch a tent?"

Everyone laughed before realizing he was dead serious. "I want a tent," he is said to have yelled, pounding his fist on the table. "I want a tent, and I'm not f__ kidding."

This case—one of those about which Mr. Artzt didn't comment—is given a positive twist by one manager who was present. "He was right," the manager says. "We'd underestimated the potential of Pert Plus, and in the end Artzt got us to increase production faster." Indeed, Pert Plus ultimately brought P&G acclaim as a leader in global marketing.

A NEW VISION

In the first 2 years of restructuring, Procter & Gamble has reorganized its marketing, sales, manufacturing, and distribution. Driving the reorganization is the long-term vision to become the market leader in each of P&G's 39 product categories.

As part of the reorganization, CEO Edwin Artzt is changing the vaunted brand management system. Only one of every three new hires ever makes it through the 4-year process to become a brand manager, a position responsible for every part of their brand's marketing, advertising, and development. But Procter & Gamble's brand managers were so focused on one single product that they often lost sight of the total market.

This led to the creation of the category manager position who has total profit and loss responsibility for an entire product line. The category manager has the authority to make quick decisions, which is an attempt to create small stand-alone businesses within the organization.

Louis Pritchett, who retired as sales vice president shortly before Mr. Artzt became CEO, says, "I told Ed he was going to lose a lot of brilliant people who were too scared to stand up to him. He thinks, 'As long as we've got these sons of bitches running scared, we'll be fine.'"

Mr. Artzt's intensity is a quality he has shown over 40 years as he climbed the Cincinnati-based company's ranks, working in virtually every division. "He was thought of as a machine in terms of work output and his almost robot-like precision in approaching the job," says Arie L. Kopelman, chairman of Chanel Inc., who worked at P&G in the 1960s. His drive stood him in good stead at P&G, a company known for a stern corporate culture that emphasizes loyalty. Mr. Artzt, now 63, clinched the top job after reviving P&G's international business in the mid-1980s.

Edwin Artzt, CEO and leader of the change, who spends 60 to 70 percent of this time on the road says, "I give everybody the opportunity for input, and—consensus or no consensus—off we go." He has earned the nickname "the prince of darkness" because he comes in, makes changes, and moves to the next problem. Artzt's goal is for a new management structure, a fresh global approach, an enduring corporate culture, and a commitment to the long term.

QUESTIONS

1. Do you see any problems in trying to change the old line culture? Why?

2. What is your opinion of Artzt's management style? Why is it effective?

at 3M, expressed this idea when he said, "Obviously, when the vision of the future is created, you have to let go of the present and the past. We have a very strong culture, and letting go was a significant challenge in itself."[22]

POWER TOOLS FOR CHANGE

HRM programs to change strategy are more likely to succeed if the factors that shape the culture can be identified and managed. In a comparison of high-innovation companies with low-innovation ones, Rosabeth Moss Kanter describes how *change masters and corporate entrepreneurs* are allowed to flourish in high-innovation companies.[23] Three organization "**power tools**" are required in the adaptive organization: information, support, and resources.

Information

The first tool is to provide employees with information or an ability to gather information. People should feel free to go outside of their own department to gather information and open communication patterns across departments. General Electric and Wang Laboratories have rules prohibiting closed meetings. Other organizations like Hewlett-Packard and Digital Equipment have information exchange meetings that cut across employee levels. "MBWA" (Management by Wandering Around) is an expression at Hewlett-Packard and is increasingly becoming a practice for managers at all levels. Making information available at all levels increases employee motivation and permits faster decision making.

Support

The second tool is to provide the corporate entrepreneur with the support and necessary go-ahead from higher management, as well as the cooperation of peers and subordinates. If the project will cut across organization lines, support and collaboration from other departments is needed. For example, interdepartment meetings and training sessions that normally bring people together can provide the opportunity to build support for projects. Organizations can remove the "fear of failure," and provide a climate that supports people in taking risks. At 3M, management encourages risk-taking and supports research—knowing that some projects will fail. They feel that an intolerant management kills initiative.

Resources

The third tool is providing the resources, including funds, staff, equipment, and materials to carry out the project. One normal process of funding innovation is through budgetary channels, but traditionally this process is too time consuming to respond to the project in a timely manner. Some organizations support projects from bootlegged funds budgeted for other projects.

Lockheed Aircraft is particularly known for its "skunk works" projects, and 3M normally requires a certain percent of a funded project be devoted to bootlegged projects. "Venture capital" and "innovation banks" also provide support for innovative projects. W. L. Gore and Associates, another example of a highly adaptive company, does not have employees; instead it has associates, and the company encourages people to develop their ideas into projects.

In one study, Don Harvey and Richard Wald investigated a program aimed at changing the culture of an old-line manufacturing company. They found that although high-tech firms operate in a more dynamic environment and require frequent

Table 16.1
Key factors in cultural change

- *Understand the old culture.* Managers can't change their course until they know where they are.

- *Encourage change in employees.* Reinforce people in changing the old culture and those with new ideas.

- *Follow outstanding units.* Recognize outstanding units in the organization and use them as a model for change.

- *Don't impose cultural change.* Let employees be involved in finding their own new approaches to change, and an improved culture will emerge.

- *Lead with a vision.* The vision provides a guiding principle for change, but must be bought into by employees.

- *Large-scale change takes time.* It may take 3 to 5 years for significant, organization-wide cultural change to take effect.

- *Live the new culture.* Top management values behaviors, and actions speak louder than words.

changes, an equally important problem involves implementing change in the old-line, traditional companies.[24] They reported that such changes are difficult and take time. Change does not take place quickly in a strongly established culture. Some of the key factors in changing an ingrained culture are shown in Table 16.1.

Any changes to the organization culture must focus on what people value and what they do. If the HR manager can get employees involved and believing in the new programs, then cultural change is possible. (See Table 16.1.)

At Pearle Vision (a retail chain providing eyewear), they changed the corporate culture to promote a more entrepreneurial and profitable operation. This involved empowering its 500 store managers through a new bonus system, a training program, and a new company culture. As they studied the problems, they realized that it was more than just a problem of money. "We had to do something about the corporate culture, too," said Deborah Flaherty, the HR manager at the organization's corporate office.

The HR team identified the three tools necessary for retail success, which centered on the ideas: *want to, can do,* and *able to.* "These became the core of our program," explains Flaherty.

"The *want to* was essentially an incentive program—a bonus plan," explains Flaherty. "The *can do* piece trained managers, and gave them the tools to manage and operate their stores better, the way independent businesspeople would. Finally, and probably most important, was the *able to.* We took a hard look at the corporate culture. Even having a new compensation program and well-trained managers, if the corporate culture didn't embrace this philosophy, we knew we weren't going to be successful."[25]

THE GOALS AND VALUES OF HRM PROGRAMS

Now that a macro approach to organizational change has been described, let us examine some of the micro issues involved in change: the underlying goals, assumptions, and values basic to most HRM programs.

The ultimate purpose of increasing an organization's ability to adapt to a changing environment is to make it more effective. What makes an organization effective or ineffective? Etzioni has suggested that effectiveness is the degree of goal achievement or, as he further elaborates, the amount of resources an organization needs to use in order to produce units of output.[26]

In general, HRM programs are aimed at three basic organizational dimensions which affect performance. **Effectiveness** refers to the accomplishment of specific organizational goals and objectives. If organizations are using their resources to attain long-term goals, the managers are effective. The closer an organization comes to achieving its strategic goals, the more effective the organization. **Efficiency** refers to the ratio of output (results) to input (resources). The higher this proportion, the more efficient the manager. When managers are able to minimize the cost of resources used to attain performance, they are managing efficiently. An organization may be efficient, but not effective, or vice versa. The third factor may be termed **motivational climate,** consisting of the set of employee attitudes and morale which influence the level of performance.

Warren Bennis proposes three other criteria as indicators of organizational effectiveness or health:[27]

- *Adaptability*—the ability to solve problems and to react with flexibility to changing environmental demands.

- *A sense of identity*—knowledge and insight on the part of the organization of what its goals are and what it is to do.

- *Capacity to test reality*—the ability to search out and accurately and correctly interpret the real properties of the environment, particularly those that have relevance for the functioning of the organization.

Richard Steers raises questions of determining what effectiveness is and how it should be measured. He does not recommend specific criteria; instead, he suggests an analysis of the major processes (goal optimization, systems perspective, and emphasis on human behavior) involved in effectiveness. Steers stresses goal identification and the need for objectively determining the reality of the environment in which the organization exists.[28]

Chris Argyris has suggested that effectiveness comes from conditions that permit the integration of organization goals with individual goals. In a similar vein, Robert Blake and Jane Mouton indicate that organizational excellence is derived from the integration of concern for production with concern for people. **Organizational effectiveness** is the end result of an HRM program. It is a multiple rather than a singular goal, involving all of these factors.

Organizations that are simply reacting to changes become increasingly slow to adapt as the rate of change increases. A renewing management system results in a source of organizational flexibility, thus allowing increased adaptation to changing conditions and a more effective organization. One of HRM's primary roles is to improve the anticipative nature of the culture and to improve the way the organization's mission is accomplished. Due to the impact of corporate culture, the HR manager must also examine the relationship between the values of change and professional values and ethics.

HRM Implementation Issues

One important factor to recognize is that the success of the HRM program is, to a large extent, dependent upon the fit between HRM values and those of the organization. One of the key issues to be resolved between the HR manager and the operating departments concerns the relative value orientations of each party. These include beliefs about people, the methods used to reach change goals, and the purpose of the HRM program.

There is a value system underlying HRM approaches. These values emphasize increasing individual growth and effectiveness by creating an organizational climate that develops human potential while achieving organizational goals.

To achieve the HRM goals, the HR manager has to consider certain ethical or value implications of his or her role in initiating an HRM change program. There are a range of these ethical issues associated with each HRM program; we now examine three important issues.[29]

The Degree of Value Congruence   The HR manager's values may not be compatible with the line managers of the organization. The HR manager brings a certain set of values to the relationship with line managers, who have their own basic values and mission. The question, then, is the degree to which the HR manager's personal values are congruent with those of other managers.

The Politics of Change   Because organizations are political systems, another ethical consideration for the HR manager is the question of choice in deciding to implement a change program. The decision to initiate an HRM program is usually made by the top management group, yet it is likely to affect all members and parts of the organization. At one major company, for example, the top executives decided on a downsizing HRM program, which involved all levels. Lower-level employees may or may not have had a real choice regarding their participation in downsizing. If organization members do not have a choice, the HR manager become the instrument for imposing change without gaining employee participation.

Organization politics are a factor in any HRM change program, because change has the potential to disrupt the current balance of power among members and departments. The HR manager cannot afford to ignore the reality of power and politics in implementing change.

The Ethics of Control   A third issue involves which of the goals of an HRM program is likely to be given precedence. As noted earlier, change programs generally are aimed at improved effectiveness, efficiency, and participant satisfaction. The question then arises: Which, or to what degree, is emphasis to be placed on each goal? Are organizational or individual goals to take precedence? Although this sounds relatively simple in theory, the executives who are supporting the HRM program are, in practice, frequently under pressure to improve efficiency and profitability, even though they may also seek increased employee satisfaction and morale. The question is: How can the HR manager help improve the productive efficiency of the organization, and at the same time improve the quality of job existence for its employees?

So the challenge for the HR manager is to try to develop a balanced program—one where employee rights and well-being are considered, as well as improvements in productivity. Underlying the challenges to the HR manager are a set of values about the nature of human beings and their positions in an organizational context as shown in Table 16.2. In this environment of change, HR managers face both exciting challenges and serious dilemmas over how to fully meet the changing values and processes of change.

SUMMARY

In this chapter, stage six of the Success System Model: changing for success is presented. Change is an inevitable consequence of operating in a dynamic environment. For HR managers, it is important to recognize that organization changes can be initiated by organization members (renewing) or as a reaction to external forces (reactive). This chapter focuses on the idea that a key aspect of implementing

Table 16.2
HRM values

- *Respect for people.* Individuals are allowed to function as human beings, perceived as being responsible, authentic, and caring. People should be treated with dignity and respect, not just as resources.

- *Trust and support.* Develop an effective and healthy organization characterized by trust, authenticity, openness, and a supportive climate.

- *Power equalization.* Provide opportunities for people to influence their work environment. Effective organizations are those with less reliance on hierarchical authority and control.

- *Confrontation.* Provide an environment of open communication where problems aren't swept under the rug. Issues and strategies should be openly confronted and decided.

- *Participation.* Provide opportunities for each individual to develop their full potential. The more that people who will be affected by changes are involved in the decisions leading to changes, the more they will be committed to implementing changes.

change is the need to institutionalize the change into organizational value systems. Consequently, one important element in implementing a change program is the corporate culture.

Whether change is anticipative or reactive, it is likely to be most successful when the organization proceeds with an HRM approach which takes into account the nature of the culture. In recent years, corporate culture has been recognized as a pervasive force influencing organization effectiveness. Culture has been defined as the shared values and behaviors of organizational members and represents a key factor in implementing planned change in organizations.

You will have an opportunity in the simulation to experience and observe a situation of organization change. You will probably find that initiating planned change is not always as easy as it looks. You may have discovered that the functioning of a group is difficult to analyze and gaining acceptance of change strategies presents difficulties. In reflecting upon the simulation, you may feel that the quality of your group's decision was not what it could have been.

In addition to helping group members work better and more harmoniously with each other, HR managers assist employees in making more effective decisions for both the organization and its members. This simulation demonstrates many of the interpersonal and organizational factors that inhibit change. If the essential task of management is to deal with change, then the HR manager must be able to initiate changes and implement HRM programs.

HRM change efforts concentrate on problems of efficiency, effectiveness, and participant satisfaction. The focus of HRM organization improvement programs include individual behavior, group and intergroup relations, and overall organization problems.

REVIEW QUESTIONS

1. Describe or compare the corporate cultures of organizations as written in magazines such as *Business Week* and *Fortune.* What makes one more effective than another?
2. Compare and contrast management efficiency and effectiveness.
3. Identify the key factors in cultural change.
4. Review a movie or novel on cultural change.

KEY WORDS AND CONCEPTS

Define and be able to use the following:

- Change
- Corporate Culture
- Cultural Resistance
- Cultural Change

- Effectiveness
- Efficiency
- Excellence
- Motivational Climate

- Organizational Effectiveness
- Three Power Tools
- Winning Culture

HRM SKILLS SIMULATION 16.1: REDUCTION IN FORCE: CONSENSUS-SEEKING CHANGE

Total time suggested: 1 hour.

A. PURPOSE

The purpose of this simulation is to examine the interdependence among team members and to provide insights into the concept of culture. To study culture, we may examine the culture of a group which share certain cultural traits. The goals include

1. Comparing decisions made by individuals with those made by the group.
2. Practicing effective consensus-seeking techniques.
3. Gaining insights into the concept of cultural values.

B. PROCEDURES

Step 1. Prior to class, form into groups of five members, each group constituting an executive committee. Assign each member of your group as one of the committee members. (Extras act as observers.) Observers use the Observer Form located at the end of this simulation.

1. Executive vice president, marketing
2. Executive vice president, finance
3. Executive vice president, manufacturing
4. Executive vice president, human resources
5. Executive vice president, research and development
6. Observers

Before class, individually read the employee profiles that follow and rank-order the 10 employees on the worksheet from "1" for least likely to "10" for most likely to be expendable. Participants are to enter their ranking in column 1 on the Executive Committee Decision Worksheet.

Step 2. Executive Committee Meeting. Through group discussion, exploration, and examination, try to reach a *consensus decision* reflecting the integrated thinking and consensus of all members. Remember, a consensus decision involves reaching mutual agreement by discussion until all agree on the final decision.

Follow these instructions for reaching consensus:

1. Try to reach the best possible decision, but at the same time defend the importance of your department.
2. Avoid changing your mind simply to reach agreement and to avoid conflict, but support solutions with which you are able to agree.
3. Avoid "conflict-reducing" techniques, such as majority vote, averaging, or trading, in reaching your decision.
4. View differences of opinion as a help rather than a hindrance in decision making.

At this point, meet together as the executive committee, and enter your results in column 2 on the Executive Committee Decision Worksheet.

Time suggested for Step 2: 40 minutes.

Step 3. Each team lists its results on the blackboard, and the instructor posts the actual performance ranking. Enter the performance ranking in column 3.

Time suggested for Step 3: 10 minutes.

Step 4. Using the answers given by the instructor, score your individual and team answers by subtracting the Personal Ranking (column 1) and Committee Ranking (column 2) each from the Actual Performance Ranking (column 3). Then record the absolute difference as the Individual Score (column 4) and Team Score (column 5), respectively. By totaling the points, an individual and a team score can be calculated. Column (4) provides an indication of the individual participant's "correctness," and column (5) provides an equivalent measure of each group's performance.

Individuals and teams can be compared based on these scores. However, individuals have varying degrees of knowledge, and the final score may not reflect how decisions were made during the team discussion.

Time suggested for Step 4: 10 minutes.

Step 5a. Team members individually complete the Values Survey and Conflict Survey Forms.

Step 5b. As a team, discuss and come to team rating on the Values Survey and Conflict Survey Forms. Observer feeds back information on team process using the Observer Form as a guide.

Time suggested for Step 5: 10 minutes.

Step 6. The instructor leads a discussion of the activity, letting each team explain its scores on the Values Survey and Conflict Survey Forms. Consider the following points and compare results for each team:

1. The consensus process within each group: things that went well and difficulties, whether the rules were followed, and the dynamics behind the posted scores.
2. The extent to which efficiency, effectiveness, and member satisfaction were emphasized in the meeting.
3. The culture that will likely develop at Delta as a result of the decisions made in the meeting.
4. How could an OD program help Delta and your management team?
5. Observers report their profile from the Observer Form.

REDUCTION IN FORCE: DELTA CORPORATION

Delta, started in 1985, is a small, family-owned firm in the microcomputer business. The company grew rapidly because of its microcomputer boards, disk drives, optical disks, tape backup drives, and innovative approaches to solving computer hardware problems. Both managers and workers have put in long hours, often sacrificing their personal time to get the company off the ground.

Unfortunately, a significant downturn in the economy has caused a reduction in sales, and it is increasingly apparent that some adjustments will have to be made if the company is to survive.

Your committee will have to make a series of recommendations for a reduction in force (layoff) of employees, all of whom are married, of the same age (28), and all with no previous experience before joining Delta.

The president has asked you to examine the personal information of the 10 employees in the company who are most expendable. They are all good employees, but because of reduced sales and earnings and a declining economy, Delta needs to be prepared for a 1 percent reduction in workforce (RIF). Therefore, you are meeting to rank-order from "1" for least likely to "10" for most likely to be "riffed." There are at least 11 employees in each of the five departments. The employees other than those on the list given to you have been with the company at least 8 years, and it is not feasible to RIF them at this time.

Among the criteria you may want to consider are:

1. Education
2. Performance
3. Seniority

4. Technical ability
5. Attitude
6. Leadership
7. Effectiveness
8. Efficiency
9. Job function
10. Social ability

EMPLOYEE PROFILES

Finance

Gwen—seniority 3½ years; 4-year college education; has performed about average on annual appraisal (75 percent); average technical abilities and leadership potential; a steady, grinding worker; works long hours; has been working on employee benefit plan for 2 years; is a non-smoker and nondrinker; has frequently complained about working with cigarette smokers.

Hal—seniority 5½ years; 4-year college education; has been rated average and above in annual appraisals (80 percent); high technical abilities; average leadership; always in on Saturday mornings; frequently works through lunch hour; has been working on committee to computerize payroll for past 18 months; is well-liked and gets along with fellow workers; is a very neat and stylish dresser.

EXECUTIVE COMMITTEE DECISION WORK SHEET

EMPLOYEE	(1) HRM RANKING	(2) COMMITTEE RANKING	(3) ACTUAL PERFORMANCE RANKING	(4) INDIVIDUAL SCORE	(5) TEAM SCORE
Gwen					
Hal					
Carole					
Dave					
Tony					
Ken					
Eduardo					
Frank					
Irv					
Jackie					

TOTAL SCORES:

VALUES SURVEY FORM

The following are several value orientations. Based on the following scale, individually rate the values at Delta based on your team's decision. Record your choice in the left column and record the team rating in the right column.

: :	:	:	:	:	:	:	: :
1	2	3	4	5	6	7	

Values	Individual Rating	Team Rating
1. High Productivity	_____	_____
2. Effective Relationships	_____	_____
3. High Quality	_____	_____
4. High Achievement	_____	_____
5. Seniority (Age)	_____	_____
6. Time Consciousness	_____	_____
7. Dress/Neatness	_____	_____
8. Amount of Education	_____	_____
9. Positive Attitudes	_____	_____
10. High Professionalism	_____	_____

CONFLICT SURVEY FORM

Rate your team, individually, on how differences were resolved during your team's meeting. Record your choice in the left column and your team rating in the right column.

1	2	3	4	5	6	7

Values	Individual Rating	Team Rating
1. Not Afraid of Conflict	_____	_____
2. Express Differences	_____	_____
3. Ignore Disagreements	_____	_____
4. Open Discussion	_____	_____
5. Analysis of Difference	_____	_____
6. Debate of Issues	_____	_____
7. Trust	_____	_____
8. Confrontation	_____	_____
9. Encourage Openness	_____	_____
10. Flexibility	_____	_____

Research and Development

Carole—seniority 2½ years; PhD in engineering; has been above-average research engineer in performance appraisal (90 percent); high technical abilities; works unusual hours (sometimes works late at night, then doesn't come in until noon the next day); developed patent on a new solid-state circuit device last year; seldom attends social events; is said to be unfriendly and often disagrees and conflicts with fellow workers.

Dave—seniority 3½ years; MS degree in engineering; has been average to above average on performance appraisal (75 percent); average technical abilities; average leadership; works steady 8 A.M. to 5 P.M.; is working on several R&D projects, but none yet completed; always ready for a coffee break or joke-telling session; is well-liked by coworkers; never complains about bad assignments.

Marketing

Tony—seniority 2 years; MBA degree; has been rated as performing better than 95 percent on performance appraisal; high technical abilities; low leadership; works erratic hours (often comes into office at 9:30 A.M., and frequently plays golf on Wednesday afternoons); sold the highest number of product units in his product line; seldom socializes with fellow workers; is often criticized because his desk is messy and disorganized, piled with correspondence and unanswered memos.

Ken—seniority 18 months; 4-year college degree; has been rated an above-average to outstanding performer (85 percent); high technical abilities; average leadership; has been criticized for not making all his sales calls, but has a good sales record and developed advertising campaign for new product line; although a good bowler, refuses to bowl on company team; has been rumored to drink quite heavily on occasion.

Human Resource Management

Eduardo—seniority 18 months; 4-year college degree; has been rated above average as performer (85 percent); average technical abilities; high leadership; is frequently away from desk and often misses meetings; has designed and implemented a new management development program; is well-liked, although frequently has differences of opinion with line managers; often takes long coffee breaks and lunch hours.

Frank—seniority 4 years; 2-year college degree; has been rated average to above average as performer (70 percent); low technical abilities; above average leadership; works long hours; regularly attends all meetings; has been redesigning performance appraisal systems for past 2 years; is involved in many company activities; belongs to Toast Masters, Inc.; is known as a friendly, easygoing guy.

Manufacturing

Irv—seniority 15 months; 4-year college degree; rated an outstanding performer (90 percent); high technical abilities; low leadership; has been criticized for not attending committee meetings; designed and implemented the computerized production control process; does not socialize with fellow employees; is known as a sloppy dresser (often wearing white or red socks with a suit).

Jackie—seniority 6 years; high school; rated an average performer (75 percent); average technical abilities; average leadership; always attends meetings; works steady 8 A.M. to 5 P.M. hours and Saturday mornings; has chaired committee to improve plant safety for past 2 years; participates in all social events; plays on company bowling and softball teams; and is known for a very neat, organized office.

OBSERVER FORM

Your role during this part of the simulation is important because your goal is to give the executive committee feedback. Rate by circling the appropriate number.

Profile

1. Level of involvement: Low 1:2:3:4:5:6:7:8:9:10 High   _____

2. Level of communication: Low 1:2:3:4:5:6:7:8:9:10 High   _____

3. Level of openness, trust: Low 1:2:3:4:5:6:7:8:9:10 High   _____

4. Level of suggesting corrective measures: Low 1:2:3:4:5:6:7:8:9:10 High   _____

5. Level of providing direction: Low 1:2:3:4:5:6:7:8:9:10 High   _____

6. Level of supportiveness: Low 1:2:3:4:5:6:7:8:9:10 High   _____

7. Level of competence: Low 1:2:3:4:5:6:7:8:9:10 High   _____

8. Overall style: Ineffective Low 1:2:3:4:5:6:7:8:9:10 High Effective   _____

Case 16.1 The Dim Lighting Company

The Dim Lighting Company is a subsidiary of a major producer of electrical products. Each subsidiary division operates as a profit center and reports to regional, group, and product vice presidents in corporate headquarters. The Dim Lighting subsidiary produces electrical lamps, employing about 2,000 workers. The general manager is Jim West, 46, an MBA from Wharton, who has been running this subsidiary successfully for the past 5 years. (See Figure 16.2.) However, last year the division failed to realize its operating targets, as profit margins dropped by 15 percent. He believes the long-term prospects are not good, and the company's salvation may be to downsize. In developing next year's budget and profit plan, Jim West feels that he is under pressure to have a good year because 2 bad years in a row might hurt his long-term potential for advancement.

DOCTOR SPINKS, DIRECTOR OF R&D

Leon Spinks, 38, director of R&D, was hired by West 3 years ago after resigning from a major competitor. Dr. Spinks has received a number of awards from various scientific societies. His group of scientists and engineers respect his technical competence and have a high level of morale. His position is to increase the R&D budget for new product development. He does not believe reducing his staff will generate any positive benefits.

Although he is recognized as a talented scientist, other managers feel that Spinks is often autocratic, strong-minded, and impatient. Dr. Spinks left his former company because management lacked creativity and innovation in R&D.

THE PROPOSAL

Dr. Spinks has submitted a budget request for a major research project: the micro-miniaturization of lighting sources, to greatly reduce energy requirements. He sees this as the "Lamp of the Future." The proposed budget would require $250,000 per year for 2 years, plus another $300,000 to begin production. Jim West immediately contacted corporate headquarters, and although his idea was highly praised, they were reluctant to expand any share in the proposed project. Dr. Spinks feels the project has a 70 percent chance of success and will develop a net cash flow of $1,000,000 by the third year.

THE BUDGET MEETING

West called a meeting of his management group on Wednesday morning to discuss the proposed budget. Dr. Spinks presented a very rational and high-powered sales pitch for his project. He suggested that the energy crunch had long-term implications, and that if the company failed to move into new technologies, they would be competitively obsolete.

Carl Preston, accounting, presented a financial analysis of the proposed project, noting the high risk, the uncertain results, and the length of time before it would contribute to operating profits. "These scientists are prima donnas, who can afford to wait for long-term results. Unfortunately, if we don't do something about the bottom line right now, we may not be here to enjoy it," he noted.

Pete Newell, marketing, agreed with Dr. Spinks: "I don't feel we can put our heads in the sand. If we don't keep up competitively, how will our salespeople be able to keep selling obsolete lighting products? Besides, I'm not sure that all of Carl's figures are completely accurate in measuring the actual return on this low-energy project."

Bill Boswell, production manager, pointed out his department had already cut back to a 35-hour week, and something had to be done soon or additional reductions would be necessary.

Bill Pendleton, human resource management, discussed the downsizing option as a serious step that would require top management's total support. Such a step would necessitate a new strategic plan, a reevaluation of all job descriptions, a wage and salary revision, new training programs, and outplacement resources. The end result would be a new corporate culture.

Thinking it over later in his office, West considered the situation. Going ahead with the micro-miniaturization project was a big gamble with high uncertainty. Proceeding with downsizing might be too radical a solution.

To resolve the issue of what Dim Lighting should do, the following steps are to be completed:

1. The class should divide into several management teams representing the Dim Lighting Company. The teams will consist of the director of R&D, director of marketing, director of manufacturing, director of human resource management, and director of accounting.
2. Each individual Dim Lighting management team will discuss the issue from their role perspective and prepare a specific action plan.
3. The individual management teams will then present to the other management teams their action plan.
4. All management teams will then attempt to consolidate their individual plans into one group action plan to be presented to general manager Jim West.

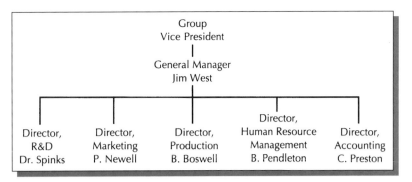

Figure 16.2
Dim Lighting Company organizational chart

ENDNOTES

1. Noel M. Tichy and Stratford Sherman, *Control Your Destiny or Someone Else Will* (New York: HarperCollins, 1994), 3–50.
2. Brian Dumaine, "The Bureaucracy Busters," *Fortune* (June 17, 1991): 36–50; and Thomas J. Peters, *Thriving on Chaos* (New York: Alfred A. Knopf, 1987), 27.
3. Peter Davoleer, "Change Leaders," *Inc.* (June 1999): 64.
4. D. B. Adams, "Facing Change or Changing Face," *Industry Week* (May 1, 1995): 17.
5. R. H. Kilmann, "Corporate Culture," *Psychology Today* (April 1985): 63.
6. P. Shrivastra, "Integrating Strategy Formulation with Organizational Culture," *Journal of Business Strategy* (Winter 1984): 103–04.
7. "The Cola Superpowers' Outrageous New Arsenals," *Business Week* (March 20, 1989): 162; Subrata N. Chakrabarty, "How Pepsi Broke Into India," *Forbes* (November 27, 1989): 43–44; Patricia Sellers, "Financial Soundness," *Fortune* (January 29, 1990): 46–47.
8. See Sonja A. Sackmann, "The Farmers of Culture." Paper presented at Academy of Management, 1989; and Christa L. Walck, "Why Organizational Culture Cannot Survive the Rational Paradigm." Paper presented at Academy of Management, 1989, for Meanings of Culture.
9. Donald F. Harvey, *Business Policy and Strategic Management* (Columbus, OH: Charles E. Merrill Publishing Co., 1982), 44.
10. Terrence E. Deal and Allan A. Kennedy, "Culture: A New Look Through Old Lenses," *Journal of Applied Behavioral Science* 19, no. 4 (1983): 108.
11. K. L. Miller, "The Factory Career at Toyota," *Business Week* (May 17, 1993): 95.
12. See Brian Dumaine, "Creating a New Company Culture," *Fortune* (January 15, 1990): 127–31.
13. Henry Migliore, R. T. Martin, Tim Baer, and Jeffrey L. Horvath, "Corporate Culture Index," Proceedings, Southern Management Association, 1989, p. 217.
14. See Richard D. Teach, R. G. Schwartz, and Fred A. Tarpley, Jr., "Small Firm Cultures," Proceedings, Southern Management Association, 1989, p. 211.
15. David Whiteside, "Roger Smith's Campaign to Change the GM Culture," *Business Week* (April 7, 1986): 84.
16. See Tom Peters, *Thriving on Chaos* (New York: Alfred A. Knopf, 1987), 27; and Robert H. Waterman, Jr., *The Renewal Factor* (New York: Bantam Books, 1987).
17. Harold Leavitt, *Corporate Pathfinders* (Homewood, IL: Dow Jones-Irwin, 1986), 10–11.
18. John Sculley, *Odyssey* (New York: Harper & Row, 1987), 83.
19. "Now, for US Air's Next Trip . . . ," *Business Week* (June 17, 1991): 58; and Michael M. Miller and Patricia Bellew Gray, "Why Businesses Often Sink in 'Decisional Quicksand'," *Wall Street Journal,* 15 December 1986, p. 29.
20. Brian Dumaine, "P&G Rewrites the Marketing Rules," *Fortune* (November 6, 1989): 35–48; and Alecia Swasy, "Slow and Steady," *Wall Street Journal,* 21 September 1989, p. 1.
21. Bro Uttal, "The Corporate Culture Vultures," *Fortune* 108, no. 8 (October 17, 1983): 66.
22. Stephanie Lawrence, "Voices of HR Experience," *Personnel Journal* (April 1989): 72.
23. Rosabeth Moss Kanter, "SMR Forum: Innovation—The Only Hope for Times Ahead?" *Sloan Management Review* 25, no. 4 (Summer 1984): 51–55.
24. Donald F. Harvey and Richard A. Wald, "Changing an Organizational Culture . . . ," Proceedings, Southern Management Association, 1989, p. 214.
25. Jennifer J. Laabs, "Pearle Vision's Managers Think Like Entrepreneurs," *Personnel Journal* (January 1993): 42.

26. A. Etzioni, *Modern Organizations* (Upper Saddle River, NJ: Prentice Hall, 1964), 8.

27. Warren Bennis, *Organization Development, Its Nature, Origins, and Prospects* (Reading, MA: Addison-Wesley Publishing Co., Inc., 1969), 26–32.

28. Richard Steers, "When Is an Organization Effective?" *Organizational Dynamics* (Autumn 1976): 50–63.

29. See Kevin C. Wooten and Louis P. White, "Ethical Problems in the Practice of Organization Development," *Training and Development Journal* (April 1983): 16–23.

Chapter 17

The Success System:
Total Quality Management

Objectives

After completing this chapter, you will be able to:

1. Define the concept of total quality management (TQM).
2. Describe the basic objectives of a TQM program.
3. Define the concept of quality.
4. Identify several approaches to implementing TQM.

Premeeting preparation

1. Read chapter 17.
2. Prepare for HRM Skills Simulation 17.1.
3. Read Case 17.1: Wengart Aircraft. Answer questions.

Background Information

There are many change programs which have been used in business environments with varying degrees of success. In today's global market competition, the most recent innovation is total quality management. TQM is the most widely used business change program whose influence is rapidly growing in the United States and the world.

Gary Tooker, CEO of Motorola, Inc., is one of the biggest fans of total quality management (TQM). In the 1980s, Motorola was trailing the Japanese. To be competitive, they turned to TQM. Today few U.S. companies can match Motorola's devotion to quality. The results of their commitment to TQM have been overwhelming. Overall product defects have been slashed from nearly 3,000 per million in 1983 to under 200, and their global sales rose 13 percent. Motorola even went one step further with its commitment to "Six Sigma" quality (statistical jargon for defect-free manufacturing), and the company appears intent to do whatever it takes to accomplish this goal.

Under its current leadership, Motorola has increased its quality 100 times and has reached a statistical margin of 3.4 defects per million parts produced—99.9997 percent perfection. Examples of the acceptance of TQM in the United States abound, but what remains to be seen is whether a company can really survive in the twenty-first century without embracing the concepts of TQM.[1]

TQM programs have been used at 3M, IBM, Xerox, Motorola, and by organizations throughout the United States, and indeed the world. In the twenty-first century, organizations that fail to change are likely to become second-class players in a rapidly changing global environment.

In this chapter, stage six of the Success System Model: changing for success will be continued. In the following sections, we will examine the concept of total quality management, and several approaches to implementing TQM will be described. The successful organization must be customer-driven and continuously developing a "high performance workplace."

Total Quality Management (TQM)

Total quality management (TQM) is a **commitment to excellence** by everyone in an organization that emphasizes excellence achieved by teamwork and a process of continuous improvement. "Now most companies have 'total quality' programs that integrate every department from manufacturing to marketing and research in the effort to improve," says Earl C. Conway of Procter & Gamble. The driving force behind TQM is a commitment to be the best and to provide the highest quality products and services which meet or exceed the needs of the customer. Organizations are being forced to change if they want to remain competitive. They are looking for ways to improve quality, increase productivity, and adopt a customer orientation. These changes are so fundamental that they must take root in a company's very essence, which means in its culture.[2] Trident Precision Manufacturing implemented a TQM program resulting in a lower turnover (41 percent to 3.5 percent) and fewer defects.[3]

TQM usually involves a major cultural change, because TQM is completely different from traditional management. This requires a new way of managing and employee involvement at all levels. Individuals throughout the organization must be motivated to change and to do things differently. They must have an awareness of what needs to be changed and why, and this takes the support and knowledge of the workers. (See cartoon.)

Source: B.C. by permission of Johnny Hart and Creators Syndicate, Inc.

A Brief History of TQM

TQM had its beginning in the 1930s with the pioneering work of Walter A. Shewart, who acted as a mentor to the late W. Edwards Deming. The concept really began during World War II when Shewart's methods made quality a science. Stewart replaced traditional end-line inspection with an "on-line" awareness of variation.[4]

Three of the leading "gurus" on TQM are W. Edwards Deming (who took his message to Japan in the 1950s), Joseph Juran, and Phil Crosby. Deming applied Shewart's principles of statistical process control in Japan and helped turn Japan into an economic power.[5] As a result, Japanese companies have improved quality and productivity and dominate many world markets.

Joseph Juran went to Japan shortly after Deming and built his own equally impressive reputation for quality planning, quality control, and quality improvement. Although Juran and Deming appear to have mutual respect for one another, Juran believes that Deming is basically a statistician, "and a bit out of place when talking about management." However, both TQM gurus have had a major influence in championing quality with similar key points, including

- Quality means conformance to requirements.
- Defect prevention—not inspection—is the way to achieve quality.
- The only acceptable quality standard is one that tolerates zero defects.
- The cost of poor quality—in warranty payments, excess inventory, engineering errors, and other money eaters—can amount to 25 percent of sales at manufacturing companies and up to 40 percent of operating costs at service companies.

The Objectives of TQM

TQM involves an entirely *new* way of doing things. Employees are asked to challenge old methods to find new and better ways of doing things and to be involved in decision making. This is usually applied to work teams and individually, including all levels of the organization. The key is to get everyone involved.

The goal of TQM is to improve **customer satisfaction,** with employees at all levels continually seeking to improve existing performance. TQM provides a strategy for eliminating the causes of poor quality and increasing productivity. (See HRM in Action.)

Douglas Aircraft, a subsidiary of McDonnell Douglas Corporation, was totally restructured in secret sessions mandated by the parent company's CEO, John McDonnell. Selected corporate executives (none from Douglas Aircraft) were picked up by chauffeurs, their destinations kept secret, and led downstairs to the basement of the home of Robert Hood, Jr., a senior executive. There they were told to "ponder the imponderables." No one at Douglas learned of the changes until a Monday morning in February, when all 5,200 managers were bussed to a hangar in Long Beach, California.

THE FIRING

CEO John McDonnell introduced the new Douglas Aircraft president, Robert Hood, and three other top managers who were new to Douglas. McDonnell then told the managers they had all lost their jobs! They could, if they wanted, reapply for their jobs. Many managers did reapply for management positions, and eventually 4,000 were rehired as managers—1,000 fewer than before the reorganization. Management levels were cut from 9 to 5. Besides cutting immediate costs, the restructuring had another objective of improving communications by tearing down barriers between companies, departments, and people.

Many insiders, even at Douglas, were convinced that something extreme had to be done to ensure Douglas's survival. Since Douglas was taken over by McDonnell over 23 years ago, Douglas had earned a reputation for extravagant offices and holding expensive ceremonies while corporate headquarters remained austere.

TOTAL QUALITY MANAGEMENT SYSTEM

The second part of the change program involved starting a total quality management system (TQMS) at Douglas and other McDonnell operations. The purpose of TQMS is that through the teamwork of production line employees with less direct supervision, quality will improve, and production mistakes will not have to be corrected at a later and more costly point. TQMS is a teamwork-based system intended to help build the highest quality products at the lowest possible competitive price. According to CEO McDonnell, "We're trying to make fundamental changes in how we conduct our business and how we work at our jobs."

TQMS seems to be getting a lot of top management support; however, production floor supervisors directly involved in the program say management needs to be more supportive of team leaders by providing more communication and leadership skills and coaching their supervisors. Other supervisors report that employees don't want to take responsibility for anything. Even TQMS's more ardent supporters on the floor say there are a lot of drawbacks and a lot of nonparticipation in the program. Bob Barnhart, a senior engineer and field service representative to the Air Force, says, "I think this TQMS is a viable start, but don't let it stop. It needs to keep growing. We've got a long way to go. . . ."

THE RESULTS

Over a year after the "Monday Morning Massacre," the change still had not paid off. Morale, particularly among managers, is still low. In a VCR tape sent to employees, John McDonnell said, "For years at DAC [Douglas Aircraft] we've tried Band-Aids as a way of patching outmoded systems and processes that were breaking down under the weight of rapid and sustained expansion . . . This time we're fixing the root causes of DAC's problems . . . But don't expect immediate bottom line results at DAC."

The success of the changes remains questionable. Recent indications suggest that management is growing increasingly concerned that the remedies are not working as well as planned. An internal memo from deputy Douglas president John Capellupo cites a problem with "people who appear to be ideal" at the job. Continuing, Mr. Capellupo says, ". . . I conclude that we have a clear lack of discipline throughout our organization including all levels of management as well as our workforce." He went on to say that the total quality management program had led to a permissive system.

Doug Griffith, president of the local UAW representing Douglas's workers, says, "You've got a cadre of people who were part of the traditional good-ol'-boy network, and now they're suddenly out of it. We've got a lot of them out on the floor, and they're a threat to what we're doing, like poison in the well."

Some workers, making fun of TQMS, say that it stands for Time to Quit and Move to Seattle, the home of its healthy competitor, Boeing. They may have an opportunity, with recently announced cutbacks of about 17,000 workers to reduce costs.

QUESTIONS

1. What types of TQM approaches were used at McDonnell Douglas?

2. How would you attempt to solve the problem of "Time to Quit and Move to Seattle?"

TQM is a commitment to excellence, emphasizing continuous improvements in quality. The level of employee involvement required by TQM creates new roles for all organizational members. Responsibility and decision making are pushed to the lower levels of the organization. Top management, middle managers, and first-level supervisors all must become involved for the team philosophy to gain acceptance throughout the organization. One of Japan's TQM gurus, Kaoru Ishikawa, says "Quality literally becomes every top manager's business." Operating level employees are involved in identifying and analyzing job problems, and then in developing proposals for reducing or eliminating them.

A cultural change is usually a first step in the introduction of the TQM approach. "Total quality is not a cookbook thing," says David K. Snekiker, a vice president who runs the quality program at Battelle Memorial Institute in Columbus, Ohio. "It's a culture-transforming approach."

However, the corporate culture required for TQM to succeed may not develop rapidly. It is estimated that it takes several years to accomplish large scale changes in an organization. TQM is not a set of rules and regulations, but is a philosophy, and cannot be forced on the employees. Because a company's culture has developed around past values and behaviors, the approach to change is usually accomplished by a TQM education and training program. In addition to training and development activities, new employee people skills are a central factor in implementing the TQM philosophy.[7] A summary of the differences between TQM and traditional management may be seen in Table 17.1.

What Is Quality?

In TQM, the definition of quality is based on customer needs being met to the maximum degree possible. "Quality means the product meets all requirements."[8] As a result of TQM, many firms have reported a positive relationship between the quality of products and services that companies produce and the profitability of those firms. Quality has two key elements: the conformance of a product or service to the internal standards of the firm; and the customer's perception of the quality of that product or service. It is important to distinguish between these two types of quality, because a number of products have conformed to internal standards but have not satisfied the market.

In the final analysis, a firm's products must be perceived as superior by the marketplace.[9] Many companies are now thinking in terms of "total quality." That means quality in the product itself and in all the services that come with it. Ford Motor Company has about 200 employees in its customer assistance center, who answer over 5,000 calls a day from customers with complaints and questions. Complaints that come in are electronically forwarded to dealers who are expected to contact the person with the complaint and start correcting the situation within 24 hours.[10]

TQM emphasizes that how a process is implemented is just as important as what the process includes. In TQM, all employees are involved in improving the quality of their product or service so that customers' needs are not only met but

Table 17.1
The characteristics of TQM/traditional management

TQM	TRADITIONAL MANAGEMENT
Customer focus	Management focus
Quality first	Profits first
Multiple quality dimensions	Single quality dimension
Management and worker involvement	No worker involvement
Process-oriented	Results-oriented

exceeded. Under Motorola's "Six Sigma" quality program, for example, everyone in the company is working toward defect-free manufacturing leading to the highest possible level of customer satisfaction.[11]

IMPLEMENTING TQM

There are several approaches to implementing TQM that have been used successfully. Like other major HRM programs, quality improvement efforts often are established for a lot of the wrong reasons. First, many companies are already doing it. Second, the chairman wants to win the Baldrige Award, a prestigious award for a successful TQM program. Third, well-meaning consultants have convinced managers that a pre-packaged, total-quality management program is all that is needed to eliminate product defects, enhance customer satisfaction, boost productivity, cut costs, and increase corporate profits.

Unfortunately, it doesn't work that way. Recently, it was reported two-thirds of all quality-improvement programs ultimately fail because organizations simply don't understand what quality really means or how to attain it. Many quality-management programs are too poorly conceived to result in improved products or services.

One difficulty is there is no right or wrong way to achieve quality. In fact, a study conducted by the American Quality Foundation, a New York City-based think tank, revealed that the 584 companies surveyed used a total of 945 different quality-management tactics.[12]

You must know where you are before you can chart a course for where you want to be. Before beginning a TQM process, it's important to assess the organization in terms of current quality levels and to define the level of quality it needs to achieve. AT&T, for example, used the Baldrige criteria to take a baseline measurement of the company and to provide a game plan toward improved quality. In a recent survey of 1,350 companies, almost half (49 percent) currently had TQM programs.[13]

The Experience of Successful Firms

As HR managers review the quality needs of their own organizations, they also should learn about quality techniques and about the quality experiences of other companies. The winners of the Malcolm Baldrige Award are good sources of quality information, because they're expected to share information about their successful quality strategies with other U.S. organizations. Texas Instruments took full advantage of this opportunity by sending executives to quality conferences hosted by Westinghouse, Motorola, and Xerox.

Create Action Plans and Set Goals

After the organization has developed a sense of how and where quality improvement should be implemented, then strategic TQM goals and action plans should be developed. At this point, an HR professional who can serve as the internal quality expert should be appointed. This person helps in defining the company's short- and long-term goals and in facilitating the TQM programs. In the early stages of TQM, HR managers need to be involved in the company's effort to analyze quality needs and develop goals and objectives. HR professionals can share their understanding of the corporate culture with top managers, who may think a certain program will work just because it worked at Federal Express or Motorola. If the program probably isn't going to be accepted, then the HR manager needs to point this out in the early stages. This is critical, because top management sometimes becomes out-of-touch with the corporate culture at the operating levels.

The Guru Approach

Another approach to implementing TQM may be termed the **Guru Approach,** because it uses the writings of TQM gurus such as Deming, Juran, or Crosby as a benchmark to identify organizational problems. The firm uses the guru's system to implement changes. Deming's 14-point model is one example of a guru's approach that has been widely used by U.S. companies, as well as in Japan.[14]

1. Create consistency of purpose for improvement of product and service.
2. Adopt the new philosophy.
3. Cease dependence on mass inspection.
4. End the practice of awarding business on price tag alone.
5. Improve constantly and forever the system of production and service.
6. Institute training.
7. Institute leadership.
8. Drive out fear.
9. Break down barriers between staff areas.
10. Eliminate slogans, exhortations, and targets for the workforce.
11. Eliminate numerical quotas.
12. Remove barriers to pride of workmanship.
13. Institute a vigorous program of education and retraining.
14. Take action to accomplish the transformation.

Organizations using the Guru method focus on these key factors as a way to develop a master plan. With this approach, corporations try to duplicate the basics of Japanese quality management (popularly known as total quality control, or "Quality is everybody's job"). This approach focuses on fine-tuning the entire firm to make it as adaptable to changes in customer demands and market conditions as possible.[15]

It is important to note that the ideas of the quality gurus involve much more than a set of techniques. Often the guru or others work as consultants during the implementation process. Regardless of the approach used, the success of TQM is based upon a commitment to excellence by everyone in an organization. TQM also requires teamwork and a process of continuous improvement.

Basic Elements of TQM

TQM uses many basic concepts with its system for creating organization-wide participation in planning and implementing a continuous improvement process that *exceeds* the expectations of the customer or client. Two of the major elements of TQM are employee involvement and self-managed teams.

Employee involvement (EI) is a strategy organizations use to allow workers more responsibility and accountability for doing their job. The term itself involves a range of activities from soliciting employees' work-improvement ideas to creating self-managed work teams who are given control over their jobs and work organization.[16]

EI is based on two factors. First, people tend to support what they helped create. For example, someone who is actively involved in developing a change in a work process is more likely to see that the changes are being carried out, it really is working, and thus will be selling it to their friends and coworkers. Second is the idea that people who know most about the job are those who actually perform the work. Gaining the participation of the workers actually performing the job often provides ideas not available to managers.[17]

Many organizations are now using these EI techniques for several reasons:[18]

1. EI provides a greater commitment to changes by employees because the employees are involved in designing those changes.
2. EI in decision making and planning gives a wider understanding of the organization's objectives and commitment to achieving those objectives.
3. EI provides increased employee satisfaction, thus reducing turnover.
4. EI increases team and organizational spirit which develops increased cooperation and coordination among employees at all levels.

Empowering

Empowerment refers to management giving greater decision making to employees, instead of keeping it for themselves.[19] Empowerment has become important for several reasons. First, globalization and competition have increased. This increased competition requires more and more innovation, which requires more freedom for the innovators. Finally, the increased competition has forced American businesses to be more productive than ever before.[20] For the managers who have empowered employees, the payoffs have been great. For example, Federal Express—the first service category recipient of the Malcolm Baldrige Award for Quality—felt it owed the award to its empowered employees.[21]

Self-Managed Teams

The **self-managed team** concept has been mainly used on assembly lines. Over 1 in 5 American employers are now using self-managed work teams and it is expected to increase to approximately 50 percent by the year 2000.[22] It works because more information and more ideas are available to a team of workers than to one individual worker. Self-managed teams also reportedly improve productivity and profits.[23]

The Adolph Coors Company, for example, uses self-managed teams. Production workers are organized in teams of 9 or 10. Each team is responsible for its own scheduling. The system permits shift trading, as long as the team's work gets done. These production teams also participate in hiring decisions, managing budgets, and improving efficiency. Have these teams improved things at Coors? Management seems to think so, and the numbers support this with companies reporting turnover rates of less than 1 percent a year.[24]

Create A Vision

In a *Fortune* magazine survey of senior executives, 98 percent of the respondents said conveying a strong sense of vision would be one of a CEO's most important characteristics in the year 2000, compared to 75 percent who described themselves or their current CEO as having this as a distinguishing characteristic.[25] In a study of effective leaders at all levels of an organization, not just CEOs, it was found that one of the most powerful impacts they can have is through communicating their vision of the organization.[26]

Some of the more competitive organizations have a well-articulated vision that all members understand. For example, Motorola's CEO, Robert Galvin, began a total quality management program and made **Six Sigma** quality a goal to attain in

5 years. Six Sigma is a quality term meaning being perfect 99.9999998 percent of the time—near-perfect manufacturing. Motorola spent $25 million in the first year on education programs to explain the complicated concepts to all employees. Six Sigma posters hung throughout every building and memos came out nearly weekly from Mr. Galvin on quality. It was a mammoth job to get 105,000 Motorola employees to adopt Six Sigma, but it was a vision CEO Robert Galvin held and he successfully communicated it to all Motorola's employees.[27]

SUMMARY

In this chapter, we have examined stage six of the Success System Model: changes in work design called TQM. Although TQM has been used over a period of several years with varying degrees of success, some approaches (such as self-managed teams) are somewhat new.

Total quality management is a commitment to excellence by everyone in an organization. Self-managed work teams represent a significantly new method of organizing and managing an organization. Most businesses that use this approach choose to apply it to specific plants or work sites, instead of the entire organization. Self-managed work teams require a major commitment from the organization—both managers and workers. The long-term effectiveness of the teams has not been clearly established, but many organizations and their members are enthusiastic about the approach. Self-managed work teams seem to be one of the most popular interventions, and one that major corporations are hoping will make them competitive in the twenty-first century.

TQM has potentially broader applications for all types of organizations. The success of TQM in organizations in the United States has been increasing. Although there is a lack of conclusive research on TQM programs, there is much information available to help HR managers carry out more successful programs.

In the simulation, you will have an opportunity to participate in a TQM implementation. Though the experiment will be limited in size and time, you will perhaps draw some conclusions of your own about the application of TQM and self-managed work teams. In the last several years, TQM has received much more attention and seems to be having a positive impact in improving organizations.

REVIEW QUESTIONS

1. How would you communicate TQM to workers?
2. What is the role of HRM in implementing TQM within a company?
3. How would you use incentives to bolster quality efforts?
4. How can the design of HRM policies assist in promoting TQM initiatives?
5. Define the key characteristics of TQM.

KEY WORDS AND CONCEPTS

Define and be able to use the following:

- Commitment to Excellence
- Customer Satisfaction
- Employee Involvement (EI)
- Empowerment
- Guru Approach
- Self-Managed Team
- Six Sigma

Total time suggested: 2 hours, 25 minutes.

A. PURPOSE

The purpose of this simulation is to provide a situation where you will need to involve others, and to observe how information affects team decision-making regarding TQM. During and after the simulation, you are encouraged to become aware of the processes you use in your attempts to influence and relate with others while designing a TQM program. You will experience

- How quality information is shared.
- How problem solving strategies influence results.
- How collaboration and competition affect team problem solving.

B. PROCEDURES

Step 1. All participants should read Sierra Manufacturing Background Information. Form groups of five to act out the TQM committee role play. (Roles should be selected prior to the class meeting.) Additional class members will serve as observers. Each player should read only their role and the background information.

1. General manager
2. Director, marketing
3. Director, production
4. Director, human resource management
5. Director, engineering
6. HRM consultant

Step 2. TQM Committee Meeting. Your team is to use the information to arrive at a decision. The meeting is scheduled to last 45 minutes.

The decisions facing the committee are:

1. What should be the basic goal—efficiency or effectiveness; short-term profit or long-term market share?
2. What should the decision be on pricing policy—to stay with the policy or to become more flexible?
3. How should people be retained—by increasing salaries, bonuses, or other ways?
4. How can a TQM program be effectively implemented?

Time suggested for Step 2: 45 minutes.

Step 3. After the executive meeting, each team completes the diagnosis, formulates a TQM program to present to the executive committee for their consideration, and fills out the Team Profile.

Time suggested for Step 3: 15 minutes.

Step 4. The consultant presents the TQM program to their group.

Time suggested for Step 4: 30 minutes.

Step 5. Each team will complete the Team Profile Form and discuss results and observations of team process and consulting style.

Time suggested for Step 5: 20 minutes.

Step 6. Each consultant should present their team's TQM program for class discussion and critique.

Time suggested for Step 6: 20 minutes.

Step 7. As a class, discuss the seven questions in the Team Profile Form.

Time suggested for Step 7: 10 minutes.

The Sierra Manufacturing Company is a leading manufacturer of industrial and military equipment. The company is divided into several major functional groups, each headed by a vice president. One of these groups is the products group, which is divided into a number of product divisions, each headed by a division general manager (see Figure 17.1).

The Sierra Division's general manager oversees the directors for engineering, marketing, production, and human resource management. Sierra's performance has been excellent, especially over the past 10 years, but with the exception of the most recent 2 years. In fact, Sierra has a record of being one of the most profitable divisions of Sierra Manufacturing in terms of amount of profit and return on investment. However, in the last 2 years, they suffered declines in sales of 6 percent and 13 percent, respectively. Sierra uses cost centers with each division autonomous in its operations; however, each division is expected to be self-supporting.

Sierra employs about 1,200 people and operates from one plant location. The increase in employees has been rapid within the past 10 years, but the increase leveled off this year because of the sales decline. So far there have not been any layoffs, but if the current sales trend continues, layoffs may have to considered as a possibility to reduce costs. The employees are unionized (as is common in this industry), but Sierra has exceptionally positive relationships with the union. This is due largely to the diligent work at corporate headquarters' human resource development department where the contracts are formulated. At the local level, leadership training has been helpful, but the quality circles had some problems after 6 months and were discontinued.

The major problem with sales has been attributed to the new major competitors who have entered the field. To date, the product line has faced little competition, probably because of the expensive and technologically advanced processes used in the fabrication. However, several quality problems have been reported, and customer quality complaints have been increasing. Because of the technological orientation of the products, it is important that Sierra be able to respond quickly to the changing demands of their customers. Also, for Sierra to be really competitive, it is increasingly necessary for it to outguess the needs of its customers and to bring in technologically superior products of the highest quality before

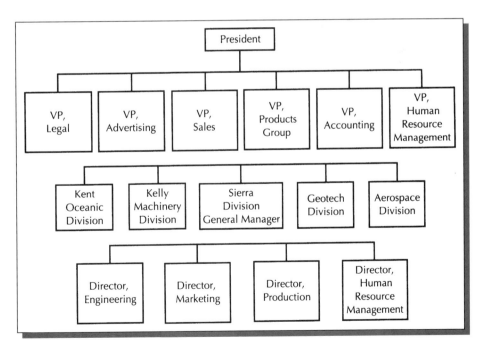

Figure 17.1
Sierra Manufacturing Company organizational chart

its competitors can respond. Most recently, Sierra's ability to effectively respond to its competitors' increasing quality standards has been diminished, because several dynamic middle managers and other key employees were lost to its competitors.

Recently, a key engineer has left Sierra and has formed a competing company, Infiniti. He has been recruiting many key people from Sierra—mainly engineers, marketing, and production specialists. Infiniti offers a bonus, but mainly recruits based on their free-form corporate culture, self-managed teams, and upon personal growth for the individual. However, they often work much longer hours than employees at Sierra.

Sierra has recently submitted a proposal to one of its major customers (a large aerospace corporation) for a very large order involving from 1,000 to 10,000 machines requiring extremely high quality standards. This order could involve more sales over the long term. This company has always used the Sierra product because of its excellent quality and fine support systems, its training and customer service. Despite this, the purchasing agent of the aerospace firm has recently informed Sierra that it has two competing bids—one of which is from Infiniti, whose prices are lower than Sierra's standard $12,900 price by as much as 20 to 25 percent. Basically, the bottom line is if Sierra cannot meet the competition, then the bid will probably go to a competitor. Infiniti's quality record is good and continues to improve.

Sierra products are used as workstations in a variety of industrial and military products requiring utmost precision. The military contracts have been declining, but not at a greater rate than the civilian sales. The products themselves are very high-tech and require strong engineering and software support. Many of the materials used in the manufacturing process are exotic metals and plastics that are very difficult to fabricate to close tolerances. In many cases, the products must be extremely lightweight and have high strength. In some cases, the composition of the products and the processes used in manufacturing are the result of inventions developed at Sierra, who owns the patent rights.

Corporate headquarters has recently formed a new TQM team. It has been suggested by the vice president of the Products Group that Sierra Division consider implementing the TQM approach. As Sierra believes it is important to allow its divisions to be fairly autonomous, Sierra has the authority to choose to participate and to help design a TQM program which best fits its own culture and needs.

ROLE DESCRIPTIONS (READ *ONLY* YOUR ROLE)

Role 1—Sierra general manager. You have been with the company for 8 years, 5 in your current job. Although you started fast, things have slowed down for the past 2 years. Your goal is to be promoted to group vice president, and to do this, you need to turn things around right now and show a good profit profile. To accomplish this, you want to cut labor costs by 10 percent, cut expenses to the bone, and get rid of any fat or dead wood that exists. You operate best in a directive, structured, and centralized situation, and feel that the current problems stem from a lack of control and coordination among departments. Your goal now is to increase short-run profits at any cost.

You basically would like to retain the pricing policy because the real question is value (which your company has always provided). But in this instance, because Infiniti is involved, you'd rather cut the price than lose the order. You feel the way to keep people from leaving is to appeal to their loyalty to Sierra.

During the meeting, you want to convince the directors to voluntarily cut costs by 10 percent, which will directly affect the bottom line. You also hope to sell them on a more centralized and controlled operation—a "taut ship." You feel that the basic causes of the current problems are the operating relations between departments and the lack of proper controls on spending.

You see the HRM manager as a possible ally in achieving your goal of promotion. A good word back at corporate headquarters would undoubtedly increase your chances. Consequently, you want to appear to be highly competent, dynamic, a "mover and a shaker," and an integrative manager.

Role 2—director of marketing. You are an MBA, and have been with the company for 4 years. You feel that a decentralized organization is most effective, and believe that dividing Sierra into major product groups (instead of the current functional form) would be best suited for the company. You are very concerned with good relationships, as well as goal accomplishment, and are known as a "super salesman." You feel strongly that what the organization needs to solve its problems is an increased marketing and promotional effort. You recognize that the established market is important, but also that a firm must be innovative and adapt to changing markets with new products and promotions. A decentralized, product-oriented organization will best allow Sierra to respond quickly to changing markets.

You feel that competitors are forcing you to change your pricing policies. Therefore, you must change, or lose business. This does not mean that Sierra will compete on price alone, but rather that you must change to meet new competition. You feel that growth and being the best is the way to hold people: You can't keep good people with the money alone—they need a challenge.

In the meeting, you wish to push strongly for an aggressive marketing campaign aimed at increasing market share as a way to solve current problems. This requires increasing the sales force by 10 percent, and a 15 to 20 percent increase in advertising. The only way to halt a sales decline is to increase the marketing effort. You feel strongly that a decentralized, product-oriented organization is the way to go, with a product manager responsible for each major product line. The past problems were largely due to high manufacturing costs and poor product quality, and to an inability to respond to the customers' demands. You hope to convince the HRM manager to support the major products group structure.

Role 3—director of production. You have been with the company for over 20 years. You worked your way up through the ranks, and have found that a structured, decisive leadership style works best. You see increased efficiency as the major goal, because excessive spending in marketing and engineering is needlessly raising costs. You are convinced that costs can be reduced drastically by limiting engineering changes, limiting the number of products, and by slowing down the introduction of new products (which marketing always wants). This will allow a more stable and efficient production-line operation, rather than the hectic, constantly changing situation you have now.

You feel that Infiniti and others will go out of business from price cutting. Therefore, Sierra should stick with its pricing policy. This policy has been critical to its success over the years. You feel employees should be loyal to Sierra, that we should keep our key people by providing bonuses or stock options, and anyone who threatens to leave should be fired for disloyalty.

In the meeting, you are going to push for some "no nonsense" cost controls on overhead, particularly in marketing and engineering. You strongly oppose any layoffs in production, because skilled workers are hard to get and you are forced to pay overtime now. You also need a more automated assembly line, which, in the long run, will cut production costs and reduce the need for overtime. You would like to cut out the employee development programs initiated by the human resource director. Although the leadership programs were helpful, the quality circles nearly caused a small rebellion when you did not approve of some production changes. You suggest a more centralized operation with tighter financial controls. For example, you feel that salespeople pad their expense reports beyond reason. You hope to get support from the HRM director for a more efficient and centralized form of operation.

Role 4—director of human resource management. You have a Master's degree in human resource management and have been with the company for 5 years. You favor a more decentralized organization and a type of leadership that is concerned with human needs, and have been working toward this goal. You feel strongly that the most important resource in the organization is people. Morale and the satisfaction of individuals are the primary goals as you see it. You have already initiated several TQM-type programs (communication, quality circles, and leadership training), and would like to see a more innovative TQM program to improve the organization's long-term quality and effectiveness. All of the programs you consider successful except for the quality circles. Some production line employees got upset when their suggestions were not implemented by the director of production. They came to see you about initiating the manufacturing changes they had proposed, but you had to explain it was the production director's decision to make.

You see a real problem in the changing, competitive market place, and feel that pricing policies may need to be changed. You wish to retain key people, and feel Infiniti is a real threat because they have informal networks to find out who the key people are and then go after them. You feel that Sierra has to offer a better culture and more personal growth for its employees (as well as financial incentives), if it is to retain and attract good people.

In the meeting, you strongly oppose any form of layoffs. The negative effects on morale would be almost irreversible. What is needed, you feel, is a raise in pay and improved coordination between departments (instead of the constant bickering and fighting which prevails). You want to urge implementation of *self-managed work teams* (SMWT), which will solve these problems. This would improve the communication and coordination between groups. Naturally, you would be designing the SMWT program. If it is successful, this could lead to the application of the teams in the whole company.

Role 5—director of engineering. You have an MSEE, and have been with the company for 3 years. You feel that a highly decentralized structure with a participative leadership is most effective. You see long-term effectiveness as the most important goal. Both profit and market share depend on the ability to remain innovative in R&D. You feel that the company must become more innovative and improve product marketability to survive.

You feel that the key to sustained performance is the relationship between Sierra and its customers—the ability to meet customer needs with innovative new products and to produce them at competitive values. You feel that we must get this order in an attempt to stop Infiniti before they can get their foot in the door. You see the key to increasing markets and retaining key people is the challenge of being on the leading edge: of designing and producing the highest quality, where new approaches and risk taking are encouraged.

In the meeting, you wish to propose increased expenditures in R&D for the next 2 years. You also need two new engineers (in stress analysis and thermal dynamics) for these advanced projects. You feel that a reduction in manufacturing costs, less overtime, and reducing advertising budgets, will allow for this. You feel that the current problems are due to stagnant, low-risk management, low-risk strategies, front-office interference, and a lack of R&D in emerging fields. The production department is old and obsolete, both in methods and equipment. You have suggested new methods, but your advice has been rejected. You hope to gain the consultant's support in creating a more innovative, TQM-oriented organizational climate. Recently, you have lost several of your key engineers to other companies. You think Sierra's lack of an incentive system tends to stifle any innovation. You would like to see the company use some of the TQM techniques you used when you were at Motorola, such as team building and self-managed teams.

Role 6—HRM consultant. You are the consultant from the company's newly formed TQM group. You hope to accomplish several things at this meeting:

1. To develop a consultant-client relationship with all the committee members.
2. To make a preliminary diagnosis of possible quality problems.
3. To assist the committee by doing process consultation during the meeting.

TEAM PROFILE FORM

Team Profile: Rate the team on their effectiveness in resolving the TQM issue.

	Low				Moderate		High			
(A) Involvement	1	2	3	4	5	6	7	8	9	10
(B) Leadership	1	2	3	4	5	6	7	8	9	10
(C) Competence	1	2	3	4	5	6	7	8	9	10
(D) Communication	1	2	3	4	5	6	7	8	9	10
(E) Goals	1	2	3	4	5	6	7	8	9	10
(F) Decision Making	1	2	3	4	5	6	7	8	9	10
(G) Collaboration	1	2	3	4	5	6	7	8	9	10
(H) Openness	1	2	3	4	5	6	7	8	9	10
(I) Listening	1	2	3	4	5	6	7	8	9	10
(J) Motivation	1	2	3	4	5	6	7	8	9	10

Did the HR manager

1. Establish a relationship?
2. Take over the problem?
3. Focus on feelings?
4. Encourage the client to be specific?
5. Allow the client to talk?
6. Lead and direct the conversation?
7. Show indications of judging the client?

Case 17.1   Wengart Aircraft

President Ralph Larsen of Wengart Aircraft has become increasingly concerned about profits. Though he is not fearful of a company takeover, he does feel an obligation to maximize shareholders' return on their investment. He and about a dozen top executives receive sizable stock bonuses, so it is to their advantage to obtain a high share price.

Wengart manufactures commercial and military aircraft. It is number two in its industry which is composed of nine companies. Its profits, however, are ranked as seventh. It is disturbing to Mr. Larsen and his top management team that they are not able to maximize profits.

QUALITY PROBLEMS

Quality has been identified by the top management team as one of the major problems at Wengart. Aircraft have to be reworked even after they are sent to the customer. The federal government, one of Wengart's largest customers, shares this concern for quality, to the extent that several letters have ben sent to Mr. Larsen from the Secretary of Defense warning him that unless quality is improved by 20 percent within 6 months, the government will exercise its contract provision to withhold partial payment as a penalty. This will place even more pressure on profits. Nongovernment customers have also expressed serious concerns about quality. There have been major stories in the *Wall Street Journal* and *Business Week* about Wengart's quality problems and its deteriorating financial condition.

The Department of Defense, in its latest letter to Mr. Larsen, said it would look favorably upon Wengart implementing a "total quality management" (TQM) program, similar to programs at other aircraft, automobile, and electronic firms. By Presidential Executive Order 12552 applying TQM to all federal executive agencies, the Department of Defense is encouraging all defense contractors to adopt TQM.

TOTAL QUALITY MANAGEMENT AND THE CONSULTANT

Mr. Larsen, in an effort to learn more about TQM, hired a management consultant to explain TQM. The consultant made several points at a 2-hour meeting with Mr. Larsen:

- Customer, engineering, production, and product support functions are integrated into a team.
- The customer is the next person in line. The customer can, therefore, be the next person on the production line for someone within the company, or it can be the purchaser of Wengart's planes. Everyone in the company is both a customer and a producer.
- Quality is giving customers what they have a right to expect.

- Substantial increases in education and training are required.
- Teamwork is a basic building block of TQM.
- Mr. Larsen, as the CEO, and his top management team must be committed to TQM, and must communicate its importance by word and deed at every opportunity.
- TQM will have to become part of Wengart's culture. The CEO must believe in humanistic work principles that include improved leadership, working conditions, and job security.

Mr. Larsen thanked the consultant and said he would take it from here. To Mr. Larsen, TQM was a matter of common sense. It was what they were doing or should be doing.

Mr. Larsen decided that they had no other choice but to implement TQM. He called a meeting of his vice presidents and explained TQM. (See Figure 17.2.) Kent Kelly, VP of production, was placed in charge of the program by Mr. Larsen. However, Mary O'Connor, VP of human resources, tried to convince him that TQM should be a joint project between human resources and production with Mr. Larsen's office coordinating the program. Mr. Larsen explained to them that he didn't have time to get involved with TQM personally, as he wanted to spend his time and energies improving profits.

PICO DURANGO F-24 PLANT

Sally Rand, a supervisor of the wire harness assembly team for the F-24 aircraft, is responsible for 11 people on the swing shift. Her people put together the thousands of color-coded electrical wires that make up a "harness." Another production team places the harness in place in the aircraft by running the harness from the aircraft's central computer to the other sections of the aircraft. The F-24 is a new and highly advanced fighter aircraft of the Air Force, using the latest in electronic and computer controls in combination with a stealth design. Ms. Rand's team, like every team on the F-24, is critical to the plane's ability to fly.

Two months ago, all managers and supervisors within the Pico Durango plant (including Ms. Rand) attended a meeting called by the plant supervisor, Allan Yoshida, where he explained TQM. Supervisors came away from the meeting with various interpretations of TQM, so line workers tended to get different ideas about TQM. Within a day after the meeting, all workers in the plant received a brief memo from Mr. Yoshida in which he outlined TQM, said that supervisors had details, and that everyone was to support the program.

Ms. Rand was very enthusiastic about TQM. She was taking a management course through a local university, and her class had recently spent several class meetings

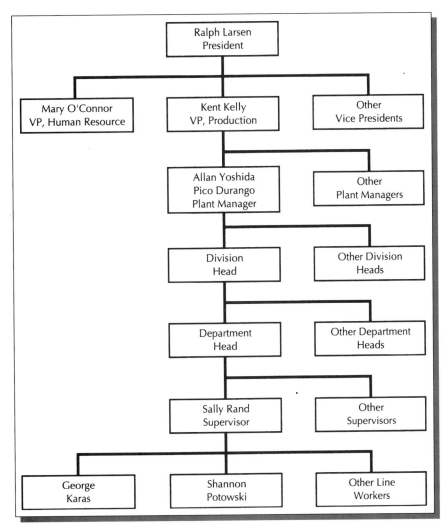

Figure 17.2
Wengart Aircraft organizational chart

learning about TQM. She was, however, confused at the brevity of the TQM information she and the other supervisors got from Mr. Yoshida.

For two of Ms. Rand's veteran workers, George Karas and Shannon Potowski, it sounded just like the other management programs where the union workers did all the work and management, especially top management, got the credit—and the bucks. Both of the workers made some rough calculations and figured that, under the old system, at least 20 percent of their time was spent reworking a defective harness after it had been installed in a plane, waiting on products coming from the previous production team, or waiting on delayed inventory items. The waiting time, which was also common with other teams, was a good opportunity to go to the company store, take a little longer coffee break, or visit with friends on other production teams. After comparing notes with other workers around the plant, plant workers generally concluded that Alan Yoshida was trying to speed up production so that the midnight shift could be cut.

This morning, Ms. Rand and several other supervisors went around their department and division heads to see Mr. Yoshida. They explained the rumors they had heard from workers about a worker plan to get the job done right the first time, but to make sure it took so long that no one would be laid off. Mr. Yoshida, unsure about what to do, referred to the seven-page memo Kent Kelly had sent him on how to implement TQM. Mr. Yoshida's knowledge about TQM was limited to the memo he had received from Mr. Kelly. The situation the supervisors were explaining was valid, Mr. Yoshida said. Unfortunately, Mr. Kelly's memo did not address the problem.

After looking at the way Mr. Kelly had set up the plant goals, Mr. Yoshida decided that quality was what mattered most. Mr. Yoshida quickly reasoned his next promotion was dependent on meeting his quality goals—not improving productivity. Getting the workers mad at you could be a sure-fire way to lose both quality and production. He told the supervisors at the meeting to pass the word that layoffs were not the purpose of TQM, and just make sure quality was top-notch.

After the meeting, Mr. Yoshida wondered if he should call Mr. Kelly and see if there was any more to TQM he should know about. But then after several minutes, he decided that if the program was very important, he surely would have heard something more. Best not to make waves.

QUESTIONS

1. Identify the driving and restraining forces toward acceptance of the TQM program at the top management level.
2. What are the driving and restraining forces of accepting the TQM program at the line worker level? Are the forces different from those at the top level?
3. Evaluate the way top management communicated the change program to the lower levels.
4. What was the vision of Wengart communicated by the president and other managers?
5. If you were an OD consultant to Wengart's top management, what would be your recommendations for implementing the TQM program?

ENDNOTES

1. Ronald Henkoff, "Keeping Motorola on a Roll," *Fortune* (April 18, 1994): 67. See also Robert Neff, "Going for the Glory," *Business Week* (October 25, 1991): 6.
2. Brian Dumaine, "Creating a New Company Culture," *Fortune* (January 15, 1990): 127.
3. J. Laabs, "Quality Drives Trident's Success," *Work Force* (February 1998): 44.
4. Ellis Pines, "The Gurus of TQM," *Aviation Week and Space Technology* 121 (May 21, 1990): S34.
5. W. Edwards Deming, *Out of Crisis* (Cambridge, MA: Massachusetts Institute of Technology Center for Advanced Engineering Study, 1986), chapter 2.
6. Ellis Pines, "The Gurus of TQM," *Aviation Week and Space Technology* 121 (May 21, 1990): S29.
7. Ellis Pines, "TQM Training: A New Culture Sparks Change at Every Level," *Aviation Week and Space Technology* 132 (May 21, 1990): S38.
8. Benjamin D. Burge, "Producing a Quality Product," *Journal of Systems Management* 41 (November 1990): 7.
9. Jeremy Main, "Under the Spell of the Quality Gurus," *Fortune* (August 18, 1986): 30.
10. Frank Rose, "Now Quality Means Service Too," *Fortune* (April 22, 1991): 97–111.
11. B. G. Yovovich, "Motorola's Quest for Quality," *Business Marketing* (September 1991): 14–29.
12. Shari Caudron, "Keys to Starting a TQM Program," *Personnel Journal* (February 1993): 29.
13. "Workforce Trends," *Training*, October 1996, p. 68.
14. Mary Walton, *The Deming Management Method* (New York: Putnam's, 1986).
15. Ibid, p. 122.
16. C. Ronald Schwisow, "Tools for Your Motivational Campaign," *HR Magazine* (November 1991): 63–64.
17. S. Bicos, "Employee Participation without Pain," *HR Magazine* (April 1990): 89.
18. N. Margulies and S. Black, "Perspectives on the Implementation of Participative Approaches," *Human Resources Management* 26, no. 3 (Fall 1987): 386.
19. A. Karr, "Empowering Workers: Is It Real or Overplayed?" *Wall Street Journal,* 18 June 1991, p. A1.
20. Jeffrey Gandz, "The Employee Empowerment Era," *Business Quarterly* (Autumn 1990): 74–79; and Peter Fleming, "Empowerment Strengthens the Rock," *Management Review* (December 1991): 34–37.
21. A. Halcrow, "Employee Participation Is a Sign of the Times," *Personnel Journal* (January 1988): 10.
22. JoAnn Lubin, "Trying to Increase Worker Productivity, More Employers Alter Management Style," *Wall Street Journal,* 13 February 1992, p. B1.
23. Jana Schilder, "Work Teams Boost Productivity," *Personnel Journal* (February 1992): 67–71.
24. "Coors, AT&T Credit Find Building Teams Isn't Easy—But It's Worth It," *Tallahassee Democrat,* 7 August 1991, p. 7D.
25. Lester B. Korn, "How the Next CEO Will Be Different," *Fortune* (May 22, 1989): 157–61.
26. W. Bennis and B. Nanus, *Leaders* (New York: Harper & Row, 1985).
27. Mark S. Gill, "Stalking Six Sigma," *Business Month* (January 1990): 42–46.

Chapter 18

The Success System: Managing Diversity

Objectives

After completing this chapter, you will be able to:

1. Define the concept of workforce diversity.
2. Recognize the trends that are changing the workforce of the twenty-first century.
3. Discuss the advantages and disadvantages in managing a diverse workforce.
4. Identify the steps an organization needs to take for managing a diverse workforce.

Premeeting preparation

1. Read chapter 18.
2. Prepare for HRM Skills Simulation 18.1. Read Parts A and B, Step 1.
3. Read Case 18.1: Precision Products, Inc. Answer questions.

Background Information

One generation back, as the nation settled into postwar prosperity, 30 percent of all women worked outside the home—even though *Leave It To Beaver* reflected the cultural ideal of family life. However, with a plentiful labor supply, few employers had to reach beyond the male Caucasian in his prime, except for the least-wanted jobs. Indeed, by the late 1960s, as employers awarded self-winding watches to 65-year-olds, the first fresh-faced baby boomers were on their way to personnel.

The last of that numerous cohort is now straggling into the world of paychecks and withholding taxes. The boss is losing that confident glow. The decline in birth rates after 1960 has slashed the numbers of young people available to fill jobs up to the year 2010 and maybe beyond.

The years of selective hiring are over. Global competition for all sorts of workers—entry-level, skilled, seasoned—has begun. Employers must now look to women, minorities, and older workers. Over the next 10 years, only 15 percent of workforce entrants will be native-born white males. Developing a new, more diverse workforce and making it work effectively will be one of corporate America's biggest challenges in the decade ahead.[1] Employers from Atlantic Richfield Company to Xerox Corporation are incorporating the ideal of workplace diversity.

Managing Cultural Diversity

Few companies can match the cultural diversity record of Ortho Pharmaceutical. The company, part of Johnson & Johnson's $4-billion pharmaceutical manufacturing sector, produces, distributes, and markets women's health-care products. They are also known as Elsie Cross' "most progressive client," and have become this diversity consultant's "showcase for the how and why of corporate culture change."

Currently, women and minorities are now being promoted in numbers representative of their numbers within the workforce. According to one report, "Women hold 25 percent of the management positions, up from 22 percent in the year prior to beginning the diversity corporate culture change program. Similarly, blacks in managerial positions increased from 6 percent to 13 percent, while other minorities jumped from 10 percent representation within managerial ranks to 18 percent." Although white males still hold a significant 63 percent of the top positions within the company, Ortho's record of upward mobility for women and minorities is still an impressive one.

An Ortho company spokesperson commented, "What we do here isn't easy. But if you value differences among people, incorporate those differences into the team, and then reward the team, change happens. Never fast enough, but it happens nonetheless."[2]

One of the biggest challenges for the HR manager will be managing a more diverse workforce effectively. Managing diversity refers to understanding and using employee differences to develop a more effective and profitable organization.[3]

In this chapter, we present the next stage of the Success System Model: managing diversity, and the strategies, skills, and processes involved in effectively managing a diverse workforce. Diversity will be emerging in many ways, including an aging workforce.[4]

Managing diversity is not a new management topic. Since the Civil Rights Act of 1964, the acceptance of various ethnic and religious groups has progressed. Currently, efforts are emerging to include a new group of "outsiders:" cultural and racial minorities and women. Today more than half of the U.S. workforce consists of people other than white, U.S.-born males, and this trend is expected to continue. Two-thirds of all global migration is to the United States.[5]

Today's immigrants often lack a high school education. Only 20 percent are admitted because their skills are in great demand. Yet the criteria could change toward more preference for skills. This year, to allay shortages, U.S. hospitals will hire 20,000 foreign nurses on 5-year visas.[6]

Many organizations are aware they will have to be more accommodating of differences. They are also beginning to find their customers are also becoming increasingly diverse, so that having a diversified workforce can be a competitive advantage in today's marketplace.

Diversity Today

Cultural diversity refers to more than just skin color and gender. Diversity refers to all kinds of differences. These differences include age, disability status, military experience, religion, and education, in addition to gender, race, and nationality. (See Figure 18.1.)

These groups share many common values, attitudes, and perceptions, but also have cultural differences. Every subculture is made up of individuals who are unique in personality, education, and life experiences. There could be more differences among a group of Asians from Thailand, Hong Kong, and Korea, than among a Caucasian, an African-American, and an Asian, all born in Los Angeles. Similarly, all white males do not share the same goals, values, or workplace behaviors. (See cartoon.)

Managing diversity, then, involves being more aware of characteristics common to different groups of employees, while also managing these employees as individuals. Managing diversity means not just tolerating differences, but supporting and using these resources to the organization's advantage. Organizations will not have a choice of whether or not to have a diverse workforce; it is happening already, and managers must learn to manage this diverse workforce if they are to be successful in the future.

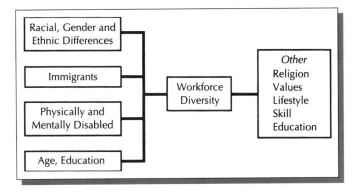

Figure 18.1
Characteristics of a diversified workforce

Source: CROCK by Rechin, Parker, and Wilder. © North America Syndicate, Inc.

Digital Equipment Corporation, a *Fortune* 500 computer manufacturer, is pioneering the move to a diverse workforce. Digital built two plants especially designed to give women and minorities the opportunity to grow and develop in a comfortable learning environment before being assigned to other Digital facilities.

Top management wanted every employee to be able to reach his or her potential. This meant developing a culture in which individual differences were not just tolerated, but valued and even celebrated. Barbara Walker was hired to expand Digital's EEO and affirmative action concepts.

Walker started Digital's Valuing Differences Program. The Valuing Differences Program and philosophy are based on the concept that the broader the spectrum of differences in the workplace, the richer the synergy among the employees, the more creative their ideas, and the more excellent the organization's performance. Walker, whose title is "Manager of Valuing Differences," was able to sell her program throughout the company.

The Valuing Differences Program is aimed at developing employee understanding of the stereotypes and assumptions associated with cultural differences. It also tries to reduce the prejudices each group may hold toward others. The company has also named a number of senior managers to various cultural boards of directors and Valuing Differences boards of directors. These groups promote openness to individual differences, encourage younger managers committed to the goal of diversity, and sponsor celebrations of racial, gender, and ethnic differences (such as Hispanic Heritage Week and Black History Month).

Digital hopes to gain the competitive advantage of a more diverse workforce, higher morale, and a reputation for being a better place to work. It wants the pick of talent in the marketplace and does not want to lose experienced employees to its competition.

QUESTIONS

1. What was Digital Equipment Corporation's top management plan to help employees achieve their potential? Do you agree or disagree?

2. How does the Valuing Differences Program work? Can you suggest any additions or deletions?

3. What does Digital hope to gain from a diverse workforce? Discuss.

CURRENT TRENDS AFFECTING WORKFORCE DIVERSITY

Several studies predict that eight major trends will change the work and the workforce of the twenty-first century (see Table 18.1). Organizations must start now to prepare for these trends if they want a high performing workforce in the coming years.[8]

Table 18.1
Trends affecting the
workforce of the
twenty-first century

1. The number of workers will decrease.

2. The average age of workers will rise.

3. More women will be on the job.

4. One-third of new workers will be minorities.

5. There will be more immigrants than at any other time since World War I.

6. Most new jobs will be in services and information.

7. The new jobs will require higher skills.

8. The challenge for business will be immense.

The Size of the Workforce

The growth of the U.S. population—almost 1.9 percent per year in the 1950s—is expected to slow to only 0.7 percent in the twenty-first century.[9] Changes in fertility, death, and immigration rates could increase the population, but probably not until later in the twenty-first century.

Using even the most conservative economic growth projections, the number of jobs that will be created is expected to equal or exceed the growth in the labor force in the year 2000.[10]

The United States has historically experienced a surplus of workers, but this scenario is rapidly changing. Organizations will be competing for the best candidates from a smaller and more diverse labor pool. To recruit effectively in the future, employers need to understand this changing workforce.

The Workforce of the Future

In the past, white American males dominated the U.S. workforce. However, it is estimated white males will constitute only 15 percent of new entrants to the labor force in the 1995–2000 period. The remaining 85 percent of those joining the workforce will be white females, immigrants, and minorities. By the year 2000, women will make up about 47 percent of workers, and minorities and immigrants will hold 26 percent of all jobs, up from 22 percent in 1990.[11]

Gender Issues

One of the most important developments in the U.S. labor market has been the increasing number of women working outside the home. Social changes during the late 1970s and early 1980s, coupled with financial necessity, caused women to enter the workforce and redefine their role to include having a career.

It is predicted that by the year 2000, women will make up 65 percent of all labor force entrants.[12] Furthermore, 61 percent of all U.S. women are expected to be working by the year 2000.[13]

In 1990, approximately 62 percent of all mothers were employed. Now, women with children under age 6 make up the fastest-growing segment of the workforce.[14] For these working women (as well as their spouses), **balancing work life** with family and parenting presents an enormous challenge.

The problem of combining a career and family life is not just a women's issue. In many ways, the changing status of women has given men the opportunity to redefine male roles, expectations, and lifestyles. Some men are deciding that there is more to life than corporate success and are choosing to scale back work hours and commitments to spend more time with families. Worker values have been shifting toward personal goals, quality of life, self-fulfillment, and family. Workers today, both men and women, are looking to achieve harmony between career and family life.

The high-performing career-and-family woman can be a major player in companies. She can provide a significant business advantage as the competition for able people escalates. The price companies must pay to retain these women is threefold: plan for and manage a **maternity program,** provide the flexibility which will allow women to be maximally productive, and take an active company role in helping to support high-quality and affordable child-care services.

Minorities

Although white workers are expected to remain the largest labor group in the United States, their numbers will increase only 15 percent, compared with a 20 percent increase for blacks and a 74 percent increase for Hispanics by the year 2000.[15]

English is expected to be the second language for the majority of California's population by the year 2000. By 2020, most of that state's entry-level workers will be Hispanic, and current projections indicate that Hispanics will surpass blacks as the largest racial minority within the next 25 years.[16]

Physically Disabled

The largest unemployed minority group in the United States are people with disabilities. Of the 13 million disabled persons of working age, only 34 percent worked full- or part-time in 1990.[17] In a survey of these disabled workers, 66 percent reported that they wanted to work.

The Americans with Disabilities Act (ADA) defines a disability as a physical or mental impairment that substantially limits one or more major life activities. Examples of such physical or mental impairments include those resulting from conditions such as orthopedic, visual, speech, and hearing impairments; cerebral palsy; epilepsy; muscular dystrophy; multiple sclerosis; HIV infections; cancer; heart disease; diabetes; mental retardation; emotional illness; specific learning disabilities; drug abuse; and alcoholism.

In the 1990s, changing laws and technology were providing greater access for the disabled to education and jobs. For most businesses, the mentally and physically disabled represented a largely unexplored labor market.[18]

Age

The **baby-boomers** (born between 1946 and 1964) are aging, causing the average age of the workforce to rise to 39 by the year 2000.[19] At that time, the age group from 16 to 24 dropped by 2 million, from 24 percent of the labor force in 1976 to 16 percent in 2000. The number of people age 50 to 65 will increase at more than twice the rate of the overall population. Within the next 20 years, 25 percent of the workforce will be 55 years of age or older.[20]

During this time, the workforce is expected to generate over 16 million new jobs. Entry-level workers will be in short supply, and fewer new workers will enter the labor force than will be lost through retirement. Many older employees are opting for **early retirement,** even though there is no longer a mandatory retirement age and life expectancies have increased. In the future, companies will need to retain and hire older, experienced workers.

Many older workers don't necessarily want to be spend time in leisure activities for 20 years. Some companies are finding ways to retrain and employ them. In Florida, where 18 percent of the population is over 65, the future is now—fast-food chains recruit workers in retirement villages. Last year, Kelly Services, Inc., in Troy, Michigan, put out a call for workers over 55. Now they're 8 percent of the "temp" rolls. In Boston, one BayBanks Inc. unit has hired 45 retirees as clericals, tellers, and clerks.[21] Retirement-age workers may need to be encouraged to continue in or to reenter the workforce on a flexible or part-time basis, whether for economic reasons, social interaction, or the need to be productive.

MANAGING DIVERSITY AND EEO

The goal of Equal Employment Opportunity was to correct the past exclusion of women and minorities from U.S. organizations. There has been a great deal of progress made in hiring women and minorities, but these groups still work in jobs disproportionately clustered at the bottom of corporate hierarchies.[22] Despite organizational efforts, equal employment opportunity (EEO) and affirmative action have not adequately improved the upward mobility of women and minorities.

EEO programs emphasize treating all employees equally. Managing diversity, however, necessitates that organizations make changes in their systems, structures, and management practices in order to eliminate any barriers that may exist to keep people from reaching their full potential. The goal should be not to treat all people the same, but rather to treat people as individuals, recognizing each employee has different needs which require different efforts to succeed.

Advantages of Diversity

For many organizations, the original impetus to diversify their workforces was equal opportunity and social responsibility. Morally and ethically, diversity was the right thing to do. In the 1990s, organizations were approaching diversity efforts from a more practical, business-oriented perspective.

Companies with a reputation for providing opportunities for diverse employees will have a competitive advantage in the labor market, and will be sought out by the most qualified employees. In addition, when employees believe their differences are not merely tolerated but valued, they may become more loyal, productive, and committed.

Challenges of a Diverse Workforce

A diverse workforce also poses many challenges. Many of these challenges can be turned into advantages if the workforce is managed effectively. Such challenges include different holidays and religious events, attitudes toward work customs and worker supervision, preferences for certain types of food, and lack of understanding of employee benefits programs.

Less Cohesiveness

Diversity can create a lessening in the level of cohesiveness. **Cohesiveness** refers to how tightly-knit the group is, and the degree to which group members perceive, interpret, and act on their environment in similar or mutually agreed-upon ways. Because of differences in language, culture, and experience, diverse work groups typically are less cohesive than homogeneous groups.

Racism, or Just Ignorance?

Welcome to a rude new world, where some faux pas are easily categorized as racist. However, many mistakes may be the result of ignorance and expressed in an inappropriate manner or context.

It's the offhand remark that cuts or injures: the request for a speaker with an "adorable" British accent "to say something in English;" the question to women of Indian descent about the **tikka or kumkum** (the red beauty mark, often made from a powder and worn on the forehead or scalp), "Does that dot wash off?;" the constant query to every Asian-American, "Are you Japanese, Chinese, or what?"[23]

Communication Problems

One of the most common challenges of diversity is communication. Communication problems may include misunderstandings, inaccuracies, errors, and slower actions. Speed is lost when group members are not all fluent in the working language, or when additional time must be taken to fully explain communication.

Diversity also increases errors and misunderstandings. Group members may assume they interpret things similarly, when in fact they do not. They may also lack a common understanding because of their different cultural value systems.

Mistrust

People tend to associate with others who are like themselves. This tendency often leads to mistrust and misunderstanding of those who are different because of low familiarity. This causes stress and tension in work groups, and often reaching agreement on decisions can be difficult.

Stereotyping

Each individual learns to see the world in a certain way based on a unique set of backgrounds and experiences. Each individual's interests, values, and culture act as filters, and leads him or her to distort, block, and select what they choose to interpret. One sees what one expects to see. Team members often stereotype those who are "different" rather than accurately perceiving those individuals' contributions and capabilities.

Ultimately, consultants say, accommodating differences can pay off. "The goal of diversity programs is to provide employers with a better sense of how these differences are actualized in the workplace, to be more sensitive to the fact that there are many roads up the mountain," said Neil Pickett, director of program management at the Hudson Institute, a think tank based in Indianapolis.

"People who conform to the very traditional, old-fashioned, bureaucratic mind-set of a large company are not good for a company, no matter what color they are," he added. "More companies are depending on the creativity . . . of their employees, and they want people who can think outside the box."[24]

Our society won't survive without the values of tolerance, and **cultural tolerance** comes to nothing without cultural understanding. The challenge facing America will be the shaping of a truly common public culture, one responsive to the long-silenced cultures of color. If we relinquish the ideal of America as a plural nation, we've abandoned the very experiment America represents. The price is too great to pay.

How Organizations Can Cultivate a Diverse Workforce

Many organizations have moved quickly to adapt to workforce diversity changes over the past 2 decades. Companies are motivated by an understanding that there are "bottom-line" advantages for companies who are developing the potential of all employees. These companies began seeking a wide range of diverse talent from every group represented within the nation's culture. Just as group decisions improve the quality of decision making, work teams drawing on this rich combination of diverse talent enlarge the amount of information and approaches available for group problem solving. Many companies are now developing programs aimed toward training managers and employees in skills necessary to work comfortably with others from differing backgrounds.

The organization's approach to becoming multicultural and taking advantage of a diverse workforce usually includes (1) top management support; (2) assessing the workforce; and (3) attracting diverse employees.

Top Management Support

In order for the diversity program to succeed, top management support is critical. One way to communicate this commitment to all employees—as well as to the external environment—is to incorporate the organization's attitudes toward diversity into the corporate mission statement and into strategic plans and objectives.

Diversity Assessment

The next step in managing diversity is to assess the organization's workforce, culture, and practices in recruitment, promotions, benefits, and compensation. In addition, the demographics of the labor pool need to be considered. The goal of assessment is to identify problems and make changes where needed.

Many women and Asians, for example, tend to be less aggressive in a corporate culture, but most organizations value this trait. After the assessment, HR managers might find the cultural values need to be changed so diverse styles are equally acceptable. The assessment also identifies existing corporate values and norms for their impact on a diverse workforce.

Attracting Employees

Companies can attract a diverse, qualified workforce through using effective recruiting practices, accommodating employees' work and family needs, and offering alternative work arrangements. Although such efforts increase costs in the short term, the expectation is they will be more than offset in the long term.

HRM STRATEGIES TO LESSEN RESISTANCE TO DIVERSITY

Norms are the organized and shared ideas of what members of an organization should do and feel. The members themselves define the norms, as well as enforce individual behavior to conform to the norms. These behaviors are developed by the team through peer pressure. Because norms generally have strong support from the team, they are often hard to change.

The organization culture includes the language, dress, patterns of behavior, value system, feelings, attitudes, interactions, and group norms of the members. Larger organizations will have **subcultures** formed around smaller work or social groups. According to the system view of organization behavior, it is difficult to change the ways of behaving in one part of the organization without influencing the other parts. Unless the HR manager begins by considering the acceptance of diversity by the organization as a whole, the ultimate acceptance of the HRM program is in serious question.

If resistance to diversity can be minimized, the chances of a successful HRM program are enhanced. Initially, two things in reducing resistance should be recognized by both the HR manager and the employee: (1) Resistance to change can be predicted; and (2) Resistance cannot be repressed effectively in the long run. Change of some type is inevitable. The task of the HR manager is to make conflict resulting from the resistance creative for organizational good. That is, as the repression of conflict is unwise and even futile, the objective is to turn the energies generated in the resistance of the change to good advantage. However, an HR manager can minimize the threat that underlies resistance. Certain actions may be implemented to make resistance creative for the organization and to reduce resistance to a more diverse organization.

Education and Communication

The uncertainty and fear of the unknown associated with change can be minimized by an effective communication program. The lack of reliable information leads to rumors and uncertainty. Information concerning the what and why involved in the HRM program should be provided to all organization members. In a survey commissioned by *Fortune* magazine of 1,500 senior executives from 20 countries, 89 percent believed the need to communicate frequently with employees will be one of a CEO's top characteristics, compared to 59 percent saying it currently was a top characteristic.[25]

Many companies, including Texas Instruments and General Motors, have shown employees commercial television programs about the ability of U.S. companies to compete internationally in an attempt to increase awareness of the need for more diversity. When employees are told of falling sales, sharply rising costs, declining profits, decreasing quality, customer complaints, high absenteeism, and other statistics that compare unfavorably with the competition or where the company would like to be, organization employees are much more likely to support changes.

Organizations, such as General Mills and Digital Equipment Computer, spend a significant amount of time training production-line employees to prepare for a more diverse workforce. A major benefit is that employees are able to analyze and understand the problems for themselves. The importance for change is appreciated directly by employees—from line workers to top executives. The longer members speculate in the absence of reliable facts, the more likely it is that resistance will emerge. Most managers underestimate the amount of communication needed, so it is better to use "overkill" than to understate the situation.

The advantages and rewards of the proposed HR programs should be emphasized in communication. Opposition to change disappears as the fears it generates are explained away. Once the reasons underlying a diversity program are made clear and how individuals will benefit, employees involved can more readily understand and accept the impact of the change.

Participation of Employees in the HRM Program

One basic technique for increasing the acceptance of diversity is to be certain that the individuals involved are allowed to share in the decision process, rather than being forced. The involvement of the individual in matters of concern increases the probability of having an acceptable program. An individual who has participated in the formation of the HR program has an interest and ownership in the program, which is likely to lead to increased motivation and understanding.

A diversity program "prepared on high and cast as pearls before swine" will most certainly be destined to failure. Captain Queeg, in the following excerpt from *The Caine Mutiny*, very enthusiastically follows the policy of dictated change which later contributed to the crew's mutiny:

> "Now, there are four ways of doing a thing aboard ship—the right way, the wrong way, the Navy way, and my way. I want things on this ship done my way. Don't worry about the other ways. Do things my way, and we'll get along—okay. Now are there any questions?" He looked around. There were no questions. He nodded with smiling satisfaction.[26]

If there is a union in the workplace, it needs to be involved and supportive of the diversity program. Some HRM programs (such as TQM and self-managed work teams, as discussed in chapter 17) directly involve the union. When potential resistors are drawn into the planning and implementation process, resistance to the change may be reduced or eliminated.

Facilitation and Support

Reinforcing the diversity program and providing support for those involved is another way HR managers can deal with resistance. If the situation allows, the HR manager can arrange promotions, monetary rewards, or public recognition for those participating in the diversity program. In one HRM program in which the authors were involved, a well-publicized promotion was arranged for a manager who had endorsed and participated in the HRM program despite considerable risk of criticism by his peers and immediate superiors when he volunteered for the program. The result was a dramatic acceptance of the HRM program by other managers.

Negotiation and Agreement

Another technique is negotiation with potential resisters. Some examples include union agreements, increasing an employee's pension benefits in exchange for early retirement, or negotiating agreement with the heads of departments that would be affected by the change.

Leadership

The leadership of key managers in the organization is critical. Other managers who are affected by the change need to be involved and supportive. Many companies provide management development seminars to open up managers to the acceptance of changes. America West Airlines' top executives demonstrate through their own work behavior how they want middle managers to behave. Managers at all levels are expected to lead with gentle persuasion, nurture talents, and draw out ideas. The chairman of the board, Edward Beauvais, and the president, Michael Conway, maintain close contact with employees by spending at least one third of their time directly with workers. They have a sacred open-door policy, an employee telephone hot line number to top management, and spend a good deal of time in the field.[27]

Other than the formal leadership in the organization, the informal leaders' support is also important. Bringing in informal leaders early in the planning stages can build "grass-roots" support for the program.

Reward Systems

Flexible reward systems that take account of individual differences in employees can help in the acceptance of changes. Profit-sharing, bonuses, skill and knowledge-based pay, gain-sharing, and stock ownership plans have recently become more common in large and small businesses.[28] Profit-sharing uses the performance of the business to calculate pay. Knowledge-based pay or skill-based pay uses the knowledge or skills a worker has to determine pay. Gain-sharing recognizes the value of a specific group based on measurable characteristics in the basis for calculating pay.

The trend toward more flexible reward systems will likely continue. In 1976, approximately 1,000 employee-owned businesses existed in the United States. Estimates now show that there are over 10,000 employee-owned businesses employing more than 10 million people. From 1988 to 1990, an estimated 200 public corporations have set up employee stock ownership plans.[29] Ford Motor Company has a profit-sharing plan in place that recently rewarded hourly employees with $2,800 for the year. At its Saturn plant, General Motors pays workers and executives 80 percent of the base pay of other plants; but employees can make up the difference and more if they meet productivity, quality, and sales targets.[30]

One study found that employee ownership "can have a positive effect on a work group's norms, cohesiveness, and cooperative behaviors; on an employee's work-related attitudes, motivation, and behavior; and on an organization's performance and profitability. Ownership per se does not, however, automatically and directly produce these social-psychological and behavioral effects." The researchers concluded that, "An employee-ownership system designed and operated with strong equity, information, and influence components will help produce psychologically experienced ownership and build employees' commitment to and integration into the organization."[31]

Explicit and Implicit Coercion

Managers may force people to go along with a program by explicit or implicit threats involving loss of jobs, loss of promotion or raises, and so forth. At one company that was introducing quality improvement teams, managers who were ordered by their president over their objections to participate sat with their backs to the conference table.[32] In some situations, managers may also dismiss or transfer employees who refuse to change. Though not uncommon, such methods pose risks and make it more difficult to gain support for future HRM programs. Organizations that have introduced team work have found a few employees can't make the transition of working cooperatively with others in teams. They have provided opportunities for these workers to transfer to work situations where they will not be working interdependently with others.

Climate Conducive to Communication

Creating a climate where everyone involved in the diversity program feels free and not threatened to communicate with others can minimize resistance in the long run. If attitudes of respect, understanding, and communication prevail, this will help to break a cycle of **reciprocal threat** and aggressiveness on the part of the resisters and the advocates of the HRM program. The manager ensures that parties do not sit in judgment of each other, but instead focuses attention on the basic issues and the relevant facts.

Capitalizing on Global Diversity

Organizational experts and multinational managers agree that managing diversity and working with people who are different is more complex than working with people who share the same attitudes, values, and behaviors.

Traditional models of organizational behavior have been replaced by diversity—a workforce of different ages, races, ethnic, nationalities, physical abilities, and lifestyles.

SUMMARY

In this chapter, we have examined managing a diverse workforce. Some approaches have been used over a period of several years with varying degrees of success, yet other methods are somewhat new.

The process of change is complex because of the interaction of social, technical, and psychological factors. People often become satisfied with the status quo and react with insecurity or anxiety when change occurs.

Diversity is a broad term that refers to differences such as religious affiliation, age, disability status, military experience, sexual orientation, economic class, educational level, and lifestyle, as well as gender, race, nationality, and ethnicity.

Managing diversity means not only hiring people who are different from the norm, but also supporting and using employee differences to the organization's advantage. Managing diversity is becoming a bottom-line issue. As the labor market is changing, organizations must be able to recruit, develop, and retain a diverse workforce.

The challenges for managers created by a diverse workforce include decreased group cohesiveness, communication problems, mistrust and tension, and stereotyping. These challenges can be turned into advantages by training and by effective management.

Managers can be trained to become aware of the myths, stereotypes, and true cultural differences (as well as organizational barriers) that prevent employees from making full contributions. Employees can be trained to better understand the corporate culture, success requirements, and career choices that affect opportunities for advancement.

An important factor to be considered prior to the implementation of any HRM program is the motivation of the employees toward change. Some resistance to proposed programs may arise from perceived (real or unreal) threats to personal security.

In the simulation, you will have an opportunity to participate in a traditional organization and in one based on using the ideas of diversity in work teams. Though the experiment is limited in size and time, you will draw some conclusions of your own about the application of diversity in work teams.

In the last several years, workforce diversity has received much more attention and seems to be having a positive impact in improving organizations. There are several approaches that will help managers in improving productivity, but there is a definite need for additional research into workforce diversity programs.

Managing diversity means enabling a heterogeneous workforce to perform to its potential in an equitable work environment where no one group has an advantage or disadvantage.

The challenges facing American business as a result of the dramatic changes in the composition of the workforce are

- How to ensure profits and growth?

- How to maintain a skilled workforce?

- How to adequately train managers to manage diversity?

These issues hardly seem new, but after 25 years of legislation, government intervention, and corporate policies, the problems associated with managing diversity have grown more acute.

REVIEW QUESTIONS

1. Describe a classroom or work example situation where you had difficulty interacting or working with someone "different" from yourself. How did you feel?
2. How would you define *workforce diversity?*
3. What is meant by *managing diversity?*
4. Describe the advantages and challenges created by a diversified workforce.
5. Describe the social and demographic changes and economic and employment shifts creating the changing workforce.
6. Read a book or review a video movie and identify managing diversity issues.

Define and be able to use the following:

- Balancing Work Life
- Baby-Boomers
- Cohesiveness
- Cultural Diversity
- Cultural Tolerance
- Early Retirement
- Flexible Reward Systems
- Maternity Program
- Reciprocal Threat
- Six Sigma
- Subcultures
- Tikka or Kumkum

HRM SKILLS SIMULATION 18.1: MANAGING DIVERSITY

A. PURPOSE

The purpose of this exercise is to experience and observe how diverse cultural values impacts effective organization functioning. You will experience how conflicting values can sometimes be resolved. The goals are

1. To increase your awareness of the feeling of "being different."
2. To better understand the context of "being different."
3. To explore group members' social values.

B. PROCEDURES

Step 1. Prior to class, individually complete the Diversity Values Worksheet.

Step 2. Form groups of five team members. Your task is to arrive at a consensus for a team ranking.

Step 3. After the class reconvenes, team spokespersons present team findings.

QUESTIONS

1. Were there individual values in situations that surprised you?
2. How would you define "being different?"
3. Can this exercise be used to improve diversity?

DIVERSITY VALUES WORKSHEET

Instructions: Your task is to rank these items in order of value. In other words, place the number 1 beside the item you think employees would welcome most as a social value, the number 2 for the second most welcomed change, and so on until you have ranked all social values, the number 13 representing the value people would welcome the least among these values.

Social Values	Your Rank	Group Rank
1. More emphasis on self-expression	_____	_____
2. Less emphasis on money	_____	_____
3. More acceptance of sexual freedom	_____	_____
4. More emphasis on technological improvements	_____	_____
5. More respect for authority	_____	_____
6. More respect for traditional family ties	_____	_____
7. Less emphasis on working hard	_____	_____
8. More acceptance of drug usage	_____	_____
9. More acceptance of smoking	_____	_____
10. More acceptance of cultural differences	_____	_____
11. More acceptance of different lifestyles	_____	_____
12. More acceptance of disabilities	_____	_____
13. More acceptance of working with AIDS	_____	_____

Case 18.1   Precision Products, Inc.

Friday morning had begun rather routinely for Helen Brown, personnel manager, until the telephone call. It was from the company CEO and President Howard J. Peterson, Jr. Apparently he had read an article about diversity and wondered where Precision Products was positioned on this issue. Peterson was not satisfied with Helen's comments and wanted a position paper on his desk in 3 days. Because this was Friday, that meant another weekend of work.

Helen quickly dialed her Affirmative Action Officer Mike Hudson to schedule a work session. In the afternoon, they finally met and began to analyze the diversity situation at Precision Products. Looking over Mike's regional demographic data, the company appeared to have a workforce which represented the ethnic composition of the community. Helen observed the legal requirements of EEO appeared to have been met, but what had the company done to ensure these people had become indoctrinated into Precision Products' culture? Mike quickly admitted there were no official company programs designed to accomplish this goal.

After a prolonged discussion, they both agreed the goal of managing diversity went beyond hiring representative numbers, and must be expanded to ensure all employees were contributing to Precision Products goals. Through such participation, the company and the employees would all prosper. For the company, this would mean increased market share and profit growth. For the employees, it would mean a more satisfying place to work and the opportunity to experience personal growth.

The next step was how to achieve such a goal through better personnel policies. It was apparent some managers and coworkers were not adequately interacting with all employees. They appeared to be uncomfortable in providing corrective training and feedback to different employee ethnic groups. There seemed to be value differences and inaccurate stereotypes which prevented the free flow of communications. Rather than appreciate how an understanding of culture differences could strengthen Precision Products, there was a wall of indifference.

Now the problem had been isolated, the logical step was to decide how to change the problem from a negative to a positive. Helen and Mike agreed to return Saturday morning with their individual change lists. The next morning, after several hours of discussion, a change program began to formalize. What was needed was an attitude change program consisting of several training sessions for all employees. The program would begin by stressing the value of becoming aware of each other's cultural and personal characteristics emphasizing differences and similarities. After this stage, the program would discuss how these factors develop into stereotypes with resulting behavioral patterns. Specific behavior incidents would be analyzed to determine the why and how of what actually took place. The final stage would be a showing of one of the many diversity videos available through private vendors. This would conclude with a small group discussion of coaching, feedback, and cross-cultural communication. The wrap-up would present the consensus of the groups.

Helen and Mike reviewed their rough draft and broke for a fast lunch. Helen said, "We can put the final touches on this in the afternoon and have the finished Managing Diversity proposal on Howard Peterson's desk early Monday morning."

QUESTIONS

1. How important is the managing diversity project for the long term success of Precision Products? Discuss.
2. What would you add or subtract to the Managing Diversity proposal? Explain.
3. For diversity to work, what are some attitudes which need to be changed? Try to be specific.

ENDNOTES

1. Marcia Forsberg, "Cultural Training," *Personnel Journal* (May 1993): 81.
2. J. P. White, "Diversity's Champion: When Elsie Cross Takes on Racism and Sexism in Corporations, She Strives to Free Everyone—Even the White Men at the Top," *Los Angeles Times Magazine* (August 9, 1992): 15.
3. See H. Fullerton, "Labor Force 2006," *Monthly Labor Review* (November 1997): 23.
4. R. Stodghill, "The Coming Bottleneck," *Business Week* (March 24, 1997): 184.
5. J. Fernandez, *Managing a Diverse Work Force* (Lexington, MA: Lexington Books, 1991).
6. Dreyfus, "Get Ready for the New Work Force," *Fortune* (April 23, 1990): 165–168.
7. C. Solomon, "The Corporate Response to Workforce Diversity," *Personnel Journal* (August 1989): 42–53; S. Overman, "Managing the Diverse Workforce," *Human Resource Magazine* (April 1991): 32–36.
8. W. Johnson and A. Packer, *Workforce 2000: Work and Workers for the 21st Century* (Indianapolis: Hudson Institute, 1987).

9. H. Fullerton, "Labor Force 2006," *Monthly Labor Review* (November 1997): 23.

10. "Four by Four," *Training and Development Journal* 34, no. 2 (February 1989): 13–21.

11. B. Nussbaum, "Needed Human Capital," *Business Week* (September 19, 1988): 100–103.

12. K. Kovach and J. Pearce, "HR Strategic Mandates for the 1990s," *Personnel* (April 1990): 50–55.

13. *Opportunity 2000* (Indianapolis: Hudson Institute, 1988).

14. T. O'Carolan, "Parenting Time: Whose Problem is It?" *Personnel Administrator* (August 1987): 58–65.

15. W. Johnson and A. Packer, *Workforce 2000: Work and Workers for the 21st Century* (Indianapolis: Hudson Institute, 1987).

16. K. Kovach and J. Pearce. "HR Strategic Mandates for the 1990s," *Personnel* (April 1990): 50–55.

17. *Opportunity 2000* (Indianapolis: Hudson Institute, 1988), 100.

18. J. Peters, "How to Bridge the Hiring Gap," *Personnel Administrator* (October 1989): 76–85.

19. M. Finney, "The ASPA Labor Shortage Survey," *Personnel Administrator* (February 1989): 35–42.

20. C. Fyock, *America's Work Force is Coming of Age* (Lexington, MA: Lexington Books, 1990).

21. Charlene Solomon, "Managing Today's Immigrants," *Personnel Journal* (February 1993): 56.

22. Dreyfus, "Get Ready for the New Work Force," *Fortune* (April 23, 1990): 165–168.

23. Itabari Njeri, "The Challenge of Diversity: When Different Groups Converge, the Ignorant and the Curious Can Be Unexpectedly Rude," *Los Angeles Times*, 2 April 1989, View, p. 6.

24. "Whose Culture Is It, Anyway?" *New York Times*, 4 May 1991, PB 1.

25. Lester B. Korn, "How the Next CEO Will Be Different," *Fortune* (May 22, 1989): 157–61.

26. Herman Wouk, *The Caine Mutiny: A Novel of World War II* (Garden City, NY: Doubleday & Co., Inc., 1951), 131.

27. Kenneth Labich, "Making Over Middle Managers," *Fortune* (May 8, 1990): 58–64.

28. For a more detailed discussion of reward system, see Kanter, *When Giants Learn to Dance*, pp. 229–66; and Henry Tosi and Lisa Tosi, "What Managers Need to Know About Knowledge-Based Pay," *Organizational Dynamics* (Winter 1986): 52–64.

29. Jon L. Pierce and Candace A. Furo, "Employee Ownership: Implications for Management," *Organizational Dynamics* (Winter 1990): 32–43.

30. James B. Treece, "Here Comes GM's Saturn," *Business Week* (April 9, 1990): 56–62.

31. Jon L. Pierce and Candace A. Furo, "Employee Ownership: Implications for Management," *Organizational Dynamics* (Winter 1990): 32–43.

32. Thomas M. Rohan, "A New Culture," *Industry Week* (April 17, 1989): 43–56.

Part VII

The Success System: Focusing on a High-Performing Workforce

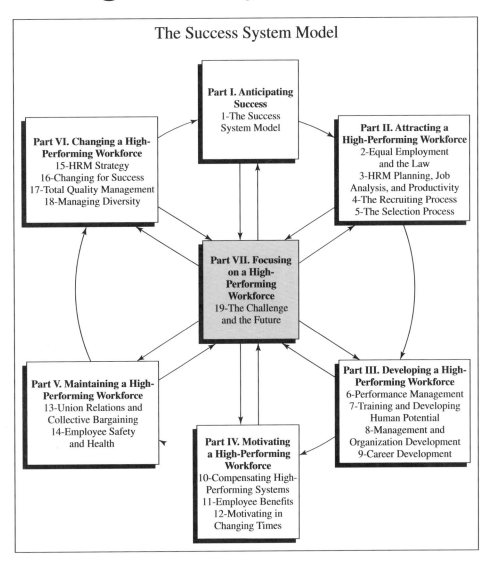

The Success System Model

Part I. Anticipating Success
1-The Success System Model

Part II. Attracting a High-Performing Workforce
2-Equal Employment and the Law
3-HRM Planning, Job Analysis, and Productivity
4-The Recruiting Process
5-The Selection Process

Part VI. Changing a High-Performing Workforce
15-HRM Strategy
16-Changing for Success
17-Total Quality Management
18-Managing Diversity

Part VII. Focusing on a High-Performing Workforce
19-The Challenge and the Future

Part V. Maintaining a High-Performing Workforce
13-Union Relations and Collective Bargaining
14-Employee Safety and Health

Part IV. Motivating a High-Performing Workforce
10-Compensating High-Performing Systems
11-Employee Benefits
12-Motivating in Changing Times

Part III. Developing a High-Performing Workforce
6-Performance Management
7-Training and Developing Human Potential
8-Management and Organization Development
9-Career Development

Chapter 19

Human Resource Management: The Challenge and the Future

Objectives

Upon completing this chapter, you will be able to:

1. Understand the basic issues in using HRM as an approach to developing an effective organization.
2. Recognize ways of maintaining, internalizing, and stabilizing an HRM program.
3. Identify some of the future trends and problems facing the HR manager.

Premeeting preparation

1. Read chapter 19.
2. Prepare for HRM Skills Simulation 19.1. Read Parts A and B, Steps 1, 2, and 3.
3. Prepare for HRM Skills Simulation 19.2. Read Parts A and B, Steps 1 and 2.
4. Read Case 19.1: The Bob Knowlton Case. Answer questions.

Tomorrow's organization will be different from today's. In a world of global competitiveness and technological innovation, organizations are reengineering, restructuring, and flattening the hierarchy to meet market pressures. Leading companies now envision an endlessly changing organization. The new term is "reconfigurable: an organization that is flexible and able to change on an annual, monthly, weekly, daily, even hourly time frame. Unchanging systems will become dinosaurs."[1]

One of the recurring themes of this book has been the movement toward a more proactive role for human resource managers. In some large corporations, the HRM department is viewed as a clerical function—keeping records, writing ads, recruiting employees—but not a real management function; like Rodney Dangerfield, "they get no *respect!*" Perhaps Derek Torrington and Laura Hall, two of our British colleagues, have best presented this view.

> That rock-hard, steely-eyed film star Clint Eastwood has appeared in several films as tough cop Harry Callaghan, whose approach to law and order is to shoot first and not bother asking too many questions afterwards. On one occasion he had killed rather a lot of people even by his own high standards, so that he was becoming politically embarrassing to the authorities. Something had to be done. The Chief of Police nerved himself and called Harry into his office, taking care that there was a large table between them, and gave him the news that he was being transferred—to Personnel. There was a moment of electric silence. A nervous tick flickered briefly on Harry Callaghan's right cheek. His jaw locked and those famous cold blue eyes gave the Chief a look that could have penetrated armor plate as he hissed his reply through clenched teeth: "Personnel is for __holes." Whereupon he left the room, slamming the door with sufficient vigor to splinter the woodwork in several places.
>
> Being a man of few words, Harry Callaghan did not explain further, but we can interpret his view as being the common one that Personnel work is not for the people who can and do, but for the people who can't and don't. It is regarded as the easy option for those who shirk the hard, competitive world of marketing, the precision of finance, or the long hours and hard knocks of manufacturing. It is soft, ineffectual and unimportant.
>
> A more benign version of that stereotype is that personnel HR is the human face of management, still avoiding the ruthless cut and thrust, but an important aspect of making the organization work effectively and ensuring that employees are well looked after. It is this second view that attracts many applicants to this area, people who feel that they could not cope with social work, but want to do something that is worthwhile and 'working with people'. Human Resource management seems to offer all that, and perhaps a company car as well, without the taint of the rat race.[2]

In the millennium, HRM needs to take an active role in developing a high-performing system and leading change. Change is happening in all organizations, but with differing degrees of rapidity and significance. Some organizations operate under highly volatile conditions causing rapid system-wide realignment and adaptation. Other organizations exist in relatively placid environments, with subsequently slower rates of change and less impact on the whole system. Tom Peters suggests that in today's world, "Excellence isn't—there are no excellent companies. The old saw, 'If it ain't broke, don't fix it' needs revision. I propose: "If it ain't broke, you just haven't looked hard enough.' Fix it anyway."[3]

There is a continuing need for long-range HR strategies to improve organizational decision making and work relationships to meet these changing conditions.

Clearly, HRM is becoming increasingly important in organizations of all types—industrial, governmental, and health care. Still, there are issues and challenges facing HR managers as they function in a changing workplace.

Change is a continuing process. Every organization exists in a continuous state of adapting to change. Some changes are caused by external competitive forces, whereas others emerge as a result of shifting forces within the organization. Many management theorists feel authoritarian or bureaucratic systems are too rigid to adapt to this increasing rate of change and therefore become reactive organizations—reacting drastically after problems emerge.

More and more organizations are finding employees are no longer satisfied with simply filling a slot in the organization chart. In a survey of American workers conducted for the U.S. Labor Department, the University of Michigan's Survey Research Center found that 41.5 percent responded "very true" when asked if they had interesting work with the freedom to decide how to do the job. This is 9.8 percent lower than the results in a similar earlier survey. Also, when asked about having enough information and authority to accomplish their job, 52.4 percent of workers responded "very true." This was down 10.9 percent from the earlier survey. It is not likely that jobs are getting worse. Rather, employees are probably getting better; that is, people are achieving higher educational levels, with a resulting increase in the level of motivational needs.

Because organizations are in a continuous state of change, HRM is also a continuing process. As one set of objectives is achieved, new standards of excellence and new challenges arise. As a result, the HR manager has two primary criteria of effectiveness. One criterion is the satisfaction and well-being of the employees in the organization; the other is the ability of the organization to maintain innovation within the system and the development of new capabilities. Because an HRM program is an approach to improving effectiveness, there is a need for an evaluation of the results. The organization members involved in the HRM process need feedback on the results of their efforts in order to determine whether to modify, continue, or discontinue these activities.

In today's changing environment, organizations must develop adaptive mechanisms and anticipative management systems. To cope with these changing conditions, the HR manager needs to take a proactive role, to be able to monitor progress toward HRM goals, and to recognize when these efforts have been effective. The individuals and teams involved in a HRM program need feedback to measure their progress toward goals and to stabilize HRM programs. This continuing assessment also acts to prevent deterioration or a return to prior behavior, attitudes, or values. An organization might implement a TQM program and initially feel that the program is successful. A year later, however, most managers may have discarded TQM and returned to prior management methods unless there is some stabilization of the TQM program.

HRM is an ongoing, continuing process. The completion of one program leads into another cycle in the process of development. In this chapter, we continue the final stage of the Success System Model: changing for success. Here we focus on a more proactive role for the HR manager. We examine the HRM evaluation process, identify several key issues, and discuss the future of the HRM field.

EVALUATION OF THE HRM PROGRAMS

After a HRM program has been implemented (such as a TQM program), the emphasis must be placed upon evaluating and **stabilizing** the new approaches so the changed behavior becomes part of the cultural norms. This stage involves three factors: (1) feedback: generating and communicating data to employees so they can measure their progress; (2) stabilizing or "freezing" the changes or desired behavior so that it will be continued; and (3) evaluating the HRM program results.

The Feedback of Information

The organization members involved in an HRM program need feedback on the results of the change in order to determine whether to modify, continue, or discontinue their activities. If employee teams obtain no feedback on the consequence of a change program, the program may be perceived as a failure and be discontinued. Therefore, part of the HR manager's job is to see that necessary information is made available to participating members and teams. In research conducted on TQM, it was found that more successful programs used early successes to encourage participants.[4]

The feedback of information is important because it also can create commitment among organization members. Commitment to change emerges from open communications and management's ability to reinforce new behaviors so that employees can see how their contribution affects outcomes.

One criterion for determining the effectiveness of an HRM program is whether or not system problems have been corrected. In certain instances, data will be readily available, particularly around operational indices of performance, quality, and productivity. In other instances, the HR manager may gather data from after-the-fact interviews or questionnaires to verify the degree of change in less tangible factors such as morale, leadership style, and job satisfaction.

At Chaparral Steel, for example, team meetings are held to share information on productivity, order backlog, and man-hours per ton produced. Monthly financial statements, including a chart tracking operating profits (their key measure for profit sharing), are posted for all team members.[5]

Work teams may also use such techniques as the "organization mirror" to gain information on how other organization groups view their changed status. A systematic and periodic appraisal of results should be designed into the HRM program to determine when desired levels have been achieved. This requires the setting of some type of "benchmark" to measure the extent or degree of change over time.

The HRM Manager and the line managers also need to provide reinforcement and support for programs by giving recognition, encouragement, and approval for positive change. Receiving information or performance data is important, but a major factor in the deterioration of performance is lack of recognition or reinforcement. (See Our Changing World.)

OUR CHANGING WORLD
DOWNSIZING—THE ROAD TO EFFICIENCY?[6]

Many companies have chosen the HRM tool of downsizing to achieve increased efficiency and bottom-line improvement. There have been many success stories, but there have also been many failures.

One success story is Sea-Land Services and its downsizing program. The company eliminated over 800 positions and five layers of management. This resulted in a decrease of $300 million in operating expenses. Perhaps of more significance is that productivity increased beyond what management thought possible. The end

result was revenues increased by 30 percent and profits soared by 35 percent. This dramatic change occurred in a global market marked by recession and without competition.

The downsizing process is being not only utilized by healthy companies, but also by unhealthy companies; not only by large companies, but also small companies. The causes of downsizing appear to be the consolidation of entire industries, replacing of jobs by new technologies, weak economies, and increased global competition.

Downsizing, as in any procedure, does not guarantee success. One survey by the American Management Association found less than half of the companies downsizing failed to report increased profits. The Conference Board reported 64 percent of downsized firms with more than 10,000 employees found lower morale among surviving employees. Overtime costs increased 30 percent, and 22 percent found they had eliminated the wrong people.

One company experiencing problems was NYNEX Corporation after its separation from AT&T. NYNEX cut 9,000 employees from a manager staff of 25,000. Although the company was successful in separating large numbers of people by using generous incentives, it became apparent there were still too many people in some departments and not enough people in other departments. NYNEX had to begin a new program to correct this problem by refilling 4,000 positions and spending millions of dollars to regain lost momentum.

What was the differences between the success of Sea-Land Services and the experience of NYNEX? For Sea-Land Services, the difference was the advanced planning which took place, utilizing the services of their human resource management department. The first step was a thorough 9-month program which examined practically every operation of the company, resulting in new job descriptions based on every position from top-level executives to janitors. This is called zero-base staffing, in which every job is at risk. The result was a new organization with the abilities and skills programmed to serve it.

Downsizing requires not only an eye to the present, but also to the future. Strategic human resource management planning is an absolute requirement to ensure success. Companies cannot afford to lose valuable high-skill employees who may be needed in the period following downsizing. This could lead to increased overtime, contract work, and temporaries, all contributing to expenses that could exceed cost savings. Eliminating the wrong positions could increase employee burnout as job responsibilities increase, negatively affecting productivity and increasing errors. Further, job cuts may result in legal action by the affected employees, especially if poorly prepared performance appraisals are relied on as the only basis for retention.

The process of downsizing requires careful planning, and the human resource department will play a key role in such a program. The HR professional must be ready to advocate a managed approach by providing education, leadership, and ensuring both fairness and equity.

QUESTIONS

1. What was the difference in downsizing approaches used by Sea-Land Services and NYNEX? Why did these differences exist?

2. What does zero-based staffing mean, how is it used, and what is your opinion of its use?

3. What responsibilities does downsizing place upon the human resource department? How can HRM respond?

THE STABILIZATION OF CHANGE

When the HRM objectives have been achieved, some means must be devised to ensure that the new operating level is stabilized. If this is not done, the tendency is for the individual, team, or the organization to deteriorate and revert to previous ineffective behaviors. As an example, an individual may desire to discontinue some habit, such as smoking, and actually change for a short period of time. However, the change objective is not accomplished if the person begins smoking again 6 months later. The use of skills on the jobs is called **transfer of training.** One criticism of off-site training is called "fade-out" or lack of transfer of training. For example, a manager may develop new management behaviors while at a seminar, but the change erodes away back on the job because the work environment has not changed and is not supportive. Fade-out, or deterioration of change, may occur in an HRM program when the change is not stabilized into the system and behavior gradually slips back into previous ineffective modes. Obviously, one measure of success is whether or not the changes are permanently accepted by the organization.

The HRM program itself may have a stabilizing effect because of its advantages and support. At TRW, team development programs have become so widely accepted that many project managers request a team-building session every time a new project is initiated. There is also a sort of 'Hawthorne effect' surrounding many HRM programs (such as self-managed work teams or TQM techniques), so participating employees feel they are an elite group and sell the benefits of the HRM program to other members, thus stabilizing the acceptance of change.

Sometimes an HRM program is initiated in one division or subsystem of an organization, and the performance results may be used to demonstrate the effectiveness of the new techniques to another division. Where results are obtainable, such as those relating to decreased turnover, quality, and costs, this recognition may act as a stabilizing force.

Once an HRM program is fully implemented, the program should become institutionalized or internalized by team members. The acceptance and adoption of a program depends upon practice and familiarity, so that the innovation becomes a routine part of organization activity.

Finally, some form of continuing assessment of the HRM program during later periods should be included to guard against a decline over time. The greater the investment in the HRM program, the more detailed the reappraisal mechanisms should be.

THE EVALUATION OF HRM PROGRAMS

One major problem in HRM programs lies in the need for the development of better research designs to measure bottom line results. The primary purpose of HRM evaluation is to measure what happens to operating variables when new programs are implemented. Unfortunately, there are usually many uncontrollable variables (such as economic conditions and technological changes) which influence the state of the organization over time.[7]

Most professionals feel that the evaluation method should be designed into the HRM program. They suggest that HRM evaluation data will be important in the future for three groups: (1) The top management decision-makers: to show them that HRM expenditures are providing the desired results; (2) The employees: to provide feedback about their performance; and (3) The HR managers: to develop their expertise and design new programs based upon their past experiences.

Evaluating HRM programs involves making an assessment about whether the program has been satisfactorily implemented, and, if so, whether it is bringing about the desired outcomes. When organizations invest large amounts in major HRM programs, there is an increasing need for data on the results. HR managers are frequently being asked to justify the HRM program in terms of basic productivity, cost savings, or other bottom line measures. Consequently, organizations are constantly seeking a more rigorous evaluation of HRM programs. (See cartoon.)

Source: B.C. by permission of Johnny Hart and Creators Syndicate, Inc.

Some Conditions for Success of HRM Programs

The conditions leading to possible success of HRM programs include the following:

1. *Pressure to Change.* The organization is generally under considerable external or internal pressure to improve. Top management has been aroused to action, and is searching for solutions.
2. *Top Management Involvement.* Top management is involved and takes a direct and responsible role in the HRM process. Several levels of management generally participate in the collection of data and the analysis of specific problems.
3. *Commitment to Change.* New ideas and methods for developing solutions are generated at a number of levels in the organization. This results in a commitment to change by most organization employees.
4. *Beta Testing.* The programs are generally developed, tested, and found acceptable before the scope of the change is expanded to include larger departments or the entire system.
5. *Results.* The HRM program is generally reinforced by positive results.[8]

HRM programs involve a long-term implementation of innovative techniques to increase organization effectiveness. They function on the idea that improving the way people work together and the way work teams cooperate leads to increasing effectiveness. The management style needed to work in an innovative manner differs from traditional concepts, and HRM programs are designed to focus upon the manager's attitudes and to develop a managerial style to encourage action in the presence of risk. HRM strategies try to increase the manager's tolerance for ambiguity and uncertainty and the ability to communicate with and motivate others.

One thing is clear: HRM is itself in the midst of changing. You must decide for yourself what rings true in terms of your own experience and what does not. HRM has been described as a process designed to increase organizational effectiveness by integrating the needs of the individual employees for growth and development with organization goals. In a changing environment, HRM provides strategies to alter beliefs, attitudes, values, and structures of organizations, making them more anticipative and adaptive to deal with problems of "future shock."

The new HRM role represents a major change from more traditional practices. HRM needs to be involved in changing organization systems and revitalizing them in line with the needs of the individuals within the system and environmental constraints. As the environment changes, it is important individual managers be aware of and understand the advantages and disadvantages of the techniques and strategies available for managing in this changing context. The new proactive role of HRM provides a dynamic and powerful methodology for helping people and organizations to collaboratively work together and become a winning team.

Emerging Issues and Values

HRM is a growing, developing, and changing field of study. Consequently, there are a number of evolving theories and concepts.

HRM is an approach for creating and seeking **organizational excellence,** which is the underlying goal of the modern manager and organization. The successful managerial organizations are seeking the need to practice "anticipative" management styles, rather than using "reactive" styles (that is, waiting until after the fact to react to change). As the rate of change has increased, so has the range of programs used in HRM.

For the foreseeable future, it is difficult to find a firm that has a solid or sustainable lead over its competitors. The rate of change is too rapid for organizations to become complacent. In fact, the cycles between winner and loser are becoming increasingly immediate and drastic.

At least 15 of the 43 excellent companies highlighted by Thomas Peters and Robert Waterman in their book, *In Search of Excellence,* lost their luster soon after the book's publication. And one—People Express, which had been considered an example of what to do right in an organization—escaped bankruptcy by being purchased by its rival, Texas Air.

Companies such as Eastman Kodak and Texas Instruments, if judged on their performance during the last decade, would not pass the financial tests for excellence laid down in the book. Others, including Atari, Avon, and Levi Strauss, have suffered significant earnings declines stemming from serious business or management problems.

Failures of U.S. businesses are at an all-time high since the Great Depression. Though the entrepreneurial drive is strong—in 1992 there were 250,456 new businesses started—57,067 businesses went bankrupt that year, and more than half of them were less than 5 years old.

EXCELLENT COMPANIES IN TROUBLE

In *In Search of Excellence,* it is suggested U.S. firms needed to regain their competitive edge by placing more emphasis on the people side of business—customer and employees—and by sticking to what they do best. Why have so many excellent companies had problems? One criticism has been that companies have ignored such fundamental factors as technology, fundamental changes in markets, and broad economic and business trends.

Companies such as Lockheed learned their lessons the hard way. In the initial stages of the L-1011 Tristar production, with high costs coupled with losses in defense contracts, Lockheed was saved from bankruptcy by federal loan guarantees. However, when the crisis was passed and it was clear to analysts that there was not a large enough market to support the Tristar, Boeing's 747, and McDonnell Douglas' DC-10, Lockheed continued production. To Lockheed, the Tristar was a symbol of getting back in the commercial aircraft business, and they hung on despite the lack of enough firm orders to see the project to the break-even point. Eventually, Lockheed gave up and took a $400 million write-off.

EXCELLENCE IN A CHANGING WORLD

The excellent companies of today do not have a guarantee on remaining excellent. Companies that have followed one set of rules, such as those espoused in *In Search of Excellence,* have tended to get into trouble just as companies did when they followed the strict rules of the financial number crunchers.

Leading management consultants, including Tom Peters, have suggested two ways to respond to this changing era of unsustainable excellence. One is reactive: to buy and sell businesses in hope of staying in front of the industry growth curve. The second strategy is proactive, and involves meeting uncertainty by becoming a "world-class competitor:" with high-quality, enhanced responsiveness, and continuous, short-cycle innovation aimed at creating new markets for both new and mature products and services.

If the word "excellence" is to be meaningful in the future, it may require major redefinition: as Tom Peters has noted, "Excellent firms don't believe in excellence—only in constant improvement and constant change. That is, excellent firms of tomorrow will cherish impermanence—and thrive on chaos."

QUESTIONS

1. For organizations in trouble, what can be done to pull them out of their problems?
2. What would be your definition of excellence?

FUTURE TRENDS IN HRM

The application of HRM programs is growing rapidly. New models, techniques, and approaches are being constantly developed and old techniques discarded. HRM itself is facing future shock.

An awareness of the complex environment in which organizations exist is evidenced by the popularity of new trend books in management, such as *Liberation Management, Teaching the Elephants to Dance,* and *Control Your Destiny or Someone*

Else Will. As shapers of change, the HR manager will play a critical role in helping organizations adjust to the changing forces and trends that affect them. These future trends include

- **Organization transformation (OT).** This recent advance in change strategies is used in situations of drastic, abrupt change when the organization's survival is at stake. These include such changes as mergers, takeovers, product changes, and plant closures, which often involve large-scale layoffs and restructuring.
- **Shared vision.** This approach requires all levels of management to identify the strategic vision of the future and decide what it takes to make it work.
- **Innovation.** Organizations are focusing more effort on innovating—creating new products, goods, and services—and also on new ways of organizing and relating among organization members. 3M, for example, is known to have a corporate culture that encourages and supports innovation.
- **Trust.** The critical factor in high-performing organizations is the development of trust within and between individuals, teams, and organizational units and levels. Without trust, there can be no sustainable excellence with an organization.
- **Empowerment.** In order to develop high-performing systems, organization members must be empowered—given the autonomy to do things their own way, to achieve recognition, involvement, and a sense of worth in their jobs. This allows for member ownership of ideas and strategies, and for "buy in" management. The payoff to employee empowerment and involvement is that it allows individuals to discover and use their own potential.

Because of the rapid changes, predicting the future trends in HRM is difficult if not impossible. However, there are several **"cutting edge" trends** which appear to be affecting the future directions of HRM.[10]

Macrosystem Trends

These trends focus on the organization system, including

- *The impact of culture change.* It will become increasingly important to understand the impact of culture on morale, productivity, competence, organizational health, and especially the relationship of culture to strategy.
- *Total resource utilization.* Another trend which has emerged is the need for a systems approach to ensure efficient use of the organization's resources. HR managers will be increasingly required to work with complex client systems.
- *Centralization versus decentralization.* In organizations of the future, it will be necessary to both centralize and decentralize functions, structure, and governance.
- *Conflict resolution.* Conflict management has become an important element in today's complex organizations, and value and goal differences are continuing problems. Future HRM activities should include helping managers to diagnose conflict and to resolve disputes.
- *Interorganization collaboration.* As limited resources and increased complexity confront the manager of the future, increased sharing, collaboration, and cooperation among organizations will be necessary. Networking offers alternative routes for organizational action.

Human Resource System Trends

These trends focus on group dynamics, including

- *Downsizing.* There is a trend toward reducing layers of management, number of employees, increasing participation, and developing temporary systems for problem solving. HR managers may be facilitating teamwork, assisting in "downsizing," and managing the transition to "do more with less" systems.

- *Resource linking.* As problems become more complex, it becomes important to develop ad hoc problem-solving groups.
- *Integrating TQM.* An increasing emphasis on productivity and quality suggest future trends for HR managers to develop links between the goals of management and improving total quality management systems.
- *Managing diversity.* There are increasing trends toward greater diversity of the workforce, including multinational corporations and a need for and integration of values and skills.
- *Networking.* In order for organizations to benefit from knowledge and innovation, efficient systems for identifying and accessing information will be needed.

The Individual Trends

These trends focus on the individual:

- *Intrinsic worth.* Evidence suggests that intrinsic, not extrinsic, motivation is a factor in stress and its symptoms. The HR manager can assist in shared understanding and training to deal with these problems.
- *Change in individuals.* With an increased emphasis on corporate training and development efforts, the HR manager will need to make this process easier and more effective.
- *The effects of thinking.* The concept of the thinking individual raises the question of corporate values and cultures as belief systems, and offers the HR manager a vehicle for creating a positive, research-based value system in the organization.
- *Health and fitness.* Currently, "fitness" models focus on organizational and individual health. Such models will provide an increase in self-selected excellence and fitness approaches for the HR manager in the future.
- *Interdependence.* Finally, the increasing complexity emphasizes the interdependent relationship between the individual and the organization. The HR manager will need to develop synergy among organizational elements.

THE FUTURE OF HRM

As a result of the accelerating rate of change in the modern environment, HRM is increasingly viewed and applied as an approach for making organizations more creative, efficient, and competent. Because of the increase in the size of organizations and their dispersion over wider geographic areas, executives are becoming more in need of a system to obtain information about their organization. A formalized information system is becoming essential for all organizational operations, and communication barriers such as intergroup rivalry and conflicts are becoming more prevalent. Although technology is becoming more complex, organizations are facing more social trauma.[11]

HRM is an expanding and vital technology. A great deal has been accomplished during its past history, and certainly much more needs to be done in the future. HRM is being applied in a multinational framework and in a variety of organizational settings, including industrial, governmental, and health-care institutions. It is agreed by most theorists that there is a need for more empirical studies on the relationship of various HRM programs to other organizational variables, and a need for a more proactive role for the HR manager.

SUMMARY

In this book, we have examined the practice and application of the Success System Model as an approach to organizational excellence. It seems fair to say that, despite criticism and controversy, HRM is a growing and developing professional field.

One problem is that much of the research supporting various HRM activities has either been biased or has failed to be replicated with similar results. Consequently, one study may suggest that a certain program has been very effective within an organization, whereas a second similar study finds just the opposite—a complete lack of positive impact. Given much conflicting data, how is one to evaluate the various methodologies, strategies, and interventions that may be utilized in an HRM program?

A second problem is that of overgeneralization on limited or short-term data. In a number of instances, very positive initial reports have initiated a "halo effect," so that everyone tries to duplicate an apparent success, only to discover later that the final outcome is not as positive as initial reports appeared.

One example of this at a food plant involved an HRM program based upon the team concept, in which self-managed work teams were assigned areas of responsibility. The program had some very positive results, but other pressures emerged, and analysts reported later that the program seemed to be deteriorating. The HRM program resulted in lower unit costs, decreased turnover, and lower accident rates, but external pressures from the power system seemed to be posing new problems, which may have affected long-term results.

We are optimistic about the future of HRM and believe that it will continue to grow and be more proactive. This growth will result because the problems of adapting to a more competitive and global environment create the need for expanded use of HRM concepts. The increasing need for organization transformation, high-performing systems, innovation, and empowerment, suggests that speed in making transitions is the critical issue facing organizations today. HR managers must be more proactive and be able to develop new and innovative ways of adapting organizations to high-speed change. As more organizations seek to achieve organizational excellence, there will be a parallel growth in the need for new HRM models, new strategies, new programs, and a more proactive HR manager role.

REVIEW QUESTIONS

1. Identify some of the conditions for success of an HRM program.
2. Is HRM becoming more proactive? Why or why not?
3. Do you agree or disagree with the criticisms of HRM?

KEY WORDS AND CONCEPTS

Define and be able to use the following:

- Cutting Edge Trends
- Empowerment
- In Search of Excellence
- Innovation
- Organization Transformation (OT)
- Organizational Excellence
- Shared Vision
- Stabilizing
- Transfer of Training
- Trust

Total time suggested: 1 hour.

A. PURPOSE

In most organizations, there is a lot of untapped human potential. In excellent, renewing organizations, this potential can be released, resulting in personal growth for the individual. Personal development and organization renewal involve changes in attitudes and behavior which are related to self-concepts, roles, goals, and values.

The purpose of this profile is to help you gauge for yourself aspects of your behavior. During this course, you have gained additional opportunities to obtain information about yourself of how you behave in organization situations. This feedback may provide the impetus for you to change, but the ultimate responsibility for that change is with you.

In this simulation, you will experience

- Developing skills in goal-setting and changing behaviors.
- Developing skill in listening and using feedback.
- Exploring the proactive role in an on-going situation.
- Increasing your self-renewal capability.

B. PROCEDURES

Part A. The HRM Profile Survey

Step 1. Before class, complete the HRM Profile Survey. How you respond reflects how you view yourself, which in turn reveals something of your behavior style. Based on the scale, select the number to indicate the degree to which you feel each description is characteristic of you. Record your choice in the blank to the right.

Step 2. Complete the HRM Profile Form by coloring in (with colored pens) the bar graph from your chapter 2 HRM Profile Form in the appropriate line (or bring in computer printout) relative to the behavior profile you have just completed. Note that the 30 item descriptions fit into the five categories: communicating skills, interpersonal skills, aspiration-achievement levels, problem-solving skills, and leadership skills. The profile provides information about your behavioral style and allows you to see where you stand in each category. It also lets you directly compare your score from prior levels (chapter 2) on these scales by looking at the differences in the bar graphs. The profile may indicate factors on which your score is less desirable than you would like. You may also find categories upon which you have made improvement during this course and guidance in assessing the kinds of changes you may wish to make in order to become a more effective HRM manager.

Step 3. The HRM Profile Form can be used as a feedback tool. You will be able to learn more about yourself by assessing the kinds of changes you may need to make in order to become more effective. Form into trios, with one person acting as the interviewer, a second as the interviewee, and the third as observer (see the HRM Profile Form and Observer Recording Form). The interviewer will help you to develop a fuller understanding of how your style plays a part in your overall effectiveness and how you have developed your strengths during this course. The Interviewer will review the Interviewee's HRM Profile Form for the following:

1. How accurate are the profile assessments relative to performance in class?
2. Were they a complete and challenging set of goals?
3. Were they realistic and feasible?
4. Did the interviewee do and demonstrate these by the end of the course?

The observer will observe the interview style using the Observer Recording Form, and try to provide feedback on the interviewing style. At the end of each interview, the observer gives feedback to the interviewer using the Observer Recording Form. Then rotate roles so that each person is in each of the three roles. Continue the simulation by switching roles until all have played each of the roles.

Time suggested for Step 3: 15–20 minutes per person (in each of the rotating roles)

Step 4. Meeting with the entire class, discuss:

1. How can we improve performance?
2. What interview skills seemed to work best?
3. Do we view change as positive or negative.
4. Was the role of the interviewer helpful? How?
5. How effective was our team?

Time suggested for Step 4: 15 minutes.

HRM PROFILE SURVEY

```
 ::   :   :   :   :   :   ::
  1   2   3   4   5   6   7
```

| Not at All | Somewhat | Very |
| Characteristic | Characteristic | Characteristic |

1. Having the ability to communicate in a clear, concise, and persuasive manner _____

2. Being spontaneous—saying and doing things that seem natural on the spur of the moment _____

3. Doing things "by the book"—noticing appropriate rules and procedures and following them _____

4. Being creative—having a lot of unusual, original ideas; thinking of new approaches to problems others do not often come up with _____

5. Being competitive—wanting to win and be the best _____

6. Being able to listen to and understand others _____

7. Being aware of other people's moods and feelings _____

8. Being careful in your work—taking pains to make sure everything is "just right" _____

9. Being resourceful in coming up with possible ways of dealing with problems _____

10. Being a leader—having other people look to you for direction taking over when things are confused _____

11. Having the ability to accept feedback without reacting defensively, becoming hostile, or withdrawing _____

12. Having the ability to deal with conflict and anger _____

13. Having written work neat and organized; making plans before starting on a difficult task; organizing details of work _____

14. Thinking clearly and logically; attempting to deal with ambiguity, complexity, and confusion in a situation which requires thoughtful, logical analysis _____

15. Having self-confidence when faced with a challenging situation _____

16. Having the ability to level with others, to give feedback to others _____

17. Doing new and different things; meeting new people; experimenting and trying out new ideas or activities _____

18. Having a high level of aspiration; setting difficult goals _____

19. Analyzing a situation carefully before acting; working out a course of action in detail before embarking on it _____

20. Being effective at initiating projects and innovative ideas _____

21. Seeking ideas from others; drawing others into discussion _____

22. Having a tendency to seek close personal relationships participating in social activities with friends; giving affection and receiving it from others _____

23. Being dependable—staying on the job; doing what is expected _____

24. Having the ability to work as a catalyst; to stimulate and encourage others to develop their own resources for solving their own problems _____

25. Taking responsibility; relying on your own abilities and judgment rather than those of others _____

26. Selling your own ideas effectively _____

27. Being the dominant person; having a strong need for control or recognition _____

28. Getting deeply involved in your work; being extremely committed to ideas or work you are doing _____

29. Having the ability to evaluate possible solutions critically _____

30. Having the ability to work in unstructured situations, with little or no support, and to continue to work effectively even if faced with lack of cooperation, resistance, or hostility _____

HRM PROFILE FORM

			SCORE	NOT AT ALL CHARACTERISTIC			SOMEWHAT CHARACTERISTIC		VERY CHARACTERISTIC	
				1	2	3	4	5	6	7
A. Communicating Skills										
Items 1. Communicates	Ch. 2									
	Ch. 19									
6. Listens	Ch. 2									
	Ch. 19									
11. Receives Feedback	Ch. 2									
	Ch. 19									
16. Gives Feedback	Ch. 2									
	Ch. 19									
21. Seeks Ideas	Ch. 2									
	Ch. 19									
26. Sells Ideas	Ch. 2									
	Ch. 19									
MEAN SCORE A	Ch. 2									
	Ch. 19									
B. Interpersonal Skills										
Items 2. Is Spontaneous	Ch. 2									
	Ch. 19									
7. Is Aware	Ch. 2									
	Ch. 19									
12. Deals with Conflict	Ch. 2									
	Ch. 19									
17. Experiments	Ch. 2									
	Ch. 19									
22. Seeks Close Relationships	Ch. 2									
	Ch. 19									
27. Is Dominant	Ch. 2									
	Ch. 19									
MEAN SCORE B	Ch. 2									
	Ch. 19									
C. Aspiration-Achievement Levels										
Items 3. Conforms	Ch. 2									
	Ch. 19									
8. Is Careful	Ch. 2									
	Ch. 19									
13. Is Organized	Ch. 2									
	Ch. 19									
18. Aspires	Ch. 2									
	Ch. 19									

		SCORE	NOT AT ALL CHARACTERISTIC			SOMEWHAT CHARACTERISTIC			VERY CHARACTERISTIC		
23. Is Dependable	Ch. 2										
	Ch. 19										
28. Is Committed to Ideas or Work	Ch. 2										
	Ch. 19										
MEAN SCORE C	Ch. 2										
	Ch. 19										
D. Problem-Solving Skills											
Items 4. Is Creative	Ch. 2										
	Ch. 19										
9. Is Resourceful	Ch. 2										
	Ch. 19										
14. Is Logical	Ch. 2										
	Ch. 19										
19. Analyzes	Ch. 2										
	Ch. 19										
24. Is Catalyst	Ch. 2										
	Ch. 19										
29. Evaluates	Ch. 2										
	Ch. 19										
MEAN SCORE D	Ch. 2										
	Ch. 19										
E. Leadership Skills											
Items 5. Is Competitive	Ch. 2										
	Ch. 19										
10. Is a Leader	Ch. 2										
	Ch. 19										
15. Is Confident	Ch. 2										
	Ch. 19										
20. Initiates	Ch. 2										
	Ch. 19										
25. Takes Responsibility	Ch. 2										
	Ch. 19										
30. Can Work in Unstructured Situations	Ch. 2										
	Ch. 19										
Mean Score E	Ch. 2										
	Ch. 19										
Overall HRM Profile Average	Ch. 2										
Total Mean (A + B + C + D + E) ÷ 5	Ch. 19										

OBSERVER RECORDING FORM

1. **Level of involvement:**
   Cautious   Low 1:2:3:4:5:6:7:8:9:10 High   Interested

2. **Level of communication:**
   Doesn't listen   Low 1:2:3:4:5:6:7:8:9:10 High   Listens

3. **Level of openness, trust:**
   Shy, uncertain   Low 1:2:3:4:5:6:7:8:9:10 High   Warm, friendly

4. **Level of collaboration:**
   Authoritative   Low 1:2:3:4:5:6:7:8:9:10 High   Seeks agreement

5. **Level of influence:**
   Gives in   Low 1:2:3:4:5:6:7:8:9:10 High   Convincing

6. **Level of supportiveness:**
   Disagrees   Low 1:2:3:4:5:6:7:8:9:10 High   Supports

7. **Level of direction:**
   Easygoing, agreeable   Low 1:2:3:4:5:6:7:8:9:10 High   Gives directions

8. **Level of competence:**
   Unsure   Low 1:2:3:4:5:6:7:8:9:10 High   Competent

9. **Other:**   Low 1:2:3:4:5:6:7:8:9:10 High

10. **Overall style:**
    Ineffective   Low 1:2:3:4:5:6:7:8:9:10 High   Effective

Case 19.1   The Bob Knowlton Case[12]

He liked to stay after the others had gone. His appointment as project head was still new enough to give him a deep sense of pleasure. His eyes were on the graphs before him but in his mind he could hear Dr. Jerrold, the project head, saying again, "There's one thing about this place that you can bank on. The sky is the limit for a man who can produce!" Knowlton felt again the tingle of happiness and embarrassment. Well, dammit, he said to himself, he had produced. He wasn't kidding anybody. He had come to the Simmons Laboratories 2 years ago. During a routine testing of some rejected Clanson components, he had stumbled on the idea of the photon correlator, and the rest just happened. Jerrold had been enthusiastic; a separate project had been set up for further research and development of the device, and he had gotten the job of running it. The whole sequence of events still seemed a little miraculous to Knowlton.

He shrugged out of the reverie and bent determinedly over the sheets when he heard someone come into the room behind him. He looked up expectantly; Jerrold often stayed late himself,and now and then dropped in for a chat. This always made the day's end especially pleasant for Bob. It wasn't Jerrold. The man who had come in was a stranger. He was tall, thin, and rather dark. He wore steel-rimmed glasses and had on a very wide leather belt with a large brass buckle. Lucy remarked later that it was the kind of belt the Pilgrims must have worn.

The stranger smiled and introduced himself, "I'm Simon Fester. Are you Bob Knowlton?" Bob said yes, and they shook hands. "Doctor Jerrold said I might find you in. We were talking about your work, and I'm very much interested in what you are doing." Bob waved to a chair.

Fester didn't seem to belong in any of the standard categories of visitors: customer, visiting fireman, stockholder. Bob pointed to the sheets on the table. "There are the preliminary results of a test we're running. We have a new gadget by the tail and we're trying to understand it. It's not finished, but I can show you the section that we're testing."

He stood up, but Fester was deep into the graphs. After a moment, he looked up with an odd grin. "These look like plots of a Jennings surface. I've been playing around with some autocorrelation functions of surfaces—you know that stuff." Bob, who had no idea what he was referring to, grinned back and nodded, and immediately felt uncomfortable. "Let me show you the monster," he said, and led the way to the workroom.

After Fester left, Knowlton slowly put the graphs away, feeling vaguely annoyed. Then, as if he had made a decision, he quickly locked up and took the long way out so that he would pass Jerrold's office. But the office was locked. Knowlton wondered whether Jerrold and Fester had left together.

The next morning, Knowlton dropped into Jerrold's office, mentioned that he had talked with Fester and asked who he was. "Sit down for a minute," Jerrold said. "I want to talk to you about him. What do you think of him?" Knowlton replied truthfully that he thought Fester was very bright and probably very competent. Jerrold looked pleased. "We're taking him on," he said. "He's had a very good background in a number of laboratories, and he seems to have ideas about the problems we're tackling here." Knowlton nodded in agreement, instantly wishing that Fester would not be placed with him. "I don't know yet where he will finally land," Jerrold continued, "but he seems interested in what you are doing. I thought he might spend a little time with you by way of getting started." Knowlton nodded thoughtfully. "If his interest in your work continues, you can add him to your group." "Well, he seemed to have some good ideas even without knowing exactly what we are doing," Knowlton answered. "I hope he stays; we'd be glad to have him."

Knowlton walked back to the lab with mixed feelings. He told himself that Fester would be good for the group. He was no dunce, he'd produce. Knowlton thought again of Jerrold's promise when he had promoted him—"the man who produces gets ahead in this outfit." The words seemed to carry the overtones of a threat now.

That day Fester didn't appear until mid-afternoon. He explained that he had had a long lunch with Jerrold, discussing his place in the lab. "Yes," said Knowlton, "I talked with Jerry this morning about it, and we both thought you might work with us for awhile." Fester smiled in the same knowing way that he had smiled when he mentioned the Jennings surfaces. "I'd like to," he said. Knowlton introduced Fester to the other members of the lab. Fester and Link, the mathematician of the group, hit it off well together and spent the rest of the afternoon discussing a method of analysis of patterns that Link had been worrying over for the last month.

It was 6:30 P.M. when Knowlton finally left the lab that night. He had waited almost eagerly for the end of the day to come—when they would all be gone and he could sit in the quiet room, relax, and think it over. "Think what over?" he asked himself. He didn't know. Shortly after 5 P.M., they had all gone except Fester, and what followed was almost a duel. Knowlton was annoyed that he was being cheated out of his quiet period, and finally resentfully determined that Fester should leave first.

Jerrold did not make any attempt to meet Knowlton. In a way, he felt aggrieved about the whole thing. Fester, too, was surprised at the suddenness of Knowlton's departure and when Jerrold, in talking to him, asked him whether he had reasons to prefer to stay with the photon group instead of the project for the Air Force which was being organized. He chose the Air Force project and went on to that job the following week. The photon lab was hard hit. The leadership of the lab was given to Link, with the understanding that this would be temporary until someone could come in to take over.

Fester was sitting at the conference table reading, and Knowlton was sitting at the desk in the little glass-enclosed cubby that he used during the day when he needed to be undisturbed. Fester had gotten the last year's progress reports out and was studying them carefully. The time dragged. Knowlton doodled on a pad, the tension growing inside him. What the hell did Fester think he was going to find in the reports?

Knowlton finally gave up and they left the lab together. Fester took several of the reports with him to study in the evening. Knowlton asked him if he thought the reports gave a clear picture of the lab's activities. "They're excellent," Fester answered with obvious sincerity. "They're not only good reports; what they report is damn good, too!" Knowlton was surprised at the relief he felt, and grew almost jovial as he said goodnight.

Driving home, Knowlton felt more optimistic about Fester's presence in the lab. He had never fully understood the analysis that Link was attempting. If there was anything wrong with Link's approach, Fester would probably spot it. "And if I'm any judge," he murmured, "he won't be especially diplomatic about it."

He described Fester to his wife, who was amused by the broad leather belt and the brass buckle. "It's the kind of belt that Pilgrims must have worn," she laughed. "I'm not worried about how he holds his pants up," he laughed at her. "I'm afraid that he's the kind that just has to make like a genius twice each day. And that can be pretty rough on the group."

Knowlton had been asleep for several hours when he was jerked awake by the telephone. He realized it had rung several times. He swung off the bed muttering about damn fools and telephones. It was Fester. Without any excuses and apparently oblivious of the time, he plunged into an excited recital of how Link's patterning problem could be solved. Knowlton covered the mouthpiece to answer his wife's stage-whispered, "Who is it?" "It's the genius," replied Knowlton.

Fester, completely ignoring the fact that it was 2:00 in the morning, proceeded in a very excited way to start in the middle of an explanation of a completely new approach to certain of the photon lab problems that he had stumbled on while analyzing past experiments. Knowlton managed to put some enthusiasm in his own voice and stood there, half-dazed and very uncomfortable, listening to Fester talk endlessly about what he had discovered. It was probably not only a new approach, but also an analysis that showed the inherent weakness of the previous experiment and how experimentation along that line would certainly have been inconclusive. The following day Knowlton spent the entire morning with Fester and Link, the customary morning meeting of Bob's group having been called off so that Fester's work of the previous night could be gone over in detail. Fester was very anxious that this be done and Knowlton was not too unhappy to call the meeting off for reasons of his own.

For the next several days, Fester sat in the back office that had been turned over to him and did nothing but read the progress reports of the work that had been done in the last 6 months. Knowlton caught himself feeling apprehensive about the reaction that Fester might have to some of his work. He was a little surprised at his own feelings. He had always been proud—although he had put on a convincingly modest face—of the way in which new ground had been broken by his group in the study of photon measuring devices. Now he wasn't sure, and it seemed to him that Fester might easily show that the line of research they had been following was unsound or even unimaginative.

The next morning, as was the custom, the members of the lab, including the secretaries, sat around the conference table. Bob always prided himself on the fact that the work of the lab was guided and evaluated by the group as a whole and he was fond of repeating that it was not a waste of time to include secretaries in such meetings. Often, what started out as a boring recital of fundamental assumptions to a naive listener, uncovered new ways of regarding these assumptions that would not have occurred to the researcher who had long ago accepted them as a necessary basis for his work.

The group meetings also served Bob in another sense. He admitted to himself that he would have felt far less secure if he had had to direct the work out of his own mind, so to speak. With the group meeting as the principle of leadership, it was always possible to justify the exploration of blind alleys because of the general educative effect on the team. Fester was there; Lucy and Martha were there; Link was sitting next to Fester, their conversation concerning Link's mathematical study apparently continuing from yesterday. The other members, Bob Davenport, George Thurlow, and Arthur Oliver, were waiting quietly.

Knowlton, for reasons that he didn't quite understand, proposed for discussion this morning a problem that all of them had spent a great deal of time on previously, with the conclusion that a solution was impossible, that there was no feasible way of treating it in an experimental fashion. When Knowlton proposed the problem, Davenport remarked that there was hardly any use of going over it again, that he was satisfied that there was no way of approaching the problem with the equipment and the physical capacities of the lab.

The statement had the effect of a shot of adrenaline on Fester. He said he would like to know what the problem was in detail and, walking to the blackboard, began setting down the "factors" as various members of the group began discussing the problem and simultaneously listing the reasons why it had been abandoned.

Very early in the description of the problem it was evident that Fester was going to disagree about the impossibility of attacking it. The group realized this and finally the descriptive materials and their recounting of the reasoning that had led to its abandonment dwindled away. Fester began his statement which, as it proceeded, might well have been prepared the previous night although Knowlton knew this was impossible. He couldn't help being impressed with the organized analogical way that Fester was presenting ideas that must have occurred to him only a few minutes before.

Fester had some things to say, however, which left Knowlton with a mixture of annoyance, irritation, and, at the same time, a rather smug feeling of superiority over Fester in at least one area. Fester was of the opinion that the way that the problem had been analyzed was really typical of group thinking and, with an air of sophistication that made it difficult for a listener to dissent, he proceeded to comment on the American emphasis on team ideas, satirically describing the ways in which they led to a "high level of mediocrity."

During this time, Knowlton observed that Link stared studiously at the floor, and he was very conscious of George Thurlow's and Bob Davenport's glances toward him at several points of Fester's little speech. Inwardly, Knowlton couldn't help feeling that this was one point at least in which Fester was off on the wrong foot. The whole lab, following Jerry's lead, talked if not practiced the theory of small research teams as the basic organization for effective research. Fester insisted that the problem could be approached and that he would like to study it for a while himself.

Knowlton ended the morning session by remarking that the meetings would continue and that the very fact that a supposedly insoluble experimental problem was now going to get another chance was another indication of the value of such meetings. Fester immediately remarked that he was not at all averse to meeting for the purpose of informing the group of the progress of its members—that the point he wanted to make was that creative advances were seldom accomplished in such meetings, that they were made by the individual "living with" the problem closely and continuously, a sort of personal relationship to it.

Knowlton went on to say to Fester that he was very glad Fester had raised these points and that he was sure the group would profit by reexamining the basis on which they had been operating. Knowlton agreed that individual effort was probably the basis for making the major advances, but that he considered the group meetings useful primarily because of the effect they had on keeping the group together and on helping the weaker members of the group keep up with the ones who were able to advance more easily and quickly in the analysis of problems.

It was clear as days went by and the meetings continued that Fester came to enjoy them because of the pattern that the meetings assumed. It became typical for Fester to hold forth and it was unquestionably clear that he was more brilliant, better prepared on the various subjects that were germane to the problems being studied, and that he was more capable of going ahead than anyone there.

Knowlton grew increasingly disturbed as he realized that his leadership of the group had been, in fact, taken over.

Whenever the subject of Fester was mentioned in his occasional meetings with Dr. Jerrold, Knowlton would comment only on the ability and obvious capacity for work that Fester had. Somehow he never felt that he could mention his own discomforts, not only because they revealed a weakness on his own part, but also because it was quite clear that Jerrold himself was considerably impressed with Fester's work and with the contacts he had with him outside the photon laboratory.

Knowlton now began to feel that perhaps the intellectual advantages that Fester had brought to the group did not quite compensate for what he felt were evidences of a breakdown in the cooperative spirit he had seen in the group before Fester's coming. More and more of the morning meetings were skipped. Fester's opinion concerning the abilities of others of the group, with the exception of Link, was obviously low. At times, during morning meetings or in smaller discussions, he had been on the point of rudeness, refusing to pursue an argument when he claimed it was based on the other person's ignorance of the facts involved. His impatience of others led him to also make similar remarks to Dr. Jerrold. Knowlton inferred this from a conversation with Jerrold in which Jerrold asked whether Davenport and Oliver were going to be continued on; and his failure to mention Link, the mathematician, led Knowlton to feel that this was the result of private conversations between Fester and Jerrold.

It was not difficult for Knowlton to make a quite convincing case on whether the brilliance of Fester was sufficient recompense for the beginning of this breaking up of the group. He took the opportunity to speak privately with Davenport and with Oliver and it was quite clear that both of them were uncomfortable because of Fester. Knowlton didn't press the discussion beyond the point of hearing them in one way or another say they did feel awkward and that it was sometimes difficult for them to understand the arguments he advanced, but often embarrassing to ask him to fill in the background on which his arguments were based. Knowlton did not interview Link in this manner.

About 6 months after Fester's arrival at the photon lab, a meeting was scheduled in which the sponsors of the research were coming in to get some idea of the work and its progress. It was customary at these meetings for project heads to present the research being conducted in their groups. The members of each group were invited to other meetings which were held later in the day and open to all, but the special meetings were usually made up only of project heads, the head of the laboratory, and the sponsors.

As the time for the special meeting approached, it seemed to Knowlton that he must avoid the presentation at all cost. His reasons for this was that he could not trust himself to present the ideas and work that Fester had advanced, because of his apprehension as to whether he could present them in sufficient detail and answer such questions about them as might be asked. On the other hand, he did not feel he could ignore these newer lines of work and present only the material that he had done or that had been started before Fester's arrival. He felt also that it would not be beyond Fester at all, in his blunt and undiplomatic way—if he were present at the meeting, that is—to make comments on his [Knowlton's] presentation and reveal Knowlton's inadequacy. It also seemed quite clear that it would not be easy to keep Fester from attending the meeting, even though he was not on the administrative level of those invited.

Knowlton found the opportunity to speak to Jerrold and raised the question. He remarked to Jerrold that, with the meetings coming up and with the interest in the work and with the contributions that Fester had been making, he would probably like to come to these meetings, but there was a question of the feelings of the others in the group if Fester alone were invited. Jerrold passed this over very lightly by saying that he didn't think the group would fail to understand Fester's rather different position and that he thought that Fester by all means should be invited. Knowlton then immediately said he had thought so, too; Fester should present the work because much of it was work he had done; and, as Knowlton put it, that this would be a nice way to recognize Fester's contributions and to reward him, as he was eager to be recognized as a productive member of the lab. Jerrold agreed, and so the matter was decided.

Fester's presentation was very successful and in some ways dominated the meeting. He attracted the interest and attention of many of those who had come, and a long discussion followed his presentation. Later in the evening—with the entire laboratory staff present—a little circle of people gathered about Fester. One of them was Jerrold himself, and a lively discussion took place concerning the application of Fester's theory. All of this disturbed Knowlton, and his reaction and behavior were characteristic. He joined the circle, praised Fester to Jerrold and to others, and remarked on the brilliance of his work.

Knowlton, without consulting anyone, began at this time to take some interest in the possibility of a job elsewhere. After a few weeks, he found that a new laboratory of considerable size was being organized in a nearby city, and that the kind of training he had would enable him to get a project head job equivalent to the one he had at the lab, with slightly more money.

He immediately accepted it and notified Jerrold by a letter, which he mailed on a Friday night to Jerrold's home. The letter was quite brief, and Jerrold was stunned. The letter merely said that he had found a better position; that there were personal reasons why he didn't want to appear at the lab any more; that he would be glad to come back at a later time from where he would be, some 40 miles away, to assist if there were any mixup at all in the past work; that he felt sure that Fester could, however, supply any leadership that was required for the group; and that his decision to leave so suddenly was based on some personal problems—he hinted at problems of health in his family, his mother and father. All of this was fictitious, of course. Jerrold took it at face value but felt his relationship with Knowlton had been warm and that Knowlton was satisfied and, as a matter of fact, quite happy and productive.

Jerrold was considered disturbed, because he had already decided to place Fester in charge of another project that was going to be set up very soon. He had been wondering how to explain this to Knowlton, in view of the obvious help Knowlton was getting from Fester and the high regard in which he held him. Jerrold had, as a matter of fact, considered the possibility that Knowlton could add to his staff another person with the kind of background and training that had been unique in Fester and had proved so valuable. Bob Knowlton was sitting alone in the conference room of the laboratory. The rest of the group had gone. One of the secretaries had stopped and talked for a while about her husband's coming induction into the Army, and had finally left. Bob, alone in the laboratory, slid a little further down in his chair, looking with satisfaction at the results of the first test run of the new photon unit.

QUESTIONS

1. Consider the problem of Fester suddenly dropping in on Knowlton. What HRM concepts did Dr. Jerrold violate? What should Dr. Jerrold have done?

2. How would you approach the issue of recruitment and selection of personnel? Consider the process considered in earlier chapters of this book.

3. Think about Dr. Jerrold's announcement to Knowlton that "We're taking him on . . . ". How does this procedure conform to HRM practices?

4. Discuss Dr. Jerrold's comment, "I don't know yet where he will finally land." What do you think of the company's HR planning? What about job descriptions?

5. What is your opinion of the company's human resource manager? Is the HR manager in control? What are your specific suggestions to the HR manager for preventing the repeat of a similar Jerrold-Knowlton situation?

A. PURPOSE

You will soon be leaving this organization, and this simulation is intended to provide you an opportunity to bring the class to a close. More specifically, it will allow you to clear up any questions you may have about the content of the subject matter.

B. PURPOSE

You are encouraged to share any thoughts, feelings, opinions, and so forth, that you may have relative to the class and its members. There is no format to this simulation. It is suggested that it be conducted as an informal discussion.

ENDNOTES

1. See Peter Drucker, "Change Leaders," *Inc.* (June 1999): 64.

2. Derek Torrington and Laura Hall, *Personnel Management: A New Approach* (Upper Saddle River, NJ: Prentice Hall, 1987).

3. Tom Peters, "Facing Up to the Need for a Management Revolution," *California Management Review* (Winter 1988): 7–37.

4. "Well-designed HR Policies Improve TQM Initiatives," *Personnel Journal* (August 1993): Special Report, 48N.

5. Brian Dumaine, "Who Needs a Boss?" *Fortune* (May 7, 1990): 52.

6. Samuel Greengard, "Don't Rush Downsizing: Plan, Plan, Plan," *Personnel Journal* (November 1993): 64.

7. See John B. Miner, "The Validity and Usefulness of Theories in an Emerging Organizational Science," *Academy of Management Review* 9, no. 2 (April 1984): 535–41; and R. J. Bullock and Patti F. Bullock, "Pure Science Versus Science—Action Models of Data Feedback," *Group and Organization Studies* 9, no. 1 (March 1984): 22–27.

8. Larry Greiner, "Patterns of Organizational Change," *Harvard Business Review* (May-June 1976): 119–230.

9. John Hulpke, California State University, Bakersfield, 1994, source: Samuel Greengard, "Don't Rush Downsizing: Plan, Plan, Plan," *Personnel Journal* 72, no. 11 (November 1993): 64.

10. Gordon Lippitt, Ronald Lippitt, and Clayton Lafferty, "Cutting Edge Trends in Organization Development," *Training and Development Journal* 38, no. 7 (July 1984): 59–62.

11. See Lynda M. Applegate, James I. Cash, Jr., and D. Quinn Mills, "Information Technology and Tomorrow's Manager," *Harvard Business Review* (November-December 1988): 128. See also W. Halal, "Organizational Development in the Future," *California Management Review* 52, no. 1 (Spring 1974).

12. We are indebted to Professor Alex Bavelas of Stanford University for the use of this case, and it is used with his permission.

INDEX

Cash balance pension plans, 278–279
Caterpillar, 336, 339
Change
    career planning for, 227–228
    as competitive necessity, 68–69, 410–411
    cultural resistance to, 415–417
    global issues of, 15
    HRM strategies for, 70, 389–391,
        418–420, 473–476
    management development for, 205–206
    organizational strategy for, 4, 16–17,
        209–212, 383, 391–399
    and Success System Model, 5
    tools for, 417–418
Checklist appraisals, 164–165
Chevron, 36, 37
Child care programs, 285–286
Child labor, 45
Chipman-Union, 281
Chrysler, 276, 338
Civil Rights Acts
    1866, 33
    1991, 37–38, 47
    1964 (Title VII), 36, 37, 41–42, 49, 144
Coaching, 185–186
Coca-Cola, 411–412
Cohesiveness, 457
Collective bargaining, 330–332, 335–341
College recruiting, 106, 109–111, 113–114
Colvin, Teresa, 209
Commissions, 299, 306
Communication
    of benefit plans, 288
    diversity issues, 458, 460, 462
    safety issues, 359
    self-managed work teams, 88
Comparable worth, 78, 262
Compensable factors, 256
Compensation. *See also* Benefits; Incentives
    commission plans, 299, 306
    definition of, 4, 251–252
    equity issues, 78, 254–255, 262–263
    flexible reward systems, 461–462
    and job analysis, 76
    and job evaluation, 256–262
    overview of, 250–251
    for performance management, 159
    program design issues, 253–255
    unemployment, 274
    variable pay, 263–264
    wage structures, 260–262
Computer-assisted instruction, 187
Computer-assisted interviews, 140–141
Computers, safety issues of, 368
Consent election, 334
Continuing education, 189
Continuous learning, 228
Contracts, labor, 336–341. *See also* Unions
        and union relations
Cooperative education, 189–190

Corporate culture. *See* Culture, corporate
Cost management issues, 193, 275–276,
        354–355
Creative individualism, 18
Credit reports, 145
Critical incidents, 166
Crosby, Phil, 435
Cross-training, 187
Cultural diversity. *See* Diversity
Cultural resistance to change, 415–417
Cultural systems (in organizations),
        397–398
Cultural tolerance, 458
Culture, corporate
    Asian, 185
    definition of, 16, 391, 392, 412–413
    diversity issues, 458, 459
    and organizational success, 413–417
    and self-managed work teams, 86–87
    and strategic change, 16–17, 209–212,
        383, 391–399, 410–411, 415–417
    strength of, 393–394
    and TQM, 437
    types of, 411–412
Cummins Engine Company, 311
Customer satisfaction, 435
Cutting edge trends (HRM), 479–480

D

Dana Corporation, 88–89
Databases, employment, 107
Deal, Terrence, 398, 413
Decertification election, 339
Defined-benefit pension plans, 278
Defined-contribution pension plans,
        278–279
Del Monte, 254–255
Delta Airlines, 343
Deming, W. Edwards, 206, 435
Depression, 367
Development, employee, 160, 180–181. *See
        also* Training and development
Dictionary of Occupational Titles (DOT), 74
Differential piece rate plans, 304
Digital Equipment Corporation (DEC), 45,
        214, 454
Direct observation, 80–81
Disabled persons
    AIDS patients as, 40–41
    interviewing of, 142
    legal issues, 39–40
    on-the-job programs, 360–361
    training of, 192
    work-related injuries, 353
    workplace trends, 456
Discipline of employees, 50–51, 167, 360
Discrimination. *See also* Diversity
    age, 38–39, 103, 262–263, 272, 279
    compensation issues, 262–263